High Performance MySQL

Other Microsoft .NET resources from O'Reilly

Related titles

Managing and Using MySQL
MySQL Cookbook™
MySQL Pocket Reference
MySQL Reference Manual
Learning PHP
PHP 5 Essentials

PHP Cookbook™
Practical PostgreSQL
Programming PHP
SQL Tuning
Web Database Applications
   with PHP and MySQL

.NET Books Resource Center

dotnet.oreilly.com is a complete catalog of O'Reilly's books on .NET and related technologies, including sample chapters and code examples.

ONDotnet.com provides independent coverage of fundamental, interoperable, and emerging Microsoft .NET programming and web services technologies.

Conferences

O'Reilly Media bring diverse innovators together to nurture the ideas that spark revolutionary industries. We specialize in documenting the latest tools and systems, translating the innovator's knowledge into useful skills for those in the trenches. Visit *conferences.oreilly.com* for our upcoming events.

Safari Bookshelf (*safari.oreilly.com*) is the premier online reference library for programmers and IT professionals. Conduct searches across more than 1,000 books. Subscribers can zero in on answers to time-critical questions in a matter of seconds. Read the books on your Bookshelf from cover to cover or simply flip to the page you need. Try it today for free.

SECOND EDITION

High Performance MySQL

Baron Schwartz, Peter Zaitsev, Vadim Tkachenko,
Jeremy D. Zawodny, Arjen Lentz,
and Derek J. Balling

O'REILLY®

Beijing · Cambridge · Farnham · Köln · Sebastopol · Taipei · Tokyo

High Performance MySQL, Second Edition

by Baron Schwartz, Peter Zaitsev, Vadim Tkachenko, Jeremy D. Zawodny, Arjen Lentz, and Derek J. Balling

Copyright © 2008 O'Reilly Media, Inc. All rights reserved.
Printed in the United States of America.

Published by O'Reilly Media, Inc., 1005 Gravenstein Highway North, Sebastopol, CA 95472.

O'Reilly books may be purchased for educational, business, or sales promotional use. Online editions are also available for most titles (*safari.oreilly.com*). For more information, contact our corporate/institutional sales department: (800) 998-9938 or *corporate@oreilly.com*.

Editor: Andy Oram	**Indexer:** Angela Howard
Production Editor: Loranah Dimant	**Cover Designer:** Karen Montgomery
Copyeditor: Rachel Wheeler	**Interior Designer:** David Futato
Proofreader: Loranah Dimant	**Illustrators:** Jessamyn Read

Printing History:

April 2004:	First Edition.
June 2008:	Second Edition.

 This book uses RepKover™, a durable and flexible lay-flat binding.

ISBN: 978-0-596-10171-8

[M]

Table of Contents

Foreword

I have known Peter, Vadim, and Arjen a long time and have witnessed their long history of both using MySQL for their own projects and tuning it for a lot of different high-profile customers. On his side, Baron has written client software that enhances the usability of MySQL.

The authors' backgrounds are clearly reflected in their complete reworking in this second edition of *High Performance MySQL: Optimizations, Replication, Backups, and More*. It's not just a book that tells you how to optimize your work to use MySQL better than ever before. The authors have done considerable extra work, carrying out and publishing benchmark results to prove their points. This will give you, the reader, a lot of valuable insight into MySQL's inner workings that you can't easily find in any other book. In turn, that will allow you to avoid a lot of mistakes in the future that can lead to suboptimal performance.

I recommend this book both to new users of MySQL who have played with the server a little and now are ready to write their first real applications, and to experienced users who already have well-tuned MySQL-based applications but need to get "a little more" out of them.

—Michael Widenius
March 2008

Preface

We had several goals in mind for this book. Many of them were derived from thinking about that mythical perfect MySQL book that none of us had read but that we kept looking for on bookstore shelves. Others came from a lot of experience helping other users put MySQL to work in their environments.

We wanted a book that wasn't just a SQL primer. We wanted a book with a title that didn't start or end in some arbitrary time frame ("...in Thirty Days," "Seven Days To a Better...") and didn't talk down to the reader. Most of all, we wanted a book that would help you take your skills to the next level and build fast, reliable systems with MySQL—one that would answer questions like "How can I set up a cluster of MySQL servers capable of handling millions upon millions of queries and ensure that things keep running even if a couple of the servers die?"

We decided to write a book that focused not just on the needs of the MySQL application developer but also on the rigorous demands of the MySQL administrator, who needs to keep the system up and running no matter what the programmers or users may throw at the server. Having said that, we assume that you are already relatively experienced with MySQL and, ideally, have read an introductory book on it. We also assume some experience with general system administration, networking, and Unix-like operating systems.

This revised and expanded second edition includes deeper coverage of all the topics in the first edition and many new topics as well. This is partly a response to the changes that have taken place since the book was first published: MySQL is a much larger and more complex piece of software now. Just as importantly, its popularity has exploded. The MySQL community has grown much larger, and big corporations are now adopting MySQL for their mission-critical applications. Since the first edition, MySQL has become recognized as ready for the enterprise.[*] People are also

---

[*] We think this phrase is mostly marketing fluff, but it seems to convey a sense of importance to a lot of people.

using it more and more in applications that are exposed to the Internet, where downtime and other problems cannot be concealed or tolerated.

As a result, this second edition has a slightly different focus than the first edition. We emphasize reliability and correctness just as much as performance, in part because we have used MySQL ourselves for applications where significant amounts of money are riding on the database server. We also have deep experience in web applications, where MySQL has become very popular. The second edition speaks to the expanded world of MySQL, which didn't exist in the same way when the first edition was written.

How This Book Is Organized

We fit a lot of complicated topics into this book. Here, we explain how we put them together in an order that makes them easier to learn.

A Broad Overview

Chapter 1, *MySQL Architecture*, is dedicated to the basics—things you'll need to be familiar with before you dig in deeply. You need to understand how MySQL is organized before you'll be able to use it effectively. This chapter explains MySQL's architecture and key facts about its storage engines. It helps you get up to speed if you aren't familiar with some of the fundamentals of a relational database, including transactions. This chapter will also be useful if this book is your introduction to MySQL but you're already familiar with another database, such as Oracle.

Building a Solid Foundation

The next four chapters cover material you'll find yourself referencing over and over as you use MySQL.

Chapter 2, *Finding Bottlenecks: Benchmarking and Profiling*, discusses the basics of benchmarking and profiling—that is, determining what sort of workload your server can handle, how fast it can perform certain tasks, and so on. You'll want to benchmark your application both before and after any major change, so you can judge how effective your changes are. What seems to be a positive change may turn out to be a negative one under real-world stress, and you'll never know what's really causing poor performance unless you measure it accurately.

In Chapter 3, *Schema Optimization and Indexing*, we cover the various nuances of data types, table design, and indexes. A well-designed schema helps MySQL perform much better, and many of the things we discuss in later chapters hinge on how well your application puts MySQL's indexes to work. A firm understanding of indexes and how to use them well is essential for using MySQL effectively, so you'll probably find yourself returning to this chapter repeatedly.

Chapter 4, *Query Performance Optimization*, explains how MySQL executes queries and how you can take advantage of its query optimizer's strengths. Having a firm grasp of how the query optimizer works will do wonders for your queries and will help you understand indexes better. (Indexing and query optimization are sort of a chicken-and-egg problem; reading Chapter 3 again after you read Chapter 4 might be useful.) This chapter also presents specific examples of virtually all common classes of queries, illustrating where MySQL does a good job and how to transform queries into forms that take advantage of its strengths.

Up to this point, we've covered the basic topics that apply to any database: tables, indexes, data, and queries. Chapter 5, *Advanced MySQL Features*, goes beyond the basics and shows you how MySQL's advanced features work. We examine the query cache, stored procedures, triggers, character sets, and more. MySQL's implementation of these features is different from other databases, and a good understanding of them can open up new opportunities for performance gains that you might not have thought about otherwise.

Tuning Your Application

The next two chapters discuss how to make changes to improve your MySQL-based application's performance.

In Chapter 6, *Optimizing Server Settings*, we discuss how you can tune MySQL to make the most of your hardware and to work as well as possible for your specific application. Chapter 7, *Operating System and Hardware Optimization*, explains how to get the most out of your operating system and hardware. We also suggest hardware configurations that may provide better performance for larger-scale applications.

Scaling Upward After Making Changes

One server isn't always enough. In Chapter 8, *Replication*, we discuss replication—that is, getting your data copied automatically to multiple servers. When combined with the scaling, load-balancing, and high availability lessons in Chapter 9, *Scaling and High Availability*, this will provide you with the groundwork for scaling your applications as large as you need them to be.

An application that runs on a large-scale MySQL backend often provides significant opportunities for optimization in the application itself. There are better and worse ways to design large applications. While this isn't the primary focus of the book, we don't want you to spend all your time concentrating on MySQL. Chapter 10, *Application-Level Optimization*, will help you discover the low-hanging fruit in your overall architecture, especially if it's a web application.

Making Your Application Reliable

The best-designed, most scalable architecture in the world is no good if it can't survive power outages, malicious attacks, application bugs or programmer mistakes, and other disasters.

In Chapter 11, *Backup and Recovery*, we discuss various backup and recovery strategies for your MySQL databases. These strategies will help minimize your downtime in the event of inevitable hardware failure and ensure that your data survives such catastrophes.

Chapter 12, *Security*, provides you with a firm grasp of some of the security issues involved in running a MySQL server. More importantly, we offer many suggestions to allow you to prevent outside parties from harming the servers you've spent all this time trying to configure and optimize. We explain some of the rarely explored areas of database security, showing both the benefits and performance impacts of various practices. Usually, in terms of performance, it pays to keep security policies simple.

Miscellaneous Useful Topics

In the last few chapters and the book's appendixes, we delve into several topics that either don't "fit" in any of the earlier chapters or are referenced often enough in multiple chapters that they deserve a bit of special attention.

Chapter 13, *MySQL Server Status* shows you how to inspect your MySQL server. Knowing how to get status information from the server is important; knowing what that information means is even more important. We cover SHOW INNODB STATUS in particular detail, because it provides deep insight into the operations of the InnoDB transactional storage engine.

Chapter 14, *Tools for High Performance* covers tools you can use to manage MySQL more efficiently. These include monitoring and analysis tools, tools that help you write queries, and so on. This chapter covers the Maatkit tools Baron created, which can enhance MySQL's functionality and make your life as a database administrator easier. It also demonstrates a program called *innotop*, which Baron wrote as an easy-to-use interface to what your MySQL server is presently doing. It functions much like the Unix *top* command and can be invaluable at all phases of the tuning process to monitor what's happening inside MySQL and its storage engines.

Appendix A, *Transferring Large Files*, shows you how to copy very large files from place to place efficiently—a must if you are going to manage large volumes of data. Appendix B, *Using EXPLAIN*, shows you how to really use and understand the all-important EXPLAIN command. Appendix C, *Using Sphinx with MySQL*, is an introduction to Sphinx, a high-performance full-text indexing system that can complement MySQL's own abilities. And finally, Appendix D, *Debugging Locks*, shows you how to decipher what's going on when queries are requesting locks that interfere with each other.

Software Versions and Availability

MySQL is a moving target. In the years since Jeremy wrote the outline for the first edition of this book, numerous releases of MySQL have appeared. MySQL 4.1 and 5.0 were available only as alpha versions when the first edition went to press, but these versions have now been in production for years, and they are the backbone of many of today's large online applications. As we completed this second edition, MySQL 5.1 and 6.0 were the bleeding edge instead. (MySQL 5.1 is a release candidate, and 6.0 is alpha.)

We didn't rely on one single version of MySQL for this book. Instead, we drew on our extensive collective knowledge of MySQL in the real world. The core of the book is focused on MySQL 5.0, because that's what we consider the "current" version. Most of our examples assume you're running some reasonably mature version of MySQL 5.0, such as MySQL 5.0.40 or newer. We have made an effort to note features or functionalities that may not exist in older releases or that may exist only in the upcoming 5.1 series. However, the definitive reference for mapping features to specific versions is the MySQL documentation itself. We expect that you'll find yourself visiting the annotated online documentation (*http://dev.mysql.com/doc/*) from time to time as you read this book.

Another great aspect of MySQL is that it runs on all of today's popular platforms: Mac OS X, Windows, GNU/Linux, Solaris, FreeBSD, you name it! However, we are biased toward GNU/Linux* and other Unix-like operating systems. Windows users are likely to encounter some differences. For example, file paths are completely different. We also refer to standard Unix command-line utilities; we assume you know the corresponding commands in Windows.†

Perl is the other rough spot when dealing with MySQL on Windows. MySQL comes with several useful utilities that are written in Perl, and certain chapters in this book present example Perl scripts that form the basis of more complex tools you'll build. Maatkit is also written in Perl. However, Perl isn't included with Windows. In order to use these scripts, you'll need to download a Windows version of Perl from ActiveState and install the necessary add-on modules (DBI and DBD::mysql) for MySQL access.

---

* To avoid confusion, we refer to Linux when we are writing about the kernel, and GNU/Linux when we are writing about the whole operating system infrastructure that supports applications.

† You can get Windows-compatible versions of Unix utilities at *http://unxutils.sourceforge.net* or *http://gnuwin32.sourceforge.net*.

Conventions Used in This Book

The following typographical conventions are used in this book:

Italic

> Used for new terms, URLs, email addresses, usernames, hostnames, filenames, file extensions, pathnames, directories, and Unix commands and utilities.

`Constant width`

> Indicates elements of code, configuration options, database and table names, variables and their values, functions, modules, the contents of files, or the output from commands.

`Constant width bold`

> Shows commands or other text that should be typed literally by the user. Also used for emphasis in command output.

`Constant width italic`

> Shows text that should be replaced with user-supplied values.

 This icon signifies a tip, suggestion, or general note.

 This icon indicates a warning or caution.

Using Code Examples

This book is here to help you get your job done. In general, you may use the code in this book in your programs and documentation. You don't need to contact us for permission unless you're reproducing a significant portion of the code. For example, writing a program that uses several chunks of code from this book doesn't require permission. Selling or distributing a CD-ROM of examples from O'Reilly books *does* require permission. Answering a question by citing this book and quoting example code doesn't require permission. Incorporating a significant amount of example code from this book into your product's documentation *does* require permission.

Examples are maintained on the site *http://www.highperfmysql.com* and will be updated there from time to time. We cannot commit, however, to updating and testing the code for every minor release of MySQL.

We appreciate, but don't require, attribution. An attribution usually includes the title, author, publisher, and ISBN. For example: *"High Performance MySQL: Optimization, Backups, Replication, and More, Second Edition*, by Baron Schwartz et al. Copyright 2008 O'Reilly Media, Inc., 9780596101718."

If you feel your use of code examples falls outside fair use or the permission given above, feel free to contact us at *permissions@oreilly.com*.

Safari® Books Online

 When you see a Safari® Books Online icon on the cover of your favorite technology book, that means the book is available online through the O'Reilly Network Safari Bookshelf.

Safari offers a solution that's better than e-books. It's a virtual library that lets you easily search thousands of top tech books, cut and paste code samples, download chapters, and find quick answers when you need the most accurate, current information. Try it for free at *http://safari.oreilly.com*.

How to Contact Us

Please address comments and questions concerning this book to the publisher:

O'Reilly Media, Inc.
1005 Gravenstein Highway North
Sebastopol, CA 95472
800-998-9938 (in the United States or Canada)
707-829-0515 (international or local)
707-829-0104 (fax)

We have a web page for this book, where we list errata, examples, and any additional information. You can access this page at:

http://www.oreilly.com/catalog/9780596101718/

To comment or ask technical questions about this book, send email to:

bookquestions@oreilly.com

For more information about our books, conferences, Resource Centers, and the O'Reilly Network, see our web site at:

http://www.oreilly.com

You can also get in touch with the authors directly. Baron's weblog is at *http://www.xaprb.com*.

Peter and Vadim maintain two weblogs, the well-established and popular *http://www.mysqlperformanceblog.com* and the more recent *http://www.webscalingblog.com*. You can find the web site for their company, Percona, at *http://www.percona.com*.

Arjen's company, OpenQuery, has a web site at *http://openquery.com.au*. Arjen also maintains a weblog at *http://arjen-lentz.livejournal.com* and a personal site at *http://lentz.com.au*.

Acknowledgments for the Second Edition

Sphinx developer Andrew Aksyonoff wrote Appendix C, *Using Sphinx with MySQL* We'd like to thank him first for his in-depth discussion.

We have received invaluable help from many people while writing this book. It's impossible to list everyone who gave us help—we really owe thanks to the entire MySQL community and everyone at MySQL AB. However, here's a list of people who contributed directly, with apologies if we've missed anyone: Tobias Asplund, Igor Babaev, Pascal Borghino, Roland Bouman, Ronald Bradford, Mark Callaghan, Jeremy Cole, Britt Crawford and the HiveDB Project, Vasil Dimov, Harrison Fisk, Florian Haas, Dmitri Joukovski and Zmanda (thanks for the diagram explaining LVM snapshots), Alan Kasindorf, Sheeri Kritzer Cabral, Marko Makela, Giuseppe Maxia, Paul McCullagh, B. Keith Murphy, Dhiren Patel, Sergey Petrunia, Alexander Rubin, Paul Tuckfield, Heikki Tuuri, and Michael "Monty" Widenius.

A special thanks to Andy Oram and Isabel Kunkle, our editor and assistant editor at O'Reilly, and to Rachel Wheeler, the copyeditor. Thanks also to the rest of the O'Reilly staff.

From Baron

I would like to thank my wife Lynn Rainville and our dog Carbon. If you've written a book, I'm sure you know how grateful I am to them. I also owe a huge debt of gratitude to Alan Rimm-Kaufman and my colleagues at the Rimm-Kaufman Group for their support and encouragement during this project. Thanks to Peter, Vadim, and Arjen for giving me the opportunity to make this dream come true. And thanks to Jeremy and Derek for breaking the trail for us.

From Peter

I've been doing MySQL performance and scaling presentations, training, and consulting for years, and I've always wanted to reach a wider audience, so I was very excited when Andy Oram approached me to work on this book. I have not written a book before, so I wasn't prepared for how much time and effort it required. We first started talking about updating the first edition to cover recent versions of MySQL, but we wanted to add so much material that we ended up rewriting most of the book.

This book is truly a team effort. Because I was very busy bootstrapping Percona, Vadim's and my consulting company, and because English is not my first language, we all had different roles. I provided the outline and technical content, then I reviewed the material, revising and extending it as we wrote. When Arjen (the former head of the MySQL documentation team) joined the project, we began to fill out the outline. Things really started to roll once we brought in Baron, who can write high-quality book content at insane speeds. Vadim was a great help with in-depth MySQL source code checks and when we needed to back our claims with benchmarks and other research.

As we worked on the book, we found more and more areas we wanted to explore in more detail. Many of the book's topics, such as replication, query optimization, InnoDB, architecture, and design could easily fill their own books, so we had to stop somewhere and leave some material for a possible future edition or for our blogs, presentations, and articles.

We got great help from our reviewers, who are the top MySQL experts in the world, from both inside and outside of MySQL AB. These include MySQL's founder, Michael Widenius; InnoDB's founder, Heikki Tuuri; Igor Babaev, the head of the MySQL optimizer team; and many others.

I would also like to thank my wife, Katya Zaytseva, and my children, Ivan and Nadezhda, for allowing me to spend time on the book that should have been Family Time. I'm also grateful to Percona's employees for handling things when I disappeared to work on the book, and of course to Andy Oram and O'Reilly for making things happen.

From Vadim

I would like to thank Peter, who I am excited to have worked with on this book and look forward to working with on other projects; Baron, who was instrumental in getting this book done; and Arjen, who was a lot of fun to work with. Thanks also to our editor Andy Oram, who had enough patience to work with us; the MySQL team that created great software; and our clients who provide me the opportunities to fine tune my MySQL understanding. And finally a special thank you to my wife, Valerie, and our sons, Myroslav and Timur, who always support me and help me to move forward.

From Arjen

I would like to thank Andy for his wisdom, guidance, and patience. Thanks to Baron for hopping on the second edition train while it was already in motion, and to Peter and Vadim for solid background information and benchmarks. Thanks also to Jeremy and Derek for the foundation with the first edition; as you wrote in my copy, Derek: "Keep 'em honest, that's all I ask."

Also thanks to all my former colleagues (and present friends) at MySQL AB, where I acquired most of what I know about the topic; and in this context a special mention for Monty, whom I continue to regard as the proud parent of MySQL, even though his company now lives on as part of Sun Microsystems. I would also like to thank everyone else in the global MySQL community.

And last but not least, thanks to my daughter Phoebe, who at this stage in her young life does not care about this thing called "MySQL," nor indeed has she any idea which of The Wiggles it might refer to! For some, ignorance is truly bliss, and they provide us with a refreshing perspective on what is really important in life; for the rest of you, may you find this book a useful addition on your reference bookshelf. And don't forget your life.

Acknowledgments for the First Edition

A book like this doesn't come into being without help from literally dozens of people. Without their assistance, the book you hold in your hands would probably still be a bunch of sticky notes on the sides of our monitors. This is the part of the book where we get to say whatever we like about the folks who helped us out, and we don't have to worry about music playing in the background telling us to shut up and go away, as you might see on TV during an awards show.

We couldn't have completed this project without the constant prodding, begging, pleading, and support from our editor, Andy Oram. If there is one person most responsible for the book in your hands, it's Andy. We really do appreciate the weekly nag sessions.

Andy isn't alone, though. At O'Reilly there are a bunch of other folks who had some part in getting those sticky notes converted to a cohesive book that you'd be willing to read, so we also have to thank the production, illustration, and marketing folks for helping to pull this book together. And, of course, thanks to Tim O'Reilly for his continued commitment to producing some of the industry's finest documentation for popular open source software.

Finally, we'd both like to give a big thanks to the folks who agreed to look over the various drafts of the book and tell us all the things we were doing wrong: our reviewers. They spent part of their 2003 holiday break looking over roughly formatted versions of this text, full of typos, misleading statements, and outright mathematical errors. In no particular order, thanks to Brian "Krow" Aker, Mark "JDBC" Matthews, Jeremy "the other Jeremy" Cole, Mike "VBMySQL.com" Hillyer, Raymond "Rainman" De Roo, Jeffrey "Regex Master" Friedl, Jason DeHaan, Dan Nelson, Steve "Unix Wiz" Friedl, and, last but not least, Kasia "Unix Girl" Trapszo.

From Jeremy

I would again like to thank Andy for agreeing to take on this project and for continually beating on us for more chapter material. Derek's help was essential for getting the last 20–30% of the book completed so that we wouldn't miss yet another target date. Thanks for agreeing to come on board late in the process and deal with my sporadic bursts of productivity, and for handling the XML grunt work, Chapter 10, Appendix C, and all the other stuff I threw your way.

I also need to thank my parents for getting me that first Commodore 64 computer so many years ago. They not only tolerated the first 10 years of what seems to be a lifelong obsession with electronics and computer technology, but quickly became supporters of my never-ending quest to learn and do more.

Next, I'd like to thank a group of people I've had the distinct pleasure of working with while spreading MySQL religion at Yahoo! during the last few years. Jeffrey Friedl and Ray Goldberger provided encouragement and feedback from the earliest stages of this undertaking. Along with them, Steve Morris, James Harvey, and Sergey Kolychev put up with my seemingly constant experimentation on the Yahoo! Finance MySQL servers, even when it interrupted their important work. Thanks also to the countless other Yahoo!s who have helped me find interesting MySQL problems and solutions. And, most importantly, thanks for having the trust and faith in me needed to put MySQL into some of the most important and visible parts of Yahoo!'s business.

Adam Goodman, the publisher and owner of *Linux Magazine*, helped me ease into the world of writing for a technical audience by publishing my first feature-length MySQL articles back in 2001. Since then, he's taught me more than he realizes about editing and publishing and has encouraged me to continue on this road with my own monthly column in the magazine. Thanks, Adam.

Thanks to Monty and David for sharing MySQL with the world. Speaking of MySQL AB, thanks to all the other great folks there who have encouraged me in writing this: Kerry, Larry, Joe, Marten, Brian, Paul, Jeremy, Mark, Harrison, Matt, and the rest of the team there. You guys rock.

Finally, thanks to all my weblog readers for encouraging me to write informally about MySQL and other technical topics on a daily basis. And, last but not least, thanks to the Goon Squad.

From Derek

Like Jeremy, I've got to thank my family, for much the same reasons. I want to thank my parents for their constant goading that I should write a book, even if this isn't anywhere near what they had in mind. My grandparents helped me learn two valuable lessons, the meaning of the dollar and how much I would fall in love with computers, as they loaned me the money to buy my first Commodore VIC-20.

I can't thank Jeremy enough for inviting me to join him on the whirlwind book-writing roller coaster. It's been a great experience and I look forward to working with him again in the future.

A special thanks goes out to Raymond De Roo, Brian Wohlgemuth, David Calafrancesco, Tera Doty, Jay Rubin, Bill Catlan, Anthony Howe, Mark O'Neal, George Montgomery, George Barber, and the myriad other people who patiently listened to me gripe about things, let me bounce ideas off them to see whether an outsider could understand what I was trying to say, or just managed to bring a smile to my face when I needed it most. Without you, this book might still have been written, but I almost certainly would have gone crazy in the process.

## CHAPTER 1

MySQL Architecture

MySQL's architecture is very different from that of other database servers, and makes it useful for a wide range of purposes. MySQL is not perfect, but it is flexible enough to work well in very demanding environments, such as web applications. At the same time, MySQL can power embedded applications, data warehouses, content indexing and delivery software, highly available redundant systems, online transaction processing (OLTP), and much more.

To get the most from MySQL, you need to understand its design so that you can work with it, not against it. MySQL is flexible in many ways. For example, you can configure it to run well on a wide range of hardware, and it supports a variety of data types. However, MySQL's most unusual and important feature is its storage-engine architecture, whose design separates query processing and other server tasks from data storage and retrieval. In MySQL 5.1, you can even load storage engines as runtime plug-ins. This separation of concerns lets you choose, on a per-table basis, how your data is stored and what performance, features, and other characteristics you want.

This chapter provides a high-level overview of the MySQL server architecture, the major differences between the storage engines, and why those differences are important. We've tried to explain MySQL by simplifying the details and showing examples. This discussion will be useful for those new to database servers as well as readers who are experts with other database servers.

MySQL's Logical Architecture

A good mental picture of how MySQL's components work together will help you understand the server. Figure 1-1 shows a logical view of MySQL's architecture.

The topmost layer contains the services that aren't unique to MySQL. They're services most network-based client/server tools or servers need: connection handling, authentication, security, and so forth.

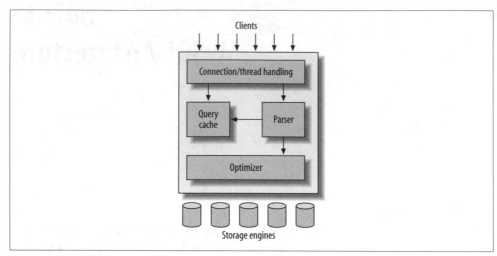

Figure 1-1. A logical view of the MySQL server architecture

The second layer is where things get interesting. Much of MySQL's brains are here, including the code for query parsing, analysis, optimization, caching, and all the built-in functions (e.g., dates, times, math, and encryption). Any functionality provided across storage engines lives at this level: stored procedures, triggers, and views, for example.

The third layer contains the storage engines. They are responsible for storing and retrieving all data stored "in" MySQL. Like the various filesystems available for GNU/Linux, each storage engine has its own benefits and drawbacks. The server communicates with them through the *storage engine API*. This interface hides differences between storage engines and makes them largely transparent at the query layer. The API contains a couple of dozen low-level functions that perform operations such as "begin a transaction" or "fetch the row that has this primary key." The storage engines don't parse SQL* or communicate with each other; they simply respond to requests from the server.

Connection Management and Security

Each client connection gets its own thread within the server process. The connection's queries execute within that single thread, which in turn resides on one core or CPU. The server caches threads, so they don't need to be created and destroyed for each new connection.†

---

* One exception is InnoDB, which does parse foreign key definitions, because the MySQL server doesn't yet implement them itself.

† MySQL AB plans to separate connections from threads in a future version of the server.

When clients (applications) connect to the MySQL server, the server needs to authenticate them. Authentication is based on username, originating host, and password. X.509 certificates can also be used across an Secure Sockets Layer (SSL) connection. Once a client has connected, the server verifies whether the client has privileges for each query it issues (e.g., whether the client is allowed to issue a SELECT statement that accesses the Country table in the world database). We cover these topics in detail in Chapter 12.

Optimization and Execution

MySQL parses queries to create an internal structure (the parse tree), and then applies a variety of optimizations. These may include rewriting the query, determining the order in which it will read tables, choosing which indexes to use, and so on. You can pass hints to the optimizer through special keywords in the query, affecting its decision-making process. You can also ask the server to explain various aspects of optimization. This lets you know what decisions the server is making and gives you a reference point for reworking queries, schemas, and settings to make everything run as efficiently as possible. We discuss the optimizer in much more detail in Chapter 4.

The optimizer does not really care what storage engine a particular table uses, but the storage engine does affect how the server optimizes query. The optimizer asks the storage engine about some of its capabilities and the cost of certain operations, and for statistics on the table data. For instance, some storage engines support index types that can be helpful to certain queries. You can read more about indexing and schema optimization in Chapter 3.

Before even parsing the query, though, the server consults the query cache, which can store only SELECT statements, along with their result sets. If anyone issues a query that's identical to one already in the cache, the server doesn't need to parse, optimize, or execute the query at all—it can simply pass back the stored result set! We discuss the query cache at length in "The MySQL Query Cache" on page 204.

Concurrency Control

Anytime more than one query needs to change data at the same time, the problem of concurrency control arises. For our purposes in this chapter, MySQL has to do this at two levels: the server level and the storage engine level. Concurrency control is a big topic to which a large body of theoretical literature is devoted, but this book isn't about theory or even about MySQL internals. Thus, we will just give you a simplified overview of how MySQL deals with concurrent readers and writers, so you have the context you need for the rest of this chapter.

We'll use an email box on a Unix system as an example. The classic *mbox* file format is very simple. All the messages in an *mbox* mailbox are concatenated together, one after another. This makes it very easy to read and parse mail messages. It also makes mail delivery easy: just append a new message to the end of the file.

But what happens when two processes try to deliver messages at the same time to the same mailbox? Clearly that could corrupt the mailbox, leaving two interleaved messages at the end of the mailbox file. Well-behaved mail delivery systems use locking to prevent corruption. If a client attempts a second delivery while the mailbox is locked, it must wait to acquire the lock itself before delivering its message.

This scheme works reasonably well in practice, but it gives no support for concurrency. Because only a single process can change the mailbox at any given time, this approach becomes problematic with a high-volume mailbox.

Read/Write Locks

Reading from the mailbox isn't as troublesome. There's nothing wrong with multiple clients reading the same mailbox simultaneously; because they aren't making changes, nothing is likely to go wrong. But what happens if someone tries to delete message number 25 while programs are reading the mailbox? It depends, but a reader could come away with a corrupted or inconsistent view of the mailbox. So, to be safe, even reading from a mailbox requires special care.

If you think of the mailbox as a database table and each mail message as a row, it's easy to see that the problem is the same in this context. In many ways, a mailbox is really just a simple database table. Modifying rows in a database table is very similar to removing or changing the content of messages in a mailbox file.

The solution to this classic problem of concurrency control is rather simple. Systems that deal with concurrent read/write access typically implement a locking system that consists of two lock types. These locks are usually known as *shared locks* and *exclusive locks*, or *read locks* and *write locks*.

Without worrying about the actual locking technology, we can describe the concept as follows. Read locks on a resource are shared, or mutually nonblocking: many clients may read from a resource at the same time and not interfere with each other. Write locks, on the other hand, are exclusive—i.e., they block both read locks and other write locks—because the only safe policy is to have a single client writing to the resource at given time and to prevent all reads when a client is writing.

In the database world, locking happens all the time: MySQL has to prevent one client from reading a piece of data while another is changing it. It performs this lock management internally in a way that is transparent much of the time.

Lock Granularity

One way to improve the concurrency of a shared resource is to be more selective about what you lock. Rather than locking the entire resource, lock only the part that contains the data you need to change. Better yet, lock only the exact piece of data you plan to change. Minimizing the amount of data that you lock at any one time lets changes to a given resource occur simultaneously, as long as they don't conflict with each other.

The problem is locks consume resources. Every lock operation—getting a lock, checking to see whether a lock is free, releasing a lock, and so on—has overhead. If the system spends too much time managing locks instead of storing and retrieving data, performance can suffer.

A locking strategy is a compromise between lock overhead and data safety, and that compromise affects performance. Most commercial database servers don't give you much choice: you get what is known as row-level locking in your tables, with a variety of often complex ways to give good performance with many locks.

MySQL, on the other hand, does offer choices. Its storage engines can implement their own locking policies and lock granularities. Lock management is a very important decision in storage engine design; fixing the granularity at a certain level can give better performance for certain uses, yet make that engine less suited for other purposes. Because MySQL offers multiple storage engines, it doesn't require a single general-purpose solution. Let's have a look at the two most important lock strategies.

Table locks

The most basic locking strategy available in MySQL, and the one with the lowest overhead, is *table locks*. A table lock is analogous to the mailbox locks described earlier: it locks the entire table. When a client wishes to write to a table (insert, delete, update, etc.), it acquires a write lock. This keeps all other read and write operations at bay. When nobody is writing, readers can obtain read locks, which don't conflict with other read locks.

Table locks have variations for good performance in specific situations. For example, READ LOCAL table locks allow some types of concurrent write operations. Write locks also have a higher priority than read locks, so a request for a write lock will advance to the front of the lock queue even if readers are already in the queue (write locks can advance past read locks in the queue, but read locks cannot advance past write locks).

Although storage engines can manage their own locks, MySQL itself also uses a variety of locks that are effectively table-level for various purposes. For instance, the server uses a table-level lock for statements such as ALTER TABLE, regardless of the storage engine.

Row locks

The locking style that offers the greatest concurrency (and carries the greatest overhead) is the use of *row locks*. Row-level locking, as this strategy is commonly known, is available in the InnoDB and Falcon storage engines, among others. Row locks are implemented in the storage engine, not the server (refer back to the logical architecture diagram if you need to). The server is completely unaware of locks implemented in the storage engines, and, as you'll see later in this chapter and throughout the book, the storage engines all implement locking in their own ways.

Transactions

You can't examine the more advanced features of a database system for very long before *transactions* enter the mix. A transaction is a group of SQL queries that are treated *atomically*, as a single unit of work. If the database engine can apply the entire group of queries to a database, it does so, but if any of them can't be done because of a crash or other reason, none of them is applied. It's all or nothing.

Little of this section is specific to MySQL. If you're already familiar with ACID transactions, feel free to skip ahead to "Transactions in MySQL" on page 10, later in this chapter.

A banking application is the classic example of why transactions are necessary. Imagine a bank's database with two tables: checking and savings. To move $200 from Jane's checking account to her savings account, you need to perform at least three steps:

1. Make sure her checking account balance is greater than $200.
2. Subtract $200 from her checking account balance.
3. Add $200 to her savings account balance.

The entire operation should be wrapped in a transaction so that if any one of the steps fails, any completed steps can be rolled back.

You start a transaction with the START TRANSACTION statement and then either make its changes permanent with COMMIT or discard the changes with ROLLBACK. So, the SQL for our sample transaction might look like this:

```
1  START TRANSACTION;
2  SELECT balance FROM checking WHERE customer_id = 10233276;
3  UPDATE checking SET balance = balance - 200.00 WHERE customer_id = 10233276;
4  UPDATE savings  SET balance = balance + 200.00 WHERE customer_id = 10233276;
5  COMMIT;
```

But transactions alone aren't the whole story. What happens if the database server crashes while performing line 4? Who knows? The customer probably just lost $200. And what if another process comes along between lines 3 and 4 and removes the entire checking account balance? The bank has given the customer a $200 credit without even knowing it.

Transactions aren't enough unless the system passes the *ACID test*. ACID stands for Atomicity, Consistency, Isolation, and Durability. These are tightly related criteria that a well-behaved transaction processing system must meet:

Atomicity
> A transaction must function as a single indivisible unit of work so that the entire transaction is either applied or rolled back. When transactions are atomic, there is no such thing as a partially completed transaction: it's all or nothing.

Consistency
> The database should always move from one consistent state to the next. In our example, consistency ensures that a crash between lines 3 and 4 doesn't result in $200 disappearing from the checking account. Because the transaction is never committed, none of the transaction's changes is ever reflected in the database.

Isolation
> The results of a transaction are usually invisible to other transactions until the transaction is complete. This ensures that if a bank account summary runs after line 3 but before line 4 in our example, it will still see the $200 in the checking account. When we discuss isolation levels, you'll understand why we said *usually* invisible.

Durability
> Once committed, a transaction's changes are permanent. This means the changes must be recorded such that data won't be lost in a system crash. Durability is a slightly fuzzy concept, however, because there are actually many levels. Some durability strategies provide a stronger safety guarantee than others, and nothing is ever 100% durable. We discuss what durability *really* means in MySQL in later chapters, especially in "InnoDB I/O Tuning" on page 283.

ACID transactions ensure that banks don't lose your money. It is generally extremely difficult or impossible to do this with application logic. An ACID-compliant database server has to do all sorts of complicated things you might not realize to provide ACID guarantees.

Just as with increased lock granularity, the downside of this extra security is that the database server has to do more work. A database server with ACID transactions also generally requires more CPU power, memory, and disk space than one without them. As we've said several times, this is where MySQL's storage engine architecture works to your advantage. You can decide whether your application needs transactions. If you don't really need them, you might be able to get higher performance with a nontransactional storage engine for some kinds of queries. You might be able to use LOCK TABLES to give the level of protection you need without transactions. It's all up to you.

Isolation Levels

Isolation is more complex than it looks. The SQL standard defines four isolation levels, with specific rules for which changes are and aren't visible inside and outside a transaction. Lower isolation levels typically allow higher concurrency and have lower overhead.

 Each storage engine implements isolation levels slightly differently, and they don't necessarily match what you might expect if you're used to another database product (thus, we won't go into exhaustive detail in this section). You should read the manuals for whichever storage engine you decide to use.

Let's take a quick look at the four isolation levels:

READ UNCOMMITTED

> In the READ UNCOMMITTED isolation level, transactions can view the results of uncommitted transactions. At this level, many problems can occur unless you really, really know what you are doing and have a good reason for doing it. This level is rarely used in practice, because its performance isn't much better than the other levels, which have many advantages. Reading uncommitted data is also known as a *dirty read*.

READ COMMITTED

> The default isolation level for most database systems (but not MySQL!) is READ COMMITTED. It satisfies the simple definition of isolation used earlier: a transaction will see only those changes made by transactions that were already committed when it began, and its changes won't be visible to others until it has committed. This level still allows what's known as a *nonrepeatable read*. This means you can run the same statement twice and see different data.

REPEATABLE READ

> REPEATABLE READ solves the problems that READ UNCOMMITTED allows. It guarantees that any rows a transaction reads will "look the same" in subsequent reads within the same transaction, but in theory it still allows another tricky problem: *phantom reads*. Simply put, a phantom read can happen when you select some range of rows, another transaction inserts a new row into the range, and then you select the same range again; you will then see the new "phantom" row. InnoDB and Falcon solve the phantom read problem with multiversion concurrency control, which we explain later in this chapter.
>
> REPEATABLE READ is MySQL's default transaction isolation level. The InnoDB and Falcon storage engines respect this setting, which you'll learn how to change in Chapter 6. Some other storage engines do too, but the choice is up to the engine.

SERIALIZABLE

> The highest level of isolation, SERIALIZABLE, solves the phantom read problem by forcing transactions to be ordered so that they can't possibly conflict. In a nutshell, SERIALIZABLE places a lock on every row it reads. At this level, a lot of timeouts and lock contention may occur. We've rarely seen people use this isolation level, but your application's needs may force you to accept the decreased concurrency in favor of the data stability that results.

Table 1-1 summarizes the various isolation levels and the drawbacks associated with each one.

Table 1-1. ANSI SQL isolation levels

Isolation level	Dirty reads possible	Nonrepeatable reads possible	Phantom reads possible	Locking reads
READ UNCOMMITTED	Yes	Yes	Yes	No
READ COMMITTED	No	Yes	Yes	No
REPEATABLE READ	No	No	Yes	No
SERIALIZABLE	No	No	No	Yes

Deadlocks

A *deadlock* is when two or more transactions are mutually holding and requesting locks on the same resources, creating a cycle of dependencies. Deadlocks occur when transactions try to lock resources in a different order. They can happen whenever multiple transactions lock the same resources. For example, consider these two transactions running against the StockPrice table:

Transaction #1
```
START TRANSACTION;
UPDATE StockPrice SET close = 45.50 WHERE stock_id = 4 and date = '2002-05-01';
UPDATE StockPrice SET close = 19.80 WHERE stock_id = 3 and date = '2002-05-02';
COMMIT;
```

Transaction #2
```
START TRANSACTION;
UPDATE StockPrice SET high  = 20.12 WHERE stock_id = 3 and date = '2002-05-02';
UPDATE StockPrice SET high  = 47.20 WHERE stock_id = 4 and date = '2002-05-01';
COMMIT;
```

If you're unlucky, each transaction will execute its first query and update a row of data, locking it in the process. Each transaction will then attempt to update its second row, only to find that it is already locked. The two transactions will wait forever for each other to complete, unless something intervenes to break the deadlock.

To combat this problem, database systems implement various forms of deadlock detection and timeouts. The more sophisticated systems, such as the InnoDB storage engine, will notice circular dependencies and return an error instantly. This is actually a very good thing—otherwise, deadlocks would manifest themselves as very slow queries. Others will give up after the query exceeds a lock wait timeout, which is not so good. The way InnoDB currently handles deadlocks is to roll back the transaction that has the fewest exclusive row locks (an approximate metric for which will be the easiest to roll back).

Lock behavior and order are storage engine-specific, so some storage engines might deadlock on a certain sequence of statements even though others won't. Deadlocks have a dual nature: some are unavoidable because of true data conflicts, and some are caused by how a storage engine works.

Deadlocks cannot be broken without rolling back one of the transactions, either partially or wholly. They are a fact of life in transactional systems, and your applications should be designed to handle them. Many applications can simply retry their transactions from the beginning.

Transaction Logging

Transaction logging helps make transactions more efficient. Instead of updating the tables on disk each time a change occurs, the storage engine can change its in-memory copy of the data. This is very fast. The storage engine can then write a record of the change to the transaction log, which is on disk and therefore durable. This is also a relatively fast operation, because appending log events involves sequential I/O in one small area of the disk instead of random I/O in many places. Then, at some later time, a process can update the table on disk. Thus, most storage engines that use this technique (known as *write-ahead logging*) end up writing the changes to disk twice.*

If there's a crash after the update is written to the transaction log but before the changes are made to the data itself, the storage engine can still recover the changes upon restart. The recovery method varies between storage engines.

Transactions in MySQL

MySQL AB provides three transactional storage engines: InnoDB, NDB Cluster, and Falcon. Several third-party engines are also available; the best-known engines right now are solidDB and PBXT. We discuss some specific properties of each engine in the next section.

---

* The PBXT storage engine cleverly avoids some write-ahead logging.

AUTOCOMMIT

MySQL operates in AUTOCOMMIT mode by default. This means that unless you've explicitly begun a transaction, it automatically executes each query in a separate transaction. You can enable or disable AUTOCOMMIT for the current connection by setting a variable:

```
mysql> SHOW VARIABLES LIKE 'AUTOCOMMIT';
+---------------+-------+
| Variable_name | Value |
+---------------+-------+
| autocommit    | ON    |
+---------------+-------+
1 row in set (0.00 sec)
mysql> SET AUTOCOMMIT = 1;
```

The values 1 and ON are equivalent, as are 0 and OFF. When you run with AUTOCOMMIT=0, you are always in a transaction, until you issue a COMMIT or ROLLBACK. MySQL then starts a new transaction immediately. Changing the value of AUTOCOMMIT has no effect on nontransactional tables, such as MyISAM or Memory tables, which essentially always operate in AUTOCOMMIT mode.

Certain commands, when issued during an open transaction, cause MySQL to commit the transaction before they execute. These are typically Data Definition Language (DDL) commands that make significant changes, such as ALTER TABLE, but LOCK TABLES and some other statements also have this effect. Check your version's documentation for the full list of commands that automatically commit a transaction.

MySQL lets you set the isolation level using the SET TRANSACTION ISOLATION LEVEL command, which takes effect when the next transaction starts. You can set the isolation level for the whole server in the configuration file (see Chapter 6), or just for your session:

```
mysql> SET SESSION TRANSACTION ISOLATION LEVEL READ COMMITTED;
```

MySQL recognizes all four ANSI standard isolation levels, and InnoDB supports all of them. Other storage engines have varying support for the different isolation levels.

Mixing storage engines in transactions

MySQL doesn't manage transactions at the server level. Instead, the underlying storage engines implement transactions themselves. This means you can't reliably mix different engines in a single transaction. MySQL AB is working on adding a higher-level transaction management service to the server, which will make it safe to mix and match transactional tables in a transaction. Until then, be careful.

If you mix transactional and nontransactional tables (for instance, InnoDB and MyISAM tables) in a transaction, the transaction will work properly if all goes well. However, if a rollback is required, the changes to the nontransactional table can't be undone. This leaves the database in an inconsistent state from which it may be difficult to recover and renders the entire point of transactions moot. This is why it is really important to pick the right storage engine for each table.

MySQL will not usually warn you or raise errors if you do transactional operations on a nontransactional table. Sometimes rolling back a transaction will generate the warning "Some nontransactional changed tables couldn't be rolled back," but most of the time, you'll have no indication you're working with nontransactional tables.

Implicit and explicit locking

InnoDB uses a two-phase locking protocol. It can acquire locks at any time during a transaction, but it does not release them until a COMMIT or ROLLBACK. It releases all the locks at the same time. The locking mechanisms described earlier are all implicit. InnoDB handles locks automatically, according to your isolation level.

However, InnoDB also supports explicit locking, which the SQL standard does not mention at all:

- SELECT ... LOCK IN SHARE MODE
- SELECT ... FOR UPDATE

MySQL also supports the LOCK TABLES and UNLOCK TABLES commands, which are implemented in the server, not in the storage engines. These have their uses, but they are not a substitute for transactions. If you need transactions, use a transactional storage engine.

We often see applications that have been converted from MyISAM to InnoDB but are still using LOCK TABLES. This is no longer necessary because of row-level locking, and it can cause severe performance problems.

 The interaction between LOCK TABLES and transactions is complex, and there are unexpected behaviors in some server versions. Therefore, we recommend that you never use LOCK TABLES unless you are in a transaction and AUTOCOMMIT is disabled, no matter what storage engine you are using.

Multiversion Concurrency Control

Most of MySQL's transactional storage engines, such as InnoDB, Falcon, and PBXT, don't use a simple row-locking mechanism. Instead, they use row-level locking in conjunction with a technique for increasing concurrency known as *multiversion concurrency control* (MVCC). MVCC is not unique to MySQL: Oracle, PostgreSQL, and some other database systems use it too.

You can think of MVCC as a twist on row-level locking; it avoids the need for locking at all in many cases and can have much lower overhead. Depending on how it is implemented, it can allow nonlocking reads, while locking only the necessary records during write operations.

MVCC works by keeping a snapshot of the data as it existed at some point in time. This means transactions can see a consistent view of the data, no matter how long they run. It also means different transactions can see different data in the same tables at the same time! If you've never experienced this before, it may be confusing, but it will become easier to understand with familiarity.

Each storage engine implements MVCC differently. Some of the variations include *optimistic* and *pessimistic* concurrency control. We'll illustrate one way MVCC works by explaining a simplified version of InnoDB's behavior.

InnoDB implements MVCC by storing with each row two additional, hidden values that record when the row was created and when it was expired (or deleted). Rather than storing the actual times at which these events occurred, the row stores the system version number at the time each event occurred. This is a number that increments each time a transaction begins. Each transaction keeps its own record of the current system version, as of the time it began. Each query has to check each row's version numbers against the transaction's version. Let's see how this applies to particular operations when the transaction isolation level is set to REPEATABLE READ:

SELECT
InnoDB must examine each row to ensure that it meets two criteria:

- InnoDB must find a version of the row that is at least as old as the transaction (i.e., its version must be less than or equal to the transaction's version). This ensures that either the row existed before the transaction began, or the transaction created or altered the row.
- The row's deletion version must be undefined or greater than the transaction's version. This ensures that the row wasn't deleted before the transaction began.

Rows that pass both tests may be returned as the query's result.

INSERT
InnoDB records the current system version number with the new row.

DELETE
InnoDB records the current system version number as the row's deletion ID.

UPDATE
InnoDB writes a new copy of the row, using the system version number for the new row's version. It also writes the system version number as the old row's deletion version.

The result of all this extra record keeping is that most read queries never acquire locks. They simply read data as fast as they can, making sure to select only rows that meet the criteria. The drawbacks are that the storage engine has to store more data with each row, do more work when examining rows, and handle some additional housekeeping operations.

MVCC works only with the REPEATABLE READ and READ COMMITTED isolation levels. READ UNCOMMITTED isn't MVCC-compatible because queries don't read the row version that's appropriate for their transaction version; they read the newest version, no matter what. SERIALIZABLE isn't MVCC-compatible because reads lock every row they return.

Table 1-2 summarizes the various locking models and concurrency levels in MySQL.

Table 1-2. Locking models and concurrency in MySQL using the default isolation level

Locking strategy	Concurrency	Overhead	Engines
Table level	Lowest	Lowest	MyISAM, Merge, Memory
Row level	High	High	NDB Cluster
Row level with MVCC	Highest	Highest	InnoDB, Falcon, PBXT, solidDB

MySQL's Storage Engines

This section gives an overview of MySQL's storage engines. We won't go into great detail here, because we discuss storage engines and their particular behaviors throughout the book. Even this book, though, isn't a complete source of documentation; you should read the MySQL manuals for the storage engines you decide to use. MySQL also has forums dedicated to each storage engine, often with links to additional information and interesting ways to use them.

If you just want to compare the engines at a high level, you can skip ahead to Table 1-3.

MySQL stores each database (also called a *schema*) as a subdirectory of its data directory in the underlying filesystem. When you create a table, MySQL stores the table definition in a *.frm* file with the same name as the table. Thus, when you create a table named MyTable, MySQL stores the table definition in *MyTable.frm*. Because MySQL uses the filesystem to store database names and table definitions, case sensitivity depends on the platform. On a Windows MySQL instance, table and database names are case insensitive; on Unix-like systems, they are case sensitive. Each storage engine stores the table's data and indexes differently, but the server itself handles the table definition.

To determine what storage engine a particular table uses, use the SHOW TABLE STATUS command. For example, to examine the user table in the mysql database, execute the following:

```
mysql> SHOW TABLE STATUS LIKE 'user' \G
*************************** 1. row ***************************
           Name: user
         Engine: MyISAM
     Row_format: Dynamic
           Rows: 6
 Avg_row_length: 59
    Data_length: 356
Max_data_length: 4294967295
   Index_length: 2048
      Data_free: 0
 Auto_increment: NULL
    Create_time: 2002-01-24 18:07:17
    Update_time: 2002-01-24 21:56:29
     Check_time: NULL
      Collation: utf8_bin
       Checksum: NULL
 Create_options:
        Comment: Users and global privileges
1 row in set (0.00 sec)
```

The output shows that this is a MyISAM table. You might also notice a lot of other information and statistics in the output. Let's briefly look at what each line means:

Name

The table's name.

Engine

The table's storage engine. In old versions of MySQL, this column was named Type, not Engine.

Row_format

The row format. For a MyISAM table, this can be Dynamic, Fixed, or Compressed. Dynamic rows vary in length because they contain variable-length fields such as VARCHAR or BLOB. Fixed rows, which are always the same size, are made up of fields that don't vary in length, such as CHAR and INTEGER. Compressed rows exist only in compressed tables; see "Compressed MyISAM tables" on page 18.

Rows

The number of rows in the table. For nontransactional tables, this number is always accurate. For transactional tables, it is usually an estimate.

Avg_row_length

How many bytes the average row contains.

Data_length

How much data (in bytes) the entire table contains.

Max_data_length

The maximum amount of data this table can hold. See "Storage" on page 16 for more details.

Index_length
> How much disk space the index data consumes.

Data_free
> For a MyISAM table, the amount of space that is allocated but currently unused. This space holds previously deleted rows and can be reclaimed by future INSERT statements.

Auto_increment
> The next AUTO_INCREMENT value.

Create_time
> When the table was first created.

Update_time
> When data in the table last changed.

Check_time
> When the table was last checked using CHECK TABLE or *myisamchk*.

Collation
> The default character set and collation for character columns in this table. See "Character Sets and Collations" on page 237 for more on these features.

Checksum
> A live checksum of the entire table's contents if enabled.

Create_options
> Any other options that were specified when the table was created.

Comment
> This field contains a variety of extra information. For a MyISAM table, it contains the comments, if any, that were set when the table was created. If the table uses the InnoDB storage engine, the amount of free space in the InnoDB tablespace appears here. If the table is a view, the comment contains the text "VIEW."

The MyISAM Engine

As MySQL's default storage engine, MyISAM provides a good compromise between performance and useful features, such as full-text indexing, compression, and spatial (GIS) functions. MyISAM doesn't support transactions or row-level locks.

Storage

MyISAM typically stores each table in two files: a data file and an index file. The two files bear *.MYD* and *.MYI* extensions, respectively. The MyISAM format is platform-neutral, meaning you can copy the data and index files from an Intel-based server to a PowerPC or Sun SPARC without any trouble.

MyISAM tables can contain either dynamic or static (fixed-length) rows. MySQL decides which format to use based on the table definition. The number of rows a MyISAM table can hold is limited primarily by the available disk space on your database server and the largest file your operating system will let you create.

MyISAM tables created in MySQL 5.0 with variable-length rows are configured by default to handle 256 TB of data, using 6-byte pointers to the data records. Earlier MySQL versions defaulted to 4-byte pointers, for up to 4 GB of data. All MySQL versions can handle a pointer size of up to 8 bytes. To change the pointer size on a MyISAM table (either up or down), you must specify values for the MAX_ROWS and AVG_ROW_LENGTH options that represent ballpark figures for the amount of space you need:

```
CREATE TABLE mytable (
   a    INTEGER  NOT NULL PRIMARY KEY,
   b    CHAR(18) NOT NULL
) MAX_ROWS = 1000000000 AVG_ROW_LENGTH = 32;
```

In this example, we've told MySQL to be prepared to store at least 32 GB of data in the table. To find out what MySQL decided to do, simply ask for the table status:

```
mysql> SHOW TABLE STATUS LIKE 'mytable' \G
*************************** 1. row ***************************
           Name: mytable
         Engine: MyISAM
     Row_format: Fixed
           Rows: 0
 Avg_row_length: 0
    Data_length: 0
Max_data_length: 98784247807
   Index_length: 1024
      Data_free: 0
 Auto_increment: NULL
    Create_time: 2002-02-24 17:36:57
    Update_time: 2002-02-24 17:36:57
     Check_time: NULL
  Create_options: max_rows=1000000000 avg_row_length=32
        Comment:
1 row in set (0.05 sec)
```

As you can see, MySQL remembers the create options exactly as specified. And it chose a representation capable of holding 91 GB of data! You can change the pointer size later with the ALTER TABLE statement, but that will cause the entire table and all of its indexes to be rewritten, which may take a long time.

MyISAM features

As one of the oldest storage engines included in MySQL, MyISAM has many features that have been developed over years of use to fill niche needs:

Locking and concurrency

MyISAM locks entire tables, not rows. Readers obtain shared (read) locks on all tables they need to read. Writers obtain exclusive (write) locks. However, you can insert new rows into the table while select queries are running against it (concurrent inserts). This is a very important and useful feature.

Automatic repair

MySQL supports automatic checking and repairing of MyISAM tables. See "MyISAM I/O Tuning" on page 281 for more information.

Manual repair

You can use the CHECK TABLE mytable and REPAIR TABLE mytable commands to check a table for errors and repair them. You can also use the *myisamchk* command-line tool to check and repair tables when the server is offline.

Index features

You can create indexes on the first 500 characters of BLOB and TEXT columns in MyISAM tables. MyISAM supports full-text indexes, which index individual words for complex search operations. For more information on indexing, see Chapter 3.

Delayed key writes

MyISAM tables marked with the DELAY_KEY_WRITE create option don't write changed index data to disk at the end of a query. Instead, MyISAM buffers the changes in the in-memory key buffer. It flushes index blocks to disk when it prunes the buffer or closes the table. This can boost performance on heavily used tables that change frequently. However, after a server or system crash, the indexes will definitely be corrupted and will need repair. You should handle this with a script that runs *myisamchk* before restarting the server, or by using the automatic recovery options. (Even if you don't use DELAY_KEY_WRITE, these safeguards can still be an excellent idea.) You can configure delayed key writes globally, as well as for individual tables.

Compressed MyISAM tables

Some tables—for example, in CD-ROM- or DVD-ROM-based applications and some embedded environments—never change once they're created and filled with data. These might be well suited to compressed MyISAM tables.

You can compress (or "pack") tables with the *myisampack* utility. You can't modify compressed tables (although you can uncompress, modify, and recompress tables if you need to), but they generally use less space on disk. As a result, they offer faster performance, because their smaller size requires fewer disk seeks to find records. Compressed MyISAM tables can have indexes, but they're read-only.

The overhead of decompressing the data to read it is insignificant for most applications on modern hardware, where the real gain is in reducing disk I/O. The rows are compressed individually, so MySQL doesn't need to unpack an entire table (or even a page) just to fetch a single row.

The MyISAM Merge Engine

The Merge engine is a variation of MyISAM. A Merge table is the combination of several identical MyISAM tables into one virtual table. This is particularly useful when you use MySQL in logging and data warehousing applications. See "Merge Tables and Partitioning" on page 253 for a detailed discussion of Merge tables.

The InnoDB Engine

InnoDB was designed for transaction processing—specifically, processing of many short-lived transactions that usually complete rather than being rolled back. It remains the most popular storage engine for transactional storage. Its performance and automatic crash recovery make it popular for nontransactional storage needs, too.

InnoDB stores its data in a series of one or more data files that are collectively known as a *tablespace*. A tablespace is essentially a black box that InnoDB manages all by itself. In MySQL 4.1 and newer versions, InnoDB can store each table's data and indexes in separate files. InnoDB can also use raw disk partitions for building its tablespace. See "The InnoDB tablespace" on page 290 for more information.

InnoDB uses MVCC to achieve high concurrency, and it implements all four SQL standard isolation levels. It defaults to the REPEATABLE READ isolation level, and it has a *next-key locking* strategy that prevents phantom reads in this isolation level: rather than locking only the rows you've touched in a query, InnoDB locks gaps in the index structure as well, preventing phantoms from being inserted.

InnoDB tables are built on a *clustered index*, which we will cover in detail in Chapter 3. InnoDB's index structures are very different from those of most other MySQL storage engines. As a result, it provides very fast primary key lookups. However, *secondary indexes* (indexes that aren't the primary key) contain the primary key columns, so if your primary key is large, other indexes will also be large. You should strive for a small primary key if you'll have many indexes on a table. InnoDB doesn't compress its indexes.

At the time of this writing, InnoDB can't build indexes by sorting, which MyISAM can do. Thus, InnoDB loads data and creates indexes more slowly than MyISAM. Any operation that changes an InnoDB table's structure will rebuild the entire table, including all the indexes.

InnoDB was designed when most servers had slow disks, a single CPU, and limited memory. Today, as multicore servers with huge amounts of memory and fast disks are becoming less expensive, InnoDB is experiencing some scalability issues.

InnoDB's developers are addressing these issues, but at the time of this writing, several of them remain problematic. See "InnoDB Concurrency Tuning" on page 296 for more information about achieving high concurrency with InnoDB.

Besides its high-concurrency capabilities, InnoDB's next most popular feature is foreign key constraints, which the MySQL server itself doesn't yet provide. InnoDB also provides extremely fast lookups for queries that use a primary key.

InnoDB has a variety of internal optimizations. These include predictive read-ahead for prefetching data from disk, an adaptive hash index that automatically builds hash indexes in memory for very fast lookups, and an insert buffer to speed inserts. We cover these extensively later in this book.

InnoDB's behavior is very intricate, and we highly recommend reading the "InnoDB Transaction Model and Locking" section of the MySQL manual if you're using InnoDB. There are many surprises and exceptions you should be aware of before building an application with InnoDB.

The Memory Engine

Memory tables (formerly called HEAP tables) are useful when you need fast access to data that either never changes or doesn't need to persist after a restart. Memory tables are generally about an order of magnitude faster than MyISAM tables. All of their data is stored in memory, so queries don't have to wait for disk I/O. The table structure of a Memory table persists across a server restart, but no data survives.

Here are some good uses for Memory tables:

- For "lookup" or "mapping" tables, such as a table that maps postal codes to state names
- For caching the results of periodically aggregated data
- For intermediate results when analyzing data

Memory tables support HASH indexes, which are very fast for lookup queries. See "Hash indexes" on page 101 for more information on HASH indexes.

Although Memory tables are very fast, they often don't work well as a general-purpose replacement for disk-based tables. They use table-level locking, which gives low write concurrency, and they do not support TEXT or BLOB column types. They also support only fixed-size rows, so they really store VARCHARs as CHARs, which can waste memory.

MySQL uses the Memory engine internally while processing queries that require a temporary table to hold intermediate results. If the intermediate result becomes too large for a Memory table, or has TEXT or BLOB columns, MySQL will convert it to a MyISAM table on disk. We say more about this in later chapters.

People often confuse Memory tables with temporary tables, which are ephemeral tables created with CREATE TEMPORARY TABLE. Temporary tables can use any storage engine; they are not the same thing as tables that use the Memory storage engine. Temporary tables are visible only to a single connection and disappear entirely when the connection closes.

The Archive Engine

The Archive engine supports only INSERT and SELECT queries, and it does not support indexes. It causes much less disk I/O than MyISAM, because it buffers data writes and compresses each row with *zlib* as it's inserted. Also, each SELECT query requires a full table scan. Archive tables are thus ideal for logging and data acquisition, where analysis tends to scan an entire table, or where you want fast INSERT queries on a replication master. Replication slaves can use a different storage engine for the same table, which means the table on the slave can have indexes for faster performance on analysis. (See Chapter 8 for more about replication.)

Archive supports row-level locking and a special buffer system for high-concurrency inserts. It gives consistent reads by stopping a SELECT after it has retrieved the number of rows that existed in the table when the query began. It also makes bulk inserts invisible until they're complete. These features emulate some aspects of transactional and MVCC behaviors, but Archive is not a transactional storage engine. It is simply a storage engine that's optimized for high-speed inserting and compressed storage.

The CSV Engine

The CSV engine can treat comma-separated values (CSV) files as tables, but it does not support indexes on them. This engine lets you copy files in and out of the database while the server is running. If you export a CSV file from a spreadsheet and save it in the MySQL server's data directory, the server can read it immediately. Similarly, if you write data to a CSV table, an external program can read it right away. CSV tables are especially useful as a data interchange format and for certain kinds of logging.

The Federated Engine

The Federated engine does not store data locally. Each Federated table refers to a table on a remote MySQL server, so it actually connects to a remote server for all operations. It is sometimes used to enable "hacks" such as tricks with replication.

There are many oddities and limitations in the current implementation of this engine. Because of the way the Federated engine works, we think it is most useful for single-row lookups by primary key, or for INSERT queries you want to affect a remote server. It does not perform well for aggregate queries, joins, or other basic operations.

The Blackhole Engine

The Blackhole engine has no storage mechanism at all. It discards every INSERT instead of storing it. However, the server writes queries against Blackhole tables to its logs as usual, so they can be replicated to slaves or simply kept in the log. That makes the Blackhole engine useful for fancy replication setups and audit logging.

The NDB Cluster Engine

MySQL AB acquired the NDB Cluster engine from Sony Ericsson in 2003. It was originally designed for high speed (real-time performance requirements), with redundancy and load-balancing capabilities. Although it logged to disk, it kept all its data in memory and was optimized for primary key lookups. MySQL has since added other indexing methods and many optimizations, and MySQL 5.1 allows some columns to be stored on disk.

The NDB architecture is unique: an NDB cluster is completely unlike, for example, an Oracle cluster. NDB's infrastructure is based on a shared-nothing concept. There is no storage area network or other big centralized storage solution, which some other types of clusters rely on. An NDB database consists of data nodes, management nodes, and SQL nodes (MySQL instances). Each data node holds a segment ("fragment") of the cluster's data. The fragments are duplicated, so the system has multiple copies of the same data on different nodes. One physical server is usually dedicated to each node for redundancy and high availability. In this sense, NDB is similar to RAID at the server level.

The management nodes are used to retrieve the centralized configuration, and for monitoring and control of the cluster nodes. All data nodes communicate with each other, and all MySQL servers connect to all data nodes. Low network latency is critically important for NDB Cluster.

A word of warning: NDB Cluster is very "cool" technology and definitely worth some exploration to satisfy your curiosity, but many technical people tend to look for excuses to use it and attempt to apply it to needs for which it's not suitable. In our experience, even after studying it carefully, many people don't really learn what this engine is useful for and how it works until they've installed it and used it for a while. This commonly results in much wasted time, because it is simply not designed as a general-purpose storage engine.

One common shock is that NDB currently performs joins at the MySQL server level, not in the storage engine layer. Because all data for NDB must be retrieved over the network, complex joins are extremely slow. On the other hand, single-table lookups can be very fast, because multiple data nodes each provide part of the result. This is just one of many aspects you'll have to consider and understand thoroughly when looking at NDB Cluster for a particular application.

NDB Cluster is so large and complex that we won't discuss it further in this book. You should seek out a book dedicated to the topic if you are interested in it. We will say, however, that it's generally not what you think it is, and for most traditional applications, it is not the answer.

The Falcon Engine

Jim Starkey, a database pioneer whose earlier inventions include Interbase, MVCC, and the BLOB column type, designed the Falcon engine. MySQL AB acquired the Falcon technology in 2006, and Jim currently works for MySQL AB.

Falcon is designed for today's hardware—specifically, for servers with multiple 64-bit processors and plenty of memory—but it can also operate in more modest environments. Falcon uses MVCC and tries to keep running transactions entirely in memory. This makes rollbacks and recovery operations extremely fast.

Falcon is unfinished at the time of this writing (for example, it doesn't yet synchronize its commits with the binary log), so we can't write about it with much authority. Even the initial benchmarks we've done with it will probably be outdated when it's ready for general use. It appears to have good potential for many online applications, but we'll know more about it as time passes.

The solidDB Engine

The solidDB engine, developed by Solid Information Technology (*http://www.soliddb.com*), is a transactional engine that uses MVCC. It supports both pessimistic and optimistic concurrency control, which no other engine currently does. solidDB for MySQL includes full foreign key support. It is similar to InnoDB in many ways, such as its use of clustered indexes. solidDB for MySQL includes an online backup capability at no charge.

The solidDB for MySQL product is a complete package that consists of the solidDB storage engine, the MyISAM storage engine, and MySQL server. The "glue" between the solidDB storage engine and the MySQL server was introduced in late 2006. However, the underlying technology and code have matured over the company's 15-year history. Solid certifies and supports the entire product. It is licensed under the GPL and offered commercially under a dual-licensing model that is identical to the MySQL server's.

The PBXT (Primebase XT) Engine

The PBXT engine, developed by Paul McCullagh of SNAP Innovation GmbH in Hamburg, Germany (*http://www.primebase.com*), is a transactional storage engine with a unique design. One of its distinguishing characteristics is how it uses its transaction logs and data files to avoid write-ahead logging, which reduces much of the overhead of transaction commits. This architecture gives PBXT the potential to deal with very high write concurrency, and tests have already shown that it can be faster than InnoDB for certain operations. PBXT uses MVCC and supports foreign key constraints, but it does not use clustered indexes.

PBXT is a fairly new engine, and it will need to prove itself further in production environments. For example, its implementation of truly durable transactions was completed only recently, while we were writing this book.

As an extension to PBXT, SNAP Innovation is working on a scalable "blob streaming" infrastructure (*http://www.blobstreaming.org*). It is designed to store and retrieve large chunks of binary data efficiently.

The Maria Storage Engine

Maria is a new storage engine being developed by some of MySQL's top engineers, including Michael Widenius, who created MySQL. The initial 1.0 release includes only some of its planned features.

The goal is to use Maria as a replacement for MyISAM, which is currently MySQL's default storage engine, and which the server uses internally for tasks such as privilege tables and temporary tables created while executing queries. Here are some highlights from the roadmap:

- The option of either transactional or nontransactional storage, on a per-table basis
- Crash recovery, even when a table is running in nontransactional mode
- Row-level locking and MVCC
- Better BLOB handling

Other Storage Engines

Various third parties offer other (sometimes proprietary) engines, and there are a myriad of special-purpose and experimental engines out there (for example, an engine for querying web services). Some of these engines are developed informally, perhaps by just one or two engineers. This is because it's relatively easy to create a storage engine for MySQL. However, most such engines aren't widely publicized, in part because of their limited applicability. We'll leave you to explore these offerings on your own.

Selecting the Right Engine

When designing MySQL-based applications, you should decide which storage engine to use for storing your data. If you don't think about this during the design phase, you will likely face complications later in the process. You might find that the default engine doesn't provide a feature you need, such as transactions, or maybe the mix of read and write queries your application generates will require more granular locking than MyISAM's table locks.

Because you can choose storage engines on a table-by-table basis, you'll need a clear idea of how each table will be used and the data it will store. It also helps to have a good understanding of the application as a whole and its potential for growth. Armed with this information, you can begin to make good choices about which storage engines can do the job.

 It's not necessarily a good idea to use different storage engines for different tables. If you can get away with it, it will usually make your life a lot easier if you choose one storage engine for all your tables.

Considerations

Although many factors can affect your decision about which storage engine(s) to use, it usually boils down to a few primary considerations. Here are the main elements you should take into account:

Transactions

If your application requires transactions, InnoDB is the most stable, well-integrated, proven choice at the time of this writing. However, we expect to see the up-and-coming transactional engines become strong contenders as time passes.

MyISAM is a good choice if a task doesn't require transactions and issues primarily either SELECT or INSERT queries. Sometimes specific components of an application (such as logging) fall into this category.

Concurrency

How best to satisfy your concurrency requirements depends on your workload. If you just need to insert and read concurrently, believe it or not, MyISAM is a fine choice! If you need to allow a mixture of operations to run concurrently without interfering with each other, one of the engines with row-level locking should work well.

Backups

The need to perform regular backups may also influence your table choices. If your server can be shut down at regular intervals for backups, the storage engines are equally easy to deal with. However, if you need to perform online backups in one form or another, the choices become less clear. Chapter 11 deals with this topic in more detail.

Also bear in mind that using multiple storage engines increases the complexity of backups and server tuning.

Crash recovery

> If you have a lot of data, you should seriously consider how long it will take to recover from a crash. MyISAM tables generally become corrupt more easily and take much longer to recover than InnoDB tables, for example. In fact, this is one of the most important reasons why a lot of people use InnoDB when they don't need transactions.

Special features

> Finally, you sometimes find that an application relies on particular features or optimizations that only some of MySQL's storage engines provide. For example, a lot of applications rely on clustered index optimizations. At the moment, that limits you to InnoDB and solidDB. On the other hand, only MyISAM supports full-text search inside MySQL. If a storage engine meets one or more critical requirements, but not others, you need to either compromise or find a clever design solution. You can often get what you need from a storage engine that seemingly doesn't support your requirements.

You don't need to decide right now. There's a lot of material on each storage engine's strengths and weaknesses in the rest of the book, and lots of architecture and design tips as well. In general, there are probably more options than you realize yet, and it might help to come back to this question after reading more.

Practical Examples

These issues may seem rather abstract without some sort of real-world context, so let's consider some common database applications. We'll look at a variety of tables and determine which engine best matches with each table's needs. We give a summary of the options in the next section.

Logging

Suppose you want to use MySQL to log a record of every telephone call from a central telephone switch in real time. Or maybe you've installed *mod_log_sql* for Apache, so you can log all visits to your web site directly in a table. In such an application, speed is probably the most important goal; you don't want the database to be the bottleneck. The MyISAM and Archive storage engines would work very well because they have very low overhead and can insert thousands of records per second. The PBXT storage engine is also likely to be particularly suitable for logging purposes.

Things will get interesting, however, if you decide it's time to start running reports to summarize the data you've logged. Depending on the queries you use, there's a good chance that gathering data for the report will significantly slow the process of inserting records. What can you do?

One solution is to use MySQL's built-in replication feature to clone the data onto a second (slave) server, and then run your time- and CPU-intensive queries against the data on the slave. This leaves the master free to insert records and lets you run any query you want on the slave without worrying about how it might affect the real-time logging.

You can also run queries at times of low load, but don't rely on this strategy continuing to work as your application grows.

Another option is to use a Merge table. Rather than always logging to the same table, adjust the application to log to a table that contains the year and name or number of the month in its name, such as web_logs_2008_01 or web_logs_2008_jan. Then define a Merge table that contains the data you'd like to summarize and use it in your queries. If you need to summarize data daily or weekly, the same strategy works; you just need to create tables with more specific names, such as web_logs_2008_01_01. While you're busy running queries against tables that are no longer being written to, your application can log records to its current table uninterrupted.

Read-only or read-mostly tables

Tables that contain data used to construct a catalog or listing of some sort (jobs, auctions, real estate, etc.) are usually read from far more often than they are written to. This makes them good candidates for MyISAM—if you don't mind what happens when MyISAM crashes. Don't underestimate how important this is; a lot of users don't really understand how risky it is to use a storage engine that doesn't even try very hard to get their data written to disk.

It's an excellent idea to run a realistic load simulation on a test server and then literally pull the power plug. The firsthand experience of recovering from a crash is priceless. It saves nasty surprises later.

Don't just believe the common "MyISAM is faster than InnoDB" folk wisdom. It is *not* categorically true. We can name dozens of situations where InnoDB leaves MyISAM in the dust, especially for applications where clustered indexes are useful or where the data fits in memory. As you read the rest of this book, you'll get a sense of which factors influence a storage engine's performance (data size, number of I/O operations required, primary keys versus secondary indexes, etc.), and which of them matter to your application.

Order processing

When you deal with any sort of order processing, transactions are all but required. Half-completed orders aren't going to endear customers to your service. Another important consideration is whether the engine needs to support foreign key constraints. At the time of this writing, InnoDB is likely to be your best bet for order-processing applications, though any of the transactional storage engines is a candidate.

Stock quotes

If you're collecting stock quotes for your own analysis, MyISAM works great, with the usual caveats. However, if you're running a high-traffic web service that has a real-time quote feed and thousands of users, a query should never have to wait. Many clients could be trying to read and write to the table simultaneously, so row-level locking or a design that minimizes updates is the way to go.

Bulletin boards and threaded discussion forums

Threaded discussions are an interesting problem for MySQL users. There are hundreds of freely available PHP and Perl-based systems that provide threaded discussions. Many of them aren't written with database efficiency in mind, so they tend to run a lot of queries for each request they serve. Some were written to be database independent, so their queries do not take advantage of the features of any one database system. They also tend to update counters and compile usage statistics about the various discussions. Many of the systems also use a few monolithic tables to store all their data. As a result, a few central tables become the focus of heavy read and write activity, and the locks required to enforce consistency become a substantial source of contention.

Despite their design shortcomings, most of the systems work well for small and medium loads. However, if a web site grows large enough and generates significant traffic, it may become very slow. The obvious solution is to switch to a different storage engine that can handle the heavy read/write volume, but users who attempt this are sometimes surprised to find that the systems run even more slowly than they did before!

What these users don't realize is that the system is using a particular query, normally something like this:

```
mysql> SELECT COUNT(*) FROM table;
```

The problem is that not all engines can run that query quickly: MyISAM can, but other engines may not. There are similar examples for every engine. Chapter 2 will help you keep such a situation from catching you by surprise and show you how to find and fix the problems if it does.

CD-ROM applications

If you ever need to distribute a CD-ROM- or DVD-ROM-based application that uses MySQL data files, consider using MyISAM or compressed MyISAM tables, which can easily be isolated and copied to other media. Compressed MyISAM tables use far less space than uncompressed ones, but they are read-only. This can be problematic in certain applications, but because the data is going to be on read-only media anyway, there's little reason not to use compressed tables for this particular task.

Storage Engine Summary

Table 1-3 summarizes the transaction- and locking-related traits of MySQL's most popular storage engines. The MySQL version column shows the minimum MySQL version you'll need to use the engine, though for some engines and MySQL versions you may have to compile your own server. The word "All" in this column indicates all versions since MySQL 3.23.

Table 1-3. MySQL storage engine summary

Storage engine	MySQL version	Transactions	Lock granularity	Key applications	Counter-indications
MyISAM	All	No	Table with concurrent inserts	SELECT, INSERT, bulk loading	Mixed read/write workload
MyISAM Merge	All	No	Table with concurrent inserts	Segmented archiving, data warehousing	Many global lookups
Memory (HEAP)	All	No	Table	Intermediate calculations, static lookup data	Large datasets, persistent storage
InnoDB	All	Yes	Row-level with MVCC	Transactional processing	None
Falcon	6.0	Yes	Row-level with MVCC	Transactional processing	None
Archive	4.1	Yes	Row-level with MVCC	Logging, aggregate analysis	Random access needs, updates, deletes
CSV	4.1	No	Table	Logging, bulk loading of external data	Random access needs, indexing
Blackhole	4.1	Yes	Row-level with MVCC	Logged or replicated archiving	Any but the intended use
Federated	5.0	N/A	N/A	Distributed data sources	Any but the intended use
NDB Cluster	5.0	Yes	Row-level	High availability	Most typical uses
PBXT	5.0	Yes	Row-level with MVCC	Transactional processing, logging	Need for clustered indexes
solidDB	5.0	Yes	Row-level with MVCC	Transactional processing	None
Maria (planned)	6.x	Yes	Row-level with MVCC	MyISAM replacement	None

Table Conversions

There are several ways to convert a table from one storage engine to another, each with advantages and disadvantages. In the following sections, we cover three of the most common ways.

ALTER TABLE

The easiest way to move a table from one engine to another is with an ALTER TABLE statement. The following command converts mytable to Falcon:

```
mysql> ALTER TABLE mytable ENGINE = Falcon;
```

This syntax works for all storage engines, but there's a catch: it can take a lot of time. MySQL will perform a row-by-row copy of your old table into a new table. During that time, you'll probably be using all of the server's disk I/O capacity, and the original table will be read-locked while the conversion runs. So, take care before trying this technique on a busy table. Instead, you can use one of the methods discussed next, which involve making a copy of the table first.

When you convert from one storage engine to another, any storage engine-specific features are lost. For example, if you convert an InnoDB table to MyISAM and back again, you will lose any foreign keys originally defined on the InnoDB table.

Dump and import

To gain more control over the conversion process, you might choose to first dump the table to a text file using the *mysqldump* utility. Once you've dumped the table, you can simply edit the dump file to adjust the CREATE TABLE statement it contains. Be sure to change the table name as well as its type, because you can't have two tables with the same name in the same database even if they are of different types—and *mysqldump* defaults to writing a DROP TABLE command before the CREATE TABLE, so you might lose your data if you are not careful!

See Chapter 11 for more advice on dumping and reloading data efficiently.

CREATE and SELECT

The third conversion technique is a compromise between the first mechanism's speed and the safety of the second. Rather than dumping the entire table or converting it all at once, create the new table and use MySQL's INSERT ... SELECT syntax to populate it, as follows:

```
mysql> CREATE TABLE innodb_table LIKE myisam_table;
mysql> ALTER TABLE innodb_table ENGINE=InnoDB;
mysql> INSERT INTO innodb_table SELECT * FROM myisam_table;
```

That works well if you don't have much data, but if you do, it's often more efficient to populate the table incrementally, committing the transaction between each chunk so the undo logs don't grow huge. Assuming that id is the primary key, run this query repeatedly (using larger values of x and y each time) until you've copied all the data to the new table:

```
mysql> START TRANSACTION;
mysql> INSFRT INTO innodb_table SELECT * FROM myisam_table
    -> WHERE id BETWEEN x AND y;
mysql> COMMIT;
```

After doing so, you'll be left with the original table, which you can drop when you're done with it, and the new table, which is now fully populated. Be careful to lock the original table if needed to prevent getting an inconsistent copy of the data!

CHAPTER 2
Finding Bottlenecks: Benchmarking and Profiling

At some point, you're bound to need more performance from MySQL. But what should you try to improve? A particular query? Your schema? Your hardware? The only way to know is to measure what your system is doing, and test its performance under various conditions. That's why we put this chapter early in the book.

The best strategy is to find and strengthen the weakest link in your application's chain of components. This is especially useful if you don't know what prevents better performance—or what will prevent better performance in the future.

Benchmarking and *profiling* are two essential practices for finding bottlenecks. They are related, but they're not the same. A benchmark measures your system's performance. This can help determine a system's capacity, show you which changes matter and which don't, or show how your application performs with different data.

In contrast, profiling helps you find where your application spends the most time or consumes the most resources. In other words, benchmarking answers the question "How well does this perform?" and profiling answers the question "Why does it perform the way it does?"

We've arranged this chapter in two parts, the first about benchmarking and the second about profiling. We begin with a discussion of reasons and strategies for benchmarking, then move on to specific benchmarking tactics. We show you how to plan and design benchmarks, design for accurate results, run benchmarks, and analyze the results. We end the first part with a look at benchmarking tools and examples of how to use several of them.

The rest of the chapter shows how to profile both applications and MySQL. We show detailed examples of real-life profiling code we've used in production to help analyze application performance. We also show you how to log MySQL's queries, analyze the logs, and use MySQL's status counters and other tools to see what MySQL and your queries are doing.

Why Benchmark?

Many medium to large MySQL deployments have staff dedicated to benchmarking. However, every developer and DBA should be familiar with basic benchmarking principles and practices, because they're broadly useful. Here are some things benchmarks can help you do:

- Measure how your application currently performs. If you don't know how fast it currently runs, you can't be sure any changes you make are helpful. You can also use historical benchmark results to diagnose problems you didn't foresee.

- Validate your system's scalability. You can use a benchmark to simulate a much higher load than your production systems handle, such as a thousand-fold increase in the number of users.

- Plan for growth. Benchmarks help you estimate how much hardware, network capacity, and other resources you'll need for your projected future load. This can help reduce risk during upgrades or major application changes.

- Test your application's ability to tolerate a changing environment. For example, you can find out how your application performs during a sporadic peak in concurrency or with a different configuration of servers, or you can see how it handles a different data distribution.

- Test different hardware, software, and operating system configurations. Is RAID 5 or RAID 10 better for your system? How does random write performance change when you switch from ATA disks to SAN storage? Does the 2.4 Linux kernel scale better than the 2.6 series? Does a MySQL upgrade help performance? What about using a different storage engine for your data? You can answer these questions with special benchmarks.

You can also use benchmarks for other purposes, such as to create a unit test suite for your application, but we focus only on performance-related aspects here.

Benchmarking Strategies

There are two primary benchmarking strategies: you can benchmark the application as a whole, or isolate MySQL. These two strategies are known as *full-stack* and *single-component* benchmarking, respectively. There are several reasons to measure the application as a whole instead of just MySQL:

- You're testing the entire application, including the web server, the application code, and the database. This is useful because you don't care about MySQL's performance in particular; you care about the whole application.

- MySQL is not always the application bottleneck, and a full-stack benchmark can reveal this.

- Only by testing the full application can you see how each part's cache behaves.

- Benchmarks are good only to the extent that they reflect your actual application's behavior, which is hard to do when you're testing only part of it.

On the other hand, application benchmarks can be hard to create and even harder to set up correctly. If you design the benchmark badly, you can end up making bad decisions, because the results don't reflect reality.

Sometimes, however, you don't really want to know about the entire application. You may just need a MySQL benchmark, at least initially. Such a benchmark is useful if:

- You want to compare different schemas or queries.

- You want to benchmark a specific problem you see in the application.

- You want to avoid a long benchmark in favor of a shorter one that gives you a faster "cycle time" for making and measuring changes.

It's also useful to benchmark MySQL when you can repeat your application's queries against a real dataset. The data itself and the dataset's size both need to be realistic. If possible, use a snapshot of actual production data.

Unfortunately, setting up a realistic benchmark can be complicated and time-consuming, and if you can get a copy of the production dataset, count yourself lucky. Of course, this might be impossible—for example, you might be developing a new application that has few users and little data. If you want to know how it'll perform when it grows very large, you'll have no option but to simulate the larger application's data and workload.

What to Measure

You need to identify your goals before you start benchmarking—indeed, before you even design your benchmarks. Your goals will determine the tools and techniques you'll use to get accurate, meaningful results. Frame your goals as a questions, such as "Is this CPU better than that one?" or "Do the new indexes work better than the current ones?"

It might not be obvious, but you sometimes need different approaches to measure different things. For example, latency and throughput might require different benchmarks.

Consider some of the following measurements and how they fit your performance goals:

Transactions per time unit
    This is one of the all-time classics for benchmarking database applications. Standardized benchmarks such as TPC-C (see *http://www.tpc.org*) are widely quoted,

and many database vendors work very hard to do well on them. These benchmarks measure online transaction processing (OLTP) performance and are most suitable for interactive multiuser applications. The usual unit of measurement is transactions per second.

The term *throughput* usually means the same thing as transactions (or another unit of work) per time unit.

Response time or latency

This measures the total time a task requires. Depending on your application, you might need to measure time in milliseconds, seconds, or minutes. From this you can derive average, minimum, and maximum response times.

Maximum response time is rarely a useful metric, because the longer the benchmark runs, the longer the maximum response time is likely to be. It's also not at all repeatable, as it's likely to vary widely between runs. For this reason, many people use *percentile response times* instead. For example, if the 95th percentile response time is 5 milliseconds, you know that the task finishes in less than 5 milliseconds 95% of the time.

It's usually helpful to graph the results of these benchmarks, either as lines (for example, the average and 95th percentile) or as a scatter plot so you can see how the results are distributed. These graphs help show how the benchmarks will behave in the long run.

Suppose your system does a checkpoint for one minute every hour. During the checkpoint, the system stalls and no transactions complete. The 95th percentile response time will not show the spikes, so the results will hide the problem. However, a graph will show periodic spikes in the response time. Figure 2-1 illustrates this.

Figure 2-1 shows the number of transactions per minute (NOTPM). This line shows significant spikes, which the overall average (the dotted line) doesn't show at all. The first spike is because the server's caches are cold. The other spikes show when the server spends time intensively flushing dirty pages to the disk. Without the graph, these aberrations are hard to see.

Scalability

Scalability measurements are useful for systems that need to maintain performance under a changing workload.

"Performance under a changing workload" is a fairly abstract concept. Performance is typically measured by a metric such as throughput or response time, and the workload may vary along with changes in database size, number of concurrent connections, or hardware.

Scalability measurements are good for capacity planning, because they can show weaknesses in your application that other benchmark strategies won't show. For

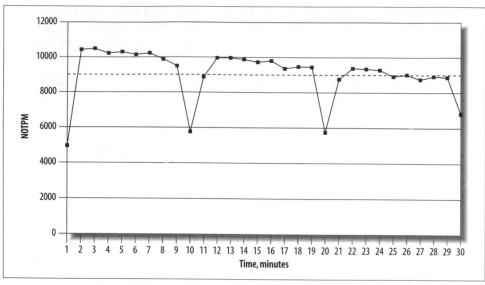

Figure 2-1. Results from a 30-minute dbt2 benchmark run

example, if you design your system to perform well on a response-time benchmark with a single connection (a poor benchmark strategy), your application might perform badly when there's any degree of concurrency. A benchmark that looks for consistent response times under an increasing number of connections would show this design flaw.

Some activities, such as batch jobs to create summary tables from granular data, just need fast response times, period. It's fine to benchmark them for pure response time, but remember to think about how they'll interact with other activities. Batch jobs can cause interactive queries to suffer, and vice versa.

Concurrency

Concurrency is an important but frequently misused and misunderstood metric. For example, it's popular to say how many users are browsing a web site at the same time. However, HTTP is stateless and most users are simply reading what's displayed in their browsers, so this doesn't translate into concurrency on the web server. Likewise, concurrency on the web server doesn't necessarily translate to the database server; the only thing it directly relates to is how much data your session storage mechanism must be able to handle. A more accurate measurement of concurrency on the web server is how many requests per second the users generate at the peak time.

You can measure concurrency at different places in the application, too. The higher concurrency on the web server may cause higher concurrency at the database level, but the language and toolset will influence this. For example, Java with a connection pool will probably cause a lower number of concurrent connections to the MySQL server than PHP with persistent connections.

More important still is the number of connections that are running queries at a given time. A well-designed application might have hundreds of connections open to the MySQL server, but only a fraction of these should be running queries at the same time. Thus, a web site with "50,000 users at a time" might require only 10 or 15 simultaneously running queries on the MySQL server!

In other words, what you should really care about benchmarking is the *working concurrency*, or the number of threads or connections doing work simultaneously. Measure whether performance drops much when the concurrency increases; if it does, your application probably can't handle spikes in load.

You need to either make sure that performance doesn't drop badly, or design the application so it doesn't create high concurrency in the parts of the application that can't handle it. You generally want to limit concurrency at the MySQL server, with designs such as application queuing. See Chapter 10 for more on this topic.

Concurrency is completely different from response time and scalability: it's not a *result*, but rather a *property* of how you set up the benchmark. Instead of measuring the concurrency your application achieves, you measure the application's performance at various levels of concurrency.

In the final analysis, you should benchmark whatever is important to your users. Benchmarks measure performance, but "performance" means different things to different people. Gather some requirements (formally or informally) about how the system should scale, what acceptable response times are, what kind of concurrency you expect, and so on. Then try to design your benchmarks to account for all the requirements, without getting tunnel vision and focusing on some things to the exclusion of others.

Benchmarking Tactics

With the general behind us, let's move on to the specifics of how to design and execute benchmarks. Before we discuss how to do benchmarks well, though, let's look at some common mistakes that can lead to unusable or inaccurate results:

- Using a subset of the real data size, such as using only one gigabyte of data when the application will need to handle hundreds of gigabytes, or using the current dataset when you plan for the application to grow much larger.
- Using incorrectly distributed data, such as uniformly distributed data when the real system's data will have "hot spots." (Randomly generated data is often unrealistically distributed.)
- Using unrealistically distributed parameters, such as pretending that all user profiles are equally likely to be viewed.
- Using a single-user scenario for a multiuser application.

- Benchmarking a distributed application on a single server.

- Failing to match real user behavior, such as "think time" on a web page. Real users request a page and then read it; they don't click on links one after another without pausing.

- Running identical queries in a loop. Real queries aren't identical, so they cause cache misses. Identical queries will be fully or partially cached at some level.

- Failing to check for errors. If a benchmark's results don't make sense—e.g., if a slow operation suddenly completes very quickly—check for errors. You might just be benchmarking how quickly MySQL can detect a syntax error in the SQL query! Always check error logs after benchmarks, as a matter of principle.

- Ignoring how the system performs when it's not warmed up, such as right after a restart. Sometimes you need to know how long it'll take your server to reach capacity after a restart, so you'll want to look specifically at the warm-up period. Conversely, if you intend to study normal performance, you'll need to be aware that if you benchmark just after a restart many caches will be cold, and the benchmark results won't reflect the results you'll get under load when the caches are warmed up.

- Using default server settings. See Chapter 6 for more on optimizing server settings.

Merely avoiding these mistakes will take you a long way toward improving the quality of your results.

All other things being equal, you should typically strive to make the tests as realistic as you can. Sometimes, though, it makes sense to use a slightly unrealistic benchmark. For example, say your application is on a different host from the database server. It would be more realistic to run the benchmarks in the same configuration, but doing so would add more variables, such as how fast and how heavily loaded the network is. Benchmarking on a single node is usually easier, and, in some cases, it's accurate enough. You'll have to use your judgment as to when this is appropriate.

Designing and Planning a Benchmark

The first step in planning a benchmark is to identify the problem and the goal. Next, decide whether to use a standard benchmark or design your own.

If you use a standard benchmark, be sure to choose one that matches your needs. For example, don't use TCP to benchmark an e-commerce system. In TCP's own words, TCP "illustrates decision support systems that examine large volumes of data." Therefore, it's not an appropriate benchmark for an OLTP system.

Designing your own benchmark is a complicated and iterative process. To get started, take a snapshot of your production data set. Make sure you can restore this data set for subsequent runs.

Next, you need queries to run against the data. You can make a unit test suite into a rudimentary benchmark just by running it many times, but that's unlikely to match how you really use the database. A better approach is to log all queries on your production system during a representative time frame, such as an hour during peak load or an entire day. If you log queries during a small time frame, you may need to choose several time frames. This will let you cover all system activities, such as weekly reporting queries or batch jobs you schedule during off-peak times.[*]

You can log queries at different levels. For example, you can log the HTTP requests on a web server if you need a full-stack benchmark. You can also enable MySQL's query log, but if you replay a query log, be sure to recreate the separate threads instead of just replaying each query linearly. It's also important to create a separate thread for each connection in the log, instead of shuffling queries among threads. The query log shows which connection ran each query.

Even if you don't build your own benchmark, you should write down your benchmarking plan. You're going to run the benchmark many times over, and you need to be able to reproduce it exactly. Plan for the future, too. You may not be the one who runs the benchmark the next time around, and even if you are, you may not remember exactly how you ran it the first time. Your plan should include the test data, the steps taken to set up the system, and the warm-up plan.

Design some method of documenting parameters and results, and document each run carefully. Your documentation method might be as simple as a spreadsheet or notebook, or as complex as a custom-designed database (keep in mind that you'll probably want to write some scripts to help analyze the results, so the easier it is to process the results without opening spreadsheets and text files, the better).

You may find it useful to make a benchmark directory with subdirectories for each run's results. You can then place the results, configuration files, and notes for each run in the appropriate subdirectory. If your benchmark lets you measure more than you think you're interested in, record the extra data anyway. It's much better to have unneeded data than to miss important data, and you might find the extra data useful in the future. Try to record as much additional information as you can during the benchmarks, such as CPU usage, disk I/O, and network traffic statistics; counters from SHOW GLOBAL STATUS; and so on.

Getting Accurate Results

The best way to get accurate results is to design your benchmark to answer the question you want to answer. Have you chosen the right benchmark? Are you capturing the data you need to answer the question? Are you benchmarking by the wrong crite-

---

[*] All this is provided that you want a perfect benchmark, of course. Real life usually gets in the way.

ria? For example, are you running a CPU-bound benchmark to predict the performance of an application you know will be I/O-bound?

Next, make sure your benchmark results will be repeatable. Try to ensure that the system is in the same state at the beginning of each run. If the benchmark is important, you should reboot between runs. If you need to benchmark on a warmed-up server, which is the norm, you should also make sure that your warm-up is long enough and that it's repeatable. If the warm-up consists of random queries, for example, your benchmark results will not be repeatable.

If the benchmark changes data or schema, reset it with a fresh snapshot between runs. Inserting into a table with a thousand rows will not give the same results as inserting into a table with a million rows! The data fragmentation and layout on disk can also make your results nonrepeatable. One way to make sure the physical layout is close to the same is to do a quick format and file copy of a partition.

Watch out for external load, profiling and monitoring systems, verbose logging, periodic jobs, and other factors that can skew your results. A typical surprise is a *cron* job that starts in the middle of a benchmark run, or a Patrol Read cycle or scheduled consistency check on your RAID card. Make sure all the resources the benchmark needs are dedicated to it while it runs. If something else is consuming network capacity, or if the benchmark runs on a SAN that's shared with other servers, your results might not be accurate.

Try to change as few parameters as possible each time you run a benchmark. This is called "isolating the variable" in science. If you must change several things at once, you risk missing something. Parameters can also be dependent on one another, so sometimes you can't change them independently. Sometimes you may not even know they are related, which adds to the complexity.*

It generally helps to change the benchmark parameters iteratively, rather than making dramatic changes between runs. For example, use techniques such as divide-and-conquer (halving the differences between runs) to hone in on a good value for a server setting.

We see a lot of benchmarks that try to predict performance after a migration, such as migrating from Oracle to MySQL. These are often troublesome, because MySQL performs well on completely different types of queries than Oracle. If you want to know how well an application built on Oracle will run after migrating it to MySQL, you usually need to redesign the schema and queries for MySQL. (In some cases, such as when you're building a cross-platform application, you might want to know how the same queries will run on both platforms, but that's unusual.)

---

* Sometimes, this doesn't really matter. For example, if you're thinking about migrating from a Solaris system on SPARC hardware to GNU/Linux on x86, there's no point in benchmarking Solaris on x86 as an intermediate step!

You can't get meaningful results from the default MySQL configuration settings either, because they're tuned for tiny applications that consume very little memory.

Finally, if you get a strange result, don't simply dismiss it as a bad data point. Investigate and try to find out what happened. You might find a valuable result, a huge problem, or a flaw in your benchmark design.

Running the Benchmark and Analyzing Results

Once you've prepared everything, you're ready to run the benchmark and begin gathering and analyzing data.

It's usually a good idea to automate the benchmark runs. Doing so will improve your results and their accuracy, because it will prevent you from forgetting steps or accidentally doing things differently on different runs. It will also help you document how to run the benchmark.

Any automation method will do; for example, a Makefile or a set of custom scripts. Choose whatever scripting language makes sense for you: shell, PHP, Perl, etc. Try to automate as much of the process as you can, including loading the data, warming up the system, running the benchmark, and recording the results.

 When you have it set up correctly, benchmarking can be a one-step process. If you're just running a one-off benchmark to check something quickly, you might not want to automate it.

You'll usually run a benchmark several times. Exactly how many runs you need depends on your scoring methodology and how important the results are. If you need greater certainty, you need to run the benchmark more times. Common practices are to look for the best result, average all the results, or just run the benchmark five times and average the three best results. You can be as precise as you want. You may want to apply statistical methods to your results, find the confidence interval, and so on, but you often don't need that level of certainty.* If it answers your question to your satisfaction, you can simply run the benchmark several times and see how much the results vary. If they vary widely, either run the benchmark more times or run it longer, which usually reduces variance.

Once you have your results, you need to analyze them—that is, turn the numbers into knowledge. The goal is to answer the question that frames the benchmark. Ideally, you'd like to be able to make a statement such as "Upgrading to four CPUs increases throughput by 50% with the same latency" or "The indexes made the queries faster."

---

* If you really need scientific, rigorous results, you should read a good book on how to design and execute controlled tests, as the subject is much larger than we can cover here.

How you "crunch the numbers" depends on how you collect the results. You should probably write scripts to analyze the results, not only to help reduce the amount of work required, but for the same reasons you should automate the benchmark itself: repeatability and documentation.

Benchmarking Tools

You don't have to roll your own benchmarking system, and in fact you shouldn't unless there's a good reason why you can't use one of the available ones. There are a wide variety of tools ready for you to use. We show you some of them in the following sections.

Full-Stack Tools

Recall that there are two types of benchmarks: full-stack and single-component. Not surprisingly, there are tools to benchmark full applications, and there are tools to stress-test MySQL and other components in isolation. Testing the full stack is usually a better way to get a clear picture of your system's performance. Existing full-stack tools include:

ab

> *ab* is a well-known Apache HTTP server benchmarking tool. It shows how many requests per second your HTTP server is capable of serving. If you are benchmarking a web application, this translates to how many requests per second the entire application can satisfy. It's a very simple tool, but its usefulness is also limited because it just hammers one URL as fast as it can. More information on *ab* is available at *http://httpd.apache.org/docs/2.0/programs/ab.html*.

http_load

> This tool is similar in concept to *ab*; it is also designed to load a web server, but it's more flexible. You can create an input file with many different URLs, and *http_load* will choose from among them at random. You can also instruct it to issue requests at a timed rate, instead of just running them as fast as it can. See *http://www.acme.com/software/http_load/* for more information.

JMeter

> JMeter is a Java application that can load another application and measure its performance. It was designed for testing web applications, but you can also use it to test FTP servers and issue queries to a database via JDBC.
>
> JMeter is much more complex than *ab* and *http_load*. For example, it has features that let you simulate real users more flexibly, by controlling such parameters as ramp-up time. It has a graphical user interface with built-in result graphing, and it offers the ability to record and replay results offline. For more information, see *http://jakarta.apache.org/jmeter/*.

Single-Component Tools

Here are some useful tools to test the performance of MySQL and the system on which it runs. We show example benchmarks with some of these tools in the next section:

mysqlslap

> *mysqlslap* (*http://dev.mysql.com/doc/refman/5.1/en/mysqlslap.html*) simulates load on the server and reports timing information. It is part of the MySQL 5.1 server distribution, but it should be possible to run it against MySQL 4.1 and newer servers. You can specify how many concurrent connections it should use, and you can give it either a SQL statement on the command line or a file containing SQL statements to run. If you don't give it statements, it can also auto-generate SELECT statements by examining the server's schema.

sysbench

> *sysbench* (*http://sysbench.sourceforge.net*) is a multithreaded system benchmarking tool. Its goal is to get a sense of system performance, in terms of the factors important for running a database server. For example, you can measure the performance of file I/O, the OS scheduler, memory allocation and transfer speed, POSIX threads, and the database server itself. *sysbench* supports scripting in the Lua language (*http://www.lua.org*), which makes it very flexible for testing a variety of scenarios.

Database Test Suite

> The Database Test Suite, designed by The Open-Source Development Labs (OSDL) and hosted on SourceForge at *http://sourceforge.net/projects/osdldbt/*, is a test kit for running benchmarks similar to some industry-standard benchmarks, such as those published by the Transaction Processing Performance Council (TPC). In particular, the *dbt2* test tool is a free (but uncertified) implementation of the TPC-C OLTP test. It supports InnoDB and Falcon; at the time of this writing, the status of other transactional MySQL storage engines is unknown.

MySQL Benchmark Suite (sql-bench)

> MySQL distributes its own benchmark suite with the MySQL server, and you can use it to benchmark several different database servers. It is single-threaded and measures how quickly the server executes queries. The results show which types of operations the server performs well.

> The main benefit of this benchmark suite is that it contains a lot of predefined tests that are easy to use, so it makes it easy to compare different storage engines or configurations. It's useful as a high-level benchmark, to compare the overall performance of two servers. You can also run a subset of its tests (for example, just testing UPDATE performance). The tests are mostly CPU-bound, but there are short periods that demand a lot of disk I/O.

The biggest disadvantages of this tool are that it's single-user, it uses a very small dataset, you can't test your site-specific data, and its results may vary between runs. Because it's single-threaded and completely serial, it will not help you assess the benefits of multiple CPUs, but it can help you compare single-CPU servers.

Perl and DBD drivers are required for the database server you wish to benchmark. Documentation is available at *http://dev.mysql.com/doc/en/mysql-benchmarks.html/*.

Super Smack

Super Smack (*http://vegan.net/tony/supersmack/*) is a benchmarking, stress-testing, and load-generating tool for MySQL and PostgreSQL. It is a complex, powerful tool that lets you simulate multiple users, load test data into the database, and populate tables with randomly generated data. Benchmarks are contained in "smack" files, which use a simple language to define clients, tables, queries, and so on.

Benchmarking Examples

In this section, we show you some examples of actual benchmarks with tools we mentioned in the preceding sections. We can't cover each tool exhaustively, but these examples should help you decide which benchmarks might be useful for your purposes and get you started using them.

http_load

Let's start with a simple example of how to use *http_load*, and use the following URLs, which we saved to a file called *urls.txt*:

```
http://www.mysqlperformanceblog.com/
http://www.mysqlperformanceblog.com/page/2/
http://www.mysqlperformanceblog.com/mysql-patches/
http://www.mysqlperformanceblog.com/mysql-performance-presentations/
http://www.mysqlperformanceblog.com/2006/09/06/slow-query-log-analyzes-tools/
```

The simplest way to use *http_load* is to simply fetch the URLs in a loop. The program fetches them as fast as it can:

```
$ http_load -parallel 1 -seconds 10 urls.txt
19 fetches, 1 max parallel, 837929 bytes, in 10.0003 seconds
44101.5 mean bytes/connection
1.89995 fetches/sec, 83790.7 bytes/sec
msecs/connect: 41.6647 mean, 56.156 max, 38.21 min
msecs/first-response: 320.207 mean, 508.958 max, 179.308 min
HTTP response codes:
  code 200 -- 19
```

MySQL's BENCHMARK( ) Function

MySQL has a handy BENCHMARK( ) function that you can use to test execution speeds for certain types of operations. You use it by specifying a number of times to execute and an expression to execute. The expression can be any scalar expression, such as a scalar subquery or a function. This is convenient for testing the relative speed of some operations, such as seeing whether MD5( ) is faster than SHA1( ):

```
mysql> SET @input := 'hello world';
mysql> SELECT BENCHMARK(1000000, MD5(@input));
+---------------------------------+
| BENCHMARK(1000000, MD5(@input)) |
+---------------------------------+
|                               0 |
+---------------------------------+
1 row in set (2.78 sec)
mysql> SELECT BENCHMARK(1000000, SHA1(@input));
+----------------------------------+
| BENCHMARK(1000000, SHA1(@input)) |
+----------------------------------+
|                                0 |
+----------------------------------+
1 row in set (3.50 sec)
```

The return value is always 0; you time the execution by looking at how long the client application reported the query took. In this case, it looks like MD5( ) is faster. However, using BENCHMARK( ) correctly is tricky unless you know what it's really doing. It simply measures how fast the server can execute the expression; it does not give any indication of the parsing and optimization overhead. And unless the expression includes a user variable, as in our example, the second and subsequent times the server executes the expression might be cache hits.[a]

Although it's handy, we don't use BENCHMARK( ) for real benchmarks. It's too hard to figure out what it really measures, and it's too narrowly focused on a small part of the overall execution process.

[a] One of the authors made this mistake and found that 10,000 executions of a certain expression ran just as fast as 1 execution. It was a cache hit. In general, this type of behavior should always make you suspect either a cache hit or an error.

The results are pretty self-explanatory; they simply show statistics about the requests. A slightly more complex usage scenario is to fetch the URLs as fast as possible in a loop, but emulate five concurrent users:

```
$ http_load -parallel 5 -seconds 10 urls.txt
94 fetches, 5 max parallel, 4.75565e+06 bytes, in 10.0005 seconds
50592 mean bytes/connection
9.39953 fetches/sec, 475541 bytes/sec
msecs/connect: 65.1983 mean, 169.991 max, 38.189 min
msecs/first-response: 245.014 mean, 993.059 max, 99.646 min
```

```
HTTP response codes:
    code 200 - 94
```

Alternatively, instead of fetching as fast as possible, we can emulate the load for a predicted rate of requests (such as five per second):

```
$ http_load -rate 5 -seconds 10 urls.txt
48 fetches, 4 max parallel, 2.50104e+06 bytes, in 10 seconds
52105 mean bytes/connection
4.8 fetches/sec, 250104 bytes/sec
msecs/connect: 42.5931 mean, 60.462 max, 38.117 min
msecs/first-response: 246.811 mean, 546.203 max, 108.363 min
HTTP response codes:
    code 200 - 48
```

Finally, we emulate even more load, with an incoming rate of 20 requests per second. Notice how the connect and response times increase with the higher load:

```
$ http_load -rate 20 -seconds 10 urls.txt
111 fetches, 89 max parallel, 5.91142e+06 bytes, in 10.0001 seconds
53256.1 mean bytes/connection
11.0998 fetches/sec, 591134 bytes/sec
msecs/connect: 100.384 mean, 211.885 max, 38.214 min
msecs/first-response: 2163.51 mean, 7862.77 max, 933.708 min
HTTP response codes:
    code 200 -- 111
```

sysbench

The *sysbench* tool can run a variety of benchmarks, which it refers to as "tests." It was designed to test not only database performance, but also how well a system is likely to perform as a database server. We start with some tests that aren't MySQL-specific and measure performance for subsystems that will determine the system's overall limits. Then we show you how to measure database performance.

The sysbench CPU benchmark

The most obvious subsystem test is the CPU benchmark, which uses 64-bit integers to calculate prime numbers up to a specified maximum. We run this on two servers, both running GNU/Linux, and compare the results. Here's the first server's hardware:

```
[server1 ~]$ cat /proc/cpuinfo
...
model name      : AMD Opteron(tm) Processor 246
stepping        : 1
cpu MHz         : 1992.857
cache size      : 1024 KB
```

And here's how to run the benchmark:

```
[server1 ~]$ sysbench --test=cpu --cpu-max-prime=20000 run
sysbench v0.4.8:  multi-threaded system evaluation benchmark
...
Test execution summary:
```

```
        total time:                              121.7404s
```

The second server has a different CPU:

```
[server2 ~]$ cat /proc/cpuinfo
...
model name      : Intel(R) Xeon(R) CPU            5130  @ 2.00GHz
stepping        : 6
cpu MHz         : 1995.005
```

Here's its benchmark result:

```
[server1 ~]$ sysbench --test=cpu --cpu-max-prime=20000 run
sysbench v0.4.8:  multi-threaded system evaluation benchmark
...
Test execution summary:
        total time:                              61.8596s
```

The result simply indicates the total time required to calculate the primes, which is very easy to compare. In this case, the second server ran the benchmark about twice as fast as the first server.

The sysbench file I/O benchmark

The fileio benchmark measures how your system performs under different kinds of I/O loads. It is very helpful for comparing hard drives, RAID cards, and RAID modes, and for tweaking the I/O subsystem.

The first stage in running this test is to prepare some files for the benchmark. You should generate much more data than will fit in memory. If the data fits in memory, the operating system will cache most of it, and the results will not accurately represent an I/O-bound workload. We begin by creating a dataset:

```
$ sysbench --test=fileio --file-total-size=150G prepare
```

The second step is to run the benchmark. Several options are available to test different types of I/O performance:

seqwr
> Sequential write

seqrewr
> Sequential rewrite

seqrd
> Sequential read

rndrd
> Random read

rndwr
> Random write

rndrw
> Combined random read/write

The following command runs the random read/write access file I/O benchmark:

```
$ sysbench --test=fileio --file-total-size=150G --file-test-mode=rndrw
--init-rnd=on --max-time=300 --max-requests=0 run
```

Here are the results:

```
sysbench v0.4.8:  multi-threaded system evaluation benchmark

Running the test with following options:
Number of threads: 1
Initializing random number generator from timer.

Extra file open flags: 0
128 files, 1.1719Gb each
150Gb total file size
Block size 16Kb
Number of random requests for random IO: 10000
Read/Write ratio for combined random IO test: 1.50
Periodic FSYNC enabled, calling fsync( ) each 100 requests.
Calling fsync( ) at the end of test, Enabled.
Using synchronous I/O mode
Doing random r/w test
Threads started!
Time limit exceeded, exiting...
Done.

Operations performed:  40260 Read, 26840 Write, 85785 Other = 152885 Total
Read 629.06Mb  Written 419.38Mb  Total transferred 1.0239Gb  (3.4948Mb/sec)
   223.67 Requests/sec executed

Test execution summary:
     total time:                     300.0004s
     total number of events:         67100
     total time taken by event execution: 254.4601
     per-request statistics:
         min:                        0.0000s
         avg:                        0.0038s
         max:                        0.5628s
         approx.  95 percentile:     0.0099s

Threads fairness:
     events (avg/stddev):        67100.0000/0.00
     execution time (avg/stddev):   254.4601/0.00
```

There's a lot of information in the output. The most interesting numbers for tuning the I/O subsystem are the number of requests per second and the total throughput. In this case, the results are 223.67 requests/sec and 3.4948 MB/sec, respectively. These values provide a good indication of disk performance.

When you're finished, you can run a cleanup to delete the files *sysbench* created for the benchmarks:

```
$ sysbench --test=fileio --file-total-size=150G cleanup
```

The sysbench OLTP benchmark

The OLTP benchmark emulates a transaction-processing workload. We show an example with a table that has a million rows. The first step is to prepare a table for the test:

```
$ sysbench --test=oltp --oltp-table-size=1000000 --mysql-db=test --mysql-user=root
prepare
sysbench v0.4.8:  multi-threaded system evaluation benchmark

No DB drivers specified, using mysql
Creating table 'sbtest'...
Creating 1000000 records in table 'sbtest'...
```

That's all you need to do to prepare the test data. Next, we run the benchmark in read-only mode for 60 seconds, with 8 concurrent threads:

```
$ sysbench --test=oltp --oltp-table-size=1000000 --mysql-db=test --mysql-user=root --
max-time=60 --oltp-read-only=on --max-requests=0 --num-threads=8 run
sysbench v0.4.8:  multi-threaded system evaluation benchmark

No DB drivers specified, using mysql
WARNING: Preparing of "BEGIN" is unsupported, using emulation
(last message repeated 7 times)
Running the test with following options:
Number of threads: 8

Doing OLTP test.
Running mixed OLTP test
Doing read-only test
Using Special distribution (12 iterations,  1 pct of values are returned in 75 pct
cases)
Using "BEGIN" for starting transactions
Using auto_inc on the id column
Threads started!
Time limit exceeded, exiting...
(last message repeated 7 times)
Done.

OLTP test statistics:
    queries performed:
        read:                  179606
        write:                 0
        other:                 25658
        total:                 205264
    transactions:              12829   (213.07 per sec.)
    deadlocks:                 0       (0.00 per sec.)
    read/write requests:       179606 (2982.92 per sec.)
    other operations:          25658   (426.13 per sec.)

Test execution summary:
    total time:                          60.2114s
    total number of events:              12829
    total time taken by event execution: 480.2086
```

```
per-request statistics:
      min:                         0.0030s
      avg:                         0.0374s
      max:                         1.9106s
      approx. 95 percentile:       0.1163s

Threads fairness:
    events (avg/stddev):        1603.6250/70.66
    execution time (avg/stddev):  60.0261/0.06
```

As before, there's quite a bit of information in the results. The most interesting parts are:

- The transaction count
- The rate of transactions per second
- The per-request statistics (minimal, average, maximal, and 95th percentile time)
- The thread-fairness statistics, which show how fair the simulated workload was

Other sysbench features

The *sysbench* tool can run several other system benchmarks that don't measure a database server's performance directly:

memory
> Exercises sequential memory reads or writes.

threads
> Benchmarks the thread scheduler's performance. This is especially useful to test the scheduler's behavior under high load.

mutex
> Measures mutex performance by emulating a situation where all threads run concurrently most of the time, acquiring mutex locks only briefly. (A mutex is a data structure that guarantees mutually exclusive access to some resource, preventing concurrent access from causing problems.)

seqwr
> Measures sequential write performance. This is very important for testing a system's practical performance limits. It can show how well your RAID controller's cache performs and alert you if the results are unusual. For example, if you have no battery-backed write cache but your disk achieves 3,000 requests per second, something is wrong, and your data is not safe.

In addition to the benchmark-specific mode parameter (*--test*), *sysbench* accepts some other common parameters, such as *--num-threads*, *--max-requests*, and *--max-time*. See the documentation for more information on these.

dbt2 TPC-C on the Database Test Suite

The Database Test Suite's *dbt2* tool is a free implementation of the TPC-C test. TPC-C is a specification published by the TPC organization that emulates a complex online transaction-processing load. It reports its results in transactions per minute (tpmC), along with the cost of each transaction (Price/tpmC). The results depend greatly on the hardware, so the published TPC-C results contain detailed specifications of the servers used in the benchmark.

 The *dbt2* test is not really TPC-C. It's not certified by TPC, and its results aren't directly comparable with TPC-C results.

Let's look at a sample of how to set up and run a *dbt2* benchmark. We used version 0.37 of *dbt2*, which is the most recent version we were able to use with MySQL (newer versions contain fixes that MySQL does not fully support). The following are the steps we took:

1. Prepare data.

   The following command creates data for 10 warehouses in the specified directory. The warehouses use a total of about 700 MB of space. The amount of space required will change in proportion to the number of warehouses, so you can change the *-w* parameter to create a dataset with the size you need.

   ```
   # src/datagen -w 10 -d /mnt/data/dbt2-w10
   warehouses = 10
   districts = 10
   customers = 3000
   items = 100000
   orders = 3000
   stock = 100000
   new_orders = 900

   Output directory of data files: /mnt/data/dbt2-w10

   Generating data files for 10 warehouse(s)...
   Generating item table data...
   Finished item table data...
   Generating warehouse table data...
   Finished warehouse table data...
   Generating stock table data...
   ```

2. Load data into the MySQL database.

   The following command creates a database named dbt2w10 and loads it with the data we generated in the previous step (*-d* is the database name and *-f* is the directory with the generated data):

   ```
   # scripts/mysql/mysql_load_db.sh -d dbt2w10 -f /mnt/data/dbt2-w10 -s /var/lib/
   mysql/mysql.sock
   ```

3. Run the benchmark.

The final step is to execute the following command from the *scripts* directory:

```
# run_mysql.sh -c 10 -w 10 -t 300 -n dbt2w10 -u root -o /var/lib/mysql/mysql.sock
-e
*************************************************************************
*                    DBT2 test for MySQL   started                      *
*                                                                        *
*            Results can be found in output/9 directory                  *
*************************************************************************
*                                                                        *
*  Test consists of 4 stages:                                            *
*                                                                        *
*  1. Start of client to create pool of databases connections            *
*  2. Start of driver to emulate terminals and transactions generation  *
*  3. Test                                                               *
*  4. Processing of results                                              *
*                                                                        *
*************************************************************************


DATABASE NAME:                  dbt2w10
DATABASE USER:                  root
DATABASE SOCKET:                /var/lib/mysql/mysql.sock
DATABASE CONNECTIONS:           10
TERMINAL THREADS:               100
SCALE FACTOR(WARHOUSES):        10
TERMINALS PER WAREHOUSE:        10
DURATION OF TEST(in sec):       300
SLEEPY in (msec)                300
ZERO DELAYS MODE:               1


Stage 1. Starting up client...
Delay for each thread - 300 msec. Will sleep for 4 sec to start 10 database
connections
CLIENT_PID = 12962


Stage 2. Starting up driver...
Delay for each thread - 300 msec. Will sleep for 34 sec to start 100 terminal
threads
All threads has spawned successfuly.


Stage 3. Starting of the test. Duration of the test 300 sec


Stage 4. Processing of results...
Shutdown clients. Send TERM signal to 12962.
  Response Time (s)
   Transaction      %  Average :  90th %  Total  Rollbacks     %
 ------------    -----  ---------------   ------  ---------   -----
      Delivery   3.53   2.224 :   3.059    1603         0    0.00
     New Order  41.24   0.659 :   1.175   18742       172    0.92
  Order Status   3.86   0.684 :   1.228    1756         0    0.00
       Payment  39.23   0.644 :   1.161   17827         0    0.00
   Stock Level   3.59   0.652 :   1.147    1630         0    0.00
```

```
3396.95 new-order transactions per minute (NOTPM)
5.5 minute duration
0 total unknown errors
31 second(s) ramping up
```

The most important result is this line near the end:

```
3396.95 new-order transactions per minute (NOTPM)
```

This shows how many transactions per minute the system can process; more is better. (The term "new-order" is not a special term for a type of transaction; it simply means the test simulated someone placing a new order on the imaginary e-commerce web site.)

You can change a few parameters to create different benchmarks:

-c The number of connections to the database. You can change this to emulate different levels of concurrency and see how the system scales.

-e This enables zero-delay mode, which means there will be no delay between queries. This stress-tests the database, but it can be unrealistic, as real users need some "think time" before generating new queries.

-t The total duration of the benchmark. Choose this time carefully, or the results will be meaningless. Too short a time for benchmarking an I/O-bound workload will give incorrect results, because the system will not have enough time to warm the caches and start to work normally. On the other hand, if you want to benchmark a CPU-bound workload, you shouldn't make the time too long, or the dataset may grow significantly and become I/O bound.

This benchmark's results can provide information on more than just performance. For example, if you see too many rollbacks, you'll know something is likely to be wrong.

MySQL Benchmark Suite

The MySQL Benchmark Suite consists of a set of Perl benchmarks, so you'll need Perl to run them. You'll find the benchmarks in the *sql-bench/* subdirectory in your MySQL installation. On Debian GNU/Linux systems, for example, they're in */usr/share/mysql/sql-bench/*.

Before getting started, read the included *README* file, which explains how to use the suite and documents the command-line arguments. To run all the tests, use commands like the following:

```
$ cd /usr/share/mysql/sql-bench/
sql-bench$ ./run-all-tests --server=mysql --user=root --log --fast
Test finished. You can find the result in:
output/RUN-mysql_fast-Linux_2.4.18_686_smp_i686
```

The benchmarks can take quite a while to run—perhaps over an hour, depending on your hardware and configuration. If you give the *--log* command-line option, you can monitor progress while they're running. Each test logs its results in a subdirectory named *output*. Each file contains a series of timings for the operations in each benchmark. Here's a sample, slightly reformatted for printing:

```
sql-bench$ tail -5 output/select-mysql_fast-Linux_2.4.18_686_smp_i686
Time for count_distinct_group_on_key (1000:6000):
   34  wallclock secs ( 0.20 usr  0.08 sys +  0.00 cusr  0.00 csys =  0.28 CPU)
Time for count_distinct_group_on_key_parts (1000:100000):
   34  wallclock secs ( 0.57 usr  0.27 sys +  0.00 cusr  0.00 csys =  0.84 CPU)
Time for count_distinct_group (1000:100000):
   34  wallclock secs ( 0.59 usr  0.20 sys +  0.00 cusr  0.00 csys =  0.79 CPU)
Time for count_distinct_big (100:1000000):
   8   wallclock secs ( 4.22 usr  2.20 sys +  0.00 cusr  0.00 csys =  6.42 CPU)
Total time:
   868 wallclock secs (33.24 usr  9.55 sys +  0.00 cusr  0.00 csys = 42.79 CPU)
```

As an example, the count_distinct_group_on_key (1000:6000) test took 34 wall-clock seconds to execute. That's the total amount of time the client took to run the test. The other values (usr, sys, cursr, csys) that added up to 0.28 seconds constitute the overhead for this test. That's how much of the time was spent running the benchmark client code, rather than waiting for the MySQL server's response. This means that the figure we care about—how much time was tied up by things outside the client's control—was 33.72 seconds.

Rather than running the whole suite, you can run the tests individually. For example, you may decide to focus on the insert test. This gives you more detail than the summary created by the full test suite:

```
sql-bench$ ./test-insert
Testing server 'MySQL 4.0.13 log' at 2003-05-18 11:02:39

Testing the speed of inserting data into 1 table and do some selects on it.
The tests are done with a table that has 100000 rows.

Generating random keys
Creating tables
Inserting 100000 rows in order
Inserting 100000 rows in reverse order
Inserting 100000 rows in random order
Time for insert (300000):
   42 wallclock secs ( 7.91 usr  5.03 sys +  0.00 cusr  0.00 csys = 12.94 CPU)
Testing insert of duplicates
Time for insert_duplicates (100000):
   16 wallclock secs ( 2.28 usr  1.89 sys +  0.00 cusr  0.00 csys =  4.17 CPU)
```

Profiling

Profiling shows you how much each part of a system contributes to the total cost of producing a result. The simplest cost metric is time, but profiling can also measure the number of function calls, I/O operations, database queries, and so forth. The goal is to understand why a system performs the way it does.

Profiling an Application

Just like with benchmarking, you can profile at the application level or on a single component, such as the MySQL server. Application-level profiling usually yields better insight into how to optimize the application and provides more accurate results, because the results include the work done by the whole application. For example, if you're interested in optimizing the application's MySQL queries, you might be tempted to just run and analyze the queries. However, if you do this, you'll miss a lot of important information about the queries, such as insights into the work the application has to do when reading results into memory and processing them.[*]

Because web applications are such a common use case for MySQL, we use a PHP web site as our example. You'll typically need to profile the application globally to see how the system is loaded, but you'll probably also want to isolate some subsystems of interest, such as the search function. Any expensive subsystem is a good candidate for profiling in isolation.

When we need to optimize how a PHP web site uses MySQL, we prefer to gather statistics at the granularity of objects (or modules) in the PHP code. The goal is to measure how much of each page's response time is consumed by database operations. Database access is often, but not always, the bottleneck in applications. Bottlenecks can also be caused by any of the following:

- External resources, such as calls to web services or search engines
- Operations that require processing large amounts of data in the application, such as parsing big XML files
- Expensive operations in tight loops, such as abusing regular expressions
- Badly optimized algorithms, such as naïve search algorithms to find items in lists

Before looking at MySQL queries, you should figure out the actual source of your performance problems. Application profiling can help you find the bottlenecks, and it's an important step in monitoring and improving overall performance.

How and what to measure

Time is an appropriate profiling metric for most applications, because the end user cares most about time. In web applications, we like to have a debug mode that

---

[*] If you're investigating a bottleneck, you might be able to take shortcuts and figure out where it is by examining some basic system statistics. If the web servers are idle and the MySQL server is at 100% CPU usage, you might not need to profile the whole application, especially if it's a crisis. You can look into the whole application after you fix the crisis.

makes each page display its queries along with their times and number of rows. We can then run EXPLAIN on slow queries (you'll find more information about EXPLAIN in later chapters). For deeper analysis, we combine this data with metrics from the MySQL server.

We recommend that you include profiling code in *every* new project you start. It might be hard to inject profiling code into an existing application, but it's easy to include it in new applications. Many libraries contain features that make it easy. For example, Java's JDBC and PHP's *mysqli* database access libraries have built-in features for profiling database access.

Profiling code is also invaluable for tracking down odd problems that appear only in production and can't be reproduced in development.

Your profiling code should gather and log at least the following:

- Total execution time, or "wall-clock time" (in web applications, this is the total page render time)
- Each query executed, and its execution time
- Each connection opened to the MySQL server
- Every call to an external resource, such as web services, *memcached*, and externally invoked scripts
- Potentially expensive function calls, such as XML parsing
- User and system CPU time

This information will help you monitor performance much more easily. It will give you insight into aspects of performance you might not capture otherwise, such as:

- Overall performance problems
- Sporadically increased response times
- System bottlenecks, which might not be MySQL
- Execution time of "invisible" users, such as search engine spiders

A PHP profiling example

To give you an idea of how easy and unobtrusive profiling a PHP web application can be, let's look at some code samples. The first example shows how to instrument the application, log the queries and other profiling data in a MySQL log table, and analyze the results.

To reduce the impact of logging, we capture all the logging information in memory, then write it to a single row when the page finishes executing. This is a better approach than logging every query individually, because logging every query doubles the number of queries you need to send to the MySQL server. Logging each bit of profiling data separately would actually make it harder to analyze bottlenecks, as you rarely have that much granularity to identify and troubleshoot problems in the application.

We start with the code you'll need to capture the profiling information. Here's a simplified example of a basic PHP 5 logging class, *class.Timer.php*, which uses built-in functions such as getrusage( ) to determine the script's resource usage:

```php
1   <?php
2   /*
3    * Class Timer, implementation of time logging in PHP
4    */
5
6   class Timer {
7     private $aTIMES = array( );
8
9     function startTime($point)
10    {
11      $dat = getrusage( );
12
13      $this->aTIMES[$point]['start'] = microtime(TRUE);
14      $this->aTIMES[$point]['start_utime'] =
15         $dat["ru_utime.tv_sec"]*1e6+$dat["ru_utime.tv_usec"];
16      $this->aTIMES[$point]['start_stime'] =
17         $dat["ru_stime.tv_sec"]*1e6+$dat["ru_stime.tv_usec"];
```

```
18    }
19
20    function stopTime($point, $comment='')
21    {
22      $dat = getrusage();
23      $this->aTIMES[$point]['end'] = microtime(TRUE);
24      $this->aTIMES[$point]['end_utime'] =
25        $dat["ru_utime.tv_sec"] * 1e6 + $dat["ru_utime.tv_usec"];
26      $this->aTIMES[$point]['end_stime'] =
27        $dat["ru_stime.tv_sec"] * 1e6 + $dat["ru_stime.tv_usec"];
28
29      $this->aTIMES[$point]['comment'] .= $comment;
30
31      $this->aTIMES[$point]['sum'] +=
32        $this->aTIMES[$point]['end'] - $this->aTIMES[$point]['start'];
33      $this->aTIMES[$point]['sum_utime'] +=
34        ($this->aTIMES[$point]['end_utime'] -
35          $this->aTIMES[$point]['start_utime']) / 1e6;
36      $this->aTIMES[$point]['sum_stime'] +=
37        ($this->aTIMES[$point]['end_stime'] -
38          $this->aTIMES[$point]['start_stime']) / 1e6;
39    }
40
41    function logdata() {
42
43      $query_logger = DBQueryLog::getInstance('DBQueryLog');
44      $data['utime'] = $this->aTIMES['Page']['sum_utime'];
45      $data['wtime'] = $this->aTIMES['Page']['sum'];
46      $data['stime'] = $this->aTIMES['Page']['sum_stime'];
47      $data['mysql_time'] = $this->aTIMES['MySQL']['sum'];
48      $data['mysql_count_queries'] = $this->aTIMES['MySQL']['cnt'];
49      $data['mysql_queries'] = $this->aTIMES['MySQL']['comment'];
50      $data['sphinx_time'] = $this->aTIMES['Sphinx']['sum'];
51
52      $query_logger->logProfilingData($data);
53
54    }
55
56    // This helper function implements the Singleton pattern
57    function getInstance() {
58      static $instance;
59
60      if(!isset($instance)) {
61        $instance = new Timer();
62      }
63
64      return($instance);
65    }
66  }
67  ?>
```

It's easy to use the Timer class in your application. You just need to wrap a timer around potentially expensive (or otherwise interesting) calls. For example, here's how to wrap a timer around every MySQL query. PHP's new `mysqli` interface lets you extend the basic `mysqli` class and redeclare the query method:

```php
68  <?php
69  class mysqlx extends mysqli {
70    function query($query, $resultmode) {
71      $timer = Timer::getInstance();
72      $timer->startTime('MySQL');
73      $res = parent::query($query, $resultmode);
74      $timer->stopTime('MySQL', "Query: $query\n");
75      return $res;
76    }
77  }
78  ?>
```

This technique requires very few code changes. You can simply change `mysqli` to `mysqlx` globally, and your whole application will begin logging all queries. You can use this approach to measure access to any external resource, such as queries to the Sphinx full-text search engine:

```php
$timer->startTime('Sphinx');
$this->sphinxres = $this->sphinx_client->Query ( $query, "index" );
$timer->stopTime('Sphinx', "Query: $query\n");
```

Next, let's see how to log the data you're gathering. This is an example of when it's wise to use the MyISAM or Archive storage engine. Either of these is a good candidate for storing logs. We use `INSERT DELAYED` when adding rows to the logs, so the `INSERT` will be executed as a background thread on the database server. This means the query will return instantly, so it won't perceptibly affect the application's response time. (Even if we don't use `INSERT DELAYED`, inserts will be concurrent unless we explicitly disable them, so external `SELECT` queries won't block the logging.) Finally, we hand-roll a date-based partitioning scheme by creating a new log table each day.

Here's a `CREATE TABLE` statement for our logging table:

```sql
CREATE TABLE logs.performance_log_template (
   ip                   INT UNSIGNED NOT NULL,
   page                 VARCHAR(255) NOT NULL,
   utime                FLOAT NOT NULL,
   wtime                FLOAT NOT NULL,
   mysql_time           FLOAT NOT NULL,
   sphinx_time          FLOAT NOT NULL,
   mysql_count_queries  INT UNSIGNED NOT NULL,
   mysql_queries        TEXT NOT NULL,
   stime                FLOAT NOT NULL,
   logged               TIMESTAMP NOT NULL
                        default CURRENT_TIMESTAMP on update CURRENT_TIMESTAMP,
   user_agent           VARCHAR(255) NOT NULL,
   referer              VARCHAR(255) NOT NULL
) ENGINE=ARCHIVE;
```

We never actually insert any data into this table; it's just a template for the CREATE TABLE LIKE statements we use to create the table for each day's data.

We explain more about this in Chapter 3, but for now, we'll just note that it's a good idea to use the smallest data type that can hold the desired data. We're using an unsigned integer to store the IP address. We're also using a 255-character column to store the page and the referrer. These values can be longer than 255 characters, but the first 255 are usually enough for our needs.

The final piece of the puzzle is logging the results when the page finishes executing. Here's the PHP code needed to log the data:

```
79  <?php
80  // Start of the page execution
81  $timer = Timer::getInstance();
82  $timer->startTime('Page');
83  // ... other code ...
84  // End of the page execution
85  $timer->stopTime('Page');
86  $timer->logdata();
87  ?>
```

The Timer class uses the DBQueryLog helper class, which is responsible for logging to the database and creating a new log table every day. Here's the code:

```
88   <?php
89   /*
90    * Class DBQueryLog logs profiling data into the database
91    */
92   class DBQueryLog {
93
94     // constructor, etc, etc...
95
96     /*
97      * Logs the data, creating the log table if it doesn't exist. Note
98      * that it's cheaper to assume the table exists, and catch the error
99      * if it doesn't, than to check for its existence with every query.
100     */
101    function logProfilingData($data) {
102      $table_name = "logs.performance_log_" . @date("ymd");
103
104      $query = "INSERT DELAYED INTO $table_name (ip, page, utime,
105              wtime, stime, mysql_time, sphinx_time, mysql_count_queries,
106              mysql_queries, user_agent, referer) VALUES  (.. data ..)";
107
108      $res = $this->mysqlx->query($query);
109      // Handle "table not found" error - create new table for each new day
110      if ((!$res) && ($this->mysqlx->errno == 1146)) { // 1146 is table not found
111        $res = $this->mysqlx->query(
112          "CREATE TABLE $table_name LIKE logs.performance_log_template");
113        $res = $this->mysqlx->query($query);
114      }
115    }
```

```
116  }
117  ?>
```

Once we've logged some data, we can analyze the logs. The beauty of using MySQL for logging is that you get the flexibility of SQL for analysis, so you can easily write queries to get any report you want from the logs. For instance, to find a few pages whose execution time was more than 10 seconds on the first day of February 2007:

```
mysql> SELECT page, wtime, mysql_time
    -> FROM performance_log_070201 WHERE wtime > 10 LIMIT 7;
+------------------------------------------------+---------+------------+
| page                                           | wtime   | mysql_time |
+------------------------------------------------+---------+------------+
| /page1.php                                     | 50.9295 |   0.000309 |
| /page1.php                                     | 32.0893 |   0.000305 |
| /page1.php                                     | 40.4209 |   0.000302 |
| /page3.php                                     | 11.5834 |   0.000306 |
| /login.php                                     | 28.5507 |    28.5257 |
| /access.php                                    | 13.0308 |    13.0064 |
| /page4.php                                     | 32.0687 |   0.000333 |
+------------------------------------------------+---------+------------+
```

(We'd normally select more data in such a query, but we've shortened it here for the purpose of illustration.)

If you compare the wtime (wall-clock time) and the query time, you'll see that MySQL query execution time was responsible for the slow response time in only two of the seven pages. Because we're storing the queries with the profiling data, we can retrieve them for examination:

```
mysql> SELECT mysql_queries
    -> FROM performance_log_070201 WHERE mysql_time > 10 LIMIT 1\G
*************************** 1. row ***************************
mysql_queries:
Query: SELECT id, chunk_id FROM domain WHERE domain = 'domain.com'
Time: 0.00022602081298828
Query: SELECT server.id sid, ip, user, password, domain_map.id as chunk_id FROM
server JOIN domain_map ON (server.id = domain_map.master_id) WHERE domain_map.id = 24
Time: 0.00020599365234375
Query: SELECT id, chunk_id, base_url,title FROM site WHERE id = 13832
Time: 0.00017690658569336
Query: SELECT server.id sid, ip, user, password, site_map.id as chunk_id FROM server
JOIN site_map ON (server.id = site_map.master_id) WHERE site_map.id = 64
Time: 0.0001990795135498
Query: SELECT from_site_id, url_from, count(*) cnt FROM link24.link_in24  FORCE INDEX
(domain_message)  WHERE domain_id=435377 AND message_day IN (...) GROUP BY from_site_
id ORDER BY cnt desc LIMIT 10
Time: 6.3193740844727
Query: SELECT revert_domain, domain_id, count(*) cnt FROM art64.link_out64 WHERE
from_site_id=13832 AND message_day IN (...)  GROUP BY domain_id ORDER BY cnt desc
LIMIT 10
Time: 21.3649559021
```

This reveals two problematic queries, with execution times of 6.3 and 21.3 seconds, that need to be optimized.

Logging all queries in this manner is expensive, so we usually either log only a fraction of the pages or enable logging only in debug mode.

How can you tell whether there's a bottleneck in a part of the system that you're not profiling? The easiest way is to look at the "lost time." In general, the wall-clock time (wtime) is the sum of the user time, system time, SQL query time, and every other time you can measure, plus the "lost time" you can't measure. There's some overlap, such as the CPU time needed for the PHP code to process the SQL queries, but this is usually insignificant. Figure 2-2 is a hypothetical illustration of how wall-clock time might be divided up.

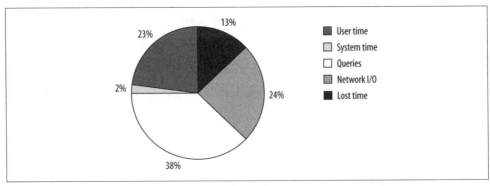

Figure 2-2. Lost time is the difference between wall-clock time and time for which you can account

Ideally, the "lost time" should be as small as possible. If you subtract everything you've measured from the wtime and you still have a lot left over, something you're not measuring is adding time to your script's execution. This may be the time needed to generate the page, or there may be a wait somewhere.*

There are two kinds of waits: waiting in the queue for CPU time, and waiting for resources. A process waits in the queue when it is ready to run, but all the CPUs are busy. It's not usually possible to figure out how much time a process spends waiting in the CPU queue, but that's generally not the problem. More likely, you're making some external resource call and not profiling it.

If your profiling is complete enough, you should be able to find bottlenecks easily. It's pretty straightforward: if your script's execution time is mostly CPU time, you probably need to look at optimizing your PHP code. Sometimes some measurements mask others, though. For example, you might have high CPU usage because you

---

* Assuming the web server buffers the result, so your script's execution ends and you don't measure the time it takes to send the result to the client.

have a bug that makes your caching system inefficient and forces your application to do too many SQL queries.

As this example demonstrates, profiling at the application level is the most flexible and useful technique. If possible, it's a good idea to insert profiling into any application you need to troubleshoot for performance bottlenecks.

As a final note, we should mention that we've shown only basic application profiling techniques here. Our goal for this section is to show you how to figure out whether MySQL is the problem. You might also want to profile your application's code itself. For example, if you decide you need to optimize your PHP code because it's using too much CPU time, you can use tools such as *xdebug*, *Valgrind*, and *cachegrind* to profile CPU usage.

Some languages have built-in support for profiling. For example, you can profile Ruby code with the *-r* command-line option, and Perl as follows:

```
$ perl -d:DProf <script file>
$ dprofpp tmon.out
```

A quick web search for "profiling *<language>*" is a good place to start.

MySQL Profiling

We go into much more detail about MySQL profiling, because it's less dependent on your specific application. Application profiling and server profiling are sometimes both necessary. Although application profiling can give you a more complete picture of the entire system's performance, profiling MySQL can provide a lot of information that isn't available when you look at the application as a whole. For example, profiling your PHP code won't show you how many rows MySQL examined to execute queries.

As with application profiling, the goal is to find out where MySQL spends most of its time. We won't go into profiling MySQL's source code; although that's useful sometimes for customized MySQL installations, it's a topic for another book. Instead, we show you some techniques you can use to capture and analyze information about the different kinds of work MySQL does to execute queries.

You can work at whatever level of granularity suits your purposes: you can profile the server as a whole or examine individual queries or batches of queries. The kinds of information you can glean include:

- Which data MySQL accesses most
- What kinds of queries MySQL executes most
- What states MySQL threads spend the most time in
- What subsystems MySQL uses most to execute a query
- What kinds of data accesses MySQL does during a query

- How much of various kinds of activities, such as index scans, MySQL does

We start at the broadest level—profiling the whole server—and work toward more detail.

Logging queries

MySQL has two kinds of query logs: the *general log* and the *slow log*. They both log queries, but at opposite ends of the query execution process. The general log writes out every query as the server receives it, so it contains queries that may not even be executed due to errors. The general log captures all queries, as well as some non-query events such as connecting and disconnecting. You can enable it with a single configuration directive:

```
log = <file_name>
```

By design, the general log does not contain execution times or any other information that's available only after a query finishes. In contrast, the slow log contains only queries that have executed. In particular, it logs queries that take more than a specified amount of time to execute. Both logs can be helpful for profiling, but the slow log is the primary tool for catching problematic queries. We usually recommend enabling it.

The following configuration sample will enable the log, capture all queries that take more than two seconds to execute, and log queries that don't use any indexes. It will also log slow administrative statements, such as OPTIMIZE TABLE:

```
log-slow-queries                = <file_name>
long_query_time                 = 2
log-queries-not-using-indexes
log-slow-admin-statements
```

You should customize this sample and place it in your *my.cnf* server configuration file. For more on server configuration, see Chapter 6.

The default value for long_query_time is 10 seconds. This is too long for most set-ups, so we usually use two seconds. However, even one second is too long for many uses. We show you how to get finer-grained logging in the next section.

In MySQL 5.1, the global slow_query_log and slow_query_log_file system variables provide runtime control over the slow query log, but in MySQL 5.0, you can't turn the slow query log on or off without restarting the MySQL server. The usual workaround for MySQL 5.0 is the long_query_time variable, which you can change dynamically. The following command doesn't really disable slow query logging, but it has practically the same effect (if any of your queries takes longer than 10,000 seconds to execute, you should optimize it anyway!):

```
mysql> SET GLOBAL long_query_time = 10000;
```

A related configuration variable, log_queries_not_using_indexes, makes the server log to the slow log any queries that don't use indexes, no matter how quickly they

---

execute. Although enabling the slow log normally adds only a small amount of logging overhead relative to the time it takes a "slow" query to execute, queries that don't use indexes can be frequent and very fast (for example, scans of very small tables). Thus, logging them can cause the server to slow down, and even use a lot of disk space for the log.

Unfortunately, you can't enable or disable logging of these queries with a dynamically settable variable in MySQL 5.0. You have to edit the configuration file, then restart MySQL. One way to reduce the burden without a restart is to make the log file a symbolic link to /dev/null when you want to disable it (in fact, you can use this trick for any log file). You just need to run FLUSH LOGS after making the change to ensure that MySQL closes its current log file descriptor and reopens the log to /dev/null.

In contrast to MySQL 5.0, MySQL 5.1 lets you change logging at runtime and lets you log to tables you can query with SQL. This is a great improvement.

Finer control over logging

The slow query log in MySQL 5.0 and earlier has a few limitations that make it useless for some purposes. One problem is that its granularity is only in seconds, and the minimum value for long_query_time in MySQL 5.0 is one second. For most interactive applications, this is way too long. If you're developing a high-performance web application, you probably want the *whole page* to be generated in much less than a second, and the page will probably issue many queries while it's being generated. In this context, a query that takes 150 milliseconds to execute would probably be considered a very slow query indeed.

Another problem is that you cannot log all queries the server executes into the slow log (in particular, the slave thread's queries aren't logged). The general log does log all queries, but it logs them before they're even parsed, so it doesn't contain information such as the execution time, lock time, and number of rows examined. Only the slow log contains that kind of information about a query.

Finally, if you enable the log_queries_not_using_indexes option, your slow log may be flooded with entries for fast, efficient queries that happen to do full table scans. For example, if you generate a drop-down list of states from SELECT * FROM STATES, that query will be logged because it's a full table scan.

When profiling for the purpose of performance optimization, you're looking for queries that cause the most work for the MySQL server. This doesn't always mean slow queries, so the notion of logging "slow" queries might not be useful. As an example, a 10-millisecond query that runs a 1,000 times per second will load the server more than a 10-second query that runs once every second. To identify such a problem, you'd need to log every query and analyze the results.

It's usually a good idea to look both at slow queries (even if they're not executed often) and at the queries that, in total, cause the most work for the server. This will help you find different types of problems, such as queries that cause a poor user experience.

We've developed a patch to the MySQL server, based on work by Georg Richter, that lets you specify slow query times in microseconds instead of seconds. It also lets you log *all* queries to the slow log, by setting long_query_time=0. The patch is available from *http://www.mysqlperformanceblog.com/mysql-patches/*. Its major drawback is that to use it you may need to compile MySQL yourself, because the patch isn't included in the official MySQL distribution in versions prior to MySQL 5.1.

At the time of this writing, the version of the patch included with MySQL 5.1 changes only the time granularity. A new version of the patch, which is not yet included in any official MySQL distribution, adds quite a bit more useful functionality. It includes the query's connection ID, as well as information about the query cache, join type, temporary tables, and sorting. It also adds InnoDB statistics, such as information on I/O behavior and lock waits.

The new patch lets you log queries executed by the slave SQL thread, which is very important if you're having trouble with replication slaves that are lagging (see "Excessive Replication Lag" on page 399 for more on how to help slaves keep up). It also lets you selectively log only some sessions. This is usually enough for profiling purposes, and we think it's a good practice.

This patch is relatively new, so you should use it with caution if you apply it yourself. We think it's pretty safe, but it hasn't been battle-tested as much as the rest of the MySQL server. If you're worried about the patched server's stability, you don't have to run the patched version all the time; you can just start it for a few hours to log some queries, and then go back to the unpatched version.

When profiling, it's a good idea to log all queries with long_query_time=0. If much of your load comes from very simple queries, you'll want to know that. Logging all these queries will impact performance a bit, and it will require lots of disk space— another reason you might not want to log every query all the time. Fortunately, you can change long_query_time without restarting the server, so it's easy to get a sample of all the queries for a little while, then revert to logging only very slow queries.

How to read the slow query log

Here's an example from a slow query log:

```
1  # Time: 030303  0:51:27
2  # User@Host: root[root] @ localhost []
3  # Query_time: 25  Lock_time: 0  Rows_sent: 3949  Rows_examined: 378036
4  SELECT ...
```

Line 1 shows when the query was logged, and line 2 shows who executed it. Line 3 shows how many seconds it took to execute, how long it waited for table locks at the MySQL server level (not at the storage engine level), how many rows the query returned, and how many rows it examined. These lines are all commented out, so they won't execute if you feed the log into a MySQL client. The last line is the query.

Here's a sample from a MySQL 5.1 server:

```
1  # Time: 070518  9:47:00
2  # User@Host: root[root] @ localhost []
3  # Query_time: 0.000652  Lock_time: 0.000109  Rows_sent: 1  Rows_examined: 1
4  SELECT ...
```

The information is mostly the same, except the times in line 3 are high precision. A newer version of the patch adds even more information:

```
1  # Time: 071031 20:03:16
2  # User@Host: root[root] @ localhost []
3  # Thread_id: 4
4  # Query_time: 0.503016  Lock_time: 0.000048  Rows_sent: 56  Rows_examined: 1113
5  # QC_Hit: No  Full_scan: No  Full_join: No  Tmp_table: Yes  Disk_tmp_table: No
6  # Filesort: Yes  Disk_filesort: No  Merge_passes: 0
7  #    InnoDB_IO_r_ops: 19  InnoDB_IO_r_bytes: 311296  InnoDB_IO_r_wait: 0.382176
8  #    InnoDB_rec_lock_wait: 0.000000  InnoDB_queue_wait: 0.067538
9  #    InnoDB_pages_distinct: 20
10 SELECT ...
```

Line 5 shows whether the query was served from the query cache, whether it did a full scan of a table, whether it did a join without indexes, whether it used a temporary table, and if so whether the temporary table was created on disk. Line 6 shows whether the query did a filesort and, if so, whether it was on disk and how many sort merge passes it performed.

Lines 7, 8, and 9 will appear if the query used InnoDB. Line 7 shows how many page read operations InnoDB scheduled during the query, along with the corresponding value in bytes. The last value on line 7 is how long it took InnoDB to read data from disk. Line 8 shows how long the query waited for row locks and how long it spent waiting to enter the InnoDB kernel.[*]

Line 9 shows approximately how many unique InnoDB pages the query accessed. The larger this grows, the less accurate it is likely to be. One use for this information is to estimate the query's working set in pages, which is how the InnoDB buffer pool caches data. It can also show you how helpful your clustered indexes really are. If the query's rows are clustered well, they'll fit in fewer pages. See "Clustered Indexes" on page 110 for more on this topic.

Using the slow query log to troubleshoot slow queries is not always straightforward. Although the log contains a lot of useful information, one very important bit of information is missing: an idea of *why* a query was slow. Sometimes it's obvious. If the log says 12,000,000 rows were examined and 1,200,000 were sent to the client, you know why it was slow to execute—it was a big query! However, it's rarely that clear.

[*] See "InnoDB Concurrency Tuning" on page 296 for more information on the InnoDB kernel.

Be careful not to read too much into the slow query log. If you see the same query in the log many times, there's a good chance that it's slow and needs optimization. But just because a query appears in the log doesn't mean it's a bad query, or even necessarily a slow one. You may find a slow query, run it yourself, and find that it executes in a fraction of a second. Appearing in the log simply means the query took a long time *then*; it doesn't mean it will take a long time now or in the future. There are many reasons why a query can be slow sometimes and fast at other times:

- A table may have been locked, causing the query to wait. The Lock_time indicates how long the query waited for locks to be released.

- The data or indexes may not have been cached in memory yet. This is common when MySQL is first started or hasn't been well tuned.

- A nightly backup process may have been running, making all disk I/O slower.

- The server may have been running other queries at the same time, slowing down this query.

As a result, you should view the slow query log as only a partial record of what's happened. You can use it to generate a list of possible suspects, but you need to investigate each of them in more depth.

The slow query log patches are specifically designed to try to help you understand why a query is slow. In particular, if you're using InnoDB, the InnoDB statistics can help a lot: you can see if the query was waiting for I/O from the disk, whether it had to spend a lot of time waiting in the InnoDB queue, and so on.

Log analysis tools

Now that you've logged some queries, it's time to analyze the results. The general strategy is to find the queries that impact the server most, check their execution plans with EXPLAIN, and tune as necessary. Repeat the analysis after tuning, because your changes might affect other queries. It's common for indexes to help SELECT queries but slow down INSERT and UPDATE queries, for example.

You should generally look for the following three things in the logs:

Long queries
    Routine batch jobs will generate long queries, but your normal queries shouldn't take very long.

High-impact queries
    Find the queries that constitute most of the server's execution time. Recall that short queries that are executed often may take up a lot of time.

New queries
    Find queries that weren't in the top 100 yesterday but are today. These might be new queries, or they might be queries that used to run quickly and are suffering because of different indexing or another change.

If your slow query log is fairly small this is easy to do manually, but if you're logging all queries (as we suggested), you really need tools to help you. Here are some of the more common tools for this purpose:

mysqldumpslow

MySQL provides *mysqldumpslow* with the MySQL server. It's a Perl script that can summarize the slow query log and show you how many times each query appears in the log. That way, you won't waste time trying to optimize a 30-second slow query that runs once a day when there are many other shorter slow queries that run thousands of time per day.

The advantage of *mysqldumpslow* is that it's already installed; the disadvantage is that it's a little less flexible than some of the other tools. It is also poorly documented, and it doesn't understand logs from servers that are patched with the microsecond slow-log patch.

mysql_slow_log_filter

This tool, available from *http://www.mysqlperformanceblog.com/files/utils/mysql_slow_log_filter*, does understand the microsecond log format. You can use it to extract queries that are longer than a given threshold or that examine more than a given number of rows. It's great for "tailing" your log file if you're running the microsecond patch, which can make your log grow too quickly to follow without filtering. You can run it with high thresholds for a while, optimize until the worst offenders are gone, then change the parameters to catch more queries and continue tuning.

Here's a command that will show queries that either run longer than half a second or examine more than 1,000 rows:

```
$ tail -f mysql-slow.log | mysql_slow_log_filter -T 0.5 -R 1000
```

mysql_slow_log_parser

This is another tool, available from *http://www.mysqlperformanceblog.com/files/utils/mysql_slow_log_parser*, that can aggregate the microsecond slow log. In addition to aggregating and reporting, it shows minimum and maximum values for execution time and number of rows analyzed, prints the "canonicalized" query, and prints a real sample you can EXPLAIN. Here's a sample of its output:

```
### 3579 Queries
### Total time: 3.348823, Average time: 0.000935686784017883
### Taking 0.000269  to 0.130820  seconds to complete
### Rows analyzed 1 - 1
SELECT id FROM forum WHERE id=XXX;
SELECT id FROM forum WHERE id=12345;
```

mysqlsla

The MySQL Statement Log Analyzer, available from *http://hackmysql.com/mysqlsla*, can analyze not only the slow log but also the general log and "raw" logs containing delimited SQL statements. Like *mysql_slow_log_parser*, it can canonicalize and summarize; it can also EXPLAIN queries (it rewrites many non-SELECT statements for EXPLAIN) and generate sophisticated reports.

You can use the slow log statistics to predict how much you'll be able to reduce the server's resource consumption. Suppose you sample queries for an hour (3,600 seconds) and find that the total combined execution time for all the queries in the log is 10,000 seconds (the total time is greater than the wall-clock time because the queries execute in parallel). If log analysis shows you that the worst query accounts for 3,000 seconds of execution time, you'll know that this query is responsible for 30% of the load. Now you know how much you can reduce the server's resource consumption by optimizing this query.

Profiling a MySQL Server

One of the best ways to profile a server—that is, to see what it spends most of its time doing—is with SHOW STATUS. SHOW STATUS returns a lot of status information, and we mention only a few of the variables in its output here.

 SHOW STATUS has some tricky behaviors that can give bad results in MySQL 5.0 and newer. Refer to Chapter 13 for more details on SHOW STATUS's behavior and pitfalls.

To see how your server is performing in near real time, periodically sample SHOW STATUS and compare the result with the previous sample. You can do this with the following command:

```
mysqladmin extended -r -i 10
```

Some of the variables are not strictly increasing counters, so you may see odd output such as a negative number of Threads_running. This is nothing to worry about; it just means the counter has decreased since the last sample.

Because the output is extensive, it might help to pass the results through *grep* to filter out variables you don't want to watch. Alternatively, you can use *innotop* or another of the tools mentioned in Chapter 14 to inspect its results. Some of the more useful variables to monitor are:

Bytes_received *and* Bytes_sent
    The traffic to and from the server

Com_*
    The commands the server is executing

Created_*
    Temporary tables and files created during query execution

Handler_*
    Storage engine operations

Select_*
> Various types of join execution plans

Sort_*
> Several types of sort information

You can use this approach to monitor MySQL's internal operations, such as number of key accesses, key reads from disk for MyISAM, rate of data access, data reads from disk for InnoDB, and so on. This can help you determine where the real or potential bottlenecks are in your system, without ever looking at a single query. You can also use tools that analyze SHOW STATUS, such as *mysqlreport*, to get a snapshot of the server's overall health.

We won't go into detail on the meaning of the status variables here, but we explain them when we use them in examples, so don't worry if you don't know what all of them mean.

Another good way to profile a MySQL server is with SHOW PROCESSLIST. This enables you not only to see what kinds of queries are executing, but also to see the state of your connections. Some things, such as a high number of connections in the Locked state, are obvious clues to bottlenecks. As with SHOW STATUS, the output from SHOW PROCESSLIST is so verbose that it's usually more convenient to use a tool such as *innotop* than to inspect it manually.

Profiling Queries with SHOW STATUS

The combination of FLUSH STATUS and SHOW SESSION STATUS is very helpful to see what happens while MySQL executes a query or batch of queries. This is a great way to optimize queries.

Let's look at an example of how to interpret what a query does. First, run FLUSH STATUS to reset your session status variables to zero, so you can see how much work MySQL does to execute the query:

```
mysql> FLUSH STATUS;
```

Next, run the query. We add SQL_NO_CACHE, so MySQL doesn't serve the query from the query cache:

```
mysql> SELECT SQL_NO_CACHE film_actor.actor_id, COUNT(*)
    -> FROM sakila.film_actor
    ->    INNER JOIN sakila.actor USING(actor_id)
    -> GROUP BY film_actor.actor_id
    -> ORDER BY COUNT(*) DESC;
...
200 rows in set (0.18 sec)
```

The query returned 200 rows, but what did it really do? SHOW STATUS can give some insight. First, let's see what kind of query plan the server chose:

```
mysql> SHOW SESSION STATUS LIKE 'Select%';
+-----------------------+-------+
```

```
| Variable_name         | Value |
+-----------------------+-------+
| Select_full_join      | 0     |
| Select_full_range_join| 0     |
| Select_range          | 0     |
| Select_range_check    | 0     |
| Select_scan           | 2     |
+-----------------------+-------+
```

It looks like MySQL did a full table scan (actually, it looks like it did two, but that's an artifact of SHOW STATUS; we come back to that later). If the query had involved more than one table, several variables might have been greater than zero. For example, if MySQL had used a range scan to find matching rows in a subsequent table, Select_full_range_join would also have had a value. We can get even more insight by looking at the low-level storage engine operations the query performed:

```
mysql> SHOW SESSION STATUS LIKE 'Handler%';
+----------------------------+-------+
| Variable_name              | Value |
+----------------------------+-------+
| Handler_commit             | 0     |
| Handler_delete             | 0     |
| Handler_discover           | 0     |
| Handler_prepare            | 0     |
| Handler_read_first         | 1     |
| Handler_read_key           | 5665  |
| Handler_read_next          | 5662  |
| Handler_read_prev          | 0     |
| Handler_read_rnd           | 200   |
| Handler_read_rnd_next      | 207   |
| Handler_rollback           | 0     |
| Handler_savepoint          | 0     |
| Handler_savepoint_rollback | 0     |
| Handler_update             | 5262  |
| Handler_write              | 219   |
+----------------------------+-------+
```

The high values of the "read" operations indicate that MySQL had to scan more than one table to satisfy this query. Normally, if MySQL read only one table with a full table scan, we'd see high values for Handler_read_rnd_next and Handler_read_rnd would be zero.

In this case, the multiple nonzero values indicate that MySQL must have used a temporary table to satisfy the different GROUP BY and ORDER BY clauses. That's why there are nonzero values for Handler_write and Handler_update: MySQL presumably wrote to the temporary table, scanned it to sort it, and then scanned it again to output the results in sorted order. Let's see what MySQL did to order the results:

```
mysql> SHOW SESSION STATUS LIKE 'Sort%';
+-------------------+-------+
| Variable_name     | Value |
+-------------------+-------+
```

```
| Sort_merge_passes | 0   |
| Sort_range        | 0   |
| Sort_rows         | 200 |
| Sort_scan         | 1   |
+-------------------+-----+
```

As we guessed, MySQL sorted the rows by scanning a temporary table containing every row in the output. If the value were higher than 200 rows, we'd suspect that it sorted at some other point during the query execution. We can also see how many temporary tables MySQL created for the query:

```
mysql> SHOW SESSION STATUS LIKE 'Created%';
+-------------------------+-------+
| Variable_name           | Value |
+-------------------------+-------+
| Created_tmp_disk_tables | 0     |
| Created_tmp_files       | 0     |
| Created_tmp_tables      | 5     |
+-------------------------+-------+
```

It's nice to see that the query didn't need to use the disk for the temporary tables, because that's very slow. But this is a little puzzling; surely MySQL didn't create five temporary tables just for this one query?

In fact, the query needs only one temporary table. This is the same artifact we noticed before. What's happening? We're running the example on MySQL 5.0.45, and in MySQL 5.0 SHOW STATUS actually selects data from the INFORMATION_SCHEMA tables, which introduces a "cost of observation."* This is skewing the results a little, as you can see by running SHOW STATUS again:

```
mysql> SHOW SESSION STATUS LIKE 'Created%';
+-------------------------+-------+
| Variable_name           | Value |
+-------------------------+-------+
| Created_tmp_disk_tables | 0     |
| Created_tmp_files       | 0     |
| Created_tmp_tables      | 6     |
+-------------------------+-------+
```

Note that the value has incremented again. The Handler and other variables are similarly affected. Your results will vary, depending on your MySQL version.

You can use this same process—FLUSH STATUS, run the query, and run SHOW STATUS—in MySQL 4.1 and older versions as well. You just need an idle server, because older versions have only global counters, which can be changed by other processes.

The best way to compensate for the "cost of observation" caused by running SHOW STATUS is to calculate the cost by running it twice and subtracting the second result from the first. You can then subtract this from SHOW STATUS to get the true cost of the

---

* The "cost of observation" problem is fixed in MySQL 5.1 for SHOW SESSION STATUS.

query. To get accurate results, you need to know the scope of the variables, so you know which have a cost of observation; some are per-session and some are global. You can automate this complicated process with *mk-query-profiler*.

You can integrate this type of automatic profiling in your application's database connection code. When profiling is enabled, the connection code can automatically flush the status before each query and log the differences afterward. Alternatively, you can profile per-page instead of per-query. Either strategy is useful to show you how much work MySQL did during the queries.

SHOW PROFILE

SHOW PROFILE is a patch Jeremy Cole contributed to the Community version of MySQL, as of MySQL 5.0.37.* Profiling is disabled by default but can be enabled at the session level. Enabling it makes the MySQL server collect information about the resources the server uses to execute a query. To start collecting statistics, set the profiling variable to 1:

```
mysql> SET profiling = 1;
```

Now let's run a query:

```
mysql> SELECT COUNT(DISTINCT actor.first_name) AS cnt_name, COUNT(*) AS cnt
    -> FROM sakila.film_actor
    -> INNER JOIN sakila.actor USING(actor_id)
    -> GROUP BY sakila.film_actor.film_id
    -> ORDER BY cnt_name DESC;
...
997 rows in set (0.03 sec)
```

This query's profiling data was stored in the session. To see queries that have been profiled, use SHOW PROFILES:

```
mysql> SHOW PROFILES\G
*************************** 1. row ***************************
Query_ID: 1
Duration: 0.02596900
   Query: SELECT COUNT(DISTINCT actor.first_name) AS cnt_name,...
```

You can retrieve the stored profiling data with the SHOW PROFILE statement. When you run it without an argument, it shows status values and durations for the most recent statement:

```
mysql> SHOW PROFILE;
+------------------------+----------+
| Status                 | Duration |
+------------------------+----------+
| (initialization)       | 0.000005 |
```

---

* At the time of this writing, SHOW PROFILE is not yet included in the Enterprise versions of MySQL, even those newer than 5.0.37.

```
| Opening tables       | 0.000033  |
| System lock          | 0.000037  |
| Table lock           | 0.000024  |
| init                 | 0.000079  |
| optimizing           | 0.000024  |
| statistics           | 0.000079  |
| preparing            | 0.00003   |
| Creating tmp table   | 0.000124  |
| executing            | 0.000008  |
| Copying to tmp table | 0.010048  |
| Creating sort index  | 0.004769  |
| Copying to group table | 0.0084880 |
| Sorting result       | 0.001136  |
| Sending data         | 0.000925  |
| end                  | 0.00001   |
| removing tmp table   | 0.00004   |
| end                  | 0.000005  |
| removing tmp table   | 0.00001   |
| end                  | 0.000011  |
| query end            | 0.00001   |
| freeing items        | 0.000025  |
| removing tmp table   | 0.00001   |
| freeing items        | 0.000016  |
| closing tables       | 0.000017  |
| logging slow query   | 0.000006  |
+----------------------+-----------+
```

Each row represents a change of state for the process and indicates how long it stayed in that state. The Status column corresponds to the State column in the output of SHOW FULL PROCESSLIST. The values come from the thd->proc_info variable, so you're looking at values that come directly from MySQL's internals. These are documented in the MySQL manual, though most of them are intuitively named and shouldn't be hard to understand.

You can specify a query to profile by giving its Query_ID from the output of SHOW PROFILES, and you can specify additional columns of output. For example, to see user and system CPU usage times for the preceding query, use the following command:

```
mysql> SHOW PROFILE CPU FOR QUERY 1;
```

SHOW PROFILE gives a lot of insight into the work the server does to execute a query, and it can help you understand what your queries really spend their time doing. Some of the limitations are its unimplemented features, the inability to see and profile another connection's queries, and the overhead caused by profiling.

Other Ways to Profile MySQL

We've shown you just enough detail in this chapter to illustrate how to use MySQL's internal status information to see what's happening inside the server. You can do some profiling with several of MySQL's other status outputs as well. Other useful commands include SHOW INNODB STATUS and SHOW MUTEX STATUS. We go into these and other commands in much more detail in Chapter 13.

When You Can't Add Profiling Code

Sometimes you can't add profiling code or patch the server, or even change the server's configuration. However, there's usually a way to do at least some type of profiling. Try these ideas:

- Customize your web server logs, so they record the wall-clock time and CPU time each request uses.
- Use packet sniffers to catch and time queries (including network latency) as they cross the network. Freely available sniffers include *mysqlsniffer* (*http:// hackmysql.com/mysqlsniffer*) and *tcpdump*; see *http://forge.mysql.com/snippets/ view.php?id=15* for an example of how to use *tcpdump*.
- Use a proxy, such as MySQL Proxy, to capture and time queries.

Operating System Profiling

It's often useful to peek into operating system statistics and try to find out what the operating system and hardware are doing. This can help not only when profiling an application, but also when troubleshooting.

This section is admittedly biased toward Unix-like operating systems, because that's what we work with most often. However, you can use the same techniques on other operating systems, as long as they provide the statistics.

The tools we use most frequently are *vmstat*, *iostat*, *mpstat*, and *strace*. Each of these shows a slightly different perspective on some combination of process, CPU, memory, and I/O activity. These tools are available on most Unix-like operating systems. We show examples of how to use them throughout this book, especially at the end of Chapter 7.

 Be careful with *strace* on GNU/Linux on production servers. It seems to have issues with multithreaded processes sometimes, and we've crashed servers with it.

Troubleshooting MySQL Connections and Processes

One set of tools we don't discuss elsewhere in detail is tools for discovering network activity and doing basic troubleshooting. As an example of how to do this, we show how you can track a MySQL connection back to its origin on another server.

Begin with the output of SHOW PROCESSLIST in MySQL, and note the Host column in one of the processes. We use the following example:

```
*************************** 21. row ***************************
      Id: 91296
    User: web
    Host: sargon.cluster3:37636
      db: main
 Command: Sleep
    Time: 10
   State:
    Info: NULL
```

The Host column shows where the connection originated and, just as importantly, the TCP port from which it came. You can use that information to find out which process opened the connection. If you have root access to sargon, you can use *netstat* and the port number to find out which process opened the connection:

```
root@sargon# netstat -ntp | grep :37636
tcp 0 0 192.168.0.12:37636 192.168.0.21:3306 ESTABLISHED 16072/apache2
```

The process number and name are in the last field of output: process 16072 started this connection, and it came from Apache. Once you know the process ID you can branch out to discover many other things about it, such as which other network connections the process owns:

```
root@sargon# netstat -ntp | grep 16072/apache2
tcp 0 0 192.168.0.12:37636 192.168.0.21:3306 ESTABLISHED 16072/apache2
tcp 0 0 192.168.0.12:37635 192.168.0.21:3306 ESTABLISHED 16072/apache2
tcp 0 0 192.168.0.12:57917 192.168.0.3:389   ESTABLISHED 16072/apache2
```

It looks like that Apache worker process has two MySQL connections (port 3306) open, and something to port 389 on another machine as well. What is port 389? There's no guarantee, but many programs do use standardized port numbers, such as MySQL's default port of 3306. A list is often in */etc/services*, so let's see what that says:

```
root@sargon# grep 389 /etc/services
ldap            389/tcp # Lightweight Directory Access Protocol
ldap            389/udp
```

We happen to know this server uses LDAP authentication, so LDAP makes sense. Let's see what else we can find out about process 16072. It's pretty easy to see what the process is doing with *ps*. The fancy pattern to *grep* we use here is so you can see the first line of output, which shows column headings:

```
root@sargon# ps -eaf | grep 'UID\|16072'
UID       PID PPID C STIME TTY     TIME CMD
apache  16072 22165 0 09:20 ?  00:00:00 /usr/sbin/apache2 -D DEFAULT_VHOST...
```

You can potentially use this information to find other problems. Don't be surprised, for example, to find that a service such as LDAP or NFS is causing problems for Apache and manifesting as slow page-generation times.

You can also list a process's open files using the *lsof* command. This is great for finding out all sorts of information, because everything is a file in Unix. We won't show the output here because it's very verbose, but you can run *lsof | grep 16072* to find the process's open files. You can also use *lsof* to find network connections when *netstat* isn't available. For example, the following command uses *lsof* to show approximately the same information we found with *netstat*. We've reformatted the output slightly for printing:

```
root@sargon# lsof -i -P | grep 16072
apache2 16072 apache  3u IPv4 25899404 TCP *:80 (LISTEN)
apache2 16072 apache 15u IPv4 33841089 TCP sargon.cluster3:37636->
                                          hammurabi.cluster3:3306 (ESTABLISHED)
apache2 16072 apache 27u IPv4 33818434 TCP sargon.cluster3:57917->
                                          romulus.cluster3:389 (ESTABLISHED)
apache2 16072 apache 29u IPv4 33841087 TCP sargon.cluster3:37635->
                                          hammurabi.cluster3:3306 (ESTABLISHED)
```

On GNU/Linux, the */proc* filesystem is another invaluable troubleshooting aid. Each process has its own directory under */proc*, and you can see lots of information about it, such as its current working directory, memory usage, and much more.

Apache actually has a feature similar to the Unix *ps* command: the */server-status/* URL. For example, if your intranet runs Apache at *http://intranet/*, you can point your web browser to *http://intranet/server-status/* to see what Apache is doing. This can be a helpful way to find out what URL a process is serving. The page has a legend that explains its output.

Advanced Profiling and Troubleshooting

If you need to dig deeper into a process to find out what it's doing—for example, why it's in uninterruptible sleep status—you can use *strace -p* and/or *gdb -p*. These commands can show system calls and backtraces, which can give more information about what the process was doing when it got stuck. Lots of things could make a process get stuck, such as NFS locking services that crash, a call to a remote web service that's not responding, and so on.

You can also profile systems or parts of systems in more detail to find out what they're doing. If you really need high performance and you start having problems, you might even find yourself profiling MySQL's internals. Although this might not seem to be your job (it's the MySQL developer team's job, right?), it can help you isolate the part of a system that's causing trouble. You may not be able or willing to fix it, but at least you can design your application to avoid a weakness.

Here are some tools you might find useful:

OProfile
    OProfile (*http://oprofile.sourceforge.net*) is a system profiler for Linux. It consists of a kernel driver and a daemon for collecting sample data, and several tools to

help you analyze the profiling data you collected. It profiles all code, including interrupt handlers, the kernel, kernel modules, applications, and shared libraries. If an application is compiled with debug symbols, OProfile can annotate the source, but this is not necessary; you can profile a system without recompiling anything. It has relatively low overhead, normally in the range of a few percent.

gprof

gprof is the GNU profiler, which can produce execution profiles of programs compiled with the *-pg* option. It calculates the amount of time spent in each routine. *gprof* can produce reports on function call frequency and durations, a call graph, and annotated source listings.

Other tools

There are many other tools, including specialized and/or proprietary programs. These include Intel VTune, the Sun Performance Analyzer (part of Sun Studio), and DTrace on Solaris and other systems.

CHAPTER 3
Schema Optimization and Indexing

Optimizing a poorly designed or badly indexed schema can improve performance by orders of magnitude. If you require high performance, you must design your schema and indexes for the specific queries you will run. You should also estimate your performance requirements for different kinds of queries, because changes to one query or one part of the schema can have consequences elsewhere. Optimization often involves tradeoffs. For example, adding indexes to speed up retrieval will slow updates. Likewise, a denormalized schema can speed up some types of queries but slow down others. Adding counter and summary tables is a great way to optimize queries, but they may be expensive to maintain.

Sometimes you may need to go beyond the role of a developer and question the business requirements handed to you. People who aren't experts in database systems often write business requirements without understanding their performance impacts. If you explain that a small feature will double the server hardware requirements, they may decide they can live without it.

Schema optimization and indexing require a big-picture approach as well as attention to details. You need to understand the whole system to understand how each piece will affect others. This chapter begins with a discussion of data types, then covers indexing strategies and normalization. It finishes with some notes on storage engines.

You will probably need to review this chapter after reading the chapter on query optimization. Many of the topics discussed here—especially indexing—can't be considered in isolation. You have to be familiar with query optimization and server tuning to make good decisions about indexes.

Choosing Optimal Data Types

MySQL supports a large variety of data types, and choosing the correct type to store your data is crucial to getting good performance. The following simple guidelines can help you make better choices, no matter what type of data you are storing:

Smaller is usually better.

In general, try to use the smallest data type that can correctly store and represent your data. Smaller data types are usually faster, because they use less space on the disk, in memory, and in the CPU cache. They also generally require fewer CPU cycles to process.

Make sure you don't underestimate the range of values you need to store, though, because increasing the data type range in multiple places in your schema can be a painful and time-consuming operation. If you're in doubt as to which is the best data type to use, choose the smallest one that you don't think you'll exceed. (If the system is not very busy or doesn't store much data, or if you're at an early phase in the design process, you can change it easily later.)

Simple is good.

Fewer CPU cycles are typically required to process operations on simpler data types. For example, integers are cheaper to compare than characters, because character sets and collations (sorting rules) make character comparisons complicated. Here are two examples: you should store dates and times in MySQL's built-in types instead of as strings, and you should use integers for IP addresses. We discuss these topics further later.

Avoid NULL *if possible.*

You should define fields as NOT NULL whenever you can. A lot of tables include nullable columns even when the application does not need to store NULL (the absence of a value), merely because it's the default. You should be careful to specify columns as NOT NULL unless you intend to store NULL in them.

It's harder for MySQL to optimize queries that refer to nullable columns, because they make indexes, index statistics, and value comparisons more complicated. A nullable column uses more storage space and requires special processing inside MySQL. When a nullable column is indexed, it requires an extra byte per entry and can even cause a fixed-size index (such as an index on a single integer column) to be converted to a variable-sized one in MyISAM.

Even when you do need to store a "no value" fact in a table, you might not need to use NULL. Consider using zero, a special value, or an empty string instead.

The performance improvement from changing NULL columns to NOT NULL is usually small, so don't make finding and changing them on an existing schema a priority unless you know they are causing problems. However, if you're planning to index columns, avoid making them nullable if possible.

The first step in deciding what data type to use for a given column is to determine what general class of types is appropriate: numeric, string, temporal, and so on. This is usually pretty straightforward, but we mention some special cases where the choice is unintuitive.

The next step is to choose the specific type. Many of MySQL's data types can store the same kind of data but vary in the range of values they can store, the precision they permit, or the physical space (on disk and in memory) they require. Some data types also have special behaviors or properties.

For example, a DATETIME and a TIMESTAMP column can store the same kind of data: date and time, to a precision of one second. However, TIMESTAMP uses only half as much storage space, is time zone–aware, and has special autoupdating capabilities. On the other hand, it has a much smaller range of allowable values, and sometimes its special capabilities can be a handicap.

We discuss base data types here. MySQL supports many aliases for compatibility, such as INTEGER, BOOL, and NUMERIC. These are only aliases. They can be confusing, but they don't affect performance.

Whole Numbers

There are two kinds of numbers: whole numbers and real numbers (numbers with a fractional part). If you're storing whole numbers, use one of the integer types: TINYINT, SMALLINT, MEDIUMINT, INT, or BIGINT. These require 8, 16, 24, 32, and 64 bits of storage space, respectively. They can store values from $-2^{(N-1)}$ to $2^{(N-1)}-1$, where N is the number of bits of storage space they use.

Integer types can optionally have the UNSIGNED attribute, which disallows negative values and approximately doubles the upper limit of positive values you can store. For example, a TINYINT UNSIGNED can store values ranging from 0 to 255 instead of from –128 to 127.

Signed and unsigned types use the same amount of storage space and have the same performance, so use whatever's best for your data range.

Your choice determines how MySQL *stores* the data, in memory and on disk. However, integer *computations* generally use 64-bit BIGINT integers, even on 32-bit architectures. (The exceptions are some aggregate functions, which use DECIMAL or DOUBLE to perform computations.)

MySQL lets you specify a "width" for integer types, such as INT(11). This is meaningless for most applications: it does not restrict the legal range of values, but simply specifies the number of characters MySQL's interactive tools (such as the command-line client) will reserve for display purposes. For storage and computational purposes, INT(1) is identical to INT(20).

 The Falcon storage engine is different from other storage engines MySQL AB provides in that it stores integers in its own internal format. The user has no control over the actual size of the stored data. Third-party storage engines, such as Brighthouse, also have their own storage formats and compression schemes.

Real Numbers

Real numbers are numbers that have a fractional part. However, they aren't just for fractional numbers; you can also use DECIMAL to store integers that are so large they don't fit in BIGINT. MySQL supports both exact and inexact types.

The FLOAT and DOUBLE types support approximate calculations with standard floating-point math. If you need to know exactly how floating-point results are calculated, you will need to research your platform's floating-point implementation.

The DECIMAL type is for storing exact fractional numbers. In MySQL 5.0 and newer, the DECIMAL type supports exact math. MySQL 4.1 and earlier used floating-point math to perform computations on DECIMAL values, which could give strange results because of loss of precision. In these versions of MySQL, DECIMAL was only a "storage type."

The server itself performs DECIMAL math in MySQL 5.0 and newer, because CPUs don't support the computations directly. Floating-point math is somewhat faster, because the CPU performs the computations natively.

Both floating-point and DECIMAL types let you specify a precision. For a DECIMAL column, you can specify the maximum allowed digits before and after the decimal point. This influences the column's space consumption. MySQL 5.0 and newer pack the digits into a binary string (nine digits per four bytes). For example, DECIMAL(18, 9) will store nine digits from each side of the decimal point, using nine bytes in total: four for the digits before the decimal point, one for the decimal point itself, and four for the digits after the decimal point.

A DECIMAL number in MySQL 5.0 and newer can have up to 65 digits. Earlier MySQL versions had a limit of 254 digits and stored the values as unpacked strings (one byte per digit). However, these versions of MySQL couldn't actually use such large numbers in computations, because DECIMAL was just a storage format; DECIMAL numbers were converted to DOUBLEs for computational purposes,

You can specify a floating-point column's desired precision in a couple of ways, which can cause MySQL to silently choose a different data type or to round values when you store them. These precision specifiers are nonstandard, so we suggest that you specify the type you want but not the precision.

Floating-point types typically use less space than DECIMAL to store the same range of values. A FLOAT column uses four bytes of storage. DOUBLE consumes eight bytes and has greater precision and a larger range of values. As with integers, you're choosing only the storage type; MySQL uses DOUBLE for its internal calculations on floating-point types.

Because of the additional space requirements and computational cost, you should use DECIMAL only when you need exact results for fractional numbers—for example, when storing financial data.

String Types

MySQL supports quite a few string data types, with many variations on each. These data types changed greatly in versions 4.1 and 5.0, which makes them even more complicated. Since MySQL 4.1, each string column can have its own character set and set of sorting rules for that character set, or *collation* (see Chapter 5 for more on these topics). This can impact performance greatly.

VARCHAR and CHAR types

The two major string types are VARCHAR and CHAR, which store character values. Unfortunately, it's hard to explain exactly how these values are stored on disk and in memory, because the implementations are storage engine-dependent (for example, Falcon uses its own storage formats for almost every data type). We assume you are using InnoDB and/or MyISAM. If not, you should read the documentation for your storage engine.

Let's take a look at how VARCHAR and CHAR values are typically stored on disk. Be aware that a storage engine may store a CHAR or VARCHAR value differently in memory from how it stores that value on disk, and that the server may translate the value into yet another storage format when it retrieves it from the storage engine. Here's a general comparison of the two types:

VARCHAR

VARCHAR stores variable-length character strings and is the most common string data type. It can require less storage space than fixed-length types, because it uses only as much space as it needs (i.e., less space is used to store shorter values). The exception is a MyISAM table created with ROW_FORMAT=FIXED, which uses a fixed amount of space on disk for each row and can thus waste space.

VARCHAR uses 1 or 2 extra bytes to record the value's length: 1 byte if the column's maximum length is 255 bytes or less, and 2 bytes if it's more. Assuming the latin1 character set, a VARCHAR(10) will use up to 11 bytes of storage space. A VARCHAR(1000) can use up to 1002 bytes, because it needs 2 bytes to store length information.

VARCHAR helps performance because it saves space. However, because the rows are variable-length, they can grow when you update them, which can cause extra work. If a row grows and no longer fits in its original location, the behavior is storage engine-dependent. For example, MyISAM may fragment the row, and InnoDB may need to split the page to fit the row into it. Other storage engines may never update data in place at all.

It's usually worth using VARCHAR when the maximum column length is much larger than the average length; when updates to the field are rare, so fragmentation is not a problem; and when you're using a complex character set such as UTF-8, where each character uses a variable number of bytes of storage.

In version 5.0 and newer, MySQL preserves trailing spaces when you store and retrieve values. In versions 4.1 and older, MySQL strips trailing spaces.

CHAR

CHAR is fixed-length: MySQL always allocates enough space for the specified number of characters. When storing a CHAR value, MySQL removes any trailing spaces. (This was also true of VARCHAR in MySQL 4.1 and older versions—CHAR and VARCHAR were logically identical and differed only in storage format.) Values are padded with spaces as needed for comparisons.

CHAR is useful if you want to store very short strings, or if all the values are nearly the same length. For example, CHAR is a good choice for MD5 values for user passwords, which are always the same length. CHAR is also better than VARCHAR for data that's changed frequently, because a fixed-length row is not prone to fragmentation. For very short columns, CHAR is also more efficient than VARCHAR; a CHAR(1) designed to hold only Y and N values will use only one byte in a single-byte character set,* but a VARCHAR(1) would use two bytes because of the length byte.

This behavior can be a little confusing, so we illustrate with an example. First, we create a table with a single CHAR(10) column and store some values in it:

```
mysql> CREATE TABLE char_test( char_col CHAR(10));
mysql> INSERT INTO char_test(char_col) VALUES
    -> ('string1'), ('  string2'), ('string3 ');
```

When we retrieve the values, the trailing spaces have been stripped away:

```
mysql> SELECT CONCAT("'", char_col, "'") FROM char_test;
+---------------------------+
| CONCAT("'", char_col, "'") |
+---------------------------+
| 'string1'                 |
| '  string2'               |
| 'string3'                 |
+---------------------------+
```

If we store the same values into a VARCHAR(10) column, we get the following result upon retrieval:

```
mysql> SELECT CONCAT("'", varchar_col, "'") FROM varchar_test;
+-----------------------------+
| CONCAT("'", varchar_col, "'") |
+-----------------------------+
| 'string1'                   |
| '  string2'                 |
| 'string3 '                  |
+-----------------------------+
```

---

* Remember that the length is specified in characters, not bytes. A multibyte character set can require more than one byte to store each character.

How data is stored is up to the storage engines, and not all storage engines handle fixed-length and variable-length data the same way. The Memory storage engine uses fixed-size rows, so it has to allocate the maximum possible space for each value even when it's a variable-length field. On the other hand, Falcon uses variable-length columns even for fixed-length CHAR fields. However, the padding and trimming behavior is consistent across storage engines, because the MySQL server itself handles that.

The sibling types for CHAR and VARCHAR are BINARY and VARBINARY, which store binary strings. Binary strings are very similar to conventional strings, but they store bytes instead of characters. Padding is also different: MySQL pads BINARY values with \0 (the zero byte) instead of spaces and doesn't strip the pad value on retrieval.*

These types are useful when you need to store binary data and want MySQL to compare the values as bytes instead of characters. The advantage of byte-wise comparisons is more than just a matter of case insensitivity. MySQL literally compares BINARY strings one byte at a time, according to the numeric value of each byte. As a result, binary comparisons can be much simpler than character comparisons, so they are faster.

Generosity Can Be Unwise

Storing the value 'hello' requires the same amount of space in a VARCHAR(5) and a VARCHAR(200) column. Is there any advantage to using the shorter column?

As it turns out, there is a big advantage. The larger column can use much more memory, because MySQL often allocates fixed-size chunks of memory to hold values internally. This is especially bad for sorting or operations that use in-memory temporary tables. The same thing happens with filesorts that use on-disk temporary tables.

The best strategy is to allocate only as much space as you really need.

BLOB and TEXT types

BLOB and TEXT are string data types designed to store large amounts of data as either binary or character strings, respectively.

In fact, they are each families of data types: the character types are TINYTEXT, SMALLTEXT, TEXT, MEDIUMTEXT, and LONGTEXT, and the binary types are TINYBLOB, SMALLBLOB, BLOB, MEDIUMBLOB, and LONGBLOB. BLOB is a synonym for SMALLBLOB, and TEXT is a synonym for SMALLTEXT.

---

* Be careful with the BINARY type if the value must remain unchanged after retrieval. MySQL will pad it to the required length with \0s.

Unlike with all other data types, MySQL handles each BLOB and TEXT value as an object with its own identity. Storage engines often store them specially; InnoDB may use a separate "external" storage area for them when they're large. Each value requires from one to four bytes of storage space in the row and enough space in external storage to actually hold the value.

The only difference between the BLOB and TEXT families is that BLOB types store binary data with no collation or character set, but TEXT types have a character set and collation.

MySQL sorts BLOB and TEXT columns differently from other types: instead of sorting the full length of the string, it sorts only the first max_sort_length bytes of such columns. If you need to sort by only the first few characters, you can either decrease the max_sort_length server variable or use ORDER BY SUBSTRING(*column*, *length*).

MySQL can't index the full length of these data types and can't use the indexes for sorting. (You'll find more on these topics later in the chapter.)

How to Avoid On-Disk Temporary Tables

Because the Memory storage engine doesn't support the BLOB and TEXT types, queries that use BLOB or TEXT columns and need an implicit temporary table will have to use on-disk MyISAM temporary tables, even for only a few rows. This can result in a serious performance overhead. Even if you configure MySQL to store temporary tables on a RAM disk, many expensive operating system calls will be required. (The Maria storage engine should alleviate this problem by caching everything in memory, not just the indexes.)

The best solution is to avoid using the BLOB and TEXT types unless you really need them. If you can't avoid them, you may be able to use the ORDER BY SUBSTRING(*column*, *length*) trick to convert the values to character strings, which will permit in-memory temporary tables. Just be sure that you're using a short enough substring that the temporary table doesn't grow larger than max_heap_table_size or tmp_table_size, or MySQL will convert the table to an on-disk MyISAM table.

If the Extra column of EXPLAIN contains "Using temporary," the query uses an implicit temporary table.

Using ENUM instead of a string type

Sometimes you can use an ENUM column instead of conventional string types. An ENUM column can store up to 65,535 distinct string values. MySQL stores them very compactly, packed into one or two bytes depending on the number of values in the list. It stores each value internally as an integer representing its position in the field definition list, and it keeps the "lookup table" that defines the number-to-string correspondence in the table's *.frm* file. Here's an example:

```
mysql> CREATE TABLE enum_test(
    ->     e ENUM('fish', 'apple', 'dog') NOT NULL
    -> );
mysql> INSERT INTO enum_test(e) VALUES('fish'), ('dog'), ('apple');
```

The three rows actually store integers, not strings. You can see the dual nature of the values by retrieving them in a numeric context:

```
mysql> SELECT e + 0 FROM enum_test;
+-------+
| e + 0 |
+-------+
|     1 |
|     3 |
|     2 |
+-------+
```

This duality can be terribly confusing if you specify numbers for your ENUM constants, as in ENUM('1', '2', '3'). We suggest you don't do this.

Another surprise is that an ENUM field sorts by the internal integer values, not by the strings themselves:

```
mysql> SELECT e FROM enum_test ORDER BY e;
+-------+
| e     |
+-------+
| fish  |
| apple |
| dog   |
+-------+
```

You can work around this by specifying ENUM members in the order in which you want them to sort. You can also use FIELD() to specify a sort order explicitly in your queries, but this prevents MySQL from using the index for sorting:

```
mysql> SELECT e FROM enum_test ORDER BY FIELD(e, 'apple', 'dog', 'fish');
+-------+
| e     |
+-------+
| apple |
| dog   |
| fish  |
+-------+
```

The biggest downside of ENUM is that the list of strings is fixed, and adding or removing strings requires the use of ALTER TABLE. Thus, it might not be a good idea to use ENUM as a string data type when the list of allowed string values is likely to change in the future. MySQL uses ENUM in its own privilege tables to store Y and N values.

Because MySQL stores each value as an integer and has to do a lookup to convert it to its string representation, ENUM columns have some overhead. This is usually offset by their smaller size, but not always. In particular, it can be slower to join a CHAR or VARCHAR column to an ENUM column than to another CHAR or VARCHAR column.

To illustrate, we benchmarked how quickly MySQL performs such a join on a table in one of our applications. The table has a fairly wide primary key:

```
CREATE TABLE webservicecalls (
    day date NOT NULL,
    account smallint NOT NULL,
    service varchar(10) NOT NULL,
    method varchar(50) NOT NULL,
    calls int NOT NULL,
    items int NOT NULL,
    time float NOT NULL,
    cost decimal(9,5) NOT NULL,
    updated datetime,
    PRIMARY KEY (day, account, service, method)
) ENGINE=InnoDB;
```

The table contains about 110,000 rows and is only about 10 MB, so it fits entirely in memory. The service column contains 5 distinct values with an average length of 4 characters, and the method column contains 71 values with an average length of 20 characters.

We made a copy of this table and converted the service and method columns to ENUM, as follows:

```
CREATE TABLE webservicecalls_enum (
    ... omitted ...
    service ENUM(...values omitted...) NOT NULL,
    method ENUM(...values omitted...) NOT NULL,
    ... omitted ...
) ENGINE=InnoDB;
```

We then measured the performance of joining the tables by the primary key columns. Here is the query we used:

```
mysql> SELECT SQL_NO_CACHE COUNT(*)
    -> FROM webservicecalls
    ->    JOIN webservicecalls USING(day, account, service, method);
```

We varied this query to join the VARCHAR and ENUM columns in different combinations. Table 3-1 shows the results.

Table 3-1. Speed of joining VARCHAR and ENUM columns

Test	Queries per second
VARCHAR joined to VARCHAR	2.6
VARCHAR joined to ENUM	1.7
ENUM joined to VARCHAR	1.8
ENUM joined to ENUM	3.5

The join is faster after converting the columns to ENUM, but joining the ENUM columns to VARCHAR columns is slower. In this case, it looks like a good idea to convert these columns, as long as they don't have to be joined to VARCHAR columns.

However, there's another benefit to converting the columns: according to the Data_length column from SHOW TABLE STATUS, converting these two columns to ENUM made the table about 1/3 smaller. In some cases, this might be beneficial even if the ENUM columns have to be joined to VARCHAR columns. Also, the primary key itself is only about half the size after the conversion. Because this is an InnoDB table, if there are any other indexes on this table, reducing the primary key size will make them much smaller too. We explain this later in the chapter.

Date and Time Types

MySQL has many types for various kinds of date and time values, such as YEAR and DATE. The finest granularity of time MySQL can store is one second. However, it can do temporal *computations* with microsecond granularity, and we show you how to work around the storage limitations.

Most of the temporal types have no alternatives, so there is no question of which one is the best choice. The only question is what to do when you need to store both the date and the time. MySQL offers two very similar data types for this purpose: DATETIME and TIMESTAMP. For many applications, either will work, but in some cases, one works better than the other. Let's take a look:

DATETIME

> This type can hold a large range of values, from the year 1001 to the year 9999, with a precision of one second. It stores the date and time packed into an integer in YYYYMMDDHHMMSS format, independent of time zone. This uses eight bytes of storage space.

> By default, MySQL displays DATETIME values in a sortable, unambiguous format, such as 2008-01-16 22:37:08. This is the ANSI standard way to represent dates and times.

TIMESTAMP

> As its name implies, the TIMESTAMP type stores the number of seconds elapsed since midnight, January 1, 1970 (Greenwich Mean Time)—the same as a Unix timestamp. TIMESTAMP uses only four bytes of storage, so it has a much smaller range than DATETIME: from the year 1970 to partway through the year 2038. MySQL provides the FROM_UNIXTIME() and UNIX_TIMESTAMP() functions to convert a Unix timestamp to a date, and vice versa.

> Newer MySQL versions format TIMESTAMP values just like DATETIME values, but older MySQL versions display them without any punctuation between the parts. This is only a display formatting difference; the TIMESTAMP storage format is the same in all MySQL versions.

> The value a TIMESTAMP displays also depends on the time zone. The MySQL server, operating system, and client connections all have time zone settings.

Thus, a TIMESTAMP that stores the value 0 actually displays as 1969-12-31 19:00:00 in Eastern Daylight Time, which has a five-hour offset from GMT.

TIMESTAMP also has special properties that DATETIME doesn't have. By default, MySQL will set the first TIMESTAMP column to the current time when you insert a row without specifying a value for the column.* MySQL also updates the first TIMESTAMP column's value by default when you update the row, unless you assign a value explicitly in the UPDATE statement. You can configure the insertion and update behaviors for any TIMESTAMP column. Finally, TIMESTAMP columns are NOT NULL by default, which is different from every other data type.

Special behavior aside, in general if you can use TIMESTAMP you should, as it is more space-efficient than DATETIME. Sometimes people store Unix timestamps as integer values, but this usually doesn't gain you anything. As that format is often less convenient to deal with, we do not recommend doing this.

What if you need to store a date and time value with subsecond resolution? MySQL currently does not have an appropriate data type for this, but you can use your own storage format: you can use the BIGINT data type and store the value as a timestamp in microseconds, or you can use a DOUBLE and store the fractional part of the second after the decimal point. Both approaches will work well.

Bit-Packed Data Types

MySQL has a few storage types that use individual bits within a value to store data compactly. All of these types are technically string types, regardless of the underlying storage format and manipulations:

BIT

> Before MySQL 5.0, BIT is just a synonym for TINYINT. But in MySQL 5.0 and newer, it's a completely different data type with special characteristics. We discuss the new behavior here.
>
> You can use a BIT column to store one or many true/false values in a single column. BIT(1) defines a field that contains a single bit, BIT(2) stores two bits, and so on; the maximum length of a BIT column is 64 bits.
>
> BIT behavior varies between storage engines. MyISAM packs the columns together for storage purposes, so 17 individual BIT columns require only 17 bits to store (assuming none of the columns permits NULL). MyISAM rounds that to three bytes for storage. Other storage engines, such as Memory and InnoDB, store each column as the smallest integer type large enough to contain the bits, so you don't save any storage space.

---

* The rules for TIMESTAMP behavior are complex and have changed in various MySQL versions, so you should verify that you are getting the behavior you want. It's usually a good idea to examine the output of SHOW CREATE TABLE after making changes to TIMESTAMP columns.

MySQL treats BIT as a string type, not a numeric type. When you retrieve a BIT(1) value, the result is a string but the contents are the binary value 0 or 1, not the ASCII value "0" or "1". However, if you retrieve the value in a numeric context, the result is the number to which the bit string converts. Keep this in mind if you need to compare the result to another value. For example, if you store the value b'00111001' (which is the binary equivalent of 57) into a BIT(8) column and retrieve it, you will get the string containing the character code 57. This happens to be the ASCII character code for "9". But in a numeric context, you'll get the value 57:

```
mysql> CREATE TABLE bittest(a bit(8));
mysql> INSERT INTO bittest VALUES(b'00111001');
mysql> SELECT a, a + 0 FROM bittest;
+------+-------+
| a    | a + 0 |
+------+-------+
| 9    |    57 |
+------+-------+
```

This can be very confusing, so we recommend that you use BIT with caution. For most applications, we think it is a better idea to avoid this type.

If you want to store a true/false value in a single bit of storage space, another option is to create a nullable CHAR(0) column. This column is capable of storing either the absence of a value (NULL) or a zero-length value (the empty string).

SET

If you need to store many true/false values, consider combining many columns into one with MySQL's native SET data type, which MySQL represents internally as a packed set of bits. It uses storage efficiently, and MySQL has functions such as FIND_IN_SET() and FIELD() that make it easy to use in queries. The major drawback is the cost of changing the column's definition: this requires an ALTER TABLE, which is very expensive on large tables (but see the workaround later in this chapter). In general, you also can't use indexes for lookups on SET columns.

Bitwise operations on integer columns

An alternative to SET is to use an integer as a packed set of bits. For example, you can pack eight bits in a TINYINT and manipulate them with bitwise operators. You can make this easier by defining named constants for each bit in your application code.

The major advantage of this approach over SET is that you can change the "enumeration" the field represents without an ALTER TABLE. The drawback is that your queries are harder to write and understand (what does it mean when bit 5 is set?). Some people are comfortable with bitwise manipulations and some aren't, so whether you'll want to try this technique is largely a matter of taste.

An example application for packed bits is an access control list (ACL) that stores permissions. Each bit or SET element represents a value such as CAN_READ, CAN_WRITE, or CAN_DELETE. If you use a SET column, you'll let MySQL store the bit-to-value mapping in the column definition; if you use an integer column, you'll store the mapping in your application code. Here's what the queries would look like with a SET column:

```
mysql> CREATE TABLE acl (
    ->     perms SET('CAN_READ', 'CAN_WRITE', 'CAN_DELETE') NOT NULL
    -> );
mysql> INSERT INTO acl(perms) VALUES ('CAN_READ,CAN_DELETE');
mysql> SELECT perms FROM acl WHERE FIND_IN_SET('CAN_READ', perms);
+---------------------+
| perms               |
+---------------------+
| CAN_READ,CAN_DELETE |
+---------------------+
```

If you used an integer, you could write that example as follows:

```
mysql> SET @CAN_READ    := 1 << 0,
    ->     @CAN_WRITE   := 1 << 1,
    ->     @CAN_DELETE  := 1 << 2;
mysql> CREATE TABLE acl (
    ->     perms TINYINT UNSIGNED NOT NULL DEFAULT 0
    -> );
mysql> INSERT INTO acl(perms) VALUES(@CAN_READ + @CAN_DELETE);
mysql> SELECT perms FROM acl WHERE perms & @CAN_READ;
+-------+
| perms |
+-------+
|     5 |
+-------+
```

We've used variables to define the values, but you can use constants in your code instead.

Choosing Identifiers

Choosing a good data type for an identifier column is very important. You're more likely to compare these columns to other values (for example, in joins) and to use them for lookups than other columns. You're also likely to use them in other tables as foreign keys, so when you choose a data type for an identifier column, you're probably choosing the type in related tables as well. (As we demonstrated earlier in this chapter, it's a good idea to use the same data types in related tables, because you're likely to use them for joins.)

When choosing a type for an identifier column, you need to consider not only the storage type, but also how MySQL performs computations and comparisons on that type. For example, MySQL stores ENUM and SET types internally as integers but converts them to strings when doing comparisons in a string context.

Once you choose a type, make sure you use the same type in all related tables. The types should match exactly, including properties such as UNSIGNED.* Mixing different data types can cause performance problems, and even if it doesn't, implicit type conversions during comparisons can create hard-to-find errors. These may even crop up much later, after you've forgotten that you're comparing different data types.

Choose the smallest size that can hold your required range of values, and leave room for future growth if necessary. For example, if you have a state_id column that stores U.S state names, you don't need thousands or millions of values, so don't use an INT. A TINYINT should be sufficient and is three bytes smaller. If you use this value as a foreign key in other tables, three bytes can make a big difference.

Integer types

Integers are usually the best choice for identifiers, because they're fast and they work with AUTO_INCREMENT.

ENUM *and* SET

The ENUM and SET types are generally a poor choice for identifiers, though they can be good for static "definition tables" that contain status or "type" values. ENUM and SET columns are appropriate for holding information such as an order's status, a product's type, or a person's gender.

As an example, if you use an ENUM field to define a product's type, you might want a lookup table primary keyed on an identical ENUM field. (You could add columns to the lookup table for descriptive text, to generate a glossary, or to provide meaningful labels in a pull-down menu on a web site.) In this case, you'll want to use the ENUM as an identifier, but for most purposes you should avoid doing so.

String types

Avoid string types for identifiers if possible, as they take up a lot of space and are generally slower than integer types. Be especially cautious when using string identifiers with MyISAM tables. MyISAM uses packed indexes for strings by default, which may make lookups much slower. In our tests, we've noted up to six times slower performance with packed indexes on MyISAM.

You should also be very careful with completely "random" strings, such as those produced by MD5( ), SHA1( ), or UUID( ). Each new value you generate with them will be distributed in arbitrary ways over a large space, which can slow INSERT and some types of SELECT queries:†

---

* If you're using the InnoDB storage engine, you may not be able to create foreign keys unless the data types match exactly. The resulting error message, "ERROR 1005 (HY000): Can't create table," can be confusing depending on the context, and questions about it come up often on MySQL mailing lists. (Oddly, you can create foreign keys between VARCHAR columns of different lengths.)

† On the other hand, for some very large tables with many writers, such pseudorandom values can actually help eliminate "hot spots."

- They slow `INSERT` queries because the inserted value has to go in a random location in indexes. This causes page splits, random disk accesses, and clustered index fragmentation for clustered storage engines.
- They slow `SELECT` queries because logically adjacent rows will be widely dispersed on disk and in memory.
- Random values cause caches to perform poorly for all types of queries because they defeat locality of reference, which is how caching works. If the entire data set is equally "hot," there is no advantage to having any particular part of the data cached in memory, and if the working set does not fit in memory, the cache will have a lot of flushes and misses.

If you do store UUID values, you should remove the dashes or, even better, convert the UUID values to 16-byte numbers with `UNHEX( )` and store them in a `BINARY(16)` column. You can retrieve the values in hexadecimal format with the `HEX( )` function.

Values generated by `UUID( )` have different characteristics from those generated by a cryptographic hash function such ash `SHA1( )`: the UUID values are unevenly distributed and are somewhat sequential. They're still not as good as a monotonically increasing integer, though.

Special Types of Data

Some kinds of data don't correspond directly to the available built-in types. A timestamp with subsecond resolution is one example; we showed you some options for storing such data earlier in the chapter.

Another example is an IP address. People often use `VARCHAR(15)` columns to store IP addresses. However, an IP address is really an unsigned 32-bit integer, not a string. The dotted-quad notation is just a way of writing it out so that humans can read it more easily. You should store IP addresses as unsigned integers. MySQL provides the `INET_ATON( )` and `INET_NTOA( )` functions to convert between the two representations. Future versions of MySQL may provide a native data type for IP addresses.

Indexing Basics

Indexes are data structures that help MySQL retrieve data efficiently. They are critical for good performance, but people often forget about them or misunderstand them, so indexing is a leading cause of real-world performance problems. That's why we put this material early in the book—even earlier than our discussion of query optimization.

Indexes (also called "keys" in MySQL) become more important as your data gets larger. Small, lightly loaded databases often perform well even without proper indexes, but as the dataset grows, performance can drop very quickly.

Beware of Autogenerated Schemas

We've covered the most important data type considerations (some with serious and others with more minor performance implications), but we haven't yet told you about the evils of autogenerated schemas.

Badly written schema migration programs and programs that autogenerate schemas can cause severe performance problems. Some programs use large VARCHAR fields for *everything*, or use different data types for columns that will be compared in joins. Be sure to double-check a schema if it was created for you automatically.

Object-relational mapping (ORM) systems (and the "frameworks" that use them) are another frequent performance nightmare. Some of these systems let you store any type of data in any type of backend data store, which usually means they aren't designed to use the strengths of any of the data stores. Sometimes they store each property of each object in a separate row, even using timestamp-based versioning, so there are multiple versions of each property!

This design may appeal to developers, because it lets them work in an object-oriented fashion without needing to think about how the data is stored. However, applications that "hide complexity from developers" usually don't scale well. We suggest you think carefully before trading performance for developer productivity, and always test on a realistically large dataset, so you don't discover performance problems too late.

The easiest way to understand how an index works in MySQL is to think about the index in a book. To find out where a particular topic is discussed in a book, you look in the index, and it tells you the page number(s) where that term appears.

MySQL uses indexes in a similar way. It searches the index's data structure for a value. When it finds a match, it can find the row that contains the match. Suppose you run the following query:

```
mysql> SELECT first_name FROM sakila.actor WHERE actor_id = 5;
```

There's an index on the actor_id column, so MySQL will use the index to find rows whose actor_id is 5. In other words, it performs a lookup on the values in the index and returns any rows containing the specified value.

An index contains values from a specified column or columns in a table. If you index more than one column, the column order is very important, because MySQL can only search efficiently on a leftmost prefix of the index. Creating an index on two columns is not the same as creating two separate single-column indexes, as you'll see.

Types of Indexes

There are many types of indexes, each designed to perform well for different purposes. Indexes are implemented in the storage engine layer, not the server layer. Thus, they are not standardized: indexing works slightly differently in each engine, and not all engines support all types of indexes. Even when multiple engines support the same index type, they may implement it differently under the hood.

That said, let's look at the index types MySQL currently supports, their benefits, and their drawbacks.

B-Tree indexes

When people talk about an index without mentioning a type, they're probably referring to a *B-Tree index*, which typically uses a B-Tree data structure to store its data.[*] Most of MySQL's storage engines support this index type. The Archive engine is the exception: it didn't support indexes at all until MySQL 5.1, when it started to allow a single indexed AUTO_INCREMENT column.

We use the term "B-Tree" for these indexes because that's what MySQL uses in CREATE TABLE and other statements. However, storage engines may use different storage structures internally. For example, the NDB Cluster storage engine uses a T-Tree data structure for these indexes, even though they're labeled BTREE.

Storage engines store B-Tree indexes in various ways on disk, which can affect performance. For instance, MyISAM uses a prefix compression technique that makes indexes smaller, while InnoDB leaves indexes uncompressed because it can't use compressed indexes for some of its optimizations. Also, MyISAM indexes refer to the indexed rows by the physical positions of the rows as stored, but InnoDB refers to them by their primary key values. Each variation has benefits and drawbacks.

The general idea of a B-Tree is that all the values are stored in order, and each leaf page is the same distance from the root. Figure 3-1 shows an abstract representation of a B-Tree index, which corresponds roughly to how InnoDB's indexes work (InnoDB uses a B+Tree structure). MyISAM uses a different structure, but the principles are similar.

A B-Tree index speeds up data access because the storage engine doesn't have to scan the whole table to find the desired data. Instead, it starts at the root node (not shown in this figure). The slots in the root node hold pointers to child nodes, and the storage engine follows these pointers. It finds the right pointer by looking at the values in the node pages, which define the upper and lower bounds of the values in the

---

[*] Many storage engines actually use a B+Tree index, in which each leaf node contains a link to the next for fast range traversals through nodes. Refer to computer science literature for a detailed explanation of B-Tree indexes.

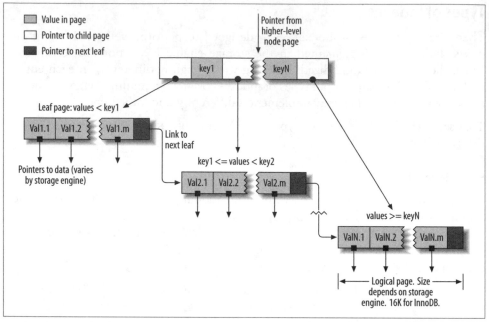

Figure 3-1. An index built on a B-Tree (technically, a B+Tree) structure

child nodes. Eventually, the storage engine either determines that the desired value doesn't exist or successfully reaches a leaf page.

Leaf pages are special, because they have pointers to the indexed data instead of pointers to other pages. (Different storage engines have different types of "pointers" to the data.) Our illustration shows only one node page and its leaf pages, but there may be many levels of node pages between the root and the leaves. The tree's depth depends on how big the table is.

Because B-Trees store the indexed columns in order, they're useful for searching for ranges of data. For instance, descending the tree for an index on a text field passes through values in alphabetical order, so looking for "everyone whose name begins with I through K" is efficient.

Suppose you have the following table:

```
CREATE TABLE People (
    last_name   varchar(50)    not null,
    first_name  varchar(50)    not null,
    dob         date           not null,
    gender      enum('m', 'f') not null,
    key(last_name, first_name, dob)
);
```

The index will contain the values from the last_name, first_name, and dob columns for every row in the table. Figure 3-2 illustrates how the index arranges the data it stores.

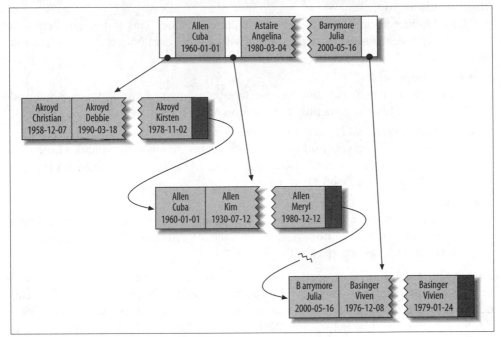

Figure 3-2. Sample entries from a B-Tree (technically, a B+Tree) index

Notice that the index sorts the values according to the order of the columns given in the index in the `CREATE TABLE` statement. Look at the last two entries: there are two people with the same name but different birth dates, and they're sorted by birth date.

Types of queries that can use a B-Tree index. B-Tree indexes work well for lookups by the full key value, a key range, or a key prefix. They are useful only if the lookup uses a leftmost prefix of the index.[*] The index we showed in the previous section will be useful for the following kinds of queries:

Match the full value
A match on the full key value specifies values for all columns in the index. For example, this index can help you find a person named Cuba Allen who was born on 1960-01-01.

Match a leftmost prefix
This index can help you find all people with the last name Allen. This uses only the first column in the index.

---

[*] This is MySQL-specific, and even version-specific. Other databases can use nonleading index parts, though it's usually more efficient to use a complete prefix. MySQL may offer this option in the future; we show workarounds later in the chapter.

Match a column prefix

You can match on the first part of a column's value. This index can help you find all people whose last names begin with J. This uses only the first column in the index.

Match a range of values

This index can help you find people whose last names are between Allen and Barrymore. This also uses only the first column.

Match one part exactly and match a range on another part

This index can help you find everyone whose last name is Allen and whose first name starts with the letter K (Kim, Karl, etc.). This is an exact match on last_name and a range query on first_name.

Index-only queries

B-Tree indexes can normally support index-only queries, which are queries that access only the index, not the row storage. We discuss this optimization in "Covering Indexes" on page 120.

Because the tree's nodes are sorted, they can be used for both lookups (finding values) and ORDER BY queries (finding values in sorted order). In general, if a B-Tree can help you find a row in a particular way, it can help you sort rows by the same criteria. So, our index will be helpful for ORDER BY clauses that match all the types of lookups we just listed.

Here are some limitations of B-Tree indexes:

- They are not useful if the lookup does not start from the leftmost side of the indexed columns. For example, this index won't help you find all people named Bill or all people born on a certain date, because those columns are not leftmost in the index. Likewise, you can't use the index to find people whose last name *ends* with a particular letter.

- You can't skip columns in the index. That is, you won't be able to find all people whose last name is Smith and who were born on a particular date. If you don't specify a value for the first_name column, MySQL can use only the first column of the index.

- The storage engine can't optimize accesses with any columns to the right of the first range condition. For example, if your query is WHERE last_name="Smith" AND first_name LIKE 'J%' AND dob='1976-12-23', the index access will use only the first two columns in the index, because the LIKE is a range condition (the server can use the rest of the columns for other purposes, though). For a column that has a limited number of values, you can often work around this by specifying equality conditions instead of range conditions. We show detailed examples of this in the indexing case study later in this chapter.

Now you know why we said the column order is extremely important: these limitations are all related to column ordering. For high-performance applications, you might need to create indexes with the same columns in different orders to satisfy your queries.

Some of these limitations are not inherent to B-Tree indexes, but are a result of how the MySQL query optimizer and storage engines use indexes. Some of them may be removed in the future.

Hash indexes

A *hash index* is built on a hash table and is useful only for exact lookups that use every column in the index.[*] For each row, the storage engine computes a *hash code* of the indexed columns, which is a small value that will probably differ from the hash codes computed for other rows with different key values. It stores the hash codes in the index and stores a pointer to each row in a hash table.

In MySQL, only the Memory storage engine supports explicit hash indexes. They are the default index type for Memory tables, though Memory tables can have B-Tree indexes too. The Memory engine supports nonunique hash indexes, which is unusual in the database world. If multiple values have the same hash code, the index will store their row pointers in the same hash table entry, using a linked list.

Here's an example. Suppose we have the following table:

```
CREATE TABLE testhash (
    fname VARCHAR(50) NOT NULL,
    lname VARCHAR(50) NOT NULL,
    KEY USING HASH(fname)
) ENGINE=MEMORY;
```

containing this data:

```
mysql> SELECT * FROM testhash;
+--------+-----------+
| fname  | lname     |
+--------+-----------+
| Arjen  | Lentz     |
| Baron  | Schwartz  |
| Peter  | Zaitsev   |
| Vadim  | Tkachenko |
+--------+-----------+
```

Now suppose the index uses an imaginary hash function called f( ), which returns the following values (these are just examples, not real values):

```
f('Arjen') = 2323
f('Baron') = 7437
f('Peter') = 8784
f('Vadim') = 2458
```

[*] See the computer science literature for more on hash tables.

The index's data structure will look like this:

Slot	Value
2323	Pointer to row 1
2458	Pointer to row 4
7437	Pointer to row 2
8784	Pointer to row 3

Notice that the slots are ordered, but the rows are not. Now, when we execute this query:

```
mysql> SELECT lname FROM testhash WHERE fname='Peter';
```

MySQL will calculate the hash of 'Peter' and use that to look up the pointer in the index. Because f('Peter') = 8784, MySQL will look in the index for 8784 and find the pointer to row 3. The final step is to compare the value in row 3 to 'Peter', to make sure it's the right row.

Because the indexes themselves store only short hash values, hash indexes are very compact. The hash value's length doesn't depend on the type of the columns you index—a hash index on a TINYINT will be the same size as a hash index on a large character column.

As a result, lookups are usually lightning-fast. However, hash indexes have some limitations:

- Because the index contains only hash codes and row pointers rather than the values themselves, MySQL can't use the values in the index to avoid reading the rows. Fortunately, accessing the in-memory rows is very fast, so this doesn't usually degrade performance.

- MySQL can't use hash indexes for sorting because they don't store rows in sorted order.

- Hash indexes don't support partial key matching, because they compute the hash from the entire indexed value. That is, if you have an index on (A,B) and your query's WHERE clause refers only to A, the index won't help.

- Hash indexes support only equality comparisons that use the =, IN( ), and <=> operators (note that <> and <=> are not the same operator). They can't speed up range queries, such as WHERE price > 100.

- Accessing data in a hash index is very quick, unless there are many collisions (multiple values with the same hash). When there are collisions, the storage engine must follow each row pointer in the linked list and compare their values to the lookup value to find the right row(s).

- Some index maintenance operations can be slow if there are many hash collisions. For example, if you create a hash index on a column with a very low selectivity (many hash collisions) and then delete a row from the table, finding the pointer from the index to that row might be expensive. The storage engine will have to examine each row in that hash key's linked list to find and remove the reference to the one row you deleted.

These limitations make hash indexes useful only in special cases. However, when they match the application's needs, they can improve performance dramatically. An example is in data-warehousing applications where a classic "star" schema requires many joins to lookup tables. Hash indexes are exactly what a lookup table requires.

In addition to the Memory storage engine's explicit hash indexes, the NDB Cluster storage engine supports unique hash indexes. Their functionality is specific to the NDB Cluster storage engine, which we don't cover in this book.

The InnoDB storage engine has a special feature called *adaptive hash indexes*. When InnoDB notices that some index values are being accessed very frequently, it builds a hash index for them in memory on top of B-Tree indexes. This gives its B-Tree indexes some properties of hash indexes, such as very fast hashed lookups. This process is completely automatic, and you can't control or configure it.

Building your own hash indexes. If your storage engine doesn't support hash indexes, you can emulate them yourself in a manner similar to that InnoDB uses. This will give you access to some of the desirable properties of hash indexes, such as a very small index size for very long keys.

The idea is simple: create a pseudohash index on top of a standard B-Tree index. It will not be exactly the same thing as a real hash index, because it will still use the B-Tree index for lookups. However, it will use the keys' hash values for lookups, instead of the keys themselves. All you need to do is specify the hash function manually in the query's WHERE clause.

An example of when this approach works well is for URL lookups. URLs generally cause B-Tree indexes to become huge, because they're very long. You'd normally query a table of URLs like this:

```
mysql> SELECT id FROM url WHERE url="http://www.mysql.com";
```

But if you remove the index on the url column and add an indexed url_crc column to the table, you can use a query like this:

```
mysql> SELECT id FROM url WHERE url="http://www.mysql.com"
    ->     AND url_crc=CRC32("http://www.mysql.com");
```

This works well because the MySQL query optimizer notices there's a small, highly selective index on the url_crc column and does an index lookup for entries with that value (1560514994, in this case). Even if several rows have the same url_crc value, it's very easy to find these rows with a fast integer comparison and then examine them to find the one that matches the full URL exactly. The alternative is to index the full URL as a string, which is much slower.

One drawback to this approach is the need to maintain the hash values. You can do this manually or, in MySQL 5.0 and newer, you can use triggers. The following example shows how triggers can help maintain the url_crc column when you insert and update values. First, we create the table:

```
CREATE TABLE pseudohash (
    id int unsigned NOT NULL auto_increment,
    url varchar(255) NOT NULL,
    url_crc int unsigned NOT NULL DEFAULT 0,
    PRIMARY KEY(id)
);
```

Now we create the triggers. We change the statement delimiter temporarily, so we can use a semicolon as a delimiter for the trigger:

```
DELIMITER |

CREATE TRIGGER pseudohash_crc_ins BEFORE INSERT ON pseudohash FOR EACH ROW BEGIN
SET NEW.url_crc=crc32(NEW.url);
END;
|

CREATE TRIGGER pseudohash_crc_upd BEFORE UPDATE ON pseudohash FOR EACH ROW BEGIN
SET NEW.url_crc=crc32(NEW.url);
END;
|

DELIMITER ;
```

All that remains is to verify that the trigger maintains the hash:

```
mysql> INSERT INTO pseudohash (url) VALUES ('http://www.mysql.com');
mysql> SELECT * FROM pseudohash;
+----+----------------------+------------+
| id | url                  | url_crc    |
+----+----------------------+------------+
|  1 | http://www.mysql.com | 1560514994 |
+----+----------------------+------------+
mysql> UPDATE pseudohash SET url='http://www.mysql.com/' WHERE id=1;
mysql> SELECT * FROM pseudohash;
+----+-----------------------+------------+
| id | url                   | url_crc    |
+----+-----------------------+------------+
|  1 | http://www.mysql.com/ | 1558250469 |
+----+-----------------------+------------+
```

If you use this approach, you should not use SHA1( ) or MD5( ) hash functions. These return very long strings, which waste a lot of space and result in slower comparisons. They are cryptographically strong functions designed to virtually eliminate collisions, which is not your goal here. Simple hash functions can offer acceptable collision rates with better performance.

If your table has many rows and CRC32( ) gives too many collisions, implement your own 64-bit hash function. Make sure you use a function that returns an integer, not a string. One way to implement a 64-bit hash function is to use just part of the value returned by MD5( ). This is probably less efficient than writing your own routine as a user-defined function (see "User-Defined Functions" on page 230), but it'll do in a pinch:

```
mysql> SELECT CONV(RIGHT(MD5('http://www.mysql.com/'), 16), 16, 10) AS HASH64;
+----------------------+
| HASH64               |
+----------------------+
| 9761173720318281581  |
+----------------------+
```

Maatkit (*http://maatkit.sourceforge.net*) includes a UDF that implements a Fowler/Noll/Vo 64-bit hash, which is very fast.

Handling hash collisions. When you search for a value by its hash, you must also include the literal value in your WHERE clause:

```
mysql> SELECT id FROM url WHERE url_crc=CRC32("http://www.mysql.com")
    ->     AND url="http://www.mysql.com";
```

The following query will *not* work correctly, because if another URL has the CRC32( ) value 1560514994, the query will return both rows:

```
mysql> SELECT id FROM url WHERE url_crc=CRC32("http://www.mysql.com");
```

The probability of a hash collision grows much faster than you might think, due to the so-called Birthday Paradox. CRC32( ) returns a 32-bit integer value, so the probability of a collision reaches 1% with as few as 93,000 values. To illustrate this, we loaded all the words in */usr/share/dict/words* into a table along with their CRC32( ) values, resulting in 98,569 rows. There is already one collision in this set of data! The collision makes the following query return more than one row:

```
mysql> SELECT word, crc FROM words WHERE crc = CRC32('gnu');
+---------+------------+
| word    | crc        |
+---------+------------+
| codding | 1774765869 |
| gnu     | 1774765869 |
+---------+------------+
```

The correct query is as follows:

```
mysql> SELECT word, crc FROM words WHERE crc = CRC32('gnu') AND word = 'gnu';
+------+------------+
| word | crc        |
+------+------------+
| gnu  | 1774765869 |
+------+------------+
```

To avoid problems with collisions, you must specify both conditions in the WHERE clause. If collisions aren't a problem—for example, because you're doing statistical queries and you don't need exact results—you can simplify, and gain some efficiency, by using only the CRC32( ) value in the WHERE clause.

Spatial (R-Tree) indexes

MyISAM supports spatial indexes, which you can use with geospatial types such as GEOMETRY. Unlike B-Tree indexes, spatial indexes don't require your WHERE clauses to operate on a leftmost prefix of the index. They index the data by all dimensions at the same time. As a result, lookups can use any combination of dimensions efficiently. However, you must use the MySQL GIS functions, such as MBRCONTAINS( ), for this to work.

Full-text indexes

FULLTEXT is a special type of index for MyISAM tables. It finds keywords in the text instead of comparing values directly to the values in the index. Full-text searching is completely different from other types of matching. It has many subtleties, such as stopwords, stemming and plurals, and Boolean searching. It is much more analogous to what a search engine does than to simple WHERE parameter matching.

Having a full-text index on a column does not eliminate the value of a B-Tree index on the same column. Full-text indexes are for MATCH AGAINST operations, not ordinary WHERE clause operations.

We discuss full-text indexing in more detail in "Full-Text Searching" on page 244.

Indexing Strategies for High Performance

Creating the correct indexes and using them properly is essential to good query performance. We've introduced the different types of indexes and explored their strengths and weaknesses. Now let's see how to really tap into the power of indexes.

There are many ways to choose and use indexes effectively, because there are many special-case optimizations and specialized behaviors. Determining what to use when and evaluating the performance implications of your choices are skills you'll learn over time. The following sections will help you understand how to use indexes effectively, but don't forget to benchmark!

Isolate the Column

If you don't isolate the indexed columns in a query, MySQL generally can't use indexes on columns unless the columns are isolated in the query. "Isolating" the column means it should not be part of an expression or be inside a function in the query.

For example, here's a query that can't use the index on actor_id:

```
mysql> SELECT actor_id FROM sakila.actor WHERE actor_id + 1 = 5;
```

A human can easily see that the WHERE clause is equivalent to actor_id = 4, but MySQL can't solve the equation for actor_id. It's up to you to do this. You should get in the habit of simplifying your WHERE criteria, so the indexed column is alone on one side of the comparison operator.

Here's another example of a common mistake:

```
mysql> SELECT ... WHERE TO_DAYS(CURRENT_DATE) - TO_DAYS(date_col) <= 10;
```

This query will find all rows where the date_col value is newer than 10 days ago, but it won't use indexes because of the TO_DAYS( ) function. Here's a better way to write this query:

```
mysql> SELECT ... WHERE date_col >= DATE_SUB(CURRENT_DATE, INTERVAL 10 DAY);
```

This query will have no trouble using an index, but you can still improve it in another way. The reference to CURRENT_DATE will prevent the query cache from caching the results. You can replace CURRENT_DATE with a literal to fix that problem:

```
mysql> SELECT ... WHERE date_col >= DATE_SUB('2008-01-17', INTERVAL 10 DAY);
```

See Chapter 5 for details on the query cache.

Prefix Indexes and Index Selectivity

Sometimes you need to index very long character columns, which makes your indexes large and slow. One strategy is to simulate a hash index, as we showed earlier in this chapter. But sometimes that isn't good enough. What can you do?

You can often save space and get good performance by indexing the first few characters instead of the whole value. This makes your indexes use less space, but it also makes them less *selective*. Index selectivity is the ratio of the number of distinct indexed values (the *cardinality*) to the total number of rows in the table (*#T*), and ranges from 1/*#T* to 1. A highly selective index is good because it lets MySQL filter out more rows when it looks for matches. A unique index has a selectivity of 1, which is as good as it gets.

A prefix of the column is often selective enough to give good performance. If you're indexing BLOB or TEXT columns, or very long VARCHAR columns, you *must* define prefix indexes, because MySQL disallows indexing their full length.

The trick is to choose a prefix that's long enough to give good selectivity, but short enough to save space. The prefix should be long enough to make the index nearly as useful as it would be if you'd indexed the whole column. In other words, you'd like the prefix's cardinality to be close to the full column's cardinality.

To determine a good prefix length, find the most frequent values and compare that list to a list of the most frequent prefixes. There's no good table to demonstrate this in the Sakila sample database, so we derive one from the city table, just so we have enough data to work with:

```
CREATE TABLE sakila.city_demo(city VARCHAR(50) NOT NULL);
INSERT INTO sakila.city_demo(city) SELECT city FROM sakila.city;
-- Repeat the next statement five times:
INSERT INTO sakila.city_demo(city) SELECT city FROM sakila.city_demo;
-- Now randomize the distribution (inefficiently but conveniently):
UPDATE sakila.city_demo
   SET city = (SELECT city FROM  sakila.city ORDER BY RAND( ) LIMIT 1);
```

Now we have an example dataset. The results are not realistically distributed, and we used RAND( ), so your results will vary, but that doesn't matter for this exercise. First, we find the most frequently occurring cities:

```
mysql> SELECT COUNT(*) AS cnt, city
    -> FROM sakila.city_demo GROUP BY city ORDER BY cnt DESC LIMIT 10;
+-----+----------------+
| cnt | city           |
+-----+----------------+
|  65 | London         |
|  49 | Hiroshima      |
|  48 | Teboksary      |
|  48 | Pak Kret       |
|  48 | Yaound         |
|  47 | Tel Aviv-Jaffa |
|  47 | Shimoga        |
|  45 | Cabuyao        |
|  45 | Callao         |
|  45 | Bislig         |
+-----+----------------+
```

Notice that there are roughly 45 to 65 occurrences of each value. Now we find the most frequently occurring city name *prefixes*, beginning with three-letter prefixes:

```
mysql> SELECT COUNT(*) AS cnt, LEFT(city, 3) AS pref
    -> FROM sakila.city_demo GROUP BY pref ORDER BY cnt DESC LIMIT 10;
+-----+------+
| cnt | pref |
+-----+------+
| 483 | San  |
| 195 | Cha  |
| 177 | Tan  |
| 167 | Sou  |
| 163 | al-  |
| 163 | Sal  |
| 146 | Shi  |
| 136 | Hal  |
| 130 | Val  |
| 129 | Bat  |
+-----+------+
```

There are many more occurrences of each prefix, so there are many fewer unique prefixes than unique full-length city names. The idea is to increase the prefix length until the prefix becomes nearly as selective as the full length of the column. A little experimentation shows that 7 is a good value:

```
mysql> SELECT COUNT(*) AS cnt, LEFT(city, 7) AS pref
    -> FROM sakila.city_demo GROUP BY pref ORDER BY cnt DESC LIMIT 10;
+-----+---------+
| cnt | pref    |
+-----+---------+
|  70 | Santiag |
|  68 | San Fel |
|  65 | London  |
|  61 | Valle d |
|  49 | Hiroshi |
|  48 | Teboksa |
|  48 | Pak Kre |
|  48 | Yaound  |
|  47 | Tel Avi |
|  47 | Shimoga |
+-----+---------+
```

Another way to calculate a good prefix length is by computing the full column's selectivity and trying to make the prefix's selectivity close to that value. Here's how to find the full column's selectivity:

```
mysql> SELECT COUNT(DISTINCT city)/COUNT(*) FROM sakila.city_demo;
+-------------------------------+
| COUNT(DISTINCT city)/COUNT(*) |
+-------------------------------+
|                        0.0312 |
+-------------------------------+
```

The prefix will be about as good, on average, if we target a selectivity near .031. It's possible to evaluate many different lengths in one query, which is useful on very large tables. Here's how to find the selectivity of several prefix lengths in one query:

```
mysql> SELECT COUNT(DISTINCT LEFT(city, 3))/COUNT(*) AS sel3,
    ->    COUNT(DISTINCT LEFT(city, 4))/COUNT(*) AS sel4,
    ->    COUNT(DISTINCT LEFT(city, 5))/COUNT(*) AS sel5,
    ->    COUNT(DISTINCT LEFT(city, 6))/COUNT(*) AS sel6,
    ->    COUNT(DISTINCT LEFT(city, 7))/COUNT(*) AS sel7
    -> FROM sakila.city_demo;
+--------+--------+--------+--------+--------+
| sel3   | sel4   | sel5   | sel6   | sel7   |
+--------+--------+--------+--------+--------+
| 0.0239 | 0.0293 | 0.0305 | 0.0309 | 0.0310 |
+--------+--------+--------+--------+--------+
```

This query shows that increasing the prefix length results in successively smaller improvements as it approaches seven characters.

It's not a good idea to look only at average selectivity. You also need to think about *worst-case* selectivity. The average selectivity might make you think a four- or five-character prefix is good enough, but if your data is very uneven, that could be a trap. If you look at the number of occurrences of the most common city name prefixes using a value of 4, you'll see the unevenness clearly:

```
mysql> SELECT COUNT(*) AS cnt, LEFT(city, 4) AS pref
    -> FROM sakila.city_demo GROUP BY pref ORDER BY cnt DESC LIMIT 5;
+-----+------+
| cnt | pref |
+-----+------+
| 205 | San  |
| 200 | Sant |
| 135 | Sout |
| 104 | Chan |
|  91 | Toul |
+-----+------+
```

With four characters, the most frequent prefixes occur quite a bit more often than the most frequent full-length values. That is, the selectivity on those values is lower than the average selectivity. If you have a more realistic dataset than this randomly generated sample, you're likely to see this effect even more. For example, building a four-character prefix index on real-world city names will give terrible selectivity on cities that begin with "San" and "New," of which there are many.

Now that we've found a good value for our sample data, here's how to create a prefix index on the column:

```
mysql> ALTER TABLE sakila.city_demo ADD KEY (city(7));
```

Prefix indexes can be a great way to make indexes smaller and faster, but they have downsides too: MySQL cannot use prefix indexes for ORDER BY or GROUP BY queries, nor can it use them as covering indexes.

 Sometimes suffix indexes make sense (e.g., for finding all email addresses from a certain domain). MySQL does not support reversed indexes natively, but you can store a reversed string and index a prefix of it. You can maintain the index with triggers; see "Building your own hash indexes" on page 103, earlier in this chapter.

Clustered Indexes

Clustered indexes[*] aren't a separate type of index. Rather, they're an approach to data storage. The exact details vary between implementations, but InnoDB's clustered indexes actually store a B-Tree index and the rows together in the same structure.

When a table has a clustered index, its rows are actually stored in the index's leaf pages. The term "clustered" refers to the fact that rows with adjacent key values are stored close to each other.[†] You can have only one clustered index per table, because you can't store the rows in two places at once. (However, *covering indexes* let you emulate multiple clustered indexes; more on this later.)

---

[*] Oracle users will be familiar with the term "index-organized table," which means the same thing.

[†] This isn't always true, as you'll see in a moment.

Because storage engines are responsible for implementing indexes, not all storage engines support clustered indexes. At present, solidDB and InnoDB are the only ones that do. We focus on InnoDB in this section, but the principles we discuss are likely to be at least partially true for any storage engine that supports clustered indexes now or in the future.

Figure 3-3 shows how records are laid out in a clustered index. Notice that the leaf pages contain full rows but the node pages contain only the indexed columns. In this case, the indexed column contains integer values.

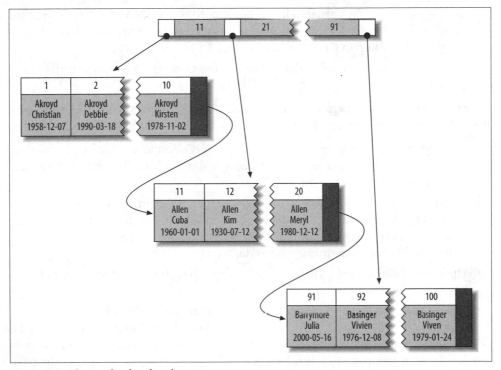

Figure 3-3. Clustered index data layout

Some database servers let you choose which index to cluster, but none of MySQL's storage engines does at the time of this writing. InnoDB clusters the data by the primary key. That means that the "indexed column" in Figure 3-3 is the primary key column.

If you don't define a primary key, InnoDB will try to use a unique nonnullable index instead. If there's no such index, InnoDB will define a hidden primary key for you and then cluster on that.* InnoDB clusters records together only within a page. Pages with adjacent key values may be distant from each other.

---

* The solidDB storage engine does this too.

A clustering primary key can help performance, but it can also cause serious performance problems. Thus, you should think carefully about clustering, especially when you change a table's storage engine from InnoDB to something else or vice versa.

Clustering data has some very important advantages:

- You can keep related data close together. For example, when implementing a mailbox, you can cluster by user_id, so you can retrieve all of a single user's messages by fetching only a few pages from disk. If you didn't use clustering, each message might require its own disk I/O.

- Data access is fast. A clustered index holds both the index and the data together in one B-Tree, so retrieving rows from a clustered index is normally faster than a comparable lookup in a nonclustered index.

- Queries that use covering indexes can use the primary key values contained at the leaf node.

These benefits can boost performance tremendously if you design your tables and queries to take advantage of them. However, clustered indexes also have disadvantages:

- Clustering gives the largest improvement for I/O-bound workloads. If the data fits in memory the order in which it's accessed doesn't really matter, so clustering doesn't give much benefit.

- Insert speeds depend heavily on insertion order. Inserting rows in primary key order is the fastest way to load data into an InnoDB table. It may be a good idea to reorganize the table with OPTIMIZE TABLE after loading a lot of data if you didn't load the rows in primary key order.

- Updating the clustered index columns is expensive, because it forces InnoDB to move each updated row to a new location.

- Tables built upon clustered indexes are subject to *page splits* when new rows are inserted, or when a row's primary key is updated such that the row must be moved. A page split happens when a row's key value dictates that the row must be placed into a page that is full of data. The storage engine must split the page into two to accommodate the row. Page splits can cause a table to use more space on disk.

- Clustered tables can be slower for full table scans, especially if rows are less densely packed or stored nonsequentially because of page splits.

- Secondary (nonclustered) indexes can be larger than you might expect, because their leaf nodes contain the primary key columns of the referenced rows.

- Secondary index accesses require two index lookups instead of one.

The last point can be a bit confusing. Why would a secondary index require two index lookups? The answer lies in the nature of the "row pointers" the secondary index stores. Remember, a leaf node doesn't store a pointer to the referenced row's physical location; rather, it stores the row's primary key values.

That means that to find a row from a secondary index, the storage engine first finds the leaf node in the secondary index and then uses the primary key values stored there to navigate the primary key and find the row. That's double work: two B-Tree navigations instead of one. (In InnoDB, the adaptive hash index can help reduce this penalty.)

Comparison of InnoDB and MyISAM data layout

The differences between clustered and nonclustered data layouts, and the corresponding differences between primary and secondary indexes, can be confusing and surprising. Let's see how InnoDB and MyISAM lay out the following table:

```
CREATE TABLE layout_test (
    col1 int NOT NULL,
    col2 int NOT NULL,
    PRIMARY KEY(col1),
    KEY(col2)
);
```

Suppose the table is populated with primary key values 1 to 10,000, inserted in random order and then optimized with OPTIMIZE TABLE. In other words, the data is arranged optimally on disk, but the rows may be in a random order. The values for col2 are randomly assigned between 1 and 100, so there are lots of duplicates.

MyISAM's data layout. MyISAM's data layout is simpler, so we illustrate that first. MyISAM stores the rows on disk in the order in which they were inserted, as shown in Figure 3-4.

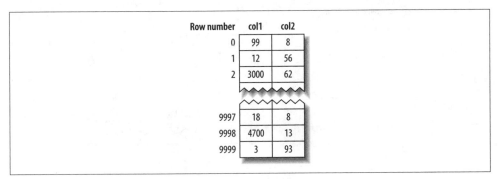

Figure 3-4. MyISAM data layout for the layout_test table

We've shown the row numbers, beginning at 0, beside the rows. Because the rows are fixed-size, MyISAM can find any row by seeking the required number of bytes from the beginning of the table. (MyISAM doesn't always use "row numbers," as we've shown; it uses different strategies depending on whether the rows are fixed-size or variable-size.)

This layout makes it easy to build an index. We illustrate with a series of diagrams, abstracting away physical details such as pages and showing only "nodes" in the index. Each leaf node in the index can simply contain the row number. Figure 3-5 illustrates the table's primary key.

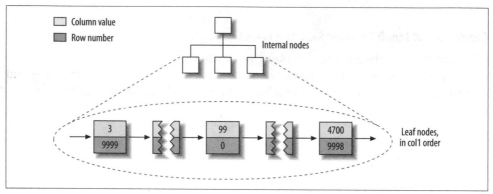

Figure 3-5. *MyISAM primary key layout for the layout_test table*

We've glossed over some of the details, such as how many internal B-Tree nodes descend from the one before, but that's not important to understanding the basic data layout of a nonclustered storage engine.

What about the index on col2? Is there anything special about it? As it turns out, no—it's just an index like any other. Figure 3-6 illustrates the col2 index.

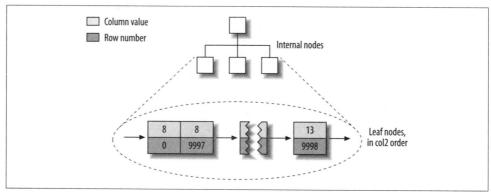

Figure 3-6. *MyISAM col2 index layout for the layout_test table*

In fact, in MyISAM, there is no structural difference between a primary key and any other index. A primary key is simply a unique, nonnullable index named PRIMARY.

InnoDB's data layout. InnoDB stores the same data very differently because of its clustered organization. InnoDB stores the table as shown in Figure 3-7.

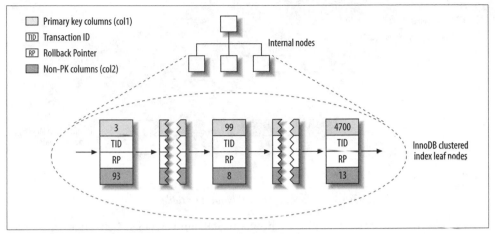

Figure 3-7. InnoDB primary key layout for the layout_test table

At first glance, that might not look very different from Figure 3-5. But look again, and notice that this illustration shows the *whole table*, not just the index. Because the clustered index "is" the table in InnoDB, there's no separate row storage as there is for MyISAM.

Each leaf node in the clustered index contains the primary key value, the transaction ID and rollback pointer InnoDB uses for transactional and MVCC purposes, and the rest of the columns (in this case, col2). If the primary key is on a column prefix, InnoDB includes the full column value with the rest of the columns.

Also in contrast to MyISAM, secondary indexes are very different from clustered indexes in InnoDB. Instead of storing "row pointers," InnoDB's secondary index leaf nodes contain the primary key values, which serve as the "pointers" to the rows. This strategy reduces the work needed to maintain secondary indexes when rows move or when there's a data page split. Using the row's primary key values as the pointer makes the index larger, but it means InnoDB can move a row without updating pointers to it.

Figure 3-8 illustrates the col2 index for the example table.

Each leaf node contains the indexed columns (in this case just col2), followed by the primary key values (col1).

These diagrams have illustrated the B-Tree leaf nodes, but we intentionally omitted details about the non-leaf nodes. InnoDB's non-leaf B-Tree nodes each contain the indexed column(s), plus a pointer to the next deeper node (which may be either another non-leaf node or a leaf node). This applies to all indexes, clustered and secondary.

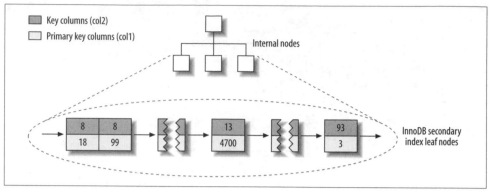

Figure 3-8. InnoDB secondary index layout for the layout_test table

Figure 3-9 is an abstract diagram of how InnoDB and MyISAM arrange the table. This illustration makes it easier to see how differently InnoDB and MyISAM store data and indexes.

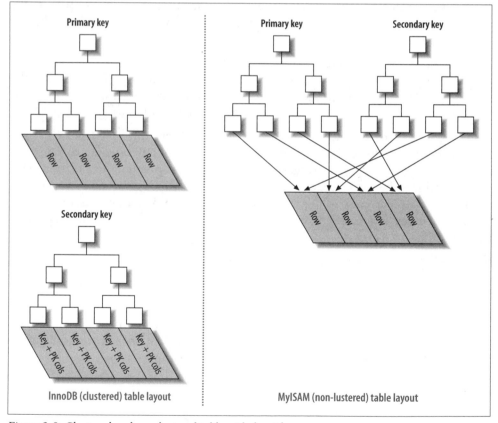

Figure 3-9. Clustered and nonclustered tables side-by-side

If you don't understand why and how clustered and nonclustered storage are different, and why it's so important, don't worry. It will become clearer as you learn more, especially in the rest of this chapter and in the next chapter. These concepts are complicated, and they take a while to understand fully.

Inserting rows in primary key order with InnoDB

If you're using InnoDB and don't need any particular clustering, it can be a good idea to define a *surrogate key*, which is a primary key whose value is not derived from your application's data. The easiest way to do this is usually with an AUTO_INCREMENT column. This will ensure that rows are inserted in sequential order and will offer better performance for joins using primary keys.

It is best to avoid random (nonsequential) clustered keys. For example, using UUID values is a poor choice from a performance standpoint: it makes clustered index insertion random, which is a worst-case scenario, and does not give you any helpful data clustering.

To demonstrate, we benchmarked two cases. The first is inserting into a userinfo table with an integer ID, defined as follows:

```
CREATE TABLE userinfo (
    id              int unsigned NOT NULL AUTO_INCREMENT,
    name            varchar(64) NOT NULL DEFAULT '',
    email           varchar(64) NOT NULL DEFAULT '',
    password        varchar(64) NOT NULL DEFAULT '',
    dob             date DEFAULT NULL,
    address         varchar(255) NOT NULL DEFAULT '',
    city            varchar(64) NOT NULL DEFAULT '',
    state_id        tinyint unsigned NOT NULL DEFAULT '0',
    zip             varchar(8) NOT NULL DEFAULT '',
    country_id      smallint unsigned NOT NULL DEFAULT '0',
    gender          ('M','F') NOT NULL DEFAULT 'M',
    account_type    varchar(32) NOT NULL DEFAULT '',
    verified        tinyint NOT NULL DEFAULT '0',
    allow_mail      tinyint unsigned NOT NULL DEFAULT '0',
    parrent_account int unsigned NOT NULL DEFAULT '0',
    closest_airport varchar(3) NOT NULL DEFAULT '',
    PRIMARY KEY (id),
    UNIQUE  KEY email (email),
    KEY     country_id (country_id),
    KEY     state_id (state_id),
    KEY     state_id_2 (state_id,city,address)
) ENGINE=InnoDB
```

Notice the autoincrementing integer primary key.

The second case is a table named userinfo_uuid. It is identical to the userinfo table, except that its primary key is a UUID instead of an integer:

```
CREATE TABLE userinfo_uuid (
   uuid varchar(36) NOT NULL,
   ...
```

We benchmarked both table designs. First, we inserted a million records into both tables on a server with enough memory to hold the indexes. Next, we inserted three million rows into the same tables, which made the indexes bigger than the server's memory. Table 3-2 compares the benchmark results.

Table 3-2. Benchmark results for inserting rows into InnoDB tables

Table	Rows	Time (sec)	Index size (MB)
userinfo	1,000,000	137	342
userinfo_uuid	1,000,000	180	544
userinfo	3,000,000	1233	1036
userinfo_uuid	3,000,000	4525	1707

Notice that not only does it take longer to insert the rows with the UUID primary key, but the resulting indexes are quite a bit bigger. Some of that is due to the larger primary key, but some of it is undoubtedly due to page splits and resultant fragmentation as well.

To see why this is so, let's see what happened in the index when we inserted data into the first table. Figure 3-10 shows inserts filling a page and then continuing on a second page.

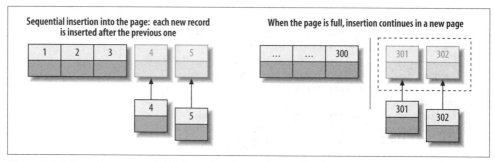

Figure 3-10. Inserting sequential index values into a clustered index

As Figure 3-10 illustrates, InnoDB stores each record immediately after the one before, because the primary key values are sequential. When the page reaches its maximum fill factor (InnoDB's initial fill factor is only 15/16 full, to leave room for modifications later), the next record goes into a new page. Once the data has been loaded in this sequential fashion, the pages are packed nearly full with in-order records, which is highly desirable.

Contrast that with what happened when we inserted the data into the second table with the UUID clustered index, as shown in Figure 3-11.

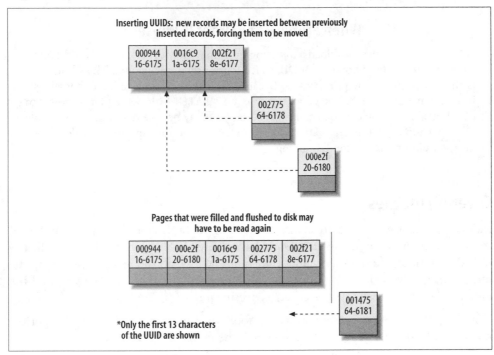

Figure 3-11. Inserting nonsequential values into a clustered index

Because each new row doesn't necessarily have a larger primary key value than the previous one, InnoDB cannot always place the new row at the end of the index. It has to find the appropriate place for the row—on average, somewhere near the middle of the existing data—and make room for it. This causes a lot of extra work and results in a suboptimal data layout. Here's a summary of the drawbacks:

- The destination page might have been flushed to disk and removed from the caches, in which case, InnoDB will have to find it and read it from the disk before it can insert the new row. This causes a lot of random I/O.

- InnoDB sometimes has to split pages to make room for new rows. This requires moving around a lot of data.

- Pages become sparsely and irregularly filled because of splitting, so the final data is fragmented.

After loading such random values into a clustered index, you should probably do an OPTIMIZE TABLE to rebuild the table and fill the pages optimally.

The moral of the story is that you should strive to insert data in primary key order when using InnoDB, and you should try to use a clustering key that will give a monotonically increasing value for each new row.

Covering Indexes

Indexes are a way to find rows efficiently, but MySQL can also use an index to retrieve a column's data, so it doesn't have to read the row at all. After all, the index's leaf nodes contain the values they index; why read the row when reading the index can give you the data you want? An index that contains (or "covers") all the data needed to satisfy a query is called a *covering index*.

Covering indexes can be a very powerful tool and can dramatically improve performance. Consider the benefits of reading only the index instead of the data:

- Index entries are usually much smaller than the full row size, so MySQL can access significantly less data if it reads only the index. This is very important for cached workloads, where much of the response time comes from copying the data. It is also helpful for I/O-bound workloads, because the indexes are smaller than the data and fit in memory better. (This is especially true for MyISAM, which can pack indexes to make them even smaller.)

- Indexes are sorted by their index values (at least within the page), so I/O-bound range accesses will need to do less I/O compared to fetching each row from a random disk location. For some storage engines, such as MyISAM, you can even OPTIMIZE the table to get fully sorted indexes, which will let simple range queries use completely sequential index accesses.

- Most storage engines cache indexes better than data. (Falcon is a notable exception.) Some storage engines, such as MyISAM, cache only the index in MySQL's memory. Because the operating system caches the data for MyISAM, accessing it typically requires a system call. This may cause a huge performance impact, especially for cached workloads where the system call is the most expensive part of data access.

- Covering indexes are especially helpful for InnoDB tables, because of InnoDB's clustered indexes. InnoDB's secondary indexes hold the row's primary key values at their leaf nodes. Thus, a secondary index that covers a query avoids another index lookup in the primary key.

In all of these scenarios, it is typically much less expensive to satisfy a query from an index instead of looking up the rows.

A covering index can't be just any kind of index. The index must store the values from the columns it contains. Hash, spatial, and full-text indexes don't store these values, so MySQL can use only B-Tree indexes to cover queries. And again, different storage engines implement covering indexes differently, and not all storage engines support them (at the time of this writing, the Memory and Falcon storage engines don't).

When you issue a query that is covered by an index (an *index-covered query*), you'll see "Using index" in the Extra column in EXPLAIN.[*] For example, the sakila. inventory table has a multicolumn index on (store_id, film_id). MySQL can use this index for a query that accesses only those two columns, such as the following:

```
mysql> EXPLAIN SELECT store_id, film_id FROM sakila.inventory\G
*************************** 1. row ***************************
           id: 1
  select_type: SIMPLE
        table: inventory
         type: index
possible_keys: NULL
          key: idx_store_id_film_id
      key_len: 3
          ref: NULL
         rows: 4673
        Extra: Using index
```

Index-covered queries have subtleties that can disable this optimization. The MySQL query optimizer decides before executing a query whether an index covers it. Suppose the index covers a WHERE condition, but not the entire query. If the condition evaluates as false, MySQL 5.1 and earlier will fetch the row anyway, even though it doesn't need it and will filter it out.

Let's see why this can happen, and how to rewrite the query to work around the problem. We begin with the following query:

```
mysql> EXPLAIN SELECT * FROM products WHERE actor='SEAN CARREY'
    -> AND title like '%APOLLO%'\G
*************************** 1. row ***************************
           id: 1
  select_type: SIMPLE
        table: products
         type: ref
possible_keys: ACTOR,IX_PROD_ACTOR
          key: ACTOR
      key_len: 52
```

---

[*] It's easy to confuse "Using index" in the Extra column with "index" in the type column. However, they are completely different. The type column has nothing to do with covering indexes; it shows the query's access type, or how the query will find rows.

```
        ref: const
       rows: 10
      Extra: Using where
```

The index can't cover this query for two reasons:

- No index covers the query, because we selected all columns from the table and no index covers all columns. There's still a shortcut MySQL could theoretically use, though: the WHERE clause mentions only columns the index covers, so MySQL could use the index to find the actor and check whether the title matches, and only then read the full row.

- MySQL can't perform the LIKE operation in the index. This is a limitation of the low-level storage engine API, which allows only simple comparisons in index operations. MySQL can perform prefix-match LIKE patterns in the index because it can convert them to simple comparisons, but the leading wildcard in the query makes it impossible for the storage engine to evaluate the match. Thus, the MySQL server itself will have to fetch and match on the row's values, not the index's values.

There's a way to work around both problems with a combination of clever indexing and query rewriting. We can extend the index to cover (artist, title, prod_id) and rewrite the query as follows:

```
mysql> EXPLAIN SELECT *
    -> FROM products
    ->    JOIN (
    ->       SELECT prod_id
    ->       FROM products
    ->       WHERE actor='SEAN CARREY' AND title LIKE '%APOLLO%'
    ->    ) AS t1 ON (t1.prod_id=products.prod_id)\G
*************************** 1. row ***************************
          id: 1
 select_type: PRIMARY
       table: <derived2>
             ...omitted...
*************************** 2. row ***************************
          id: 1
 select_type: PRIMARY
       table: products
             ...omitted...
*************************** 3. row ***************************
          id: 2
 select_type: DERIVED
       table: products
        type: ref
possible_keys: ACTOR,ACTOR_2,IX_PROD_ACTOR
         key: ACTOR_2
     key_len: 52
         ref:
        rows: 11
       Extra: Using where; Using index
```

Now MySQL uses the covering index in the first stage of the query, when it finds matching rows in the subquery in the FROM clause. It doesn't use the index to cover the whole query, but it's better than nothing.

The effectiveness of this optimization depends on how many rows the WHERE clause finds. Suppose the products table contains a million rows. Let's see how these two queries perform on three different datasets, each of which contains a million rows:

1. In the first, 30,000 products have Sean Carrey as the actor, and 20,000 of those contain Apollo in the title.

2. In the second, 30,000 products have Sean Carrey as the actor, and 40 of those contain Apollo in the title.

3. In the third, 50 products have Sean Carrey as the actor, and 10 of those contain Apollo in the title.

We used these three datasets to benchmark the two variations on the query and got the results shown in Table 3-3.

Table 3-3. Benchmark results for index-covered queries versus non-index-covered queries

Dataset	Original query	Optimized query
Example 1	5 queries per sec	5 queries per sec
Example 2	7 queries per sec	35 queries per sec
Example 3	2400 queries per sec	2000 queries per sec

Here's how to interpret these results:

- In example 1 the query returns a big result set, so we can't see the optimization's effect. Most of the time is spent reading and sending data.

- Example 2, where the second condition filter leaves only a small set of results after index filtering, shows how effective the proposed optimization is: performance is five times better on our data. The efficiency comes from needing to read only 40 full rows, instead of 30,000 as in the first query.

- Example 3 shows the case when the subquery is inefficient. The set of results left after index filtering is so small that the subquery is more expensive than reading all the data from the table.

This optimization is sometimes an effective way to help avoid reading unnecessary rows in MySQL 5.1 and earlier. MySQL 6.0 may avoid this extra work itself, so you might be able to simplify your queries when you upgrade.

In most storage engines, an index can cover only queries that access columns that are part of the index. However, InnoDB can actually take this optimization a little bit further. Recall that InnoDB's secondary indexes hold primary key values at their leaf nodes. This means InnoDB's secondary indexes effectively have "extra columns" that InnoDB can use to cover queries.

For example, the `sakila.actor` table uses InnoDB and has an index on `last_name`, so the index can cover queries that retrieve the primary key column `actor_id`, even though that column isn't technically part of the index:

```
mysql> EXPLAIN SELECT actor_id, last_name
    -> FROM sakila.actor WHERE last_name = 'HOPPER'\G
*************************** 1. row ***************************
           id: 1
  select_type: SIMPLE
        table: actor
         type: ref
possible_keys: idx_actor_last_name
          key: idx_actor_last_name
      key_len: 137
          ref: const
         rows: 2
        Extra: Using where; Using index
```

Using Index Scans for Sorts

MySQL has two ways to produce ordered results: it can use a filesort, or it can scan an index in order.* You can tell when MySQL plans to scan an index by looking for "index" in the type column in EXPLAIN. (Don't confuse this with "Using index" in the Extra column.)

Scanning the index itself is fast, because it simply requires moving from one index entry to the next. However, if MySQL isn't using the index to cover the query, it will have to look up each row it finds in the index. This is basically random I/O, so reading data in index order is usually much slower than a sequential table scan, especially for I/O-bound workloads.

MySQL can use the same index for both sorting and finding rows. If possible, it's a good idea to design your indexes so that they're useful for both tasks at once.

Ordering the results by the index works only when the index's order is exactly the same as the ORDER BY clause and all columns are sorted in the same direction (ascending or descending). If the query joins multiple tables, it works only when all columns in the ORDER BY clause refer to the first table. The ORDER BY clause also has the same limitation as lookup queries: it needs to form a leftmost prefix of the index. In all other cases, MySQL uses a filesort.

One case where the ORDER BY clause doesn't have to specify a leftmost prefix of the index is if there are constants for the leading columns. If the WHERE clause or a JOIN clause specifies constants for these columns, they can "fill the gaps" in the index.

---

* MySQL has two filesort algorithms; you can read more about them in "Sort optimizations" on page 176.

For example, the rental table in the standard Sakila sample database has an index on (rental_date, inventory_id, customer_id):

```
CREATE TABLE rental (
    ...
    PRIMARY KEY (rental_id),
    UNIQUE KEY rental_date (rental_date,inventory_id,customer_id),
    KEY idx_fk_inventory_id (inventory_id),
    KEY idx_fk_customer_id (customer_id),
    KEY idx_fk_staff_id (staff_id),
    ...
);
```

MySQL uses the rental_date index to order the following query, as you can see from the lack of a filesort in EXPLAIN:

```
mysql> EXPLAIN SELECT rental_id, staff_id FROM sakila.rental
    -> WHERE rental_date = '2005-05-25'
    -> ORDER BY inventory_id, customer_id\G
*************************** 1. row ***************************
         type: ref
possible_keys: rental_date
          key: rental_date
         rows: 1
        Extra: Using where
```

This works, even though the ORDER BY clause isn't itself a leftmost prefix of the index, because we specified an equality condition for the first column in the index.

Here are some more queries that can use the index for sorting. This one works because the query provides a constant for the first column of the index and specifies an ORDER BY on the second column. Taken together, those two form a leftmost prefix on the index:

```
... WHERE rental_date = '2005-05-25' ORDER BY inventory_id DESC;
```

The following query also works, because the two columns in the ORDER BY are a leftmost prefix of the index:

```
... WHERE rental_date > '2005-05-25' ORDER BY rental_date, inventory_id;
```

Here are some queries that *cannot* use the index for sorting:

- This query uses two different sort directions, but the index's columns are all sorted ascending:

  ```
  ... WHERE rental_date = '2005-05-25' ORDER BY inventory_id DESC, customer_id ASC;
  ```

- Here, the ORDER BY refers to a column that isn't in the index:

  ```
  ... WHERE rental_date = '2005-05-25' ORDER BY inventory_id, staff_id;
  ```

- Here, the WHERE and the ORDER BY don't form a leftmost prefix of the index:

  ```
  ... WHERE rental_date = '2005-05-25' ORDER BY customer_id;
  ```

- This query has a range condition on the first column, so MySQL doesn't use the rest of the index:

  ```
  ... WHERE rental_date > '2005-05-25' ORDER BY inventory_id, customer_id;
  ```

- Here there's a multiple equality on the `inventory_id` column. For the purposes of sorting, this is basically the same as a range:

  ```
  ... WHERE rental_date = '2005-05-25' AND inventory_id IN(1,2) ORDER BY customer_id;
  ```

- Here's an example where MySQL could theoretically use an index to order a join, but doesn't because the optimizer places the `film_actor` table second in the join (Chapter 4 shows ways to change the join order):

  ```
  mysql> EXPLAIN SELECT actor_id, title FROM sakila.film_actor
      -> INNER JOIN sakila.film USING(film_id) ORDER BY actor_id\G
  +------------+------------------------------------------------+
  | table      | Extra                                          |
  +------------+------------------------------------------------+
  | film       | Using index; Using temporary; Using filesort   |
  | film_actor | Using index                                    |
  +------------+------------------------------------------------+
  ```

One of the most important uses for ordering by an index is a query that has both an `ORDER BY` and a `LIMIT` clause. We explore this in more detail later.

Packed (Prefix-Compressed) Indexes

MyISAM uses prefix compression to reduce index size, allowing more of the index to fit in memory and dramatically improving performance in some cases. It packs string values by default, but you can even tell it to compress integer values.

MyISAM packs each index block by storing the block's first value fully, then storing each additional value in the block by recording the number of bytes that have the same prefix, plus the actual data of the suffix that differs. For example, if the first value is "perform" and the second is "performance," the second value will be stored analogously to "7,ance". MyISAM can also prefix-compress adjacent row pointers.

Compressed blocks use less space, but they make certain operations slower. Because each value's compression prefix depends on the value before it, MyISAM can't do binary searches to find a desired item in the block and must scan the block from the beginning. Sequential forward scans perform well, but reverse scans—such as `ORDER BY DESC`—don't work as well. Any operation that requires finding a single row in the middle of the block will require scanning, on average, half the block.

Our benchmarks have shown that packed keys make index lookups on MyISAM tables perform several times more slowly for a CPU-bound workload, because of the scans required for random lookups. Reverse scans of packed keys are even slower. The tradeoff is one of CPU and memory resources versus disk resources.

Packed indexes can be about one-tenth the size on disk, and if you have an I/O-bound workload they can more than offset the cost for certain queries.

You can control how a table's indexes are packed with the PACK_KEYS option to CREATE TABLE.

Redundant and Duplicate Indexes

MySQL allows you to create multiple indexes on the same column; it does not "notice" and protect you from your mistake. MySQL has to maintain each duplicate index separately, and the query optimizer will consider each of them when it optimizes queries. This can cause a serious performance impact.

Duplicate indexes are indexes of the same type, created on the same set of columns in the same order. You should try to avoid creating them, and you should remove them if you find them.

Sometimes you can create duplicate indexes without knowing it. For example, look at the following code:

```
CREATE TABLE test (
    ID INT NOT NULL PRIMARY KEY,
    UNIQUE(ID),
    INDEX(ID)
);
```

An inexperienced user might think this identifies the column's role as a primary key, adds a UNIQUE constraint, and adds an index for queries to use. In fact, MySQL implements UNIQUE constraints and PRIMARY KEY constraints with indexes, so this actually creates three indexes on the same column! There is typically no reason to do this, unless you want to have different types of indexes on the same column to satisfy different kinds of queries.[*]

Redundant indexes are a bit different from duplicated indexes. If there is an index on (A, B), another index on (A) would be redundant because it is a prefix of the first index. That is, the index on (A, B) can also be used as an index on (A) alone. (This type of redundancy applies only to B-Tree indexes.) However, an index on (B, A) would not be redundant, and neither would an index on (B), because B is not a leftmost prefix of (A, B). Furthermore, indexes of different types (such as hash or full-text indexes) are not redundant to B-Tree indexes, no matter what columns they cover.

Redundant indexes usually appear when people add indexes to a table. For example, someone might add an index on (A, B) instead of extending an existing index on (A) to cover (A, B).

---

[*] An index is not necessarily a duplicate if it's a different type of index; there are often good reasons to have KEY(col) and FULLTEXT KEY(col).

In most cases you don't want redundant indexes, and to avoid them you should extend existing indexes rather than add new ones. Still, there are times when you'll need redundant indexes for performance reasons. The main reason to use a redundant index is when extending an existing index, the redundant index will make it much larger.

For example, if you have an index on an integer column and you extend it with a long VARCHAR column, it may become significantly slower. This is especially true if your queries use the index as a covering index, or if it's a MyISAM table and you perform a lot of range scans on it (because of MyISAM's prefix compression).

Consider the userinfo table, which we described in "Inserting rows in primary key order with InnoDB" on page 117, earlier in this chapter. This table contains 1,000,000 rows, and for each state_id there are about 20,000 records. There is an index on state_id, which is useful for the following query. We refer to this query as Q1:

```
mysql> SELECT count(*) FROM userinfo WHERE state_id=5;
```

A simple benchmark shows an execution rate of almost 115 queries per second (QPS) for this query. We also have a related query that retrieves several columns instead of just counting rows. This is Q2:

```
mysql> SELECT state_id, city, address FROM userinfo WHERE state_id=5;
```

For this query, the result is less than 10 QPS.* The simple solution to improve its performance is to extend the index to (state_id, city, address), so the index will cover the query:

```
mysql> ALTER TABLE userinfo DROP KEY state_id,
    ->     ADD KEY state_id_2 (state_id, city, address);
```

After extending the index, Q2 runs faster, but Q1 runs more slowly. If we really care about making both queries fast, we should leave both indexes, even though the single-column index is redundant. Table 3-4 shows detailed results for both queries and indexing strategies, with MyISAM and InnoDB storage engines. Note that InnoDB's performance doesn't degrade as much for Q1 with only the state_id_2 index, because InnoDB doesn't use key compression.

Table 3-4. Benchmark results in QPS for SELECT queries with various index strategies

	state_id only	state_id_2 only	Both state_id and state_id_2
MyISAM, Q1	114.96	25.40	112.19
MyISAM, Q2	9.97	16.34	16.37
InnoDB, Q1	108.55	100.33	107.97
InnoDB, Q2	12.12	28.04	28.06

* We've used an in-memory example here. When the table is bigger and the workload becomes I/O-bound, the difference between the numbers will be much larger.

The drawback of having two indexes is the maintenance cost. Table 3-5 shows how long it takes to insert a million rows into the table.

Table 3-5. *Speed of inserting a million rows with various index strategies*

	state_id only	Both state_id and state_id_2
InnoDB, enough memory for both indexes	80 seconds	136 seconds
MyISAM, enough memory for only one index	72 seconds	470 seconds

As you can see, inserting new rows into the table with more indexes is dramatically slower. This is true in general: adding new indexes may have a large performance impact for INSERT, UPDATE, and DELETE operations, especially if a new index causes you to hit memory limits.

Indexes and Locking

Indexes play a very important role for InnoDB, because they let queries lock fewer rows. This is an important consideration, because in MySQL 5.0 InnoDB never unlocks a row until the transaction commits.

If your queries never touch rows they don't need, they'll lock fewer rows, and that's better for performance for two reasons. First, even though InnoDB's row locks are very efficient and use very little memory, there's still some overhead involved in row locking. Secondly, locking more rows than needed increases lock contention and reduces concurrency.

InnoDB locks rows only when it accesses them, and an index can reduce the number of rows InnoDB accesses and therefore locks. However, this works only if InnoDB can filter out the undesired rows *at the storage engine level*. If the index doesn't permit InnoDB to do that, the MySQL server will have to apply a WHERE clause after InnoDB retrieves the rows and returns them to the server level. At this point, it's too late to avoid locking the rows: InnoDB will already have locked them, and the server won't be able to unlock them.

This is easier to see with an example. We use the Sakila sample database again:

```
mysql> SET AUTOCOMMIT=0;
mysql> BEGIN;
mysql> SELECT actor_id FROM sakila.actor WHERE actor_id < 5
    ->     AND actor_id <> 1 FOR UPDATE;
+----------+
| actor_id |
+----------+
|        2 |
|        3 |
|        4 |
+----------+
```

This query returns only rows 2 through 4, but it actually gets exclusive locks on *rows 1 through 4*. InnoDB locked row 1 because the plan MySQL chose for this query was an index range access:

```
mysql> EXPLAIN SELECT actor_id FROM sakila.actor
    -> WHERE actor_id < 5 AND actor_id <> 1 FOR UPDATE;
+----+-------------+-------+-------+---------+-------------------------+
| id | select_type | table | type  | key     | Extra                   |
+----+-------------+-------+-------+---------+-------------------------+
|  1 | SIMPLE      | actor | range | PRIMARY | Using where; Using index |
+----+-------------+-------+-------+---------+-------------------------+
```

In other words, the low-level storage engine operation was "begin at the start of the index and fetch all rows until actor_id < 5 is false." The server didn't tell InnoDB about the WHERE condition that eliminated row 1. Note the presence of "Using where" in the Extra column in EXPLAIN. This indicates that the MySQL server is applying a WHERE filter after the storage engine returns the rows.

Summary of Indexing Strategies

Now that you've learned more about indexing, perhaps you're wondering where to get started with your own tables. The most important thing to do is examine the queries you're going to run most often, but you should also think about less-frequent operations, such as inserting and updating data. Try to avoid the common mistake of creating indexes without knowing which queries will use them, and consider whether all your indexes together will form an optimal configuration.

Sometimes you can just look at your queries, and see which indexes they need, add them, and you're done. But sometimes you'll have enough different kinds of queries that you can't add perfect indexes for them all, and you'll need to compromise. To find the best balance, you should benchmark and profile.

The first thing to look at is response time. Consider adding an index for any query that's taking too long. Then examine the queries that cause the most load (see Chapter 2 for more on how to measure this), and add indexes to support them. If your system is approaching a memory, CPU, or disk bottleneck, take that into account. For example, if you do a lot of long aggregate queries to generate summaries, your disks might benefit from covering indexes that support GROUP BY queries.

Where possible, try to extend existing indexes rather than adding new ones. It is usually more efficient to maintain one multicolumn index than several single-column indexes. If you don't yet know your query distribution, strive to make your indexes as selective as you can, because highly selective indexes are usually more beneficial.

Here's a second query that proves row 1 is locked, even though it didn't appear in the results from the first query. Leaving the first connection open, start a second connection and execute the following:

```
mysql> SET AUTOCOMMIT=0;
mysql> BEGIN;
mysql> SELECT actor_id FROM sakila.actor WHERE actor_id = 1 FOR UPDATE;
```

The query will hang, waiting for the first transaction to release the lock on row 1. This behavior is necessary for statement-based replication (discussed in Chapter 8) to work correctly.

As this example shows, InnoDB can lock rows it doesn't really need even when it uses an index. The problem is even worse when it can't use an index to find and lock the rows: if there's no index for the query, MySQL will do a full table scan and lock every row, whether it "needs" it or not.*

Here's a little-known detail about InnoDB, indexes, and locking: InnoDB can place shared (read) locks on secondary indexes, but exclusive (write) locks require access to the primary key. That eliminates the possibility of using a covering index and can make SELECT FOR UPDATE much slower than LOCK IN SHARE MODE or a nonlocking query.

An Indexing Case Study

The easiest way to understand indexing concepts is with an illustration, so we've prepared a case study in indexing.

Suppose we need to design an online dating site with user profiles that have many different columns, such as the user's country, state/region, city, sex, age, eye color, and so on. The site must support searching the profiles by various combinations of these properties. It must also let the user sort and limit results by the last time the profile's owner was online, ratings from other members, etc. How do we design indexes for such complex requirements?

Oddly enough, the first thing to decide is whether we have to use index-based sorting, or whether filesorting is acceptable. Index-based sorting restricts how the indexes and queries need to be built. For example, we can't use an index for a WHERE clause such as WHERE age BETWEEN 18 AND 25 if the same query uses an index to sort users by the ratings other users have given them. If MySQL uses an index for a range criterion in a query, it cannot also use another index (or a suffix of the same index) for ordering. Assuming this will be one of the most common WHERE clauses, we'll take for granted that many queries will need a filesort.

Supporting Many Kinds of Filtering

Now we need to look at which columns have many distinct values and which columns appear in WHERE clauses most often. Indexes on columns with many distinct

---

* This is supposed to be fixed in MySQL 5.1 with row-based binary logging and the READ COMMITTED transaction isolation level, but it applies to all MySQL versions we tested, up to and including 5.1.22.

values will be very selective. This is generally a good thing, because it lets MySQL filter out undesired rows more efficiently.

The country column may or may not be selective, but it'll probably be in most queries anyway. The sex column is certainly not selective, but it'll probably be in every query. With this in mind, we create a series of indexes for many different combinations of columns, prefixed with (sex,country).

The traditional wisdom is that it's useless to index columns with very low selectivity. So why would we place a nonselective column at the beginning of every index? Are we out of our minds?

We have two reasons for doing this. The first reason is that, as stated earlier, almost every query will use sex. We might even design the site such that users can choose to search for only one sex at a time. But more importantly, there's not much downside to adding the column, because we have a trick up our sleeves.

Here's the trick: even if a query that doesn't restrict the results by sex is issued, we can ensure that the index is usable anyway by adding AND sex IN('m', 'f') to the WHERE clause. This won't actually filter out any rows, so it's functionally the same as not including the sex column in the WHERE clause at all. However, we *need* to include this column, because it'll let MySQL use a larger prefix of the index. This trick is useful in situations like this one, but if the column had many distinct values, it wouldn't work well because the IN( ) list would get too large.

This case illustrates a general principle: keep all options on the table. When you're designing indexes, don't just think about the kinds of indexes you need for existing queries, but consider optimizing the queries, too. If you see the need for an index but you think some queries might suffer because of it, ask yourself whether you can change the queries. You should optimize queries and indexes together to find the best compromise; you don't have to design the perfect indexing scheme in a vacuum.

Next, we think about what other combinations of WHERE conditions we're likely to see and consider which of those combinations would be slow without proper indexes. An index on (sex, country, age) is an obvious choice, and we'll probably also need indexes on (sex, country, region, age) and (sex, country, region, city, age).

That's getting to be a lot of indexes. If we want to reuse indexes and it won't generate too many combinations of conditions, we can use the IN( ) trick, and scrap the (sex, country, age) and (sex, country, region, age) indexes. If they're not specified in the search form, we can ensure the index prefix has equality constraints by specifying a list of all countries, or all regions for the country. (Combined lists of all countries, all regions, and all sexes would probably be too large.)

These indexes will satisfy the most frequently specified search queries, but how can we design indexes for less common options, such as has_pictures, eye_color, hair_color, and education? If these columns are not very selective and are not used a lot, we can simply skip them and let MySQL scan a few extra rows. Alternatively, we can add them before the age column and use the IN( ) technique described earlier to handle the case where they are not specified.

You may have noticed that we're keeping the age column at the end of the index. What makes this column so special, and why should it be at the end of the index? We're trying to make sure that MySQL uses as many columns of the index as possible, because it uses only the leftmost prefix, up to and including the first condition that specifies a range of values. All the other columns we've mentioned can use equality conditions in the WHERE clause, but age is almost certain to be a range (e.g., age BETWEEN 18 AND 25).

We could convert this to an IN( ) list, such as age IN(18, 19, 20, 21, 22, 23, 24, 25), but this won't always be possible for this type of query. The general principle we're trying to illustrate is to keep the range criterion at the end of the index, so the optimizer will use as much of the index as possible.

We've said that you can add more and more columns to the index and use IN( ) lists to cover cases where those columns aren't part of the WHERE clause, but you can overdo this and get into trouble. Using more than a few such lists explodes the number of combinations the optimizer has to evaluate, and this can ultimately reduce query speed. Consider the following WHERE clause:

```
WHERE  eye_color  IN('brown','blue','hazel')
   AND hair_color IN('black','red','blonde','brown')
   AND sex        IN('M','F')
```

The optimizer will convert this into 4*3*2 = 24 combinations, and the WHERE clause will then have to check for each of them. Twenty-four is not an extreme number of combinations, but be careful if that number approaches thousands. Older MySQL versions had more problems with large numbers of IN( ) combinations: query optimization could take longer than execution and consume a lot of memory. Newer MySQL versions stop evaluating combinations if the number of combinations gets too large, but this limits how well MySQL can use the index.

Avoiding Multiple Range Conditions

Let's assume we have a last_online column and we want to be able to show the users who were online during the previous week:

```
WHERE  eye_color   IN('brown','blue','hazel')
   AND hair_color  IN('black','red','blonde','brown')
   AND sex         IN('M','F')
   AND last_online > DATE_SUB('2008-01-17', INTERVAL 7 DAY)
   AND age         BETWEEN 18 AND 25
```

There's a problem with this query: it has two range conditions. MySQL can use either the last_online criterion or the age criterion, but not both.

What Is a Range Condition?

EXPLAIN's output can sometimes make it hard to tell whether MySQL is really looking for a range of values, or for a list of values. EXPLAIN uses the same term, "range," to indicate both. For example, MySQL calls the following a "range" query, as you can see in the type column:

```
mysql> EXPLAIN SELECT actor_id FROM sakila.actor
    -> WHERE actor_id > 45\G
*********************** 1. row ************************
           id: 1
  select_type: SIMPLE
        table: actor
         type: range
```

But what about this one?

```
mysql> EXPLAIN SELECT actor_id FROM sakila.actor
    -> WHERE actor_id IN(1, 4, 99)\G
*********************** 1. row ************************
           id: 1
  select_type: SIMPLE
        table: actor
         type: range
```

There's no way to tell the difference by looking at EXPLAIN, but we draw a distinction between ranges of values and multiple equality conditions. The second query is a multiple equality condition, in our terminology.

We're not just being picky: these two kinds of index accesses perform differently. The range condition makes MySQL ignore any further columns in the index, but the multiple equality condition doesn't have that limitation.

If the last_online restriction appears without the age restriction, or if last_online is more selective than age, we may wish to add another set of indexes with last_online at the end. But what if we can't convert the age to an IN( ) list, and we really need the speed boost of restricting by last_online and age simultaneously? At the moment there's no way to do this directly, but we can convert one of the ranges to an equality comparison. To do this, we add a precomputed active column, which we'll maintain with a periodic job. We'll set the column to 1 when the user logs in, and the job will set it back to 0 if the user doesn't log in for seven consecutive days.

This approach lets MySQL use indexes such as (active, sex, country, age). The column may not be absolutely accurate, but this kind of query might not require a high degree of accuracy. If we do need accuracy, we can leave the last_online condition in the WHERE clause, *but not index it*. This technique is similar to the one we used to simulate HASH indexes for URL lookups earlier in this chapter. The condition won't use any index, but because it's unlikely to throw away many of the rows that an index would find an index wouldn't really be beneficial anyway. Put another way, the lack of an index won't hurt the query noticeably.

By now, you can probably see the pattern: if a user wants to see both active and inactive results, we can add an `IN()` list. We've added a lot of these lists, but the alternative is to create separate indexes that can satisfy every combination of columns on which we need to filter. We'd have to use at least the following indexes: `(active,sex,country,age)`, `(active,country,age)`, `(sex,country,age)`, and `(country,age)`. Although such indexes might be more optimal for each specific query, the overhead of maintaining them all, combined with all the extra space they'd require, would likely make this a poor strategy overall.

This is a case where optimizer changes can really affect the optimal indexing strategy. If a future version of MySQL can do a true loose index scan, it should be able to use multiple range conditions on a single index, so we won't need the `IN()` lists for the kinds of queries we're considering here.

Optimizing Sorts

The last issue we want to cover in this case study is sorting. Sorting small result sets with filesorts is fast, but what if millions of rows match a query? For example, what if only sex is specified in the `WHERE` clause?

We can add special indexes for sorting these low-selectivity cases. For example, an index on `(sex,rating)` can be used for the following query:

```
mysql> SELECT <cols> FROM profiles WHERE sex='M' ORDER BY rating LIMIT 10;
```

This query has both `ORDER BY` and `LIMIT` clauses, and it would be very slow without the index.

Even with the index, the query can be slow if the user interface is paginated and someone requests a page that's not near the beginning. This case creates a bad combination of `ORDER BY` and `LIMIT` with an offset:

```
mysql> SELECT <cols> FROM profiles WHERE sex='M' ORDER BY rating LIMIT 100000, 10;
```

Such queries can be a serious problem no matter how they're indexed, because the high offset requires them to spend most of their time scanning a lot of data that they will then throw away. Denormalizing, precomputing, and caching are likely to be the only strategies that work for queries like this one. An even better strategy is to limit the number of pages you let the user view. This is unlikely to impact the user's experience, because no one really cares about the 10,000th page of search results.

Another good strategy for optimizing such queries is to use a covering index to retrieve just the primary key columns of the rows you'll eventually retrieve. You can then join this back to the table to retrieve all desired columns. This helps minimize the amount of work MySQL must do gathering data that it will only throw away. Here's an example that requires an index on `(sex, rating)` to work efficiently:

```
mysql> SELECT <cols> FROM profiles INNER JOIN (
    ->    SELECT <primary key cols> FROM profiles
    ->    WHERE x.sex='M' ORDER BY rating LIMIT 100000, 10
    -> ) AS x USING(<primary key cols>);
```

Index and Table Maintenance

Once you've created tables with proper data types and added indexes, your work isn't over: you still need to maintain your tables and indexes to make sure they perform well. The three main goals of table maintenance are finding and fixing corruption, maintaining accurate index statistics, and reducing fragmentation.

Finding and Repairing Table Corruption

The worst thing that can happen to a table is corruption. With the MyISAM storage engine, this often happens due to crashes. However, all storage engines can experience index corruption due to hardware problems or internal bugs in MySQL or the operating system.

Corrupted indexes can cause queries to return incorrect results, raise duplicate-key errors when there is no duplicated value, or even cause lockups and crashes. If you experience odd behavior—such as an error that you think shouldn't be happening— run CHECK TABLE to see if the table is corrupt. (Note that some storage engines don't support this command, and others support multiple options to specify how thoroughly they check the table.) CHECK TABLE usually catches most table and index errors.

You can fix corrupt tables with the REPAIR TABLE command, but again, not all storage engines support this. In these cases you can do a "no-op" ALTER, such as altering a table to use the same storage engine it currently uses. Here's an example for an InnoDB table:

```
mysql> ALTER TABLE innodb_tbl ENGINE=INNODB;
```

Alternatively, you can either use an offline engine-specific repair utility, such as *myisamchk*, or dump the data and reload it. However, if the corruption is in the system area, or in the table's "row data" area instead of the index, you may be unable to use any of these options. In this case, you may need to restore the table from your backups or attempt to recover data from the corrupted files (see Chapter 11).

Updating Index Statistics

The MySQL query optimizer uses two API calls to ask the storage engines how index values are distributed when deciding how to use indexes. The first is the records_in_range( ) call, which accepts range end points and returns the (possibly estimated) number of records in that range. The second is info( ), which can return various types of data, including index cardinality (how many records there are for each key value).

When the storage engine doesn't provide the optimizer with accurate information about the number of rows a query will examine, the optimizer uses the index statistics, which you can regenerate by running ANALYZE TABLE, to estimate the number of rows. MySQL's optimizer is cost-based, and the main cost metric is how much data the query will access. If the statistics were never generated, or if they are out of date, the optimizer can make bad decisions. The solution is to run ANALYZE TABLE.

Each storage engine implements index statistics differently, so the frequency with which you'll need to run ANALYZE TABLE differs, as does the cost of running the statement:

- The Memory storage engine does not store index statistics at all.
- MyISAM stores statistics on disk, and ANALYZE TABLE performs a full index scan to compute cardinality. The entire table is locked during this process.
- InnoDB does not store statistics on disk, but rather estimates them with random index dives the first time a table is opened. ANALYZE TABLE uses random dives for InnoDB, so InnoDB statistics are less accurate, but they may not need manual updates unless you keep your server running for a very long time. Also, ANALYZE TABLE is nonblocking and relatively inexpensive in InnoDB, so you can update the statistics online without affecting the server much.

You can examine the cardinality of your indexes with the SHOW INDEX FROM command. For example:

```
mysql> SHOW INDEX FROM sakila.actor\G
*************************** 1. row ***************************
        Table: actor
   Non_unique: 0
     Key_name: PRIMARY
 Seq_in_index: 1
  Column_name: actor_id
    Collation: A
  Cardinality: 200
     Sub_part: NULL
       Packed: NULL
         Null:
   Index_type: BTREE
      Comment:
*************************** 2. row ***************************
        Table: actor
   Non_unique: 1
     Key_name: idx_actor_last_name
 Seq_in_index: 1
  Column_name: last_name
    Collation: A
  Cardinality: 200
     Sub_part: NULL
       Packed: NULL
         Null:
   Index_type: BTREE
      Comment:
```

This command gives quite a lot of index information, which the MySQL manual explains in detail. We do want to call your attention to the Cardinality column, though. This shows how many distinct values the storage engine estimates are in the index. You can also get this data from the INFORMATION_SCHEMA.STATISTICS table in MySQL 5.0 and newer, which can be quite handy. For example, you can write queries against the INFORMATION_SCHEMA tables to find indexes with very low selectivity.

Reducing Index and Data Fragmentation

B-Tree indexes can become fragmented, which reduces performance. Fragmented indexes may be poorly filled and/or nonsequential on disk.

By design B-Tree indexes require random disk accesses to "dive" to the leaf pages, so random access is the rule, not the exception. However, the leaf pages can still perform better if they are physically sequential and tightly packed. If they are not, we say they are fragmented, and range scans or full index scans can be many times slower. This is especially true for index-covered queries.

The table's data storage can also become fragmented. However, data storage fragmentation is more complex than index fragmentation. There are two types of data fragmentation:

Row fragmentation
: This type of fragmentation occurs when the row is stored in multiple pieces in multiple locations. Row fragmentation reduces performance even if the query needs only a single row from the index.

Intra-row fragmentation
: This kind of fragmentation occurs when logically sequential pages or rows are not stored sequentially on disk. It affects operations such as full table scans and clustered index range scans, which normally benefit from a sequential data layout on disk.

MyISAM tables may suffer from both types of fragmentation, but InnoDB never fragments short rows.

To defragment data, you can either run OPTIMIZE TABLE or dump and reload the data.

These approaches work for most storage engines. For some, such as MyISAM, they also defragment indexes by rebuilding them with a sort algorithm, which creates the indexes in sorted order. There is currently no way to defragment InnoDB indexes, as InnoDB can't build indexes by sorting in MySQL 5.0.[*] Even dropping and recreating InnoDB indexes may result in fragmented indexes, depending on the data.

For storage engines that don't support OPTIMIZE TABLE, you can rebuild the table with a no-op ALTER TABLE. Just alter the table to have the same engine it currently uses:

---

[*] The InnoDB developers are working on this problem at the time of this writing.

```
mysql> ALTER TABLE <table> ENGINE=<engine>;
```

Normalization and Denormalization

There are usually many ways to represent any given data, ranging from fully normalized to fully denormalized and anything in between. In a normalized database, each fact is represented once and only once. Conversely, in a denormalized database, information is duplicated, or stored in multiple places.

If you're not familiar with normalization, you should study it. There are many good books on the topic and resources online; here, we just give a brief introduction to the aspects you need to know for this chapter. Let's start with the classic example of employees, departments, and department heads:

EMPLOYEE	DEPARTMENT	HEAD
Jones	Accounting	Jones
Smith	Engineering	Smith
Brown	Accounting	Jones
Green	Engineering	Smith

The problem with this schema is that abnormalities can occur while the data is being modified. Say Brown takes over as the head of the Accounting department. We need to update multiple rows to reflect this change, and while those updates are being made the data is in an inconsistent state. If the "Jones" row says the head of the department is something different from the "Brown" row, there's no way to know which is right. It's like the old saying, "A person with two watches never knows what time it is." Furthermore, we can't represent a department without employees—if we delete all employees in the Accounting department, we lose all records about the department itself. To avoid these problems, we need to normalize the table by separating the employee and department entities. This process results in the following two tables for employees:

EMPLOYEE_NAME	DEPARTMENT
Jones	Accounting
Smith	Engineering
Brown	Accounting
Green	Engineering

and departments:

DEPARTMENT	HEAD
Accounting	Jones
Engineering	Smith

These tables are now in second normal form, which is good enough for many purposes. However, second normal form is only one of many possible normal forms.

 We're using the last name as the primary key here for purposes of illustration, because it's the "natural identifier" of the data. In practice, however, we wouldn't do that. It's not guaranteed to be unique, and it's usually a bad idea to use a long string for a primary key.

Pros and Cons of a Normalized Schema

People who ask for help with performance issues are frequently advised to normalize their schemas, especially if the workload is write-heavy. This is often good advice. It works well for the following reasons:

- Normalized updates are usually faster than denormalized updates.
- When the data is well normalized, there's little or no duplicated data, so there's less data to change.
- Normalized tables are usually smaller, so they fit better in memory and perform better.
- The lack of redundant data means there's less need for DISTINCT or GROUP BY queries when retrieving lists of values. Consider the preceding example: it's impossible to get a distinct list of departments from the denormalized schema without DISTINCT or GROUP BY, but if DEPARTMENT is a separate table, it's a trivial query.

The drawbacks of a normalized schema usually have to do with retrieval. Any nontrivial query on a well-normalized schema will probably require at least one join, and perhaps several. This is not only expensive, but it can make some indexing strategies impossible. For example, normalizing may place columns in different tables that would benefit from belonging to the same index.

Pros and Cons of a Denormalized Schema

A denormalized schema works well because everything is in the same table, which avoids joins.

If you don't need to join tables, the worst case for most queries—even the ones that don't use indexes—is a full table scan. This can be much faster than a join when the data doesn't fit in memory, because it avoids random I/O.

A single table can also allow more efficient indexing strategies. Suppose you have a web site where users post their messages, and some users are premium users. Now say you want to view the last 10 messages from each of the premium users. If you've normalized the schema and indexed the publishing dates of the messages, the query might look like this:

```
mysql> SELECT message_text, user_name
    -> FROM message
    ->     INNER JOIN user ON message.user_id=user.id
    -> WHERE user.account_type='premium'
    -> ORDER BY message.published DESC LIMIT 10;
```

To execute this query efficiently, MySQL will need to scan the published index on the message table. For each row it finds, it will need to probe into the user table and check whether the user is a premium user. This is inefficient if only a small fraction of users have premium accounts.

The other possible query plan is to start with the user table, select all premium users, get all messages for them, and do a filesort. This will probably be even worse.

The problem is the join, which is keeping you from sorting and filtering simultaneously with a single index. If you denormalize the data by combining the tables and add an index on (account_type, published), you can write the query without a join. This will be very efficient:

```
mysql> SELECT message_text,user_name
    -> FROM user_messages
    -> WHERE account_type='premium'
    -> ORDER BY published DESC
    -> LIMIT 10;
```

A Mixture of Normalized and Denormalized

Given that both normalized and denormalized schemas have benefits and drawbacks, how can you choose the best design?

The truth is, fully normalized and fully denormalized schemas are like laboratory rats: they usually have little to do with the real world. In the real world, you often need to mix the approaches, possibly using a partially normalized schema, cache tables, and other techniques.

The most common way to denormalize data is to duplicate, or cache, selected columns from one table in another table. In MySQL 5.0 and newer, you can use triggers to update the cached values, which makes the implementation easier.

In our web site example, for instance, instead of denormalizing fully you can store account_type in both the user and message tables. This avoids the insert and delete problems that come with full denormalization, because you never lose information about the user, even when there are no messages. It won't make the user_message table much larger, but it will let you select the data efficiently.

However, it's now more expensive to update a user's account type, because you have to change it in both tables. To see whether that's a problem, you must consider how frequently you'll have to make such changes and how long they will take, compared to how often you'll run the SELECT query.

Another good reason to move some data from the parent table to the child table is for sorting. For example, it would be extremely expensive to sort messages by the author's name on a normalized schema, but you can perform such a sort very efficiently if you cache the author_name in the message table and index it.

It can also be useful to cache derived values. If you need to display how many messages each user has posted (as many forums do), either you can run an expensive subquery to count the data every time you display it, or you can have a num_messages column in the user table that you update whenever a user posts a new message.

Cache and Summary Tables

Sometimes the best way to improve performance is to keep redundant data in the same table as the data from which was derived. However, sometimes you'll need to build completely separate summary or cache tables, specially tuned for your retrieval needs. This approach works best if you can tolerate slightly stale data, but sometimes you really don't have a choice (for instance, when you need to avoid complex and expensive real-time updates).

The terms "cache table" and "summary table" don't have standardized meanings. We use the term "cache tables" to refer to tables that contain data that can be easily, if more slowly, retrieved from the schema (i.e., data that is logically redundant). When we say "summary tables," we mean tables that hold aggregated data from GROUP BY queries (i.e., data that is not logically redundant). Some people also use the term "roll-up tables" for these tables, because the data has been "rolled up."

Staying with the web site example, suppose you need to count the number of messages posted during the previous 24 hours. It would be impossible to maintain an accurate real-time counter on a busy site. Instead, you could generate a summary table every hour. You can often do this with a single query, and it's more efficient than maintaining counters in real time. The drawback is that the counts are not 100% accurate.

If you need to get an accurate count of messages posted during the previous 24-hour period (with no staleness), there is another option. Begin with a per-hour summary table. You can then count the exact number of messages posted in a given 24-hour period by adding the number of messages in the 23 whole hours contained in that period, the partial hour at the beginning of the period, and the partial hour at the end of the period. Suppose your summary table is called msg_per_hr and is defined as follows:

```
CREATE TABLE msg_per_hr (
   hr DATETIME NOT NULL,
   cnt INT UNSIGNED NOT NULL,
   PRIMARY KEY(hr)
);
```

You can find the number of messages posted in the previous 24 hours by adding the results of the following three queries:[*]

```
mysql> SELECT SUM(cnt) FROM msg_per_hr
    -> WHERE hr BETWEEN
    ->    CONCAT(LEFT(NOW( ), 14), '00:00') - INTERVAL 23 HOUR
    ->    AND CONCAT(LEFT(NOW( ), 14), '00:00') - INTERVAL 1 HOUR;
mysql> SELECT COUNT(*) FROM message
    -> WHERE posted >= NOW( ) - INTERVAL 24 HOUR
    ->    AND posted < CONCAT(LEFT(NOW( ), 14), '00:00') - INTERVAL 23 HOUR;
mysql> SELECT COUNT(*) FROM message
    -> WHERE posted >= CONCAT(LEFT(NOW( ), 14), '00:00');
```

Either approach—an inexact count or an exact count with small range queries to fill in the gaps—is more efficient than counting all the rows in the message table. This is the key reason for creating summary tables. These statistics are expensive to compute in real time, because they require scanning a lot of data, or queries that will only run efficiently with special indexes that you don't want to add because of the impact they will have on updates. Computing the most active users or the most frequent "tags" are typical examples of such operations.

Cache tables, in turn, are useful for optimizing search and retrieval queries. These queries often require a particular table and index structure that is different from the one you would use for general online transaction processing (OLTP) operations.

For example, you might need many different index combinations to speed up various types of queries. These conflicting requirements sometimes demand that you create a cache table that contains only some of the columns from the main table. A useful technique is to use a different storage engine for the cache table. If the main table uses InnoDB, for example, by using MyISAM for the cache table you'll gain a smaller index footprint and the ability to do full-text search queries. Sometimes you might even want to take the table completely out of MySQL and into a specialized system that can search more efficiently, such as the Lucene or Sphinx search engines.

When using cache and summary tables, you have to decide whether to maintain their data in real time or with periodic rebuilds. Which is better will depend on your application, but a periodic rebuild not only can save resources but also can result in a more efficient table that's not fragmented and has fully sorted indexes.

When you rebuild summary and cache tables, you'll often need their data to remain available during the operation. You can achieve this by using a "shadow table," which is a table you build "behind" the real table. When you're done building it, you can swap the tables with an atomic rename. For example, if you need to rebuild my_summary, you can create my_summary_new, fill it with data, and swap it with the real table:

---

[*] We're using LEFT(NOW( ), 14) to round the current date and time to the nearest hour.

```
mysql> DROP TABLE IF EXISTS my_summary_new, my_summary_old;
mysql> CREATE TABLE my_summary_new LIKE my_summary;
-- populate my_summary_new as desired
mysql> RENAME TABLE my_summary TO my_summary_old, my_summary_new TO my_summary;
```

If you rename the original my_summary table my_summary_old before assigning the name my_summary to the newly rebuilt table, as we've done here, you can keep the old version until you're ready to overwrite it at the next rebuild. It's handy to have it for a quick rollback if the new table has a problem.

Counter tables

An application that keeps counts in a table can run into concurrency problems when updating the counters. Such tables are very common in web applications. You can use them to cache the number of friends a user has, the number of downloads of a file, and so on. It's often a good idea to build a separate table for the counters, to keep it small and fast. Using a separate table can help you avoid query cache invalidations and lets you use some of the more advanced techniques we show in this section.

To keep things as simple as possible, suppose you have a counter table with a single row that just counts hits on your web site:

```
mysql> CREATE TABLE hit_counter (
    ->    cnt int unsigned not null
    -> ) ENGINE=InnoDB;
```

Each hit on the web site updates the counter:

```
mysql> UPDATE hit_counter SET cnt = cnt + 1;
```

The problem is that this single row is effectively a global "mutex" for any transaction that updates the counter. It will serialize those transactions. You can get higher concurrency by keeping more than one row and updating a random row. This requires the following change to the table:

```
mysql> CREATE TABLE hit_counter (
    ->    slot tinyint unsigned not null primary key,
    ->    cnt int unsigned not null
    -> ) ENGINE=InnoDB;
```

Prepopulate the table by adding 100 rows to it. Now the query can just choose a random slot and update it:

```
mysql> UPDATE hit_counter SET cnt = cnt + 1 WHERE slot = RAND() * 100;
```

To retrieve statistics, just use aggregate queries:

```
mysql> SELECT SUM(cnt) FROM hit_counter;
```

A common requirement is to start new counters every so often (for example, once a day). If you need to do this, you can change the schema slightly:

```
mysql> CREATE TABLE daily_hit_counter (
    ->     day date not null,
    ->     slot tinyint unsigned not null,
    ->     cnt int unsigned not null,
    ->     primary key(day, slot)
    -> ) ENGINE=InnoDB;
```

You don't want to pregenerate rows for this scenario. Instead, you can use ON
DUPLICATE KEY UPDATE:

```
mysql> INSERT INTO daily_hit_counter(day, slot, cnt)
    ->     VALUES(CURRENT_DATE, RAND( ) * 100, 1)
    ->     ON DUPLICATE KEY UPDATE cnt = cnt + 1;
```

If you want to reduce the number of rows to keep the table smaller, you can write a
periodic job that merges all the results into slot 0 and deletes every other slot:

```
mysql> UPDATE daily_hit_counter as c
    ->     INNER JOIN (
    ->         SELECT day, SUM(cnt) AS cnt, MIN(slot) AS mslot
    ->         FROM daily_hit_counter
    ->         GROUP BY day
    ->     ) AS x USING(day)
    -> SET c.cnt  = IF(c.slot = x.mslot, x.cnt, 0),
    ->     c.slot = IF(c.slot = x.mslot, 0, c.slot);
mysql> DELETE FROM daily_hit_counter WHERE slot <> 0 AND cnt = 0;
```

Faster Reads, Slower Writes

You'll often need extra indexes, redundant fields, or even cache and summary tables
to speed up read queries. These add work to write queries and maintenance jobs, but
this is still a technique you'll see a lot when you design for high performance: you
amortize the cost of the slower writes by speeding up reads significantly.

However, this isn't the only price you pay for faster read queries. You also increase
development complexity for both read and write operations.

Speeding Up ALTER TABLE

MySQL's ALTER TABLE performance can become a problem with very large tables.
MySQL performs most alterations by making an empty table with the desired new
structure, inserting all the data from the old table into the new one, and deleting the
old table. This can take a very long time, especially if you're short on memory and
the table is large and has lots of indexes. Many people have experience with ALTER
TABLE operations that have taken hours or days to complete.

MySQL AB is working on improving this. Some of the upcoming improvements include support for "online" operations that won't lock the table for the whole operation. The InnoDB developers are also working on support for building indexes by sorting. MyISAM already supports this technique, which makes building indexes much faster and results in a compact index layout. (InnoDB currently builds its indexes one row at a time in primary key order, which means the index trees aren't built in optimal order and are fragmented.)

Not all ALTER TABLE operations cause table rebuilds. For example, you can change or drop a column's default value in two ways (one fast, and one slow). Say you want to change a film's default rental duration from 3 to 5 days. Here's the expensive way:

```
mysql> ALTER TABLE sakila.film
    -> MODIFY COLUMN rental_duration TINYINT(3) NOT NULL DEFAULT 5;
```

Profiling that statement with SHOW STATUS shows that it does 1,000 handler reads and 1,000 inserts. In other words, it copied the table to a new table, even though the column's type, size, and nullability didn't change.

In theory, MySQL could have skipped building a new table. The default value for the column is actually stored in the table's *.frm* file, so you should be able to change it without touching the table itself. MySQL doesn't yet use this optimization, however: any MODIFY COLUMN will cause a table rebuild.

You can change a column's default with ALTER COLUMN,* though:

```
mysql> ALTER TABLE sakila.film
    -> ALTER COLUMN rental_duration SET DEFAULT 5;
```

This statement modifies the *.frm* file and leaves the table alone. As a result, it is very fast.

Modifying Only the .frm File

We've seen that modifying a table's *.frm* file is fast and that MySQL sometimes rebuilds a table when it doesn't have to. If you're willing to take some risks, you can convince MySQL to do several other types of modifications without rebuilding the table.

 The technique we're about to demonstrate is unsupported, undocumented, and may not work. Use it at your own risk. We advise you to back up your data first!

You can potentially do the following types of operations without a table rebuild:

---

* ALTER TABLE lets you modify columns with ALTER COLUMN, MODIFY COLUMN, and CHANGE COLUMN. All three do different things.

- Remove (but not add) a column's `AUTO_INCREMENT` attribute.
- Add, remove, or change `ENUM` and `SET` constants. If you remove a constant and some rows contain that value, queries will return the value as the empty string.

The basic technique is to create a *.frm* file for the desired table structure and copy it into the place of the existing table's *.frm* file, as follows:

1. Create an empty table with *exactly the same layout*, except for the desired modification (such as added `ENUM` constants).
2. Execute `FLUSH TABLES WITH READ LOCK`. This will close all tables in use and prevent any tables from being opened.
3. Swap the *.frm* files.
4. Execute `UNLOCK TABLES` to release the read lock.

As an example, we add a constant to the rating column in `sakila.film`. The current column looks like this:

```
mysql> SHOW COLUMNS FROM sakila.film LIKE 'rating';
+--------+-------------------------------------+------+-----+---------+-------+
| Field  | Type                                | Null | Key | Default | Extra |
+--------+-------------------------------------+------+-----+---------+-------+
| rating | enum('G','PG','PG-13','R','NC-17')  | YES  |     | G       |       |
+--------+-------------------------------------+------+-----+---------+-------+
```

We add a PG-14 rating for parents who are just a little bit more cautious about films:

```
mysql> CREATE TABLE sakila.film_new LIKE sakila.film;
mysql> ALTER TABLE sakila.film_new
    -> MODIFY COLUMN rating ENUM('G','PG','PG-13','R','NC-17', 'PG-14')
    -> DEFAULT 'G';
mysql> FLUSH TABLES WITH READ LOCK;
```

Notice that we're adding the new value *at the end of the list of constants*. If we placed it in the middle, after PG-13, we'd change the meaning of the existing data: existing R values would become PG-14, NC-17 would become R, and so on.

Now we swap the *.frm* files from the operating system's command prompt:

```
root:/var/lib/mysql/sakila# mv film.frm film_tmp.frm
root:/var/lib/mysql/sakila# mv film_new.frm film.frm
root:/var/lib/mysql/sakila# mv film_tmp.frm film_new.frm
```

Back in the MySQL prompt, we can now unlock the table and see that the changes took effect:

```
mysql> UNLOCK TABLES;
mysql> SHOW COLUMNS FROM sakila.film LIKE 'rating'\G
*************************** 1. row ***************************
Field: rating
 Type: enum('G','PG','PG-13','R','NC-17','PG-14')
```

The only thing left to do is drop the table we created to help with the operation:

```
mysql> DROP TABLE sakila.film_new;
```

Building MyISAM Indexes Quickly

The usual trick for loading MyISAM tables efficiently is to disable keys, load the data, and reenable the keys:

```
mysql> ALTER TABLE test.load_data DISABLE KEYS;
-- load the data
mysql> ALTER TABLE test.load_data ENABLE KEYS;
```

This works because it lets MyISAM delay building the keys until all the data is loaded, at which point, it can build the indexes by sorting. This is much faster and results in a defragmented, compact index tree.[*]

Unfortunately, it doesn't work for unique indexes, because DISABLE KEYS applies only to nonunique indexes. MyISAM builds unique indexes in memory and checks the uniqueness as it loads each row. Loading becomes extremely slow as soon as the index's size exceeds the available memory.

As with the ALTER TABLE hacks in the previous section, you can speed up this process if you're willing to do a little more work and assume some risk. This can be useful for loading data from backups, for example, when you already know all the data is valid and there's no need for uniqueness checks.

 Again, this is an undocumented, unsupported technique. Use it at your own risk, and back up your data first.

Here are the steps you'll need to take:

1. Create a table of the desired structure, but without any indexes.
2. Load the data into the table to build the *.MYD* file.
3. Create another empty table with the desired structure, this time including the indexes. This will create the *.frm* and *.MYI* files you need.
4. Flush the tables with a read lock.
5. Rename the second table's *.frm* and *.MYI* files, so MySQL uses them for the first table.
6. Release the read lock.
7. Use REPAIR TABLE to build the table's indexes. This will build all indexes by sorting, including the unique indexes.

This procedure can be much faster for very large tables.

---

[*] MyISAM will also build indexes by sorting when you use LOAD DATA INFILE and the table is empty.

Notes on Storage Engines

We close this chapter with some storage engine-specific schema design choices you should keep in mind. We're not trying to write an exhaustive list; our goal is just to present some key factors that are relevant to schema design.

The MyISAM Storage Engine

Table locks

MyISAM tables have table-level locks. Be careful this doesn't become a bottleneck.

No automated data recovery

If the MySQL server crashes or power goes down, you should check and possibly repair your MyISAM tables before using them. If you have large tables, this could take hours.

No transactions

MyISAM tables don't support transactions. In fact, MyISAM doesn't even guarantee that a single statement will complete; if there's an error halfway through a multirow UPDATE, for example, some of the rows will be updated and some won't.

Only indexes are cached in memory

MyISAM caches only the index inside the MySQL process, in the key buffer. The operating system caches the table's data, so in MySQL 5.0 an expensive operating system call is required to retrieve it.

Compact storage

Rows are stored jam-packed one after another, so you get a small disk footprint and fast full table scans for on-disk data.

The Memory Storage Engine

Table locks

Like MyISAM tables, Memory tables have table locks. This isn't usually a problem though, because queries on Memory tables are normally fast.

No dynamic rows

Memory tables don't support dynamic (i.e., variable-length) rows, so they don't support BLOB and TEXT fields at all. Even a VARCHAR(5000) turns into a CHAR(5000)—a huge memory waste if most values are small.

Hash indexes are the default index type

Unlike for other storage engines, the default index type is hash if you don't specify it explicitly.

No index statistics

Memory tables don't support index statistics, so you may get bad execution plans for some complex queries.

Content is lost on restart

Memory tables don't persist any data to disk, so the data is lost when the server restarts, even though the tables' definitions remain.

The InnoDB Storage Engine

Transactional

InnoDB supports transactions and four transaction isolation levels.

Foreign keys

As of MySQL 5.0, InnoDB is the only stock storage engine that supports foreign keys. Other storage engines will accept them in CREATE TABLE statements, but won't enforce them. Some third-party engines, such as solidDB for MySQL and PBXT, support them at the storage engine level too; MySQL AB plans to add support at the server level in the future.

Row-level locks

Locks are set at the row level, with no escalation and nonblocking selects—standard selects don't set any locks at all, which gives very good concurrency.

Multiversioning

InnoDB uses multiversion concurrency control, so by default your selects may read stale data. In fact, its MVCC architecture adds a lot of complexity and possibly unexpected behaviors. You should read the InnoDB manual thoroughly if you use InnoDB.

Clustering by primary key

All InnoDB tables are clustered by the primary key, which you can use to your advantage in schema design.

All indexes contain the primary key columns

Indexes refer to the rows by the primary key, so if you don't keep your primary key short, the indexes will grow very large.

Optimized caching

InnoDB caches both data and memory in the buffer pool. It also automatically builds hash indexes to speed up row retrieval.

Unpacked indexes

Indexes are not packed with prefix compression, so they can be much larger than for MyISAM tables.

Slow data load

As of MySQL 5.0, InnoDB does not specially optimize data load operations. It builds indexes a row at a time, instead of building them by sorting. This may result in significantly slower data loads.

Blocking AUTO_INCREMENT

In versions earlier than MySQL 5.1, InnoDB uses a table-level lock to generate each new AUTO_INCREMENT value.

No cached COUNT(*) *value*

Unlike MyISAM or Memory tables, InnoDB tables don't store the number of rows in the table, which means COUNT(*) queries without a WHERE clause can't be optimized away and require full table or index scans. See "Optimizing COUNT() Queries" on page 188 for more on this topic.

Query Performance Optimization

In the previous chapter, we explained how to optimize a schema, which is one of the necessary conditions for high performance. But working with the schema isn't enough—you also need to design your queries well. If your queries are bad, even the best-designed schema will not perform well.

Query optimization, index optimization, and schema optimization go hand in hand. As you gain experience writing queries in MySQL, you will come to understand how to design schemas to support efficient queries. Similarly, what you learn about optimal schema design will influence the kinds of queries you write. This process takes time, so we encourage you to refer back to this chapter and the previous one as you learn more.

This chapter begins with general query design considerations—the things you should consider first when a query isn't performing well. We then dig much deeper into query optimization and server internals. We show you how to find out how MySQL executes a particular query, and you'll learn how to change the query execution plan. Finally, we look at some places MySQL doesn't optimize queries well and explore query optimization patterns that help MySQL execute queries more efficiently.

Our goal is to help you understand deeply how MySQL really executes queries, so you can reason about what is efficient or inefficient, exploit MySQL's strengths, and avoid its weaknesses.

Slow Query Basics: Optimize Data Access

The most basic reason a query doesn't perform well is because it's working with too much data. Some queries just have to sift through a lot of data and can't be helped. That's unusual, though; most bad queries can be changed to access less data. We've found it useful to analyze a poorly performing query in two steps:

1. Find out whether your *application* is retrieving more data than you need. That usually means it's accessing too many rows, but it might also be accessing too many columns.

2. Find out whether the *MySQL server* is analyzing more rows than it needs.

Are You Asking the Database for Data You Don't Need?

Some queries ask for more data than they need and then throw some of it away. This demands extra work of the MySQL server, adds network overhead,* and consumes memory and CPU resources on the application server.

Here are a few typical mistakes:

Fetching more rows than needed

One common mistake is assuming that MySQL provides results on demand, rather than calculating and returning the full result set. We often see this in applications designed by people familiar with other database systems. These developers are used to techniques such as issuing a SELECT statement that returns many rows, then fetching the first *N* rows, and closing the result set (e.g., fetching the 100 most recent articles for a news site when they only need to show 10 of them on the front page). They think MySQL will provide them with these 10 rows and stop executing the query, but what MySQL really does is generate the complete result set. The client library then fetches all the data and discards most of it. The best solution is to add a LIMIT clause to the query.

Fetching all columns from a multitable join

If you want to retrieve all actors who appear in *Academy Dinosaur*, don't write the query this way:

```
mysql> SELECT * FROM sakila.actor
    -> INNER JOIN sakila.film_actor USING(actor_id)
    -> INNER JOIN sakila.film USING(film_id)
    -> WHERE sakila.film.title = 'Academy Dinosaur';
```

That returns all columns from all three tables. Instead, write the query as follows:

```
mysql> SELECT sakila.actor.* FROM sakila.actor...;
```

Fetching all columns

You should always be suspicious when you see SELECT *. Do you really need all columns? Probably not. Retrieving all columns can prevent optimizations such as covering indexes, as well as adding I/O, memory, and CPU overhead for the server.

Some DBAs ban SELECT * universally because of this fact, and to reduce the risk of problems when someone alters the table's column list.

---

* Network overhead is worst if the application is on a different host from the server, but transferring data between MySQL and the application isn't free even if they're on the same server.

Of course, asking for more data than you really need is not always bad. In many cases we've investigated, people tell us the wasteful approach simplifies development, as it lets the developer use the same bit of code in more than one place. That's a reasonable consideration, as long as you know what it costs in terms of performance. It may also be useful to retrieve more data than you actually need if you use some type of caching in your application, or if you have another benefit in mind. Fetching and caching full objects may be preferable to running many separate queries that retrieve only parts of the object.

Is MySQL Examining Too Much Data?

Once you're sure your queries *retrieve* only the data you need, you can look for queries that *examine* too much data while generating results. In MySQL, the simplest query cost metrics are:

- Execution time
- Number of rows examined
- Number of rows returned

None of these metrics is a perfect way to measure query cost, but they reflect roughly how much data MySQL must access internally to execute a query and translate approximately into how fast the query runs. All three metrics are logged in the slow query log, so looking at the slow query log is one of the best ways to find queries that examine too much data.

Execution time

As discussed in Chapter 2, the standard slow query logging feature in MySQL 5.0 and earlier has serious limitations, including lack of support for fine-grained logging. Fortunately, there are patches that let you log and measure slow queries with microsecond resolution. These are included in the MySQL 5.1 server, but you can also patch earlier versions if needed. Beware of placing too much emphasis on query execution time. It's nice to look at because it's an objective metric, but it's not consistent under varying load conditions. Other factors—such as storage engine locks (table locks and row locks), high concurrency, and hardware—can also have a considerable impact on query execution times. This metric is useful for finding queries that impact the application's response time the most or load the server the most, but it does not tell you whether the actual execution time is reasonable for a query of a given complexity. (Execution time can also be both a symptom and a cause of problems, and it's not always obvious which is the case.)

Rows examined and rows returned

It's useful to think about the number of rows examined when analyzing queries, because you can see how efficiently the queries are finding the data you need.

However, like execution time, it's not a perfect metric for finding bad queries. Not all row accesses are equal. Shorter rows are faster to access, and fetching rows from memory is much faster than reading them from disk.

Ideally, the number of rows examined would be the same as the number returned, but in practice this is rarely possible. For example, when constructing rows with joins, multiple rows must be accessed to generate each row in the result set. The ratio of rows examined to rows returned is usually small—say, between 1:1 and 10:1—but sometimes it can be orders of magnitude larger.

Rows examined and access types

When you're thinking about the cost of a query, consider the cost of finding a single row in a table. MySQL can use several access methods to find and return a row. Some require examining many rows, but others may be able to generate the result without examining any.

The access method(s) appear in the type column in EXPLAIN's output. The access types range from a full table scan to index scans, range scans, unique index lookups, and constants. Each of these is faster than the one before it, because it requires reading less data. You don't need to memorize the access types, but you should understand the general concepts of scanning a table, scanning an index, range accesses, and single-value accesses.

If you aren't getting a good access type, the best way to solve the problem is usually by adding an appropriate index. We discussed indexing at length in the previous chapter; now you can see why indexes are so important to query optimization. Indexes let MySQL find rows with a more efficient access type that examines less data.

For example, let's look at a simple query on the Sakila sample database:

```
mysql> SELECT * FROM sakila.film_actor WHERE film_id = 1;
```

This query will return 10 rows, and EXPLAIN shows that MySQL uses the ref access type on the idx_fk_film_id index to execute the query:

```
mysql> EXPLAIN SELECT * FROM sakila.film_actor WHERE film_id = 1\G
*************************** 1. row ***************************
           id: 1
  select_type: SIMPLE
        table: film_actor
         type: ref
possible_keys: idx_fk_film_id
          key: idx_fk_film_id
      key_len: 2
          ref: const
         rows: 10
        Extra:
```

EXPLAIN shows that MySQL estimated it needed to access only 10 rows. In other words, the query optimizer knew the chosen access type could satisfy the query efficiently. What would happen if there were no suitable index for the query? MySQL would have to use a less optimal access type, as we can see if we drop the index and run the query again:

```
mysql> ALTER TABLE sakila.film_actor DROP FOREIGN KEY fk_film_actor_film;
mysql> ALTER TABLE sakila.film_actor DROP KEY idx_fk_film_id;
mysql> EXPLAIN SELECT * FROM sakila.film_actor WHERE film_id = 1\G
*************************** 1. row ***************************
           id: 1
  select_type: SIMPLE
        table: film_actor
         type: ALL
possible_keys: NULL
          key: NULL
      key_len: NULL
          ref: NULL
         rows: 5073
        Extra: Using where
```

Predictably, the access type has changed to a full table scan (ALL), and MySQL now estimates it'll have to examine 5,073 rows to satisfy the query. The "Using where" in the Extra column shows that the MySQL server is using the WHERE clause to discard rows after the storage engine reads them.

In general, MySQL can apply a WHERE clause in three ways, from best to worst:

- Apply the conditions to the index lookup operation to eliminate nonmatching rows. This happens at the storage engine layer.

- Use a covering index ("Using index" in the Extra column) to avoid row accesses, and filter out nonmatching rows after retrieving each result from the index. This happens at the server layer, but it doesn't require reading rows from the table.

- Retrieve rows from the table, then filter nonmatching rows ("Using where" in the Extra column). This happens at the server layer and requires the server to read rows from the table before it can filter them.

This example illustrates how important it is to have good indexes. Good indexes help your queries get a good access type and examine only the rows they need. However, adding an index doesn't always mean that MySQL will access and return the same number of rows. For example, here's a query that uses the COUNT( ) aggregate function:[*]

```
mysql> SELECT actor_id, COUNT(*) FROM sakila.film_actor GROUP BY actor_id;
```

This query returns only 200 rows, but it needs to read thousands of rows to build the result set. An index can't reduce the number of rows examined for a query like this one.

---

[*] See "Optimizing COUNT( ) Queries" on page 188 for more on this topic.

Unfortunately, MySQL does not tell you how many of the rows it accessed were used to build the result set; it tells you only the total number of rows it accessed. Many of these rows could be eliminated by a WHERE clause and end up not contributing to the result set. In the previous example, after removing the index on sakila.film_actor, the query accessed every row in the table and the WHERE clause discarded all but 10 of them. Only the remaining 10 rows were used to build the result set. Understanding how many rows the server accesses and how many it really uses requires reasoning about the query.

If you find that a huge number of rows were examined to produce relatively few rows in the result, you can try some more sophisticated fixes:

- Use covering indexes, which store data so that the storage engine doesn't have to retrieve the complete rows. (We discussed these in the previous chapter.)

- Change the schema. An example is using summary tables (discussed in the previous chapter).

- Rewrite a complicated query so the MySQL optimizer is able to execute it optimally. (We discuss this later in this chapter.)

Ways to Restructure Queries

As you optimize problematic queries, your goal should be to find alternative ways to get the result you want—but that doesn't necessarily mean getting the same result set back from MySQL. You can sometimes transform queries into equivalent forms and get better performance. However, you should also think about rewriting the query to retrieve different results, if that provides an efficiency benefit. You may be able to ultimately do the same work by changing the application code as well as the query. In this section, we explain techniques that can help you restructure a wide range of queries and show you when to use each technique.

Complex Queries Versus Many Queries

One important query design question is whether it's preferable to break up a complex query into several simpler queries. The traditional approach to database design emphasizes doing as much work as possible with as few queries as possible. This approach was historically better because of the cost of network communication and the overhead of the query parsing and optimization stages.

However, this advice doesn't apply as much to MySQL, because it was designed to handle connecting and disconnecting very efficiently and to respond to small and simple queries very quickly. Modern networks are also significantly faster than they used to be, reducing network latency. MySQL can run more than 50,000 simple queries per second on commodity server hardware and over 2,000 queries per second from a single correspondent on a Gigabit network, so running multiple queries isn't necessarily such a bad thing.

Connection response is still slow compared to the number of rows MySQL can traverse per second internally, though, which is counted in millions per second for in-memory data. All else being equal, it's still a good idea to use as few queries as possible, but sometimes you can make a query more efficient by decomposing it and executing a few simple queries instead of one complex one. Don't be afraid to do this; weigh the costs, and go with the strategy that causes less work. We show some examples of this technique a little later in the chapter.

That said, using too many queries is a common mistake in application design. For example, some applications perform 10 single-row queries to retrieve data from a table when they could use a single 10-row query. We've even seen applications that retrieve each column individually, querying each row many times!

Chopping Up a Query

Another way to slice up a query is to divide and conquer, keeping it essentially the same but running it in smaller "chunks" that affect fewer rows each time.

Purging old data is a great example. Periodic purge jobs may need to remove quite a bit of data, and doing this in one massive query could lock a lot of rows for a long time, fill up transaction logs, hog resources, and block small queries that shouldn't be interrupted. Chopping up the DELETE statement and using medium-size queries can improve performance considerably, and reduce replication lag when a query is replicated. For example, instead of running this monolithic query:

```
mysql> DELETE FROM messages WHERE created < DATE_SUB(NOW( ),INTERVAL 3 MONTH);
```

you could do something like the following pseudocode:

```
rows_affected = 0
do {
   rows_affected = do_query(
       "DELETE FROM messages WHERE created < DATE_SUB(NOW( ),INTERVAL 3 MONTH)
       LIMIT 10000")
} while rows_affected > 0
```

Deleting 10,000 rows at a time is typically a large enough task to make each query efficient, and a short enough task to minimize the impact on the server[*] (transactional storage engines may benefit from smaller transactions). It may also be a good idea to add some sleep time between the DELETE statements to spread the load over time and reduce the amount of time locks are held.

---

[*] Maatkit's *mk-archiver* tool makes these types of jobs easy.

Join Decomposition

Many high-performance web sites use *join decomposition*. You can decompose a join by running multiple single-table queries instead of a multitable join, and then performing the join in the application. For example, instead of this single query:

```
mysql> SELECT * FROM tag
    ->     JOIN tag_post ON tag_post.tag_id=tag.id
    ->     JOIN post ON tag_post.post_id=post.id
    -> WHERE tag.tag='mysql';
```

You might run these queries:

```
mysql> SELECT * FROM  tag WHERE tag='mysql';
mysql> SELECT * FROM  tag_post WHERE tag_id=1234;
mysql> SELECT * FROM  post WHERE  post.id in (123,456,567,9098,8904);
```

This looks wasteful at first glance, because you've increased the number of queries without getting anything in return. However, such restructuring can actually give significant performance advantages:

- Caching can be more efficient. Many applications cache "objects" that map directly to tables. In this example, if the object with the tag `mysql` is already cached, the application can skip the first query. If you find posts with an `id` of 123, 567, or 9098 in the cache, you can remove them from the `IN( )` list. The query cache might also benefit from this strategy. If only one of the tables changes frequently, decomposing a join can reduce the number of cache invalidations.

- For MyISAM tables, performing one query per table uses table locks more efficiently: the queries will lock the tables individually and relatively briefly, instead of locking them all for a longer time.

- Doing joins in the application makes it easier to scale the database by placing tables on different servers.

- The queries themselves can be more efficient. In this example, using an `IN( )` list instead of a join lets MySQL sort row IDs and retrieve rows more optimally than might be possible with a join. We explain this in more detail later.

- You can reduce redundant row accesses. Doing a join in the application means you retrieve each row only once, whereas a join in the query is essentially a denormalization that might repeatedly access the same data. For the same reason, such restructuring might also reduce the total network traffic and memory usage.

- To some extent, you can view this technique as manually implementing a hash join instead of the nested loops algorithm MySQL uses to execute a join. A hash join may be more efficient. (We discuss MySQL's join strategy later in this chapter.)

Summary: When Application Joins May Be More Efficient

Doing joins in the application may be more efficient when:

- You cache and reuse a lot of data from earlier queries
- You use multiple MyISAM tables
- You distribute data across multiple servers
- You replace joins with IN( ) lists on large tables
- A join refers to the same table multiple times

Query Execution Basics

If you need to get high performance from your MySQL server, one of the best ways to invest your time is in learning how MySQL optimizes and executes queries. Once you understand this, much of query optimization is simply a matter of reasoning from principles, and query optimization becomes a very logical process.

 This discussion assumes you've read Chapter 2, which provides a foundation for understanding the MySQL query execution engine.

Figure 4-1 shows how MySQL generally executes queries.

Follow along with the illustration to see what happens when you send MySQL a query:

1. The client sends the SQL statement to the server.
2. The server checks the query cache. If there's a hit, it returns the stored result from the cache; otherwise, it passes the SQL statement to the next step.
3. The server parses, preprocesses, and optimizes the SQL into a query execution plan.
4. The query execution engine executes the plan by making calls to the storage engine API.
5. The server sends the result to the client.

Each of these steps has some extra complexity, which we discuss in the following sections. We also explain which states the query will be in during each step. The query optimization process is particularly complex and important to understand.

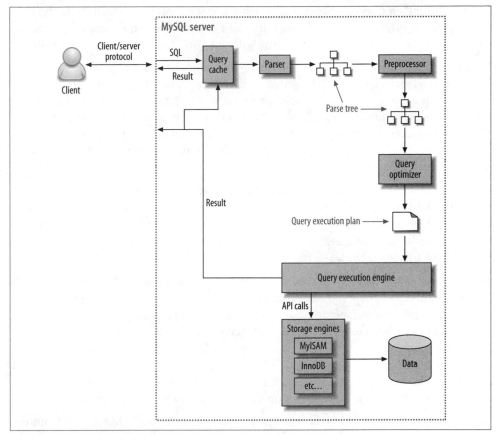

Figure 4-1. Execution path of a query

The MySQL Client/Server Protocol

Though you don't need to understand the inner details of MySQL's client/server protocol, you do need to understand how it works at a high level. The protocol is half-duplex, which means that at any given time the MySQL server can be either sending or receiving messages, but not both. It also means there is no way to cut a message short.

This protocol makes MySQL communication simple and fast, but it limits it in some ways too. For one thing, it means there's no flow control; once one side sends a message, the other side must fetch the entire message before responding. It's like a game of tossing a ball back and forth: only one side has the ball at any instant, and you can't toss the ball (send a message) unless you have it.

The client sends a query to the server as a single packet of data. This is why the max_
packet_size configuration variable is important if you have large queries.* Once the
client sends the query, it doesn't have the ball anymore; it can only wait for results.

In contrast, the response from the server usually consists of many packets of data.
When the server responds, the client has to receive the *entire* result set. It cannot
simply fetch a few rows and then ask the server not to bother sending the rest. If the
client needs only the first few rows that are returned, it either has to wait for all of
the server's packets to arrive and then discard the ones it doesn't need, or disconnect ungracefully. Neither is a good idea, which is why appropriate LIMIT clauses are
so important.

Here's another way to think about this: when a client fetches rows from the server, it
thinks it's *pulling* them. But the truth is, the MySQL server is *pushing* the rows as it
generates them. The client is only receiving the pushed rows; there is no way for it to
tell the server to stop sending rows. The client is "drinking from the fire hose," so to
speak. (Yes, that's a technical term.)

Most libraries that connect to MySQL let you either fetch the whole result set and
buffer it in memory, or fetch each row as you need it. The default behavior is generally to fetch the whole result and buffer it in memory. This is important because until
all the rows have been fetched, the MySQL server will not release the locks and other
resources required by the query. The query will be in the "Sending data" state
(explained in the following section, "Query states" on page 163). When the client
library fetches the results all at once, it reduces the amount of work the server needs
to do: the server can finish and clean up the query as quickly as possible.

Most client libraries let you treat the result set as though you're fetching it from the
server, although in fact you're just fetching it from the buffer in the library's memory. This works fine most of the time, but it's not a good idea for huge result sets
that might take a long time to fetch and use a lot of memory. You can use less memory, and start working on the result sooner, if you instruct the library not to buffer
the result. The downside is that the locks and other resources on the server will
remain open while your application is interacting with the library.†

Let's look at an example using PHP. First, here's how you'll usually query MySQL
from PHP:

```php
<?php
$link   = mysql_connect('localhost', 'user', 'p4ssword');
$result = mysql_query('SELECT * FROM HUGE_TABLE', $link);
while ( $row = mysql_fetch_array($result) ) {
    // Do something with result
}
?>
```

---

* If the query is too large, the server will refuse to receive any more data and throw an error.

† You can work around this with SQL_BUFFER_RESULT, which we see a bit later.

The code seems to indicate that you fetch rows only when you need them, in the while loop. However, the code actually fetches the entire result into a buffer with the mysql_query( ) function call. The while loop simply iterates through the buffer. In contrast, the following code doesn't buffer the results, because it uses mysql_unbuffered_query( ) instead of mysql_query( ):

```php
<?php
$link   = mysql_connect('localhost', 'user', 'p4ssword');
$result = mysql_unbuffered_query('SELECT * FROM HUGE_TABLE', $link);
while ( $row = mysql_fetch_array($result) ) {
   // Do something with result
}
?>
```

Programming languages have different ways to override buffering. For example, the Perl DBD::mysql driver requires you to specify the C client library's mysql_use_result attribute (the default is mysql_buffer_result). Here's an example:

```perl
#!/usr/bin/perl
use DBI;
my $dbh = DBI->connect('DBI:mysql:;host=localhost', 'user', 'p4ssword');
my $sth = $dbh->prepare('SELECT * FROM HUGE_TABLE', { mysql_use_result => 1 });
$sth->execute();
while ( my $row = $sth->fetchrow_array() ) {
   # Do something with result
}
```

Notice that the call to prepare( ) specified to "use" the result instead of "buffering" it. You can also specify this when connecting, which will make every statement unbuffered:

```perl
my $dbh = DBI->connect('DBI:mysql:;mysql_use_result=1', 'user', 'p4ssword');
```

Query states

Each MySQL connection, or *thread*, has a state that shows what it is doing at any given time. There are several ways to view these states, but the easiest is to use the SHOW FULL PROCESSLIST command (the states appear in the Command column). As a query progresses through its lifecycle, its state changes many times, and there are dozens of states. The MySQL manual is the authoritative source of information for all the states, but we list a few here and explain what they mean:

Sleep
:   The thread is waiting for a new query from the client.

Query
:   The thread is either executing the query or sending the result back to the client.

Locked
:   The thread is waiting for a table lock to be granted at the server level. Locks that are implemented by the storage engine, such as InnoDB's row locks, do not cause the thread to enter the Locked state.

Analyzing *and* statistics
> The thread is checking storage engine statistics and optimizing the query.

Copying to tmp table [on disk]
> The thread is processing the query and copying results to a temporary table, probably for a GROUP BY, for a filesort, or to satisfy a UNION. If the state ends with "on disk," MySQL is converting an in-memory table to an on-disk table.

Sorting result
> The thread is sorting a result set.

Sending data
> This can mean several things: the thread might be sending data between stages of the query, generating the result set, or returning the result set to the client.

It's helpful to at least know the basic states, so you can get a sense of "who has the ball" for the query. On very busy servers, you might see an unusual or normally brief state, such as statistics, begin to take a significant amount of time. This usually indicates that something is wrong.

The Query Cache

Before even parsing a query, MySQL checks for it in the query cache, if the cache is enabled. This operation is a case sensitive hash lookup. If the query differs from a similar query in the cache by even a single byte, it won't match, and the query processing will go to the next stage.

If MySQL does find a match in the query cache, it must check privileges before returning the cached query. This is possible without parsing the query, because MySQL stores table information with the cached query. If the privileges are OK, MySQL retrieves the stored result from the query cache and sends it to the client, bypassing every other stage in query execution. The query is never parsed, optimized, or executed.

You can learn more about the query cache in Chapter 5.

The Query Optimization Process

The next step in the query lifecycle turns a SQL query into an execution plan for the query execution engine. It has several sub-steps: parsing, preprocessing, and optimization. Errors (for example, syntax errors) can be raised at any point in the process. We're not trying to document the MySQL internals here, so we're going to take some liberties, such as describing steps separately even though they're often combined wholly or partially for efficiency. Our goal is simply to help you understand how MySQL executes queries so that you can write better ones.

The parser and the preprocessor

To begin, MySQL's *parser* breaks the query into tokens and builds a "parse tree" from them. The parser uses MySQL's SQL grammar to interpret and validate the query. For instance, it ensures that the tokens in the query are valid and in the proper order, and it checks for mistakes such as quoted strings that aren't terminated.

The *preprocessor* then checks the resulting parse tree for additional semantics that the parser can't resolve. For example, it checks that tables and columns exist, and it resolves names and aliases to ensure that column references aren't ambiguous.

Next, the preprocessor checks privileges. This is normally very fast unless your server has large numbers of privileges. (See Chapter 12 for more on privileges and security.)

The query optimizer

The parse tree is now valid and ready for the *optimizer* to turn it into a query execution plan. A query can often be executed many different ways and produce the same result. The optimizer's job is to find the best option.

MySQL uses a cost-based optimizer, which means it tries to predict the cost of various execution plans and choose the least expensive. The unit of cost is a single random four-kilobyte data page read. You can see how expensive the optimizer estimated a query to be by running the query, then inspecting the Last_query_cost session variable:

```
mysql> SELECT SQL_NO_CACHE COUNT(*) FROM sakila.film_actor;
+----------+
| count(*) |
+----------+
|     5462 |
+----------+
mysql> SHOW STATUS LIKE 'last_query_cost';
+-----------------+-------------+
| Variable_name   | Value       |
+-----------------+-------------+
| Last_query_cost | 1040.599000 |
+-----------------+-------------+
```

This result means that the optimizer estimated it would need to do about 1,040 random data page reads to execute the query. It bases the estimate on statistics: the number of pages per table or index, the *cardinality* (number of distinct values) of indexes, the length of rows and keys, and key distribution. The optimizer does not include the effects of any type of caching in its estimates—it assumes every read will result in a disk I/O operation.

The optimizer may not always choose the best plan, for many reasons:

- The statistics could be wrong. The server relies on storage engines to provide statistics, and they can range from exactly correct to wildly inaccurate. For example, the InnoDB storage engine doesn't maintain accurate statistics about the number of rows in a table, because of its MVCC architecture.

- The cost metric is not exactly equivalent to the true cost of running the query, so even when the statistics are accurate, the query may be more or less expensive than MySQL's approximation. A plan that reads more pages might actually be cheaper in some cases, such as when the reads are sequential so the disk I/O is faster, or when the pages are already cached in memory.

- MySQL's idea of optimal might not match yours. You probably want the fastest execution time, but MySQL doesn't really understand "fast"; it understands "cost," and as we've seen, determining cost is not an exact science.

- MySQL doesn't consider other queries that are running concurrently, which can affect how quickly the query runs.

- MySQL doesn't always do cost-based optimization. Sometimes it just follows the rules, such as "if there's a full-text MATCH( ) clause, use a FULLTEXT index if one exists." It will do this even when it would be faster to use a different index and a non-FULLTEXT query with a WHERE clause.

- The optimizer doesn't take into account the cost of operations not under its control, such as executing stored functions or user-defined functions.

- As we'll see later, the optimizer can't always estimate every possible execution plan, so it may miss an optimal plan.

MySQL's query optimizer is a highly complex piece of software, and it uses many optimizations to transform the query into an execution plan. There are two basic types of optimizations, which we call *static* and *dynamic*. *Static optimizations* can be performed simply by inspecting the parse tree. For example, the optimizer can transform the WHERE clause into an equivalent form by applying algebraic rules. Static optimizations are independent of values, such as the value of a constant in a WHERE clause. They can be performed once and will always be valid, even when the query is reexecuted with different values. You can think of these as "compile-time optimizations."

In contrast, *dynamic optimizations* are based on context and can depend on many factors, such as which value is in a WHERE clause or how many rows are in an index. They must be reevaluated each time the query is executed. You can think of these as "runtime optimizations."

The difference is important in executing prepared statements or stored procedures. MySQL can do static optimizations once, but it must reevaluate dynamic optimizations every time it executes a query. MySQL sometimes even reoptimizes the query as it executes it.[*]

---

[*] For example, the range check query plan reevaluates indexes for each row in a JOIN. You can see this query plan by looking for "range checked for each record" in the Extra column in EXPLAIN. This query plan also increments the Select_full_range_join server variable.

Here are some types of optimizations MySQL knows how to do:

Reordering joins

Tables don't always have to be joined in the order you specify in the query. Determining the best join order is an important optimization; we explain it in depth in "The join optimizer" on page 173.

Converting OUTER JOINs to INNER JOINs

An OUTER JOIN doesn't necessarily have to be executed as an OUTER JOIN. Some factors, such as the WHERE clause and table schema, can actually cause an OUTER JOIN to be equivalent to an INNER JOIN. MySQL can recognize this and rewrite the join, which makes it eligible for reordering.

Applying algebraic equivalence rules

MySQL applies algebraic transformations to simplify and canonicalize expressions. It can also fold and reduce constants, eliminating impossible constraints and constant conditions. For example, the term (5=5 AND a>5) will reduce to just a>5. Similarly, (a<b AND b=c) AND a=5 becomes b>5 AND b=c AND a=5. These rules are very useful for writing conditional queries, which we discuss later in the chapter.

COUNT( ), MIN( ), and MAX( ) optimizations

Indexes and column nullability can often help MySQL optimize away these expressions. For example, to find the minimum value of a column that's left-most in a B-Tree index, MySQL can just request the first row in the index. It can even do this in the query optimization stage, and treat the value as a constant for the rest of the query. Similarly, to find the maximum value in a B-Tree index, the server reads the last row. If the server uses this optimization, you'll see "Select tables optimized away" in the EXPLAIN plan. This literally means the optimizer has removed the table from the query plan and replaced it with a constant.

Likewise, COUNT(*) queries without a WHERE clause can often be optimized away on some storage engines (such as MyISAM, which keeps an exact count of rows in the table at all times). See "Optimizing COUNT() Queries" on page 188, later in this chapter, for details.

Evaluating and reducing constant expressions

When MySQL detects that an expression can be reduced to a constant, it will do so during optimization. For example, a user-defined variable can be converted to a constant if it's not changed in the query. Arithmetic expressions are another example.

Perhaps surprisingly, even something you might consider to be a query can be reduced to a constant during the optimization phase. One example is a MIN( ) on an index. This can even be extended to a constant lookup on a primary key or unique index. If a WHERE clause applies a constant condition to such an index, the optimizer knows MySQL can look up the value at the beginning of the query. It will then treat the value as a constant in the rest of the query. Here's an example:

```
mysql> EXPLAIN SELECT film.film_id, film_actor.actor_id
    -> FROM sakila.film
    ->    INNER JOIN sakila.film_actor USING(film_id)
    -> WHERE film.film_id = 1;
+----+-------------+------------+-------+----------------+-------+------+
| id | select_type | table      | type  | key            | ref   | rows |
+----+-------------+------------+-------+----------------+-------+------+
|  1 | SIMPLE      | film       | const | PRIMARY        | const |    1 |
|  1 | SIMPLE      | film_actor | ref   | idx_fk_film_id | const |   10 |
+----+-------------+------------+-------+----------------+-------+------+
```

MySQL executes this query in two steps, which correspond to the two rows in
the output. The first step is to find the desired row in the film table. MySQL's
optimizer knows there is only one row, because there's a primary key on the
film_id column, and it has already consulted the index during the query optimization stage to see how many rows it will find. Because the query optimizer has a
known quantity (the value in the WHERE clause) to use in the lookup, this table's
ref type is const.

In the second step, MySQL treats the film_id column from the row found in the
first step as a known quantity. It can do this because the optimizer knows that
by the time the query reaches the second step, it will know all the values from
the first step. Notice that the film_actor table's ref type is const, just as the film
table's was.

Another way you'll see constant conditions applied is by propagating a value's
constant-ness from one place to another if there is a WHERE, USING, or ON clause
that restricts them to being equal. In this example, the optimizer knows that the
USING clause forces film_id to have the same value everywhere in the query—it
must be equal to the constant value given in the WHERE clause.

Covering indexes

MySQL can sometimes use an index to avoid reading row data, when the index
contains all the columns the query needs. We discussed covering indexes at
length in Chapter 3.

Subquery optimization

MySQL can convert some types of subqueries into more efficient alternative
forms, reducing them to index lookups instead of separate queries.

Early termination

MySQL can stop processing a query (or a step in a query) as soon as it fulfills the
query or step. The obvious case is a LIMIT clause, but there are several other
kinds of early termination. For instance, if MySQL detects an impossible condition, it can abort the entire query. You can see this in the following example:

```
mysql> EXPLAIN SELECT film.film_id FROM sakila.film WHERE film_id = -1;
+----+...+----------------------------------------------------+
| id |...| Extra                                              |
+----+...+----------------------------------------------------+
|  1 |...| Impossible WHERE noticed after reading const tables |
+----+...+----------------------------------------------------+
```

This query stopped during the optimization step, but MySQL can also terminate execution sooner in some cases. The server can use this optimization when the query execution engine recognizes the need to retrieve distinct values, or to stop when a value doesn't exist. For example, the following query finds all movies without any actors:[*]

```
mysql> SELECT film.film_id
    -> FROM sakila.film
    ->    LEFT OUTER JOIN sakila.film_actor USING(film_id)
    -> WHERE film_actor.film_id IS NULL;
```

This query works by eliminating any films that have actors. Each film might have many actors, but as soon as it finds one actor, it stops processing the current film and moves to the next one because it knows the WHERE clause prohibits outputting that film. A similar "Distinct/not-exists" optimization can apply to certain kinds of DISTINCT, NOT EXISTS( ), and LEFT JOIN queries.

Equality propagation

MySQL recognizes when a query holds two columns as equal—for example, in a JOIN condition—and propagates WHERE clauses across equivalent columns. For instance, in the following query:

```
mysql> SELECT film.film_id
    -> FROM sakila.film
    ->    INNER JOIN sakila.film_actor USING(film_id)
    -> WHERE film.film_id > 500;
```

MySQL knows that the WHERE clause applies not only to the film table but to the film_actor table as well, because the USING clause forces the two columns to match.

If you're used to another database server that can't do this, you may have been advised to "help the optimizer" by manually specifying the WHERE clause for both tables, like this:

```
... WHERE film.film_id > 500 AND film_actor.film_id > 500
```

This is unnecessary in MySQL. It just makes your queries harder to maintain.

IN( ) *list comparisons*

In many database servers, IN( ) is just a synonym for multiple OR clauses, because the two are logically equivalent. Not so in MySQL, which sorts the values in the IN( ) list and uses a fast binary search to see whether a value is in the list. This is $O(\log n)$ in the size of the list, whereas an equivalent series of OR clauses is $O(n)$ in the size of the list (i.e., much slower for large lists).

The preceding list is woefully incomplete, as MySQL performs more optimizations than we could fit into this entire chapter, but it should give you an idea of the optimizer's complexity and intelligence. If there's one thing you should take away from

---

[*] We agree, a movie without actors is strange, but the Sakila sample database lists no actors for "SLACKER LIAISONS," which it describes as "A Fast-Paced Tale of a Shark And a Student who must Meet a Crocodile in Ancient China."

this discussion, it's *don't try to outsmart the optimizer*. You may end up just defeating it, or making your queries more complicated and harder to maintain for zero benefit. In general, you should let the optimizer do its work.

Of course, as smart as the optimizer is, there are times when it doesn't give the best result. Sometimes you may know something about the data that the optimizer doesn't, such as a fact that's guaranteed to be true because of application logic. Also, sometimes the optimizer doesn't have the necessary functionality, such as hash indexes; at other times, as mentioned earlier, its cost estimates may prefer a query plan that turns out to be more expensive than an alternative.

If you know the optimizer isn't giving a good result, and you know why, you can help it. Some of the options are to add a hint to the query, rewrite the query, redesign your schema, or add indexes.

Table and index statistics

Recall the various layers in the MySQL server architecture, which we illustrated in Figure 1-1. The server layer, which contains the query optimizer, doesn't store statistics on data and indexes. That's a job for the storage engines, because each storage engine might keep different kinds of statistics (or keep them in a different way). Some engines, such as Archive, don't keep statistics at all!

Because the server doesn't store statistics, the MySQL query optimizer has to ask the engines for statistics on the tables in a query. The engines may provide the optimizer with statistics such as the number of pages per table or index, the cardinality of tables and indexes, the length of rows and keys, and key distribution information. The optimizer can use this information to help it decide on the best execution plan. We see how these statistics influence the optimizer's choices in later sections.

MySQL's join execution strategy

MySQL uses the term "join" more broadly than you might be used to. In sum, it considers every query a join—not just every query that matches rows from two tables, but every query, period (including subqueries, and even a SELECT against a single table). Consequently, it's very important to understand how MySQL executes joins.

Consider the example of a UNION query. MySQL executes a UNION as a series of single queries whose results are spooled into a temporary table, then read out again. Each of the individual queries is a join, in MySQL terminology—and so is the act of reading from the resulting temporary table.

At the moment, MySQL's join execution strategy is simple: it treats every join as a nested-loop join. This means MySQL runs a loop to find a row from a table, then runs a nested loop to find a matching row in the next table. It continues until it has found a matching row in each table in the join. It then builds and returns a row from the columns named in the SELECT list. It tries to build the next row by looking for more matching rows in the last table. If it doesn't find any, it backtracks one table and looks for more rows there. It keeps backtracking until it finds another row in some table, at which point, it looks for a matching row in the next table, and so on.[*]

This process of finding rows, probing into the next table, and then backtracking can be written as nested loops in the execution plan—hence the name "nested-loop join." As an example, consider this simple query:

```
mysql> SELECT tbl1.col1, tbl2.col2
    -> FROM tbl1 INNER JOIN tbl2 USING(col3)
    -> WHERE tbl1.col1 IN(5,6);
```

Assuming MySQL decides to join the tables in the order shown in the query, the following pseudocode shows how MySQL might execute the query:

```
outer_iter = iterator over tbl1 where col1 IN(5,6)
outer_row  = outer_iter.next
while outer_row
    inner_iter = iterator over tbl2 where col3 = outer_row.col3
    inner_row  = inner_iter.next
    while inner_row
        output [ outer_row.col1, inner_row.col2 ]
        inner_row = inner_iter.next
    end
    outer_row = outer_iter.next
end
```

This query execution plan applies as easily to a single-table query as it does to a many-table query, which is why even a single-table query can be considered a join—the single-table join is the basic operation from which more complex joins are composed. It can support OUTER JOINs, too. For example, let's change the example query as follows:

```
mysql> SELECT tbl1.col1, tbl2.col2
    -> FROM tbl1 LEFT OUTER JOIN tbl2 USING(col3)
    -> WHERE tbl1.col1 IN(5,6);
```

Here's the corresponding pseudocode, with the changed parts in bold:

```
outer_iter = iterator over tbl1 where col1 IN(5,6)
outer_row  = outer_iter.next
while outer_row
    inner_iter = iterator over tbl2 where col3 = outer_row.col3
    inner_row  = inner_iter.next
    if inner_row
        while inner_row
            output [ outer_row.col1, inner_row.col2 ]
            inner_row = inner_iter.next
        end
    else
```

---

[*] As we show later, MySQL's query execution isn't quite this simple; there are many optimizations that complicate it.

```
        output [ outer_row.col1, NULL ]
    end
    outer_row = outer_iter.next
end
```

Another way to visualize a query execution plan is to use what the optimizer folks call a "swim-lane diagram." Figure 4-2 contains a swim-lane diagram of our initial INNER JOIN query. Read it from left to right and top to bottom.

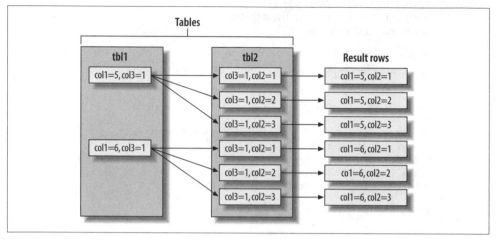

Figure 4-2. Swim-lane diagram illustrating retrieving rows using a join

MySQL executes every kind of query in essentially the same way. For example, it handles a subquery in the FROM clause by executing it first, putting the results into a temporary table,* and then treating that table just like an ordinary table (hence the name "derived table"). MySQL executes UNION queries with temporary tables too, and it rewrites all RIGHT OUTER JOIN queries to equivalent LEFT OUTER JOIN. In short, MySQL coerces every kind of query into this execution plan.

It's not possible to execute every legal SQL query this way, however. For example, a FULL OUTER JOIN can't be executed with nested loops and backtracking as soon as a table with no matching rows is found, because it might begin with a table that has no matching rows. This explains why MySQL doesn't support FULL OUTER JOIN. Still other queries can be executed with nested loops, but perform very badly as a result. We look at some of those later.

The execution plan

MySQL doesn't generate byte-code to execute a query, as many other database products do. Instead, the query execution plan is actually a tree of instructions that the

---

* There are no indexes on the temporary table, which is something you should keep in mind when writing complex joins against subqueries in the FROM clause. This applies to UNION queries, too.

query execution engine follows to produce the query results. The final plan contains enough information to reconstruct the original query. If you execute EXPLAIN EXTENDED on a query, followed by SHOW WARNINGS, you'll see the reconstructed query.[*]

Any multitable query can conceptually be represented as a tree. For example, it might be possible to execute a four-table join as shown in Figure 4-3.

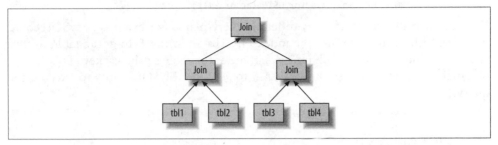

Figure 4-3. One way to join multiple tables

This is what computer scientists call a *balanced tree*. This is not how MySQL executes the query, though. As we described in the previous section, MySQL always begins with one table and finds matching rows in the next table. Thus, MySQL's query execution plans always take the form of a *left-deep tree*, as in Figure 4-4.

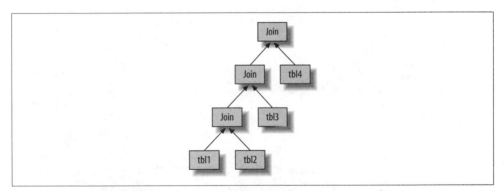

Figure 4-4. How MySQL joins multiple tables

The join optimizer

The most important part of the MySQL query optimizer is the *join optimizer*, which decides the best order of execution for multitable queries. It is often possible to join the tables in several different orders and get the same results. The join optimizer estimates the cost for various plans and tries to choose the least expensive one that gives the same result.

---

[*] The server generates the output from the execution plan. It thus has the same semantics as the original query, but not necessarily the same text.

Here's a query whose tables can be joined in different orders without changing the results:

```
mysql> SELECT film.film_id, film.title, film.release_year, actor.actor_id,
    ->     actor.first_name, actor.last_name
    ->     FROM sakila.film
    ->     INNER JOIN sakila.film_actor USING(film_id)
    ->     INNER JOIN sakila.actor USING(actor_id);
```

You can probably think of a few different query plans. For example, MySQL could begin with the film table, use the index on film_id in the film_actor table to find actor_id values, and then look up rows in the actor table's primary key. This should be efficient, right? Now let's use EXPLAIN to see how MySQL wants to execute the query:

```
*************************** 1. row ***************************
           id: 1
  select_type: SIMPLE
        table: actor
         type: ALL
possible_keys: PRIMARY
          key: NULL
      key_len: NULL
          ref: NULL
         rows: 200
        Extra:
*************************** 2. row ***************************
           id: 1
  select_type: SIMPLE
        table: film_actor
         type: ref
possible_keys: PRIMARY,idx_fk_film_id
          key: PRIMARY
      key_len: 2
          ref: sakila.actor.actor_id
         rows: 1
        Extra: Using index
*************************** 3. row ***************************
           id: 1
  select_type: SIMPLE
        table: film
         type: eq_ref
possible_keys: PRIMARY
          key: PRIMARY
      key_len: 2
          ref: sakila.film_actor.film_id
         rows: 1
        Extra:
```

This is quite a different plan from the one suggested in the previous paragraph. MySQL wants to start with the actor table (we know this because it's listed first in the EXPLAIN output) and go in the reverse order. Is this really more efficient? Let's find out. The STRAIGHT_JOIN keyword forces the join to proceed in the order specified in the query. Here's the EXPLAIN output for the revised query:

```
mysql> EXPLAIN SELECT STRAIGHT_JOIN film.film_id...\G
*************************** 1. row ***************************
           id: 1
  select_type: SIMPLE
        table: film
         type: ALL
possible_keys: PRIMARY
          key: NULL
      key_len: NULL
          ref: NULL
         rows: 951
        Extra:
*************************** 2. row ***************************
           id: 1
  select_type: SIMPLE
        table: film_actor
         type: ref
possible_keys: PRIMARY,idx_fk_film_id
          key: idx_fk_film_id
      key_len: 2
          ref: sakila.film.film_id
         rows: 1
        Extra: Using index
*************************** 3. row ***************************
           id: 1
  select_type: SIMPLE
        table: actor
         type: eq_ref
possible_keys: PRIMARY
          key: PRIMARY
      key_len: 2
          ref: sakila.film_actor.actor_id
         rows: 1
        Extra:
```

This shows why MySQL wants to reverse the join order: doing so will enable it to examine fewer rows in the first table.[*] In both cases, it will be able to perform fast indexed lookups in the second and third tables. The difference is how many of these indexed lookups it will have to do:

- Placing film first will require about 951 probes into film_actor and actor, one for each row in the first table.
- If the server scans the actor table first, it will have to do only 200 index lookups into later tables.

---

[*] Strictly speaking, MySQL doesn't try to reduce the number of rows it reads. Instead, it tries to optimize for fewer page reads. But a row count can often give you a rough idea of the query cost.

In other words, the reversed join order will require less backtracking and rereading. To double-check the optimizer's choice, we executed the two query versions and looked at the Last_query_cost variable for each. The reordered query had an estimated cost of 241, while the estimated cost of forcing the join order was 1,154.

This is a simple example of how MySQL's join optimizer can reorder queries to make them less expensive to execute. Reordering joins is usually a very effective optimization. There are times when it won't result in an optimal plan, and for those times you can use STRAIGHT_JOIN and write the query in the order you think is best—but such times are rare. In most cases, the join optimizer will outperform a human.

The join optimizer tries to produce a query execution plan tree with the lowest achievable cost. When possible, it examines all potential combinations of subtrees, beginning with all one-table plans.

Unfortunately, a join over *n* tables will have *n*-factorial combinations of join orders to examine. This is called the *search space* of all possible query plans, and it grows very quickly—a 10-table join can be executed up to 3,628,800 different ways! When the search space grows too large, it can take far too long to optimize the query, so the server stops doing a full analysis. Instead, it resorts to shortcuts such as "greedy" searches when the number of tables exceeds the optimizer_search_depth limit.

MySQL has many heuristics, accumulated through years of research and experimentation, that it uses to speed up the optimization stage. This can be beneficial, but it can also mean that MySQL may (on rare occasions) miss an optimal plan and choose a less optimal one because it's trying not to examine every possible query plan.

Sometimes queries can't be reordered, and the join optimizer can use this fact to reduce the search space by eliminating choices. A LEFT JOIN is a good example, as are correlated subqueries (more about subqueries later). This is because the results for one table depend on data retrieved from another table. These dependencies help the join optimizer reduce the search space by eliminating choices.

Sort optimizations

Sorting results can be a costly operation, so you can often improve performance by avoiding sorts or by performing them on fewer rows.

We showed you how to use indexes for sorting in Chapter 3. When MySQL can't use an index to produce a sorted result, it must sort the rows itself. It can do this in memory or on disk, but it always calls this process a *filesort*, even if it doesn't actually use a file.

If the values to be sorted will fit into the sort buffer, MySQL can perform the sort entirely in memory with a *quicksort*. If MySQL can't do the sort in memory, it performs it on disk by sorting the values in chunks. It uses a quicksort to sort each chunk and then merges the sorted chunk into the results.

There are two filesort algorithms:

Two passes (old)

Reads row pointers and ORDER BY columns, sorts them, and then scans the sorted list and rereads the rows for output.

The two-pass algorithm can be quite expensive, because it reads the rows from the table twice, and the second read causes a lot of random I/O. This is especially expensive for MyISAM, which uses a system call to fetch each row (because MyISAM relies on the operating system's cache to hold the data). On the other hand, it stores a minimal amount of data during the sort, so if the rows to be sorted are completely in memory, it can be cheaper to store less data and reread the rows to generate the final result.

Single pass (new)

Reads all the columns needed for the query, sorts them by the ORDER BY columns, and then scans the sorted list and outputs the specified columns.

This algorithm is available only in MySQL 4.1 and newer. It can be much more efficient, especially on large I/O-bound datasets, because it avoids reading the rows from the table twice and trades random I/O for more sequential I/O. However, it has the potential to use a lot more space, because it holds all desired columns from each row, not just the columns needed to sort the rows. This means fewer tuples will fit into the sort buffer, and the filesort will have to perform more sort merge passes.

MySQL may use much more temporary storage space for a filesort than you'd expect, because it allocates a fixed-size record for each tuple it will sort. These records are large enough to hold the largest possible tuple, including the full length of each VARCHAR column. Also, if you're using UTF-8, MySQL allocates three bytes for each character. As a result, we've seen cases where poorly optimized schemas caused the temporary space used for sorting to be many times larger than the entire table's size on disk.

When sorting a join, MySQL may perform the filesort at two stages during the query execution. If the ORDER BY clause refers only to columns from the first table in the join order, MySQL can filesort this table and then proceed with the join. If this happens, EXPLAIN shows "Using filesort" in the Extra column. Otherwise, MySQL must store the query's results into a temporary table and then filesort the temporary table after the join finishes. In this case, EXPLAIN shows "Using temporary; Using filesort" in the Extra column. If there's a LIMIT, it is applied after the filesort, so the temporary table and the filesort can be very large.

See "Optimizing for filesorts" on page 300 for more on how to tune the server for filesorts and how to influence which algorithm the server uses.

The Query Execution Engine

The parsing and optimizing stage outputs a query execution plan, which MySQL's query execution engine uses to process the query. The plan is a data structure; it is not executable byte-code, which is how many other databases execute queries.

In contrast to the optimization stage, the execution stage is usually not all that complex: MySQL simply follows the instructions given in the query execution plan. Many of the operations in the plan invoke methods implemented by the storage engine interface, also known as the *handler API*. Each table in the query is represented by an instance of a handler. If a table appears three times in the query, for example, the server creates three handler instances. Though we glossed over this before, MySQL actually creates the handler instances early in the optimization stage. The optimizer uses them to get information about the tables, such as their column names and index statistics.

The storage engine interface has lots of functionality, but it needs only a dozen or so "building-block" operations to execute most queries. For example, there's an operation to read the first row in an index, and one to read the next row in an index. This is enough for a query that does an index scan. This simplistic execution method makes MySQL's storage engine architecture possible, but it also imposes some of the optimizer limitations we've discussed.

> Not everything is a handler operation. For example, the server manages table locks. The handler may implement its own lower-level locking, as InnoDB does with row-level locks, but this does not replace the server's own locking implementation. As explained in Chapter 1, anything that all storage engines share is implemented in the server, such as date and time functions, views, and triggers.

To execute the query, the server just repeats the instructions until there are no more rows to examine.

Returning Results to the Client

The final step in executing a query is to reply to the client. Even queries that don't return a result set still reply to the client connection with information about the query, such as how many rows it affected.

If the query is cacheable, MySQL will also place the results into the query cache at this stage.

The server generates and sends results incrementally. Think back to the single-sweep multijoin method we mentioned earlier. As soon as MySQL processes the last table and generates one row successfully, it can and should send that row to the client.

This has two benefits: it lets the server avoid holding the row in memory, and it means the client starts getting the results as soon as possible.*

Limitations of the MySQL Query Optimizer

MySQL's "everything is a nested-loop join" approach to query execution isn't ideal for optimizing every kind of query. Fortunately, there are only a limited number of cases where the MySQL query optimizer does a poor job, and it's usually possible to rewrite such queries more efficiently.

> The information in this section applies to the MySQL server versions to which we have access at the time of this writing—that is, up to MySQL 5.1. Some of these limitations will probably be eased or removed entirely in future versions, and some have already been fixed in versions not yet released as GA (generally available). In particular, there are a number of subquery optimizations in the MySQL 6 source code, and more are in progress.

Correlated Subqueries

MySQL sometimes optimizes subqueries very badly. The worst offenders are `IN()` subqueries in the `WHERE` clause. As an example, let's find all films in the Sakila sample database's `sakila.film` table whose casts include the actress Penelope Guiness (`actor_id=1`). This feels natural to write with a subquery, as follows:

```
mysql> SELECT * FROM sakila.film
    -> WHERE film_id IN(
    ->    SELECT film_id FROM sakila.film_actor WHERE actor_id = 1);
```

It's tempting to think that MySQL will execute this query from the inside out, by finding a list of `actor_id` values and substituting them into the `IN()` list. We said an `IN()` list is generally very fast, so you might expect the query to be optimized to something like this:

```
-- SELECT GROUP_CONCAT(film_id) FROM sakila.film_actor WHERE actor_id = 1;
-- Result: 1,23,25,106,140,166,277,361,438,499,506,509,605,635,749,832,939,970,980
SELECT * FROM sakila.film
WHERE film_id
IN(1,23,25,106,140,166,277,361,438,499,506,509,605,635,749,832,939,970,980);
```

Unfortunately, exactly the opposite happens. MySQL tries to "help" the subquery by pushing a correlation into it from the outer table, which it thinks will let the subquery find rows more efficiently. It rewrites the query as follows:

```
SELECT * FROM sakila.film
```

---

* You can influence this behavior if needed—for example, with the `SQL_BUFFER_RESULT` hint. See the "Query Optimizer Hints" on page 195, later in this chapter.

```
WHERE EXISTS (
    SELECT * FROM sakila.film_actor WHERE actor_id = 1
    AND film_actor.film_id = film.film_id);
```

Now the subquery requires the film_id from the outer film table and can't be executed first. EXPLAIN shows the result as DEPENDENT SUBQUERY (you can use EXPLAIN EXTENDED to see exactly how the query is rewritten):

```
mysql> EXPLAIN SELECT * FROM sakila.film ...;
+----+--------------------+------------+--------+-----------------------+
| id | select_type        | table      | type   | possible_keys         |
+----+--------------------+------------+--------+-----------------------+
|  1 | PRIMARY            | film       | ALL    | NULL                  |
|  2 | DEPENDENT SUBQUERY | film_actor | eq_ref | PRIMARY,idx_fk_film_id |
+----+--------------------+------------+--------+-----------------------+
```

According to the EXPLAIN output, MySQL will table-scan the film table and execute the subquery for each row it finds. This won't cause a noticeable performance hit on small tables, but if the outer table is very large, the performance will be extremely bad. Fortunately, it's easy to rewrite such a query as a JOIN:

```
mysql> SELECT film.* FROM sakila.film
    ->     INNER JOIN sakila.film_actor USING(film_id)
    -> WHERE actor_id = 1;
```

Another good optimization is to manually generate the IN( ) list by executing the subquery as a separate query with GROUP_CONCAT( ). Sometimes this can be faster than a JOIN.

MySQL has been criticized thoroughly for this particular type of subquery execution plan. Although it definitely needs to be fixed, the criticism often confuses two different issues: execution order and caching. Executing the query from the inside out is one way to optimize it; caching the inner query's result is another. Rewriting the query yourself lets you take control over both aspects. Future versions of MySQL should be able to optimize this type of query much better, although this is no easy task. There are very bad worst cases for any execution plan, including the inside-out execution plan that some people think would be simple to optimize.

When a correlated subquery is good

MySQL doesn't always optimize correlated subqueries badly. If you hear advice to always avoid them, don't listen! Instead, benchmark and make your own decision. Sometimes a correlated subquery is a perfectly reasonable, or even optimal, way to get a result. Let's look at an example:

```
mysql> EXPLAIN SELECT film_id, language_id FROM sakila.film
    -> WHERE NOT EXISTS(
    ->     SELECT * FROM sakila.film_actor
    ->     WHERE film_actor.film_id = film.film_id
    -> )\G
*************************** 1. row ***************************
          id: 1
```

```
   select_type: PRIMARY
        table: film
         type: ALL
possible_keys: NULL
          key: NULL
      key_len: NULL
          ref: NULL
         rows: 951
        Extra: Using where
*************************** 2. row ***************************
           id: 2
   select_type: DEPENDENT SUBQUERY
        table: film_actor
         type: ref
possible_keys: idx_fk_film_id
          key: idx_fk_film_id
      key_len: 2
          ref: film.film_id
         rows: 2
        Extra: Using where; Using index
```

The standard advice for this query is to write it as a LEFT OUTER JOIN instead of using a subquery. In theory, MySQL's execution plan will be essentially the same either way. Let's see:

```
mysql> EXPLAIN SELECT film.film_id, film.language_id
    -> FROM sakila.film
    ->     LEFT OUTER JOIN sakila.film_actor USING(film_id)
    -> WHERE film_actor.film_id IS NULL\G
*************************** 1. row ***************************
           id: 1
   select_type: SIMPLE
        table: film
         type: ALL
possible_keys: NULL
          key: NULL
      key_len: NULL
          ref: NULL
         rows: 951
        Extra:
*************************** 2. row ***************************
           id: 1
   select_type: SIMPLE
        table: film_actor
         type: ref
possible_keys: idx_fk_film_id
          key: idx_fk_film_id
      key_len: 2
          ref: sakila.film.film_id
         rows: 2
        Extra: Using where; Using index; Not exists
```

The plans are nearly identical, but there are some differences:

- The SELECT type against `film_actor` is DEPENDENT SUBQUERY in one query and SIMPLE in the other. This difference simply reflects the syntax, because the first query uses a subquery and the second doesn't. It doesn't make much difference in terms of handler operations.

- The second query doesn't say "Using where" in the Extra column for the `film` table. That doesn't matter, though: the second query's USING clause is the same thing as a WHERE clause anyway.

- The second query says "Not exists" in the `film_actor` table's Extra column. This is an example of the early-termination algorithm we mentioned earlier in this chapter. It means MySQL is using a not-exists optimization to avoid reading more than one row in the `film_actor` table's `idx_fk_film_id` index. This is equivalent to a NOT EXISTS( ) correlated subquery, because it stops processing the current row as soon as it finds a match.

So, in theory, MySQL will execute the queries almost identically. In reality, benchmarking is the only way to tell which approach is really faster. We benchmarked both queries on our standard setup. The results are shown in Table 4-1.

Table 4-1. NOT EXISTS versus LEFT OUTER JOIN

Query	Result in queries per second (QPS)
NOT EXISTS subquery	360 QPS
LEFT OUTER JOIN	425 QPS

Our benchmark found that the subquery is quite a bit slower!

However, this isn't always the case. Sometimes a subquery can be faster. For example, it can work well when you just want to see rows from one table that match rows in another table. Although that sounds like it describes a join perfectly, it's not always the same thing. The following join, which is designed to find every film that has an actor, will return duplicates because some films have multiple actors:

```
mysql> SELECT film.film_id FROM sakila.film
    ->     INNER JOIN sakila.film_actor USING(film_id);
```

We need to use DISTINCT or GROUP BY to eliminate the duplicates:

```
mysql> SELECT DISTINCT film.film_id FROM sakila.film
    ->     INNER JOIN sakila.film_actor USING(film_id);
```

But what are we really trying to express with this query, and is it obvious from the SQL? The EXISTS operator expresses the logical concept of "has a match" without producing duplicated rows and avoids a GROUP BY or DISTINCT operation, which might require a temporary table. Here's the query written as a subquery instead of a join:

```
mysql> SELECT film_id FROM sakila.film
    ->     WHERE EXISTS(SELECT * FROM sakila.film_actor
```

```
    ->    WHERE film.film_id = film_actor.film_id);
```

Again, we benchmarked to see which strategy was faster. The results are shown in Table 4-2.

Table 4-2. EXISTS versus INNER JOIN

Query	Result in queries per second (QPS)
INNER JOIN	185 QPS
EXISTS subquery	325 QPS

In this example, the subquery performs much faster than the join.

We showed this lengthy example to illustrate two points: you should not heed categorical advice about subqueries, and you should use benchmarks to prove your assumptions about query plans and execution speed.

UNION limitations

MySQL sometimes can't "push down" conditions from the outside of a UNION to the inside, where they could be used to limit results or enable additional optimizations.

If you think any of the individual queries inside a UNION would benefit from a LIMIT, or if you know they'll be subject to an ORDER BY clause once combined with other queries, you need to put those clauses inside each part of the UNION. For example, if you UNION together two huge tables and LIMIT the result to the first 20 rows, MySQL will store both huge tables into a temporary table and then retrieve just 20 rows from it. You can avoid this by placing LIMIT 20 on each query inside the UNION.

Index merge optimizations

Index merge algorithms, introduced in MySQL 5.0, let MySQL use more than one index per table in a query. Earlier versions of MySQL could use only a single index, so when no single index was good enough to help with all the restrictions in the WHERE clause, MySQL often chose a table scan. For example, the film_actor table has an index on film_id and an index on actor_id, but neither is a good choice for both WHERE conditions in this query:

```
mysql> SELECT film_id, actor_id FROM sakila.film_actor
    -> WHERE actor_id = 1 OR film_id = 1;
```

In older MySQL versions, that query would produce a table scan unless you wrote it as the UNION of two queries:

```
mysql> SELECT film_id, actor_id FROM sakila.film_actor WHERE actor_id = 1
    -> UNION ALL
    -> SELECT film_id, actor_id FROM sakila.film_actor WHERE film_id = 1
    ->    AND actor_id <> 1;
```

In MySQL 5.0 and newer, however, the query can use both indexes, scanning them simultaneously and merging the results. There are three variations on the algorithm: union for OR conditions, intersection for AND conditions, and unions of intersections for combinations of the two. The following query uses a union of two index scans, as you can see by examining the Extra column:

```
mysql> EXPLAIN SELECT film_id, actor_id FROM sakila.film_actor
    -> WHERE actor_id = 1 OR film_id = 1\G
*************************** 1. row ***************************
           id: 1
  select_type: SIMPLE
        table: film_actor
         type: index_merge
possible_keys: PRIMARY,idx_fk_film_id
          key: PRIMARY,idx_fk_film_id
      key_len: 2,2
          ref: NULL
         rows: 29
        Extra: Using union(PRIMARY,idx_fk_film_id); Using where
```

MySQL can use this technique on complex WHERE clauses, so you may see nested operations in the Extra column for some queries. This often works very well, but sometimes the algorithm's buffering, sorting, and merging operations use lots of CPU and memory resources. This is especially true if not all of the indexes are very selective, so the parallel scans return lots of rows to the merge operation. Recall that the optimizer doesn't account for this cost—it optimizes just the number of random page reads. This can make it "underprice" the query, which might in fact run more slowly than a plain table scan. The intensive memory and CPU usage also tends to impact concurrent queries, but you won't see this effect when you run the query in isolation. This is another reason to design realistic benchmarks.

If your queries run more slowly because of this optimizer limitation, you can work around it by disabling some indexes with IGNORE INDEX, or just fall back to the old UNION tactic.

Equality propagation

Equality propagation can have unexpected costs sometimes. For example, consider a huge IN( ) list on a column the optimizer knows will be equal to some columns on other tables, due to a WHERE, ON, or USING clause that sets the columns equal to each other.

The optimizer will "share" the list by copying it to the corresponding columns in all related tables. This is normally helpful, because it gives the query optimizer and execution engine more options for where to actually execute the IN( ) check. But when the list is very large, it can result in slower optimization and execution. There's no built-in workaround for this problem at the time of this writing—you'll have to change the source code if it's a problem for you. (It's not a problem for most people.)

Parallel execution

MySQL can't execute a single query in parallel on many CPUs. This is a feature offered by some other database servers, but not MySQL. We mention it so that you won't spend a lot of time trying to figure out how to get parallel query execution on MySQL!

Hash joins

MySQL can't do true hash joins at the time of this writing—everything is a nested-loop join. However, you can emulate hash joins using hash indexes. If you aren't using the Memory storage engine, you'll have to emulate the hash indexes, too. We showed you how to do this in "Building your own hash indexes" on page 103.

Loose index scans

MySQL has historically been unable to do loose index scans, which scan noncontiguous ranges of an index. MySQL's index scans generally require a defined start point and a defined end point in the index, even if only a few noncontiguous rows in the middle are really desired for the query. MySQL will scan the entire range of rows within these end points.

An example will help clarify this. Suppose we have a table with an index on columns (a, b), and we want to run the following query:

```
mysql> SELECT ... FROM tbl WHERE b BETWEEN 2 AND 3;
```

Because the index begins with column a, but the query's WHERE clause doesn't specify column a, MySQL will do a table scan and eliminate the nonmatching rows with a WHERE clause, as shown in Figure 4-5.

It's easy to see that there's a faster way to execute this query. The index's structure (but not MySQL's storage engine API) lets you seek to the beginning of each range of values, scan until the end of the range, and then backtrack and jump ahead to the start of the next range. Figure 4-6 shows what that strategy would look like if MySQL were able to do it.

Notice the absence of a WHERE clause, which isn't needed because the index alone lets us skip over the unwanted rows. (Again, MySQL can't do this yet.)

This is admittedly a simplistic example, and we could easily optimize the query we've shown by adding a different index. However, there are many cases where adding another index can't solve the problem. One example is a query that has a range condition on the index's first column and an equality condition on the second column.

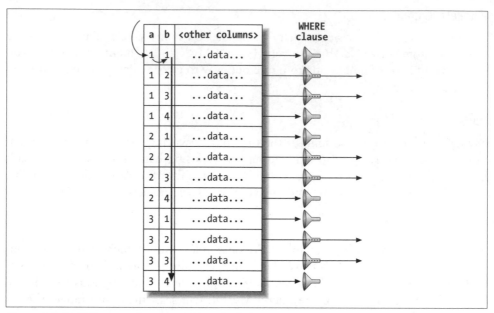

Figure 4-5. MySQL scans the entire table to find rows

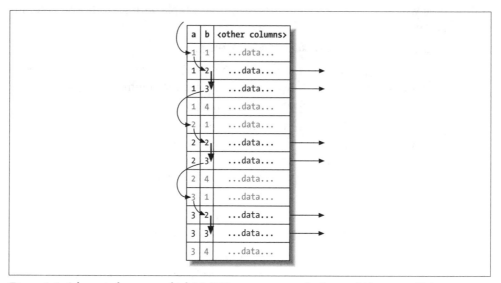

Figure 4-6. A loose index scan, which MySQL cannot currently do, would be more efficient

Beginning in MySQL 5.0, loose index scans are possible in certain limited circumstances, such as queries that find maximum and minimum values in a grouped query:

```
mysql> EXPLAIN SELECT actor_id, MAX(film_id)
    -> FROM sakila.film_actor
    -> GROUP BY actor_id\G
```

```
*************************** 1. row ***************************
           id: 1
  select_type: SIMPLE
        table: film_actor
         type: range
possible_keys: NULL
          key: PRIMARY
      key_len: 2
          ref: NULL
         rows: 396
        Extra: Using index for group-by
```

The "Using index for group-by" information in this EXPLAIN plan indicates a loose index scan. This is a good optimization for this special purpose, but it is not a general-purpose loose index scan. It might be better termed a "loose index probe."

Until MySQL supports general-purpose loose index scans, the workaround is to supply a constant or list of constants for the leading columns of the index. We showed several examples of how to get good performance with these types of queries in our indexing case study in the previous chapter.

MIN( ) and MAX( )

MySQL doesn't optimize certain MIN( ) and MAX( ) queries very well. Here's an example:

```
mysql> SELECT MIN(actor_id) FROM sakila.actor WHERE first_name = 'PENELOPE';
```

Because there's no index on first_name, this query performs a table scan. If MySQL scans the primary key, it can theoretically stop after reading the first matching row, because the primary key is strictly ascending and any subsequent row will have a greater actor_id. However, in this case, MySQL will scan the whole table, which you can verify by profiling the query. The workaround is to remove the MIN( ) and rewrite the query with a LIMIT, as follows:

```
mysql> SELECT actor_id FROM sakila.actor USE INDEX(PRIMARY)
    -> WHERE first_name = 'PENELOPE' LIMIT 1;
```

This general strategy often works well when MySQL would otherwise choose to scan more rows than necessary. If you're a purist, you might object that this query is missing the point of SQL. We're supposed to be able to tell the server *what* we want and it's supposed to figure out *how* to get that data, whereas, in this case, we're telling MySQL *how* to execute the query and, as a result, it's not clear from the query that *what* we're looking for is a minimal value. True, but sometimes you have to compromise your principles to get high performance.

SELECT and UPDATE on the same table

MySQL doesn't let you SELECT from a table while simultaneously running an UPDATE on it. This isn't really an optimizer limitation, but knowing how MySQL executes queries can help you work around it. Here's an example of a query that's disallowed, even though it is standard SQL. The query updates each row with the number of similar rows in the table:

```
mysql> UPDATE tbl AS outer_tbl
    ->    SET cnt = (
    ->        SELECT count(*) FROM tbl AS inner_tbl
    ->        WHERE inner_tbl.type = outer_tbl.type
    ->    );
ERROR 1093 (HY000): You can't specify target table 'outer_tbl' for update in FROM
clause
```

To work around this limitation, you can use a derived table, because MySQL materializes it as a temporary table. This effectively executes two queries: one SELECT inside the subquery, and one multitable UPDATE with the joined results of the table and the subquery. The subquery opens and closes the table before the outer UPDATE opens the table, so the query will now succeed:

```
mysql> UPDATE tbl
    ->    INNER JOIN(
    ->        SELECT type, count(*) AS cnt
    ->        FROM tbl
    ->        GROUP BY type
    ->    ) AS der USING(type)
    -> SET tbl.cnt = der.cnt;
```

Optimizing Specific Types of Queries

In this section, we give advice on how to optimize certain kinds of queries. We've covered most of these topics in detail elsewhere in the book, but we wanted to make a list of common optimization problems that you can refer to easily.

Most of the advice in this section is version-dependent, and it may not hold for future versions of MySQL. There's no reason why the server won't be able to do some or all of these optimizations itself someday.

Optimizing COUNT( ) Queries

The COUNT( ) aggregate function and how to optimize queries that use it is probably one of the top 10 most misunderstood topics in MySQL. You can do a web search and find more misinformation on this topic than we care to think about.

Before we get into optimization, it's important that you understand what COUNT( ) really does.

What COUNT( ) does

COUNT( ) is a special function that works in two very different ways: it counts *values* and *rows*. A value is a non-NULL expression (NULL is the absence of a value). If you specify a column name or other expression inside the parentheses, COUNT( ) counts how many times that expression has a value. This is confusing for many people, in part because values and NULL are confusing. If you need to learn how this works in SQL, we suggest a good book on SQL fundamentals. (The Internet is not necessarily a good source of accurate information on this topic, either.)

The other form of COUNT( ) simply counts the number of rows in the result. This is what MySQL does when it knows the expression inside the parentheses can never be NULL. The most obvious example is COUNT(*), which is a special form of COUNT( ) that does not expand the * wildcard into the full list of columns in the table, as you might expect; instead, it ignores columns altogether and counts rows.

One of the most common mistakes we see is specifying column names inside the parentheses when you want to count rows. When you want to know the number of rows in the result, you should *always* use COUNT(*). This communicates your intention clearly and avoids poor performance.

Myths about MyISAM

A common misconception is that MyISAM is extremely fast for COUNT( ) queries. It is fast, but only for a very special case: COUNT(*) without a WHERE clause, which merely counts the number of rows in the entire table. MySQL can optimize this away because the storage engine always knows how many rows are in the table. If MySQL knows col can never be NULL, it can also optimize a COUNT(col) expression by converting it to COUNT(*) internally.

MyISAM does not have any magical speed optimizations for counting rows when the query has a WHERE clause, or for the more general case of counting values instead of rows. It may be faster than other storage engines for a given query, or it may not be. That depends on a lot of factors.

Simple optimizations

You can sometimes use MyISAM's COUNT(*) optimization to your advantage when you want to count all but a very small number of rows that are well indexed. The following example uses the standard World database to show how you can efficiently find the number of cities whose ID is greater than 5. You might write this query as follows:

```
mysql> SELECT COUNT(*) FROM world.City WHERE ID > 5;
```

If you profile this query with SHOW STATUS, you'll see that it scans 4,079 rows. If you negate the conditions and subtract the number of cities whose IDs are less than or equal to 5 from the total number of cities, you can reduce that to five rows:

```
mysql> SELECT (SELECT COUNT(*) FROM world.City) - COUNT(*)
    -> FROM world.City WHERE ID <= 5;
```

This version reads fewer rows because the subquery is turned into a constant during the query optimization phase, as you can see with EXPLAIN:

```
+----+-------------+-------+...+------+------------------------------+
| id | select_type | table |...| rows | Extra                        |
+----+-------------+-------+...+------+------------------------------+
|  1 | PRIMARY     | City  |...|    6 | Using where; Using index     |
|  2 | SUBQUERY    | NULL  |...| NULL | Select tables optimized away |
+----+-------------+-------+...+------+------------------------------+
```

A frequent question on mailing lists and IRC channels is how to retrieve counts for several different values in the same column with just one query, to reduce the number of queries required. For example, say you want to create a single query that counts how many items have each of several colors. You can't use an OR (e.g., SELECT COUNT(color = 'blue' OR color = 'red') FROM items;), because that won't separate the different counts for the different colors. And you can't put the colors in the WHERE clause (e.g., SELECT COUNT(*) FROM items WHERE color = 'blue' AND color = 'red';), because the colors are mutually exclusive. Here is a query that solves this problem:

```
mysql> SELECT SUM(IF(color = 'blue', 1, 0)) AS blue,
    SUM(IF(color = 'red', 1, 0))    -> AS red FROM items;
```

And here is another that's equivalent, but instead of using SUM( ) uses COUNT( ) and ensures that the expressions won't have values when the criteria are false:

```
mysql> SELECT COUNT(color = 'blue' OR NULL) AS blue, COUNT(color = 'red' OR NULL)
    -> AS red FROM items;
```

More complex optimizations

In general, COUNT( ) queries are hard to optimize because they usually need to count a lot of rows (i.e., access a lot of data). Your only other option for optimizing within MySQL itself is to use a covering index, which we discussed in Chapter 3. If that doesn't help enough, you need to make changes to your application architecture. Consider summary tables (also covered in Chapter 3), and possibly an external caching system such as *memcached*. You'll probably find yourself faced with the familiar dilemma, "fast, accurate, and simple: pick any two."

Optimizing JOIN Queries

This topic is actually spread throughout most of the book, but we mention a few highlights:

- Make sure there are indexes on the columns in the ON or USING clauses. See "Indexing Basics" on page 95 for more about indexing. Consider the join order when adding indexes. If you're joining tables A and B on column c and the query optimizer decides to join the tables in the order B, A, you don't need to index the column on table B. Unused indexes are extra overhead. In general, you need to add indexes only on the second table in the join order, unless they're needed for some other reason.

- Try to ensure that any GROUP BY or ORDER BY expression refers only to columns from a single table, so MySQL can try to use an index for that operation.
- Be careful when upgrading MySQL, because the join syntax, operator precedence, and other behaviors have changed at various times. What used to be a normal join can sometimes become a cross product, a different kind of join that returns different results, or even invalid syntax.

Optimizing Subqueries

The most important advice we can give on subqueries is that you should usually prefer a join where possible, at least in current versions of MySQL. We covered this topic extensively earlier in this chapter.

Subqueries are the subject of intense work by the optimizer team, and upcoming versions of MySQL may have more subquery optimizations. It remains to be seen which of the optimizations we've seen will end up in released code, and how much difference they'll make. Our point here is that "prefer a join" is not future-proof advice. The server is getting smarter all the time, and the cases where you have to tell it how to do something instead of what results to return are becoming fewer.

Optimizing GROUP BY and DISTINCT

MySQL optimizes these two kinds of queries similarly in many cases, and in fact converts between them as needed internally during the optimization process. Both types of queries benefit from indexes, as usual, and that's the single most important way to optimize them.

MySQL has two kinds of GROUP BY strategies when it can't use an index: it can use a temporary table or a filesort to perform the grouping. Either one can be more efficient for any given query. You can force the optimizer to choose one method or the other with the SQL_BIG_RESULT and SQL_SMALL_RESULT optimizer hints.

If you need to group a join by a value that comes from a lookup table, it's usually more efficient to group by the lookup table's identifier than by the value. For example, the following query isn't as efficient as it could be:

```
mysql> SELECT actor.first_name, actor.last_name, COUNT(*)
    -> FROM sakila.film_actor
    ->    INNER JOIN sakila.actor USING(actor_id)
    -> GROUP BY actor.first_name, actor.last_name;
```

The query is more efficiently written as follows:

```
mysql> SELECT actor.first_name, actor.last_name, COUNT(*)
```

```
-> FROM sakila.film_actor
->    INNER JOIN sakila.actor USING(actor_id)
-> GROUP BY film_actor.actor_id;
```

Grouping by actor.actor_id could be more efficient than grouping by film_actor.actor_id. You should profile and/or benchmark on your specific data to see.

This query takes advantage of the fact that the actor's first and last name are dependent on the actor_id, so it will return the same results, but it's not always the case that you can blithely select nongrouped columns and get the same result. You may even have the server's SQL_MODE configured to disallow it. You can use MIN( ) or MAX( ) to work around this when you know the values within the group are distinct because they depend on the grouped-by column, or if you don't care which value you get:

```
mysql> SELECT MIN(actor.first_name), MAX(actor.last_name), ...;
```

Purists will argue that you're grouping by the wrong thing, and they're right. A spurious MIN( ) or MAX( ) is a sign that the query isn't structured correctly. However, sometimes your only concern will be making MySQL execute the query as quickly as possible. The purists will be satisfied with the following way of writing the query:

```
mysql> SELECT actor.first_name, actor.last_name, c.cnt
    -> FROM sakila.actor
    ->    INNER JOIN (
    ->       SELECT actor_id, COUNT(*) AS cnt
    ->       FROM sakila.film_actor
    ->       GROUP BY actor_id
    ->    ) AS c USING(actor_id) ;
```

But sometimes the cost of creating and filling the temporary table required for the subquery is high compared to the cost of fudging pure relational theory a little bit. Remember, the temporary table created by the subquery has no indexes.

It's generally a bad idea to select nongrouped columns in a grouped query, because the results will be nondeterministic and could easily change if you change an index or the optimizer decides to use a different strategy. Most such queries we see are accidents (because the server doesn't complain), or are the result of laziness rather than being designed that way for optimization purposes. It's better to be explicit. In fact, we suggest that you set the server's SQL_MODE configuration variable to include ONLY_FULL_GROUP_BY so it produces an error instead of letting you write a bad query.

MySQL automatically orders grouped queries by the columns in the GROUP BY clause, unless you specify an ORDER BY clause explicitly. If you don't care about the order and you see this causing a filesort, you can use ORDER BY NULL to skip the automatic sort. You can also add an optional DESC or ASC keyword right after the GROUP BY clause to order the results in the desired direction by the clause's columns.

Optimizing GROUP BY WITH ROLLUP

A variation on grouped queries is to ask MySQL to do superaggregation within the results. You can do this with a WITH ROLLUP clause, but it might not be as well optimized as you need. Check the execution method with EXPLAIN, paying attention to whether the grouping is done via filesort or temporary table; try removing the WITH ROLLUP and seeing if you get the same group method. You may be able to force the grouping method with the hints we mentioned earlier in this section.

Sometimes it's more efficient to do superaggregation in your application, even if it means fetching many more rows from the server. You can also nest a subquery in the FROM clause or use a temporary table to hold intermediate results.

The best approach may be to move the WITH ROLLUP functionality into your application code.

Optimizing LIMIT and OFFSET

Queries with LIMITs and OFFSETs are common in systems that do pagination, nearly always in conjunction with an ORDER BY clause. It's helpful to have an index that supports the ordering; otherwise, the server has to do a lot of filesorts.

A frequent problem is having a high value for the offset. If your query looks like LIMIT 10000, 20, it is generating 10,020 rows and throwing away the first 10,000 of them, which is very expensive. Assuming all pages are accessed with equal frequency, such queries scan half the table on average. To optimize them, you can either limit how many pages are permitted in a pagination view, or try to make the high offsets more efficient.

One simple technique to improve efficiency is to do the offset on a covering index, rather than the full rows. You can then join the result to the full row and retrieve the additional columns you need. This can be much more efficient. Consider the following query:

```
mysql> SELECT film_id, description FROM sakila.film ORDER BY title LIMIT 50, 5;
```

If the table is very large, this query is better written as follows:

```
mysql> SELECT film.film_id, film.description
    -> FROM sakila.film
    ->    INNER JOIN (
    ->       SELECT film_id FROM sakila.film
    ->       ORDER BY title LIMIT 50, 5
    ->    ) AS lim USING(film_id);
```

This works because it lets the server examine as little data as possible in an index without accessing rows, and then, once the desired rows are found, join them against the full table to retrieve the other columns from the row. A similar technique applies to joins with LIMIT clauses.

Sometimes you can also convert the limit to a positional query, which the server can execute as an index range scan. For example, if you precalculate and index a position column, you can rewrite the query as follows:

```
mysql> SELECT film_id, description FROM sakila.film
    -> WHERE position BETWEEN 50 AND 54 ORDER BY position;
```

Ranked data poses a similar problem, but usually mixes GROUP BY into the fray. You'll almost certainly need to precompute and store ranks.

If you really need to optimize pagination systems, you should probably use precomputed summaries. As an alternative, you can join against redundant tables that contain only the primary key and the columns you need for the ORDER BY. You can also use Sphinx; see Appendix C for more information.

Optimizing SQL_CALC_FOUND_ROWS

Another common technique for paginated displays is to add the SQL_CALC_FOUND_ROWS hint to a query with a LIMIT, so you'll know how many rows would have been returned without the LIMIT. It may seem that there's some kind of "magic" happening here, whereby the server predicts how many rows it would have found. But unfortunately, the server doesn't really do that; it can't count rows it doesn't actually find. This option just tells the server to generate and throw away the rest of the result set, instead of stopping when it reaches the desired number of rows. That's very expensive.

A better design is to convert the pager to a "next" link. Assuming there are 20 results per page, the query should then use a LIMIT of 21 rows and display only 20. If the 21st row exists in the results, there's a next page, and you can render the "next" link.

Another possibility is to fetch and cache many more rows than you need—say, 1,000—and then retrieve them from the cache for successive pages. This strategy lets your application know how large the full result set is. If it's fewer than 1,000 rows, the application knows how many page links to render; if it's more, the application can just display "more than 1,000 results found." Both strategies are much more efficient than repeatedly generating an entire result and discarding most of it.

Even when you can't use these tactics, using a separate COUNT(*) query to find the number of rows can be much faster than SQL_CALC_FOUND_ROWS, if it can use a covering index.

Optimizing UNION

MySQL always executes UNION queries by creating a temporary table and filling it with the UNION results. MySQL can't apply as many optimizations to UNION queries as you might be used to. You might have to help the optimizer by manually "pushing down" WHERE, LIMIT, ORDER BY, and other conditions (i.e., copying them, as appropriate, from the outer query into each SELECT in the UNION).

It's important to *always* use UNION ALL, unless you need the server to eliminate duplicate rows. If you omit the ALL keyword, MySQL adds the distinct option to the temporary table, which uses the full row to determine uniqueness. This is quite expensive. Be aware that the ALL keyword doesn't eliminate the temporary table, though. MySQL always places results into a temporary table and then reads them out again, even when it's not really necessary (for example, when the results could be returned directly to the client).

Query Optimizer Hints

MySQL has a few optimizer hints you can use to control the query plan if you're not happy with the one MySQL's optimizer chooses. The following list identifies these hints and indicates when it's a good idea to use them. You place the appropriate hint in the query whose plan you want to modify, and it is effective for only that query. Check the MySQL manual for the exact syntax of each hint. Some of them are version-dependent. The options are:

HIGH_PRIORITY *and* LOW_PRIORITY

These hints tell MySQL how to prioritize the statement relative to other statements that are trying to access the same tables.

HIGH_PRIORITY tells MySQL to schedule a SELECT statement before other statements that may be waiting for locks, so they can modify data. In effect, it makes the SELECT go to the front of the queue instead of waiting its turn. You can also apply this modifier to INSERT, where it simply cancels the effect of a global LOW_PRIORITY server setting.

LOW_PRIORITY is the reverse: it makes the statement wait at the very end of the queue if there are any other statements that want to access the tables—even if the other statements are issued after it. It's rather like an overly polite person holding the door at a restaurant: as long as there's anyone else waiting, it will starve itself! You can apply this hint to SELECT, INSERT, UPDATE, REPLACE, and DELETE statements.

These hints are effective on storage engines with table-level locking, but you should never need them on InnoDB or other engines with fine-grained locking and concurrency control. Be careful when using them on MyISAM, because they can disable concurrent inserts and greatly reduce performance.

The HIGH_PRIORITY and LOW_PRIORITY hints are a frequent source of confusion. They do not allocate more or fewer resources to queries to make them "work harder" or "not work as hard"; they simply affect how the server queues statements that are waiting for access to a table.

DELAYED

This hint is for use with INSERT and REPLACE. It lets the statement to which it is applied return immediately and places the inserted rows into a buffer, which will be inserted in bulk when the table is free. This is most useful for logging and similar applications where you want to insert a lot of rows without making the client wait, and without causing I/O for each statement. There are many limitations; for example, delayed inserts are not implemented in all storage engines, and LAST_INSERT_ID( ) doesn't work with them.

STRAIGHT_JOIN

This hint can appear either just after the SELECT keyword in a SELECT statement, or in any statement between two joined tables. The first usage forces all tables in the query to be joined in the order in which they're listed in the statement. The second usage forces a join order on the two tables between which the hint appears.

The STRAIGHT_JOIN hint is useful when MySQL doesn't choose a good join order, or when the optimizer takes a long time to decide on a join order. In the latter case, the thread will spend a lot of time in "Statistics" state, and adding this hint will reduce the search space for the optimizer.

You can use EXPLAIN to see what order the optimizer would choose, then rewrite the query in that order and add STRAIGHT_JOIN. This is a good idea as long as you don't think the fixed order will result in bad performance for some WHERE clauses. You should be careful to revisit such queries after upgrading MySQL, however, because new optimizations may appear that will be defeated by STRAIGHT_JOIN.

SQL_SMALL_RESULT *and* SQL_BIG_RESULT

These hints are for SELECT statements. They tell the optimizer how and when to use temporary tables and sort in GROUP BY or DISTINCT queries. SQL_SMALL_RESULT tells the optimizer that the result set will be small and can be put into indexed temporary tables to avoid sorting for the grouping, whereas SQL_BIG_RESULT indicates that the result will be large and that it will be better to use temporary tables on disk with sorting.

SQL_BUFFER_RESULT

This hint tells the optimizer to put the results into a temporary table and release table locks as soon as possible. This is different from the client-side buffering we described in "The MySQL Client/Server Protocol" on page 161, earlier in this chapter. Server-side buffering can be useful when you don't use buffering on the client, as it lets you avoid consuming a lot of memory on the client and still release locks quickly. The tradeoff is that the server's memory is used instead of the client's.

SQL_CACHE *and* SQL_NO_CACHE

These hints instruct the server that the query either is or is not a candidate for caching in the query cache. See the next chapter for details on how to use them.

SQL_CALC_FOUND_ROWS

This hint tells MySQL to calculate a full result set when there's a LIMIT clause, even though it returns only LIMIT rows. You can retrieve the total number of rows it found via FOUND_ROWS( ) (but see "Optimizing SQL_CALC_FOUND_ROWS" on page 194, earlier in this chapter, for reasons why you shouldn't use this hint).

FOR UPDATE *and* LOCK IN SHARE MODE

These hints control locking for SELECT statements, but only for storage engines that have row-level locks. They enable you to place locks on the matched rows, which can be useful when you want to lock rows you know you are going to update later, or when you want to avoid lock escalation and just acquire exclusive locks as soon as possible.

These hints are not needed for INSERT ... SELECT queries, which place read locks on the source rows by default in MySQL 5.0. (You can disable this behavior, but it's not a good idea—we explain why in Chapters 8 and 11.) MySQL 5.1 may lift this restriction under certain conditions.

At the time of this writing, only InnoDB supports these hints, and it's too early to say whether other storage engines with row-level locks will support them in the future. When using these hints with InnoDB, be aware that they may disable some optimizations, such as covering indexes. InnoDB can't lock rows exclusively without accessing the primary key, which is where the row versioning information is stored.

USE INDEX, IGNORE INDEX, *and* FORCE INDEX

These hints tell the optimizer which indexes to use or ignore for finding rows in a table (for example, when deciding on a join order). In MySQL 5.0 and earlier, they don't influence which indexes the server uses for sorting and grouping; in MySQL 5.1 the syntax can take an optional FOR ORDER BY or FOR GROUP BY clause.

FORCE INDEX is the same as USE INDEX, but it tells the optimizer that a table scan is extremely expensive compared to the index, even if the index is not very useful. You can use these hints when you don't think the optimizer is choosing the right index, or when you want to take advantage of an index for some reason, such as implicit ordering without an ORDER BY. We gave an example of this in "Optimizing LIMIT and OFFSET" on page 193, earlier in this chapter, where we showed how to get a minimum value efficiently with LIMIT.

In MySQL 5.0 and newer, there are also some system variables that influence the optimizer:

optimizer_search_depth

This variable tells the optimizer how exhaustively to examine partial plans. If your queries are taking a very long time in the "Statistics" state, you might try lowering this value.

```
optimizer_prune_level
```
This variable, which is enabled by default, lets the optimizer skip certain plans based on the number of rows examined.

Both options control optimizer shortcuts. These shortcuts are valuable for good performance on complex queries, but they can cause the server to miss optimal plans for the sake of efficiency. That's why it sometimes makes sense to change them.

User-Defined Variables

It's easy to forget about MySQL's user-defined variables, but they can be a powerful technique for writing efficient queries. They work especially well for queries that benefit from a mixture of procedural and relational logic. Purely relational queries treat everything as unordered sets that the server somehow manipulates all at once. MySQL takes a more pragmatic approach. This can be a weakness, but it can be a strength if you know how to exploit it, and user-defined variables can help.

User-defined variables are temporary containers for values, which persist as long as your connection to the server lives. You define them by simply assigning to them with a SET or SELECT statement:[*]

```
mysql> SET @one      := 1;
mysql> SET @min_actor := (SELECT MIN(actor_id) FROM sakila.actor);
mysql> SET @last_week := CURRENT_DATE-INTERVAL 1 WEEK;
```

You can then use the variables in most places an expression can go:

```
mysql> SELECT ... WHERE col <= @last_week;
```

Before we get into the strengths of user-defined variables, let's take a look at some of their peculiarities and disadvantages and see what things you *can't* use them for:

- They prevent query caching.
- You can't use them where a literal or identifier is needed, such as for a table or column name, or in the LIMIT clause.
- They are connection-specific, so you can't use them for interconnection communication.
- If you're using connection pooling or persistent connections, they can cause seemingly isolated parts of your code to interact.
- They are case sensitive in MySQL versions prior to 5.0, so beware of compatibility issues.
- You can't explicitly declare these variables' types, and the point at which types are decided for undefined variables differs across MySQL versions. The best thing to do is initially assign a value of 0 for variables you want to use for inte-

---

[*] In some contexts you can assign with a plain = sign, but we think it's better to avoid ambiguity and always use :=.

gers, 0.0 for floating-point numbers, or ' ' (the empty string) for strings. A variable's type changes when it is assigned to; MySQL's user-defined variable typing is dynamic.

- The optimizer might optimize away these variables in some situations, preventing them from doing what you want.

- Order of assignment, and indeed even the time of assignment, can be nondeterministic and depend on the query plan the optimizer chose. The results can be very confusing, as you'll see later.

- The := assignment operator has lower precedence than any other operator, so you have to be careful to parenthesize explicitly.

- Undefined variables do not generate a syntax error, so it's easy to make mistakes without knowing it.

One of the most important features of variables is that you can assign a value to a variable and use the resulting value at the same time. In other words, an assignment is an *L-value*. Here's an example that simultaneously calculates and outputs a "row number" for a query:

```
mysql> SET @rownum := 0;
mysql> SELECT actor_id, @rownum := @rownum + 1 AS rownum
    -> FROM sakila.actor LIMIT 3;
+----------+--------+
| actor_id | rownum |
+----------+--------+
|        1 |      1 |
|        2 |      2 |
|        3 |      3 |
+----------+--------+
```

This example isn't terribly interesting, because it just shows that we can duplicate the table's primary key. Still, it has its uses; one of which is ranking. Let's write a query that returns the 10 actors who have played in the most movies, with a rank column that gives actors the same rank if they're tied. We start with a query that finds the actors and the number of movies:

```
mysql> SELECT actor_id, COUNT(*) as cnt
    -> FROM sakila.film_actor
    -> GROUP BY actor_id
    -> ORDER BY cnt DESC
    -> LIMIT 10;
+----------+-----+
| actor_id | cnt |
+----------+-----+
|      107 |  42 |
|      102 |  41 |
|      198 |  40 |
|      181 |  39 |
|       23 |  37 |
|       81 |  36 |
```

```
|       106 |  35 |
|        60 |  35 |
|        13 |  35 |
|       158 |  35 |
+-----------+-----+
```

Now let's add the rank, which should be the same for all the actors who played in 35 movies. We use three variables to do this: one to keep track of the current rank, one to keep track of the previous actor's movie count, and one to keep track of the current actor's movie count. We change the rank when the movie count changes. Here's a first try:

```
mysql> SET @curr_cnt := 0, @prev_cnt := 0, @rank := 0;
mysql> SELECT actor_id,
    ->     @curr_cnt := COUNT(*) AS cnt,
    ->     @rank     := IF(@prev_cnt <> @curr_cnt, @rank + 1, @rank) AS rank,
    ->     @prev_cnt := @curr_cnt AS dummy
    -> FROM sakila.film_actor
    -> GROUP BY actor_id
    -> ORDER BY cnt DESC
    -> LIMIT 10;
+-----------+-----+------+-------+
| actor_id  | cnt | rank | dummy |
+-----------+-----+------+-------+
|       107 |  42 |    0 |     0 |
|       102 |  41 |    0 |     0 |
...
```

Oops—the rank and count never got updated from zero. Why did this happen?

It's impossible to give a one-size-fits-all answer. The problem could be as simple as a misspelled variable name (in this example it's not), or something more involved. In this case, EXPLAIN shows there's a temporary table and filesort, so the variables are being evaluated at a different time from when we expected.

This is the type of inscrutable behavior you'll often experience with MySQL's user-defined variables. Debugging such problems can be tough, but it can really pay off. Ranking in SQL normally requires quadratic algorithms, such as counting the distinct number of actors who played in a greater number of movies. A user-defined variable solution can be a linear algorithm—quite an improvement.

An easy solution in this case is to add another level of temporary tables to the query, using a subquery in the FROM clause:

```
mysql> SET @curr_cnt := 0, @prev_cnt := 0, @rank := 0;
    -> SELECT actor_id,
    ->     @curr_cnt := cnt AS cnt,
    ->     @rank     := IF(@prev_cnt <> @curr_cnt, @rank + 1, @rank) AS rank,
    ->     @prev_cnt := @curr_cnt AS dummy
    -> FROM (
    ->     SELECT actor_id, COUNT(*) AS cnt
    ->     FROM sakila.film_actor
```

```
    ->    GROUP BY actor_id
    ->    ORDER BY cnt DESC
    ->    LIMIT 10
    -> ) as der;
+----------+-----+------+-------+
| actor_id | cnt | rank | dummy |
+----------+-----+------+-------+
|      107 |  42 |    1 |    42 |
|      102 |  41 |    2 |    41 |
|      198 |  40 |    3 |    40 |
|      181 |  39 |    4 |    39 |
|       23 |  37 |    5 |    37 |
|       81 |  36 |    6 |    36 |
|      106 |  35 |    7 |    35 |
|       60 |  35 |    7 |    35 |
|       13 |  35 |    7 |    35 |
|      158 |  35 |    7 |    35 |
+----------+-----+------+-------+
```

Most problems with user variables come from assigning to them and reading them at different stages in the query. For example, it doesn't work predictably to assign them in the SELECT statement and read from them in the WHERE clause. The following query might look like it will just return one row, but it doesn't:

```
mysql> SET @rownum := 0;
mysql> SELECT actor_id, @rownum := @rownum + 1 AS cnt
    -> FROM sakila.actor
    -> WHERE @rownum <= 1;
+----------+------+
| actor_id | cnt  |
+----------+------+
|        1 |    1 |
|        2 |    2 |
+----------+------+
```

This happens because the WHERE and SELECT are different stages in the query execution process. This is even more obvious when you add another stage to execution with an ORDER BY:

```
mysql> SET @rownum := 0;
mysql> SELECT actor_id, @rownum := @rownum + 1 AS cnt
    -> FROM sakila.actor
    -> WHERE @rownum <= 1
    -> ORDER BY first_name;
```

This query returns every row in the table, because the ORDER BY added a filesort and the WHERE is evaluated before the filesort. The solution to this problem is to assign and read in the *same* stage of query execution:

```
mysql> SET @rownum := 0;
mysql> SELECT actor_id, @rownum AS rownum
    -> FROM sakila.actor
    -> WHERE (@rownum := @rownum + 1) <= 1;
+----------+--------+
| actor_id | rownum |
```

```
+----------+--------+
|        1 | 1      |
+----------+--------+
```

Pop quiz: what will happen if you add the ORDER BY back to this query? Try it and see. If you didn't get the results you expected, why not? What about the following query, where the ORDER BY changes the variable's value and the WHERE clause evaluates it?

```
mysql> SET @rownum := 0;
mysql> SELECT actor_id, first_name, @rownum AS rownum
    -> FROM sakila.actor
    -> WHERE @rownum <= 1
    -> ORDER BY first_name, LEAST(0, @rownum := @rownum + 1);
```

The answer to most unexpected user-defined variable behavior can be found by running EXPLAIN and looking for "Using where," "Using temporary," or "Using filesort" in the Extra column.

The last example introduced another useful hack: we placed the assignment in the LEAST( ) function, so its value is effectively masked and won't skew the results of the ORDER BY (as we've written it, the LEAST( ) function will always return 0). This trick is very helpful when you want to do variable assignments solely for their side effects: it lets you hide the return value and avoid extra columns, such as the dummy column we showed in a previous example. The GREATEST( ), LENGTH( ), ISNULL( ), NULLIF( ), COALESCE( ), and IF( ) functions are also useful for this purpose, alone and in combination, because they have special behaviors. For instance, COALESCE( ) stops evaluating its arguments as soon as one has a defined value.

You can put variable assignments in all types of statements, not just SELECT statements. In fact, this is one of the best uses for user-defined variables. For example, you can rewrite expensive queries, such as rank calculations with subqueries, as cheap once-through UPDATE statements.

It can be a little tricky to get the desired behavior, though. Sometimes the optimizer decides to consider the variables compile-time constants and refuses to perform assignments. Placing the assignments inside a function like LEAST( ) will usually help. Another tip is to check whether your variable has a defined value before executing the containing statement. Sometimes you want it to, but other times you don't.

With a little experimentation, you can do all sorts of interesting things with user-defined variables. Here are some ideas:

- Run totals and averages
- Emulate FIRST( ) and LAST( ) functions for grouped queries
- Do math on extremely large numbers
- Reduce an entire table to a single MD5 hash value

- "Unwrap" a sampled value that wraps when it increases beyond a certain boundary
- Emulate read/write cursors

Be Careful with MySQL Upgrades

As we've said, trying to outsmart the MySQL optimizer usually is not a good idea. It generally creates more work and increases maintenance costs for very little benefit. This is especially relevant when you upgrade MySQL, because optimizer hints used in your queries might prevent new optimizer strategies from being used.

The MySQL optimizer uses indexes as a moving target. New MySQL versions change how existing indexes can be used, and you should adjust your indexing practices as these new versions become available. For example, we've mentioned that MySQL 4.0 and older could use only one index per table per query, but MySQL 5.0 and newer can use index merge strategies.

Besides the big changes MySQL occasionally makes to the query optimizer, each incremental release typically includes many tiny changes. These changes usually affect small things, such as the conditions under which an index is excluded from consideration, and let MySQL optimize more special cases.

Although all this sounds good in theory, in practice some queries perform *worse* after an upgrade. If you've used a certain version for a long time, you have likely tuned certain queries just for that version, whether you know it or not. These optimizations may no longer apply in newer versions, or may degrade performance.

If you care about high performance you should have a benchmark suite that represents your particular workload, which you can run against the new version on a development server before you upgrade the production servers. Also, before upgrading, you should read the release notes and the list of known bugs in the new version. The MySQL manual includes a user-friendly list of known serious bugs.

Most MySQL upgrades bring better performance overall; we don't mean to imply otherwise. However, you should still be careful.

Advanced MySQL Features

MySQL 5.0 and 5.1 introduced many features, such as stored procedures, views, and triggers, that are familiar to users with a background in other database servers. The addition of these features attracted many new users to MySQL. However, their performance implications did not really become clear until people began to use them widely.

This chapter covers these recent additions and other advanced topics, including some features that were available in MySQL 4.1 and even earlier. We focus on performance, but we also show you how to get the most from these advanced features.

The MySQL Query Cache

Many database products can cache query execution plans, so the server can skip the SQL parsing and optimization stages for repeated queries. MySQL can do this in some circumstances, but it also has a different type of cache (known as the *query cache*) that stores *complete result sets* for SELECT statements. This section focuses on that cache.

The MySQL query cache holds the exact bits that a completed query returned to the client. When a query cache hit occurs, the server can simply return the stored results immediately, skipping the parsing, optimization, and execution steps.

The query cache keeps track of which tables a query uses, and if any of those tables changes, it invalidates the cache entry. This coarse invalidation policy may seem inefficient—because the changes made to the tables might not affect the results stored in the cache—but it's a simple approach with low overhead, which is important on a busy system.

The query cache is designed to be completely transparent to the application. The application does not need to know whether MySQL returned data from the cache or actually executed the query. The result should be the same either way. In other words, the query cache doesn't change semantics; the server appears to behave the same way with it enabled or disabled.[*]

How MySQL Checks for a Cache Hit

The way MySQL checks for a cache hit is simple and quite fast: the cache is a lookup table. The lookup key is a hash of the query text itself, the current database, the client protocol version, and a handful of other things that might affect the actual bytes in the query's result.

MySQL does not parse, "normalize," or parameterize a statement when it checks for a cache hit; it uses the statement and other bits of data exactly as the client sends them. Any difference in character case, spacing, or comments—any difference at all—will prevent a query from matching a previously cached version. This is something to keep in mind while writing queries. Using consistent formatting and style is a good habit anyway, but in this case it can even make your system faster.

Another caching consideration is that the query cache will not store a result unless the query that generated it was deterministic. Thus, any query that contains a nondeterministic function, such as NOW( ) or CURRENT_DATE( ), will not be cached. Similarly, functions such as CURRENT_USER( ) or CONNECTION_ID( ) may vary when executed by different users, thereby preventing a cache hit. In fact, the query cache does not work for queries that refer to user-defined functions, stored functions, user variables, temporary tables, tables in the mysql database, or any table that has a column-level privilege. (For a list of everything that makes a query uncacheable, see the MySQL manual.)

We often hear statements such as "MySQL doesn't check the cache if the query contains a nondeterministic function." This is incorrect. MySQL cannot know whether a query contains a nondeterministic function unless it parses the query, and the cache lookup happens *before* parsing. The server performs a case insensitive check to verify that the query begins with the letters SEL, but that's all.

However, it is correct to say "The server will find no results in the cache if the query contains a function such as NOW( )," because even if the server executed the same query earlier, it will not have cached the results. MySQL marks a query as uncacheable as soon as it notices a construct that forbids caching, and the results generated by such a query are not stored.

A useful technique to enable the caching of queries that refer to the current date is to include the date as a literal value, instead of using a function. For example:

---

[*] The query cache actually does change semantics in one subtle way: by default, a query can still be served from the cache when one of the tables to which it refers is locked with LOCK TABLES. You can disable this with the query_cache_wlock_invalidate variable.

```
... DATE_SUB(CURRENT_DATE, INTERVAL 1 DAY) -- Not cacheable!
... DATE_SUB('2007-07-14', INTERVAL 1 DAY) -- Cacheable
```

Because the query cache works at the level of a complete SELECT statement when the server first receives it from the client connection, identical queries made inside a subquery or view cannot use the query cache, and neither can queries in stored procedures. Prepared statements also cannot use the query cache in versions prior to MySQL 5.1.

MySQL's query cache can improve performance, but there are a few issues you should be aware of when using it. First, enabling the query cache adds some overhead for both reads and writes:

- Read queries must check the cache before beginning.
- If the query is cacheable and isn't in the cache yet, there's some overhead due to storing the result after generating it.
- Finally, there's overhead for write queries, which must invalidate the cache entries for queries that use tables they change.

This overhead is relatively minimal, so the query cache can still be a net gain. However, as we explain later, the extra overhead can add up.

For InnoDB users, another problem is that transactions limit the query cache's usefulness. When a statement inside a transaction modifies a table, the server invalidates any cached queries that refer to the table, even though InnoDB's multiversioning might hide the transaction's changes from other statements. The table is also globally uncacheable until the transaction commits, so no further queries against that table—whether inside or outside the transaction—can be cached until the transaction commits. Long-running transactions can, therefore, increase the number of query cache misses.

Invalidation can also become a problem with a large query cache. If there are many queries in the cache, the invalidation can take a long time and cause the entire system to stall while it works. This is because there's a single global lock on the query cache, which will block all queries that need to access it. Accessing happens both when checking for a hit and when checking whether there are any queries to invalidate.

How the Cache Uses Memory

MySQL stores the query cache completely in memory, so you need to understand how it uses memory before you can tune it correctly. The cache stores more than just query results in its memory. It's a lot like a filesystem in some ways: it keeps structures that help it figure out which memory in its pool is free, mappings between tables and query results, query text, and the query results.

Aside from some basic housekeeping structures, which require about 40 KB, the query cache's memory pool is available to be used in variable-sized *blocks*. Every block knows what type it is, how large it is, and how much data it contains, and it holds pointers to the next and previous logical and physical blocks. Blocks can be of several types: they can store cache results, lists of tables used by a query, query text, and so on. However, the different types of blocks are treated in much the same way, so there's no need to distinguish among them for purposes of tuning the query cache.

When the server starts, it initializes the memory for the query cache. The memory pool is initially a single free block. This block is as large as the entire amount of memory the cache is configured to use, minus the housekeeping structures.

When the server caches a query's results, it allocates a block to store those results. This block must be a minimum of query_cache_min_res_unit bytes, though it may be larger if the server knows it is storing a larger result. Unfortunately, the server cannot allocate a block of precisely the right size, because it makes its initial allocation before the result set is complete. The server does not build the entire result set in memory and then send it—it's much more efficient to send each row as it's generated. Consequently, when it begins caching the result set, the server has no way of knowing how large it will eventually be.

Allocating blocks is a relatively slow process, because it requires the server to look at its lists of free blocks to find one that's big enough. Therefore, the server tries to minimize the number of allocations it makes. When it needs to cache a result set, it allocates a block of at least the minimum size and begins placing the results in that block. If the block becomes full while there is still data left to store, the server allocates a new block—again of at least the minimum size—and continues storing the data in that block. When the result is finished, if there is space left in the last block the server trims it to size and merges the leftover space into the adjacent free block. Figure 5-1 illustrates this process.*

When we say the server "allocates a block," we don't mean it is asking the operating system to allocate memory with malloc( ) or a similar call. It does that only once, when it creates the query cache. What we mean is that the server is examining its list of blocks and either choosing the best place to put a new block or, if necessary, removing the oldest cached query to make room. In other words, the MySQL server manages its own memory; it does not rely on the operating system to do it.

So far, this is all pretty straightforward. However, the picture can become quite a bit more complicated than it appeared in Figure 5-1. Let's suppose the average result is quite small, and the server is sending results to two client connections simultaneously. Trimming the results can leave a free block that's smaller than query_cache_min_res_

---

* We've simplified the diagrams in this section for the purposes of illustration. The server really allocates query cache blocks in a more complicated fashion than we've shown here. If you're interested in how it works, the comments at the top of *sql/sql_cache.cc* in the server's source code explain it very clearly.

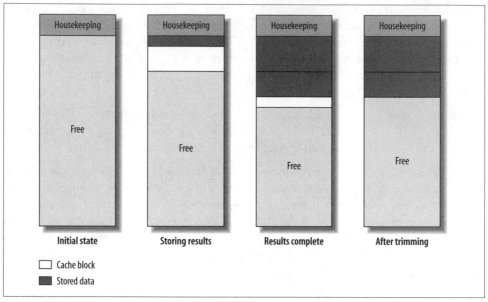

Figure 5-1. How the query cache allocates blocks to store a result

unit and cannot be used for storing future cache results. The block allocation might end up looking something like Figure 5-2.

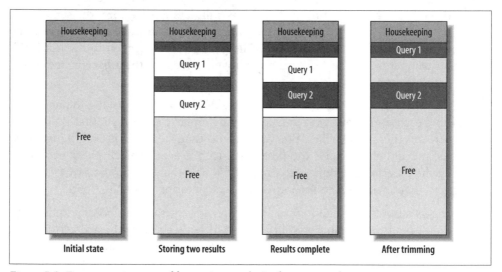

Figure 5-2. Fragmentation caused by storing results in the query cache

Trimming the first result to size left a gap between the two results—a block too small to use for storing a different query result. The appearance of such gaps is called *frag-*

mentation, and it's a classic problem in memory and filesystem allocation. Fragmentation can happen for a number of reasons, including cache invalidations, which can leave blocks that are too small to reuse later.

When the Query Cache Is Helpful

Caching queries isn't automatically more efficient than not caching them. Caching takes work, and the query cache results in a net gain only if the savings are greater than the overhead. This will depend on your server's workload.

In theory, you can tell whether the cache is helpful by comparing the amount of work the server has to do with the cache enabled and disabled. With the cache disabled, each read query has to execute and return its results, and each write query has to execute. With the cache enabled, each read query has to first check the cache and then either return the stored result or, if there isn't one, execute, generate the result, store it, and return it. Each write query has to execute and then check whether there are any cached queries that must be invalidated.

Although this may sound straightforward, it's not—it's hard to accurately calculate or predict the query cache's benefit. External factors must also be taken into account. For example, the query cache can reduce the amount of time required to come up with a query's result, but not the time it takes to send the result to the client program, which may be the dominating factor.

The type of query that benefits most from caching is one whose result is expensive to generate but doesn't take up much space in the cache, so it's cheap to store, return to the client, and invalidate. Aggregate queries, such as small COUNT( ) results from large tables, fit into this category. However, many other types of queries might be worth caching too.

One of the easiest ways to tell if you are benefiting from the query cache is to examine the query cache hit rate. This is the number of queries that are served from the cache instead of being executed by the server. When the server receives a SELECT statement, it increments either the Qcache_hits or the Com_select status variable, depending on whether the query was cached. Thus, the query cache hit rate is given by the formula Qcache_hits / (Qcache_hits+Com_select).

What's a good cache hit rate? It depends. Even a 30% hit rate can be very helpful, because the work saved by not executing queries is typically much more (per query) than the overhead of invalidating entries and storing results in the cache. It is also important to know which queries are cached. If the cache hits represent the most expensive queries, even a low hit rate can save work for the server.

Any SELECT query that MySQL doesn't serve from the cache is a *cache miss*. A cache miss can occur for any of the following reasons:

- The query is not cacheable, either because it contains a nondeterministic construct (such as CURRENT_DATE) or because its result set is too large to store. Both types of uncacheable queries increment the Qcache_not_cached status variable.

- The server has never seen the query before, so it never had a chance to cache its result.

- The query's result was previously cached, but the server removed it. This can happen because there wasn't enough memory to keep it, because someone instructed the server to remove it, or because it was invalidated (more on invalidations in a moment).

If your server has a lot of cache misses but very few uncacheable queries, one of the following must be true:

- The query cache is not warmed up yet. That is, the server hasn't had a chance to fill the cache with result sets.

- The server is seeing queries it hasn't seen before. If you don't have a lot of repeated queries, this can happen even after the cache is warmed up.

- There are a lot of cache invalidations.

Cache invalidations can happen because of fragmentation, insufficient memory, or data modifications. If you have allocated enough memory to the cache and tuned the query_cache_min_res_unit value properly, most cache invalidations should be due to data modifications. You can see how many queries have modified data by examining the Com_* status variables (Com_update, Com_delete, and so forth), and you can see how many queries have been invalidated due to low memory by checking the Qcache_lowmem_prunes status variable.

It's a good idea to consider the overhead of invalidation separately from the hit rate. As an extreme example, suppose you have one table that gets all the reads and has a 100% query cache hit rate, and another table that gets only updates. If you simply calculate the hit rate from the status variables, you will see a 100% hit rate. However, the query cache can still be inefficient, because it will slow down the update queries. All update queries will have to check whether any of the queries in the query cache need to be invalidated as a result of their modifications, but since the answer will always be "no," this is wasted work. You may not spot a problem such as this unless you check the number of uncacheable queries as well as the hit rate.

A server that handles a balanced blend of writes and cacheable reads on the same tables also may not benefit much from the query cache. The writes will constantly invalidate cached results, while at the same time the cacheable reads will constantly insert new results into the cache. These will be beneficial only if they are subsequently served from the cache.

If a cached result is invalidated before the server receives the same SELECT statement again, storing it was a waste of time and memory. Examine the relative sizes of Com_select and Qcache_inserts to see whether this is happening. If nearly every SELECT is a cache miss (thus incrementing `Com_select`) and subsequently stores its result into the cache, `Qcache_inserts` will be nearly as large as `Com_select`. Thus, you'd like `Qcache_inserts` to be much smaller than `Com_select`, at least when the cache is properly warmed up.

Every application has a finite *potential cache size*, even if there are no write queries. The potential cache size is the amount of memory required to store every possible cacheable query the application will ever issue. In theory, this is an extremely large number for most applications. In practice, many applications have a much smaller usable cache size than you might expect, because of the number of invalidations. Even if you make the query cache very large, it will never fill up more than the potential cache size.

You should monitor how much of the query cache your server actually uses. If it doesn't use as much memory as you've given it, make it smaller, and if memory restrictions are causing excessive invalidations, make it bigger. Don't worry about the cache size too much, though; giving it a little more or a little less memory than you think it'll really use affect impact performance that much. It's only a problem when there's a lot of wasted memory or so many cache invalidations that caching is a net loss.

You also have to balance the query cache with the other server caches, such as the InnoDB buffer pool or MyISAM key cache. It's not possible to just give a ratio or a simple formula for this, because the right balance depends on the application.

How to Tune and Maintain the Query Cache

Once you understand how the query cache works, it's easy to tune. It has only a few "moving parts":

query_cache_type
> Whether the query cache is enabled. Possible values are OFF, ON, or DEMAND, where the latter means that only queries containing the SQL_CACHE modifier are eligible for caching. This is both a session-level and a global variable. (See Chapter 6 for details on session and global variables.)

query_cache_size
> The total memory to allocate to the query cache, in bytes. This must be a multiple of 1,024 bytes, so MySQL may use a slightly different value than the one you specify.

query_cache_min_res_unit
> The minimum size when allocating a block. We explained this setting earlier in "How the Cache Uses Memory" on page 206; it's discussed further in the next section.

`query_cache_limit`

The largest result set that MySQL will cache. Queries whose results are larger than this setting will not be cached. Remember that the server caches results as it generates them, so it doesn't know in advance when a result will be too large to cache. If the result exceeds the specified limit, MySQL will increment the `Qcache_not_cached` status variable and discard the results cached so far. If you know this happens a lot, you can add the `SQL_NO_CACHE` hint to queries you don't want to incur this overhead.

`query_cache_wlock_invalidate`

Whether to serve cached results that refer to tables other connections have locked. The default value is `OFF`, which makes the query cache change the server's semantics because it lets you read cached data from a table another connection has locked, which you wouldn't normally be able to do. Changing it to `ON` will keep you from reading this data, but it might increase lock waits. This really doesn't matter for most applications, so the default is generally fine.

In principle, tuning the cache is pretty simple, but understanding the effects of your changes is more complicated. In the following sections, we show you how to reason about the query cache, so you can make good decisions.

Reducing fragmentation

There's no way to avoid all fragmentation, but choosing your `query_cache_min_res_unit` value carefully can help you avoid wasting a lot of memory in the query cache. The trick is to balance the size of each new block against the number of allocations the server has to do while storing results. If you make this value too small, the server will waste less memory, but it will have to allocate blocks more frequently, which is more work for the server. If you make it too large, you'll get too much fragmentation. The tradeoff is wasting memory versus using more CPU cycles during allocation.

The best setting varies with the size of your typical query result. You can see the average size of the queries in the cache by dividing the memory used (approximately `query_cache_size − Qcache_free_memory`) by the `Qcache_queries_in_cache` status variable. If you have a mixture of large and small results, you might not be able to choose a size that avoids fragmentation while also avoiding too many allocations. However, you may have reason to believe that it's not beneficial to cache the larger results (this is frequently true). You can keep large results from being cached by lowering the `query_cache_limit` variable, which can sometimes help achieve a better balance between fragmentation and the overhead of storing results in the cache.

You can detect query cache fragmentation by examining the `Qcache_free_blocks` status variable, which shows you how many blocks in the query cache are of type `FREE`. In the final configuration shown in Figure 5-2, there are two free blocks. The worst possible fragmentation is when there's a slightly-too-small free block between every pair of blocks used to store data, so every other block is a free block. Thus, if `Qcache_free_blocks` approaches `Qcache_total_blocks / 2`, your query cache is severely fragmented. If the `Qcache_lowmem_prunes` status variable is increasing and you have a lot of free blocks, fragmentation is causing queries to be deleted from the cache prematurely.

You can defragment the query cache with `FLUSH QUERY CACHE`. This command compacts the query cache by moving all blocks "upward" and removing the free space between them, leaving a single free block at the bottom. It blocks access to the query cache while it runs, which pretty much locks the whole server, but it's usually fast unless your cache is very large. Contrary to its name, it does not remove queries from the cache. That's what `RESET QUERY CACHE` does.

Improving query cache usage

If your query cache isn't fragmented but you're still not getting a good hit rate, you might have given it too little memory. If the server can't find any free blocks that are large enough to use for a new block, it must "prune" some queries from the cache.

When the server prunes cache entries, it increments the `Qcache_lowmem_prunes` status variable. If this value increases rapidly, there are two possible causes:

- If there are many free blocks, fragmentation is the likely culprit (see the previous section).
- If there are few free blocks, it might mean that your workload can use a larger cache size than you're giving it. You can see the amount of unused memory in the cache by examining `Qcache_free_memory`.

If there are many free blocks, fragmentation is low, there are few prunes due to low memory, and the hit rate is *still* low, your workload probably won't benefit much from the query cache. Something is keeping it from being used. If you have a lot of updates, that's probably the culprit; it's also possible that your queries are not cacheable.

If you've measured the cache hit ratio and you're still not sure whether the server is benefiting from the query cache, you can disable it and monitor performance, then reenable it and see how performance changes. To disable the query cache, set `query_cache_size` to 0. (Changing `query_cache_type` globally won't affect connections that are already open, and it won't return the memory to the server.) You can also benchmark, but it's sometimes tricky to get a realistic combination of cached queries, uncached queries, and updates.

Figure 5-3 shows a flowchart with a basic example of the process you can use to analyze and tune your server's query cache.

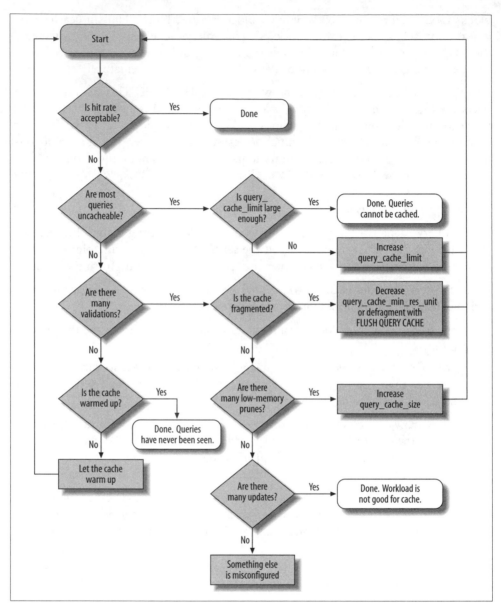

Figure 5-3. How to analyze and tune the query cache

InnoDB and the Query Cache

InnoDB interacts with the query cache in a more complex way than other storage engines, because of its implementation of MVCC. In MySQL 4.0, the query cache is disabled entirely within transactions, but in MySQL 4.1 and newer, InnoDB indicates to the server, on a per-table basis, whether a transaction can access the query cache. It controls access to the query cache for both reads (retrieving results from the cache) and writes (saving results to the cache).

The factors that determine access are the transaction ID and whether there are any locks on the table. Each table in InnoDB's in-memory data dictionary has an associated transaction ID counter. Transactions whose IDs are less than the counter value are forbidden to read from or write to the query cache for queries that involve that table. Any locks on a table also make queries that access it uncacheable. For example, if a transaction performs a SELECT FOR UPDATE query on a table, no other transactions will be able to read from or write to the query cache for queries involving that table until the locks are released

When a transaction commits, InnoDB updates the counters for the tables upon which the transaction has locks. A lock is a rough heuristic for determining whether the transaction has modified a table; it is possible for a transaction to lock rows in a table and not update them, but it is not possible for it to modify the table's contents without acquiring any locks. InnoDB sets each table's counter to the system's transaction ID, which is the maximum transaction ID in existence.

This has the following consequences:

- The table's counter is an absolute lower bound on which transactions can use the query cache. If the system's transaction ID is 5 and a transaction acquires locks on rows in a table and then commits, transactions 1 through 4 can never read from or write to the query cache for queries involving that table again.

- The table's counter is updated not to the transaction ID of the transaction that locked rows in it, but to the system's transaction ID. As a result, transactions that lock rows in tables may find themselves blocked from reading from or writing to the query cache for queries involving that table in the future.

Query cache storage, retrieval, and invalidation are handled at the server level, and InnoDB cannot bypass or delay this. However, InnoDB can tell the server explicitly to invalidate queries that involve specific tables. This is necessary when a foreign key constraint, such as ON DELETE CASCADE, alters the contents of a table that isn't mentioned in a query.

In principle, InnoDB's MVCC architecture could let queries be served from the cache when modifications to a table don't affect the consistent read view other transactions see. However, implementing this would be complex. InnoDB's algorithm takes some shortcuts for simplicity, at the cost of locking transactions out of the query cache when this might not really be necessary.

General Query Cache Optimizations

Many schema, query, and application design decisions affect the query cache. In addition to what we discussed in the previous sections, here are some points to keep in mind:

- Having multiple smaller tables instead of one huge one can help the query cache. This design effectively makes the invalidation strategy work at a finer level of granularity. Don't let this unduly influence your schema design, though, as other factors can easily outweigh the benefit.

- It's more efficient to batch writes than to do them singly, because this method invalidates cached cache entries only once.

- We've noticed that the server can stall for a long time while invalidating entries in or pruning a very large query cache. This is the case at least up to MySQL 5.1. The easy solution is to not make query_cache_size too big; about 256 MB should be more than enough.

- You cannot control the query cache on a per-database or per-table basis, but you can include or exclude individual queries with the SQL_CACHE and SQL_NO_CACHE modifiers in the SELECT statement. You can also enable or disable the query cache on a per-connection basis by setting the session-level query_cache_type server variable to the appropriate value.

- For a write-heavy application, disabling the query cache completely may improve performance. Doing so eliminates the overhead of caching queries that would be invalidated soon anyway. Remember to set query_cache_size to 0 when you disable it, so it doesn't consume any memory.

If you want to avoid the query cache for most queries, but you know that some will benefit significantly from caching, you can set the global query_cache_type to DEMAND and then add the SQL_CACHE hint to those queries you want to cache. Although this requires you to do more work, it gives you very fine-grained control over the cache. Conversely, if you want to cache most queries and exclude just a few, you can add SQL_NO_CACHE to them.

Alternatives to the Query Cache

The MySQL query cache works on the principle that the fastest query is the one you don't have to execute, but you still have to issue the query, and the server still needs to do a little bit of work. What if you really didn't have to talk to the database server at all for particular queries? Client-side caching can help ease the workload on your MySQL server even more. We explain caching more in Chapter 10.

Storing Code Inside MySQL

MySQL lets you store code inside the server in the form of triggers, stored procedures, and stored functions. In MySQL 5.1, you can also store code in periodic jobs called *events*. Stored procedures and stored functions are collectively known as "stored routines."

All four types of stored code use a special extended SQL language that contains procedural structures such as loops and conditionals.[*] The biggest difference between the types of stored code is the context in which they operate—that is, their inputs and outputs. Stored procedures and stored functions can accept parameters and return results, but triggers and events do not.

In principle, stored code is a good way to share and reuse code. Giuseppe Maxia and others have created a library of useful general-purpose stored routines at *http://mysql-sr-lib.sourceforge.net*. However, it's hard to reuse stored routines from other database systems, because most have their own language (the exception is DB2, which has a fairly similar language based on the same standard).[†]

We focus more on the performance implications of stored code than on how to write it. O'Reilly's *MySQL Stored Procedure Programming* (by Guy Harrison and Steven Feuerstein) may be useful if you plan to write stored procedures in MySQL.

It's easy to find both advocates and opponents of stored code. Without taking sides, we list some of the pros and cons of using it in MySQL. First, the advantages:

- It runs where the data is, so you can save bandwidth and reduce latency by running tasks on the database server.
- It's a form of code reuse. It can help centralize business rules, which can enforce consistent behavior and provide more safety and peace of mind.
- It can ease release policies and maintenance.
- It can provide some security advantages and a way to control privileges more finely. A common example is a stored procedure for funds transfer at a bank: the procedure transfers the money within a transaction and logs the entire operation for auditing. You can let applications call the stored procedure without granting access to the underlying tables.
- The server caches stored procedure execution plans, which lowers the overhead of repeated calls.

---

[*] The language is a subset of SQL/PSM, the Persistent Stored Modules part of the SQL standard. It is defined in ISO/IEC 9075-4:2003 (E).

[†] There are also some porting utilities, such as the *tsql2mysql* project (*http://sourceforge.net/projects/tsql2mysql*) for porting from Microsoft SQL Server.

- Because it's stored in the server and can be deployed, backed up, and maintained with the server, stored code is well suited for maintenance jobs. It doesn't have any external dependencies, such as Perl libraries or other software that you might not want to place on the server.

- It enables division of labor between application programmers and database programmers. It can be preferable for a database expert to write the stored procedures, as not every application programmer is good at writing efficient SQL queries.

Disadvantages include the following:

- MySQL doesn't provide good developing and debugging tools, so it's harder to write stored code in MySQL than it is in some other database servers.

- The language is slow and primitive compared to application languages. The number of functions you can use is limited, and it's hard to do complex string manipulations and write intricate logic.

- Stored code can actually add complexity to deploying your application. Instead of just application code and database schema changes, you'll need to deploy code that's stored inside the server, too.

- Because stored routines are stored with the database, they can create a security vulnerability. Having nonstandard cryptographic functions inside a stored routine, for example, will not protect your data if the database is compromised. If the cryptographic function were in the code, the attacker would have to compromise both the code and the database.

- Storing routines moves the load to the database server, which is typically harder to scale and more expensive than application or web servers.

- MySQL doesn't give you much control over the resources stored code can allocate, so a mistake can bring down the server.

- MySQL's implementation of stored code is pretty limited—execution plan caches are per-connection, cursors are materialized as temporary tables, and so on. (We mention the limitations of various features as we describe them.)

- It's hard to profile code with stored procedures in MySQL. It's difficult to analyze the slow query log when it just shows CALL XYZ('A'), because you have to go and find that procedure and look at the statements inside it.

- Stored code is a way to hide complexity, which simplifies development but is often very bad for performance.

When you're thinking about using stored code, you should ask yourself where you want your business logic to live: in application code, or in the database? Both approaches are popular. You just need to be aware that you're placing logic into the database when you use stored code.

Stored Procedures and Functions

MySQL's architecture and query optimizer place some limits on how you can use stored routines and how efficient they can be. The following restrictions apply at the time of this writing:

- The optimizer doesn't use the DETERMINISTIC modifier in stored functions to optimize away multiple calls within a single query.

- The optimizer cannot currently estimate how much it will cost to execute a stored function.

- Each connection has its own stored procedure execution plan cache. If many connections call the same procedure, they'll waste resources caching the same execution plan over and over. (If you use connection pooling or persistent connections, the execution plan cache can have a longer useful life.)

- Stored routines and replication are a tricky combination. You may not want to replicate the call to the routine. Instead, you may want to replicate the exact changes made to your dataset. Row-based replication, introduced in MySQL 5.1, helps alleviate this problem. If binary logging is enabled in MySQL 5.0, the server will insist that you either define all stored procedures as DETERMINISTIC or enable the elaborately named server option log_bin_trust_function_creators.

We usually prefer to keep stored routines small and simple. We like to perform complex logic outside the database in a procedural language, which is more expressive and versatile. It can also give you access to more computational resources and potentially to different forms of caching.

However, stored procedures can be much faster for certain types of operations—especially small queries. If a query is small enough, the overhead of parsing and network communication becomes a significant fraction of the overall work required to execute it. To illustrate this, we created a simple stored procedure that inserts a specified number of rows into a table. Here's the procedure's code:

```
1   DROP PROCEDURE IF EXISTS insert_many_rows;
2
3   delimiter //
4
5   CREATE PROCEDURE insert_many_rows (IN loops INT)
6   BEGIN
7      DECLARE v1 INT;
8      SET v1=loops;
9      WHILE v1 > 0 DO
10        INSERT INTO test_table values(NULL,0,
11                'qqqqqqqqqqwwwwwwwwwweeeeeeeeeeerrrrrrrrrrttttttttttt',
12                'qqqqqqqqqqwwwwwwwwwweeeeeeeeeeerrrrrrrrrrttttttttttt');
13      SET v1 = v1 - 1;
14    END WHILE;
```

```
15  END;
16  //
17
18  delimiter ;
```

We then benchmarked how quickly this stored procedure could insert a million rows into a table, as compared to inserting one row at a time via a client application. The table structure and hardware we used doesn't really matter—what is important is the relative speed of the different approaches. Just for fun, we also measured how long the same queries took to execute when we connected through a MySQL Proxy. To keep things simple, we ran the entire benchmark on a single server, including the client application and the MySQL Proxy instance. Table 5-1 shows the results.

Table 5-1. Total time to insert one million rows one at a time

Method	Total time
Stored procedure	101 sec
Client application	279 sec
Client application with MySQL Proxy	307 sec

The stored procedure is much faster, mostly because it avoids the overhead of network communication, parsing, optimizing, and so on.

We show a typical stored procedure for maintenance jobs in the "The SQL Interface to Prepared Statements" on page 227, later in this chapter.

Triggers

Triggers let you execute code when there's an INSERT, UPDATE, or DELETE statement. You can direct MySQL to execute them before and/or after the triggering statement executes. They cannot return values, but they can read and/or change the data that the triggering statement changes. Thus, you can use triggers to enforce constraints or business logic that you'd otherwise need to write in client code. A good example is emulating foreign keys on a storage engine that doesn't support them, such as MyISAM.

Triggers can simplify application logic and improve performance, because they save round-trips between the client and the server. They can also be helpful for automatically updating denormalized and summary tables. For example, the Sakila sample database uses them to maintain the film_text table.

MySQL's trigger implementation is not very complete at the time of this writing. If you're used to relying on triggers extensively in another database product, you shouldn't assume they will work the same way in MySQL. In particular:

- You can have only one trigger per table for each event (in other words, you can't have two triggers that fire AFTER INSERT).
- MySQL supports only row-level triggers—that is, triggers always operate FOR EACH ROW rather than for the statement as a whole. This is a much less efficient way to process large datasets.

The following universal cautions about triggers apply in MySQL, too:

- They can obscure what your server is really doing, because a simple statement can make the server perform a lot of "invisible" work. For example, if a trigger updates a related table, it can double the number of rows a statement affects.
- Triggers can be hard to debug, and it's often difficult to analyze performance bottlenecks when triggers are involved.
- Triggers can cause nonobvious deadlocks and lock waits. If a trigger fails the original query will fail, and if you're not aware the trigger exists, it can be hard to decipher the error code.

In terms of performance, the most severe limitation in MySQL's trigger implementation is the FOR EACH ROW design. This sometimes makes it impractical to use triggers for maintaining summary and cache tables, because they might be too slow. The main reason to use triggers instead of a periodic bulk update is that they keep your data consistent at all times.

Triggers also may not guarantee atomicity. For example, a trigger that updates a MyISAM table cannot be rolled back if there's an error in the statement that fires it. It is possible for a trigger to cause an error, too. Suppose you attach an AFTER UPDATE trigger to a MyISAM table and use it to update another MyISAM table. If the trigger has an error that causes the second table's update to fail, the first table's update will not be rolled back.

Triggers on InnoDB tables all operate within the same transaction, so the actions they take will be atomic, together with the statement that fired them. However, if you're using a trigger with InnoDB to check another table's data when validating a constraint, be careful about MVCC, as you can get incorrect results if you're not careful. For example, suppose you want to emulate foreign keys, but you don't want to use InnoDB's foreign keys. You can write a BEFORE INSERT trigger that verifies the existence of a matching record in another table, but if you don't use SELECT FOR UPDATE in the trigger when reading from the other table, concurrent updates to that table can cause incorrect results.

We don't mean to scare you away from triggers. On the contrary, they can be very useful, particularly for constraints, system maintenance tasks, and keeping denormalized data in sync.

You can also use triggers to log changes to rows. This can be handy for custom-built replication setups where you want to disconnect systems, make data changes, and then merge the changes back together. A simple example is a group of users who take laptops onto a job site. Their changes need to be synchronized to a master database, and then the master data needs to be copied back to the individual laptops. Accomplishing this requires two-way synchronization. Triggers are a good way to build such systems. Each laptop can use triggers to log every data modification to tables that indicate which rows have been changed. The custom synchronization tool can then apply these changes to the master database. Finally, ordinary MySQL replication can sync the laptops with the master, which will have the changes from all the laptops.

Sometimes you can even work around the FOR EACH ROW limitation. Roland Bouman found that ROW_COUNT( ) always reports 1 inside a trigger, except for the first row of a BEFORE trigger. You can use this to prevent a trigger's code from executing for every row affected and run it only once per statement. It's not the same as a per-statement trigger, but it is a useful technique for emulating a per-statement BEFORE trigger in some cases. This behavior may actually be a bug that will get fixed at some point, so you should use it with care and verify that it still works when you upgrade your server. Here's a sample of how to use this hack:

```
CREATE TRIGGER fake_statement_trigger
BEFORE INSERT ON sometable
FOR EACH ROW
BEGIN
   DECLARE v_row_count INT DEFAULT ROW_COUNT( );
   IF v_row_count <> 1 THEN
      -- Your code here
   END IF;
END;
```

Events

Events are a new form of stored code in MySQL 5.1. They are akin to *cron* jobs but are completely internal to the MySQL server. You can create events that execute SQL code once at a specific time, or frequently at a specified interval. The usual practice is to wrap the complex SQL in a stored procedure, so the event merely needs to perform a CALL.

Events run in a separate event scheduler thread, because they have nothing to do with connections. They accept no inputs and return no values—there's no connection for them to get inputs from or return values to. You can see the commands they execute in the server log, if it's enabled, but it can be hard to tell that those commands were executed from an event. You can also look in the INFORMATION_SCHEMA. EVENTS table to see an event's status, such as the last time it was executed.

Similar considerations to those that apply to stored procedures apply to events: you are giving the server additional work to do. The event overhead itself is minimal, but the SQL it calls can have a potentially serious impact on performance. Good uses for events include periodic maintenance tasks, rebuilding cache and summary tables to emulate materialized views, or saving status values for monitoring and diagnostics.

The following example creates an event that will run a stored procedure for a specific database, once a week:*

```
CREATE EVENT optimize_somedb ON SCHEDULE EVERY 1 WEEK
DO
CALL optimize_tables('somedb');
```

You can specify whether events should be replicated to slave servers. In some cases this is appropriate, whereas in others it's not. Take the previous example, for instance: you probably want to run the OPTIMIZE TABLE operation on all slaves, but keep in mind that it could impact overall server performance (with table locks, for instance) if all slaves were to execute this operation at the same time.

Finally, if a periodic event can take a long time to complete, it might be possible for the event to fire again while its earlier execution is still running. MySQL doesn't protect against this, so you'll have to write your own mutual exclusivity code. You can use GET_LOCK( ) to make sure that only one event runs at a time:

```
CREATE EVENT optimize_somedb ON SCHEDULE EVERY 1 WEEK
DO
BEGIN
    DECLARE CONTINUE HANLDER FOR SQLEXCEPTION
        BEGIN END;
    IF GET_LOCK('somedb', 0) THEN
        DO CALL optimize_tables('somedb');
    END IF;
    DO RELEASE_LOCK('somedb');
END
```

The "dummy" continue handler ensures that the event will release the lock, even if the stored procedure throws an exception.

Although events are dissociated from connections, they are still associated with threads. There's a main event scheduler thread, which you must enable in your server's configuration file or with a SET command:

```
mysql> SET GLOBAL event_scheduler := 1;
```

When enabled, this thread creates a new thread to execute each event. Within the event's code, a call to CONNECTION_ID( ) will return a unique value, as usual—even though there is no "connection" per se. (The return value of CONNECTION_ID( ) is really just the thread ID.) You can watch the server's error log for information about event execution.

---

* We'll show you how to create this stored procedure later.

Preserving Comments in Stored Code

Stored procedures, stored functions, triggers, and events can all have significant amounts of code, and it's useful to add comments. But the comments may not be stored inside the server, because the command-line client can strip them out. (This "feature" of the command-line client can be a nuisance, but *c'est la vie*.)

A useful trick for preserving comments in your stored code is to use version-specific comments, which the server sees as potentially executable code (i.e., code to be executed only if the server's version number is that high or higher). The server and client programs know these aren't ordinary comments, so they won't discard them. To prevent the "code" from being executed, you can just use a very high version number, such as 99999. For example, let's add some documentation to our trigger example to demystify what it does:

```
CREATE TRIGGER fake_statement_trigger
BEFORE INSERT ON sometable
FOR EACH ROW
BEGIN
   DECLARE v_row_count INT DEFAULT ROW_COUNT( );
   /*!99999
      ROW_COUNT( ) is 1 except for the first row, so this executes
      only once per statement.
   */
   IF v_row_count <> 1 THEN
      -- Your code here
   END IF;
END;
```

Cursors

MySQL currently provides read-only, forward-only server-side cursors that you can use only from within a MySQL stored procedure. They let you iterate over query results row by row and fetch each row into variables for further processing. A stored procedure can have multiple cursors open at once, and you can "nest" cursors in loops.

MySQL may provide updatable cursors in the future, but they're not in any current release. Cursors are read-only because they iterate over temporary tables rather than the tables where the data originated.

MySQL's cursor design holds some snares for the unwary. Because they're implemented with temporary tables, they can give developers a false sense of efficiency. The most important thing to know is that *a cursor executes the entire query when you open it*. Consider the following procedure:

```
1  CREATE PROCEDURE bad_cursor( )
2  BEGIN
3     DECLARE film_id INT;
```

```
4     DECLARE f CURSOR FOR SELECT film_id FROM sakila.film;
5     OPEN f;
6     FETCH f INTO film_id;
7     CLOSE f;
8 END
```

This example shows that you can close a cursor before iterating through all of its results. A developer used to Oracle or Microsoft SQL Server might see nothing wrong with this procedure, but in MySQL it causes a lot of unnecessary work. Profiling this procedure with SHOW STATUS shows that it does 1,000 index reads and 1,000 inserts. That's because there are 1,000 rows in sakila.film. All 1,000 reads and writes occur when line 5 executes, before line 6 executes.

The moral of the story is that if you close a cursor that fetches data from a large result set early, you won't actually save work. If you need only a few rows, use LIMIT.

Cursors can cause MySQL to perform extra I/O operations too, and they can be very slow. Because in-memory temporary tables do not support the BLOB and TEXT types, MySQL has to create an on-disk temporary table for cursors over results that include these types. Even when that's not the case, if the temporary table is larger than tmp_table_size, MySQL will create it on disk.

MySQL doesn't support client-side cursors, but the client API has functions that emulate client-side cursors by fetching the entire result into memory. This is really no different from putting the result in an array in your application and manipulating it there. See "The MySQL Client/Server Protocol" on page 161 for more on the performance implications of fetching the entire result into client-side memory.

Prepared Statements

MySQL 4.1 and newer support server-side *prepared statements* that use an enhanced binary client/server protocol to send data efficiently between the client and server. You can access the prepared statement functionality through a programming library that supports the new protocol, such as the MySQL C API. The MySQL Connector/J and MySQL Connector/NET libraries provide the same capability to Java and .NET, respectively. There's also a SQL interface to prepared statements, which we discuss later.

When you create a prepared statement, the client library sends the server a prototype of the actual query you want to use. The server parses and processes this "skeleton" query, stores a structure representing the partially optimized query, and returns a *statement handle* to the client. The client library can execute the query repeatedly by specifying the statement handle.

Prepared statements can have parameters, which are question-mark placeholders for values that you can specify when you execute them. For example, you might prepare the following query:

```
mysql> INSERT INTO tbl(col1, col2, col3) VALUES (?, ?, ?) ;
```

You could then execute this query by sending the statement handle to the server, with values for each of the question-mark placeholders. You can repeat this as many times as desired. Exactly how you send the statement handle to the server will depend on your programming language. One way is to use the MySQL connectors for Java and .NET. Many client libraries that link to the MySQL C libraries also provide some interface to the binary protocol; you should read the documentation for your chosen MySQL API.

Using prepared statements can be more efficient than executing a query repeatedly, for several reasons:

- The server has to parse the query only once, which saves some parsing and other work.

- The server has to perform some query optimization steps only once, as it caches a partial query execution plan.

- Sending parameters via the binary protocol is more efficient than sending them as ASCII text. For example, a DATE value can be sent in just 3 bytes, instead of the 10 bytes required in ASCII. The biggest savings are for BLOB and TEXT values, which can be sent to the server in chunks rather than as a single huge piece of data. The binary protocol therefore helps save memory on the client, as well as reducing network traffic and the overhead of converting between the data's native storage format and the non-binary protocol's format.

- Only the parameters—not the entire query text—need to be sent for each execution, which reduces network traffic.

- MySQL stores the parameters directly into buffers on the server, which eliminates the need for the server to copy values around in memory.

Prepared statements can also help with security. There is no need to escape or quote values in the application, which is more convenient and reduces vulnerability to SQL injection or other attacks. (You should never trust user input, even when you're using prepared statements.)

You can use the binary protocol *only* with prepared statements. Issuing queries through the normal mysql_query( ) API function will *not* use the binary protocol. Many client libraries let you "prepare" statements with question-mark placeholders and then specify the values for each execution, but these libraries are often only emulating the prepare-execute cycle in client-side code and are actually sending each query to the server with mysql_query( ).

Prepared Statement Optimization

MySQL caches partial query execution plans for prepared statements, but some optimizations depend on the actual values that are bound to each parameter and therefore can't be precomputed and cached. The optimizations can be separated into three types, based on when they must be performed. The following list applies at the time of this writing, but it may change in the future:

At preparation time
> The server parses the query text, eliminates negations, and rewrites subqueries.

At first execution
> The server simplifies nested joins and converts OUTER JOIN to INNER JOIN where possible.

At every execution
> The server does the following:
>
> - Prunes partitions
> - Eliminates COUNT( ), MIN( ), and MAX( ) where possible
> - Removes constant subexpressions
> - Detects constant tables
> - Propagates equalities
> - Analyzes and optimizes ref, range, and index_merge access methods
> - Optimizes the join order

See Chapter 4 for more information on these optimizations.

The SQL Interface to Prepared Statements

A SQL interface to prepared statements is available in MySQL 4.1 and newer. Here's an example of how to use a prepared statement through SQL:

```
mysql> SET @sql := 'SELECT actor_id, first_name, last_name
    -> FROM sakila.actor WHERE first_name = ?';
mysql> PREPARE stmt_fetch_actor FROM @sql;
mysql> SET @actor_name := 'Penelope';
mysql> EXECUTE stmt_fetch_actor USING @actor_name;
+----------+------------+-----------+
| actor_id | first_name | last_name |
+----------+------------+-----------+
|        1 | PENELOPE   | GUINESS   |
|       54 | PENELOPE   | PINKETT   |
|      104 | PENELOPE   | CRONYN    |
|      120 | PENELOPE   | MONROE    |
+----------+------------+-----------+
mysql> DEALLOCATE PREPARE stmt_fetch_actor;
```

When the server receives these statements, it translates them into the same operations that would have been invoked by the client library. This means that you don't have to use the special binary protocol to create and execute prepared statements.

As you can see, the syntax is a little awkward compared to just typing the SELECT statement directly. So what's the advantage of using a prepared statement this way?

The main use case is for stored procedures. In MySQL 5.0, you can use prepared statements in stored procedures, and the syntax is similar to the SQL interface. This means you can build and execute "dynamic SQL" in stored procedures by concatenating strings, which makes stored procedures much more flexible. For example, here's a sample stored procedure that can call OPTIMIZE TABLE on each table in a specified database:

```
DROP PROCEDURE IF EXISTS optimize_tables;
DELIMITER //
CREATE PROCEDURE optimize_tables(db_name VARCHAR(64))
BEGIN
   DECLARE t VARCHAR(64);
   DECLARE done INT DEFAULT 0;
   DECLARE c CURSOR FOR
      SELECT table_name FROM INFORMATION_SCHEMA.TABLES
      WHERE TABLE_SCHEMA = db_name AND TABLE_TYPE = 'BASE TABLE';
   DECLARE CONTINUE HANDLER FOR SQLSTATE '02000' SET done = 1;
   OPEN c;
   tables_loop: LOOP
      FETCH c INTO t;
      IF done THEN
         CLOSE c;
         LEAVE tables_loop;
      END IF;
      SET @stmt_text := CONCAT("OPTIMIZE TABLE ", db_name, ".", t);
      PREPARE stmt FROM @stmt_text;
      EXECUTE stmt;
      DEALLOCATE PREPARE stmt;
   END LOOP;
   CLOSE c;
END//
DELIMITER ;
```

You can use this stored procedure as follows:

```
mysql> CALL optimize_tables('sakila');
```

Another way to write the loop in the procedure is as follows:

```
REPEAT
   FETCH c INTO t;
   IF NOT done THEN
      SET @stmt_text := CONCAT("OPTIMIZE TABLE ", db_name, ".", t);
      PREPARE stmt FROM @stmt_text;
      EXECUTE stmt;
      DEALLOCATE PREPARE stmt;
   END IF;
UNTIL done END REPEAT;
```

There is an important difference between the two loop constructs: REPEAT checks the loop condition twice for each loop. This probably won't cause a big performance problem in this example because we're merely checking an integer's value, but with more complex checks it could be costly.

Concatenating strings to refer to tables and databases is a good use for the SQL interface to prepared statements, because it lets you write statements that won't work with parameters. You can't parameterize database and table names because they are identifiers. Another scenario is dynamically setting a LIMIT clause, which you can't specify with a parameter either.

The SQL interface is useful for testing a prepared statement by hand, but it's otherwise not all that useful outside of stored procedures. Because the interface is through SQL, it doesn't use the binary protocol, and it doesn't really reduce network traffic because you have to issue extra queries to set the variables when there are parameters. You can benefit from using this interface in special cases, such as when preparing an enormous string of SQL that you'll execute many times without parameters. However, you should benchmark if you think using the SQL interface for prepared statements will save work.

Limitations of Prepared Statements

Prepared statements have a few limitations and caveats:

- Prepared statements are local to a connection, so another connection cannot use the same handle. For the same reason, a client that disconnects and reconnects loses the statements. (Connection pooling or persistent connections can alleviate this problem.)

- Prepared statements cannot use the MySQL query cache in MySQL versions prior to 5.1.

- It's not always more efficient to use prepared statements. If you use a prepared statement only once, you may spend more time preparing it than you would just executing it as normal SQL. Preparing a statement also requires an extra round-trip to the server.

- You cannot currently use a prepared statement inside a stored function (but you can use prepared statements inside stored procedures).

- You can accidentally "leak" a prepared statement by forgetting to deallocate it. This can consume a lot of resources on the server. Also, because there is a single global limit on the number of prepared statements, a mistake such as this can interfere with other connections' use of prepared statements.

User-Defined Functions

MySQL has supported *user-defined functions* (UDFs) for a long time. Unlike stored functions, which are written in SQL, you can write UDFs in any programming language that supports C calling conventions.

UDFs must be compiled and then dynamically linked with the server, making them platform-specific and giving you a lot of power. UDFs can be very fast and can access a large range of functionality in the operating system and available libraries. SQL stored functions are good for simple operations, such as calculating the great-circle distance between two points on the globe, but if you want to send network packets, you need a UDF. Also, while you can't currently build aggregate functions in SQL, you can do this easily with a UDF.

With great power comes great responsibility. A mistake in your UDF can crash your whole server, corrupt the server's memory and/or your data, and generally wreak all the havoc that any misbehaving C code can potentially cause.

Unlike stored functions written in SQL, UDFs cannot currently read and write tables—at least, not in the same transactional context as the statement that calls them. This means they're more helpful for pure computation, or interaction with the outside world. MySQL is gaining more and more possibilities for interaction with resources outside of the server. The functions Brian Aker and Patrick Galbraith have created to communicate with *memcached* (*http://tangent.org/586/ Memcached_Functions_for_MySQL.html*) are a good example of how this can be done with UDFs.

If you use UDFs, check carefully for changes between MySQL versions when you upgrade, because they may need to be recompiled or even changed to work correctly with the new MySQL server. Also make sure your UDFs are absolutely thread-safe, because they execute within the MySQL server process, which is a pure multi-threaded environment.

There are good libraries of prebuilt UDFs for MySQL, and many good examples of how to implement your own. The biggest repository of UDFs is at *http://www. mysqludf.org*.

The following is the code for the NOW_USEC( ) UDF we'll use to measure replication speed (see "How Fast Is Replication?" on page 405):

```
#include <my_global.h>
#include <my_sys.h>
#include <mysql.h>
```

```
#include <stdio.h>
#include <sys/time.h>
#include <time.h>
#include <unistd.h>

extern "C" {
   my_bool now_usec_init(UDF_INIT *initid, UDF_ARGS *args, char *message);
   char *now_usec(
                   UDF_INIT *initid,
                   UDF_ARGS *args,
                   char *result,
                   unsigned long *length,
                   char *is_null,
                   char *error);
}

my_bool now_usec_init(UDF_INIT *initid, UDF_ARGS *args, char *message) {
   return 0;
}

char *now_usec(UDF_INIT *initid, UDF_ARGS *args, char *result,
               unsigned long *length, char *is_null, char *error) {

   struct timeval tv;
   struct tm* ptm;
   char time_string[20]; /* e.g. "2006-04-27 17:10:52" */
   char *usec_time_string = result;
   time_t t;

   /* Obtain the time of day, and convert it to a tm struct. */
   gettimeofday (&tv, NULL);
   t = (time_t)tv.tv_sec;
   ptm = localtime (&t);

   /* Format the date and time, down to a single second. */
   strftime (time_string, sizeof (time_string), "%Y-%m-%d %H:%M:%S", ptm);

   /* Print the formatted time, in seconds, followed by a decimal point
    * and the microseconds. */
   sprintf(usec_time_string, "%s.%06ld\n", time_string, tv.tv_usec);

   *length = 26;

   return(usec_time_string);
}
```

Views

Views are a popular database feature that were added in MySQL 5.0. A *view* in
MySQL is a table that doesn't store any data itself. Instead, the data "in" the table is
derived from a SQL query.

This book does not explain how to create or use views; you can read the appropriate section of the MySQL manual for that and find descriptions of uses for views in other documentation. MySQL treats a view exactly like a table for many purposes, and views and tables share the same namespace in MySQL; however, MySQL doesn't treat them identically. For example, you can't have triggers on views, and you can't drop a view with the DROP TABLE command.

It's important to understand the internal implementation of views and how they interact with the query optimizer, or you may not get good performance from them. We use the world sample database to demonstrate how views work:

```
mysql> CREATE VIEW Oceania AS
    ->     SELECT * FROM Country WHERE Continent = 'Oceania'
    ->     WITH CHECK OPTION;
```

The easiest way for the server to implement a view is to execute its SELECT statement and place the result into a temporary table. It can then refer to the temporary table where the view's name appears in the query. To see how this would work, consider the following query:

```
mysql> SELECT Code, Name FROM Oceania WHERE Name = 'Australia';
```

Here's how the server might execute it. The temporary table's name is for demonstration purposes only:

```
mysql> CREATE TEMPORARY TABLE TMP_Oceania_123 AS
    ->     SELECT * FROM Country WHERE Continent = 'Oceania';
mysql> SELECT Code, Name FROM TMP_Oceania_123 WHERE Name = 'Australia';
```

There are obvious performance and query optimization problems with this approach. A better way to implement views is to rewrite a query that refers to the view, merging the view's SQL with the query's SQL. The following example shows how the query might look after MySQL has merged it into the view definition:

```
mysql> SELECT Code, Name FROM Country
    -> WHERE Continent = 'Oceania' AND Name = 'Australia';
```

MySQL can use both methods. It calls the two algorithms MERGE and TEMPTABLE,* and it tries to use the MERGE algorithm when possible. MySQL can even merge nested view definitions when a view is based upon another view. You can see the results of the query rewrite with EXPLAIN EXTENDED, followed by SHOW WARNINGS.

If a view uses the TEMPTABLE algorithm, EXPLAIN will usually show it as a DERIVED table. Figure 5-4 illustrates the two implementations.

MySQL uses TEMPTABLE when the view definition contains GROUP BY, DISTINCT, aggregate functions, UNION, subqueries, or any other construct that doesn't preserve a one-to-one relationship between the rows in the underlying base tables and the rows

---

* That's "temp table," not "can be tempted."

returned from the view. This is not a complete list, and it might change in the future. If you want to know whether a view will use MERGE or TEMPTABLE, you should EXPLAIN a trivial SELECT query against the view:

```
mysql> EXPLAIN SELECT * FROM <view_name>;
+----+-------------+
| id | select_type |
+----+-------------+
|  1 | PRIMARY     |
|  2 | DERIVED     |
+----+-------------+
```

The presence of a DERIVED select type indicates that the view will use the TEMPTABLE algorithm.

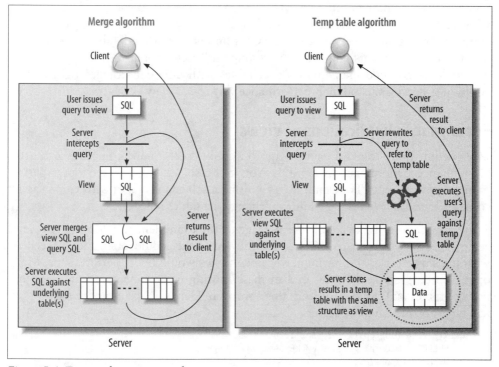

Figure 5-4. Two implementations of views

Updatable Views

An *updatable view* lets you update the underlying base tables via the view. As long as certain conditions hold, you can UPDATE, DELETE, and even INSERT into a view as you would with a normal table. For example, the following is a valid operation:

```
mysql> UPDATE Oceania SET Population = Population * 1.1 WHERE Name = 'Australia';
```

A view is not updatable if it contains GROUP BY, UNION, an aggregate function, or any of a few other exceptions. A query that changes data may contain a join, but the columns to be changed must all be in a single table. Any view that uses the TEMPTABLE algorithm is not updatable.

The CHECK OPTION clause, which we included when we created the view in the previous section, ensures that any rows changed through the view continue to match the view's WHERE clause after the change. So, we can't change the Continent column, nor can we insert a row that has a different Continent. Either would cause the server to report an error:

```
mysql> UPDATE Oceania SET Continent = 'Atlantis';
ERROR 1369 (HY000): CHECK OPTION failed 'world.Oceania'
```

Some database products allow INSTEAD OF triggers on views so you can define exactly what happens when a statement tries to modify a view's data, but MySQL does not support triggers on views. Some of MySQL's limitations on updatable views may be lifted in the future, enabling some interesting and useful applications. One possibility would be to build merge tables over tables with different storage engines. This could be a very useful and high-performance way to use views.

Performance Implications of Views

Most people don't think of using views to improve performance, but they can actually enhance performance in MySQL. You can also use them to aid other performance improvements. For example, refactoring a schema in stages with views can let some code continue working while you change the tables it accesses.

Some applications use one table per user, generally to implement a form of row-level security. A view similar to the one we showed earlier could offer similar security within a single table, and having fewer open tables would boost performance. Many open source projects that are used in mass hosting environments accumulate millions of tables and can benefit from this approach. Here's an example for a hypothetical blog-hosting database server:

```
CREATE VIEW blog_posts_for_user_1234 AS
    SELECT * FROM blog_posts WHERE user_id = 1234
    WITH CHECK OPTION;
```

You can also use views to implement column privileges without the overhead of actually creating those privileges, which can be significant. Column privileges prevent queries against the table from being cached in the query cache, too. A view can restrict access to the desired columns without causing these problems:

```
CREATE VIEW public.employeeinfo AS
    SELECT firstname, lastname -- but not socialsecuritynumber
    FROM private.employeeinfo;
GRANT SELECT ON public.* TO public_user;
```

You can also sometimes use pseudotemporary views to good effect. You can't actually create a truly temporary view that persists only for your current connection, but you can create a view under a special name, perhaps in a database reserved for it, that you know you can drop later. You can then use the view in the FROM clause, much the same way you'd use a subquery in the FROM clause. The two approaches are theoretically the same, but MySQL has a different codebase for views, so you may get better performance from the temporary view. Here's an example:

```
-- Assuming 1234 is the result of CONNECTION_ID( )
CREATE VIEW temp.cost_per_day_1234 AS
    SELECT DATE(ts) AS day, sum(cost) AS cost
    FROM logs.cost
    GROUP BY day;

SELECT c.day, c.cost, s.sales
FROM temp.cost_per_day_1234 AS c
    INNER JOIN sales.sales_per_day AS s USING(day);

DROP VIEW temp.cost_per_day_1234;
```

Note that we've used the connection ID as a unique suffix to avoid name clashes. This approach can make it easier to clean up in case the application crashes and doesn't drop the temporary view. See "Missing Temporary Tables" on page 394 for more about this technique.

Views that use the TEMPTABLE algorithm can perform very badly (although they may still perform *better* than an equivalent query that doesn't use a view). MySQL executes them as a recursive step in optimizing the outer query, before the outer query is even fully optimized, so they don't get a lot of the optimizations you might be used to from other database products. The query that builds the temporary table doesn't get WHERE conditions pushed down from the outer query, and the temporary table does not have any indexes. Here's an example, again using the temp.cost_per_day_1234 view:

```
mysql> SELECT c.day, c.cost, s.sales
    -> FROM temp.cost_per_day_1234 AS c
    ->     INNER JOIN sales.sales_per_day AS s USING(day)
    ->     WHERE day BETWEEN '2007-01-01' AND '2007-01-31';
```

What really happens in this query is that the server executes the view and places the result into a temporary table, then joins the sales_per_day table against this temporary table. The BETWEEN restriction in the WHERE clause is not "pushed into" the view, so the view will create a result set for all dates in the table, not just the one month desired. The temporary table also lacks any indexes. In this example, this isn't a problem: the server will place the temporary table first in the join order, so the join can use the index on the sales_per_day table. However, if we were joining two such views against each other, the join would not be optimized with any indexes.

You should always benchmark, or at least profile in detail, if you're trying to use views to improve performance. Even MERGE views add overhead, and it's hard to predict how a view will impact performance. If performance matters, never guess—always measure.

Views introduce some issues that aren't MySQL-specific. Views may trick developers into thinking they're simple, when in fact they're very complicated under the hood. A developer who doesn't understand the underlying complexity might think nothing of repeatedly querying what looks like a table but is in fact an expensive view. We've seen cases where an apparently simple query produced hundreds of lines of EXPLAIN output because one or more of the "tables" it referenced was actually a view that referred to many other tables and views.

Limitations of Views

MySQL does not support the materialized views that you may be used to if you've worked with other database servers. (A *materialized view* generally stores its results in an invisible table behind the scenes, with periodic updates to refresh the invisible table from the source data.) MySQL also doesn't support indexed views. You can simulate materialized and/or indexed views by building cache and summary tables, however, and in MySQL 5.1, you can use events to schedule these tasks.

MySQL's implementation of views also has a few annoyances. The biggest is that MySQL doesn't preserve your original view SQL, so if you ever try to edit a view by executing SHOW CREATE VIEW and changing the resulting SQL, you're in for a nasty surprise. The query will be expanded to the fully canonicalized and quoted internal format, without the benefit of formatting, comments, and indenting.

If you need to edit a view and you've lost the pretty-printed query you originally used to create it, you can find it in the last line of the view's *.frm* file. If you have the FILE privilege and the *.frm* file is readable by all users, you can even load the file's contents through SQL with the LOAD_FILE( ) function. A little string manipulation can retrieve your original code intact, thanks again to Roland Bouman's creativity:

```
mysql> SELECT
    ->    REPLACE(REPLACE(REPLACE(REPLACE(REPLACE(REPLACE(
    ->    REPLACE(REPLACE(REPLACE(REPLACE(REPLACE(
    ->      SUBSTRING_INDEX(LOAD_FILE('/var/lib/mysql/world/Oceania.frm'),
    ->      '\nsource=', -1),
    ->    '\\_','\_'), '\\%','\%'), '\\\\','\\'), '\\Z','\Z'), '\\t','\t'),
    ->    '\\r','\r'), '\\n','\n'), '\\b','\b'), '\\\"','\"'), '\\\'','\''),
    ->    '\\0','\0')
    -> AS source;
```

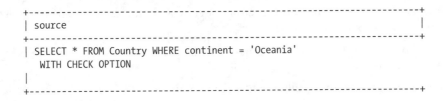

```
+-----------------------------------------------------------------+
| source                                                          |
+-----------------------------------------------------------------+
| SELECT * FROM Country WHERE continent = 'Oceania'               |
|   WITH CHECK OPTION                                             |
|                                                                 |
+-----------------------------------------------------------------+
```

Character Sets and Collations

A *character set* is a mapping from binary encodings to a defined set of symbols; you can think of it as how to represent a particular alphabet in bits. A *collation* is a set of sorting rules for a character set. In MySQL 4.1 and later, every character-based value can have a character set and a collation.* MySQL's support for character sets and collations is world-class, but it can add complexity, and in some cases it has a performance cost.

This section explains the settings and functionality you'll need for most situations. If you need to know the more esoteric details, you should consult the MySQL manual.

How MySQL Uses Character Sets

Character sets can have several collations, and each character set has a default collation. Collations belong to a particular character set and cannot be used with any other. You use a character set and a collation together, so we'll refer to them collectively as a character set from now on.

MySQL has a variety of options that control character sets. The options and the character sets are easy to confuse, so keep this distinction in mind: only character-based values can truly "have" a character set. Everything else is just a setting that specifies which character set to use for comparisons and other operations. A character-based value can be the value stored in a column, a literal in a query, the result of an expression, a user variable, and so on.

MySQL's settings can be divided into two classes: defaults for creating objects, and settings that control how the server and the client communicate.

Defaults for creating objects

MySQL has a default character set and collation for the server, for each database, and for each table. These form a hierarchy of defaults that influences the character set that's used when you create a column. That, in turn, tells the server what character set to use for values you store in the column.

---

* MySQL 4.0 and earlier used a global setting for the entire server, and you could choose from among several 8-bit character sets.

At each level in the hierarchy, you can either specify a character set explicitly or let the server use the applicable default:

- When you create a database, it inherits from the server-wide character_set_server setting.
- When you create a table, it inherits from the database.
- When you create a column, it inherits from the table.

Remember, columns are the only place MySQL stores values, so the higher levels in the hierarchy are only defaults. A table's default character set doesn't affect values stored in the tables; it just tells MySQL which character set to use when you create a column without specifying a character set explicitly.

Settings for client/server communication

When the server and the client communicate with each other, they may send data back and forth in different character sets. The server will translate as needed:

- The server assumes the client is sending statements in the character set specified by character_set_client.
- After the server receives a statement from the client, it translates it into the character set specified by character_set_connection. It also uses this setting to determine how to convert numbers into strings.
- When the server returns results or error messages back to the client, it translates them into character_set_result.

Figure 5-5 illustrates this process.

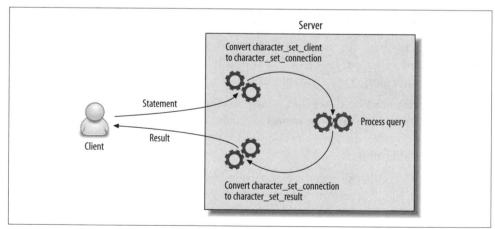

Figure 5-5. Client and server character sets

You can use the SET NAMES statement and/or the SET CHARACTER SET statement to change these three settings as needed. However, note that this command affects *only the server's settings.* The client program and the client API also need to be set correctly to avoid communication problems with the server.

Suppose you open a client connection with latin1 (the default character set, unless you've used `mysql_options()` to change it) and then use `SET NAMES utf8` to tell the server to assume the client is sending data in UTF-8. You've created a character set mismatch, which can cause errors and even security problems. You should set the client's character set and use `mysql_real_escape_string()` when escaping values. In PHP, you can change the client's character set with `mysql_set_charset()`.

How MySQL compares values

When MySQL compares two values with different character sets, it must convert them to the same character set for the comparison. If the character sets aren't compatible, this can cause an error, such as "ERROR 1267 (HY000): Illegal mix of collations." In this case, you'll generally need to use the `CONVERT()` function explicitly to force one of the values into a character set that's compatible with the other. MySQL 5.0 and newer often do this conversion implicitly, so this error is more common in MySQL 4.1.

MySQL also assigns a *coercibility* to values. This determines the priority of a value's character set and influences which value MySQL will convert implicitly. You can use the `CHARSET()`, `COLLATION()`, and `COERCIBILITY()` functions to help debug errors related to character sets and collations.

You can use *introducers* and *collate clauses* to specify the character set and/or collation for literal values in your SQL statements. For example:

```
mysql> SELECT _utf8 'hello world' COLLATE utf8_bin;
+--------------------------------------+
| _utf8 'hello world' COLLATE utf8_bin |
+--------------------------------------+
| hello world                          |
+--------------------------------------+
```

Special-case behaviors

MySQL's character set behavior holds a few surprises. Here are some things you should watch out for:

The magical `character_set_database` *setting*
> The `character_set_database` setting defaults to the default database's setting. As you change your default database, it will change too. If you connect to the server without a default database, it defaults to `character_set_server`.

`LOAD DATA INFILE`
> `LOAD DATA INFILE` interprets incoming data according to the current setting of `character_set_database`. Some versions of MySQL accept an optional `CHARACTER SET` clause in the `LOAD DATA INFILE` statement, but you shouldn't rely on this.

We've found that the best way to get reliable results is to USE the desired database, execute SET NAMES to select a character set, and only then load the data. MySQL interprets all the loaded data as having the same character set, regardless of the character sets specified for the destination columns.

SELECT INTO OUTFILE

MySQL writes all data from SELECT INTO OUTFILE without converting it. There is currently no way to specify a character set for the data without wrapping each column in a CONVERT( ) function.

Embedded escape sequences

MySQL interprets escape sequences in statements according to character_set_client, even when there's an introducer or collate clause. This is because the parser interprets the escape sequences in literal values. The parser is not collation-aware—as far as it is concerned, an introducer isn't an instruction, it's just a token.

Choosing a Character Set and Collation

MySQL 4.1 and later support a large range of character sets and collations, including support for multibyte characters with the UTF-8 encoding of the Unicode character set (MySQL supports a three-byte subset of full UTF-8 that can store most characters in most languages). You can see the supported character sets with the SHOW CHARACTER SET and SHOW COLLATION commands.

The most common choices for collations are whether letters should sort in a case sensitive or case insensitive manner, or according to the encoding's binary value. The collation names generally end with _cs, _ci, or _bin, so you can tell which is which easily.

When you specify a character set explicitly, you don't have to name both a character set and a collation. If you omit one or both, MySQL fills in the missing pieces from the applicable default. Table 5-2 shows how MySQL decides which character set and collation to use.

Table 5-2. How MySQL determines character set and collation defaults

If you specify	Resulting character set	Resulting collation
Both character set and collation	As specified	As specified
Character set only	As specified	Character set's default collation
Collation only	Character set to which collation belongs	As specified
Neither	Applicable default	Applicable default

The following commands show how to create a database, table, and column with explicitly specified character sets and collations:

```
CREATE DATABASE d CHARSET latin1;
CREATE TABLE d.t(
    col1 CHAR(1),
    col2 CHAR(1) CHARSET utf8,
    col3 CHAR(1) COLLATE latin1_bin
) DEFAULT CHARSET=cp1251;
```

The resulting table's columns have the following collations:

```
mysql> SHOW FULL COLUMNS FROM d.t;
+-------+---------+-------------------+
| Field | Type    | Collation         |
+-------+---------+-------------------+
| col1  | char(1) | cp1251_general_ci |
| col2  | char(1) | utf8_general_ci   |
| col3  | char(1) | latin1_bin        |
+-------+---------+-------------------+
```

Keep It Simple

A mixture of character sets in your database can be a real mess. Incompatible character sets tend to be terribly confusing. They may even work fine until certain characters appear in your data, at which point, you'll start getting problems in all sorts of operations (such as joins between tables). You can solve the errors only by using ALTER TABLE to convert columns to compatible character sets, or casting values to the desired character set with introducers and collate clauses in your SQL statements.

For sanity's sake, it's best to choose sensible defaults on the server level, and perhaps on the database level. Then you can deal with special exceptions on a case-by-case basis, probably at the column level.

How Character Sets and Collations Affect Queries

Some character sets may require more CPU operations, consume more memory and storage space, or even defeat indexing. Therefore, you should choose character sets and collations carefully.

Converting between character sets or collations can add overhead for some operations. For example, the sakila.film table has an index on the title column, which can speed up ORDER BY queries:

```
mysql> EXPLAIN SELECT title, release_year FROM sakila.film ORDER BY title\G
*************************** 1. row ***************************
           id: 1
  select_type: SIMPLE
        table: film
         type: index
possible_keys: NULL
          key: idx_title
```

```
       key_len: 767
           ref: NULL
          rows: 953
         Extra:
```

However, the server can use the index for sorting only if it's sorted by the same collation as the one the query specifies. The index is sorted by the column's collation, which in this case is utf8_general_ci. If you want the results ordered by another collation, the server will have to do a filesort:

```
mysql> EXPLAIN SELECT title, release_year
    -> FROM sakila.film ORDER BY title COLLATE utf8_bin\G
*************************** 1. row ***************************
           id: 1
  select_type: SIMPLE
        table: film
         type: ALL
possible_keys: NULL
          key: NULL
      key_len: NULL
          ref: NULL
         rows: 953
        Extra: Using filesort
```

In addition to accommodating your connection's default character set and any preferences you specify explicitly in queries, MySQL has to convert character sets so that it can compare them when they're not the same. For example, if you join two tables on character columns that don't have the same character set, MySQL has to convert one of them. This conversion can make it impossible to use an index, because it is just like a function enclosing the column.

The UTF-8 multibyte character set stores each character in a varying number of bytes (between one and three). MySQL uses fixed-size buffers internally for many string operations, so it must allocate enough space to accommodate the maximum possible length. For example, a CHAR(10) encoded with UTF-8 requires 30 bytes to store, even if the actual string contains no so-called wide characters. Variable-length fields (VARCHAR, TEXT) do not suffer from this on disk, but in-memory temporary tables used for processing and sorting queries will always allocate the maximum length needed.

In multibyte character sets a character is no longer the same as a byte. Consequently, MySQL has separate LENGTH( ) and CHAR_LENGTH( ) functions, which don't return the same results on multibyte characters. When you're working with multibyte character sets, be sure to use the CHAR_LENGTH( ) function when you want to count characters (e.g., when you're doing SUBSTRING( ) operations). The same caution holds for multibyte characters in application languages.

Another possible surprise is index limitations. If you index a UTF-8 column, MySQL has to assume each character can take up to three bytes, so the usual length restrictions are suddenly shortened by a factor of three:

```
mysql> CREATE TABLE big_string(str VARCHAR(500), KEY(str)) DEFAULT CHARSET=utf8;
Query OK, 0 rows affected, 1 warning (0.06 sec)
mysql> SHOW WARNINGS;
+---------+------+-------------------------------------------------------------+
| Level   | Code | Message                                                     |
+---------+------+-------------------------------------------------------------+
| Warning | 1071 | Specified key was too long; max key length is 999 bytes     |
+---------+------+-------------------------------------------------------------+
```

Notice that MySQL shortened the index to a 333-character prefix automatically:

```
mysql> SHOW CREATE TABLE big_string\G
*************************** 1. row ***************************
       Table: big_string
Create Table: CREATE TABLE `big_string` (
  `str` varchar(500) default NULL,
  KEY `str` (`str`(333))
) ENGINE=MyISAM DEFAULT CHARSET=utf8
```

If you didn't notice the warning and check the table definition, you might not have spotted that the index was created on only a prefix of the column. This will have side effects such as disabling covering indexes.

Some people recommend that you just use UTF-8 globally to "make your life simpler." However, this is not necessarily a good idea if you care about performance. Many applications don't need to use UTF-8 at all, and depending on your data, UTF-8 can use much more storage space on disk.

When deciding on a character set, it's important to consider the kind of data you will store. For example, if you store mostly English text UTF-8 will add practically no storage penalty, because most characters in the English language fit in one byte in UTF-8. On the other hand, you may see a big difference if you store non-Latin languages such as Russian or Arabic. An application that needs to store *only* Arabic could use the cp1256 character set, which can represent all Arabic characters in one byte. But if the application needs to store many different languages and you choose UTF-8 instead, the very same Arabic characters will use more space. Likewise, if you convert a column from a national character set to UTF-8, you can increase the required storage space dramatically. If you're using InnoDB, you might increase the data size to the point that the values don't fit on the page and require external storage, which can cause a lot of wasted storage space and fragmentation. See "Optimizing for BLOB and TEXT Workloads" on page 298 for more on this topic.

Sometimes you don't need to use a character set at all. Character sets are mostly useful for case insensitive comparison, sorting, and string operations that need to be character-aware, such as SUBSTRING( ). If you don't need the database server to be aware of characters, you can store anything you want in BINARY columns, including UTF-8 data. If you do this, you can also add a column that tells you what character set you used to encode the data. Although this is an approach some people have used for a long time, it does require you to be more careful. It can cause hard-to-catch mistakes, such as errors with SUBSTRING( ) and LENGTH( ), if you forget that a byte is not necessarily a character. We recommend you avoid this practice if possible.

Full-Text Searching

Most of the queries you'll write will probably have WHERE clauses that compare values for equality, filter out ranges of rows, and so on. However, you may also need to perform keyword searches, which are based on relevance instead of comparing values to each other. Full-text search systems are designed for this purpose.

Full-text searches require a special query syntax. They can work with or without indexes, but indexes can speed up the matching. The indexes used for full-text searches have a special structure to help find documents that contain the desired keywords.

You may not know it, but you're already familiar with at least one type of full-text search system: Internet search engines. Although they operate at a massive scale and don't usually have a relational database for a backend, the principles are similar.

In MySQL, only the MyISAM storage engine supports full-text indexing. It lets you search character-based content (CHAR, VARCHAR, and TEXT columns), and it supports both natural-language and Boolean searching. The full-text search implementation has a number of restrictions and limitations[*] and is quite complicated, but it's still widely used because it's included with the server and is adequate for many applications. In this section, we take a general look at how to use it and how to design for performance with full-text searching.

A MyISAM full-text index operates on a *full-text collection*, which is made up of one or more character columns from a single table. In effect, MySQL builds the index by concatenating the columns in the collection and indexing them as one long string of text.

A MyISAM full-text index is a special type of B-Tree index with two levels. The first level holds keywords. Then, for each keyword, the second level holds a list of associated *document pointers* that point to full-text collections that contain that keyword. The index doesn't contain every word in the collection. It prunes it as follows:

- A list of *stopwords* weeds out "noise" words by preventing them from being indexed. The stopword list is based on common English usage by default, but you can use the ft_stopword_file option to replace it with a list from an external file.

- The index ignores words unless they're longer than ft_min_word_len characters and shorter than ft_max_word_len characters.

---

[*] You may find that MySQL's full-text limitations make it impractical or impossible to use for your application. We discuss using Sphinx as an external full-text search engine in Appendix C.

Full-text indexes don't store information about which column in the collection a keyword occurs in, so if you need to search on different combinations of columns, you will need to create several indexes.

This also means you can't instruct a MATCH AGAINST clause to regard words from a particular column as more important than words from other columns. This is a common requirement when building search engines for web sites. For example, you might want search results to appear first when the keywords appear in an item's title. If you need this, you'll have to write more complicated queries. (We show an example later.)

Natural-Language Full-Text Searches

A natural-language search query determines each document's relevance to the query. Relevance is based on the number of matched words and the frequency with which they occur in the document. Words that are less common in the entire index make a match more relevant. In contrast, extremely common words aren't worth searching for at all. A natural-language full-text search excludes words that exist in more than 50% of the rows in the table, even if they're not in the stopword list.[*]

The syntax of a full-text search is a little different from other types of queries. You tell MySQL to do full-text matching with MATCH AGAINST in the WHERE clause. Let's look at an example. In the standard Sakila sample database, the film_text table has a full-text index on the title and description columns:

```
mysql> SHOW INDEX FROM sakila.film_text;
+-----------+----------------------+-------------+------------+
| Table     | Key_name             | Column_name | Index_type |
+-----------+----------------------+-------------+------------+
| ...
| film_text | idx_title_description | title       | FULLTEXT   |
| film_text | idx_title_description | description | FULLTEXT   |
+-----------+----------------------+-------------+------------+
```

Here's an example natural-language full-text search query:

```
mysql> SELECT film_id, title, RIGHT(description, 25),
    ->     MATCH(title, description) AGAINST('factory casualties') AS relevance
    -> FROM sakila.film_text
    -> WHERE MATCH(title, description) AGAINST('factory casualties');
+---------+---------------------+---------------------------+----------------+
| film_id | title               | RIGHT(description, 25)    | relevance      |
+---------+---------------------+---------------------------+----------------+
|     831 | SPIRITED CASUALTIES | a Car in A Baloon Factory | 8.4692449569702 |
|     126 | CASUALTIES ENCINO   | Face a Boy in A Monastery | 5.2615661621094 |
|     193 | CROSSROADS CASUALTIES | a Composer in The Outback | 5.2072987556458 |
|     369 | GOODFELLAS SALUTE   | d Cow in A Baloon Factory | 3.1522686481476 |
|     451 | IGBY MAKER          | a Dog in A Baloon Factory | 3.1522686481476 |
```

---

[*] A common mistake during testing is to put a few rows of sample data into a full-text search index, only to find that no queries match. The problem is that every word appears in more than half the rows.

MySQL performed the full-text search by breaking the search string into words and matching each of them against the title and description fields, which are combined in the full-text collection upon which the index is built. Notice that only one of the results contains both words, and that the three results that contain "casualties" (there are only three in the entire table) are listed first. That's because the index sorts the results by decreasing relevance.

 Unlike normal queries, the full-text search results are automatically ordered by relevance. MySQL cannot use an index for sorting when you perform a full-text search. Therefore, you shouldn't specify an ORDER BY clause if you want to avoid a filesort.

The MATCH( ) function actually returns the relevance as a floating-point number, as you can see from our example. You can use this to filter by relevance or to present the relevance in a user interface. There is no extra overhead from specifying the MATCH( ) function twice; MySQL recognizes they are the same and does the operation only once. However, if you put the MATCH( ) function in an ORDER BY clause, MySQL will use a filesort to order the results.

You have to specify the columns in the MATCH( ) clause exactly as they're specified in a full-text index, or MySQL can't use the index. This is because the index doesn't record in which column a keyword appeared.

This also means you can't use a full-text search to specify that a keyword should appear in a particular column of the index, as we mentioned previously. However, there's a workaround: you can do custom sorting with several full-text indexes on different combinations of columns to compute the desired ranking. Suppose we want the title column to be more important. We can add another index on this column, as follows:

```
mysql> ALTER TABLE film_text ADD FULLTEXT KEY(title) ;
```

Now we can make the title twice as important for purposes of ranking:

```
mysql> SELECT film_id, title, RIGHT(description, 25),
    -> ROUND(MATCH(title, description) AGAINST('factory casualties'), 3)
    ->     AS full_rel,
    -> ROUND(MATCH(title) AGAINST('factory casualties'), 3) AS title_rel
    -> FROM sakila.film_text
    -> WHERE MATCH(title, description) AGAINST('factory casualties')
    -> ORDER BY (2 * MATCH(title) AGAINST('factory casualties'))
    ->     + MATCH(title, description) AGAINST('factory casualties') DESC;
```

title	RIGHT(description, 25)	full_rel	title_rel
831	a Car in A Baloon Factory	8.469	5.676
126	Face a Boy in A Monastery	5.262	5.676
299	jack in The Sahara Desert	3.056	6.751
193	a Composer in The Outback	5.207	5.676

```
|     369 | d Cow in A Baloon Factory |  3.152 |   0.000 |
|     451 | a Dog in A Baloon Factory |  3.152 |   0.000 |
|     595 | a Cat in A Baloon Factory |  3.152 |   0.000 |
|     649 | nizer in A Baloon Factory |  3.152 |   0.000 |
```

However, this is usually an inefficient approach, because it causes filesorts.

Boolean Full-Text Searches

In Boolean searches, the query itself specifies the relative relevance of each word in a match. Boolean searches use the stopword list to filter out noise words, but the requirement that words be longer than ft_min_word_len characters and shorter than ft_max_word_len characters is disabled. The results are unsorted.

When constructing a Boolean search query, you can use prefixes to modify the relative ranking of each keyword in the search string. The most commonly used modifiers are shown in Table 5-3.

Table 5-3. Common modifiers for Boolean full-text searches

Example	Meaning
dinosaur	Rows containing "dinosaur" rank higher.
~dinosaur	Rows containing "dinosaur" rank lower.
+dinosaur	Rows *must* contain "dinosaur".
-dinosaur	Rows *must not* contain "dinosaur".
dino*	Rows containing words that begin with "dino" rank higher.

You can also use other operators, such as parentheses for grouping. You can construct complex searches in this way.

As an example, let's again search the sakila.film_text table for films that contain both "factory" and "casualties." A natural-language search returns results that match either or both of these terms, as we saw before. If we use a Boolean search, however, we can insist that both must appear:

```
mysql> SELECT film_id, title, RIGHT(description, 25)
    -> FROM sakila.film_text
    -> WHERE MATCH(title, description)
    ->    AGAINST('+factory +casualties' IN BOOLEAN MODE);
+---------+-------------------+---------------------------+
| film_id | title             | right(description, 25)    |
+---------+-------------------+---------------------------+
|     831 | SPIRITED CASUALTIES | a Car in A Baloon Factory |
+---------+-------------------+---------------------------+
```

You can also do a *phrase search* by quoting multiple words, which requires them to appear exactly as specified:

```
mysql> SELECT film_id, title, RIGHT(description, 25)
    -> FROM sakila.film_text
    -> WHERE MATCH(title, description)
    ->    AGAINST('"spirited casualties"' IN BOOLEAN MODE);
+---------+-------------------+---------------------------+
| film_id | title             | right(description, 25)    |
+---------+-------------------+---------------------------+
|     831 | SPIRITED CASUALTIES | a Car in A Baloon Factory |
+---------+-------------------+---------------------------+
```

Phrase searches tend to be quite slow. The full-text index alone can't answer a query like this one, because it doesn't record where words are located relative to each other in the original full-text collection. Consequently, the server actually has to look inside the rows to do a phrase search.

To execute such a search, the server will find all documents that contain both "spirited" and "casualties." It will then fetch the rows from which the documents were built, and check for the exact phrase in the collection. Because it uses the full-text index to find the initial list of documents that match, you might think this will be very fast—much faster than an equivalent LIKE operation. In fact, it *is* very fast, as long as the words in the phrase aren't common and not many results are returned from the full-text index to the Boolean matcher. If the words in the phrase *are* common, LIKE can actually be much faster, because it fetches rows sequentially instead of in quasirandom index order, and it doesn't need to read a full-text index.

A Boolean full-text search doesn't actually require a full-text index to work. It will use a full-text index if there is one, but if there isn't, it will just scan the entire table. You can even use a Boolean full-text search on columns from multiple tables, such as the results of a join. In all of these cases, though, it will be slow.

Full-Text Changes in MySQL 5.1 and Beyond

MySQL 5.1 introduced quite a few changes related to full-text searching. These include performance improvements and the ability to build pluggable parsers that can enhance the built-in capabilities. For example, plug-ins can change the way indexing works. They can split text into words more flexibly than the defaults (you can specify that "C++" is a single word, for example), do preprocessing, index different content types (such as PDF), or do custom word stemming. The plug-ins can also influence the way searches work—for example, by stemming search terms.

InnoDB developers are currently working on support for full-text indexing, but we don't know when it will be available.

Full-Text Tradeoffs and Workarounds

MySQL's implementation of full-text searching has several design limitations. These can be contradictions for specific purposes, but there are also many ways to work around them.

For example, there is only one form of relevance ranking in MySQL's full-text indexing: frequency. The index doesn't record the indexed word's position in the string, so proximity doesn't contribute to relevance. Although that's fine for many purposes—especially for small amounts of data—it might not be what you need, and MySQL's full-text indexing doesn't give you the flexibility to choose a different ranking algorithm. (It doesn't even store the data you'd need for proximity-based ranking.)

Size is another issue. MySQL's full-text indexing performs well when the index fits in memory, but if the index is not in memory, it can be very slow, especially when the fields are large. When you're using phrase searches, the data and indexes must both fit in memory for good performance. Compared to other index types, it can be very expensive to insert, update, or delete rows in a full-text index:

- Modifying a piece of text with 100 words requires not 1 but up to 100 index operations.
- The field length doesn't usually affect other index types much, but with full-text indexing, text with 3 words and text with 10,000 words will have performance profiles that differ by orders of magnitude.
- Full-text search indexes are also much more prone to fragmentation, and you may find you need to use OPTIMIZE TABLE more frequently.

Full-text indexes affect how the server optimizes queries, too. Index choice, WHERE clauses, and ORDER BY all work differently from how you might expect:

- If there's a full-text index and the query has a MATCH AGAINST clause that can use it, MySQL will use the full-text index to process the query. It will not compare the full-text index to the other indexes that might be used for the query. Some of these other indexes might actually be better for the query, but MySQL will not consider them.
- The full-text search index can perform only full-text matches. Any other criteria in the query, such as WHERE clauses, must be applied after MySQL reads the row from the table. This is different from the behavior of other types of indexes, which can be used to check several parts of a WHERE clause at once.
- Full-text indexes don't store the actual text they index. Thus, you can never use a full-text index as a covering index.
- Full-text indexes cannot be used for any type of sorting, other than sorting by relevance in natural-language mode. If you need to sort by something other than relevance, MySQL will use a filesort.

Let's see how these constraints affect queries. Suppose you have a million documents, with an ordinary index on the document's author and a full-text index on the content. You want to do a full-text search on the document content, but only for author 123. You might write the query as follows:

```
... WHERE MATCH(content) AGAINST ('High Performance MySQL')
    AND author = 123;
```

However, this query will be very inefficient. MySQL will search all one million documents first, because it prefers the full-text index. It will then apply the WHERE clause to restrict the results to the given author, but this filtering operation won't be able to use the index on the author.

One workaround is to include the author IDs in the full-text index. You can choose a prefix that's very unlikely to appear in the text, then append the author's ID to it, and include this "word" in a filters column that's maintained separately (perhaps by a trigger).

You can then extend the full-text index to include the filters column and rewrite the query as follows:

```
... WHERE MATCH(content, filters)
    AGAINST ('High Performance MySQL +author_id_123' IN BOOLEAN MODE);
```

This may be more efficient if the author ID is very selective, because MySQL will be able to narrow the list of documents very quickly by searching the full-text index for "author_id_123." If it's not selective, though, the performance might be worse. Be careful with this approach.

Sometimes you can use full-text indexes for bounding-box searches. For instance, if you want to restrict searches to a range of coordinates (for geographically constrained searches), you can encode the coordinates into the full-text collection. Suppose the coordinates for a given row are X=123 and Y=456. You can interleave the coordinates with the most significant digits first, as in XY142536, and place them in a column that is included in the full-text index. Now if you want to limit searches to, for example, a rectangle bounded by X between 100 and 199 and Y between 400 and 499, you can add "+XY14*" to the search query. This can be much faster than filtering with a WHERE clause.

A technique that sometimes works well with full-text indexes, especially for paginated displays, is to select a list of primary keys by a full-text query and cache the results. When the application is ready to render some results, it can issue another query that fetches the desired rows by their IDs. This second query can include more complicated criteria or joins that need to use other indexes to work well.

Even though only MyISAM supports full-text indexes, if you need to use InnoDB or another storage engine instead, don't worry: you can have your cake and eat it too. A common method is to replicate your tables to a slave whose tables use the MyISAM storage engine, then use the slave to serve full-text queries. If you don't want to serve some queries from a different server, you can partition a table vertically by breaking it into two, keeping textual columns separate from the rest of the data.

You can also duplicate some columns into a table that's full-text indexed. You can see this strategy in action in the sakila.film_text table, which is maintained with triggers. Yet another alternative is to use an external full-text engine, such as Lucene or Sphinx. You can read more about Sphinx in Appendix C.

GROUP BY queries with full-text searches can be performance killers, again because the full-text query typically finds a lot of matches; these cause random disk I/O, followed by a temporary table or filesort for the grouping. Because such queries are often just looking for the top items per group, a good optimization is to sample the results instead of trying for complete accuracy. For example, select the first 1,000 rows into a temporary table, then return the top result per group from that.

Full-Text Tuning and Optimization

Regular maintenance of your full-text indexes is one of the most important things you can do to enhance performance. The double-B-Tree structure of full-text indexes, combined with the large number of keywords in typical documents, means they suffer from fragmentation much more than normal indexes. Use OPTIMIZE TABLE frequently to defragment the indexes. If your server is I/O-bound, it may be much faster to just drop and recreate the full-text indexes periodically.

A server that must perform well for full-text searches needs key buffers that are large enough to hold the full-text indexes, because they work much better when they're in memory. You can use dedicated key buffers to make sure other indexes don't flush your full-text indexes from the key buffer. See "The MyISAM Key Cache" on page 274 for more details on MyISAM key buffers.

It's also important to provide a good stopword list. The defaults will work well for English prose, but they may not be good for other languages or for specialized texts, such as technical documents. For example, if you're indexing a document about MySQL, you might want "mysql" to be a stopword, because it's too common to be helpful.

You can often improve performance by skipping short words. The length is configurable with the ft_min_word_len parameter. Increasing the default value will skip more words, making your index smaller and faster, but less accurate. Also bear in mind that for special purposes, you might need very short words. For example, a full-text search of consumer electronics products for the query "cd player" is likely to produce lots of irrelevant results unless short words are allowed in the index. A user searching for "cd player" won't want to see MP3 and DVD players in the results, but if the minimum word length is the default four characters, the search will actually be for just "player," so all types of players will be returned.

The stopword list and the minimum word length can improve search speeds by keeping some words out of the index, but the search quality can suffer as a result. The right balance is application-dependent. If you need good performance and good quality results, you'll have to customize both parameters for your application. It's a good idea to build in some logging and then investigate common searches, uncommon searches, searches that don't return results, and searches that return a lot of results. You can gain insight about your users and your searchable content this way, and then use that insight to improve performance and the quality of your search results.

 Be aware that if you change the minimum word length, you'll have to rebuild the index with OPTIMIZE TABLE for the change to take effect. A related parameter is ft_max_word_len, which is mainly a safeguard to avoid indexing very long keywords.

If you're importing a lot of data into a server and you want full-text indexing on some columns, disable the full-text indexes before the import with DISABLE KEYS and enable them afterward with ENABLE KEYS. This is usually much faster because of the high cost of updating the index for each row inserted, and you'll get a defragmented index as a bonus.

For large datasets, you might need to manually partition the data across many nodes and search them in parallel. This is a difficult task, and you might be better off using an external full-text search engine, such as Lucene or Sphinx. Our experience shows they can have orders of magnitude better performance.

Foreign Key Constraints

InnoDB is currently the main storage engine that supports foreign keys in MySQL, limiting your choice of storage engines if you require them.[*] MySQL AB has promised that the server itself will someday provide storage engine-independent foreign keys, but at present it looks like InnoDB will be the main engine with foreign key support for some time to come. We therefore focus on foreign keys in InnoDB.

Foreign keys aren't free. They typically require the server to do a lookup in another table every time you change some data. Although InnoDB requires an index to make this operation faster, this doesn't eliminate the impact of these checks. It can even result in a very large index with virtually zero selectivity. For example, suppose you have a status column in a huge table and you want to constrain the status to valid values, but there are only three such values. The extra index required can add

[*] PBXT supports them, too.

significantly to the table's total size—even if the column itself is small, and especially if the primary key is large—and is useless for anything but the foreign key checks.

Still, foreign keys can actually improve performance in some cases. If you must guarantee that two related tables have consistent data, it can be more efficient to let the server perform this check than to do it in your application. Foreign keys are also useful for cascading deletes or updates, although they do operate row by row, so they're slower than multitable deletes or batch operations.

Foreign keys cause your query to "reach into" other tables, which means acquiring locks. If you insert a row into a child table, for example, the foreign key constraint will cause InnoDB to check for a corresponding value in the parent. It must also lock the row in the parent, to ensure it doesn't get deleted before the transaction completes. This can cause unexpected lock waits and even deadlocks on tables you're not touching directly. Such problems can be very unintuitive and frustrating to debug.

You can sometimes use triggers instead of foreign keys. Foreign keys tend to outperform triggers for tasks such as cascading updates, but a foreign key that's just used as a constraint, as in our status example, can be more efficiently rewritten as a trigger with an explicit list of allowable values. (You can also just use an ENUM data type.)

Instead of using foreign keys as constraints, it's often a good idea to constrain the values in the application.

Merge Tables and Partitioning

Merge tables and partitioning are related concepts, and the difference can be confusing. *Merge tables* are a MySQL feature that combines multiple MyISAM tables into a single "virtual table," much like a view that does a UNION over the tables. You create a merge table with the Merge storage engine. A merge table is not really a table *per se*; it's more like a container for similarly defined tables.

In contrast, *partitioned tables* appear to be normal tables with special sets of instructions that tell MySQL where to physically store the rows. The dirty little secret is that the storage code for partitioned tables is a lot like the code for merge tables! In fact, at a low level, each partition is just a separate table with its own separate indexes, and the partitioned table is a wrapper around a collection of Handler objects. A partitioned table looks and acts like a single table, but under the hood it's a bunch of separate tables. However, there's no way to access the underlying tables directly, which you can do with merge tables.

Partitioning is a new feature in MySQL 5.1, but merge tables have been around a long time. Both features share some of the same benefits. They enable you to do the following:

- Separate static and changing data
- Use the physical proximity of related data to optimize queries

- Design your tables so queries access less data
- Maintain very large data volumes more easily (this is one area where merge tables have some advantages over partitioned tables)

Because MySQL's implementations of partitioning and merge tables have a lot in common, they share some limitations, too. For example, there are practical limits on how many underlying tables or partitions you can have in a single merge or partitioned table. In most cases, a few hundred is the point at which you're likely to begin seeing inefficiencies. We mention each system's limitations as we explore them in more detail.

Merge Tables

You can think of merge tables as an older, more limited version of partitioning if you wish, but they are useful in their own right and even provide some features you can't get with partitions.

The merge table is really just a container that holds the real tables. You specify which tables to include with a special UNION syntax to CREATE TABLE. Here's an example that demonstrates many aspects of merge tables:

```
mysql> CREATE TABLE t1(a INT NOT NULL PRIMARY KEY)ENGINE=MyISAM;
mysql> CREATE TABLE t2(a INT NOT NULL PRIMARY KEY)ENGINE=MyISAM;
mysql> INSERT INTO t1(a) VALUES(1),(2);
mysql> INSERT INTO t2(a) VALUES(1),(2);
mysql> CREATE TABLE mrg(a INT NOT NULL PRIMARY KEY)
    -> ENGINE=MERGE UNION=(t1, t2) INSERT_METHOD=LAST;
mysql> SELECT a FROM mrg;
+------+
| a    |
+------+
|    1 |
|    1 |
|    2 |
|    2 |
+------+
```

Notice that the underlying tables have exactly the same number and types of columns, and that all indexes that exist on the merge table also exist on the underlying tables. These are requirements when creating a merge table. Notice also that there's a primary key on the sole column of each table, yet the resulting merge table has duplicate rows. This is one of the limitations of merge tables: each table inside the merge behaves normally, but the merge table doesn't enforce constraints over the entire set of tables.

The INSERT_METHOD=LAST instruction to the table tells MySQL to send all INSERT statements to the last table in the merge. Specifying FIRST or LAST is the only control you have over where rows inserted into the merge table are placed (you can still insert into the underlying tables directly, though). Partitioned tables give more control over where data is stored.

The results of an INSERT are visible in both the merge table and the underlying table:

```
mysql> INSERT INTO mrg(a) VALUES(3);
mysql> SELECT a FROM t2;
+---+
| a |
+---+
| 1 |
| 2 |
| 3 |
+---+
```

Merge tables have some other interesting features and limitations, such as what happens when you drop a merge table or one of its underlying tables. Dropping a merge table leaves its "child" tables untouched, but dropping one of the child tables has a different effect, which is operating system-specific. On GNU/Linux, for example, the underlying table's file descriptor stays open and the table continues to exist, but only via the merge table:

```
mysql> DROP TABLE t1, t2;
mysql> SELECT a FROM mrg;
+------+
| a    |
+------+
|    1 |
|    1 |
|    2 |
|    2 |
|    3 |
+------+
```

A variety of other limitations and special behaviors exist. We'll let you read the manual for the details, but we'll just note that REPLACE doesn't work at all on a merge table, and AUTO_INCREMENT won't work as you might expect.

Merge table performance impacts

The way MySQL implements merge tables has some important performance implications. As with any other MySQL feature, this makes them better suited for some uses than others. Here are some aspects of merge tables you should keep in mind:

- A merge table requires more open file descriptors than a non-merge table containing the same data. Even though a merge table looks like a single table, it actually opens the underlying tables separately. As a result, a single table cache entry can create many file descriptors. Therefore, even if you have configured the table cache to protect your server against exceeding the operating system's per-process file-descriptor limits, merge tables can cause you to exceed that limit anyway.

- The CREATE statement that creates a merge table doesn't check that the underlying tables are compatible. If the underlying tables are defined slightly differently, MySQL may create a merge table that it can't use later. Also, if you alter one of the underlying tables after creating a valid merge table, it will stop working and you'll see this error: "ERROR 1168 (HY000): Unable to open underlying table which is differently defined or of non-MyISAM type or doesn't exist."

- Queries that access a merge table access every underlying table. This can make single-row key lookups relatively slow, compared to a lookup in a single table. Therefore, it's a good idea to limit the number of underlying tables in a merge table, especially if it is the second or later table in a join. The less data you access with each operation, the more important the cost of accessing each table becomes, relative to the entire operation. Here are a few things to keep in mind when planning how to use merge tables:

  - Range lookups are less affected by the overhead of accessing all the underlying tables than individual item lookups.

  - Table scans are just as fast on merge tables as they are on normal tables.

  - Unique key and primary key lookups stop as soon as they succeed. In this case, the server accesses the underlying merge tables one at a time until the lookup finds a value, and then it accesses no further tables.

  - The underlying tables are read in the order specified in the CREATE TABLE statement. If you frequently need data in a specific order, you can exploit this to make the merge-sorting operation faster.

Merge table strengths

Merge tables excel for data that naturally has an active and an inactive part. The classic example is logging. Logs are append-only, so you can use a scheme such as a table per day. Each day you can create a new underlying table and alter the merge table to include it. You can also remove the preceding day's table from the merge table, convert it to compressed MyISAM, and then add it back.

That's not the only use for merge tables, though. They're used frequently in data warehousing applications, because another strength is the way they help manage huge volumes of data. It's practically impossible to manage a single table with terabytes of data, but the task is much easier if it's just a merged collection of 50 GB tables.

When you're managing extremely large databases, you don't just have to think about ordinary operations; you have to plan for crash and recovery scenarios, too. Keeping tables small is a very good idea, if you can do it. It's much faster to check and repair a collection of small tables than one huge one, especially if the huge table doesn't fit in memory. You can also parallelize checking and repairing when you have multiple tables.

Another concern in data warehousing is how to purge old data. Using DELETE to remove rows from a huge table is inefficient at best and disastrous at worst, but it's very simple to alter a merge table's definition and use DROP TABLE to get rid of old data. You can automate this easily.

Merge tables aren't just useful for logging and for huge datasets. They're also very handy for creating on-the-fly tables as needed. Creating and dropping merge tables is cheap, so you can use them as you'd use views with UNION ALL; however, the overhead is lower because the server doesn't spool the results into a temporary table before sending them to the client. This makes them very useful for reporting and data warehousing needs. For example, you can create a nightly job that merges yesterday's data with data from 8 days ago, 15 days ago, and so on for week-over-week reporting queries. This will enable your regular reporting queries to run without modification and automatically access the appropriate data. You can even create temporary merge tables—something you cannot do with views.

Because merge tables don't hide the underlying MyISAM tables, they offer some features that partitions don't:

- A MyISAM table can be a member of many merge tables.
- You can copy underlying tables between servers by copying the *.frm*, *.MYI*, and *.MYD* files.
- You can add more tables to a merge collection easily; just create a new table and alter the merge definition.
- You can create temporary merge tables that include only the data you want, such as data from a specific time period, which you can't do with partitions.
- You can remove a table from the merge if you want to back it up, restore it, alter it, repair it, or perform other operations on it. You can then add it back when you're done.
- You can use *myisampack* to compress some or all of the underlying tables.

In contrast, a partitioned table's partitions are hidden by the MySQL server and are accessible only through the partitioned table.

Partitioned Tables

MySQL's partitioning implementation looks much like its merge table implementation under the hood. However, it is tightly integrated into the server, and it has one crucial difference from merge tables: any given row of data is eligible to be stored in one and only one of the partitions. The table's definition specifies which rows map to which partitions, based on a *partitioning function*, which we explain more later. This means primary keys and unique keys work as expected over the whole table, and the MySQL query optimizer can optimize queries against partitioned tables more intelligently than with merge tables.

Here are some important benefits of partitioned tables:

- You can specify that certain rows are stored together in one partition, which can reduce the amount of data the server has to examine and make queries faster. For example, if you partition by date range and then query on a date range that accesses only one partition, the server will read only that partition.

- Partitioned data is easier to maintain than non-partitioned data, and it's easier to discard old data by dropping an entire partition.

- Partitioned data can be distributed physically, enabling the server to use multiple hard drives more efficiently.

MySQL's implementation of partitioning is still in flux, and it's too complicated to explore in full detail here. We want to concentrate on its performance implications, so we recommend that for the basics you turn to the MySQL manual, which has a lot of material on partitioning. You should read the entire partitioning chapter, and look at the sections on `CREATE TABLE`, `SHOW CREATE TABLE`, `ALTER TABLE`, the `INFORMATION_SCHEMA.PARTITIONS` table, and `EXPLAIN`. Partitioning has made the `CREATE TABLE` and `ALTER TABLE` commands much more complex.

Like a merge table, a partitioned table actually consists of a collection of separate tables (the partitions) with separate indexes on the storage engine level. This means that a partitioned table's memory and file descriptor requirements are similar to those of a merge table. However, the partitions cannot be accessed independently from the table, and each partition can belong to only one table.

As stated earlier, MySQL uses a partitioning function to decide which rows are stored in which partitions. The function must return a nonconstant, deterministic integer. There are several kinds of partitioning. *Range* partitioning sets up a range of values for each partition, then assigns rows to partitions on the basis of the ranges into which they fall. MySQL also supports *key*, *hash*, and *list* partitioning methods. Each type has its strengths and weaknesses, and there are limitations to some of the types, especially when dealing with primary keys.

Why partitioning works

The key to designing partitioned tables in MySQL is to think of partitioning as a coarse-grained type of indexing. Suppose you have a table with a billion rows of historical per-day, per-item sales data, and each row is fairly large—say, 500 bytes. You insert new rows, but you never update existing rows, and you mostly run queries that examine ranges of dates. The main problem with running queries against this table is that it's huge: it will be nearly half a terabyte without any indexes at all, unless you compress the data.

One approach to speeding up the per-day queries could be to add a primary key on (day, itemno) and use InnoDB. This will group each day's data together physically, so the range queries will have to examine less data. Alternatively, you could use MyISAM and insert the rows in the desired order, so an index scan won't cause a lot of random I/O.

Another option would be to omit the primary key and partition the data by day. Each query that accesses ranges of days will have to scan entire partitions, but that could be much better than doing index lookups in such a huge table. The partitioning is a little like an index: it tells MySQL approximately where to find a given row, if you know the day. However, it uses virtually no disk space or memory, precisely because the partitioning doesn't point exactly to the row (as an index does).

Don't be tempted to try to add a primary key *and* partition the table, though—you might actually decrease performance, especially if you run queries that need to access all partitions. When considering partitioning, you should benchmark carefully, because partitioned tables don't always improve performance.

Partitioning examples

We give two brief examples where partitioning is helpful. First, let's see how to design a partitioned table to store date-based data. Suppose you have aggregated performance statistics for orders and sales by product. Because you frequently run queries on ranges of dates, you place the order date first in the primary key and use the InnoDB storage engine to cluster the data by date. You can now "cluster" the data at a higher level by partitioning ranges of dates. Here's the basic table definition, without any partitioning specification:

```
CREATE TABLE sales_by_day (
    day DATE NOT NULL,
    product INT NOT NULL,
    sales DECIMAL(10, 2) NOT NULL,
    returns DECIMAL(10, 2) NOT NULL,
    PRIMARY KEY(day, product)
) ENGINE=InnoDB;
```

Partitioning by year is a common way to deal with date-based data, as is partitioning by day. The YEAR( ) and TO_DAYS( ) functions work well as partition functions for these cases. In general, a good function for range partitioning will have a linear relationship to the values by which you want to partition, and these functions match that description. Let's partition by year:

```
mysql> ALTER TABLE sales_by_day
    -> PARTITION BY RANGE(YEAR(day)) (
    ->     PARTITION p_2006 VALUES LESS THAN (2007),
    ->     PARTITION p_2007 VALUES LESS THAN (2008),
    ->     PARTITION p_2008 VALUES LESS THAN (2009),
    ->     PARTITION p_catchall VALUES LESS THAN MAXVALUE );
```

Now when we insert rows they'll be stored in the appropriate partition, depending on the value of the day column:

```
mysql> INSERT INTO sales_by_day(day, product, sales, returns) VALUES
    -> ('2007-01-15', 19, 50.00, 52.00),
    -> ('2008-09-23', 11, 41.00, 42.00);
```

We use this data in an example a bit later. Before we move on, though, we'd like to point out that there's an important limitation here: adding more years later will require altering the table, which will be expensive if the table is big (and we assume it will be, or we wouldn't be using partitions). It might be a good idea to just go ahead and define more years than you think you'll need. Even if you don't use them for a long time, including them up front should not affect performance.

Another common use for partitioned tables is simply to distribute the rows in a large table. For example, suppose you run a large number of queries against a huge table. If you want different physical disks to serve the data while multiple queries are running against the table, you might want MySQL to distribute the rows across the disks. In this case, you don't care about keeping related data close together; you just want to distribute the data evenly without having to think about it. The following will make MySQL distribute the rows by the modulus of the primary key. This is a fine way to spread data uniformly among the partitions:

```
mysql> ALTER TABLE mydb.very_big_table
    -> PARTITION BY KEY(<primary key columns>) (
    ->    PARTITION p0 DATA DIRECTORY='/data/mydb/big_table_p0/',
    ->    PARTITION p1 DATA DIRECTORY='/data/mydb/big_table_p1/');
```

You can achieve the same goal in a different way with a RAID controller. This can sometimes be better: because it is implemented in hardware, it hides the details of how it works, so it doesn't introduce more complexity into your schema and queries. It also may provide better, more uniform performance if your only goal is to distribute your data physically.

Partitioned table limitations

Partitioned tables are not a "silver bullet" solution. Here are some of the limitations in the current implementation:

- At present, all partitions have to use the same storage engine. For example, you cannot compress only some partitions the way you can compress some underlying tables in a merge table.

- Every unique index on a partitioned table must contain the columns referred to by the partition function. As a result, many instructional examples avoid using a primary key. Although it's common for data warehouses to contain tables without primary keys or unique indexes, this is less common in OLTP systems. Consequently, your choices of how to partition your data might be more limited than you'd think at first.

- Although MySQL may be able to avoid accessing all of the partitions in a partitioned table during a query, it still locks all the partitions.

- There are quite a few limitations on the functions and expressions you can use in a partitioning function.
- Some storage engines don't work with partitioning.
- Foreign keys don't work.
- You can't use LOAD INDEX INTO CACHE.

There are many other limitations as well (at least at the time of this writing, when MySQL 5.1 is not yet generally available). Partitioned tables actually provide less flexibility than merge tables in some ways. For example, if you want to add an index to a partitioned table, you can't do it a bit at a time; the ALTER will lock and rebuild the entire table. Merge tables give you more possibilities, such as adding the index one underlying table at a time. Similarly, you can't back up or restore just one partition at a time, which you can do with the underlying tables in a merge table.

Whether a table will benefit from partitioning depends on many factors, and you'll need to benchmark your own application to determine whether it is a good solution for you.

Optimizing queries against partitioned tables

Partitioning introduces new ways to optimize queries (and corresponding pitfalls). The optimizer can use the partitioning function to *prune* partitions, or remove them from a query entirely. It does this by deducing that the desired rows can be found only in certain partitions. Pruning therefore lets queries access much less data than they'd otherwise need to (in the best case).

It's very important to specify the partitioned key in the WHERE clause, even if it's otherwise redundant, so the optimizer can prune unneeded partitions. If you don't do this, the query execution engine will have to access all partitions in the table, just as it does with merge tables, and this can be extremely slow on large tables.

You can use EXPLAIN PARTITIONS to see whether the optimizer is pruning partitions. Let's return to the sample data from before:

```
mysql> EXPLAIN PARTITIONS SELECT * FROM sales_by_day\G
*************************** 1. row ***************************
           id: 1
  select_type: SIMPLE
        table: sales_by_day
   partitions: p_2006,p_2007,p_2008
         type: ALL
possible_keys: NULL
          key: NULL
      key_len: NULL
          ref: NULL
         rows: 3
        Extra:
```

As you can see, the query will access all partitions. Look at the difference when we add a constraint to the WHERE clause:

```
mysql> EXPLAIN PARTITIONS SELECT * FROM sales_by_day WHERE day > '2007-01-01'\G
*************************** 1. row ***************************
          id: 1
 select_type: SIMPLE
       table: sales_by_day
  partitions: p_2007,p_2008
```

The optimizer is quite smart about determining how to prune. It can even convert ranges into lists of discrete values and prune on each item in the list. However, it's not all-knowing. For example, the following WHERE clause is theoretically prunable, but MySQL can't prune it:

```
mysql> EXPLAIN PARTITIONS SELECT * FROM sales_by_day WHERE YEAR(day) = 2007\G
*************************** 1. row ***************************
          id: 1
 select_type: SIMPLE
       table: sales_by_day
  partitions: p_2006,p_2007,p_2008
```

At present, MySQL can prune only on comparisons to the partitioning function's columns. It cannot prune on the result of an expression, even if the expression is the same as the partitioning function. You can convert the query into an equivalent form, though:

```
mysql> EXPLAIN PARTITIONS SELECT * FROM sales_by_day
    -> WHERE day BETWEEN '2007-01-01' AND '2007-12-31'\G
*************************** 1. row ***************************
          id: 1
 select_type: SIMPLE
       table: sales_by_day
  partitions: p_2007
```

Because the WHERE clause now refers directly to the partitioning column, not to an expression, the optimizer can do some very beneficial pruning.

The optimizer is smart enough to prune partitions during query processing, too. For example, if a partitioned table is the second table in a join, and the join condition is the partitioned key, MySQL will search for matching rows only in the relevant partition(s). This is an important difference from merge tables, which will always query all underlying tables in this scenario.

Distributed (XA) Transactions

Whereas storage engine transactions give ACID properties inside the storage engine, a distributed (XA) transaction is a higher-level transaction that can extend some ACID properties outside the storage engine—and even outside the database—with a two-phase commit. MySQL 5.0 and newer have partial support for XA transactions.

An XA transaction requires a transaction coordinator, which asks all participants to prepare to commit (phase one). When the coordinator receives a "ready" from all participants, it tells them all to go ahead and commit. This is phase two. MySQL can act as a participant in XA transactions, but not as a coordinator.

There are actually two kinds of XA transactions in MySQL. The MySQL server can participate in an externally managed distributed transaction, but it also uses XA internally to coordinate storage engines and binary logging.

Internal XA Transactions

The reason for MySQL's internal use of XA transactions is the architectural separation between the server and the storage engines. Storage engines are completely independent from and unaware of each other, so any cross-engine transaction is distributed by nature and requires a third party to coordinate it. That third party is the MySQL server. Were it not for XA transactions, for example, a cross-engine transaction commit would require sequentially asking each engine involved to commit. That would introduce the possibility of a crash after one engine had committed but before another did, which would break the rules of transactions (recall that transactions are supposed to be all-or-nothing operations).

If you consider the binary log to be a "storage engine" for log events, you can see why XA transactions are necessary even when only a single transactional engine is involved. Synchronizing a storage engine commit with "committing" an event to the binary log is a distributed transaction, because the server—not the storage engine—handles the binary log.

XA currently creates a performance dilemma. It has broken InnoDB's support for *group commit* (a technique that can commit several transactions with a single I/O operation) since MySQL 5.0, so it causes many more fsync( ) calls than it should. It also causes each transaction to require a binary log sync if binary logs are enabled and requires two log flushes per commit instead of one. In other words, if you want the binary log to be safely synchronized with your transactions, each transaction will require a total of at least three fsync( ) calls. The only way to prevent this is to disable the binary log and set innodb_support_xa to 0.

These settings are incompatible with replication. Replication requires binary logging and XA support, and in addition—to be as safe as possible—you need sync_binlog set to 1, so the storage engine and the binary log are synchronized. (The XA support is worthless otherwise, because the binary log might not be "committed" to disk.) This is one of the reasons we strongly recommend using a RAID controller with a battery-backed write cache: the cache can speed up the extra fsync( ) calls and restore performance.

The next chapter goes into more detail on how to configure transaction logging and binary logging.

External XA Transactions

MySQL can participate in, but not manage, external distributed transactions. It doesn't support the full XA specification. For example, the XA specification allows connections to be joined in a single transaction, but that's not possible in MySQL at this time.

External XA transactions are even more expensive than internal ones, due to the added latency and the greater likelihood of a participant failing. Using XA over a WAN, or even over the Internet, is a common trap because of unpredictable network performance. It's generally best to avoid XA transactions when there's an unpredictable component, such as a slow network or a user who might not click the "Save" button for a long time. Anything that delays the commit has a heavy cost, because it's causing delays on not just one system, but potentially on many.

You can design high-performance distributed transactions in other ways, though. For instance, you can insert and queue data locally, then distribute it atomically in a much smaller, faster transaction. You can also use MySQL replication to ship data from one place to another. We've found that some applications that use distributed transactions really don't need to use them at all.

That said, XA transactions can be a useful way to synchronize data between servers. This method works well when you can't use replication for some reason, or when the updates are not performance-critical.

Optimizing Server Settings

People often ask, "What's the optimal configuration file for my server with 16 GB of RAM and 100 GB of data?" The truth is, there's no such file. Servers need very different configurations depending on hardware, data size, the types of queries they will run, and the system's requirements—response time, transactional durability and consistency, and so on.

The default configuration is designed not to use a lot of resources, because MySQL is intended to be very versatile, and it does not assume it is the only thing running on the server on which it is installed. By default, this configuration uses just enough resources to start MySQL and run simple queries with a little bit of data. You'll certainly need to customize it if you have more than a few megabytes of data. You can start with one of the sample configuration files included with the MySQL server distribution and tweak it as needed.

You shouldn't expect large performance gains from every configuration change. Depending on your workload, you can usually improve performance two- or three-fold by choosing appropriate values for a handful of configuration settings (exactly which options make this difference depends on a variety of factors). After that, the improvements are incremental. You might notice a particular query that runs slowly and make it better by tweaking a setting or two, but you won't usually make your server perform an order of magnitude better. To get that kind of benefit, you'll generally have to examine your schema, queries, and application architecture.

This chapter begins by showing you how MySQL's configuration options work and how you can change them. We move from that to a discussion of how MySQL uses memory and how to optimize its memory usage. Then we cover I/O and disk storage at a similar level of detail. We follow that with a section on workload-based tuning, which will help you customize MySQL to perform best for your workload. Finally, we provide some notes on tuning variables dynamically for specific queries that need customized settings.

A note on terminology: because many of MySQL's command-line options correspond to server variables, we sometimes use the terms *option* and *variable* interchangeably.

Configuration Basics

This section presents an overview of how to configure MySQL successfully. First we explain how MySQL configuration actually works, then we mention some best practices. MySQL is generally pretty forgiving about its configuration, but following these suggestions might save you a lot of work and time.

The first thing you need to know is where MySQL gets configuration information: from command-line arguments and settings in its configuration file. On Unix-like systems, the configuration file is typically located at */etc/my.cnf* or */etc/mysql/my.cnf*. If you use your operating system's startup scripts, this is typically the only place you'll specify configuration settings. If you start MySQL manually, as you might do when you're running a test installation, you can also specify settings on the command line.

 Most variables have the same names as their corresponding command-line options, but there are a few exceptions. For example, *--memlock* sets the `locked_in_memory` variable.

Any settings you decide to use permanently should go into the global configuration file, instead of being specified at the command line. Otherwise, you risk accidentally starting the server without them. It's also a good idea to keep all of your configuration files in a single place so that you can inspect them easily.

Be sure you know where your server's configuration file is located! We've seen people try unsuccessfully to tune a server with a file it doesn't read, such as */etc/my.cnf* on Debian GNU/Linux servers, which look in */etc/mysql/my.cnf* for their configuration. Sometimes there are files in several places, perhaps because a previous system administrator was confused as well. If you don't know which files your server reads, you can ask it:

```
$ which mysqld
/usr/sbin/mysqld
$ /usr/sbin/mysqld --verbose --help | grep -A 1 'Default options'
Default options are read from the following files in the given order:
/etc/mysql/my.cnf ~/.my.cnf /usr/etc/my.cnf
```

This applies to typical installations, where there's a single server on a host. You can design more complicated configurations, but there's no standard way to do this. The MySQL server distribution includes a program called *mysqlmanager*, which can run multiple instances from a single configuration with separate sections. (This is a replacement for the older *mysqld_multi* script.) However, many operating system distributions don't include or use this program in their startup scripts. In fact, many don't use the MySQL-provided startup script at all.

The configuration file is divided into sections, each of which begins with a line that contains the section name in square brackets. A MySQL program will generally read the section that has the same name as that program, and many client programs also read the client section, which gives you a place to put common settings. The server usually reads the mysqld section. Be sure you place your settings in the correct section in the file, or they will have no effect.

Syntax, Scope, and Dynamism

Configuration settings are written in all lowercase, with words separated by underscores or dashes. The following are equivalent, and you might see both forms in command lines and configuration files:

```
/usr/sbin/mysqld --auto-increment-offset=5
/usr/sbin/mysqld --auto_increment_offset=5
```

We suggest that you pick a style and use it consistently. This makes it a lot easier to search for settings in your files.

Configuration settings can have several scopes. Some settings are server-wide (global scope); others are different for each connection (session scope); and others are per-object. Many session-scoped variables have global equivalents, which you can think of as defaults. If you change the session-scoped variable, it affects only the connection from which you changed it, and the changes are lost when the connection closes. Here are some examples of the variety of behaviors of which you should be aware:

- The query_cache_size variable is globally scoped.
- The sort_buffer_size variable has a global default, but you can set it per-session as well.
- The join_buffer_size variable has a global default and can be set per-session, but a single query that joins several tables can allocate one join buffer *per join*, so there might be several join buffers per query.

In addition to setting variables in the configuration files, you can also change many (but not all) of them while the server is running. MySQL refers to these as *dynamic* configuration variables. The following statements show different ways to change the session and global values of sort_buffer_size dynamically:

```
SET          sort_buffer_size  = <value>;
SET GLOBAL   sort_buffer_size  = <value>;
SET          @@sort_buffer_size := <value>;
```

```
SET @@session.sort_buffer_size := <value>;
SET  @@global.sort_buffer_size := <value>;
```

If you set variables dynamically, be aware that those settings will be lost when MySQL shuts down. If you want to keep the settings, you'll have to update your configuration file as well.

If you set a variable's global value while the server is running , the values for the current session and any other existing sessions are not affected. This is because the session values are initialized from the global value when the connections are created. You should inspect the output of SHOW GLOBAL VARIABLES after each change to make sure it's had the desired effect.

Variables use different kinds of units, and you have to know the correct unit for each variable. For example, the table_cache variable specifies the number of tables that can be cached, not the size of the table cache in bytes. The key_buffer_size is specified in bytes, whereas still other variables may be specified in number of pages or other units, such as percentages.

Many variables can be specified with a suffix, such as 1M for one megabyte. However, this works only in the configuration file or as a command-line argument. When you use the SQL SET command, you must use the literal value 1048576, or an expression such as 1024 * 1024. You can't use expressions in configuration files.

There is also a special value you can assign to variables with the SET command: the keyword DEFAULT. Assigning this value to a session-scoped variable sets that variable to the corresponding globally scoped variable's value; assigning it to a globally scoped variable sets the variable to the compiled-in default (not the value specified in the configuration file). This is useful for resetting session-scoped variables back to the values they had when you opened the connection. We advise you not to use it for global variables, because it probably won't do what you want—that is, it doesn't set the values back to what they were when you started the server.

Side Effects of Setting Variables

Setting variables dynamically can have unexpected side effects, such as flushing dirty blocks from buffers. Be careful which settings you change online, as this can cause the server to do a lot of work.

Sometimes you can infer a variable's behavior from its name. For example, max_heap_table_size does what it sounds like: it specifies the *maximum* size to which implicit in-memory temporary tables are allowed to grow. However, the naming conventions aren't completely consistent, so you can't always guess what a variable will do by looking at its name.

Let's take a look at some important variables and the effects of changing them dynamically:

key_buffer_size

Setting this variable allocates the designated amount of space for key buffer (or key cache) all at once. However, the operating system doesn't actually commit memory to it until it is used. Setting the key buffer size to one gigabyte, for example, doesn't mean you've instantly caused the server to actually commit a gigabyte of memory to it. (We discuss how to watch the server's memory usage in the next chapter.)

MySQL lets you create multiple key caches, as we explain later in this chapter. If you set this variable to 0 for a nondefault key cache, MySQL moves any indexes from the specified cache to the default cache and deletes the specified cache when nothing is using it anymore. Setting this variable for a nonexistent cache creates it.

Setting the variable to a nonzero value for an existing cache will flush the specified cache's memory. This is technically an online operation, but it blocks all operations that try to access the cache until the flush is finished.

table_cache_size

Setting this variable has no immediate effect—the effect is delayed until the next time a thread opens a table. When this happens, MySQL checks the variable's value. If the value is larger than the number of tables in the cache, the thread can insert the newly opened table into the cache. If the value is smaller than the number of tables in the cache, MySQL deletes unused tables from the cache.

thread_cache_size

Setting this variable has no immediate effect—the effect is delayed until the next time a connection is closed. At that time, MySQL checks whether there is space in the cache to store the thread. If so, it caches the thread for future reuse by another connection. If not, it kills the thread instead of caching it. In this case, the number of threads in the cache, and hence the amount of memory the thread cache uses, does not immediately decrease; it decreases only when a new connection removes a thread from the cache to use it. (MySQL adds threads to the cache only when connections close and removes them from the cache only when new connections are created.)

query_cache_size

MySQL allocates and initializes the specified amount of memory for the query cache all at once when the server starts. If you update this variable (even if you set it to its current value), MySQL immediately deletes all cached queries, resizes the cache to the specified size, and reinitializes the cache's memory.

read_buffer_size

MySQL doesn't allocate any memory for this buffer until a query needs it, but then it immediately allocates the entire chunk of memory specified here.

read_rnd_buffer_size
> MySQL doesn't allocate any memory for this buffer until a query needs it, and then it allocates only as much memory as needed. (The name max_read_rnd_ buffer_size would describe this variable more accurately.)

sort_buffer_size
> MySQL doesn't allocate any memory for this buffer until a query needs to do a sort. However, when there's a sort, MySQL allocates the entire chunk of memory immediately, whether the full size is required or not.

We explain what these variables do in more detail elsewhere. Our goal here is simply to show you what behavior to expect when you change these important variables.

Getting Started

Be careful when setting variables. More is not always better, and if you set the values too high, you can easily cause problems: you may run out of memory, causing your server to swap, or run out of address space.

We suggest that you develop a benchmark suite before you begin tuning your server (we discussed benchmarking in Chapter 2). For the purposes of optimizing your server's configuration, you need a benchmark suite that represents your overall workload and includes edge cases such as very large and complex queries. If you have identified a particular problem spot—such as a single query that runs slowly— you can also try to optimize for that case, but you risk impacting other queries negatively without knowing it.

You should always have a monitoring system in place to measure whether a change improves or hurts your server's overall performance in real life. Benchmarks aren't enough, because they're not comprehensive. If you don't measure your server's overall performance, you might actually hurt performance without knowing it. We've seen many cases where someone changed a server's configuration and thought it improved performance, when in fact the server's performance worsened overall because of a different workload at a different time of day or day of the week. We discuss some monitoring systems in Chapter 14.

The best way to proceed is to change one or two variables, a little at a time, and run the benchmarks after each change. Sometimes the results will surprise you; you might increase a variable a little and see an improvement, then increase it a little more and see a sharp drop in performance. If performance suffers after a change, you might be asking for too much of some resource, such as too much memory for a buffer that's frequently allocated and deallocated. You might also have created a mismatch between MySQL and your operating system or hardware. For example, we've found that the optimal sort_buffer_size may be affected by how the CPU cache works, and the read_buffer_size needs to be matched to how the server's read-ahead and general I/O subsystem is configured. Larger is not always better. Some variables

---

are also dependent on others, which is something you learn with experience and by understanding the system's architecture. For example, the best `innodb_log_file_size` depends on your `innodb_buffer_pool_size`.

If you take notes, perhaps with comments in the configuration file, you might save yourself (and your successors) a lot of work. An even better idea is to place your configuration file under version control. This is a good practice anyway, as it lets you undo changes. To reduce the complexity of managing many configuration files, simply create a symbolic link from the configuration file to a central version control repository. You can read more about this in a good book about system administration.

Before you start tuning your configuration, you should tune your queries and your schema, addressing at least the obvious optimizations such as adding indexes. If you get deep into tweaking configuration and then change your queries or schema, you might need to retune the configuration. Keep in mind that tuning is an ongoing, iterative process. Unless your hardware, workload, and data are completely static, chances are you'll need to revisit your configuration later. This means you don't need to tune every last ounce of performance out of your server; in fact, the return for such an investment of time will probably be very small. We suggest that you tune your configuration until it's "good enough," then leave it alone unless you have reason to believe you're forgoing a significant performance improvement. You might also want to revisit it when you change your queries or schema.

We generally develop sample configuration files for various purposes and use them as our own defaults, especially if we manage many similar servers in an installation. But, as we warned at the beginning of this chapter, we don't have a one-size-fits-all "best configuration file" for, say, a four-CPU server with 16 GB of memory and 12 hard drives. You really do need to develop your own configurations, because even a good starting point will vary widely depending on how you're using the server.

General Tuning

You can look at configuration as a two-step process: use some basic facts about your installation to create a sensible starting point, then modify that based on the details of your workload.

You should probably use one of the samples MySQL provides as a starting point. Consider your server hardware to help you choose. How many hard drives and CPUs do you have, and how much memory? The samples have helpful names such as *my-huge.cnf*, *my-large.cnf*, and *my-small.cnf*, so which one to start with should be pretty obvious. However, the sample files apply only if you're using just MyISAM tables. If you're using another storage engine, you'll need to create your own configuration.

Tuning Memory Usage

Configuring MySQL to use memory correctly is vital to good performance. You'll almost certainly need to customize MySQL's memory usage for your needs. You can think of MySQL's memory consumption as falling into two categories: the memory you can control, and the memory you can't. You can't control how much memory MySQL uses merely to run the server, parse queries, and manage its internals, but you have a lot of control over how much memory it uses for specific purposes. Making good use of the memory you can control is not hard, but it does require you to know what you're configuring.

You can approach memory tuning in steps:

1. Determine the absolute upper limit of memory MySQL can possibly use.
2. Determine how much memory MySQL will use for per-connection needs, such as sort buffers and temporary tables.
3. Determine how much memory the operating system needs to run well. Include memory for other programs that run on the same machine, such as periodic jobs.
4. Assuming that it makes sense to do so, use the rest of the memory for MySQL's caches, such as the InnoDB buffer pool.

We go over each of these steps in the following sections, and then we take a more detailed look at the various MySQL caches' requirements.

How much memory can MySQL use?

There is a hard upper limit on the amount of memory that can possibly be available to MySQL on any given system. The starting point is the amount of physically installed memory. If your server doesn't have it, MySQL can't use it.

You also need to think about operating system or architecture limits, such as restrictions 32-bit operating systems place on how much memory a given process can address. Because MySQL runs in a single process with multiple threads, the amount of memory it can use overall may be severely limited by such restrictions—for example, 32-bit Linux kernels limit the amount of memory any one process can address to a value that is typically between 2.5 and 2.7 GB. Running out of address space is very dangerous and can cause MySQL to crash.

There are many other operating system-specific parameters and oddities that must be taken into account, including not just the per-process limits, but also stack sizes and other settings. The system's *glibc* libraries can also impose limits per single allocation. For example, you might not be able to set `innodb_buffer_pool` larger than 2 GB if that's all your *glibc* libraries support in a single allocation.

Even on 64-bit servers, some limitations still apply. For example, many of the buffers we discuss, such as the key buffer, are limited to 4 GB on a 64-bit server. Some of these restrictions are lifted in MySQL 5.1, and there will probably be more changes in the future because MySQL AB is actively working to make MySQL take advantage of more powerful hardware. The MySQL manual documents each variable's maximum values.

Per-connection memory needs

MySQL needs a small amount of memory just to hold a connection (thread) open. It also requires a certain base amount of memory to execute any given query. You'll need to set aside enough memory for MySQL to execute queries during peak load times. Otherwise, your queries will be starved for memory, and they will run poorly or fail.

It's useful to know how much memory MySQL will consume during peak usage, but some usage patterns can unexpectedly consume a lot of memory, which makes this hard to predict. Prepared statements are one example, because you can have many of them open at once. Another example is the InnoDB table cache (more about this later).

You don't need to assume a worst-case scenario when trying to predict peak memory consumption. For example, if you configure MySQL to allow a maximum of 100 connections, it theoretically might be possible to simultaneously run large queries on all 100 connections, but in reality this probably won't happen. For example, if you set `myisam_sort_buffer_size` to 256M, your worst-case usage is at least 25 GB, but this level of consumption is highly unlikely to actually occur.

Rather than calculating worst cases, a better approach is to watch your server under a real workload and see how much memory it uses, which you can see watching the process's virtual memory size. In many Unix-like systems, this is reported in the VIRT column in *top*, or VSZ in *ps*. The next chapter has more information on how to monitor memory usage.

Reserving memory for the operating system

Just as with queries, you need to reserve enough memory for the operating system to do its work. The best indication that the operating system has enough memory is that it's not actively swapping (paging) virtual memory to disk. (See "Swapping" on page 334 for more on this topic.)

You should not need to reserve more than a gigabyte or two for the operating system, even for machines with a lot of memory. Add in some extra for safety, and add in some more if you'll be running periodic memory-intensive jobs on the machine (such as backups). Don't add any memory for the operating system's caches, because they can be very large. The operating system will generally use any leftover memory for these caches, and we consider them separately from the operating system's own needs in the following sections.

Allocating memory for caches

If the server is dedicated to MySQL, any memory you don't reserve for the operating system or for query processing is available for caches.

MySQL needs more memory for caches than anything else. It uses caches to avoid disk access, which is orders of magnitude slower than accessing data in memory. The operating system may cache some data on MySQL's behalf (especially for MyISAM), but MySQL needs lots of memory for itself too.

The following are the most important caches to consider for the majority of installations:

- The operating system caches for MyISAM data
- MyISAM key caches
- The InnoDB buffer pool
- The query cache

There are other caches, but they generally don't use much memory. We discussed the query cache in detail in the previous chapter, so the following sections concentrate on the caches MyISAM and InnoDB need to work well.

It is much easier to tune a server if you're using only one storage engine. If you're using only MyISAM tables, you can disable InnoDB completely, and if you're using only InnoDB, you need to allocate only minimal resources for MyISAM (MySQL uses MyISAM tables internally for some operations). But if you're using a mixture of storage engines, it can be very hard to figure out the right balance between them. The best approach we've found is to make an educated guess and then benchmark.

The MyISAM Key Cache

The MyISAM key caches are also referred to as *key buffers*; there is one by default, but you can create more. Unlike InnoDB and some other storage engines, MyISAM itself caches only indexes, not data (it lets the operating system cache the data). If you use mostly MyISAM, you should allocate a lot of memory to the key caches.

 Much of the advice in this section assumes you're using only MyISAM tables. If you're using a mixture of MyISAM and another engine, such as InnoDB, you will have to consider the needs of both storage engines.

The most important option is the key_buffer_size, which you should try setting to between 25% and 50% of the amount of memory you reserved for caches. The remainder will be available for the operating system caches, which the operating system will usually fill with data from MyISAM's *.MYD* files. MySQL 5.0 has a hard upper limit of 4 GB for this variable, no matter what architecture you're running.

MySQL 5.1 allows larger sizes. Check the current documentation for your version of the server.

By default MyISAM caches all indexes in the default key buffer, but you can create multiple named key buffers. This lets you keep more than 4 GB of indexes in memory at once. To create key buffers named key_buffer_1 and key_buffer_2, each sized at 1 GB, place the following in the configuration file:

```
key_buffer_1.key_buffer_size = 1G
key_buffer_2.key_buffer_size = 1G
```

Now there are three key buffers: the two explicitly created by those lines and the default buffer. You can use the CACHE INDEX command to map tables to caches. You can also tell MySQL to use key_buffer_1 for the indexes from tables t1 and t2 with the following SQL statement:

```
mysql> CACHE INDEX t1, t2 IN key_buffer_1;
```

Now when MySQL reads blocks from the indexes on these tables, it will cache the blocks in the specified buffer. You can also preload the tables' indexes into the cache with the LOAD INDEX command:

```
mysql> LOAD INDEX INTO CACHE t1, t2;
```

You can place this SQL into a file that's executed when MySQL starts up. The filename must be specified in the init_file option, and the file can include multiple SQL commands, each on a single line (no comments are allowed). Any indexes you don't explicitly map to a key buffer will be assigned to the default buffer the first time MySQL needs to access the .*MYI* file.

You can monitor the performance and usage of the key buffers with information from SHOW STATUS and SHOW VARIABLES. You can calculate the hit ratio and the percentage of the buffer in use with these equations:

Cache hit ratio

    100 - ((Key_reads * 100) / Key_read_requests)

Percentage of buffer in use

    100 - ((Key_blocks_unused * key_cache_block_size) * 100 / key_buffer_size)

 In Chapter 14, we examine some tools, such as *innotop*, that can make performance monitoring more convenient.

It's good to know the cache hit rate, but this number can be misleading. For example, the difference between 99% and 99.9% looks small, but it really represents a tenfold increase. The cache hit rate is also application-dependent: some applications might work fine at 95%, whereas others might be I/O-bound at 99.9%. You might even be able to get a 99.99% hit rate with properly sized caches.

The number of cache *misses* per second is generally much more empirically useful. Suppose you have a single hard drive that can do 100 random reads per second. Five misses per second will not cause your workload to be I/O-bound, but 80 per second will likely cause problems. You can use the following equation to calculate this value:

```
Key_reads / Uptime
```

Calculate the number of misses incrementally over intervals of 10 to 100 seconds, so you can get an idea of the current performance. The following command will show the incremental values every 10 seconds:

```
$ mysqladmin extended-status -r -i 10 | grep Key_reads
```

When you're deciding how much memory to allocate to the key caches, it might help to know how much space your MyISAM indexes are actually using on disk. You don't need to make the key buffers larger than the data they will cache. If you have a Unix-like system, you can find out the size of the files storing the indexes with a command like the following:

```
$ du -sch `find /path/to/mysql/data/directory/ -name "*.MYI"`
```

Remember that MyISAM uses the operating system cache for the data files, which are often larger than the indexes. Therefore, it often makes sense to leave more memory for the operating system cache than for the key caches. Finally, even if you don't have any MyISAM tables, bear in mind that you still need to set key_buffer_size to a small amount of memory, such as 32M. The MySQL server sometimes uses MyISAM tables for internal purposes, such as temporary tables for GROUP BY queries.

The MyISAM key block size

The key block size is important (especially for write-intensive workloads) because of the way it causes MyISAM, the operating system cache, and the filesystem to interact. If the key block size is too small, you may encounter *read-around writes*, which are writes that the operating system cannot perform without first reading some data from the disk. Here's how a read-around write happens, assuming the operating system's page size is 4 KB (typically true on the x86 architecture) and the key block size is 1 KB:

1. MyISAM requests a 1 KB key block from disk.
2. The operating system reads 4 KB of data from the disk and caches it, then passes the desired 1 KB of data to MyISAM.
3. The operating system discards the cached data in favor of some other data.
4. MyISAM modifies the 1 KB key block and asks the operating system to write it back to disk.
5. The operating system reads the same 4 KB of data from the disk into the operating system cache, modifies the 1 KB that MyISAM changed, and writes the entire 4 KB back to disk.

The read-around write happened in step 5, when MyISAM asked the operating system to write only part of a 4 KB page. If MyISAM's block size had matched the operating system's, the disk read in step 5 could have been avoided.[*]

Unfortunately, in MySQL 5.0 and earlier, there's no way to configure the key block size. However, in MySQL 5.1 and later, you can avoid read-around writes by making MyISAM's key block size the same as the operating system's. The `myisam_block_size` variable controls the key block size. You can also specify the size for each key with the `KEY_BLOCK_SIZE` option in a `CREATE TABLE` or `CREATE INDEX` statement, but because all keys are stored in the same file, you really need all of them to have blocks as large as or larger than the operating system's to avoid alignment issues that could still cause read-around writes. (For example, if one key has 1 KB blocks and another has 4 KB blocks, the 4 KB block boundaries might not match the operating system's page boundaries.)

The InnoDB Buffer Pool

If you use mostly InnoDB tables, the InnoDB buffer pool probably needs more memory than anything else. Unlike the MyISAM key cache, the InnoDB buffer pool doesn't just cache indexes: it also holds row data, the adaptive hash index (see "Hash indexes" on page 101), the insert buffer, locks, and other internal structures. InnoDB also uses the buffer pool to help it delay writes, so it can merge many writes together and perform them sequentially. In short, InnoDB relies *heavily* on the buffer pool, and you should be sure to allocate enough memory to it. The MySQL manual suggests using up to 80% of the machine's physical memory for the buffer pool on a dedicated server; in reality, you can use more than that if the machine has a lot of memory. As with the MyISAM key buffers, you can use variables from `SHOW` commands or tools such as *innotop* to monitor your InnoDB buffer pool's memory usage and performance.

There's no equivalent of `LOAD INDEX INTO CACHE` for InnoDB tables. However, if you're trying to warm up a server and get it ready to handle a heavy load, you can issue queries that perform full table scans or full index scans.

In most cases, you should make the InnoDB buffer pool as large as your available memory allows. However, in rare circumstances, very large buffer pools (say, 50 GB) can cause long stalls. For example, a large buffer pool may become slow during checkpoints or insert buffer merge operations, and concurrency can drop as a result of locking. If you experience these problems, you may have to reduce the buffer pool size.

---

[*] Theoretically, if you could ensure that the original 4 KB of data was still in the operating system's cache, the read wouldn't be needed. However, you have no control over which blocks the operating system decides to keep in its cache. You can find out which blocks are in the cache with the *fincore* tool, available at *http://net.doit.wisc.edu/~plonka/fincore/*.

You can change the innodb_max_dirty_pages_pct variable to instruct InnoDB to keep more or fewer dirty (modified) pages in the buffer pool. If you allow a lot of dirty pages, InnoDB can take a long time to shut down, because it writes the dirty pages to the data files upon shutdown. You can force it to shut down quickly, but then it just has to do more recovery when it restarts, so you can't actually speed up the shutdown and restart cycle time. If you know in advance when you need to shut down, you can set the variable to a lower value, wait for the flush thread to clean up the buffer pool, and then shut down once the number of dirty pages becomes small. You can monitor the number of dirty pages by watching the Innodb_buffer_pool_pages_dirty server status variable or using *innotop* to monitor SHOW INNODB STATUS.

Lowering the value of the innodb_max_dirty_pages_pct variable doesn't actually guarantee that InnoDB will keep fewer dirty pages in the buffer pool. Instead, it controls the threshold at which InnoDB stops being "lazy." InnoDB's default behavior is to flush dirty pages with a background thread, merging writes together and performing them sequentially for efficiency. This behavior is called "lazy" because it lets InnoDB delay flushing dirty pages in the buffer pool, unless it needs to use the space for some other data. When the percentage of dirty pages exceeds the threshold, InnoDB will flush pages as quickly as it can to try to keep the dirty page count lower. The variable's default value is 90, so by default InnoDB will flush lazily until the buffer pool is 90% full of dirty pages.

You can tweak the threshold for your workload if you wish to spread out the writes a bit more. For example, lowering it to 50 will generally cause InnoDB to do more write operations, because it will flush pages sooner and therefore be unable to batch the writes as well. However, if your workload has a lot of write spikes, using a lower value may help InnoDB absorb the spikes better: it will have more "spare" memory to hold dirty pages, so it won't have to wait for other dirty pages to be flushed to disk.

The Thread Cache

The thread cache holds threads that aren't currently associated with a connection but are ready to serve new connections. When there's a thread in the cache and a new connection is created, MySQL removes the thread from the cache and gives it to the new connection. When the connection is closed, MySQL places the thread back into the cache, if there's room. If isn't room, MySQL destroys the thread. As long as MySQL has a free thread in the cache, it can respond very rapidly to connect requests, because it doesn't have to create a new thread for each connection.

The thread_cache_size variable specifies the number of threads MySQL can keep in the cache. You probably won't need to tune this value, unless your server gets many connection requests. To check whether the thread cache is large enough, watch the Threads_created status variable. We generally try to keep the thread cache large enough that we see fewer than 10 new threads created each second, but it's often pretty easy to get this number lower than 1 per second.

A good approach is to watch the Threads_connected variable and try to set thread_cache_size large enough to handle the typical fluctuation in your workload. For example, if Threads_connected usually stays between 100 and 200, you can set the cache size to 100. If it stays between 500 and 700, a thread cache of 200 should be large enough. Think of it this way: at 700 connections, there are probably no threads in the cache; at 500 connections, there are 200 cached threads ready to be used if the load increases to 700 again.

Making the thread cache very large is probably not necessary for most uses, but keeping it small doesn't save much memory, so there's little benefit in doing so. Each thread that's in the thread cache or sleeping typically uses around 256 KB of memory. This is very little compared to the amount of memory a thread can use when a connection is actively processing a query. In general, you should keep your thread cache large enough that Threads_created doesn't increase very often. If this is a very large number, however (e.g., many thousand threads), you might want to set it lower because some operating systems don't handle very large numbers of threads well, even when most of them are sleeping.

The Table Cache

The table cache is similar in concept to the thread cache, but it stores objects that represent tables. Each object in the cache contains the associated table's parsed .frm file, plus other data. Exactly what else is in the object depends on the table's storage engine. For example, for MyISAM, it holds the table data and/or index file descriptors. For merge tables it may hold many file descriptors, because merge tables can have many underlying tables.

The table cache can help you reuse resources. For instance, when a query requests access to a MyISAM table, MySQL might be able to give it a file descriptor from the cached object instead of opening the file. The table cache can also help avoid some of the I/O required for marking a MyISAM table as "in use" in the index headers.*

The table cache's design is a little MyISAM-centric—this is one of the areas where the separation between the server and the storage engines is not completely clean, for historical reasons. The table cache is a little less important for InnoDB, because InnoDB doesn't rely on it for as many purposes (such as holding file descriptors; it has its own version of a table cache for this purpose). However, even InnoDB benefits from caching the parsed .frm files.

---

* The concept of an "opened table" can be a little confusing. MySQL counts a table as opened many times when different queries are accessing it simultaneously, or even when a single query refers to the same table more than once, as in a subquery or a self-join. MyISAM's index files contain a counter that MyISAM increments when the table is opened and decrements when it is closed. This lets MyISAM see when the table wasn't closed cleanly: if it opens a table for the first time and the counter is not zero, the table wasn't closed cleanly.

In MySQL 5.1, the table cache is separated into two parts: a cache of open tables and a table definition cache (configured via the `table_open_cache` and `table_definition_cache` variables). Thus, the table definitions (the parsed *.frm* files) are separated from the other resources, such as file descriptors. Opened tables are still per-thread, per-table-used, but the table definitions are global and can be shared among all connections efficiently. You can generally set `table_definition_cache` high enough to cache all your table definitions. Unless you have tens of thousands of tables, this is likely to be the easiest approach.

If the `Opened_tables` status variable is large or increasing, the table cache isn't large enough, and you should increase the `table_cache` system variable (or `table_open_cache`, in MySQL 5.1). The only real downside to making the table cache very large is that it might cause longer shutdown times when your server has a lot of MyISAM tables, because the key blocks have to be flushed and the tables have to be marked as no longer open. It can also make `FLUSH TABLES WITH READ LOCK` take a long time to complete, for the same reason.

If you get errors indicating that MySQL can't open any more files (use the *perror* utility to check what the error number means), you might also need to increase the number of files MySQL is allowed to keep open. You can do this with the `open_files_limit` server variable in your *my.cnf* file.

The thread and table caches don't really use much memory, and they are beneficial because they conserve resources. Although creating a new thread and opening a new file aren't really expensive compared to other things MySQL might do, the overhead can add up quickly under a high-concurrency workload. Caching threads and tables can improve efficiency.

The InnoDB Data Dictionary

InnoDB has its own per-table cache, variously called a *table definition cache* or *data dictionary*, which you cannot configure. When InnoDB opens a table, it adds a corresponding object to the data dictionary. Each table can take up 4 KB or more of memory (although much less space is required in MySQL 5.1). Tables are not removed from the data dictionary when they are closed.

The main performance issue—besides memory requirements—is opening and computing statistics for the tables, which is expensive because it requires a lot of I/O. In contrast to MyISAM, InnoDB doesn't store statistics in the tables permanently; it recomputes them each time it starts. This operation is serialized by a global mutex in current versions of MySQL, so it can't be done in parallel. If you have a lot of tables, your server can take hours to start and fully warm up, during which time it might not be doing much other than waiting for one I/O operation after another. We mention this to make sure you know about it, even though there's nothing you can do to change it. It's normally a problem only when you have many (thousands or tens of thousands) large tables, which cause the process to be I/O-bound.

If you use InnoDB's `innodb_file_per_table` option (described later in "Configuring the tablespace" on page 291), there's also a separate limit on the number of *.ibd* files InnoDB can keep open at any time. This is handled by the InnoDB storage engine, not the MySQL server, and is controlled by `innodb_open_files`. InnoDB doesn't open files the same way MyISAM does: whereas MyISAM uses the table cache to hold file descriptors for open tables, in InnoDB there is no direct relationship between open tables and open files. InnoDB uses a single, global file descriptor for each *.ibd* file. If you can afford it, it's best to set `innodb_open_files` large enough that the server can keep all *.ibd* files open simultaneously.

Tuning MySQL's I/O Behavior

A few configuration options affect how MySQL synchronizes data to disk and performs recovery. These can affect performance dramatically, because they involve expensive I/O operations. They also represent a tradeoff between performance and data safety. In general, it's expensive to ensure that your data is written to disk immediately and consistently. If you're willing to risk the danger that a disk write won't really make it to permanent storage, you can increase concurrency and/or reduce I/O waits, but you'll have to decide for yourself how much risk you can tolerate.

MyISAM I/O Tuning

Let's begin by considering how MyISAM performs I/O for its indexes. MyISAM normally flushes index changes to disk after every write. If you're going to make many modifications to a table, however, it may be faster to batch these writes together.

One way to do this is with `LOCK TABLES`, which defers writes until you unlock the tables. This can be a valuable technique for improving performance, as it lets you control exactly which writes are deferred and when the writes are flushed to disk. You can defer writes for precisely the statements you want.

You can also defer index writes by using the `delay_key_write` variable. If you do this, modified key buffer blocks are not flushed until the table is closed.[*] The possible settings are as follows:

OFF

MyISAM flushes modified blocks in the key buffer (key cache) to disk after every write, unless the table is locked with `LOCK TABLES`.

---

[*] The table can be closed for several reasons. For example, the server might close the table because there's not enough room in the table cache, or someone might execute `FLUSH TABLES`.

ON

Delayed key writes are enabled, but only for tables created with the DELAY_KEY_ WRITE option.

ALL

All MyISAM tables use delayed key writes.

Delaying key writes can be helpful in some cases, but it doesn't usually create a big performance boost. It's most useful with smaller data sizes, when the key cache's read hit ratio is good but the write hit ratio is bad. It also has quite a few drawbacks:

- If the server crashes and the blocks haven't been flushed to disk, the index will be corrupt.

- If many writes are delayed, it'll take longer for MySQL to close a table, because it will have to wait for the buffers to be flushed to disk. This can cause long table cache locks in MySQL 5.0.

- FLUSH TABLES can take a long time, for the reason just mentioned. This in turn can increase the time it takes to run FLUSH TABLES WITH READ LOCK for an LVM snapshot or other backup operation.

- Unflushed dirty blocks in the key buffer might not leave any room in the buffer for new blocks to be read from disk. Therefore, queries might stall while waiting for MyISAM to free up some space in the key buffer.

In addition to tuning MyISAM's index I/O, you can configure how MyISAM tries to recover from corruption. The myisam_recover option controls how MyISAM looks for and repairs errors. You have to set this option in the configuration file or at the command line. You can view, but not change, the option's value with this SQL statement (this is not a typo—the system variable has a different name from the corresponding command-line option):

```
mysql> SHOW VARIABLES LIKE 'myisam_recover_options';
```

Enabling this option instructs MySQL to check MyISAM tables for corruption when it opens them, and to repair them if problems are found. You can set the following values:

DEFAULT *(or no setting)*

MySQL will try to repair any table that is marked as having crashed or not marked as having been closed cleanly. The default setting performs no other actions upon recovery. In contrast to how most variables work, this DEFAULT value is not an instruction to reset the variable to its compiled-in value; it essentially means "no setting."

BACKUP

Makes MySQL write a backup of the data file into a *.BAK* file, which you can examine afterward.

FORCE

> Makes recovery continue even if more than one row will be lost from the .*MYD* file.

QUICK

> Skips recovery unless there are delete blocks. These are blocks of deleted rows that are still occupying space and can be reused for future INSERT statements. This can be useful because MyISAM recovery can take a very long time on large tables.

You can use multiple settings, separated by commas. For example, BACKUP,FORCE will force recovery and create a backup.

We recommend that you enable this option, especially if you have just a few small MyISAM tables. Running a server with corrupted MyISAM tables is dangerous, as they can sometimes cause more data corruption and even server crashes. However, if you have large tables, automatic recovery might be impractical: it causes the server to check and repair all MyISAM tables when they're opened, which is inefficient. During this time, MySQL tends to block connections from performing any work. If you have a lot of MyISAM tables, it might be a good idea to use a less intrusive process that runs CHECK TABLES and REPAIR TABLES after startup. Either way, it is very important to check and repair the tables.

Enabling memory-mapped access to data files is another useful MyISAM tuning option. Memory mapping lets MyISAM access the .*MYD* files directly via the operating system's page cache, avoiding costly system calls. In MySQL 5.1 and newer, you can enable memory mapping with the myisam_use_mmap option. Older versions of MySQL use memory mapping for compressed MyISAM tables only.

InnoDB I/O Tuning

InnoDB is more complex than MyISAM. As a result, you can control not only how it recovers, but also how it opens and flushes its data, which greatly affects recovery and overall performance. InnoDB's recovery process is automatic and always runs when InnoDB starts, though you can influence what actions it takes. For more on this, see Chapter 11.

Leaving aside recovery and assuming nothing ever crashes or goes wrong, there's still a lot to configure for InnoDB. It has a complex chain of buffers and files designed to increase performance and guarantee ACID properties, and each piece of the chain is configurable. Figure 6-1 illustrates these files and buffers.

A few of the most important things to change for normal usage are the InnoDB log file size, how InnoDB flushes its log buffer, and how InnoDB performs I/O.

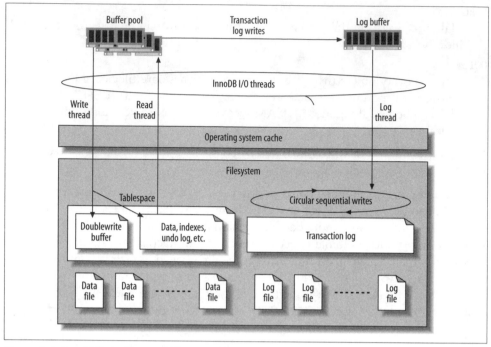

Figure 6-1. InnoDB's buffers and files

The InnoDB transaction log

InnoDB uses its log to reduce the cost of committing transactions. Instead of flushing the buffer pool to disk after each transaction commits, it logs the transactions. The changes transactions make to data and indexes often map to random locations in the tablespace, so flushing these changes to disk would require random I/O. As a rule, random I/O is much more expensive than sequential I/O because of the time it takes to seek the correct location on disk and wait for the desired part of the disk to rotate under the head.

InnoDB uses its log to convert this random disk I/O into sequential I/O. Once the log is safely on disk, the transactions are permanent, even though the changes haven't been written to the data files yet. If something bad happens (such as a power failure), InnoDB can replay the log and recover the committed transactions.

Of course, InnoDB does ultimately have to write the changes to the data files, because the log has a fixed size. It writes to the log in a circular fashion: when it reaches the end of the log, it wraps around to the beginning. It can't overwrite a log record if the changes contained there haven't been applied to the data files, because this would erase the only permanent record of the committed transaction.

InnoDB uses a background thread to flush the changes to the data files intelligently. This thread can group writes together and make the data writes sequential, for improved efficiency. In effect, the transaction log converts random data file I/O into mostly sequential log file and data file I/O. Moving flushes into the background makes queries complete more quickly and helps cushion the I/O system from spikes in the query load.

The overall log file size is controlled by innodb_log_file_size and innodb_log_files_in_group, and it's very important for write performance. The total size is the sum of each file's size. By default there are two 5 MB files, for a total of 10 MB. This is not enough for a high performance workload. The upper limit for the total log size is 4 GB, but typical sizes for extremely write-intensive workloads are only in the hundreds of megabytes (perhaps 256 MB total). The following sections explain how to find a good size for your workload.

InnoDB uses multiple files as a single circular log. You usually don't need to change the default number of logs, just the size of each log file. To change the log file size, shut down MySQL cleanly, move the old logs away, reconfigure, and restart. Be sure MySQL shuts down cleanly, or the log files will actually have entries that need to be applied to the data files! Watch the MySQL error log when you restart the server. After you've restarted successfully, you can delete the old log files.

Log file size and the log buffer. To determine the ideal size for your log files, you'll have to weigh the overhead of routine data changes against the recovery time required in the event of a crash. If the log is too small, InnoDB will have to do more checkpoints, causing more log writes. In extreme cases, write queries might stall and have to wait for changes to be applied to the data files before there is room to write into the log. On the other hand, if the log is too large, InnoDB might have to do a lot of work when it recovers. This can greatly increase recovery time.

Your data size and access patterns will influence the recovery time, too. Suppose you have a terabyte of data and 16 GB of buffer pool, and your total log size is 128 MB. If you have a lot of dirty pages (i.e., pages whose changes have not yet been flushed to the data files) in the buffer pool and they are uniformly spread across your terabyte of data, recovery after a crash might take a long time. InnoDB will have to scan through the log, examine the data files, and apply changes to the data files as needed. That's a lot of reading and writing! On the other hand, if the changes are localized— say, if only a few gigabytes of data are updated frequently—recovery might be fast, even when your data and log files are huge. Recovery time also depends on the size of a typical modification, which is related to your average row length. Short rows let more modifications fit in the log, so InnoDB might need to replay more modifications on recovery.

When InnoDB changes any data, it writes a record of the change into its *log buffer*, which it keeps in memory. InnoDB flushes the buffer to the log files on disk when the buffer gets full, when a transaction commits, or once per second—whichever comes first. Increasing the buffer size, which is 1 MB by default, can help reduce I/O if you have large transactions. The variable that controls the buffer size is called innodb_log_buffer_size.

You shouldn't need to make the buffer very large. The recommended range is 1 to 8 MB, and this should be more than enough unless you write a lot of huge BLOB records. The log entries are very compact compared to InnoDB's normal data. They are not page-based, so they don't waste space storing whole pages at a time. InnoDB also makes log entries as short as possible. They are sometimes even stored as the function number and parameters of a C function!

You can monitor InnoDB's log and log buffer I/O performance by inspecting the LOG section of the output of SHOW INNODB STATUS, and by watching the Innodb_os_log_written status variable to see how much data InnoDB writes to the log files. A good rule of thumb is to watch it over intervals of 10 to 100 seconds and note the peak value. You can use this to judge whether your log buffer is sized right. For example, if you see a peak of 100 KB written to the log per second, a 1 MB log buffer is probably plenty.

You can also use this metric to decide on a good size for your log files. If the peak is 100 KB per second, a 256 MB log file is enough to store at least 2,560 seconds of log entries, which is likely to be enough. See "SHOW INNODB STATUS" on page 565 for more on how to monitor and interpret the log and buffer status.

How InnoDB flushes the log buffer. When InnoDB flushes the log buffer to the log files on disk, it locks the buffer with a mutex, flushes it up to the desired point, and then moves any remaining entries to the front of the buffer. It is possible that more than one transaction will be ready to flush its log entries when the mutex is released. InnoDB has a group commit feature that can commit all of them to the log in a single I/O operation, but this is broken in MySQL 5.0 when the binary log is enabled.

The log buffer *must* be flushed to durable storage to ensure that committed transactions are fully durable. If you care more about performance than durability, you can change innodb_flush_log_at_trx_commit to control where and how often the log buffer is flushed. Possible settings are as follows:

0   Write the log buffer to the log file and flush the log file every second, but do nothing at transaction commit.

1   Write the log buffer to the log file and flush it to durable storage every time a transaction commits. This is the default (and safest) setting; it guarantees that you won't lose any committed transactions, unless the disk or operating system "fakes" the flush operation.

2   Write the log buffer to the log file at every commit, but don't flush it. InnoDB schedules a flush once every second. The most important difference from the 0 setting (and what makes 2 the preferable setting) is that 2 won't lose any transactions if the MySQL process crashes. If the entire server crashes or loses power, however, you can still lose transactions.

It's important to know the difference between *writing* the log buffer to the log file and *flushing* the log to durable storage. In most operating systems, writing the buffer to the log simply moves the data from InnoDB's memory buffer to the operating system's cache, which is also in memory. It doesn't actually write the data to durable storage. Thus, settings 0 and 2 *usually* result in at most one second of lost data if there's a crash or a power outage, because the data might exist only in the operating system's cache. We say "usually" because InnoDB tries to flush the log file to disk about once per second no matter what, but it is possible to lose more than a second of transactions in some cases, such as when a flush gets stalled.

In contrast, flushing the log to durable storage means InnoDB asks the operating system to actually flush the data out of the cache and ensure it is *written to the disk*. This is a blocking I/O call that doesn't complete until the data is completely written. Because writing data to a disk is slow, this can dramatically reduce the number of transactions InnoDB can commit per second when `innodb_flush_log_at_trx_commit` is set to 1. Today's high-speed drives* can perform only a couple of hundred real disk transactions per second, simply because of the limitations of drive rotation speed and seek time.

Sometimes the hard disk controller or operating system fakes a flush by putting the data into yet *another* cache, such as the hard disk's own cache. This is faster but very dangerous, because the data might still be lost if the drive loses power. This is even worse than setting `innodb_flush_log_at_trx_commit` to something other than 1, because it can cause data corruption, not just lost transactions.

Setting `innodb_flush_log_at_trx_commit` to anything other than 1 can cause you to lose transactions. However, you might find the other settings useful if you don't care about durability (the D in ACID). Maybe you just want some of InnoDB's other features, such as clustered indexes, resistance to data corruption, and row-level locking. This is not uncommon when using InnoDB to replace MyISAM solely for performance reasons.

The best configuration for high-performance transactional needs is to leave `innodb_flush_log_at_trx_commit` set to 1 and place the log files on a RAID volume with a battery-backed write cache. This is both safe and very fast. See "RAID Performance Optimization" on page 317 for more about RAID.

---

* We're talking about spindle-based disk drives with rotating platters, not solid-state hard drives, which have completely different performance characteristics.

How InnoDB opens and flushes log and data files

The `innodb_flush_method` option lets you configure how InnoDB actually interacts with the filesystem. Despite its name, it can affect how InnoDB reads data, not just how it writes it. The Windows and non-Windows values for this option are mutually exclusive: you can use `async_unbuffered`, `unbuffered`, and `normal` only on Windows, and you cannot use any other values on Windows. The default value is `unbuffered` on Windows and `fdatasync` on all other systems. (If `SHOW GLOBAL VARIABLES` shows the variable with an empty value, that means it's set to the default.)

 Changing how InnoDB performs I/O operations can change performance greatly. Benchmark carefully!

Here are the possible values:

`fdatasync`

> The default value on non-Windows systems: InnoDB uses `fsync( )` to flush both data and log files.
>
> InnoDB generally uses `fsync( )` instead of `fdatasync( )`, even though this value seems to indicate the contrary. `fdatasync( )` is like `fsync( )`, except it flushes only the file's data, not its metadata (last modified time, etc.). Therefore, `fsync( )` can cause more I/O. However, the InnoDB developers are very conservative, and they found that `fdatasync( )` caused corruption in some cases. InnoDB determines which methods can be used safely; some options are set at compile time and some are discovered at runtime. It uses the fastest safe method it can.
>
> The disadvantage of using `fsync( )` is that the operating system buffers at least some of the data in its own cache. In theory, this is wasteful double buffering, because InnoDB manages its own buffers more intelligently than the operating system can. However, the ultimate effect is very system- and filesystem-dependent. The double buffering might not be a bad thing if it lets the filesystem do smarter I/O scheduling and batching. Some filesystems and operating systems can accumulate writes and execute them together, reorder them for efficiency, or write to multiple devices in parallel. They might also do read-ahead optimizations, such as instructing the disk to preread the next sequential block if several have been requested in sequence.
>
> Sometimes these optimizations help, and sometimes they don't. You can read your system's manpage for `fsync(2)` if you're curious about exactly what your version of `fsync( )` does.
>
> `innodb_file_per_table` causes each file to be `fsync( )`ed separately, which means writes to multiple tables can't be combined into a single I/O operation. This may require InnoDB to perform a higher total number of `fsync( )` operations.

O_DIRECT

InnoDB uses the O_DIRECT flag, or directio( ), depending on the system, on the data files. This option does not affect the log files and is not necessarily available on all Unix-like operating systems. At least Linux, FreeBSD, and Solaris (late 5.0 and newer) support it. Unlike the O_DSYNC flag, it affects both reads and writes.

This setting still uses fsync( ) to flush the files to disk, but it instructs the operating system not to cache the data and not to use read-ahead. This disables the operating system's caches completely and makes all reads and writes go directly to the storage device, avoiding double buffering.

On most systems, this is implemented with a call to fcntl( ) to set the O_DIRECT flag on the file descriptor, so you can read the fcntl(2) manpage for your system's details. On Solaris, this option uses directio( ).

If your RAID card does read-ahead, this setting will not disable that. It disables only the operating system's and/or filesystem's read-ahead capabilities.

You generally won't want to disable your RAID card's write cache if you use O_DIRECT, because that's typically the only thing that keeps performance good. Using O_DIRECT when there is no buffer between InnoDB and the actual storage device, such as when you have no write cache on your RAID card, can cause performance to degrade greatly.

This setting can cause the server's warm-up time to increase significantly, especially if the operating system's cache is very large. It can also make a small buffer pool (e.g., a buffer pool of the default size) much slower than a buffered I/O would. This is because the operating system won't "help out" by keeping more of the data in its own cache. If the desired data isn't in the buffer pool, InnoDB will have to read it directly from disk.

This setting does not impose any extra penalty on the use of innodb_file_per_table.

O_DSYNC

This option sets the O_SYNC flag on the open( ) call for the log files. It makes all writes synchronous—in other words, writes do not return until the data is written to disk. This option does not affect the data files.

The difference between the O_SYNC flag and the O_DIRECT flag is that O_SYNC doesn't disable caching at the operating system level. Therefore, it doesn't avoid double buffering, and it doesn't make writes go directly to disk. With O_SYNC, writes modify the data in the cache, and then it is sent to the disk.

While synchronous writes with O_SYNC may sound very similar to what fsync( ) does, the two can be implemented very differently on both the operating system and hardware levels. When the O_SYNC flag is used, the operating system might pass a "use synchronous I/O" flag down to the hardware level, telling the device not to use caches. On the other hand, fsync( ) tells the operating system to flush modified buffers to the device, followed by an instruction for the device to flush its own caches, if applicable, so it is certain that the data has been recorded on the physical media. Another difference is that with O_SYNC, every write( ) or pwrite( ) operation syncs data to disk before it finishes, blocking the calling process. In contrast, writing without the O_SYNC flag and then calling fsync( ) allows writes to accumulate in the cache (which makes each write fast), and then flushes them all at once.

Again, despite its name, this option sets the O_SYNC flag, not the O_DSYNC flag, because the InnoDB developers found bugs with O_DSYNC. O_SYNC and O_DSYNC are similar to fysnc( ) and fdatasync( ): O_SYNC syncs both data and metadata, whereas O_DSYNC syncs data only.

async_unbuffered
This is the default value on Windows. This option causes InnoDB to use unbuffered I/O for most writes; the exception is that it uses buffered I/O to the log files when innodb_flush_log_at_trx_commit is set to 2.

This setting causes InnoDB to use the operating system's native asynchronous (overlapped) I/O for both reads and writes on Windows 2000, XP, and newer. On older Windows versions, InnoDB uses its own asynchronous I/O, which is implemented with threads.

unbuffered
Windows-only. This option is similar to async_unbuffered but does not use native asynchronous I/O.

normal
Windows-only. This option causes InnoDB not to use native asynchronous I/O or unbuffered I/O.

nosync *and* littlesync
For development use only. These options are undocumented and unsafe for production; they should *not* be used.

If your RAID controller has a battery-backed write cache, we recommend that you use O_DIRECT. If not, either the default or O_DIRECT will probably be the best choice, depending on your application.

You can configure the number of I/O threads on Windows, but not on any other platform. Setting innodb_file_io_threads to a value higher than 4 will cause InnoDB to create more read and write threads for data I/O. There will be only one insert buffer thread and one log thread, so, for example, the value 8 means there will be one insert buffer thread, one log thread, three read threads, and three write threads.

The InnoDB tablespace

InnoDB keeps its data in a *tablespace*, which is essentially a virtual filesystem spanning one or many files on disk. InnoDB uses the tablespace for many purposes, not just for storing tables and indexes. It keeps its undo log (old row versions), insert buffer, doublewrite buffer (described in an upcoming section), and other internal structures in the tablespace.

Configuring the tablespace. You specify the tablespace files with the `innodb_data_file_path` configuration option. The files are all contained in the directory given by `innodb_data_home_dir`. Here's an example:

```
innodb_data_home_dir = /var/lib/mysql/
innodb_data_file_path = ibdata1:1G;ibdata2:1G;ibdata3:1G
```

That creates a 3 GB tablespace in three files. Sometimes people wonder whether they can use multiple files to spread load across drives, like this:

```
innodb_data_file_path = /disk1/ibdata1:1G;/disk2/ibdata2:1G;...
```

While that does indeed place the files in different directories, which represent different drives in this example, InnoDB concatenates the files end-to-end. Thus, you usually don't gain much this way. InnoDB will fill the first file, then the second when the first is full, and so on; the load isn't really spread in the fashion you need for higher performance. A RAID controller is a smarter way to spread load.

To allow the tablespace to grow if it runs out of space, you can make the last file autoextend as follows:

```
...ibdata3:1G:autoextend
```

The default behavior is to create a single 10 MB autoextending file. If you make the file autoextend, it's a good idea to place an upper limit on the tablespace's size to keep it from growing very large, because once it grows, it doesn't shrink. For example, the following example limits the autoextending file to 2 GB:

```
...ibdata3:1G:autoextend:max:2G
```

Managing a single tablespace can be a hassle, especially if it autoextends and you want to reclaim the space (for this reason, we recommend disabling the autoextend feature). The only way to reclaim space is to dump your data, shut down MySQL, delete all the files, change the configuration, restart, let InnoDB create new empty files, and restore your data. InnoDB is completely unforgiving about its tablespace—you cannot simply remove files or change their sizes. It will refuse to start if you corrupt its tablespace. It is likewise very strict about its log files. If you're used to casually moving files around with MyISAM, take heed!

The `innodb_file_per_table` option lets you configure InnoDB to use one file per table in MySQL 4.1 and later. It stores the data in the database directory as *tablename.ibd* files. This makes it easier to reclaim space when you drop a table, and it can be useful for spreading tables across multiple disks. However, placing the data in multiple files can actually result in more wasted space overall, because it trades internal fragmentation in the single InnoDB tablespace for wasted space in the *.ibd* files. This is more of an issue for very small tables, because InnoDB's page size is 16 KB. Even if your table has only 1 KB of data, it will still require at least 16 KB on disk.

Even if you enable the innodb_file_per_table option, you'll still need the main tablespace for the undo logs and other system data. (It will be smaller if you're not storing all the data in it, but it's still a good idea to disable autoextend, because you can't shrink the file without reloading all your data.) Also, you still won't be able to move, back up, or restore tables by simply copying the files. It's possible to do, but it requires some extra steps, and you can't copy tables between servers at all. See "Restoring Raw Files" on page 500 for more on this topic.

Some people like to use innodb_file_per_table just because of the extra manageability and visibility it gives you. For example, it's much faster to find a table's size by examining a single file than it is to use SHOW TABLE STATUS, which has to lock and scan the buffer pool to determine how many pages are allocated to a table.

We should also note that you don't actually have to store your InnoDB files in a traditional filesystem. Like many traditional database servers, InnoDB offers the option of using a raw device—i.e., an unformatted partition—for its storage. However, today's filesystems can handle sufficiently large files that you shouldn't need to use this option. Using raw devices may improve performance by a few percentage points, but we don't think this small increase justifies the disadvantages of not being able to manipulate the data as files. When you store your data on a raw partition, you can't use *mv*, *cp*, or any other tools on it. We also think snapshot capabilities, such as those provided by GNU/Linux's Logical Volume Manager (LVM), are a huge boon. You can place a raw device on a logical volume, but this defeats the point—it's not really raw. Ultimately, the tiny performance gains you get from using raw devices aren't worth the extra hassle.

Old row versions and the tablespace. InnoDB's tablespace can grow very large in a write-heavy environment. If transactions stay open for a long time (even if they're not doing any work) and they're using the default REPEATABLE READ transaction isolation level, InnoDB won't be able to remove old row versions, because the uncommitted transactions will still need to be able to see them. InnoDB stores the old versions in the tablespace, so the it continues to grow as more data is updated. Sometimes the problem isn't uncommitted transactions, but just the workload: the purge process is only a single thread, and it might not be able to keep up with the number of old row versions that need to be purged.

In either case, the output of SHOW INNODB STATUS can help you pinpoint the problem. Look at the first and second lines of the TRANSACTIONS section, which show the current transaction number and the point to which the purge has completed. If the difference is large, you may have a lot of unpurged transactions. Here's an example:

```
------------
TRANSACTIONS
------------
```

```
Trx id counter 0 80157601
Purge done for trx's n:o <0 80154573 undo n:o <0 0
```

The transaction identifier is a 64-bit number composed of two 32-bit numbers, so you might have to do a little math to compute the difference. In this case it's easy, because the high bits are just zeros: there are 80157601 − 80154573 = 3028 potentially unpurged transactions (*innotop* can do this math for you). We said "potentially" because a large difference doesn't necessarily mean there are a lot of unpurged rows. Only transactions that change data will create old row versions, and there may be many transactions that haven't changed any data (conversely, a single transaction could have changed many rows).

If you have a lot of unpurged transactions and your tablespace is growing because of it, you can force MySQL to slow down enough for InnoDB's purge thread to keep up. This may not sound attractive, but there's no alternative. Otherwise, InnoDB will keep writing data and filling up your disk until the disk runs out of space or the tablespace reaches the limits you've defined.

To throttle the writes, set the `innodb_max_purge_lag` variable to a value other than 0. This value indicates the maximum number of transactions that can be waiting to be purged before InnoDB starts to delay further queries that update data. You'll have to know your workload to decide on a good value. As an example, if your average transaction affects 1 KB of rows and you can tolerate 100 MB of unpurged rows in your tablespace, you could set the value to 100000.

Bear in mind that unpurged row versions impact all queries, because they effectively make your tables and indexes larger. If the purge thread simply can't keep up, performance can decrease dramatically. Setting the `innodb_max_purge_lag` variable will slow down performance too, but it's the lesser of the two evils.

The doublewrite buffer

InnoDB uses a *doublewrite buffer* to avoid data corruption in case of partial page writes. A partial page write occurs when a disk write doesn't complete fully, and only a portion of a 16 KB page is written to disk. There are a variety of reasons (crashes, bugs, and so on) that a page might be partially written to disk. The doublewrite buffer guards against data corruption if this happens.

The doublewrite buffer is a special reserved area of the tablespace, large enough to hold 100 pages in a contiguous block. It is essentially a backup copy of recently written pages. When InnoDB flushes pages from the buffer pool to the disk, it writes (and flushes) them first to the doublewrite buffer, then to the main data area where they really belong. This ensures that every page write is atomic and durable.

Doesn't this mean that every page is written twice? Yes, it does, but because InnoDB writes several pages to the doublewrite buffer sequentially and only then calls `fsync()` to sync them to disk the performance impact is relatively small—generally a few percentage points. More importantly, this strategy allows the log files to be much more efficient. Because the doublewrite buffer gives InnoDB a very strong guarantee that the data pages are not corrupt, InnoDB's log records don't have to contain full pages; they are more like binary deltas to pages.

If there's a partial page write to the doublewrite buffer itself, the original page will still be on disk in its real location. When InnoDB recovers, it will use the original page instead of the corrupted copy in the doublewrite buffer. However, if the doublewrite buffer succeeds and the write to the page's real location fails, InnoDB will use the copy in the doublewrite buffer during recovery. InnoDB knows when a page is corrupt because each page has a checksum at the end; the checksum is the last thing to be written, so if the page's contents don't match the checksum, the page is corrupt. Upon recovery, therefore, InnoDB just reads each page in the doublewrite buffer and verifies the checksums. If a page's checksum is incorrect, it reads the page from its original location.

In some cases, the doublewrite buffer really isn't necessary—for example, you might want to disable it on slaves. Also, some filesystems (such as ZFS) do the same thing themselves, so it is redundant for InnoDB to do it. You can disable the doublewrite buffer by setting `innodb_doublewrite` to 0.

Other I/O tuning options

The `sync_binlog` option controls how MySQL flushes the binary log to disk. Its default value is 0, which means MySQL does no flushing, and it's up to the operating system to decide when to flush its cache to durable storage. If the value is greater than 0, it specifies how many binary log writes happen between flushes to disk (each write is a single statement if `autocommit` is set, and otherwise a transaction). It's rare to set this option to anything other than 0 or 1.

If you don't set `sync_binlog` to 1, it's likely that a crash will cause your binary log to be out of sync with your transactional data. This can easily break replication and make point-in-time recovery impossible. However, the safety provided by setting this option to 1 comes at high price. Synchronizing the binary log and the transaction log requires MySQL to flush two files in two distinct locations. This might require a disk seek, which is relatively slow.

 If you're using binary logging and InnoDB in MySQL 5.0 or later, and especially if you're upgrading from an earlier version, you should be very careful about the new XA transaction support. It is designed to synchronize transaction commits between storage engines and the binary log, but it also disables InnoDB's group commit. This can reduce performance dramatically by requiring many more fsync() calls when committing transactions. You can ease the problem by disabling the binary log *and* disabling InnoDB's XA support with `innodb_support_xa=0`. If you have a battery-backed RAID cache, each fsync() call will be fast, so it might not be an issue.

As with the InnoDB log file, placing the binary log on a RAID volume with a battery-backed write cache can give a huge performance boost.

A non-performance-related note on the binary logs: if you want to use the expire_logs_days option to remove old binary logs automatically, don't remove them with *rm*. The server will get confused and refuse to remove them automatically, and PURGE MASTER LOGS will stop working. The solution, should you find yourself entangled in this situation, is to manually resync the *hostname-bin.index* file with the list of files that still exist on disk.

We cover RAID in more depth in Chapter 7, but it's worth repeating here that good-quality RAID controllers, with battery-backed write caches set to use the write back policy, can handle *thousands* of writes per second and still give you durable storage. The data gets written to a fast cache with a battery, so it will survive even if the system loses power. When the power comes back, the RAID controller will write the data from the cache to the disk before making the disk available for use. Thus, a good RAID controller with a large enough battery-backed write cache can improve performance dramatically and is a very good investment.

Tuning MySQL Concurrency

When you're running MySQL in a high-concurrency workload, you may run into bottlenecks you wouldn't otherwise experience. The following sections explain how to detect these problems when they happen, and how to get the best performance possible under these workloads for MyISAM and InnoDB.

MyISAM Concurrency Tuning

Simultaneous reading and writing has to be controlled carefully so that readers don't see inconsistent results. MyISAM allows concurrent inserts and reads under some conditions, and it lets you "schedule" some operations to try to block as little as possible.

Before we look at MyISAM's concurrency settings, it's important to understand how MyISAM deletes and inserts rows. Delete operations don't rearrange the entire table; they just mark rows as deleted, leaving "holes" in the table. MyISAM prefers to fill the holes if it can, reusing the spaces for inserted rows. If there are no holes, it appends new rows to the end of the table.

Even though MyISAM has table-level locks, it can append new rows concurrently with reads. It does this by stopping the reads at the last row that existed when they began. This avoids inconsistent reads.

However, it is much more difficult to provide consistent reads when something is changing the middle of the table. MVCC is the most popular way to solve this problem: it lets readers read old versions of data while writers create new versions.

MyISAM doesn't support MVCC, so it doesn't support concurrent inserts unless they go at the end of the table.

You can configure MyISAM's concurrent insert behavior with the concurrent_insert variable, which can have the following values:

0   MyISAM allows no concurrent inserts; every insert locks the table exclusively.

1   This is the default value. MyISAM allows concurrent inserts, as long as there are no holes in the table.

2   This value is available in MySQL 5.0 and newer. It forces concurrent inserts to append to the end of the table, even when there are holes. If there are no threads reading from the table, MySQL will place the new rows in the holes. The table can become more fragmented than usual with this setting, so you may need to optimize your tables more frequently, depending on your workload.

You can also configure MySQL to delay some operations to a later time, when they can be combined for greater efficiency. For instance, you can delay index writes with the delay_key_write variable, which we mentioned earlier in this chapter. This involves the familiar tradeoff: write the index right away (safe but expensive), or wait and hope the power doesn't fail before the write happens (faster, but likely to cause massive index corruption in the event of a crash because the index file will be very out-of-date). You can also give INSERT, REPLACE, DELETE, and UPDATE queries lower priority than SELECT queries with the low_priority_updates option. This is equivalent to globally applying the LOW_PRIORITY modifier to UPDATE queries. See "Query Optimizer Hints" on page 195 for more on this.

Finally, even though InnoDB's scalability issues are more often talked about, MyISAM has also had problems with mutexes for a long time. In MySQL 4.0 and earlier, a global mutex protected any I/O to the key buffer, which caused scalability problems with multiple CPUs and multiple disks. MySQL 4.1's key buffer code is improved and doesn't have this problem anymore, but it still holds a mutex on each key buffer. This is an issue when a thread copies key blocks from the key buffer into its local storage, rather than reading from the disk. The disk bottleneck is gone, but there's still a bottleneck when accessing data in the key buffer. You can sometimes work around this problem with multiple key buffers, but this approach isn't always successful. For example, there's no way to solve the problem when it involves only a single index. As a result, concurrent SELECT queries can perform significantly worse on multi-CPU machines than on a single-CPU machine, even when these are the only queries running.

InnoDB Concurrency Tuning

InnoDB is designed for high concurrency, but it's not perfect. The InnoDB architecture still shows its roots in limited memory, single-CPU, single-disk systems. Some aspects of InnoDB's performance degrade badly in high-concurrency situations, and your only recourse is to limit concurrency. You can often see whether InnoDB is having concurrency issues by inspecting the SEMAPHORES section of the SHOW INNODB STATUS output. See "SEMAPHORES" on page 566 for more information.

InnoDB has its own "thread scheduler" that controls how threads enter its kernel to access data, and what they can do once they're inside the kernel. The most basic way to limit concurrency is with the innodb_thread_concurrency variable, which limits how many threads can be in the kernel at once. A value of 0 means there is no limit on the number of threads. If you are having InnoDB concurrency problems, this variable is the most important one to configure.

It's impossible to name a good value for any given architecture and workload. In theory, the following formula gives a good value:

```
concurrency = Number of CPUs * Number of Disks * 2
```

But in practice, it can be better to use a much smaller value. You will have to experiment and benchmark to find the best value for your system.

If more than the allowed number of threads are already in the kernel, a thread can't enter the kernel. InnoDB uses a two-phase process to try to let threads enter as efficiently as possible. The two-phase policy reduces the overhead of context switches caused by the operating system scheduler. The thread first sleeps for innodb_thread_sleep_delay microseconds, and then tries again. If it still can't enter, it goes into a queue of waiting threads and yields to the operating system.

The default sleep time in the first phase is 10,000 microseconds. Changing this value can help in high-concurrency environments, when the CPU is underused with a lot of threads in the "sleeping before entering queue" status. The default value can also be much too large if you have a lot of small queries, because it adds 10 milliseconds to query latency.

Once a thread is inside the kernel, it has a certain number of "tickets" that let it back into the kernel for "free," without any concurrency checks. This limits how much work it can do before it has to get back in line with other waiting threads. The innodb_concurrency_tickets option controls the number of tickets. It rarely needs to be changed unless you have a lot of extremely long-running queries. Tickets are granted per-query, not per-transaction. Once a query finishes, its unused tickets are discarded.

In addition to the bottlenecks in the buffer pool and other structures, there's another concurrency bottleneck at the commit stage, which is largely I/O-bound because of flush operations. The innodb_commit_concurrency variable governs how many threads can commit at the same time. Configuring this option may help if there's a lot of thread thrashing even when innodb_thread_concurrency is set to a low value.

The InnoDB team is working on solving these issues, and there were major improvements in MySQL 5.0.30 and 5.0.32.

Workload-Based Tuning

The ultimate goal of tuning your server is to customize it for your specific workload. This requires intimate knowledge of the number, type, and frequency of all kinds of server activities—not just queries, but other activities too, such as connecting to the server and flushing tables. You also need to know how to monitor and interpret the status and activity of MySQL and the operating system; see Chapters 7 and 14 for more on these topics.

The first thing you should do, if you haven't done it already, is become familiar with your server. Know what kinds of queries run on it. Monitor it with *innotop* or other tools. It's helpful to know not only what your server is doing overall, but what each MySQL query spends a lot of time doing. One way to glean this knowledge is by aggregating the output of SHOW PROCESSLIST by the Command column with a script (*innotop* has this ability built in), or just by inspecting it visually. Look for threads that spend a lot of time in a particular state.

If there's a time when your server is running at full capacity, try to look at the process list then, because that's the best way to see what kinds of queries suffer most. For example, are there a lot of queries copying results to temporary tables, or sorting results? If so, you know you need to look at the configuration settings for temporary tables and sort buffers. (You'll probably also need to optimize the queries themselves.)

We usually recommend using the patches we've developed for the MySQL logs, which can give you a great deal of information on what each query does and let you analyze your workload in much more detail. These patches are included in recent official MySQL server distributions, so they may already be in your server. See "Finer control over logging" on page 65 for more details.

Optimizing for BLOB and TEXT Workloads

BLOB and TEXT columns are a special type of workload for MySQL. (We refer to all of the BLOB and TEXT types as BLOB for simplicity, because they belong to the same class of data types.) There are several restrictions on BLOB values that make the server treat them differently from other types. One of the most important considerations is that the server cannot use in-memory temporary tables for BLOB values. Thus, if a query involving BLOB values requires a temporary table—no matter how small—it will go to disk immediately. This is very inefficient, especially for otherwise small and fast queries. The temporary table could be most of the query's cost.

There are two ways to ease this penalty: convert the values to VARCHAR with the SUBSTRING( ) function (see "String Types" on page 84 for more on this), or make temporary tables faster.

The best way to make temporary tables faster is to place them on a memory-based filesystem (tmpfs on GNU/Linux). This removes some overhead, although it's still much slower than using in-memory tables. Using a memory-based filesystem is helpful because the operating system tries to avoid writing data to disk.* Normal filesystems are cached in memory too, but the operating system might flush normal filesystem data every few seconds. A tmpfs filesystem never gets flushed. The tmpfs filesystem is also designed for low overhead and simplicity. For example, there's no need for the filesystem to make any provisions for recovery. That makes it faster.

The server setting that controls where temporary tables are placed is tmpdir. Monitor how full the filesystem gets to ensure you have enough space for temporary tables. If necessary, you can even specify several temporary table locations, which MySQL will use in a round-robin fashion.

If your BLOB columns are very large and you use InnoDB, you might also want to increase InnoDB's log buffer size. We wrote more about this earlier in this chapter.

For long variable-length columns (e.g., BLOB, TEXT, and long character columns), InnoDB stores a 768-byte prefix in-page with the rest of the row.† If the column's value is longer than this prefix length, InnoDB may allocate external storage space outside the row to store the rest of the value. It allocates this space in whole 16 KB pages, just like all other InnoDB pages, and each column gets its own page (columns do not share external storage space). InnoDB allocates external storage space to a column a page at a time until 32 pages are used; then it allocates 64 pages at a time.

Note that we said InnoDB *may* allocate external storage. If the total length of the row, including the full value of the long column, is shorter than InnoDB's maximum row length (a little less than 8 KB), InnoDB will not allocate external storage even if the long column's value exceeds the prefix length.

Finally, when InnoDB updates a long column that is placed in external storage, it doesn't update it in place. Instead, it writes the new value to a new location in external storage and deletes the old value.

All of this has the following consequences:

- Long columns can waste a lot of space in InnoDB. For example, if you store a column value that is one byte too long to fit in the row, it will use an entire page to store the remaining byte, wasting most of the page. Likewise, if you have a value that is slightly more than 32 pages long, it may actually use 96 pages on disk.

- External storage disables the adaptive hash index, which needs to compare the full length of columns to verify that it found the right data. (The hash helps InnoDB find "guesses" very quickly, but it must check that its "guess" is correct.)

---

* Data can still go to disk if the operating system swaps it.

† This is long enough to create a 255-character index on a column, even if it's utf8, which might require up to 3 bytes per character.

Because the adaptive hash index is completely in-memory and is built directly "on top of" frequently accessed pages in the buffer pool, it doesn't work with external storage.

- Long values can make queries with a WHERE clause that doesn't use an index run slowly. MySQL reads all columns before it applies the WHERE clause, so it might ask InnoDB to read a lot of external storage, then check the WHERE clause and throw away all the data it read. It's never a good idea to select columns you don't need, but this is a special case where it's even more important to avoid doing so. If you find your queries are suffering from this limitation, you can try to use covering indexes to help. See "Covering Indexes" on page 120 for more information.

- If you have many long columns in a single table, it might be better to combine the data they store into a single column, perhaps as an XML document. That lets all the values share external storage, rather than using their own pages.

- You can sometimes gain significant space and performance benefits by storing long columns in a BLOB and compressing them with COMPRESS( ), or compressing them in the application before sending them to MySQL.

Optimizing for filesorts

MySQL has two variables that can help you control how it performs filesorts.

Recall from "Sort optimizations" on page 176 that MySQL has two filesort algorithms. It uses the two-pass algorithm if the total size of all the columns needed for the query, plus the ORDER BY columns, exceeds max_length_for_sort_data bytes. It also uses this algorithm when any of the required columns—even those not used for the ORDER BY—is a BLOB or TEXT column. (You can use SUBSTRING( ) to convert such columns to types that can work with the single-pass algorithm.)

You can influence MySQL's choice of algorithm by changing the value of the max_length_for_sort_data variable. Because the single-pass algorithm creates a fixed-size buffer for each row it will sort, the maximum length of VARCHAR columns is what counts toward max_length_for_sort_data, not the actual size of the stored data. This is one of the reasons why we recommend you make these columns only as large as necessary.

When MySQL has to sort on BLOB or TEXT columns, it uses only a prefix and ignores the remainder of the values. This is because it has to allocate a fixed-size structure to hold the values and copy the prefix from external storage into that structure. You can specify how large this prefix should be with the max_sort_length variable.

Unfortunately, MySQL doesn't really give you any visibility into which sort algorithm it uses. If you increase the max_length_for_sort_data variable and your disk usage goes up, your CPU usage goes down, and the Sort_merge_passes status variable begins to grow more quickly than it did before the change, you've probably forced more sorts to use the single-pass algorithm.

For more on the BLOB and TEXT types, see "String Types" on page 84.

Inspecting MySQL Server Status Variables

One of the most productive ways to tune MySQL for your workload is to examine the output from SHOW GLOBAL STATUS to see which settings might need changing. If you are just getting started tuning a server and you're familiar with *mysqlreport*, running it and examining the easy-to-read report it generates can save you a lot of time. This report will help you locate potential trouble spots, and you can then inspect the relevant variables more carefully with SHOW GLOBAL STATUS. If you see something that looks like it could be improved, you can tune it. Then take a look at the incremental output of *mysqladmin extended -r -i60* to see the effects of your changes. For the best results, look both at absolute values and at how the values change over time.

There's a more detailed list of the variables you can inspect with SHOW GLOBAL STATUS in Chapter 13. The following list shows only the variables that are most productive to examine:

Aborted_clients
> If this variable's value increases over time, are you closing your connections gracefully? If not, check your network performance, and examine the max_allowed_packet configuration variable. Queries that exceed max_allowed_packet will abort ungracefully.

Aborted_connects
> This should be very close to zero; if it's not, you may have network problems. A few aborted connects are normal. For example, they may occur when someone tries to connect from the wrong host, uses the wrong username or password, or specifies an invalid database.

Binlog_cache_disk_use *and* Binlog_cache_use
> If the ratio of Binlog_cache_disk_use to Binlog_cache_use is large, increase the binlog_cache_size. You want most transactions to fit into the binary log cache, but it's OK if one occasionally spills onto disk.
>
> Reducing binary log cache misses isn't an exact science. The best approach is to increase the binlog_cache_size setting and see whether the cache miss rate decreases. Once you get it down to a certain point, you may not benefit from making the cache size larger. Suppose you have one miss per second, and you increase the size and it goes to one per minute. That's good enough—you are unlikely to get it down much lower, and even if you do, there's very little benefit, so save the memory for something else instead.

Bytes_received *and* Bytes_sent

> These values can help you determine whether a problem with the server is because of too much traffic to or from the server.* They may also point out a problem elsewhere in your code, such as a query that is fetching more data than it needs. (See "The MySQL Client/Server Protocol" on page 161 for more on this topic.)

Com_*

> You should check that you're not getting higher than expected values for unusual variables such as Com_rollback. A quick way to check for reasonable values here is *innotop*'s Command Summary mode (see Chapter 14 for more on *innotop*).

Connections

> This variable represents the number of connection attempts (not the number of current connections, which is Threads_connected). If its value increases rapidly— i.e., to hundreds per second—you may need to look into connection pooling or tuning the operating system's networking stack (see the next chapter for more on network configuration).

Created_tmp_disk_tables

> If this value is high, one of two things could be wrong: your queries might create temporary tables while selecting BLOB or TEXT columns, or your tmp_table_size and/or max_heap_table_size might not be large enough.

Created_tmp_tables

> The only way to deal with a high value for this variable is by optimizing your queries. See Chapters 3 and 4 for tips on optimization.

Handler_read_rnd_next

> Handler_read_rnd_next / Handler_read_rnd gives you the approximate average size of a full table scan. If it's large, you may need to optimize your schema, indexing, or queries.

Key_blocks_used

> If Key_blocks_used * key_cache_block_size is much smaller than key_buffer_size on a warmed-up server, your key_buffer_size is larger than you need and you're wasting memory.

Key_reads

> Watch how many reads per second you see, and match the value against your I/O system to see how closely you're approaching your I/O limits. See Chapter 7 for more information.

---

* Even if your network has enough capacity, don't rule it out as a performance bottleneck. Network latency can contribute to slow performance.

Max_used_connections

If this value is the same as `max_connections`, either `max_connections` is set too low or you had a peak in demand that exceeded your server's configured limits. Don't automatically assume you should increase `max_connections`, though! It's there as an emergency limit to keep your server from being swamped under too much load. If you see a spike in demand, you should check to make sure that your application isn't misbehaving, your server is tuned correctly, and your schema is well designed. It's better to fix the application than to simply increase the server's `max_connections` limit.

Open_files

Be careful that this doesn't approach the value of `open_files_limit`. If it does, you should probably increase the limit.

Open_tables *and* **Opened_tables**

Check this value against your `table_cache` value. If you see many `Opened_tables` per second, your `table_cache` value might not be large enough. Explicit temporary tables can also cause a growing number of opened tables even when the table cache isn't fully used, though, so it might be nothing to worry about.

Qcache_*

See "The MySQL Query Cache" on page 204 for more on the query cache.

Select_full_join

Full joins are joins without indexes, which are a real performance killer. It's best to eliminate these; even one per minute can be too much. You should optimize your queries and indexes if you have joins without indexes.

Select_full_range_join

If this number is high, you run many queries that use a range lookup strategy to join tables. These can be slow and are a good place to optimize.

Select_range_check

This variable tracks query plans that reexamine key selections for each row in a join, which has high overhead. If the value is high or increasing, you have some queries that can't find good indexes to use.

Slow_launch_threads

A large value for this status variable means that something is delaying new threads upon connection. This is a clue that something is wrong with your server, but it doesn't really indicate what. It usually means there's a system overload, causing the operating system not to schedule any CPU time for newly created threads.

Sort_merge_passes

A high value for this variable means you might need to increase the `sort_buffer_size`, perhaps just for certain queries. Check your queries and find out which ones are causing filesorts. You might be able to optimize them.

Table_locks_waited

This variable tells you how many tables were locked and caused lock waits on the server level (waits for storage engine locks, such as InnoDB's row-level locks, do not increment this variable). If this value is high and increasing, you may have a serious concurrency bottleneck. You might consider using InnoDB or another storage engine that uses row-level locking, partitioning large tables manually or with MySQL's built-in partitioning in MySQL 5.1 and later, optimizing your queries, enabling concurrent inserts, or tuning lock settings.

MySQL doesn't tell you how long the waits were. At the time of this writing, perhaps the best way to find out is with the microsecond-resolution slow query log. See "MySQL Profiling" on page 63 for more on this.

Threads_created

If this value is large or increasing, you probably need to increase the thread_cache_size variable. Check Threads_cached to see how many threads are in the cache already.

Tuning Per-Connection Settings

You should *not* raise the value of a per-connection setting globally unless you know it's the right thing to do. Some buffers are allocated all at once, even if they're not needed, so a large global setting can be a huge waste. Instead, you can raise the value when a query needs it.

The most common example of a variable that you should probably keep small and raise only for certain queries is sort_buffer_size, which controls how large the sort buffer should be for filesorts. It is allocated to its full size even for very small sorts, so if you make it much larger than the average sort requires, you'll be wasting memory and adding allocation cost.

When you find a query that needs a larger sort buffer to perform well, you can raise the sort_buffer_size value just before the query and then restore it to DEFAULT afterward. Here's an example of how to do this:

```
SET @@session.sort_buffer_size := <value>;
-- Execute the query...
SET @@session.sort_buffer_size := DEFAULT;
```

Wrapper functions can be handy for this type of code. Other variables you might set on a per-connection basis are read_buffer_size, read_rnd_buffer_size, tmp_table_size, and myisam_sort_buffer_size (if you're repairing tables).

If you need to save and restore a possibly customized value, you can do something like the following:

```
SET @saved_<unique_variable_name> := @@session.sort_buffer_size;
SET @@session.sort_buffer_size := <value>;
-- Execute the query...
SET @@session.sort_buffer_size := @saved_<unique_variable_name>;
```

Operating System and Hardware Optimization

Your MySQL server can perform only as well as its weakest link, and the operating system and hardware on which it runs are often limiting factors. The disk size, the available memory and CPU resources, the network, and the components that link them all limit the system's ultimate capacity.

In the earlier chapters, we concentrated on optimizing the MySQL server and your application. This kind of tuning is crucial, but you also need to consider your hardware and configure the operating system appropriately. For example, if your workload is I/O-bound, one approach is to design your application to minimize MySQL's I/O workload. However, it's often smarter to upgrade the I/O subsystem, install more memory, or reconfigure existing disks.

Hardware changes very rapidly, so we won't compare different products or mention particular components in this chapter. Instead, our goal is to give you a set of guidelines and approaches for solving hardware and operating system bottlenecks.

We begin by looking at what limits MySQL's performance. The most common problems are CPU, memory, and I/O bottlenecks, but they may not be what they appear at first glance. We explore how to choose CPUs for MySQL servers, and then we consider how to balance memory and disk resources. We examine different types of I/O (random versus sequential, reads versus writes) and explain how to understand your working set. That knowledge will help you choose an effective memory-to-disk ratio. We move from there to tips for choosing disks for MySQL servers, and we follow that section with the all-important topic of RAID optimization. We finish our discussion of storage with a look at external storage options (such as SANs) and some advice on how and when to use multiple disk volumes for MySQL data and logs.

From storage, we move on to network performance and how to choose an operating system and filesystem. Then we examine the threading support MySQL needs to work well, and how to avoid swapping. We close the chapter with examples of operating system status output.

What Limits MySQL's Performance?

Many different hardware components can affect MySQL's performance, but the two most frequent bottlenecks we see are CPU saturation and I/O saturation. CPU saturation happens when MySQL works with data that either fits in memory or can be read from disk as fast as needed. Examples are intensive cryptographic operations and joins without indexes that end up being cross-products.

I/O saturation, on the other hand, generally happens when you need to work with much more data than you can fit in memory. If your application is distributed across a network, or if you have a huge number of queries and/or low latency requirements, the bottleneck may shift to the network instead.

Look beyond the obvious when you think you've found a bottleneck. A weakness in one area often puts pressure on another subsystem, which then appears to be the problem. For example, if you don't have enough memory, MySQL might have to flush caches to make room for data it needs—and then, an instant later, read back the data it just flushed (this is true for both read and write operations). The memory scarcity can thus appear to be a lack of I/O capacity. Similarly, a saturated memory bus can appear to be a CPU problem. In fact, when we say that an application has a "CPU bottleneck" or is "CPU-bound," what we really mean is that there is a computational bottleneck. We delve into this issue next.

How to Select CPUs for MySQL

You should consider whether your workload is CPU-bound when upgrading current hardware or purchasing new hardware.

You can identify a CPU-bound workload by checking the CPU utilization, but instead of looking only at how heavily your CPUs are loaded overall, try to look at the balance of CPU usage and I/O for your most important queries, and notice whether the CPUs are loaded evenly. You can use tools such as *mpstat*, *iostat*, and *vmstat* (see the end of this chapter for examples) to figure out what limits your server's performance.

Which Is Better: Fast CPUs or Many CPUs?

When you have a CPU-bound workload, MySQL generally benefits most from *faster* CPUs (as opposed to more CPUs).

This isn't always true, because it depends on the workload and the number of CPUs. However, MySQL's current architecture has scaling issues with multiple CPUs, and MySQL cannot run a single query in parallel across many CPUs. As a result, the CPU speed limits the response time for each individual CPU-bound query.

Broadly speaking, there are two types of performance you might desire:

Low latency (fast response time)
> To achieve this you need fast CPUs, because each query will use only a single CPU.

High throughput
> If you can run many queries at the same time, you may benefit from multiple CPUs to service the queries. However, whether this works in practice depends on many factors. Because MySQL scales poorly on multiple CPUs, it's often better to use fewer fast CPUs instead.

If you have multiple CPUs and you're not running queries concurrently, MySQL can still use the extra CPUs for background tasks such as purging InnoDB buffers, network operations, and so on. However, these jobs are usually minor compared to executing queries. If you have a dual-CPU system running a single CPU-bound query constantly, the second CPU will probably be idle around 90% of the time.

MySQL replication (discussed in the next chapter) also works best with fast CPUs, not many CPUs. If your workload is CPU-bound, a parallel workload on the master can easily serialize into a workload the slave can't keep up with, even if the slave is more powerful than the master. That said, the I/O subsystem, not the CPU, is usually the bottleneck on a slave.

If you have a CPU-bound workload, another way to approach the question of whether you need fast CPUs or many CPUs is to consider what your queries are really doing. At the hardware level, a query can either be executing or waiting. The most common causes of waiting are waiting in the run queue (when the process is runnable, but all the CPUs are busy), waiting for latches or locks, and waiting for the disk or network. What do you expect your queries to be waiting for? If they'll be waiting in the run queue or waiting for latches or locks, you generally need faster CPUs. (There might be exceptions, such as a query waiting for the InnoDB log buffer mutex, which doesn't become free until the I/O completes—this might indicate that you actually need more I/O capacity.)

That said, MySQL can use many CPUs effectively on some workloads. For example, suppose you have many connections querying distinct tables (and thus not contending for table locks, which can be a problem with MyISAM and Memory tables), and the server's total throughput is more important than any individual query's response time. Throughput can be very high in this scenario because the threads can all run concurrently without contending with each other. Again, this may work better in theory than in practice: InnoDB has scaling issues regardless of whether queries are reading from distinct tables or not, and MyISAM has global locks on each key buffer. Full table scans on MyISAM tables are an example of queries that can run concurrently without interfering.

MySQL advertises the Falcon storage engine as being designed to take advantage of servers with at least eight CPUs, so in the future MySQL might be able to use many CPUs more effectively than it does now. However, only time and experience will reveal Falcon's true scalability.

CPU Architecture

Sixty-four-bit architectures are much more prevalent today than they were just a few years ago. MySQL works well on 64-bit architectures, though some of its internals are not yet 64-bit capable. For example, in MySQL 5.0 each MyISAM key buffer is limited to 4 GB, the size addressable by a 32-bit integer. (You can create multiple key buffers to work around this, though.)

It's a good idea to choose a 64-bit architecture for all new hardware you purchase. If you don't use a 64-bit CPU and 64-bit operating system, you won't be able to use a lot of memory efficiently: even though some 32-bit systems can support large amounts of memory, they can't use it as efficiently as a 64-bit system, and MySQL won't be able to use it well.

Scaling to Many CPUs and Cores

One place where multiple CPUs can be quite helpful is an online transaction processing system. These systems generally do many small operations, which can run on multiple CPUs because they're coming from multiple connections. In this environment, concurrency can become a bottleneck. Most web applications fall into this category.

Online transaction proccessing (OLTP) servers generally use InnoDB, which has some unresolved concurrency issues with many CPUs. However, it's not just InnoDB that can become a bottleneck. Any shared resource is a potential point of contention. InnoDB gets a lot of attention because it's the most common storage engine for high-concurrency environments, but MyISAM is no better when you really stress it, even when you're not changing any data. Many of the concurrency bottlenecks, such as InnoDB's row-level locks and MyISAM's table locks, can't be optimized away internally—there's no solution except to do the work as fast as possible, so the locks can be granted to whatever is waiting for them. It doesn't matter how many CPUs you have if a single lock is causing them all to wait. Thus, even some high-concurrency workloads benefit from faster CPUs.

There are actually two types of concurrency problems in databases, and you need different approaches to solve them:

Logical concurrency issues
> Contention for resources that are visible to the application, such as table or row locks. These problems usually require tactics such as changing your application, using a different storage engine, changing the server configuration, or using different locking hints or transaction isolation levels.

Internal concurrency issues

Contention for resources such as semaphores, access to pages in the InnoDB buffer pool, and so on. You can try to work around these problems by changing server settings, changing your operating system, or using different hardware, but you might just have to live with them. In some cases, using a different storage engine or a patch to a storage engine can help ease these problems.

The number of CPUs MySQL can use effectively and how it scales under increasing load—its "scaling pattern"—depend on both the workload and the system architecture. By "system architecture," we mean the operating system and hardware, not the application that uses MySQL. The CPU architecture (RISC, CISC, depth of pipeline, etc.), CPU model, and operating system all affect MySQL's scaling pattern. This is why benchmarking is so important: some systems may continue to perform very well under increasing concurrency, while others perform much worse.

Some systems can even give lower total performance with more processors. This is quite common; we know of many people who have tried to upgrade from four-core systems to eight-core systems, only to be forced to revert to four-core systems (or bind the MySQL process to only four of the eight cores) because of lower performance. You'll have to benchmark and see how your system does with your workload.

Some MySQL scalability bottlenecks are in the server, whereas others are in the storage engine layer. How the storage engine is designed is crucial, and you can sometimes switch to a different storage engine and get more from multiple CPUs.

The processor-speed wars we saw around the turn of the century have subsided to some extent, and CPU vendors are now focusing more on multicore CPUs and variations such as multithreading. The future of CPU design may well be hundreds of processor cores; quad-core CPUs are common today. Internal architectures vary so widely across vendors that it's impossible to generalize about the interaction between threads, CPUs, and cores. How the memory and bus are designed is also very important. In the final analysis, whether it's better to have multiple cores or multiple physical CPUs is also architecture-specific.

Balancing Memory and Disk Resources

The biggest reason to have a lot of memory isn't so you can hold a lot of data in memory: it's ultimately so you can avoid disk I/O, which is orders of magnitude slower than accessing data in memory. The trick is to balance the memory and disk size, speed, cost, and other qualities so you get good performance for your workload. Before we look at how to do that, let's go back to the basics for a moment.

Computers contain a pyramid of smaller, faster, more expensive caches, one upon the other, as depicted in Figure 7-1.

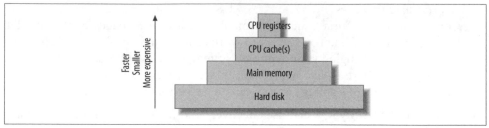

Figure 7-1. The cache hierarchy

Every level in this cache hierarchy is best used to cache "hot" data, so it can be accessed more quickly, usually using heuristics such as "recently used data is likely to be used again soon" and "data that's near recently used data is likely to be used soon." These heuristics work because of spatial and temporal *locality of reference*.

From the programmer's point of view, CPU registers and caches are transparent and architecture-specific. It is the compiler's and CPU's job to manage these. However, programmers are very conscious of the difference between main memory and the hard disk, and programs usually treat these very differently.*

This is especially true of database servers, whose behavior often goes against the predictions made by the heuristics we just mentioned. A well-designed database cache (such as the InnoDB buffer pool) is usually more efficient than an operating system's cache, which is tuned for general-purpose tasks. The database cache has much more knowledge about its data needs, and it has special-purpose logic that helps meet those needs. Also, a system call is not required to access the data in the database cache.

These special-purpose cache requirements are why you'll have to balance your cache hierarchy to suit the particular access patterns of a database server. Because the registers and on-chip caches are not user-configurable, memory and the hard disk are the only things you can change.

Random Versus Sequential I/O

Database servers use both sequential and random I/O, and random I/O benefits the most from caching. You can convince yourself of this by thinking about a typical mixed workload, with some balance of single-row lookups and multirow range scans. The typical pattern is for the "hot" data to be randomly distributed; caching this data will therefore help avoid expensive disk seeks. In contrast, sequential reads generally go through the data only once, so it's useless to cache it unless it fits completely in memory.

---

* However, programs may rely on the operating system to cache in memory a lot of data that's conceptually "on disk." This is what MyISAM does, for example.

Another reason sequential reads don't benefit much from caching is because they are faster than random reads. There are two reasons for this:

Sequential I/O is faster than random I/O.

Sequential operations are performed faster than random operations, both in memory and on disk. Suppose your disks can do 100 random I/O operations per second and can read 50 MB per second sequentially (that's roughly what a consumer-grade disk can achieve today). If you have 100-byte rows, that's 100 rows per second randomly, versus 500,000 rows per second sequentially—a difference of 5,000 times, or several orders of magnitude. Thus, the random I/O benefits more from caching in this scenario.

Accessing in-memory rows sequentially is also faster than accessing in-memory rows randomly. Today's memory chips can typically access about 250,000 100-byte rows per second randomly, and 5 million per second sequentially. Note that random accesses are some 2,500 times faster in memory than on disk, while sequential accesses are only 10 times faster in memory.

Storage engines can perform sequential reads faster than random reads.

A random read generally means that the storage engine must perform index operations. (There are exceptions to this rule, but it's true for InnoDB and MyISAM.) That usually requires navigating a B-Tree data structure and comparing values to other values. In contrast, sequential reads generally require traversing a simpler data structure, such as a linked list. That's a lot less work, so again, sequential reads are faster.

You can save work by caching sequential reads, but you can save much more work by caching random reads instead. In other words, *adding memory is the best solution for random-read I/O problems* if you can afford it.

Caching, Reads, and Writes

If you have enough memory, you can insulate the disk from read requests completely. If all your data fits in memory, every read will be a cache hit once the server's caches are warmed up. There will still be *logical reads*, but no *physical reads*. Writes are a different matter, though. A write can be performed in memory just as a read can, but sooner or later it has to be written to the disk so it's permanent. In other words, a cache can delay writes, but caching cannot eliminate writes as it can reads.

In fact, in addition to allowing writes to be delayed, caching can permit them to be grouped together in two important ways:

Many writes, one flush

A single piece of data can be changed many times in memory without all of the new values being written to disk. When the data is eventually flushed to disk, all the modifications that happened since the last physical write are made permanent. For example, many statements could update an in-memory counter. If the counter is incremented 100 times and then written to disk, 100 modifications have been grouped into one write.

I/O merging

Many different pieces of data can be modified in memory, and the modifications can be collected together, so the physical writes can be performed as a single disk operation.

This is why many transactional systems use a *write-ahead logging* strategy. Write-ahead logging lets them make changes to the pages in memory without flushing the changes to disk, which usually involves random I/O and is very slow. Instead, they write a record of the changes to a sequential log file, which is much faster. A background thread can flush the modified pages to disk later; when it does, it can optimize the writes.

Writes benefit greatly from buffering, because it converts random I/O into more sequential I/O. Asynchronous (buffered) writes are typically handled by the operating system and are batched so they can be flushed to disk more optimally. Synchronous (unbuffered) writes have to be written to disk before they finish. That's why they benefit from buffering in a RAID controller's battery-backed write-back cache (we discuss RAID a bit later).

What's Your Working Set?

Every application has a "working set" of data—that is, the data that it really needs to do its work. A lot of databases also have plenty of data that's not in the working set. You can imagine the database as a desk with filing drawers. The working set consists of the papers you need to have on the desktop to get your work done. The desktop is main memory in this analogy, while the filing drawers are the hard disks.

Just as you don't need to have *every* piece of paper on the desktop to get your work done, you don't need the whole database to fit in memory for optimal performance—just the working set.

The working set's size varies greatly depending on the application. For some applications the working set may be 1% of the total data size, while for others it could be close to 100%. When the working set doesn't fit in memory, the database server will have to shuffle data between the disk and memory to get its work done. This is why a memory shortage may look like an I/O problem. Sometimes there's no way you can fit your entire working set in memory, and sometimes you don't actually want to (for example, if your application needs a lot of sequential I/O). Your application architecture can change a lot depending on whether you can fit the working set in memory.

In the final analysis, "working set" is an ambiguous term. For example, you might need to access only 1% of your data every hour, but over a 24-hour period that might mean 20% of your data. What's the working set in this situation? It might be more helpful to think of the working set in terms of how much data you need to have cached, so your workload is mostly CPU-bound. If you can't cache enough data, your working set doesn't fit in memory.

The working set and the cache unit

The working set contains both data and indexes, and you should count it in *cache units*. A cache unit is the smallest unit of data that the storage engine works with.

The size of the cache unit varies between storage engines, and therefore so does the size of the working set. For example, InnoDB always works in pages of 16 KB. If you do a single-row lookup and InnoDB has to go to disk to get it, it'll read the entire page containing that row into the buffer pool and cache it there. This can be wasteful. Suppose you have 100-byte rows that you access randomly. InnoDB will use a lot of extra memory in the buffer pool for these rows, because it will have to read and cache a complete 16 KB page for each row. Because the working set includes indexes too, InnoDB will also read and cache the parts of the index tree it needed to find the row. InnoDB's index pages are also 16 KB in size, which means it may have to store a total of 32 KB (or more, depending on how deep the index tree is) to access a single 100-byte row. The cache unit is, therefore, another reason why well-chosen clustered indexes are so important in InnoDB. Clustered indexes not only let you optimize disk accesses, they also help you keep related data on the same pages, so you can fit more of your working set in your cache.

In contrast, the Falcon storage engine's cache unit is a row, not a page. Thus, Falcon may be more efficient at caching small, randomly accessed, widely scattered rows. To continue the desk metaphor, InnoDB requires you to take an entire file folder (database page) out of a drawer every time you need one of the sheets of paper in it. Without clustered indexes (or with poorly chosen clustered indexes), that would be very inefficient indeed. Falcon, on the other hand, lets you take any sheet of paper out of a file folder and put it on your desk, without requiring you to move the whole folder.

Both approaches have benefits and drawbacks. For example, InnoDB keeps the entire 16 KB page in memory, so if you need to access another row from the same page in the future, it's already there. Falcon has both a row cache and a page cache, which give a combination of benefits: the page cache reduces disk accesses, while the row cache uses memory efficiently. However, dual caches are inherently wasteful because they cause some data to be stored twice in memory. This is known as *double buffering*.

In theory, both strategies can be much more efficient for specific workloads, and much less efficient for others. As always, your choice will depend on what you need the storage engine to do best.

Finding an Effective Memory-to-Disk Ratio

A good memory-to-disk ratio is best discovered by experimentation and/or bench-marking. If you can fit everything into memory, you're done—there's no need to think about it further. But most of the time you can't, so you have to benchmark with a subset of your data and see what happens. What you're aiming for is an acceptable *cache miss rate*. A cache miss is when your queries request some data that's not cached in main memory, and the server has to get it from disk.

The cache miss rate really governs how much of your CPU is used, so the best way to assess your cache miss rate is to look at your CPU usage. For example, if your CPU is used 90% of the time and waiting for I/O 10% of the time, your cache miss rate is good.

Let's consider how your working set influences your cache miss rate. It's important to realize that your working set isn't just a number: it's actually a statistical distribution, and your cache miss rate is nonlinear with regard to the distribution. For example, if you have 10 GB of memory and you're getting a 10% cache miss rate, you might think you just need to add 11% more memory* to get the cache miss rate to zero. But in reality, inefficiencies such as the size of the cache unit might mean you'd theoretically need 50 GB of memory just to get a 1% miss rate. And even with a perfect cache unit match, the theoretical prediction can be wrong: factors such as data access patterns can complicate things even more. A 1% cache miss rate might require 500 GB of memory!

It's easy to get sidetracked focusing on optimizing something that might not give you much benefit. For example, a 10% miss rate may already result in 80% CPU usage, which is pretty good. Suppose you add memory and are able to get the cache miss rate down to 5%. As a gross oversimplification, you'll be delivering approximately another 6% data to the CPUs. Making another gross oversimplification, we could say that you've increased your CPU usage to 84.8%. However, this isn't a very big win, considering how much memory you might have purchased to get that result. And in reality, because of the differences between the speed of memory and disk accesses, what the CPU is really doing with the data, and many other factors, lowering the cache miss rate by 5% might not change your CPU usage much at all.

This is why we said you should strive for an *acceptable* cache miss rate, not a zero cache miss rate. There's no single number you should target, because what's considered "acceptable" will depend on your application and your workload. Some applications might do very well with a 1% cache miss rate, while others really need a rate as low as 0.01% to perform well. (A "good cache miss rate," like a "working set," is a fuzzy concept, and the fact that there are many ways to count the miss rate further complicates matters.)

---

* The right number is 11%, not 10%. A 10% miss rate is a 90% hit rate, so you need to divide 10 GB by 90%, which is 11.111 GB.

The best memory-to-disk ratio also depends on other components in your system. Suppose you have a system with 16 GB of memory, 20 GB of data, and lots of unused disk space. The system is performing nicely at 80% CPU usage. If you wish to place twice as much data on this system and maintain the same level of performance, you might think you can just double the number of CPUs and the amount of memory. However, even if every component in the system scaled perfectly with the increased load (an unrealistic assumption), this probably wouldn't work. The system with 20 GB of data is likely to be using more than 50% of some component's capacity—for example, it might already be performing 80% of its maximum number of I/O operations per second. It won't be able to handle twice as much load. Thus, the best memory-to-disk ratio depends on the system's weakest component.

Choosing Hard Disks

If you can't fit enough data in memory—for example, if you estimate you would need 500 GB of memory to fully load your CPUs with your current I/O system—you should consider a more powerful I/O subsystem, sometimes even at the expense of memory. And you should design your application to handle I/O wait.

This might seem counterintuitive. After all, we just said that more memory can ease the pressure on your I/O subsystem and reduce I/O waits. Why would you want to beef up the I/O subsystem if adding memory could solve the problem? The answer lies in the balance between the factors involved, such as the number of reads versus writes, the size of each I/O operation, and how many such operations happen every second. For example, if you need fast log writes, you can't shield the disk from these writes by increasing the amount of available memory. In this case, it might be a better idea to invest in a high-performance I/O system with a battery-backed write cache.

As a brief refresher, reading data from a conventional hard disk is a three-step process:

1. Move the read head to the right position on the disk's surface.
2. Wait for the disk to rotate, so the desired data is under the read head.
3. Wait for the disk to rotate all the desired data past the read head.

How quickly the disk can perform these operations can be condensed to two numbers: *access time* (steps 1 and 2 combined) and *transfer speed*. These two numbers also determine *latency* and *throughput*. Whether you need fast access times or fast transfer speeds—or a mixture of the two—depends on the kinds of queries you're running. In terms of total time needed to complete a disk read, small random lookups are dominated by steps 1 and 2, while big sequential reads are dominated by step 3.

Several other factors can also influence the choice of disks and which are important will depend on your application. Let's imagine you're choosing disks for an online application such as a popular news site, which does a lot of small, random reads. You might consider the following factors:

Storage capacity

This is rarely an issue for online applications, as today's disks are usually more than big enough. If they're not, combining smaller disks with RAID is standard practice.*

Transfer speed

Modern disks can usually transfer data very quickly, as we saw earlier. Exactly how quickly depends mostly on the spindle rotation speed and how densely the data is stored on the disk's surface, plus the limitations of the interface with the host system (many modern disks can read data faster than the interface can transfer it). Regardless, transfer speed is usually not a limiting factor for online applications, because they generally do a lot of small, random lookups.

Access time

This is usually the dominating factor in how fast your random lookups will perform, so you should look for fast access time.

Spindle rotation speed

Common rotation speeds today are 7,200 RPM, 10,000 RPM, and 15,000 RPM. The rotation speed contributes quite a bit to the speed of both random lookups and sequential scans.

Physical size

All other things being equal, the physical size of the disk makes a difference too: the smaller the disk is, the less time it takes to move the read head. Server-grade 2.5-inch disks are often faster than their larger cousins. They also use less power, and you can usually fit more of them into the chassis.

Disk technology changes often, so this advice may become outdated rather quickly. For example, solid-state drives are a hot topic at the time of this writing. They perform quite differently from spindle-based drives. However, they're still very expensive and are not yet used widely. We know of some projects that are using them successfully, but we don't have enough hands-on experience to give particular advice about them.

Just as with CPUs, how MySQL scales to multiple disks depends on the storage engine and the workload. InnoDB typically scales well to between 10 and 20 hard drives. However, MyISAM's table locks limit its write scalability, so a write-heavy workload on MyISAM probably won't benefit much from having many drives. Operating-system buffering and parallel background writes help somewhat, but MyISAM's write scalability is inherently more limited than InnoDB's.

As with CPUs, more disks is not always better. Some applications that demand low latency need faster drives, not more drives. For example, replication usually performs better with faster drives, because updates on a slave are single-threaded.

---

* Interestingly, some people deliberately buy larger-capacity disks, then use only 20–30% of their capacity. This increases the data locality and decreases the seek time, which can sometimes justify the higher price.

To determine whether your workload can benefit from more drives, look at *iostat* to see how the drives are loaded. A large number of outstanding requests indicates your workload might be able to use more drives efficiently. We included some *iostat* examples at the end of this chapter.

Choosing Hardware for a Slave

Choosing hardware for a replication slave is generally similar to choosing hardware for a master, though there are some differences. If you're planning to use a replication slave for failover, it usually needs to be at least as powerful as the master. And regardless of whether the slave is acting as a standby to replace the master, it must be powerful enough to perform all the writes that occur on the master, with the extra handicap that it must perform them serially. (There's more information about this in the next chapter.)

The main consideration for a slave's hardware is cost: do you need to spend as much on your slave's hardware as you do on the master? Can you configure the slave differently, so you can get more performance from it?

It depends. If the slave is a standby, you probably want the master and slave to have the same hardware and configuration. But if you're using replication solely as a cheap way to get more overall read capacity from your system, you can take a variety of shortcuts on a slave. You may want to use a different storage engine on the slave, for example, and some people use cheaper hardware or use RAID (Redundant Arrays of Inexpensive Disks) 0 instead of RAID 5 or RAID 10. You can also disable some consistency and durability guarantees to let the slave do less work. See "Tuning MySQL's I/O Behavior" on page 281 for more on this.

These measures can be cost-efficient on a large scale, but they might just make things more complex on a small scale.

RAID Performance Optimization

Storage engines often keep their data and/or indexes in single large files, which means RAID is usually the most feasible option for storing a lot of data.* RAID can help with redundancy, storage size, caching, and speed. But as with the other optimizations we've been looking at, there are many variations on RAID configurations, and it's important to choose one that's appropriate for your needs.

---

* Partitioning (see Chapter 5) is another good practice, because it usually splits the file into many files, which you can place on different devices. However, even compared to partitioning, RAID is a simple solution for very large data volumes. It doesn't require you to balance the load manually or intervene when the load distribution changes, and it gives redundancy, which you won't get by assigning partitions to different disks.

We won't cover every RAID level here, or go into the specifics of exactly how the different RAID levels store data. Good material on this topic is widely available in books and online.* Instead, we focus on how RAID configurations satisfy a database server's needs. The most important RAID levels are:

RAID 0

> RAID 0 is the cheapest and highest-performance RAID configuration, at least when you measure cost and performance simplistically (if you include data recovery, for example, it starts to look more expensive). Because it offers no redundancy, we recommend RAID 0 only for servers you don't care about, such as slaves or servers that are "disposable" for some reason. The typical scenario is a slave server that can easily be cloned from another slave.

> Again, note that *RAID 0 does not provide any redundancy*, even though "redundant" is the first letter in the RAID acronym. In fact, the probability of a RAID 0 array failing is actually *higher* than the probability of any single disk failing, not lower!

RAID 1

> RAID 1 offers good read performance for many scenarios, and it duplicates your data across disks, so there's good redundancy. RAID 1 is a little bit faster than RAID 0 for reads. It's good for servers that handle logging and similar workloads, because sequential writes rarely need many underlying disks to perform well (as opposed to random writes, which can benefit from parallelization). It is also a typical choice for low-end servers that need redundancy but have only two hard drives.

> RAID 0 and RAID 1 are very simple, and they can often be implemented well in software. Most operating systems will let you create software RAID 0 and RAID 1 volumes easily.

RAID 5

> RAID 5 is a little scary, but it's the inevitable choice for some applications because of price constraints and/or constraints on the number of disks that can physically fit in the server. It spreads the data across many disks, with distributed parity blocks so that if any one disk fails the data can be rebuilt from the parity blocks. In terms of cost per unit of storage, it's the most economical redundant configuration, because you lose only one disk's worth of storage space across the entire array.

> Random writes are expensive in RAID 5, because they require two writes and two RAID operations for the parity blocks. Writes can perform a little better if they are sequential, or if there are many physical disks. On the other hand, both random and sequential reads perform decently. RAID 5 is an acceptable choice for data volumes, or data and logs, for many workloads.

---

* Two good learning resources are the Wikipedia article on RAID (*http://en.wikipedia.org/wiki/RAID*) and the AC&NC tutorial at *http://www.acnc.com/04_00.html*.

The biggest performance cost with RAID 5 occurs if a disk fails, because the data has to be reconstructed by reading all the other disks. This affects performance severely. If you're trying to keep the server online during the rebuild, don't expect either the rebuild or the array's performance to be good. Other performance costs include limited scalability because of the parity blocks—RAID 5 doesn't scale well past 10 disks or so—and caching issues. Good RAID 5 performance depends heavily on the RAID controller's cache, which can conflict with the database server's needs. We discuss caching a bit later.

One of the mitigating factors for RAID 5 is that it's so popular. As a result, RAID controllers are often highly optimized for RAID 5, and despite the theoretical limits, smart controllers that use caches well can sometimes perform nearly as well as RAID 10 controllers for some workloads. This may actually reflect that the RAID 10 controllers are less highly optimized, but regardless of the reason, this is what we've seen.

RAID 10

RAID 10 is a very good choice for data storage, if you can afford it. It consists of mirrored pairs that are striped, so it scales both reads and writes well. It is fast and easy to rebuild, in comparison to RAID 5. It can also be implemented in software fairly well.

The performance loss when one hard drive goes out can still be significant, because that stripe can become a bottleneck. Performance can degrade by up to 50%, depending on the workload. One thing to watch out for is RAID controllers that use a "concatenated mirror" implementation for RAID 10. This is suboptimal because of the absence of striping: your most frequently accessed data might be placed on only one pair of spindles, instead of being spread across many, so you'll get poor performance.

RAID 50

RAID 50 consists of RAID 5 arrays that are striped, and it can be a good compromise between the economy of RAID 5 and the performance of RAID 10, if you have many disks. This is mainly useful for very large datasets, such as data warehouses or extremely large OLTP systems.

Table 7-1 summarizes various RAID configurations.

Table 7-1. Comparison of RAID levels

Level	Synopsis	Redundancy	Disks required	Faster reads	Faster writes
RAID 0	Cheap, fast, dangerous	No	N	Yes	Yes
RAID 1	Fast reads, simple, safe	Yes	2 (usually)	Yes	No
RAID 5	A compromise between safety, speed, and cost	Yes	N + 1	Yes	Depends

Table 7-1. Comparison of RAID levels (continued)

Level	Synopsis	Redundancy	Disks required	Faster reads	Faster writes
RAID 10	Expensive, fast, safe	Yes	2N	Yes	Yes
RAID 50	For very large data stores	Yes	2(N + 1)	Yes	Yes

RAID Failure, Recovery, and Monitoring

RAID configurations (with the exception of RAID 0) offer redundancy. This is important, but it's easy to underestimate the likelihood of concurrent disk failures. You shouldn't think of RAID as a strong guarantee of data safety.

RAID doesn't eliminate—or even reduce—the need for backups. When there is a problem, the recovery time will depend on your controller, the RAID level, the array size, the disk speed, and whether you need to keep the server online while you rebuild the array.

There is a chance of disks failing at exactly the same time. For example, a power spike or overheating can easily kill two or more disks. What's more common, however, is two disk failures happening close together. Many such issues can go unnoticed. A common case is corruption on the physical media holding data that's seldom accessed. This might go undetected for months, until either you try to read the data, or another drive fails and the RAID controller tries to use the corrupted data to rebuild the array. The larger the hard drive is, the more likely this is.

That's why it's important to monitor your RAID arrays. Most controllers offer some software to report on the array's status, and you need to keep track of this because you might otherwise be totally ignorant of a drive failure. You might miss your opportunity to recover the data and discover the problem only when a second drive fails, when it's too late.

You can mitigate this risk by actively checking your arrays for consistency at regular intervals. Background Patrol Read, a feature of some controllers that checks for damaged media and fixes it while all the drives are online, can also help avert such problems. As with recovery, extremely large arrays can be slow to check, so make sure you plan accordingly when you create large arrays.

You can also add a hot spare drive, which is unused and configured as a standby for the controller to automatically use for recovery. This is a good idea if you depend on every server. It's expensive with servers that have only a few hard drives, because the cost of having an idle disk is proportionately higher, but if you have many disks, it's almost foolish not to have a hot spare. Remember that the probability of a drive failure increases rapidly with more disks.

Balancing Hardware RAID and Software RAID

The interaction between the operating system, the filesystem, and the number of drives the operating system sees can be complicated. Bugs or limitations—or just misconfigurations—can reduce performance well below what is theoretically possible.

If you have 10 hard disks, ideally they should be able to serve 10 requests in parallel, but sometimes the filesystem, the operating system, or the RAID controller will serialize requests. One possible solution to this problem is to try different RAID configurations. For example, if you have 10 disks and want to use mirroring for redundancy and performance, you could configure them in several ways:

- Configure a single RAID 10 volume consisting of five mirrored pairs. The operating system will see a single large disk volume, and the RAID controller will hide the 10 underlying disks.

- Configure five RAID 1 mirrored pairs in the RAID controller, and let the operating system address five volumes instead of one.

- Configure five RAID 1 mirrored pairs in the RAID controller, and then use software RAID 0 to make the five volumes appear as one logical volume, effectively implementing RAID 10 partially in hardware and partially in software.

Which option is best? It depends on how all the components in your system interact. The configurations might perform identically, or they might not.

We've noticed serialization in various configurations. One example we saw (on an obsolete GNU/Linux distribution) was with the combination of the ext3 filesystem and InnoDB with `innodb_flush_method=O_DIRECT`. This appeared to cause inode-level locking in the filesystem, so only one I/O request could be sent to a file at once. In this case, serialization was per-file, and the bug was fixed in a later software version.

In another case, requests to each *device* were serialized with a 10-disk RAID 10 volume, the ReiserFS filesystem, and InnoDB with `innodb_file_per_table` enabled. Switching to software RAID 0 on top of hardware RAID 1 gave five times more throughput, because the storage system began to behave like five spindles instead of one. This situation was also caused by a bug that has since been fixed, but it's a good illustration of the sort of thing that can happen.

Serialization can happen on any layer in the software or hardware stack. If you see this problem occurring, you might try changing the filesystem, upgrading your kernel, exposing more devices to the operating system, or using a different mixture of software or hardware RAID. You should also use *iostat* to check your device's concurrency and make sure it really is doing concurrent I/O (see "How to Read iostat Output" on page 338, later in this chapter, for more on that).

Finally, don't forget to benchmark! This will help you verify that you're getting the performance you expect. For example, if one hard drive can do 200 random reads per second, a RAID 10 volume with 8 hard drives should do close to 1,600 random reads per second. If you're observing a much lower number, such as 500 random reads per second, you should research the problem. Make sure your benchmarks exercise the I/O subsystem in the same way MySQL will—for example, use the O_ DIRECT flag and test I/O performance to a single file if you're using InnoDB without innodb_file_per_table enabled. SysBench is a great tool for this. (See Chapter 2 for more on benchmarking.)

RAID Configuration and Caching

You can usually configure the RAID controller itself by entering its setup utility during the machine's boot sequence. While most controllers offer a lot of options, the two we focus on are the *chunk size* for striped arrays, and the *on-controller cache* (also known as the *RAID cache*; we use the terms interchangeably).

The RAID stripe chunk size

The optimal stripe chunk size is workload- and hardware-specific. In theory, it's good to have a large chunk size for random I/O, because it means more reads can be satisfied from a single drive.

To see why this is so, consider the size of a typical random I/O operation for your workload. If the chunk size is at least that large, and the data doesn't span the border between chunks, only a single drive needs to participate in the read. But if the chunk size is smaller than the amount of data to be read, there's no way to get around involving more than one drive in the read.

So much for theory. In practice, many RAID controllers don't work well with large chunks. For example, the controller might use the chunk size as the cache unit in its cache, which could be wasteful. The controller might also match the chunk size, cache size, and read-unit size (the amount of data it reads in a single operation). If the read unit is too large, its cache might be less effective, and it might end up reading a lot more data than it really needs, even for tiny requests.

Also, in practice it's hard to know whether any given piece of data will span multiple drives. Even if the chunk size is 16 KB, which matches InnoDB's page size, you can't be certain all of the reads will be aligned on 16 KB boundaries. The filesystem may fragment the file, and it will typically align the fragments on the filesystem block size, which is often 4 KB. Some filesystems might be smarter, but you shouldn't count on it.

The RAID cache

The RAID cache is a (relatively) small amount of memory that is physically installed on the RAID controller. It can be used to buffer data as it travels between the disks and the host system. Here are some of the reasons a RAID card might use the cache:

Caching reads
> After the controller reads some data from the disks and sends it to the host system, it can store the data; this will enable it to satisfy future requests for the same data without having to go to disk again.

> This is usually a very poor use of the RAID cache. Why? Because the operating system and the database server have their own, much larger, caches. If there's a cache hit in one of these caches, the data in the RAID cache won't be used. Conversely, if there's a miss in one of the higher-level caches, the chance that there'll be a hit in the RAID cache is vanishingly small. Because the RAID cache is so much smaller, it will almost certainly have been flushed and filled with other data too. Either way you look at it, it's a waste of memory to cache reads in the RAID cache.

Caching read-ahead data
> If the RAID controller notices sequential requests for data, it might decide to do a read-ahead read—that is, to prefetch data it predicts will be needed soon. It has to have somewhere to put the data until it's requested, though. It can use the RAID cache for this. The performance impact of this can vary widely, and you should check to ensure it's actually helping. Read-ahead operations might not help if the database server is doing its own smart read-ahead (as InnoDB does), and it might interfere with the all-important buffering of synchronous writes.

Caching writes
> The RAID controller can buffer writes in its cache and schedule them for a later time. The advantage to doing this is twofold: first, it can return "success" to the host system much more quickly than it would be able to if it had to actually perform the writes on the physical disks, and second, it can accumulate writes and do them more efficiently.

Internal operations
> Some RAID operations are very complex—especially RAID 5 writes, which have to calculate parity bits that can be used to rebuild data in the event of a failure. The controller needs to use some memory for this type of internal operation.

> This is one reason why RAID 5 can perform poorly on some controllers: it needs to read a lot of data into the cache for good performance. Some controllers can't balance caching writes with caching for the RAID 5 parity operations.

In general, the RAID controller's memory is a scarce resource that you should try to use wisely. Using it for reads is usually a waste, but using it for writes is an important way to speed up your I/O performance. Many controllers let you choose how to allocate the memory. For example, you can choose how much of it to use for caching writes and how much for reads. For RAID 0, RAID 1, and RAID 10, you should probably allocate 100% of the controller's memory for caching writes. For RAID 5, you should reserve some of the controller's memory for its internal operations. This is generally good advice, but it doesn't always apply—different RAID cards require different configurations.

When you're using the RAID cache for write caching, many controllers let you configure how long it's acceptable to delay the writes (1 second, 5 seconds, and so on). A longer delay means more writes can be grouped together and flushed to the disks optimally. The downside is that your writes will be more "bursty." That's not a bad thing, unless your application happens to make a bunch of write requests just as the controller's cache fills up, when it's about to be flushed to disk. If there's not enough room for your application's write requests, it'll have to wait. Keeping the delay shorter means you'll have more write operations and they'll be less efficient, but it smoothes out the spikiness and helps keep more of the cache free to handle bursts from the application. (We're simplifying here—controllers often have complex, vendor-specific balancing algorithms, so we're just trying to cover the basic principles.)

The write cache is very helpful for synchronous writes, such as issuing fsync( ) calls on the transaction logs and creating binary logs with sync_binlog enabled, but you shouldn't enable it unless your controller has a battery backup unit (BBU). Doing so is likely to corrupt your database, and even your transactional filesystem, in the event of power loss. If you have a BBU, however, enabling the write cache can increase performance by a factor of 20 or more for workloads that do a lot of log flushes, such as flushing the transaction log when a transaction commits.

A final consideration is that many hard drives have write caches of their own, which can "fake" fsync( ) operations by lying to the controller that the data has been written to physical media. Hard drives that are attached directly (as opposed to being attached to a RAID controller) can sometimes let their caches be managed by the operating system, but this doesn't always work either. These caches are typically flushed for an fsync( ) and bypassed for synchronous I/O, but again, the hard drive can lie. You should either ensure that these caches are flushed on fsync( ) or disable them, because they are not battery-backed. Hard drives that aren't managed properly by the operating system or RAID firmware have caused many instances of data loss.

For this and other reasons, it's always a good idea to do genuine crash testing (literally pulling the power plug out of the wall) when you install new hardware. This is often the only way to find subtle misconfigurations or sneaky hard drive behaviors. A handy script that can help you with this can be found at *http://brad.livejournal.com/2116715.html*.

If you really need to rely on your RAID controller's BBU, make sure you leave the power cord unplugged for a realistic amount of time when you test the BBU. Some units don't last as long without power as they're supposed to. Here again, one bad link can render your whole chain of storage components useless.

Storage Area Networks and Network-Attached Storage

Storage area networks (SANs) and network-attached storage (NAS) are two related, but very different, ways to attach external file storage devices to a server. A SAN exposes a block-level interface that a server sees as being directly attached, while a NAS device exposes a file-based protocol such as NFS or SMB. A SAN is usually connected to the server via the Fibre Channel Protocol (FCP) or iSCSI, while a NAS device is connected via a standard network connection.

Storage Area Networks

The benefits of using a SAN include more flexible storage management and the ability to scale storage. Many SAN solutions also have special features such as a snapshot capability and support for integrated continuous backups. They permit a server to access a very large number of hard drives—often 50 or more—and typically have very large, intelligent caches to buffer writes. The block-level interface they export appears to the server as logical unit numbers (LUNs), or virtual volumes. Many SANs also allow multiple nodes to be "clustered" to get better performance.

Although SANs work well when you have a lot of concurrent requests and need high throughput, you should not expect magic. A SAN is still ultimately a collection of hard drives that can do only a limited number of I/O operations per second, and because a SAN is external to the server and does its own processing, it adds latency to each I/O request. The extra latency makes SANs less efficient when you need very high performance for synchronous I/O, so keeping your transaction logs on a SAN is usually not as good as using a directly attached RAID controller.

In general, directly attached storage is faster than the LUNs on a SAN with the same number of similar hard drives. Sharing hard drives across LUNs also complicates performance analysis, because the LUNs affect each other in ways that are hard to measure. When you place the hard drives on separate LUNs, the effect is less noticeable, but sometimes you can still see it—for example, if you're using iSCSI, you may see contention on the network segment. The software inside the SAN has its limitations, too, and that can make the actual performance somewhat different from the theoretical or expected performance.

SANs have one big disadvantage: their cost is typically much higher than the cost of comparable directly attached storage (especially internal storage).

Most web applications don't use SANs, but they're very popular for so-called enterprise applications. There are several reasons for this:

- Enterprise applications are usually less constrained by budget, while many web applications can't afford "luxury items" such as SANs.

- Enterprises often run many applications, or many instances of a single application, and have unpredictable growth requirements. A SAN gives you the ability to buy a lot of storage, share it, and grow it on demand.

- A SAN's large buffers can help absorb write spikes and provide fast access to "hot" data, and SANs typically balance load across a very large number of hard drives. All this is usually required for clustered applications that are vertically scaled, but it doesn't help web applications much. Web applications usually don't have periods of low activity followed by huge write spikes; most of them are writing a lot of data almost constantly, so buffering writes isn't helpful. Read buffering isn't needed either, because databases tend to have their own (large, smart) caches. And the most common and successful strategy for building a very large web application is to use application partitioning (sharding), so web applications are already balancing the load across a large number of hard drives.

Network-Attached Storage

A NAS device is essentially a stripped-down file server appliance, typically with a web interface instead of a physical mouse, monitor, and keyboard. It's an economical and hassle-free way to provide a lot of storage space and is generally built upon a RAID array for redundancy.

However, NAS devices are not very fast, because they're mounted over the network. They also have a long history of problems with synchronous I/O support and locking, so we don't recommend them for general database storage. You can use them in special cases that aren't susceptible to their weaknesses, though, such as for shared read-only MyISAM tables.

Using Multiple Disk Volumes

Sooner or later, the question of where to place files will come up. MySQL creates a variety of files:

- Data and index files
- Transaction log files
- Binary log files
- General log files (e.g., for the error log, query log, and slow query log)
- Temporary files and tables

MySQL doesn't have many features for complex tablespace management. By default, it simply places all files for each database (schema) into a single directory. You have a few options to control where the data goes. For example, you can specify an index location for MyISAM tables, and you can use MySQL 5.1's partitioned tables.

If you're using InnoDB's default configuration, all data and indexes go in a single set of files, and only the table definition files are placed in the database directory. As a result, most people place all data and indexes on a single volume.

Sometimes, however, using multiple volumes can help you manage a heavy I/O load. For example, a batch job that writes data to a massive table can benefit from being on a separate volume, so it doesn't starve other queries for I/O. Ideally, you should analyze the I/O access to the different parts of your data, so you can place the data appropriately, but this is hard to do unless you already have the data on different volumes.

You've probably heard the standard advice to place your transaction logs and data files on different volumes, so the sequential I/O of the logs doesn't interfere with the random I/O of the data. But unless you have many hard drives (20 or so), you should think carefully before doing this.

The real advantage of separating the log and data files is the reduced likelihood of losing both your data and your log files in the event of a crash. Separating them is good practice if you don't have a battery-backed write cache on your RAID controller. But if you have a battery backup unit, a separate volume isn't needed as often as you might think. Performance is rarely a determining factor. This is because even though there are lots of writes to transaction logs, most of them are small. As a result, the RAID cache will usually merge the requests together, and you'll typically get just a couple of sequential physical write requests per second. This won't really interfere with the random I/O to your data files. The general logs, which have sequential asynchronous writes and low load, can also share a volume with the data comfortably.

There's another way to look at it, though, which a lot of people don't consider. Does placing logs on separate volumes improve performance? Typically, yes—but is it worth it? The answer is frequently no.

Here's why: it's *expensive* to dedicate hard drives to transaction logs. Suppose you have six hard drives. The obvious choices are to place all six into one RAID volume, or split them into four for the data and two for the transaction logs. If you do this, though, you've reduced the number of drives available for the data files by a third, which is a significant decrease; also, you're dedicating two drives to a possibly trivial workload (assuming that your RAID controller has a battery-backed write cache).

On the other hand, if you have many hard drives, dedicating some to the transaction logs is proportionately less expensive and can be beneficial. If you have a total of 30 hard drives, for example, you can ensure that the log writes are as fast as possible by dedicating 2 drives (configured as a RAID 1 volume) to the logs. For extra performance, you might also dedicate some write cache space for this RAID volume in the RAID controller.

Cost effectiveness isn't the only consideration. Another reason why you may want to keep InnoDB data and transaction logs on the same volume is that this strategy lets you use LVM snapshots for lock-free backups. Some filesystems allow consistent multivolume snapshots, and for those filesystems it might not be a big deal, but it's something to keep in mind for ext3.

If you have enabled sync_binlog, binary logs are similar to transaction logs in terms of performance. However, it's actually a *good* idea to store binary logs on a different volume from your data—it's safer to have them stored separately, so they can survive even if the data is lost. That way, you can use them for point-in-time recovery. This consideration doesn't apply to the InnoDB transaction logs, because they're useless without the data files; you can't apply transaction logs to last night's backup. (This distinction between transaction logs and binary logs might seem artificial to DBAs used to other databases, where they are one and the same.)

The only other common scenario for separating out files is the temporary directory, which MySQL uses for filesorts and on-disk temporary tables. If these won't be too big to fit, it's probably best to put them in a temporary memory-only filesystem such as tmpfs. This will be the fastest choice. If that isn't feasible on your system, put them on the same device as the operating system.

A typical disk layout is to have the operating system, swap partition, and binary logs on a RAID 1 volume, and a separate RAID 5 or RAID 10 volume that holds everything else.

Network Configuration

Just as latency and throughput are limiting factors for a hard drive, latency and bandwidth (which really means the same thing as throughput) are limiting factors for a network connection. The biggest problem for most applications is latency; a typical application does a lot of small network transfers, and the slight delay for each transfer adds up.

A network that's not operating correctly is a major performance bottleneck, too. Packet loss is a common problem. Even 1% loss is enough to cause significant performance degradation, because various layers in the protocol stack will try to fix the problems with strategies such as waiting a while and then resending packets, which adds extra time. Another common problem is broken or slow Domain Name System (DNS) resolution.

DNS is enough of an Achilles heel that enabling `skip_name_resolve` is a good idea for production servers. Broken or slow DNS resolution is a problem for lots of applications, but it's particularly severe for MySQL. When MySQL receives a connection request, it does both a forward and a reverse DNS lookup. There are lots of reasons that this could go wrong. When it does, it will cause connections to be denied, slow down the process of connecting to the server, and generally wreak havoc, up to and including denial of service attacks. If you enable the `skip_name_resolve` option, MySQL won't do any DNS lookups at all. However, this also means that your user accounts must have only IP addresses, "localhost," or IP address wildcards in the host column. Any user account that has a hostname in the host column will not be able to log in.

You need to design your network for good performance, rather than just accepting whatever you get by default. To begin, analyze how many hops are between the nodes, and map the physical network layout. For instance, suppose you have 10 web servers connected to a "Web" switch via Gigabit Ethernet (1 GigE), and this switch is connected to the "Database" switch via 1 GigE as well. If you don't take the time to trace the connections, you might never realize that your total bandwidth from all database servers to all web servers is limited to a gigabit! Each hop adds latency, too.

It's a good idea to monitor network performance and errors on all network ports. Monitor every port on servers, on routers, and on switches. The Multi Router Traffic Grapher, or MRTG (*http://oss.oetiker.ch/mrtg/*), is the tried-and-true solution for device monitoring. Other common tools for monitoring network performance (as opposed to devices) are Smokeping (*http://oss.oetiker.ch/smokeping/*) and Cacti (*http://www.cacti.net*).

Physical separation matters a lot in networking. Inter-city networks will have much worse latency than your data center's LAN, even if the bandwidth is technically the same. If the nodes are really widely separated, the speed of light actually matters. For example, if you have data centers on the west and east coasts of the U.S., they'll be separated by about 3,000 miles. The speed of light is 186,000 mps, so a one-way trip cannot be any faster than 16 ms, and a round-trip takes at least 32 ms. The physical distance is not the only performance consideration, either: there are devices in between as well. Repeaters, routers, and switches all degrade performance somewhat. Again, the more widely separated the network nodes are, the more unpredictable and unreliable the links will be.

It's a good idea to try to avoid real-time cross-data center operations as much as possible.* If it's not possible, you should make sure your application handles network failures gracefully. For example, you don't want your web servers to fork too many

---

* Replication doesn't count as a real-time cross-data center operation. It's not real-time, and it's often a good idea to replicate your data to a remote location for safety. We cover this more in the next chapter.

Apache processes because they are all stalled trying to connect to a remote data center over a link that has significant packet loss.

At the local level, use at least 1 GigE if you're not already. You might need to use a 10 GigE connection for the backbone between switches. If you need more bandwidth than that, you can use network trunking: connecting multiple network interface cards (NICs) to get more bandwidth. Trunking is essentially parallelization of networking, and it can be very helpful as part of a high-availability strategy.

When you need very high throughput, you might be able to improve performance by tuning your operating system's networking configuration. If you don't have many connections but you have large queries or result sets, you can increase the TCP buffer size. How you do this varies from system to system, but in most GNU/Linux systems you can change the values in */etc/sysctl.conf* and execute *sysctl -p*, or use the */proc* filesystem by echoing new values into the files found at */proc/sys/net/*. You can find good tutorials on this topic online with a search for "TCP tuning guide."

It's usually more important, though, to adjust your settings to deal efficiently with a lot of connections and small queries. One of the more common tweaks is to change your local port range. Here's a system that is configured to default values:

```
[root@caw2 ~]# cat /proc/sys/net/ipv4/ip_local_port_range
32768   61000
```

Sometimes you might need to change these values to a larger range. For example:

```
[root@caw2 ~]# echo 1024 65535 > /proc/sys/net/ipv4/ip_local_port_range
```

You can allow more connections to queue up as follows:

```
[root@caw2 ~]# echo 4096 > /proc/sys/net/ipv4/tcp_max_syn_backlog
```

For database servers that are used only locally, you can shorten the timeout that comes after closing a socket in the event that the peer is broken and doesn't close its side of the connection. The default is one minute on most systems, which is rather long:

```
[root@caw2 ~]# echo <value> > /proc/sys/net/ipv4/tcp_fin_timeout
```

Most of the time these settings can be left at their defaults. You'll typically need to change them only when something unusual is happening, such as extremely poor network performance or very large numbers of connections. An Internet search for "TCP variables" will turn up lots of good reading about these and many more variables.

Choosing an Operating System

GNU/Linux is the most common operating system for high-performance MySQL installations today, but MySQL will run on many operating systems.

Solaris is the leader on SPARC hardware, and it's frequently used in applications that demand high reliability. Solaris has a reputation for being slightly more difficult to work with than GNU/Linux in some ways, but it's a solid, high-performance operating system with many advanced features. In particular, Solaris 10 is gaining popularity. It has its own filesystem (ZFS), a lot of advanced troubleshooting tools (such as DTrace), good threading performance, and a virtualization technology called Solaris Zones that helps with resource management. Sun also provides good MySQL support.

FreeBSD is another option. It has historically had a number of problems with MySQL, mostly related to threading support, but newer versions are much better. Today, it's not uncommon to see MySQL deployed at a large scale on FreeBSD.

Windows is typically used for development and when MySQL is used with desktop applications. There are enterprise MySQL deployments on Windows, but Unix-like operating systems are more commonly used for these purposes. While we don't want to start any debates about operating systems, we will point out that there are no problems using a heterogeneous environment with MySQL. It's perfectly reasonable to run your MySQL server on a Unix-like operating system and run Windows on your web servers, connecting them via the high-quality ADO.NET connector (which is freely available from MySQL). It's just as easy to connect from Unix to a MySQL server hosted on Windows as it is to connect to another Unix server.

When you choose an operating system, make sure you install the 64-bit version if you're using a 64-bit architecture. It sounds silly, but we often see 32-bit operating systems mistakenly installed on 64-bit processors. The processors will often run them without complaint, but all the ordinary 32-bit limitations (such as addressable memory size restrictions) will prevent the 64-bit chips from being used to their full advantage.

When it comes to GNU/Linux distributions, personal preference is often the deciding factor. We think the best policy is to use a distribution explicitly designed for server applications, as opposed to a desktop distribution. Consider the distribution's lifecycle, release and update policies, and check whether vendor support is available. Red Hat Enterprise Linux is a good-quality, stable distribution; CentOS is a popular (and free) binary-compatible alternative; and Ubuntu is also gaining popularity.

Choosing a Filesystem

Your filesystem choices are pretty dependent on your operating system. In many systems, such as Windows, you really have only one or two choices. GNU/Linux, on the other hand, supports many filesystems.

Many people want to know which filesystems will give the best performance for MySQL on GNU/Linux, or, even more specifically, which of the choices is best for InnoDB and which for MyISAM. The benchmarks actually show that most of them are very close in most respects, but looking to the filesystem for performance is really a distraction. The filesystem's performance is very workload-specific, and no file-system is a magic bullet. Most of the time, a given filesystem won't perform significantly better or worse than any other filesystem. The exception is if you run into some filesystem limit, such as how it deals with concurrency, working with many files, fragmentation, and so on.

It's more important to consider crash recovery time and whether you'll run into specific limits, such as slow performance on directories with many files (a notorious problem with ext2 and ext3, though ext3 is getting better these days). The filesystem you choose is very important in ensuring your data's safety, so we strongly recommend you don't experiment on production systems.

When possible, it's best to use a journaling filesystem, such as ext3, ReiserFS, XFS, ZFS, or JFS. If you don't, a filesystem check after a crash can take a long time. If the system is not very important, nonjournaling filesystems may perform better than transactional ones. For example, ext2 may perform better than ext3, or you can use *tunefs* to disable the journaling feature on ext3. Mount time is also a factor for some filesystems. ReiserFS, for instance, can take a long time to mount and perform journal recovery on multiterabyte partitions.

If you use ext3, you have three options for how the data is journaled, which you can place in the */etc/fstab* mount options:

data=writeback

> This option means only metadata writes are journaled. Writes to the metadata are not synchronized with the data writes. This is the fastest configuration, and it's *usually* safe to use with InnoDB because it has its own transaction log. The exception is that a crash at just the right time could cause corruption in a *.frm* file.

> Here's an example of how this configuration could cause problems. Say a program decides to extend a file to make it larger. The metadata (the file's size) will be logged and written before the data is actually written to the (now larger) file. The result is that the file's tail—the newly extended area—contains garbage.

data=ordered

> This option also journals only the metadata, but it provides some consistency by writing the data before the metadata so that they stay consistent. It's only slightly slower than the writeback option, and it's much safer when there's a crash.

> In this configuration, if we suppose again that a program wants to extend a file, the file's metadata won't reflect the file's new size until the data that resides in the newly extended area has been written.

data=journal

> This option provides atomic journaled behavior, writing the data to the journal before it's written to the final location. It is usually unnecessary and has much

higher overhead than the other two options. However, in some cases, it can improve performance because the journaling lets the filesystem delay the writes to the data's final location.

Regardless of the filesystem, there are some specific options that it's best to disable, because they don't provide any benefit and can add quite a bit of overhead. The most famous is recording access time, which requires a write even when you're reading a file. To disable this option, add the `noatime` mount option to your */etc/fstab*; this can sometimes boost performance by as much as 5–10%, depending on the workload and the filesystem (although, it may not make much difference in other cases). Here's a sample */etc/fstab* line for the ext3 options we mentioned:

```
/dev/sda2 /usr/lib/mysql ext3 noatime,data=writeback 0 1
```

You can also tune the filesystem's read-ahead behavior, because it might be redundant. For example, InnoDB does its own read-ahead prediction. Disabling or limiting read-ahead is especially beneficial on Solaris's UFS. Using O_DIRECT automatically disables read-ahead.

Some filesystems don't support features you might need. For example, support for direct I/O may be important if you're using the O_DIRECT flush method for InnoDB (see "How InnoDB opens and flushes log and data files" on page 288 for more on this). Also, some filesystems handle a large number of underlying drives better than others; XFS is often much better at this than ext3, for instance. Finally, if you plan to use LVM snapshots for initializing slaves or taking backups, you should verify that your chosen filesystem and LVM version work well together.

Table 7-2 summarizes the characteristics of some common filesystems.

Table 7-2. Common filesystem characteristics

Filesystem	Operating system	Journaling	Large directories
ext2	GNU/Linux	No	No
ext3	GNU/Linux	Optional	Optional/partial
HFS Plus	Mac OS	Optional	Yes
JFS	GNU/Linux	Yes	No
NTFS	Windows	Yes	Yes
ReiserFS	GNU/Linux	Yes	Yes
UFS (Solaris)	Solaris	Yes	Tunable
UFS (FreeBSD)	FreeBSD	No	Optional/partial
UFS2	FreeBSD	No	Optional/partial
XFS	GNU/Linux	Yes	Yes
ZFS	Solaris, FreeBSD	Yes	Yes

Threading

As of version 5.0, MySQL uses one thread per connection, plus housekeeping threads, special-purpose threads, and any threads the storage engine creates. Therefore, MySQL requires efficient support for a large number of threads. It really needs support for kernel-level threads, as opposed to userland threads, so it can use multiple CPUs efficiently. It also needs efficient synchronization primitives, such as mutexes. The operating system's threading libraries must provide all of these.

GNU/Linux offers two thread libraries: LinuxThreads and the newer Native POSIX Threads Library (NPTL). LinuxThreads is still used in some cases, but most modern distributions have made the switch to NPTL, and many don't ship LinuxThreads at all anymore. NPTL is usually lighter and more efficient, and it doesn't suffer from a lot of the problems LinuxThreads had. It has had some performance bugs, but most of the kinks have been worked out by now.

FreeBSD also ships a number of threading libraries. Historically, it had weak support for threading, but it has gotten a lot better, and in some tests it even outperforms GNU/Linux on SMP systems. In FreeBSD 6 and newer, the recommended threading library is *libthr*; earlier versions should use *linuxthreads*, which is a FreeBSD port of GNU/Linux's LinuxThreads.

Solaris has very good support for threads.

Swapping

Swapping occurs when the operating system writes some virtual memory to disk because it doesn't have enough physical memory to hold it.* Swapping is transparent to processes running on the operating system. Only the operating system knows whether a particular virtual memory address is in physical memory or on disk.

Swapping is very bad for MySQL's performance. It defeats the purpose of caching in memory, and it results in *lower* efficiency than using too little memory for the caches. MySQL and its storage engines have many algorithms that treat in-memory data differently from data on disk, as they assume that in-memory data is cheap to access. Because swapping is invisible to user processes, MySQL (or the storage engine) won't know when data it thinks is in memory is actually moved onto the disk.

The result can be very poor performance. For example, if the storage engine thinks the data is still in memory, it might decide it's OK to lock a global mutex (such as the InnoDB buffer pool mutex) for a "short" memory operation. If this operation actually causes disk I/O, it can stall everything until the I/O completes. This means swapping is much worse than simply doing I/O as needed.

---

* Swapping is sometimes called *paging*. Technically, they are different things, but people often use them as synonyms.

On GNU/Linux, you can monitor swapping with *vmstat* (we show some examples in the next section). You need to look at the swap I/O activity, reported in the si and so columns, rather than the swap usage, which is reported in the swpd column. The swpd column can show processes that have been loaded but aren't being used, which are not really problematic. We like the si and so column values to be 0, and they should definitely be less than 10 blocks per second.

In extreme cases, too much swapping can cause the operating system to run out of swap space. If this happens, the resulting lack of virtual memory will usually crash MySQL. But even if it doesn't run out of swap space, very active swapping can cause the entire operating system to become unresponsive, to the point that you can't even log in and kill the MySQL process.

You can solve most swapping problems by configuring your MySQL buffers correctly, but sometimes the operating system's virtual memory system decides to swap MySQL anyway. This usually happens when the operating system sees a lot of I/O from MySQL, so it tries to increase the file cache to hold more data. If there's not enough memory, something must be swapped out, and that something might be MySQL itself. Some older Linux kernel versions also have counterproductive priorities that swap things when they shouldn't, but this has been alleviated in more recent kernels.

Some people advocate disabling the swap file entirely. While this sometimes works in extreme cases where the kernel just refuses to behave, it can degrade the operating system's performance. (It shouldn't in theory, but in practice it can.) It's also dangerous, because disabling swapping places an inflexible limit on virtual memory. If MySQL has a temporary spike in memory requirements, or if there are memory-hungry processes running on the same machine (nightly batch jobs, for example), MySQL can run out of memory, crash, or be killed by the operating system.

Operating systems usually allow some control over virtual memory and I/O. We mention a few ways to control them on GNU/Linux. The most basic is to change the value of */proc/sys/vm/swappiness* to a low value, such as 0 or 1. This tells the kernel not to swap unless the need for virtual memory is extreme. For example, here's how to check the current value and set it to something else:

```
$ cat /proc/sys/vm/swappiness
60
$ echo 0 > /proc/sys/vm/swappiness
```

Another option is to change how the storage engines read and write data. For example, using innodb_flush_method=O_DIRECT relieves I/O pressure. Direct I/O is not cached, so the operating system doesn't see it as a reason to increase the size of the file cache. This parameter works only for InnoDB, although Falcon has support for direct I/O too. You can also use large pages, which are not swappable. This works for MyISAM and InnoDB.

Another option is to use MySQL's `memlock` configuration option, which locks MySQL in memory. This will avoid swapping, but it can be dangerous: if there's not enough lockable memory left, MySQL can crash when it tries to allocate more memory. Problems can also be caused if too much memory is locked and there's not enough left for the operating system.

Many of the tricks are specific to a kernel version, so be careful, especially when you upgrade. In some workloads, it's hard to make the operating system behave sensibly, and your only recourse might be to lower the buffer sizes to suboptimal values.

Operating System Status

Your operating system probably provides tools to help you find out what the operating system and hardware are doing. We show you examples of how to use two widely available tools, *iostat* and *vmstat*.* If your system doesn't provide either of these tools, chances are it will provide something similar. Thus, our goal isn't to make you an expert at using *iostat* or *vmstat*, but simply to show you what to look for when you're trying to diagnose problems with tools such as these.

In addition to these tools, your operating system may provide others, such as *mpstat* or *sar*. If you're interested in other parts of your system, such as the network, you may want to instead use tools such as *ifconfig* (which shows how many network errors have occurred, among other things) or *netstat*.

By default, *vmstat* and *iostat* produce just one report showing the average values of various counters since the server was started, which is not very useful. However, you can give both tools an interval argument. This makes them generate incremental reports showing what the server is doing right now, which is much more relevant for tuning. (The first line shows the statistics since the system was started; you can just ignore this line.)

How to Read vmstat Output

Let's look at an example of *vmstat* first. To make it print out a new report every five seconds, use the following command:

```
$ vmstat 5
procs -----------memory---------- ---swap-- -----io---- -system-- ----cpu----
 r  b   swpd   free   buff  cache   si   so    bi    bo   in   cs us sy id wa
 0  0   2632  25728  23176 740244    0    0   527   521   11    3 10  1 86  3
 0  0   2632  27808  23180 738248    0    0     2   430  222   66  2  0 97  0
```

---

* We've shown *vmstat* and *iostat* here because they're widely available , and at least *vmstat* is usually installed by default on many Unix-like operating systems. However, each of these tools has its limitations, such as confusing units of measurement, sampling at intervals that don't correspond to when the operating system updates the statistics, and the inability to see all of the metrics at once. If these tools don't meet your needs, you might be interested in *dstat* (*http://dag.wieers.com/home-made/dstat/*) or *collectl* (*http://collectl. sourceforge.net/*).

You can stop *vmstat* with Ctrl-C. The output you see may vary depending on your operating system, so you may need to read the manual page to figure it out.

As stated earlier, even though we asked for incremental output, the first line of values shows the averages since the server was booted. The second line shows what's happening right now, and subsequent lines will show what's happening at five-second intervals. The columns are grouped by headers:

procs
> The r column shows how many processes are waiting for CPU time. The b column shows how many are in uninterruptible sleep, which generally means they're waiting for I/O (disk, network, user input, and so on).

memory
> The swpd column shows how many blocks are swapped out to disk (paged). The remaining three columns show how many blocks are free (unused), how many are being used for buffers, and how many are being used for the operating system's cache.

swap
> These columns show swap activity: how many blocks per second the operating system is swapping in (from disk) and out (to disk). They are much more important to monitor than the swpd column.

> We like to see si and so at 0 most of the time, and we definitely don't like to see more than 10 blocks per second. Bursts are also bad.

io
> These columns show how many blocks per second are read in from (bi) and written out to (bo) block devices. This usually reflects disk I/O.

system
> These columns show the number of interrupts per second (in) and the number of context switches per second (cs).

cpu
> These columns show the percentages of total CPU time spent running user (non-kernel) code, running system (kernel) code, idle, and waiting for I/O. A possible fifth column (st) shows the percent "stolen" from a virtual machine if you're using virtualization. This refers to the time during which something was runnable on the virtual machine, but the hypervisor chose to run something else instead. If the virtual machine doesn't want to run anything and the hypervisor runs something else, that doesn't count as stolen time.

The *vmstat* output is system-dependent, so you should read your system's vmstat(8) manpage if yours looks different from the sample we've shown. One important note: the memory, swap, and I/O statistics are in blocks, not in bytes. In Linux, blocks are usually 1,024 bytes.

How to Read iostat Output

Now let's move on to *iostat*.[*] By default, it shows some of the same CPU usage information as *vmstat*. We're usually interested in just the I/O statistics, though, so we use the following command to show only extended device statistics:

```
$ iostat -dx 5
Device:  rrqm/s wrqm/s r/s w/s rsec/s wsec/s avgrq-sz avgqu-sz await svctm %util
sda        1.6    2.8 2.5 1.8  138.8   36.9     40.7      0.1  23.2   6.0   2.6
```

As with *vmstat*, the first report shows averages since the server was booted (we generally omit it to save space), and the subsequent reports show incremental averages. There's one line per device.

There are various options that show or hide columns. The columns we've shown are the following:

rrqm/s *and* wrqm/s
> The number of merged read and write requests queued per second. "Merged" means the operating system took multiple logical requests and grouped them into a single request to the actual device.

r/s *and* w/s
> The number of read and write requests sent to the device per second.

rsec/s *and* wsec/s
> The number of sectors read and written per second. Some systems also output rkB/s and wkB/s, the number of kilobytes read and written per second. We omit those for brevity.

avgrq-sz
> The request size in sectors.

avgqu-sz
> The number of requests waiting in the device's queue.

await
> The number of milliseconds required to respond to requests, including queue time and service time. Unfortunately, *iostat* doesn't show separate service time statistics for read and write requests, which are so different that they really shouldn't be averaged together. However, you can probably chalk up high I/O waits to reads, because writes can often be buffered but reads usually have to be served directly from the spindles.

svctm
> The number of milliseconds spent servicing requests, from beginning to end, including queue time and the time the device actually takes to fulfill the request.

---

[*] The *iostat* examples we've shown in this book were slightly reformatted for printing. We've reduced the number of decimal places in the values to avoid line wrapping.

```
%util
```
The percentage of CPU time during which requests were issued. This really shows the device utilization, as the name implies, because when the value approaches 100%, the device is saturated.

You can use the output to deduce some facts about a machine's I/O subsystem. One important metric is the number of requests served concurrently. Because the reads and writes are per second and the service time's unit is thousandths of a second, the dimensions in the following formula cancel out to show the number of concurrent requests the device is serving:[*]

```
concurrency = (r/s + w/s) * (svctm/1000)
```

Here's a sample of *iostat* output:

```
Device: rrqm/s wrqm/s r/s w/s rsec/s wsec/s avgrq-sz avgqu-sz await svctm %util
sda       105   311  298 820   3236   9052      10      127   113     9    96
```

Plugging the numbers into the concurrency formula gives a concurrency of about 9.6.[†] This means that on average, the device was serving 9.6 requests at a time during the sampling interval. The sample is from a 10-disk RAID 10 volume, so the operating system is parallelizing requests to this device quite well. On the other hand, here's a device that appears to be serializing requests instead:

```
Device: rrqm/s wrqm/s r/s w/s rsec/s wsec/s avgrq-sz avgqu-sz await svctm %util
sdc        81     0  280   0   3164      0      11        2     7     3    99
```

The concurrency formula shows that this device is handling just one request per second. Both devices are close to fully utilized, but they're giving very different performances. If your device is busy nearly all the time, as these samples show, you should check the concurrency and note whether it is close to the number of physical spindles included in the device. A lower number can indicate problems.

A CPU-Bound Machine

The *vmstat* output for a CPU-bound server usually shows a high value in the us column, which reports time spent running non-kernel code. In most cases, there will also be several processes queued up for CPU time (reported in the r column). Here's a sample:

```
$ vmstat 5
procs -----------memory----------   ---swap-- -----io---- --system-- ----cpu----
 r  b   swpd   free  buff   cache    si  so   bi    bo    in    cs us sy id wa
10  2 740880 19256 46068 13719952     0   0 2788 11047 1423 14508 89  4  4  3
11  0 740880 19692 46144 13702944     0   0 2907 14073 1504 23045 90  5  2  3
```

---

[*] Another way to calculate concurrency is by the average queue size, service time, and average wait: (avuqu_sz * svctm) / await.

[†] If you do the math, you'll get about 10, because we've rounded the *iostat* output for formatting purposes. Trust us, it's really 9.6.

```
 7  1 740880 20460 46264 13683852    0    0 3554 15567 1513 24182 88  5  3  3
10  2 740880 22292 46324 13670396    0    0 2640 16351 1520 17436 88  4  4  3
```

Notice that there are also lots of context switches (the cs column). A context switch is when the operating system stops one process from running and replaces it with another.

If we take a look at the *iostat* output for the same machine (again omitting the first sample, which shows averages since boot), you can see that disk utilization is less than 50%:

```
$ iostat -dx 5
Device: rrqm/s wrqm/s r/s w/s rsec/s wsec/s avgrq-sz avgqu-sz await svctm %util
sda          0   3859  54 458   2063  34546       71        3     6     1    47
dm-0         0      0  54 4316  2063  34532        8       18     4     0    47

Device: rrqm/s wrqm/s r/s w/s rsec/s wsec/s avgrq-sz avgqu-sz await svctm %util
sda          0   2898  52 363   1767  26090       67        3     7     1    45
dm-0         0      0  52 3261  1767  26090        8       15     5     0    45
```

This machine is not I/O-bound, but it's still doing a fair amount of I/O, which is not unusual for a database server. On the other hand, a typical web server will consume a lot of CPU resources but do very little I/O, so a web server's output will not usually look like this sample.

An I/O-Bound Machine

In an I/O-bound workload, the CPUs spend a lot of time waiting for I/O requests to complete. That means *vmstat* will show many processes in uninterruptible sleep (the b column), and a high value in the wa column. Here's an example:

```
$ vmstat 5
procs -----------memory----------   ---swap-- -----io---- --system-- ----cpu----
 r  b   swpd   free   buff   cache    si   so    bi    bo   in    cs us sy id wa
 5  7 740632  22684  43212 13466436    0    0  6738 17222 1738 16648 19  3 15 63
 5  7 740632  22748  43396 13465436    0    0  6150 17025 1731 16713 18  4 21 58
 1  8 740632  22380  43416 13464192    0    0  4582 21820 1693 15211 16  4 24 56
 5  6 740632  22116  43512 13463484    0    0  5955 21158 1732 16187 17  4 23 56
```

This machine's *iostat* output shows that the disks are completely saturated:

```
$ iostat -dx 5
Device: rrqm/s wrqm/s r/s w/s rsec/s wsec/s avgrq-sz avgqu-sz await svctm %util
sda          0   5396 202 626   7319  48187       66       12    14     1   101
dm-0         0      0 202 6016  7319  48130        8       57     9     0   101

Device: rrqm/s wrqm/s r/s w/s rsec/s wsec/s avgrq-sz avgqu-sz await svctm %util
sda          0   5810 184 665   6441  51825       68       11    13     1   102
dm-0         0      0 183 6477  6441  51817        8       54     7     0   102
```

The %util value can be greater than 100% because of rounding errors.

What does it mean for a machine to be I/O-bound? If there's enough buffer capacity to serve write requests, it generally—but not always—means the disks can't keep up with *read* requests, even if the machine is doing a lot of writes. That may seem counter-intuitive until you think about the nature of reads and writes:

- Write requests can be either buffered or synchronous. They can be buffered at any of the levels we've discussed elsewhere in this book: the operating system, the RAID controller, and so on.

- Read requests are synchronous by nature. It's possible for a program to predict that it'll need some data and issue an asynchronous *prefetch* (read-ahead) request for it. However, it's more common for programs to discover they need data before they can continue working. That forces the request to be synchronous: the program must block until the request completes.

Think of it this way: you can issue a write request that goes into a buffer somewhere and completes at a later time. You can even issue many of these per second. If the buffer is working correctly and has enough space, each request can complete very quickly, and the actual writes to the physical disk can be batched and reordered for efficiency.

However, there's no way to do that with a read—no matter how few or how small the requests are, it's impossible for the disk to respond with "Here's your data, I'll do the read later." That's why reads are usually responsible for I/O wait.

A Swapping Machine

A machine that's swapping may or may not show a high value in the `swpd` column. However, you'll see high values in the `si` and `so` columns, which you don't want. Here's what the *vmstat* output looks like on a machine that's swapping heavily:

```
$ vmstat 5
procs -----------memory------------ ---swap---- -----io---- --system-- ----cpu----
 r  b   swpd   free   buff    cache    si    so    bi    bo   in    cs us sy id wa
 0 10 3794292  24436  27076 14412764 19853  9781 57874  9833 4084  8339  6 14 58 22
 4 11 3797936  21268  27068 14519324 15913 30870 40513 30924 3600  7191  6 11 36 47
 0 37 3847364  20764  27112 14547112   171 38815 22358 39146 2417  4640  6  8  9 77
```

An Idle Machine

For the sake of completeness, here's the *vmstat* output on an idle machine. Notice that there are no runnable or blocked processes, and the `idle` column shows that the CPUs are 100% idle. This sample comes from a machine running Red Hat Enterprise Linux 5, and it shows the `st` column, which is time "stolen" from a virtual machine:

```
$ vmstat 5
procs -----------memory---------- ---swap-- -----io---- --system-- -----cpu-----
 r  b   swpd   free   buff  cache   si   so    bi    bo   in   cs us sy  id wa st
 0  0    108 492556   6768 360092    0    0   345   209    2   65  2  0  97  1  0
 0  0    108 492556   6772 360088    0    0     0    14  357   19  0  0 100  0  0
 0  0    108 492556   6776 360084    0    0     0     6  355   16  0  0 100  0  0
```

Replication

MySQL's built-in replication capability is the foundation for building large, high-performance applications on top of MySQL. Replication lets you configure one or more servers as slaves, or replicas, of another server. This is not just useful for high-performance applications—it is also handy for many other tasks, such as sharing data with a remote office, keeping a "hot spare," or keeping a server with a copy of the data for testing or training purposes.

In this chapter, we examine all aspects of replication. We begin with an overview of how it works, then look at basic server setup, designing more advanced replication configurations, and managing and optimizing your replicated servers. Although we generally focus a lot on performance in this book, we are equally concerned with correctness and reliability when it comes to replication, so we show you how to make replication work well. We also look at some of the upcoming changes and improvements in MySQL replication, such as some interesting patches created by Google.

Replication Overview

The basic problem replication solves is keeping one server's data synchronized with another's. Many slaves can connect to a single master, and a slave can, in turn, act as a master. You can arrange masters and slaves in many different topologies. You can replicate the entire server, replicate only certain databases, or even choose which tables you want to replicate.

MySQL supports two kinds of replication: statement-based replication and row-based replication. Statement-based (or "logical") replication has been available since MySQL 3.23, and it's what most people are using in production today. Row-based replication is new in MySQL 5.1. Both kinds work by recording changes in the master's binary log* and replaying the log on the slave, and both are *asynchronous—*

---

* If you're new to the binary log, you can find more information in Chapter 6, the rest of this chapter, and Chapter 11.

that is, the slave's copy of the data isn't guaranteed to be up-to-date at any given instant.* There are no guarantees how large the latency on the slave might be. Large queries can make the slave fall seconds, minutes, or even hours behind the master.

MySQL's replication is mostly backward compatible. That is, a newer server can usually be a slave of an older server without trouble. However, older versions of the server are often unable to serve as slaves of newer versions: they may not understand new features or SQL syntax the newer server uses, and there may be differences in the file formats replication uses. For example, you can't replicate from a MySQL 5.0 master to a MySQL 4.0 slave. It's a good idea to test your replication setup before upgrading from one major version to another, such as from 4.1 to 5.0, or 5.0 to 5.1.

Replication generally doesn't add much overhead on the master. It requires binary logging to be enabled on the master, which can have significant overhead, but you need that for proper backups anyway. Aside from binary logging, each attached slave also adds a little load (mostly network I/O) on the master during normal operation.

Replication is relatively good for scaling reads, which you can direct to a slave, but it's not a good way to scale writes unless you design it right. Attaching many slaves to a master simply causes the writes to be done many times, once on each slave. The entire system is limited to the number of writes the weakest part can perform.

Replication is also wasteful with more than a few slaves, because it essentially duplicates a lot of data needlessly. For example, a single master with 10 slaves has 11 copies of the same data and duplicates most of the same data in 11 different caches. This is analogous to 11-way RAID 1 at the server level. This is not an economical use of hardware, yet it's surprisingly common to see this type of replication setup. We discuss ways to alleviate this problem throughout the chapter.

Problems Solved by Replication

Here are some of the more common uses for replication:

Data distribution
    MySQL's replication is usually not very bandwidth-intensive,† and you can stop and start it at will. Thus, it's useful for maintaining a copy of your data in a geographically distant location, such as a different data center. The distant slave can even work with a connection that's intermittent (intentionally or otherwise). However, if you want your slaves to have very low replication lag, you'll need a stable, low-latency link.

---

* See ""Synchronous MySQL replication" on page 451 for more on this.

† Although, as we'll see later, the row-based replication introduced in MySQL 5.1 may use much more band- width than the more traditional statement-based replication.

Load balancing

MySQL replication can help you distribute read queries across several servers, which works very well for read-intensive applications. You can do basic load balancing with a few simple code changes. On a small scale, you can use simplistic approaches such as hardcoded hostnames or round-robin DNS (which points a single hostname to multiple IP addresses). You can also take more sophisticated approaches. Standard load-balancing solutions, such as network load-balancing products, can work well for distributing load among MySQL servers. The Linux Virtual Server (LVS) project also works well. We cover load balancing in Chapter 9.

Backups

Replication is a valuable technique for helping with backups. However, a slave is neither a backup nor a substitute for backups.

High availability and failover

Replication can help avoid making MySQL a single point of failure in your application. A good failover system involving replicated slaves can help reduce downtime significantly. We also cover failover in Chapter 9.

Testing MySQL upgrades

It's common practice to set up a slave server with an upgraded MySQL version and use it to ensure that your queries work as expected, before upgrading every instance.

How Replication Works

Before we get into the details of setting up replication, let's look at how MySQL actually replicates data. At a high level, replication is a simple three-part process:

1. The master records changes to its data in its binary log. (These records are called *binary log events*.)
2. The slave copies the master's binary log events to its relay log.
3. The slave replays the events in the relay log, applying the changes to its own data.

That's just the overview—each of those steps is quite complex. Figure 8-1 illustrates replication in more detail.

The first part of the process is binary logging on the master (we show you how to set this up a bit later). Just before each transaction that updates data completes on the master, the master records the changes in its binary log. MySQL writes transactions serially in the binary log, even if the statements in the transactions were interleaved during execution. After writing the events to the binary log, the master tells the storage engine(s) to commit the transactions.

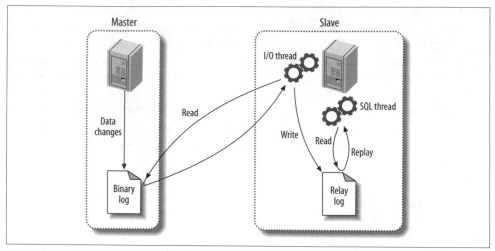

Figure 8-1. How MySQL replication works

The next step is for the slave to copy the master's binary log to its own hard drive, into the so-called *relay log*. To begin, it starts a worker thread, called the *I/O slave thread*. The I/O thread opens an ordinary client connection to the master, then starts a special *binlog dump* process (there is no corresponding SQL command). The binlog dump process reads events from the master's binary log. It doesn't poll for events. If it catches up to the master, it goes to sleep and waits for the master to signal it when there are new events. The I/O thread writes the events to the slave's relay log.

> Prior to MySQL 4.0, replication worked quite differently in many ways. For example, MySQL's first replication functionality didn't use a relay log, so replication used only two threads, not three. Most people are running more recent versions of the server, so we won't mention any further details about very old versions of MySQL in this chapter.

The *SQL slave thread* handles the last part of the process. This thread reads and replays events from the relay log, thus updating the slave's data to match the master's. As long as this thread keeps up with the I/O thread, the relay log usually stays in the operating system's cache, so relay logs have very low overhead. The events the SQL thread executes can optionally go into the slave's own binary log, which is useful for scenarios we mention later in this chapter.

Figure 8-1 showed only the two replication threads that run on the slave, but there's also a thread on the master: like any connection to a MySQL server, the connection that the slave opens to the master starts a thread on the master.

This replication architecture decouples the processes of fetching and replaying events on the slave, which allows them to be asynchronous. That is, the I/O thread can work independently of the SQL thread. It also places constraints on the replication process, the most important of which is that *replication is serialized on the slave*. This means updates that might have run in parallel (in different threads) on the master cannot be parallelized on the slave. As we'll see later, this is a performance bottleneck for many workloads.

Setting Up Replication

Setting up replication is a fairly simple process in MySQL, but there are many variations on the basic steps, depending on the scenario. The most basic scenario is a freshly installed master and slave. At a high level, the process is as follows:

1. Set up replication accounts on each server.
2. Configure the master and slave.
3. Instruct the slave to connect to and replicate from the master.

This assumes that many default settings will suffice, which is true if you've just installed the master and slave and they have the same data (the default `mysql` database). We show you how to do each step in turn, assuming your servers are called `server1` (IP address 192.168.0.1) and `server2` (IP address 192.168.0.2). We then explain how to initialize a slave from a server that's already up and running and explore the recommended replication configuration.

Creating Replication Accounts

MySQL has a few special privileges that let the replication processes run. The slave I/O thread, which runs on the replication slave server, makes a TCP/IP connection to the master. This means you must create a user account on the master and give it the proper privileges, so the I/O thread can connect as that user and read the master's binary log. Here's how to create that user account, which we'll call *repl*:

```
mysql> GRANT REPLICATION SLAVE, REPLICATION CLIENT ON *.*
    -> TO repl@'192.168.0.%' IDENTIFIED BY 'p4ssword';
```

We create this user account on both the master and the slave. Note that we restricted the user to the local network, because the replication account is insecure. (See Chapter 12 for more information on security.)

The replication user actually needs only the REPLICATION CLIENT privilege on the master and doesn't really need the REPLICATION SLAVE privilege on either server. So why did we grant these privileges on both servers? There are two reasons:

- The account you use to monitor and manage replication will need the REPLICATION SLAVE privilege, and it's easier to use the same account for both purposes (rather than create a separate user account for this purpose).

- If you set up the account on the master and then clone the slave from it, the slave will be set up correctly to act as a master, in case you want the slave and master to switch roles.

Configuring the Master and Slave

The next step is to enable a few settings on the master, which we assume is named server1. You need to enable binary logging and specify a server ID. Enter (or verify the presence of) the following lines in the master's *my.cnf* file:

```
log_bin     = mysql-bin
server_id   = 10
```

The exact values are up to you. We're taking the simplest route here, but you can do something more elaborate.

You must explicitly specify a unique server ID. We chose to use 10 instead of 1, because 1 is the default value a server will typically choose when no value is specified. (This is version-dependent; some MySQL versions just won't work at all.) Therefore, using 1 can easily cause confusion and conflicts with servers that have no explicit server IDs. A common practice is to use the final octet of the server's IP address, assuming it doesn't change and is unique (i.e., the servers belong to only one subnet).

If binary logging wasn't already specified in the master's configuration file, you'll need to restart MySQL. To verify that the binary log file is created on the master, run SHOW MASTER STATUS and check that you get output similar to the following (MySQL will append some digits to the filename, so you won't see a file with the exact name you specified):

```
mysql> SHOW MASTER STATUS;
+------------------+----------+--------------+------------------+
| File             | Position | Binlog_Do_DB | Binlog_Ignore_DB |
+------------------+----------+--------------+------------------+
| mysql-bin.000001 |       98 |              |                  |
+------------------+----------+--------------+------------------+
1 row in set (0.00 sec)
```

The slave requires a configuration in its *my.cnf* file similar to the master, and you'll also need to restart MySQL on the slave:

```
log_bin             = mysql-bin
server_id           = 2
relay_log           = mysql-relay-bin
log_slave_updates = 1
read_only           = 1
```

Several of these options are not technically necessary, and for some we're just making defaults explicit. In reality, only the `server_id` parameter is required on a slave, but we enabled `log_bin` too, and we gave the binary log file an explicit name. By default it is named after the server's hostname, but that can cause problems if the hostname changes. Also, we want every server's logs to be named the same thing to enable easy slave-to-master promotions. Thus, just as we created the same replication user account on both the master and the slave, we are using the same settings for the master and slave.

We also added two other optional configuration parameters: `relay_log` (to specify the location and name of the relay log) and `log_slave_updates` (to make the slave log the replicated events to its own binary log). The latter option causes extra work for the slaves, but as you'll see later, we have good reasons for adding these optional settings on every slave.

Some people enable just the binary log and not `log_slave_updates`, so they can see whether anything, such as a misconfigured application, is modifying data on the slave. If possible, it's better to use the `read_only` configuration setting, which prevents anything but specially privileged threads from changing data. (Don't grant your users more privileges than they need!) However, `read_only` is often not practical, especially for applications that need to be able to create tables on slaves.

 Don't place replication configuration options such as `master_host` and `master_port` into the slave's *my.cnf* file. This is an old, deprecated way to configure a slave. It can cause problems and has no benefits.

Starting the Slave

The next step is to tell the slave how to connect to the master and begin replaying its binary logs. You should not use the *my.cnf* file for this; instead, use the CHANGE MASTER TO statement. This statement replaces the corresponding *my.cnf* settings completely. It also lets you point the slave at a different master in the future, without stopping the server. Here's the basic statement you'll need to run on the slave to start replication:

```
mysql> CHANGE MASTER TO MASTER_HOST='server1',
    -> MASTER_USER='repl',
    -> MASTER_PASSWORD='p4ssword',
    -> MASTER_LOG_FILE='mysql-bin.000001',
    -> MASTER_LOG_POS=0;
```

The MASTER_LOG_POS parameter is set to 0 because this is the beginning of the log. After you run this, you should be able to inspect the output of SHOW SLAVE STATUS and see that the slave's settings are correct:

```
mysql> SHOW SLAVE STATUS\G
*************************** 1. row ***************************
              Slave_IO_State:
                 Master_Host: server1
                 Master_User: repl
                 Master_Port: 3306
               Connect_Retry: 60
             Master_Log_File: mysql-bin.000001
         Read_Master_Log_Pos: 4
              Relay_Log_File: mysql-relay-bin.000001
               Relay_Log_Pos: 4
       Relay_Master_Log_File: mysql-bin.000001
            Slave_IO_Running: No
           Slave_SQL_Running: No
                       ...omitted...
       Seconds_Behind_Master: NULL
```

The Slave_IO_State, Slave_IO_Running, and Slave_SQL_Running columns show that the slave processes are not running. Astute readers will also notice that the log position is 4 instead of 0. That's because 0 isn't really a log position; it just means "at the start of the log file." MySQL knows that the first event is really at position 4.[*]

To start replication, run the following command:

```
mysql> START SLAVE;
```

This command should produce no errors or output. Now inspect SHOW SLAVE STATUS again:

```
mysql> SHOW SLAVE STATUS\G
*************************** 1. row ***************************
              Slave_IO_State: Waiting for master to send event
                 Master_Host: server1
                 Master_User: repl
                 Master_Port: 3306
               Connect_Retry: 60
             Master_Log_File: mysql-bin.000001
         Read_Master_Log_Pos: 164
              Relay_Log_File: mysql-relay-bin.000001
               Relay_Log_Pos: 164
       Relay_Master_Log_File: mysql-bin.000001
            Slave_IO_Running: Yes
           Slave_SQL_Running: Yes
                       ...omitted...
       Seconds_Behind_Master: 0
```

---

[*] Actually, as you can see in the earlier output from SHOW MASTER STATUS, it's really at position 98. The master and slave will work that out together once the slave connects to the master, which hasn't yet happened.

Notice that the slave I/O and SQL threads are both running, and Seconds_Behind_Master is no longer NULL (we examine what Seconds_Behind_Master means later). The I/O thread is waiting for an event from the master, which means it has fetched all of the master's binary logs. The log positions have incremented, which means some events have been fetched and executed (your results will vary). If you make a change on the master, you should see the various file and position settings increment on the slave. You should also see the changes in the databases on the slave!

You will also be able to see the replication threads in the process list on both the master and the slave. On the master, you should see a connection created by the slave's I/O thread:

```
mysql> SHOW PROCESSLIST\G
*************************** 1. row ***************************
     Id: 55
   User: repl
   Host: slave1.webcluster_1:54813
     db: NULL
Command: Binlog Dump
   Time: 610237
  State: Has sent all binlog to slave; waiting for binlog to be updated
   Info: NULL
```

On the slave, you should see two threads. One is the I/O thread, and the other is the SQL thread:

```
mysql> SHOW PROCESSLIST\G
*************************** 1. row ***************************
     Id: 1
   User: system user
   Host:
     db: NULL
Command: Connect
   Time: 611116
  State: Waiting for master to send event
   Info: NULL
*************************** 2. row ***************************
     Id: 2
   User: system user
   Host:
     db: NULL
Command: Connect
   Time: 33
  State: Has read all relay log; waiting for the slave I/O thread to update it
   Info: NULL
```

The sample output we've shown comes from servers that have been running for a long time, which is why the I/O thread's Time column on the master and slave has a large value. The SQL thread has been idle for 33 seconds on the slave, which means no events have been replayed for 33 seconds.

These processes will always run under the "system user" user account, but the other column values may vary. For example, when the SQL thread is replaying an event on the slave, the Info column will show the query it is executing.

 If you just want to experiment with MySQL replication, Giuseppe Maxia's MySQL Sandbox script (*http://sourceforge.net/projects/mysql-sandbox/*) can quickly start a throwaway installation from a freshly downloaded MySQL tarball. It takes just a few keystrokes and about 15 seconds to get a running master and two running slaves:

> ```
> $ ./set_replication.pl ~/mysql-5.0.45-linux-x86_64-glibc23.
> tar.gz
> ```

Initializing a Slave from Another Server

The previous setup instructions assumed that you started the master and slave with the default initial data after a fresh installation, so you implicitly had the same data on both servers and you knew the master's binary log coordinates. This is not typically the case. You'll usually have a master that has been up and running for some time, and you'll want to synchronize a freshly installed slave with the master, even though it doesn't have the master's data.

There are several ways to initialize, or "clone," a slave from another server. These include copying data from the master, cloning a slave from another slave, and starting a slave from a recent backup. You need three things to synchronize a slave with a master:

- A snapshot of the master's data at some point in time.
- The master's current log file, and the byte offset within that log at the exact point in time you took the snapshot. We refer to these two values as the *log file coordinates*, because together they identify a binary log position. You can find the master's log file coordinates with the SHOW MASTER STATUS command.
- The master's binary log files from that time to the present.

Here are some ways to clone a slave from another server:

With a cold copy

One of the most basic ways to start a slave is to shut down the master-to-be and copy its files to the slave (see Appendix A for more on how to copy files efficiently). You can then start the master again, which begins a new binary log, and use CHANGE MASTER TO to start the slave at the beginning of that binary log. The disadvantage of this technique is obvious: you need to shut down the master while you make the copy.

With a warm copy

If you use only MyISAM tables, you can use *mysqlhotcopy* to copy files while the server is still running. See Chapter 11 for details.

Using mysqldump

If you use only InnoDB tables, you can use the following command to dump everything from the master, load it all into the slave, and change the slave's coordinates to the corresponding position in the master's binary log:

```
$ mysqldump --single-transaction --all-databases --master-data=1
--host=server1 | mysql --host=server2
```

The *--single-transaction* option causes the dump to read the data as it existed at the beginning of the transaction. This option may work with other transactional storage engines as well, but we haven't tested it. If you're not using transactional tables, you can use the *--lock-all-tables* option to get a consistent dump of all tables.

With an LVM snapshot or backup

As long as you know the corresponding binary log coordinates, you can use an LVM snapshot from the master or a backup to initialize the slave (if you use a backup, this method requires that you've kept all of the master's binary logs since the time of the backup). Just restore the backup or snapshot onto the slave, then use the appropriate binary log coordinates in CHANGE MASTER TO. There's more detail about this in Chapter 11.

InnoDB Hot Backup, also covered in Chapter 11, is a good way to initialize a slave if you use only InnoDB tables.

From another slave

You can use any of the snapshot or copy techniques just mentioned to clone one slave from another. However, if you use *mysqldump*, the *--master-data* option doesn't work.

Also, instead of using SHOW MASTER STATUS to get the master's binary log coordinates, you'll need to use SHOW SLAVE STATUS to find the position at which the slave was executing on the master when you snapshotted it.

The biggest disadvantage of cloning one slave from another is that if your slave has become out of sync with the master, you'll be cloning bad data.

 Don't use LOAD DATA FROM MASTER or LOAD TABLE FROM MASTER! They are obsolete, slow, and very dangerous. They also work only with MyISAM.

No matter what technique you choose, get comfortable with it, and document or script it. You will probably be doing it more than once, and you need to be able to do it in a pinch if something goes wrong.

Recommended Replication Configuration

There are many replication parameters, and most of them have at least some effect on data safety and performance. We explain later which rules to break and when.

In this section, we show a recommended, "safe" replication configuration that minimizes the opportunities for problems.

The most important setting for binary logging on the master is sync_binlog:

```
sync_binlog=1
```

This makes MySQL synchronize the binary log's contents to disk each time it commits a transaction, so you don't lose log events if there's a crash. If you disable this option, the server will do a little less work, but binary log entries could be corrupted or missing after a server crash. On a slave that doesn't need to act as a master, this option creates unnecessary overhead. It applies only to the binary log, not to the relay log.

We also recommend using InnoDB if you can't tolerate corrupt tables after a crash. MyISAM is fine if table corruption isn't a big deal, but MyISAM tables are likely to be in an inconsistent state after a slave server crashes. Chances are good that a statement will have been incompletely applied to one or more tables, and the data will be inconsistent even after you've repaired the tables.

If you use InnoDB, we strongly recommend setting the following options on the master:

```
innodb_flush_logs_at_trx_commit=1 # Flush every log write
innodb_support_xa=1               # MySQL 5.0 and newer only
innodb_safe_binlog               # MySQL 4.1 only, roughly equivalent to
                                  # innodb_support_xa
```

These are the default settings in MySQL 5.0. On the slave, we recommend enabling the following configuration options:

```
skip_slave_start
read_only
```

The skip_slave_start option will prevent the slave from starting automatically after a crash, which can give you a chance to repair a server if it has problems. If the slave starts automatically after a crash and is in an inconsistent state, it might cause so much additional corruption that you'll have to throw away its data and start fresh. Even if you've enabled all the options we suggested, a slave can easily break after a crash, because the relay logs and *master.info* file aren't crash-safe. They're not even flushed to disk, and there's no configuration option to control that behavior. (The Google patches we discuss later address this problem.)

The read_only option prevents most users from changing non-temporary tables. The exceptions are the slave SQL thread and threads with the SUPER privilege. This is one reason you should try to avoid giving your normal accounts the SUPER privilege (more on privileges in Chapter 12).

If a slave server is very far behind its master, the slave I/O thread can write many relay logs. The slave SQL thread will remove them as soon as it finishes replaying them (you can change this with the `relay_log_purge` option), but if it is running far behind, the I/O thread could actually fill up the disk. The solution to this problem is the `relay_log_space_limit` configuration variable. If the total size of all the relay logs grows larger than this variable's size, the I/O thread will stop and wait for the SQL thread to free up some more disk space.

Although this sounds nice, it can actually be a hidden problem. If the slave hasn't fetched all the relay logs from the master, those logs may be lost forever if the master crashes. Unless you're worried about disk space, it's probably a good idea to let the slave use as much space as it needs for relay logs. That's why we haven't included the `relay_log_space_limit` setting in our recommended configuration.

Replication Under the Hood

Now that we've explained some replication basics, let's dive deeper into it. Let's take a look at how replication really works, see what strengths and weaknesses it has as a result, and examine some more advanced replication configuration options.

Statement-Based Replication

MySQL 5.0 and earlier support only *statement-based replication* (also called *logical replication*). This is unusual in the database world. Statement-based replication works by recording the query that changed the data on the master. When the slave reads the event from the relay log and executes it, it is reexecuting the actual SQL query that the master executed. This arrangement has both benefits and drawbacks.

The most obvious benefit is that it's fairly simple to implement. Simply logging and replaying any statement that changes data will, in theory, keep the slave in sync with the master. Another benefit of statement-based replication is that the binary log events tend to be reasonably compact. So, relatively speaking, statement-based replication doesn't use a lot of bandwidth—a query that updates gigabytes of data might use only a few dozen bytes in the binary log. Also, the *mysqlbinlog* tool, which we mention throughout the chapter, is most convenient to use with statement-based logging.

In practice, however, statement-based replication is not as simple as it might seem, because many changes on the master can depend on factors besides just the query text. For example, the statements will execute at slightly—or possibly greatly—different times on the master and slave. As a result, MySQL's binary log format includes more than just the query text; it also transmits several bits of metadata, such as the current timestamp. Even so, there are some statements that MySQL can't replicate correctly, such as queries that use the `CURRENT_USER()` function. Stored routines and triggers are also problematic with statement-based replication.

Another issue with statement-based replication is that the modifications must be serializable. This requires a great deal of special-case code, configuration settings, and extra server features, including InnoDB's next-key locks and autoincrementing lock behavior. Not all storage engines work with statement-based replication, although those provided with the official MySQL server distribution up to and including MySQL 5.1 do.

You can find a complete list of statement-based replication's disadvantages in the MySQL manual's chapter on replication.

Row-Based Replication

MySQL 5.1 added support for *row-based replication*, which records the actual data changes in the binary log and is similar to how most other database products implement replication. This scheme has several advantages and drawbacks of its own. The biggest advantages are that MySQL can replicate every statement correctly, and some statements can be replicated much more efficiently. The main drawbacks are that the binary log can become much larger and that there's less visibility into what statements updated the data, so you can't use the binary log for auditing with *mysqlbinlog*.

 Row-based logging is not backward compatible. The *mysqlbinlog* utility distributed with MySQL 5.1 can read binary logs that contain events logged in row-based format (they are not human-readable, but the MySQL server can interpret them). However, versions of *mysqlbinlog* from earlier MySQL distributions will fail to recognize such log events and will exit with an error upon encountering them.

MySQL can replicate some changes more efficiently using row-based replication, because the slave doesn't have to replay the queries that changed the rows on the master. Replaying some queries can be very expensive. For example, here's a query that summarizes data from a very large table into a smaller table:

```
mysql> INSERT INTO summary_table(col1, col2, sum_col3)
    -> SELECT col1, col2, sum(col3)
    -> FROM enormous_table
    -> GROUP BY col1, col2;
```

Imagine that there are only three unique combinations of col1 and col2 in the enormous_table table. This query will scan many rows in the source table but will result in only three rows in the destination table. Replicating this event as a statement will make the slave repeat all that work just to generate a few rows, but replicating it with row-based replication will be trivially cheap on the slave. In this case, row-based replication is much more efficient.

On the other hand, the following event is much cheaper to replicate with statement-based replication:

```
mysql> UPDATE enormous_table SET col1 = 0;
```

Using row-based replication for this query would be very expensive because it changes every row: every row would have to be written to the binary log, making the binary log event extremely large. This would place more load on the master both during logging and replication, and the slower logging might reduce concurrency.

Because neither format is perfect for every situation, MySQL 5.1 switches between statement-based and row-based replication dynamically. By default, it uses statement-based replication, but when it detects an event that cannot be replicated correctly with a statement, it switches to row-based replication. You can also control the format as needed by setting the binlog_format session variable.

It's harder to do point-in-time recovery with a binary log that has events in row-based format, but not impossible. A log server can be helpful—more on that later.

In theory, row-based replication solves several problems we mention later. But in practice, most people we know who are using MySQL 5.1 in production are still using statement-based replication. Thus, it's still too early to say anything conclusive about row-based replication.

Replication Files

Let's take a look at some of the files replication uses. You already know about the binary log and the relay log, but there are several other files too. Where MySQL places them depends mostly on your configuration settings. Different MySQL versions place them in different directories by default. You can probably find them either in the data directory or in the directory that contains the server's *.pid* file (possibly */var/run/mysqld/* on Unix-like systems). Here they are:

mysql-bin.index
> A server that has binary logging enabled will also have a file named the same as the binary logs, but with a *.index* suffix. This file keeps track of the binary log files that exist on disk. It is not an index in the sense of a table's index; rather, each line in the file contains the filename of a binary log file.
>
> You might be tempted to think that this file is redundant and can be deleted (after all, MySQL could just look at the disk to find its files), but don't. MySQL relies on this index file, and it will not recognize a binary log file unless it's mentioned here.

mysql-relay-bin.index
> This file serves the same purpose for the relay logs as the binary log index file does for the binary logs.

master.info
> This file contains the information a slave server needs to connect to its master. The format is plain text (one value per line) and varies between MySQL versions.

Don't delete it, or your slave will not know how to connect to its master after it restarts. This file contains the replication user's password, in plain text, so you may want to restrict its permissions.

relay-log.info

This file contains the slave's current binary log and relay log coordinates (i.e., the slave's position on the master). Don't delete this either, or the slave will forget where it was replicating from after a restart and might try to replay statements it has already executed.

These files are a rather crude way of recording MySQL's replication and logging state. Unfortunately, they are not written synchronously, so if your server loses power and the files haven't yet been flushed to disk, they can be inaccurate when the server restarts.

By default, the binary logs are named after the server's hostname with a numeric suffix, but it's a good idea to name them explicitly in *my.cnf*, as in the following example:

```
log_bin             # Don't do this, or files will be named after the hostname
log_bin = mysql-bin # This is safe
```

This matters because replication might break if the server's hostname changes. We also suggest you don't name the log files after the hostname—in other words, don't just make the defaults explicit. Instead, choose a name for your binary logs and use it universally. This will make it much easier to move a server's files to another machine and to automate failover.

You should also name the relay logs (which are likewise named after the server's hostname by default) and the corresponding *.index* files explicitly. Here are our suggested *my.cnf* settings for all of these options:

```
log_bin         = mysql-bin
log_bin_index   = mysql-bin.index
relay_log       = mysql-relay-bin
relay_log_index = mysql-relay-bin.index
```

The *.index* files actually inherit their names from the log files, but it doesn't hurt to name them explicitly.

The *.index* files also interact with another setting, expire_logs_days, which specifies how MySQL should purge expired binary logs. If the *mysql-bin.index* files mention files that don't exist on disk, automatic purging will not work; in fact, even the PURGE MASTER LOGS statement won't work. The solution to this problem is generally to use the MySQL server to manage the binary logs, so it doesn't get confused.

You need to implement some log purging strategy explicitly, either with expire_logs_days or another means, or MySQL will fill up the disk with binary logs. You should consider your backup policy when you do this. See "The Binary Log Format" on page 487 for more on the binary log.

Sending Replication Events to Other Slaves

The `log_slave_updates` option lets you use a slave as a master of other slaves. It instructs MySQL to write the events the slave SQL thread executes into its own binary log, which its own slaves can then retrieve and execute. Figure 8-2 illustrates this.

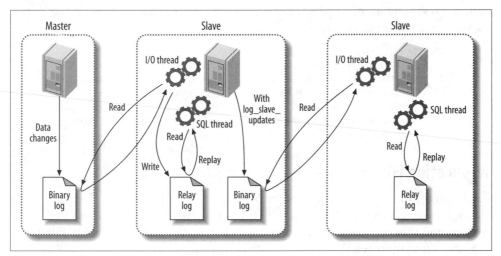

Figure 8-2. Passing on a replication event to further slaves

In this scenario, a change on the master causes an event to be written to its binary log. The first slave then fetches and executes the event. At this point, the event's life would normally be over, but because `log_slave_updates` is enabled, the slave writes it to its binary log instead. Now the second slave can retrieve the event into its own relay log and execute it. This configuration means that changes on the original master can propagate to slaves that are not attached to it directly. We prefer setting `log_slave_updates` by default because it lets you connect a slave without having to restart the server.

When the first slave writes a binary log event from the master into its own binary log, that event will almost certainly be at a different position in the log from its position on the master—that is, it could be in a different log file or at a different numerical position within the log file. This means you can't assume all servers that are at the same logical point in replication will have the same log coordinates. As we'll see later, this makes it quite complicated to do some tasks, such as changing slaves to a different master or promoting a slave to be the master.

Unless you've taken care to give each server a unique server ID, configuring a slave in this manner can cause subtle errors and may even cause replication to complain and stop. One of the more common questions about replication configuration is why one needs to specify the server ID. Shouldn't MySQL be able to replicate statements without knowing where they originated? Why does MySQL care whether the server ID is globally unique? The answer to this question lies in how MySQL prevents an infinite loop in replication. When the slave SQL thread reads the relay log, it discards any event whose server ID matches its own. This breaks infinite loops in replication. Preventing infinite loops is important for some of the more useful replication topologies, such as master-master replication.

> If you're having trouble getting replication set up, the server ID is one of the things you should check. It's not enough to just inspect the @@server_id variable. It has a default value, but replication won't work unless it's explicitly set, either in *my.cnf* or via a SET command. If you use a SET command, be sure you update the configuration file too, or your settings won't survive a server restart.

Replication Filters

Replication filtering options let you replicate just part of a server's data. There are two kinds of replication filters: those that filter events out of the binary log on the master, and those that filter events coming from the relay log on the slave. Figure 8-3 illustrates the two types.

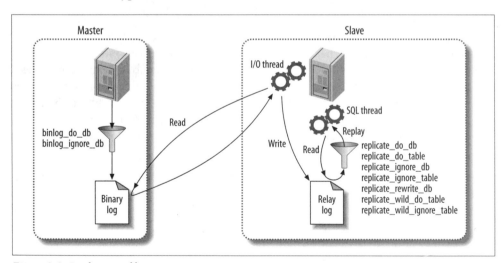

Figure 8-3. Replication filtering options

The options that control binary log filtering are binlog_do_db and binlog_ignore_db. You usually do *not* want to enable these, as we explain in a moment.

On the slave, the replicate_* options filter events as the slave SQL thread reads them from the relay log. You can replicate or ignore one or more databases, rewrite one database to another database, and replicate or ignore tables based on LIKE pattern matching syntax.

The most important thing to understand about these options is that the *_do_db and *_ignore_db options, both on the master and on the slave, do not work as you might expect. You might think they filter on the object's database name, but they actually filter *on the current default database*. That is, if you execute the following statements on the master:

```
mysql> USE test;
mysql> DELETE FROM sakila.film;
```

the *_do_db and *_ignore_db parameters will filter the DELETE statement on test, not on sakila. This is not usually what you want, and it can cause the wrong statements to be replicated or ignored. The *_do_db and *_ignore_db parameters have uses, but they're limited and rare, and you should be very careful with them. If you use these parameters, it's very easy to for replication to get out of sync.

> The binlog_do_db and binlog_ignore_db options don't just have the potential to break replication; they also make it impossible to do point-in-time recovery from a backup. For most situations, you should never use them. We show some safe ways to filter replication with Blackhole tables later in the chapter.

Stopping GRANT and REVOKE statements from replicating to slaves is a common use for replication filters.* The usual problem is that an administrator uses GRANT to give a user some write privilege on the master, and then finds it has propagated to the slave, where the user shouldn't be allowed to change any data. The following replication options on the slave will prevent this:

```
replicate_ignore_table=mysql.columns_priv
replicate_ignore_table=mysql.db
replicate_ignore_table=mysql.host
replicate_ignore_table=mysql.procs_priv
replicate_ignore_table=mysql.tables_priv
replicate_ignore_table=mysql.user
```

You may see advice to simply filter out all tables in the mysql database, with a rule such as the following:

```
replicate_wild_ignore_table=mysql.%
```

This will certainly prevent GRANT statements from replicating, but it will prevent events and routines from replicating too. Such unforeseen consequences are the reason we said you need to be careful with filters. It might be a better idea to prevent specific statements from being replicated, usually with SET SQL_LOG_BIN=0, though

---

* A better way to limit privileges on slaves is to use read_only and keep the privileges the same on the master and the slaves.

that practice has its own hazards. In general, you should use replication filters very carefully, and only if you really need them, because they make it so easy to break statement-based replication. (Row-based replication might solve some of these problems, but it's not fully proven yet.)

The filtering options are well documented in the MySQL manual, so we won't repeat the details here.

Replication Topologies

You can set up MySQL replication for almost any configuration of masters and slaves, with the limitation that a given MySQL slave instance can have only one master. Many complex topologies are possible, but even the simple ones can be very flexible. A single topology can have many different uses. Keep this in mind as you read through our descriptions, because we describe only simple uses. The variety of ways you can use replication could easily fill its own book.

We've already seen how to set up a master with a single slave. In this section, we look at some other common topologies and discuss their strengths and limitations. As we go, remember these basic rules:

- A MySQL slave instance can have only one master.
- Every slave must have a unique server ID.
- A master can have many slaves (or, correspondingly, a slave can have many siblings).
- A slave can propagate changes from its master, and be the master of other slaves, if you enable log_slave_updates.

Master and Multiple Slaves

Aside from the basic two-server master-slave setup we've already mentioned, this is the simplest replication topology. In fact, it's just as simple as the basic setup, because the slaves don't interact with each other at all; they each connect only to the master. Figure 8-4 shows this arrangement.

This configuration is most useful when you have few writes and many reads. You can spread reads across any number of slave servers, up to the point where the slaves put too much load on the master or network bandwidth from the master to the slaves becomes a problem. You can set up many slaves at once, or add slaves as you need them, using the same steps we showed earlier in this chapter.

Although this is a very simple topology, it is flexible enough to fill many needs. Here are just a few ideas:

- Use different slaves for different roles (for example, add different indexes or use different storage engines).

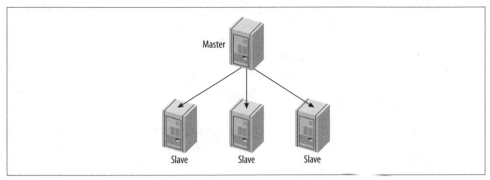

Figure 8-4. A master with multiple slaves

- Set up one of the slaves as a standby master, with no traffic other than replication.
- Put one of the slaves in a remote data center for disaster recovery.
- Time-delay one or more of the slaves for disaster recovery.
- Use one of the slaves for backups, for training, or as a development or staging server.

One of the reasons this topology is popular is that it avoids many of the complexities that come with other configurations. Here's an example: it's easy to compare one slave to another in terms of binary log positions on the master, because they'll all be the same. In other words, if you stop all the slaves at the same logical point in replication, they'll all be reading from the same physical position in the master's logs. This is a nice property that simplifies many administrative tasks, such as promoting a slave to be the master.

This property holds only among "sibling" slaves. It's more complicated to compare log positions between servers that aren't in a direct master-slave or sibling relationship. Many of the topologies we mention later, such as tree replication or distribution masters, make it harder to figure out where in the logical sequence of events a slave is really replicating.

Master-Master in Active-Active Mode

Master-master replication (also known as dual-master or bidirectional replication) involves two servers, each configured as both a master and a slave of the other—in other words, a pair of co-masters. Figure 8-5 shows the setup.

Master-master replication in active-active mode has uses, but they're generally special-purpose. One possible use is for geographically separated offices, where each office needs its own locally writable copy of data.

The biggest problem with such a configuration is how to handle conflicting changes. The list of possible problems caused by having two writable co-masters is very long.

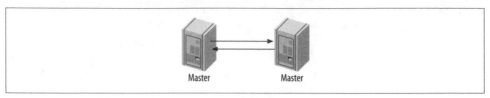

Master   Master

Figure 8-5. Master-master replication

Problems usually show up when a query changes the same row simultaneously on both servers or inserts into a table with an AUTO_INCREMENT column at the same time on both servers.

MySQL Does Not Support Multimaster Replication

We use the term *multimaster replication* very specifically to describe a slave with more than one master. Regardless of what you may have been told, MySQL (unlike some other database servers) does not support the configuration illustrated in Figure 8-6 at present. However, we show you some ways to emulate multimaster replication later in this chapter.

Unfortunately, many people use this term casually to describe any setup where there is more than one master in the entire replication topology, such as the "tree" topology we show later in this chapter. Other people use it to describe what we call master-master replication, where the servers are mutually master and slave.

These terminology problems cause a lot of confusion and even arguments, so we think it's best to be careful with names. Just imagine how hard it will be to communicate if MySQL adds support for a slave with two masters! What term will you use to describe that if you haven't reserved "multimaster replication" for the purpose?

MySQL 5.0 added some replication features that make this type of replication setup slightly safer: the auto_increment_increment and auto_increment_offset settings. These settings let servers autogenerate nonconflicting values for INSERT queries. However, allowing writes to both masters is still dangerous. Updates that happen in a different order on the two machines can still cause the data to become out of sync silently. For example, imagine you have a single-column, single-row table containing the value 1. Now suppose these two statements execute simultaneously:

- On the first co-master:

    ```
    mysql> UPDATE tbl SET col=col + 1;
    ```
- On the second:

    ```
    mysql> UPDATE tbl SET col=col * 2;
    ```

The result? One server has the value 4, and the other has the value 3. And yet, there are no replication errors at all.

Data getting out of sync is only the beginning. What if normal replication stops with an error, but applications keep writing to both servers? You can't just clone one of the servers from the other, because both of them will have changes that you need to copy to the other. Solving this problem is likely to be very hard.

If you set up a master-master active-active configuration carefully, perhaps with well-partitioned data and privileges, you can avoid some of these problems.* However, it's hard to do well, and there's usually a better way to achieve what you need.

In general, allowing writes on both servers can cause more trouble than it's worth. However, an active-passive configuration is very useful indeed, as you'll see in the next section

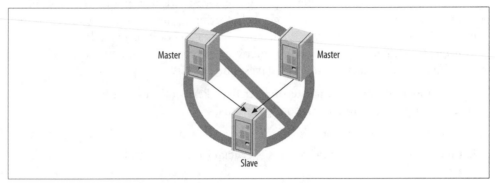

Figure 8-6. MySQL does not support multimaster replication

Master-Master in Active-Passive Mode

There's a variation on master-master replication that avoids the pitfalls we just discussed and is, in fact, a very powerful way to design fault-tolerant and highly available systems. The main difference is that one of the servers is a read-only "passive" server, as shown in Figure 8-7.

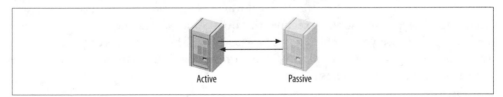

Figure 8-7. Master-master replication in active-passive mode

This configuration lets you swap the active and passive server roles back and forth very easily, because the servers' configurations are symmetrical. This makes failover and failback easy. It also lets you perform maintenance, optimize tables, upgrade

---

* Some, but not all—we can play devil's advocate and show you flaws in just about any setup you can imagine.

your operating system (or application, or hardware), and do other tasks without any downtime.

For example, running an ALTER TABLE statement locks the entire table, blocking reads and writes to it. This can take a long time and disrupt service. However, the master-master configuration lets you stop the slave threads on the active server, so it doesn't process any updates from the passive server, alter the table on the passive server, switch the roles, and restart the slave process on the formerly active server.* That server then reads its relay log and executes the same ALTER TABLE statement. Again, this may take a long time, but it doesn't matter because the server isn't serving any live queries.

The active-passive master-master topology lets you sidestep many other problems and limitations in MySQL. You can get help setting up and managing such a system with the MySQL Master-Master Replication Manager tool (*http://code.google.com/p/ mysql-master-master/*). It automates many tricky tasks, such as recovering and resyncing replication, setting up new slaves, and so on.

Let's see how to configure a master-master pair. Perform these steps on *both* servers, so they end up with symmetrical configurations:

1. Enable binary logging, choose unique server IDs, and add replication accounts.
2. Enable logging slave updates. This is crucial for failover and failback, as we'll see later.
3. Optionally configure the passive server to be read-only to prevent changes that might conflict with changes on the active server.
4. Ensure that the servers have exactly the same data.
5. Start each server's MySQL instance.
6. Configure each server as a slave of the other, beginning with the newly created binary log.

Now let's trace what happens when there's a change to the active server. The change gets written to its binary log and flows through replication to the passive server's relay log. The passive server executes the query and writes the event to its own binary log, because you enabled log_slave_updates. The active server then retrieves the same change via replication into its own relay log, but it ignores it because the server ID in the event matches its own.

See "Changing Masters" on page 382, later in this chapter, to learn how to switch roles.

---

* You can also disable binary logging temporarily with SET SQL_LOG_BIN=0, instead of stopping replication. Some commands, such as OPTIMIZE TABLE, also support a LOCAL or NO_WRITE_TO_BINLOG option that prevents logging.

Setting up an active-passive master-master topology is a little like creating a hot spare in some ways, except that you can use the "spare" to boost performance. You can use it for read queries, backups, "offline" maintenance, upgrades, and so on—things you can't do with a true hot spare. However, you cannot use it to gain better write performance than you can get with a single server (more about that later).

As we discuss more scenarios and uses for replication, we'll come back to this configuration. It is a very important and common replication topology.

Master-Master with Slaves

A related configuration is to add one or more slaves to each co-master, as shown in Figure 8-8.

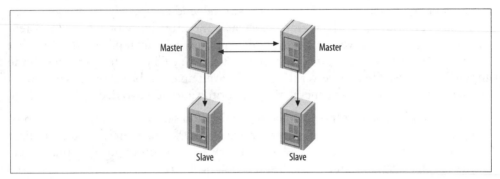

Figure 8-8. Master-master replication with slaves

The advantage of this configuration is extra redundancy. In a geographically distributed replication topology, it removes the single point of failure at each site. You can also offload read-intensive queries to the slaves, as usual.

If you're using a master-master topology locally for fast failover, this configuration is still useful. Promoting one of the slaves to replace a failed master is possible, although it's a little more complex. The same is true of moving one of the slaves to point to a different master. The added complexity is an important consideration.

Ring

The dual-master configuration is really just a special case[*] of the ring replication configuration, shown in Figure 8-9. A ring has three or more masters. Each server is a slave of the server before it in the ring, and a master of the server after it. This topology is also called *circular replication*.

---

[*] A slightly more sane special case, we might add.

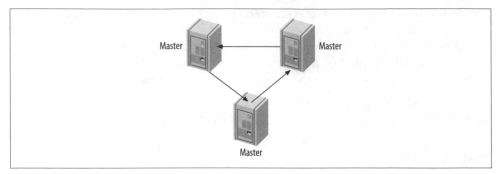

Figure 8-9. A replication ring topology

Rings don't have some of the key benefits of a master-master setup, such as symmetrical configuration and easy failover. They also depend completely on every node in the ring being available, which greatly increases the probability of the entire system failing. And if you remove one of the nodes from the ring, any replication events that originated at that node can go into an infinite loop. They'll cycle forever through the topology, because the only server that will filter out an event based on its server ID is the server that created it. In general, rings are brittle and best avoided.

You can mitigate some of the risk of a ring replication setup by adding slaves to provide redundancy at each site, as shown in Figure 8-10. This merely protects against the risk of a server failing, though. A loss of power or any other problem that affects any connection between the sites will still break the entire ring.

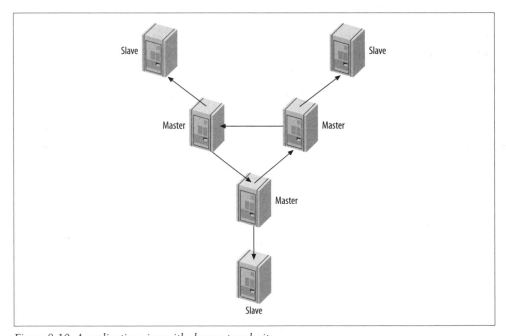

Figure 8-10. A replication ring with slaves at each site

Master, Distribution Master, and Slaves

We've mentioned that slaves can place quite a load on the master if there are enough of them. Each slave creates a new thread on the master, which executes the special *binlog dump* command. This command reads the data from the binary log and sends it to the slave. The work is repeated for each slave thread; they don't share the resources required for a binlog dump.

If there are many slaves and there's a particularly large binary log event, such as a huge `LOAD DATA INFILE`, the master's load can go up significantly. The master may even run out of memory and crash because of all the slaves requesting the same huge event at the same time. On the other hand, if the slaves are all requesting *different* binlog events that aren't in the filesystem cache anymore, that can cause a lot of disk seeks, which might also interfere with the master's performance.

For this reason, if you need many slaves, it's often a good idea to remove the load from the master and use a *distribution master*. A distribution master is a slave whose only purpose is to read and serve the binary logs from the master. Many slaves can connect to the distribution master, which insulates the original master from the load. To remove the work of actually executing the queries on the distribution master, you should change its tables to the Blackhole storage engine, as shown in Figure 8-11.

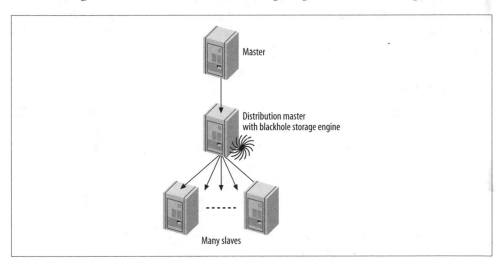

Figure 8-11. A master, a distribution master, and many slaves

It's hard to say exactly how many slaves a master can handle before it needs a distribution master. As a very general rule of thumb, if your master is running near its full capacity, you might not want to put more than about 10 slaves on it. If there's very little write activity, or you're replicating only a fraction of the tables, the master can probably serve many more slaves. Additionally, you don't have to limit yourself to just one distribution master. You can use several if you need to replicate to a really large number of slaves, or you can even use a pyramid of distribution masters.

You can also use the distribution master for other purposes, such as applying filters and rewrite rules to the binary log events. This is much more efficient than repeating the logging, rewriting, and filtering on each slave.

If you use Blackhole tables on the distribution master, it will be able to serve more slaves than it could otherwise. The distribution master will execute the queries, but the queries will be extremely cheap, because the Blackhole tables will not have any data.

A common question is how to ensure that all tables on the distribution master use the Blackhole storage engine. What if someone creates a new table on the master and specifies a different storage engine? Indeed, the same issue arises whenever you want to use a different storage engine on a slave. The usual solution is to set the server's `storage_engine` option:

```
storage_engine = blackhole
```

This will affect only `CREATE TABLE` statements that don't specify a storage engine explicitly. If you have an existing application that you can't control, this topology might be fragile. You can disable InnoDB and make tables fall back to MyISAM with the `skip_innodb` option, but you can't disable the MyISAM or Memory engines.

The other major drawback is the difficulty of replacing the master with one of the (ultimate) slaves. It's hard to promote one of the slaves into its place, because the intermediate master ensures that they will almost always have different binary log coordinates than the original master does.

Tree or Pyramid

If you're replicating a master to a very large number of slaves—whether you're distributing data geographically or just trying to build in more read capacity—it can be more manageable to use a pyramid design, as illustrated in Figure 8-12.

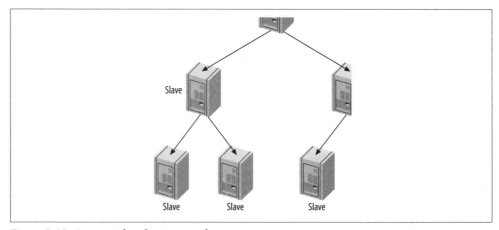

Figure 8-12. A pyramid replication topology

The advantage of this design is that it eases the load on the master, just as the distribution master did in the previous section. The disadvantage is that any failure in an intermediate level will affect multiple servers, which wouldn't happen if the slaves were each attached to the master directly. Also, the more intermediate levels you have, the harder and more complicated it is to handle failures.

Custom Replication Solutions

MySQL replication is flexible enough that you can often design a custom solution for your application's needs. You'll typically use some combination of filtering, distribution, and replicating to different storage engines. You can also use "hacks," such as replicating to and from servers that use the Blackhole storage engine (as discussed in "Master, Distribution Master, and Slaves" on page 369, earlier in this chapter). Your design can be as elaborate as you want. The biggest limitations are what you can monitor and administer reasonably and what resource constraints you have (network bandwidth, CPU power, etc.).

Selective replication

To take advantage of locality of reference and keep your working set in memory for reads, you can replicate a small amount of data to each of many slaves. If each slave has a fraction of the master's data and you direct reads to the slaves, you can make much better use of the memory on each slave. Each slave will also have only a fraction of the master's write load, so the master can become more powerful without making the slaves fall behind.

This scenario is similar in some respects to the horizontal data partitioning we talk more about in the next chapter, but it has the advantage that one server still hosts *all* the data—the master. This means you never have to look on more than one server for the data needed for a write query, and if you have read queries that need data that doesn't all exist on any single slave server, you have the option of doing those reads on the master instead. Even if you can't do all reads on the slaves, you should be able to move many of them off the master.

The simplest way to do this is to partition the data into different databases on the master, and then replicate each database to a different slave server. For example, if you want to replicate data for each department in your company to a different slave, you can create databases called sales, marketing, procurement, and so on. Each slave should then have a replicate_wild_do_table configuration option that limits its data to the given database. Here's the configuration option for the sales database:

```
replicate_wild_do_table = sales.%
```

Filtering with a distribution master is also useful. For example, if you want to replicate just part of a heavily loaded server across a slow or very expensive network, you can use a local distribution master with Blackhole tables and filtering rules. The distribution master can have replication filters that remove undesired entries from its logs. This can help avoid dangerous logging settings on the master, and it doesn't require you to transfer all the logs across the network to the remote slaves.

Separating functions

Many applications have a mixture of online transaction processing (OLTP) and online analytical processing (OLAP) queries. OLTP queries tend to be short and transactional. OLAP queries are usually large and slow and don't require absolutely up-to-date data. The two types of queries also place very different stresses on the server. Thus, they perform best on servers that are configured differently and perhaps even use different storage engines and hardware.

A common solution to this problem is to replicate the OLTP server's data to slaves specifically designed for the OLAP workload. These slaves can have different hardware, configurations, indexes, and/or storage engines. If you dedicate a slave to OLAP queries, you might also be able to tolerate more replication lag or otherwise degraded quality of service on that slave. That might mean you can use it for tasks that would result in unacceptable performance on a nondedicated slave, such as executing very long-running queries.

No special replication setup is required, although you might choose to omit some of the data from the master if you'll achieve significant savings by not having it on the slave. Remember, filtering out even a small amount of data with replication filters on the relay log might help reduce I/O and cache activity.

Data archiving

You can archive data on a slave server—that is, keep it on the slave but remove it from the master—by running delete queries on the master and ensuring that those queries don't execute on the slave. There are two common ways to do this: one is to selectively disable binary logging on the master, and the other is to use replicate_ignore_db rules on the slave.

The first method requires executing SET SQL_LOG_BIN=0 in the process that purges the data on the master, then purging the data. This has the advantage of not requiring any special replication configuration on the slave, and because the statements aren't even logged to the master's binary log, it's slightly more efficient there too. The main disadvantage is that you won't be able to use the binary log on the master for auditing or point-in-time recovery anymore, as it won't contain every modification made to the master's data. It also requires the SUPER privilege.

The second technique is to USE a certain database on the master before executing the statements that purge the data. For example, you can create a database named purge, and then specify replicate_ignore_db=purge in the slave's *my.cnf* file and restart the slave. The slave will ignore statements that USE this database. This approach doesn't have the first technique's weaknesses, but it has the (minor) drawback of making the slave fetch binary log events it doesn't need. There's also a potential for someone to mistakenly execute non-purge queries in the purge database, thus causing the slave not to replay events you want it to.

Maakit's *mk-archiver* tool supports both methods.

 A third option is to use binlog_ignore_db to filter out replication events, but as we stated earlier, we consider this dangerous for most purposes.

Using slaves for full-text searches

Many applications require a combination of transactions and full-text searches. However, only MyISAM tables offer built-in full-text search capabilities, and MyISAM doesn't support transactions. A common workaround is to configure a slave for full-text searches by changing the storage engine for certain tables to MyISAM on the slave. You can then add full-text indexes and perform full-text search queries on the slave. This avoids potential replication problems with transactional and nontransactional storage engines in the same query on the master, and it relieves the master of the extra work of maintaining the full-text indexes.

Read-only slaves

Many organizations prefer slaves to be read-only, so unintended changes don't break replication. You can achieve this with the read_only configuration variable. It disables most writes: the exceptions are the slave processes, users who have the SUPER privilege, and temporary tables. This is perfect as long as you don't give the SUPER privilege to ordinary users, which you shouldn't do anyway.

Emulating multimaster replication

MySQL does not currently support multimaster replication (i.e., a slave with more than one master). However, you can emulate this topology by changing a slave to point at different masters in turn. For example, you can point the slave at master A and let it run for a while, then point it at master B for a while, and then switch it back to master A again. How well this will work depends on your data and how much work the two masters will cause the single slave to do. If your masters are relatively lightly loaded and their updates won't conflict at all, it might work very well.

You'll need to do a little work to keep track of the binary log coordinates for each master. You also might want to ensure that the slave's I/O thread doesn't fetch more data than you intend it to execute on each cycle; otherwise, you could increase the network traffic significantly by fetching and throwing away a lot of data on each cycle.

A ready-to-use script for this purpose is available at *http://code.google.com/p/mysql-mmre/*.

You can also emulate multimaster replication using master-master (or ring) replication and the Blackhole storage engine with a slave, as depicted in Figure 8-13.

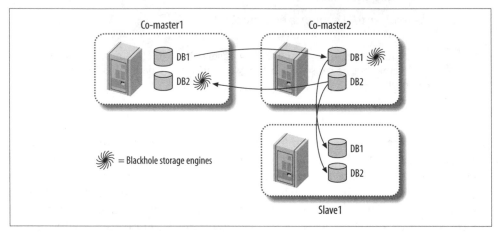

Figure 8-13. Emulating multimaster replication with dual masters and the Blackhole storage engine

In this configuration, the two masters each contain their own data. They each also contain the tables from the other master, but use the Blackhole storage engine to avoid actually storing the data in those tables. A slave is attached to one of the co-masters—it doesn't matter which one. This slave does not use the Blackhole storage engine at all, so it is effectively a slave of both masters.

In fact, it's not really necessary to use a master-master topology to achieve this. You can simply replicate from server1 to server2 to the slave. If server2 uses the Blackhole storage engine for tables replicated from server1, it will not contain any data from server1, as shown in Figure 8-14.

Either of these configurations can suffer from the usual problems, such as conflicting updates and CREATE TABLE statements that explicitly specify a storage engine.

Creating a log server

One of the things you can do with MySQL replication is create a "log server" with no data, whose only purpose is to make it easy to replay and/or filter binary log events. As you'll see later in this chapter, this is very useful for restarting replication after crashes. It's also useful for point-in-time recovery, which we discuss in Chapter 11.

Imagine you have a set of binary logs or relay logs—perhaps from a backup, perhaps from a server that crashed—and you want to replay the events in them. You could use *mysqlbinlog* to extract the events, but it's more convenient and efficient to just set

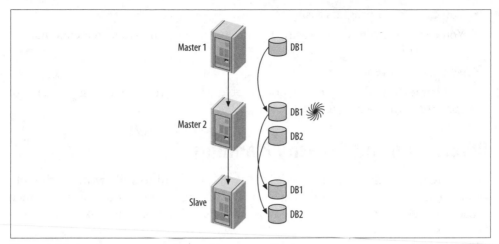

Figure 8-14. Another way to emulate multimaster replication

up a MySQL instance without any data and let it think the binary logs are its own. You can use the MySQL Sandbox script available at *http://sourceforge.net/projects/ mysql-sandbox/* to create the log server if you'll need it only temporarily. The log server *does not need any data* because it won't be executing the logs—it will only be serving the logs to other servers. (It does need to have a replication user, however.)

Let's take a look at how this technique works (we show some applications for it later). Suppose the logs are called *somelog-bin.000001*, *somelog-bin.000002*, and so on. Place these files into your log server's binary log directory. We'll assume it's */var/ log/mysql*. Then, before you start the log server, edit its *my.cnf* file as follows:

```
log_bin       = /var/log/mysql/somelog-bin
log_bin_index = /var/log/mysql/somelog-bin.index
```

The server doesn't automatically discover log files, so you'll also need to update the server's log index file. The following command will accomplish this on Unix-like systems:*

```
# /bin/ls -1 /var/log/mysql/somelog-bin.[0-9]* > /var/log/mysql/somelog-bin.index
```

Make sure the user account under which MySQL runs can read and write the log index file. Now you can start your log server and verify that it sees the log files with SHOW MASTER LOGS.

Why is a log server better than using *mysqlbinlog* for recovery? There are several reasons:

- It's faster, because it eliminates the need to extract statements from the log and pipe them into *mysql*.

---

* We use */bin/ls* explicitly to avoid invoking common aliases that add terminal escape codes for coloring.

- You can see the progress easily.

- You can work with errors easily. For example, you can skip statements that fail to replicate.

- You can filter replication events easily.

- Sometimes *mysqlbinlog* might not be able to read the binary log, because of changes to the logging format.

Replication and Capacity Planning

Writes are usually the replication bottleneck, and it's hard to scale writes with replication. You need to make sure you do the math right when you plan how much capacity slaves will add to your system overall. It's easy to make mistakes where replication is concerned.

For example, imagine your workload is 20% writes and 80% reads. To make the math easy, let's grossly oversimplify and assume the following are true:

- Read and write queries involve an identical amount of work.

- All servers are exactly equal and have a capacity of exactly 1,000 queries per second.

- Slaves and masters have the same performance characteristics.

- You can move all read queries to the slaves.

If you currently have one server handling 1,000 queries per second, how many slaves will you need to add so that you can handle twice your current load and move all read queries to the slaves?

It might seem that you could add 2 slaves and split the 1,600 reads between them. However, don't forget that your write workload has increased to 400 queries per second, and this cannot be divided between the master and slaves. Each slave must perform 400 writes per second. That means each slave is 40% busy with writes and can serve only 600 reads per second. Thus, you'll need not two but *three* slaves to handle twice the traffic.

What if your traffic doubles again? There will be 800 writes per second, so the master will still be able to keep up. But the slaves will each be 80% busy with writes too, so you'll need 16 slaves to handle the 3,200 reads per second. And if the traffic increases just a little more, it will be too much for the master.

This is far from linear scalability: you need 17 times as many servers to handle 4 times as many queries. This illustrates that you quickly reach a point of diminishing returns when adding slaves to a single master. And this is even with our unrealistic assumptions, which ignore, for example, the fact that single-threaded statement-based replication usually causes slaves to have lower capacity than the master. A real replication setup is likely to perform even worse than our theoretical one.

Why Replication Doesn't Help Scale Writes

The fundamental problem with the poor server-to-capacity ratio we just discussed is that you cannot distribute the writes equally among the machines, as you can with the reads. Another way to say this is that replication scales reads, but it doesn't scale writes.

You might wonder whether there's a way to add write capacity with replication. The answer is no—not even a little. Sharding (partitioning) your data is the only way you can scale writes, which we cover in the next chapter.

Some readers may have thought about using a master-master topology (see "Master-Master in Active-Active Mode" on page 363, earlier in this chapter) and writing to both masters. This configuration can handle slightly more writes as compared to a master-slave topology, because you can share the serialization penalty equally between the two servers. If you do 50% of the writes on each server, only the 50% that execute via replication from the other server must be serialized. In theory, that's better than doing 100% of the writes in parallel on one machine (the master) and 100% of the writes serially on the other machine (the slave).

This may seem attractive. However, such a configuration still can't handle as many writes as a single server. A server whose write workload is 50% serialized is slower than a single server that can do all its writes in parallel.

That's why this tactic does not scale writes. It's only a way to share the serialized-write disadvantage over two servers, so the "weakest link in the chain" isn't quite so weak. It provides only a relatively small improvement over an active-passive setup, adding a lot of risk for a small gain—and it generally won't benefit you anyway, as we explain in the next section.

Plan to Underutilize

Intentionally underutilizing your servers can be a smart and cost-effective way to build a large application, especially when you use replication. Servers that have spare capacity can tolerate surges better, have more power to handle slow queries and maintenance jobs (such as OPTIMIZE TABLE operations), and will be better able to keep up in replication.

Trying to reduce the replication penalty a little by writing to both nodes in a master-master topology is typically a false economy. You should usually load the master-master pair less than 50% with reads, because if you add more load, there won't be enough capacity if one of the servers fails. If both servers can handle the load by themselves, you probably won't need to worry much about the single-threaded replication penalty.

Building in excess capacity is also one of the best ways to achieve high availability, although there are other ways, such as running your application in "degraded" mode when there's a failure. The next chapter covers this in more detail.

Replication Administration and Maintenance

Setting up replication probably isn't something you'll do constantly, unless you have many servers. But once it's in place, monitoring and administering your replication topology will be a regular job, no matter how many servers you have.

You should try to automate this work as much as possible. You might not need to write your own tools for this purpose, though: in Chapter 14, we discuss several productivity tools for MySQL, many of which have built-in replication monitoring capabilities or plug-ins. Some of the more useful offerings include Nagios, MySQL Enterprise Monitor, and MonYOG.

Monitoring Replication

Replication increases the complexity of MySQL monitoring. Although replication actually happens on both the master and the slave, most of the work is done on the slave, and that is where the most common problems occur. Are all the slaves replicating? Has any slave had errors? How far behind is the slowest slave? MySQL provides most of the information you need to answer these questions, but automating the monitoring process and making replication robust is left up to you.

On the master, you can use the SHOW MASTER STATUS command to see the master's current binary log position and configuration (see "Configuring the Master and Slave" on page 348, earlier in this chapter). You can also ask the master which binary logs exist on disk:

```
mysql> SHOW MASTER LOGS;
+------------------+-----------+
| Log_name         | File_size |
+------------------+-----------+
| mysql-bin.000220 |    425605 |
| mysql-bin.000221 |   1134128 |
| mysql-bin.000222 |     13653 |
| mysql-bin.000223 |     13634 |
+------------------+-----------+
```

This information is useful in determining what parameters to give the PURGE MASTER LOGS command. You can also view replication events in the binary log with the SHOW BINLOG EVENTS command. For example, after running the previous command, we created a table on an otherwise unused server. Because we knew this was the only statement that changed any data, we knew the statement's offset in the binary log was 13634, so we were able to view it as follows:

```
mysql> SHOW BINLOG EVENTS IN 'mysql-bin.000223' FROM 13634\G
*************************** 1. row ***************************
   Log_name: mysql-bin.000223
        Pos: 13634
 Event_type: Query
  Server_id: 1
End_log_pos: 13723
       Info: use `test`; CREATE TABLE test.t(a int)
```

Measuring Slave Lag

One of the most common things you'll need to monitor is how far behind the master a slave is running. Although the Seconds_behind_master column in SHOW SLAVE STATUS theoretically shows the slave's lag, in fact it's not always accurate, for a variety of reasons:

- The slave calculates Seconds_behind_master by comparing the server's current timestamp to the timestamp recorded in the binary log event, so the slave can't even report its lag unless it is processing a query.

- The slave will usually report NULL if the slave processes aren't running.

- Some errors (for example, mismatched max_allowed_packet settings between the master and slave, or an unstable network) can break replication and/or stop the slave threads, but Seconds_behind_master will report 0 rather than indicate an error.

- The slave sometimes can't calculate the lag even if the slave processes *are* running. If this happens, the slave might report either 0 or NULL.

- A very long transaction can cause the reported lag to fluctuate. For example, if you have a transaction that updates data, stays open for an hour, and then commits, the update will go into the binary log an hour after it actually happened. When the slave processes the statement, it will temporarily report that it is an hour behind the master, and then it will jump back to zero seconds behind.

- If a distribution master is falling behind and has slaves of its own, the slaves will report that they are zero seconds behind if they are caught up with the distribution master, even if there is lag relative to the ultimate master.

The solution to these problems is to ignore Seconds_behind_master and measure slave lag with something you can observe and measure directly. One good solution is a *heartbeat record*, which is a timestamp that you update once per second on the master. To calculate the lag, you can simply subtract the heartbeat from the current timestamp on the slave. This method is immune to all the problems we just mentioned, and it has the added benefit of creating a handy timestamp that shows to what point in time the slave's data is current. The *mk-heartbeat* script, included in Maatkit, is one implementation of a replication heartbeat.

None of the lag metrics we just mentioned gives a sense of how long it will take for a slave to actually catch up to the master. This depends upon many factors, such as how powerful the slave is and how many write queries the master continues to process.

Determining Whether Slaves Are Consistent with the Master

In a perfect world, a slave would always be an exact copy of its master. But in the real world, errors in replication can cause the slave's data to "drift" out of sync with the master. Even if there are apparently no errors, slaves still get out of sync because of MySQL features that don't replicate correctly, bugs in MySQL, network corruption, crashes, ungraceful shutdowns, or other failures.*

Our experience is that this is the rule, not the exception, which means checking your slaves for consistency with their masters should probably be a routine task. This is especially important if you use replication for backups, because you don't want to take backups from a corrupted slave.

The first edition of this book had a sample script to compare the number of rows in the tables on the master and the slave. This can certainly reveal some differences, but row count isn't a very strong assurance of identical data. What you really need is an efficient method of comparing the tables' actual contents.

MySQL has no built-in method of determining whether one server has the same data as another server. It does provide some building blocks for checksumming tables and data, such as CHECKSUM TABLE. However, it's nontrivial to compare a slave to its master while replication is working.

Maatkit has a tool called *mk-table-checksum* that solves this and several other problems. The tool has several functions, including fast parallel comparisons of many servers at once, but its main feature is that it can verify that a slave's data is in sync with its master. It works by running INSERT ... SELECT queries on the master.

These queries checksum the data and insert the results into a table. The statements flow through replication and execute again on the slave. You can then compare the results on the master to the results on the slave and see whether the data differs. Because this process works through replication, it gives consistent results without needing to lock tables on both servers simultaneously.

A typical way to use the tool is to run it on the master, with parameters similar to the following:

```
$ mk-table-checksum --replicate=test.checksum --chunksize 100000 --sleep-coef=2
<master_host>
```

---

* If you're using a nontransactional storage engine, shutting down the server without first running STOP SLAVE is ungraceful.

This command checksums all tables, attempting to process them in chunks of approximately 100,000 rows, and inserts the results into the test.checksum table. It pauses between every chunk, sleeping twice as long as the last chunk took to checksum. This helps ensure that the queries don't block normal database operation.

Once the queries have replicated to the slaves, a simple query can check the slave for differences from the master. *mk-table-checksum* can discover the server's slaves, run the query on each slave, and output the results automatically. The following command will descend to a depth of 10 in the slave hierarchy, beginning at the same master server, and print out tables that differ from the master:

```
$ mk-table-checksum --replicate=test.checksum --replcheck 10 <master_host>
```

MySQL AB plans to implement a similar feature in the server itself at some point. This will probably be better than an external script, but at the time of this writing, *mk-table-checksum* is the only tool available for reliably and easily comparing a slave's data to its master's.

Resyncing a Slave from the Master

You'll probably have to deal with an out-of-sync slave more than once in your career. Perhaps you used the checksum technique and found differences; perhaps you know that the slave skipped a query or that someone changed the data on the slave.

The traditional advice for fixing an out-of-sync slave is to stop it and reclone it from the master. If an inconsistent slave is a critical problem, you should probably stop it and remove it from production as soon as you find it. You can then reclone the slave or restore it from a backup.

The drawback to this approach is the inconvenience factor, especially if you have a lot of data. If you can find out which data is different, you can probably do it more efficiently than by recloning the entire server. And if the inconsistency you discovered isn't critical, you may be able to leave it online and resync only the affected data.

The simplest fix is to dump and reload only the affected data with *mysqldump*. This can work very well if your data isn't changing while you do it. You can simply lock the table on the master, dump the table, wait for the slave to catch up to the master, and then import the table on the slave. (You need to wait for the slave to catch up, so you don't introduce more inconsistencies in other tables, such as those that might be updated in joins against the out-of-sync table.)

Although this works acceptably for many scenarios, it's often impossible to do on a busy server. It also has the disadvantage of changing the slave's data outside of replication. Changing a slave's data through replication (by making changes on the master) is usually the safest technique, because it avoids nasty race conditions and other surprises. If the table is very large or network bandwidth is limited, dumping and reloading is also prohibitively expensive. What if only every thousandth row in a million-row table is different? Dumping and reloading the whole table is wasteful in this case.

mk-table-sync is another tool from Maatkit that solves some of these problems. It can find and resolve differences between tables efficiently. It can also operate through replication, resynchronizing the slave by executing queries on the master, so there are no race conditions. It doesn't work in all scenarios, though: it requires that replication is running in order to sync a master and slave correctly, so it won't work when there's a replication error. *mk-table-sync* is designed to be efficient, but it still may be impractical for extremely large data sizes. Comparing a terabyte of data on the master and the slave inevitably causes extra work for both servers. Still, for those cases where it works, it can save you a great deal of time and effort.

Changing Masters

Sooner or later, you'll need to point a slave at a new master. Maybe you're rotating servers for an upgrade, maybe there was a failure and you need to promote a slave to be the master, or maybe you're just reallocating capacity. Regardless of the reason, you have to inform the slave about its new master.

When the process is planned, it's easy (or at least easier than it is in a crisis). You simply need to issue the CHANGE MASTER TO command on the slave, using the appropriate values. Most of the values are optional; you can specify just the ones you're changing. The slave will discard its current configuration and relay logs and begin replicating from the new master. It will also update the *master.info* file with the new parameters, so the change will persist across a slave restart.

The hardest part of this process is figuring out the desired position on the new master, so the slave begins at the same logical position at which it stopped on the old master.

Promoting a slave to a master is a little harder. There are two basic scenarios for replacing a master with one of its slaves. The first is when it's a planned promotion; the second is when it's unplanned.

Planned promotions

Promoting a slave to a master is conceptually simple. Briefly, here are the steps involved:

1. Stop writes to the old master.
2. Optionally let its slaves catch up in replication (this makes the subsequent steps simpler).
3. Configure a slave to be the new master.
4. Point slaves and write traffic to the new master, then enable writes on it.

The devil is in the details, however. Several scenarios are possible, depending on your replication topology. For example, the steps are slightly different in a master-master topology from a master-slave setup.

In more depth, here are the steps you'll probably need to take for most setups:

1. Stop all writes on the current master. If possible, you might even want to force all client programs (not replication connections) to quit. It helps if you've built your client programs with a "do not run" flag you can set. If you use virtual IP addresses, you can simply shut off the virtual IP, and then kill all client connections to close their open transactions.

2. Optionally stop all write activity on the master with FLUSH TABLES WITH READ LOCK. You can also set the master to be read-only with the read_only option. From this point on, you should forbid any writes to the soon-to-be-replaced master, because once it's no longer a master, writing to it means losing data!

3. Choose one of the slaves to be the new master, and ensure it is completely caught up in replication (i.e., let it finish executing all the relay logs it fetched from the old master).

4. Optionally verify that the new master contains the same data as the old master.

5. Execute STOP SLAVE on the new master.

6. Execute CHANGE MASTER TO MASTER_HOST='' followed by RESET SLAVE on the new master, to make it disconnect from the old master and discard the connection information in its *master.info* file. (This will not work correctly if connection information is specified in *my.cnf*, which is one reason we recommend you don't put it there.)

7. Note the new master's binary log coordinates with SHOW MASTER STATUS.

8. Make sure all other slaves are caught up.

9. Shut down the old master.

10. In MySQL 5.1 and newer, activate events on the new master if necessary.

11. Let clients connect to the new master.

12. Issue a CHANGE MASTER TO command on each slave, pointing it to the new master. Use the binary log coordinates you gathered from SHOW MASTER STATUS.

> When you promote a slave to a master, be sure to remove from it any slave-specific databases, tables, and privileges. You also need to change any slave-specific configuration parameters, such as a relaxed innodb_flush_log_at_trx_commit option. Likewise, if you demote a master to a slave, be sure to reconfigure it as needed.
>
> If you configure your masters and slaves identically, you won't need to change anything.

Unplanned promotions

If the master crashes and you have to promote a slave to replace it, the process might not be as easy. If there's only one slave, you just use the slave. But if there's more than one, you'll have to do a few extra steps to promote a slave to be the new master.

There's also the added problem of potentially lost replication events. It's possible that some updates that have happened on the master will not yet have been replicated to any of its slaves. It's even possible that a statement was executed and then rolled back on the master, but not rolled back on the slave—so the slave could actually be *ahead* of the master's logical replication position.[*] If you can recover the master's data at some point, you might be able to retrieve the lost statements and apply them manually.

In all of the following steps, be sure to use the `Master_Log_File` and `Read_Master_Log_Pos` values in your calculations. Here is the procedure to promote a slave in a master-and-slaves topology:

1. Determine which slave has the most up-to-date data. Check the output of `SHOW SLAVE STATUS` on each slave and choose the one whose `Master_Log_File`/`Read_Master_Log_Pos` coordinates are newest.

2. Let all slaves finish executing the relay logs they fetched from the old master before it crashed. If you change a slave's master before it's done executing the relay log, it will throw away the remaining log events and you won't know where it stopped.

3. Perform steps 5–7 from the list in the preceding section.

4. Compare every slave's `Master_Log_File`/`Read_Master_Log_Pos` coordinates to those of the new master.

5. Perform steps 10–12 from the list in the preceding section.

We're assuming you have `log_bin` and `log_slave_updates` enabled on all your slaves, as we advised you to do in the beginning of this chapter. Enabling this logging lets you recover all slaves to a consistent point in time, which you can't reliably do otherwise.

Locating the desired log positions

If any slave isn't at the same position as the new master, you'll have to find the position in the new master's binary logs corresponding to the last event that slave replicated, and use it for `CHANGE MASTER TO`. You can use the *mysqlbinlog* tool to examine the last query the slave executed and find that same query in the new master's binary log. A little math can often help, too.

---

[*] This is actually possible, even though MySQL doesn't log any events until the transaction commits. See "Mixing Transactional and Nontransactional Tables" on page 391, later in this chapter for the details.

To illustrate this, let's assume that log events have increasing ID numbers and that the most up-to-date slave—the new master—had just retrieved event 100 when the old master crashed. Now let's assume that there are two more slaves, slave2 and slave3; slave2 had retrieved event 99, and slave3 had retrieved event 98. If you point both slaves at the new master's current binary log position, they will begin replicating event 101, so they'll be out of sync. However, as long as the new master's binary log was enabled with log_slave_updates, you can find events 99 and 100 in the new master's binary log, so you can bring the slaves back to a consistent state.

Because of server restarts, different configurations, log rotations, or FLUSH LOGS commands, the same events can exist at different byte offsets in different servers. Finding the events can be slow and tedious, but it's usually not hard. Just examine the last event executed on each slave by running *mysqlbinlog* on the slave's binary log or relay log. Then find the same query in the new master's binary log, also with *mysqlbinlog*; it will print the byte offset of the query, and you can use this offset in the CHANGE MASTER TO query.

You can make the process faster by subtracting the byte offsets at which the new master and the slave stopped, which tells you the difference in their byte positions. If you then subtract this value from the new master's current binary log position, chances are the desired query will be at that position. You just need to verify that it is, and you've found the position at which you need to start the slave.

Let's look at a concrete example. Suppose server1 is the master of server2 and server3, and it crashes. According to Master_Log_File/Read_Master_Log_Pos in SHOW SLAVE STATUS, server2 has managed to replicate all the events that were in server1's binary log, but server3 isn't as up-to-date. Figure 8-15 illustrates this scenario (the log events and byte offsets are for demonstration purposes only).

As Figure 8-15 illustrates, we can be sure that server2 has replicated all the events in the master's binary log because its Master_Log_File and Read_Master_Log_Pos match the last positions on server1. Therefore, we can promote server2 to be the new master, and make server3 a slave of it.

But what parameters should we use in the CHANGE MASTER TO command on server3? This is where we need to do a little math and investigation. server3 stopped at offset 1493, which is 89 bytes behind offset 1582, the last command server2 executed. server2 is currently writing to position 8167 in its binary log. 8167 − 89 = 8078, so in theory we need to point server3 at that offset in server2's logs. It's a good idea to investigate the log events around this position and verify that server2 really has the right events at that offset in its logs, though. It might have something else there because of a data update that happened only on server2, for example.

Assuming that the events are the same upon inspection, the following command will switch server3 to be a slave of server2:

```
server2> CHANGE MASTER TO MASTER_HOST="server2", MASTER_LOG_FILE="mysql-bin.000009",
MASTER_LOG_POS=8078;
```

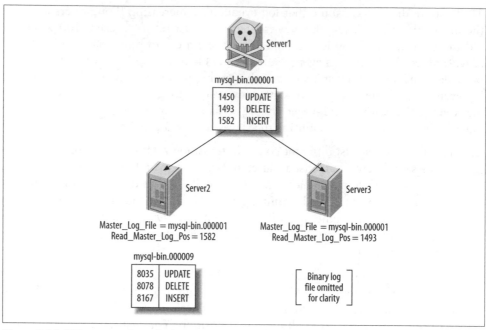

Figure 8-15. When server1 crashed, server2 was caught up, but server3 was behind in replication

What if `server1` had actually finished executing and logging one more event, beyond offset 1582, when it crashed? Because `server2` had read and executed only up to off-set 1582, you might have lost one event forever. However, if the old master's disk isn't damaged, you can still recover the missing event from its binary log with *mysql-binlog* or with a log server.

If you need to recover missing events from the old master, we recommend that you do so *after* you promote the new master, but *before* you let clients connect to it. This way, you won't have to execute the missing events on every slave; replication will take care of that for you. If the failed master is totally unavailable, however, you might have to wait and do this work later.

A variation on this procedure is to use a reliable way to store the master's binary log files, such as a SAN or a distributed replicated block device (DRBD). Even if the master has a complete failure, you'll still have its binary log files. You can set up a log server, point the slaves to it, and then let them all catch up to the point at which the master failed. This makes it trivial to promote one of the slaves to be a new master—it's essentially the same process we showed for a planned promotion. We discuss these storage options further in the next chapter.

When you promote a slave to master, don't change its server ID to match the old master's. If you do, you won't be able to use a log server to replay events from the old master. This is one of many reasons it's a good idea to treat server IDs as fixed.

Switching Roles in a Master-Master Configuration

One of the advantages of master-master replication is that you can switch the active and passive roles easily, because of the symmetrical configuration. In this section, we show you how to accomplish the switch.

When switching the roles in a master-master configuration, the most important thing is to ensure that only one of the co-masters is written to at any time. If writes from one master are interleaved with writes from the other, the writes can conflict. In other words, the passive server must not receive any binary log events from the active server after the roles are switched. You can guarantee this doesn't happen by ensuring that the passive server's slave thread is caught up to the active server before you make it writable.

The following steps switch the roles without danger of conflicting updates:

1. Stop all writes on the active server.

2. Execute SET @@global.read_only := 1 on the active server, and set the read_only option in its configuration file for safety in case of a restart. Remember, this won't stop users with the SUPER privilege from making changes. If you want to prevent changes from all users, use FLUSH TABLES WITH READ LOCK. If you don't do this, you must kill all client connections to make sure there are no long-running statements or uncommitted transactions.

3. Execute SHOW MASTER STATUS on the active server and note the binary log coordinates.

4. Execute SELECT MASTER_POS_WAIT( ) on the passive server with the active server's binary log coordinates. This command will block until the slave processes catch up to the active server.

5. Execute SET @@global.read_only := 0 on the passive server, thus making it the active server.

6. Reconfigure your applications to write to the newly active server.

Depending on your application's configuration, you may need to do other tasks as well, including changing the IP addresses on the two servers. We discuss this in the next chapter.

Replication Problems and Solutions

Breaking MySQL's replication isn't hard. The simple implementation that makes it easy to set up also means there are many ways to stop, confuse, and otherwise disrupt it. This section shows common problems, how they manifest themselves, and how you can solve or even prevent them.

Errors Caused by Data Corruption or Loss

For a variety of reasons, MySQL replication is not very resilient to crashes, power outages, and corruption caused by disk, memory, or network errors. You'll almost certainly have to restart replication at some point due to one of these problems.

Most of the problems you'll have with replication after an unexpected shutdown stem from one of the servers not flushing something to disk. Here are the issues you may encounter in the event of an unexpected shutdown:

Unexpected master shutdown

If the master isn't configured with sync_binlog, it might not have flushed its last several binary log events to disk before crashing. The slave's I/O thread may, therefore, have been in the middle of reading from an event that never made it to disk. When the master restarts, the slave will reconnect and try to read that event again, but the master will respond by telling it that there's no such binlog offset. The binlog dump process is typically almost instantaneous, so this is not uncommon.

The solution to this problem is to instruct the slave to begin reading from the beginning of the next binary log. However, some log events will have been lost permanently, which could have been prevented by configuring the master with sync_binlog.

Even if you've configured sync_binlog, MyISAM data can still get corrupted when there's a crash, and so can InnoDB data if innodb_flush_logs_at_trx_commit is not set to 1.

Unexpected slave shutdown

When the slave restarts after an unplanned shutdown, it reads its *master.info* file to determine where it stopped replicating. Unfortunately, this file is not synchronized to disk, so the information it contains is likely to be wrong. The slave will probably try to reexecute a few binary log events. This could cause some unique index violations. Unless you can determine where the slave really stopped, which is unlikely, you'll have no choice but to skip the errors that result. The *mk-slave-restart* tool, part of Maatkit, can help you with this.

If you use all InnoDB tables, you can look at the MySQL error log after restarting the slave. The InnoDB recovery process prints the binary log coordinates up to the point where it recovered, and you can use them to determine where to point the slave on the master.

In addition to data losses resulting from MySQL being shut down uncleanly, it's not uncommon for binary logs or relay logs to be corrupted on disk. The following are some of the more common scenarios:

Binary logs corrupted on the master
If the binary log is corrupted on the master, you'll have no choice but to try to skip the corrupted portion. You can run FLUSH LOGS on the master, so it starts a new log file and point the slave at the beginning of the new log, or you can try to find the end of the bad region. Sometimes you can use SET GLOBAL SQL_SLAVE_ SKIP_COUNTER = 1 to skip a single corrupt event. If there is more than one corrupt event, just repeat the process until they've all been skipped.

Relay logs corrupted on the slave
If the master's binary logs are intact, you can use CHANGE MASTER TO to discard and refetch the corrupt relay logs. Just point the slave at the same position from which it's currently replicating (Relay_Master_Log_File/Exec_Master_Log_Pos). This will cause it to throw away any relay logs on disk.

Binary log out of sync with the InnoDB transaction log
If the master crashes, InnoDB might record a transaction as committed even if it didn't get written to the binary log on disk. There's no way to recover the missing transaction, unless it's in a slave's relay log. You can prevent this with the sync_binlog parameter in MySQL 5.0, or the sync_binlog and safe_binlog parameters in MySQL 4.1.

When a binary log is corrupt, how much data you can recover depends on the type of corruption. There are several common types:

Bytes changed, but the event is still valid SQL
Unfortunately, MySQL cannot even detect this type of corruption. This is why it can be a good idea to routinely check that your slaves have the right data.

Bytes changed and the event is invalid SQL
You may be able to extract the event with *mysqlbinlog* and see garbled data, such as the following:

```
UPDATE tbl SET col?????????????????
```

Try to find the beginning of the next event, which you can find by adding the offset and length, and print it. You might be able to skip just this event.

Bytes omitted and/or the event's length is wrong
In this case, *mysqlbinlog* will sometimes exit with an error or crash because it can't read the event and can't find the beginning of the next event.

Several events corrupted or were overwritten, or offsets have shifted and the next event starts at the wrong offset
Again, *mysqlbinlog* will not be much use.

When the corruption is bad enough that *mysqlbinlog* can't read the log events, you'll have to resort to some hex editing or other tedious techniques to find the boundaries between log events. This usually isn't hard to do, because recognizable markers separate the events.

Here's an example. First, let's look at log event offsets for a sample log, as reported by *mysqlbinlog*:

```
$ mysqlbinlog mysql-bin.000113 | egrep '^# at '
# at 4
# at 98
# at 185
# at 277
# at 369
# at 447
```

A simple way to find offsets in the log is to compare the offsets to the output of the following *strings* command:

```
$ strings -n 2 -t d mysql-bin.000113
    1 binpC'G
   25 5.0.38-Ubuntu_0ubuntu1.1-log
   99 C'G
  146 std
  156 test
  161 create table test(a int)
  186 C'G
  233 std
  243 test
  248 insert into test(a) values(1)
  278 C'G
  325 std
  335 test
  340 insert into test(a) values(2)
  370 C'G
  417 std
  427 test
  432 drop table test
  448 D'G
  474 mysql-bin.000114
```

There's a pretty recognizable pattern that should allow you to locate the beginnings of events. Notice that the strings that end with 'G are located one byte after the beginning of the log event. They are part of the fixed-length log event header.

The exact value will vary from server to server, so your results will vary depending on the server whose log you're examining. With a little sleuthing, you should be able to find the pattern in your binary log and determine the next intact log event's offset. You can then try to skip past the bad event(s) with the *--start-position* argument to *mysqlbinlog*, or use the MASTER_LOG_POS parameter to CHANGE MASTER TO.

Using Nontransactional Tables

If all goes well, statement-based replication usually works fine with nontransactional tables. However, if there's an error in an update to a nontransactional table, such as the statement being killed before it is complete, the master and slave will end up with different data.

For example, suppose you're updating a MyISAM table with 100 rows. If the statement updates 50 of the rows and then someone kills it, what happens? Half of the rows will have been changed, but not the other half. Replication is bound to get out of sync as a result, because the statement will replay on the slave and change all 100 rows. (MySQL will then notice that the statement caused an error on the master but not the slave, and replication will stop with an error.)

If you're using MyISAM tables, be sure to run STOP SLAVE before stopping the MySQL server, or the shutdown will kill any running queries (including any incomplete update statements). Transactional storage engines don't have this problem. If you're using transactional tables, the failed update will be rolled back on the master and not logged to the binary log.

Mixing Transactional and Nontransactional Tables

When you use a transactional storage engine, MySQL doesn't log the statements you execute to the binary log until the transactions commit. Thus, if a transaction is rolled back, MySQL won't log the statements, so they won't get replayed on the slave.

However, if you mix transactional and nontransactional tables and there's a rollback, MySQL will be able to roll back the changes to the transactional tables, but the nontransactional ones will be changed permanently. As long as there are no errors, such as an update being killed partway through execution, this is not a problem: instead of just not logging the statements, MySQL logs the statements and then logs a ROLLBACK statement to the binary log. The result is that the same statements execute on the slave, and all is well. It's a little less efficient, because the slave must do some work and then throw it away, but the slave will theoretically still be in sync with the master.

So far, so good. The problem is when the slave has a deadlock that didn't happen on the master. The tables that use a transactional storage engine will roll back on the slave, but the slave won't be able to roll back the nontransactional tables. As a result, the slave's data will be different from the master's.

The only way to prevent this problem is to avoid mixing transactional and nontransactional tables. If you do encounter the problem, the only way to fix it is to skip the error on the slave and resync the involved tables.

In principle, row-based replication should not suffer from this problem. Row-based replication logs changes to rows, not SQL statements. If a statement changes some rows in a MyISAM table and an InnoDB table and then deadlocks on the master and rolls back the InnoDB table, the changes to the MyISAM table should still be logged to the binary log and replayed on the slave. We tested simple cases and found this to work correctly; however, at the time of this writing, we have not had enough experience with row-based replication to say for sure whether it completely avoids problems that mixing transactional and nontransactional tables causes.

Nondeterministic Statements

Any statement that changes data in a nondeterministic way can cause a slave's data to become different from its master's. For example, an UPDATE with a LIMIT relies on the order in which the statement finds rows in the table. Unless the order is guaranteed to be the same on the master and the slave—for example, if the rows are ordered by primary key—the statement may change different rows on the two servers. Such problems can be subtle and difficult to notice, so some people make a policy of never using LIMIT with any statement that changes data.

Watch out for statements that involve INFORMATION_SCHEMA tables, too. These can easily differ between the master and the slave, so the results may vary as well. Finally, be aware that most server variables, such as @@server_id and @@hostname, will not replicate correctly before MySQL 5.1.

Row-based replication does not have these limitations.

Different Storage Engines on the Master and Slave

It's often handy to have different storage engines on a slave, as we've mentioned throughout this chapter. However, in some circumstances, statement-based replication may produce different results on a slave with different storage engines. For example, nondeterministic statements (such as the ones mentioned in the previous section) are more likely to cause problems if the storage engines differ on the slave.

If you find that your slave's data is falling out of sync with the master in specific tables, you should examine the storage engines used on both servers, as well as the queries that update those tables.

Data Changes on the Slave

Statement-based replication relies upon the slave having the same data as the master, so you should not make or allow any changes on the slave (using the read_only configuration variable accomplishes this nicely). Consider the following statement:

```
mysql> INSERT INTO table1 SELECT * FROM table2;
```

If `table2` contains different data on the slave, `table1` will end up with different data, too. In other words, data differences tend to propagate from table to table. This happens with all types of queries, not just `INSERT ... SELECT` queries. There are two possible outcomes: you'll get an error such as a duplicate index violation on the slave, or you won't get any error at all. Getting an error is a blessing, because at least it alerts you that your data isn't the same on the slave. Invisibly different data can silently wreak all kinds of havoc.

The only solution to this problem is to resync the data from the master.

Nonunique Server IDs

This is one of the more elusive problems you might encounter with replication. If you accidentally configure two slaves with the same server ID, they might seem to work just fine if you're not watching closely. But if you watch their error logs, or watch the master with *innotop*, you'll notice something very odd.

On the master, you'll see only one of the two slaves connected at any time. (Usually, all slaves are connected and replicating all the time.) On the slave, you'll see frequent disconnect and reconnect error messages in the error log, but no mention of a misconfigured server ID.

Depending on the MySQL version, the slaves might replicate correctly but slowly, or they might not actually replicate correctly—any given slave might miss binary log events, or even repeat them, causing duplicate key errors (or silent data corruption). You can also crash or corrupt data on the master because of the increased load from the slaves fighting amongst themselves. And if slaves are fighting each other badly enough, the error logs can grow enormous in a very short time.

The only solution to this problem is to be careful when setting up your slaves. You may find it helpful to create a master list of slave-to-server-ID mappings so that you don't lose track of which ID belongs to each slave.* If your slaves live entirely within one network subnet, you can choose unique IDs by using the last octet of each machine's IP address.

Undefined Server IDs

If you don't define the server ID in the *my.cnf* file, MySQL will appear to set up replication with `CHANGE MASTER TO`, but will not let you start the slave:

```
mysql> START SLAVE;
ERROR 1200 (HY000): The server is not configured as slave; fix in config file or with
CHANGE MASTER TO
```

---

* Perhaps you'd like to store it in a database table? We're only half joking...you can add a unique index on the ID column.

This error is especially confusing if you've just used CHANGE MASTER TO and verified your settings with SHOW SLAVE STATUS. You might get a value from SELECT @@server_id, but it's just a default. You have to set the value explicitly.

Dependencies on Nonreplicated Data

If you have databases or tables on the master that don't exist on the slave, it's quite easy to accidentally break replication. Suppose there's a scratch database on the master that doesn't exist on the slave. If any data updates on the master refer to a table in this database, replication will break when the slave tries to replay the updates.

There's no way around this problem. The only way to prevent it is to avoid creating tables on the master that don't exist on the slave.

How does such a table get created? There are many possible ways, and some are harder to prevent than others. For example, suppose you originally created a scratch database on the slave that didn't exist on the master, and then you switched the master and slave for some reason. When you did this, you might have forgotten to remove the scratch database and its privileges. Now someone might connect to the new master and run a query in that database, or a periodic job might discover the tables and run OPTIMIZE TABLE on each of them.

This is one of the things to keep in mind when promoting a slave to master, or when deciding how to configure slaves. Anything that makes slaves different from masters, or vice versa, is a potential future problem.

Row-based replication should solve some of these problems, but it's too soon to be sure.

Missing Temporary Tables

Temporary tables are handy for some uses, but unfortunately they're incompatible with statement-based replication. If a slave crashes, or if you shut it down, any temporary tables the slave thread was using disappear. When you restart the slave, any further statements that refer to the missing temporary tables will fail.

There's no safe way to use temporary tables on the master with statement-based replication. Many people love temporary tables dearly, so it can be hard to convince them of this, but it's true. No matter how briefly they exist, temporary tables potentially make it impossible to stop and start slaves and to recover from crashes. This is true even if you use them only within a single transaction. (It's slightly less problematic to use temporary tables on a slave, where they can be convenient, but if the slave is itself a master, the problem still exists.)

If replication stops because the slave can't find a temporary table after a restart, there are really only a couple of things to do. You can skip the errors that occur, or you can manually create a table that has the same name and structure as the now-vanished temporary table. Either way, your data will likely become different on the slave if any write queries refer to the temporary table.

It's not as hard as it seems to eliminate temporary tables. The two most useful properties of a temporary table are as follows:

- They're visible only to the connection that created them, so they don't conflict with other connections' temporary tables of the same name.
- They go away when the connection closes, so you don't have to remove them explicitly.

You can emulate these properties easily by reserving a database exclusively for pseudotemporary tables, where you'll create permanent tables instead. You just have to choose unique names for them. Fortunately, that's pretty easy to do: simply append the connection ID to the table name. For example, where you used to execute CREATE TEMPORARY TABLE top_users(...), now you can execute CREATE TABLE temp. top_users_1234(...), where 1234 is the value returned by CONNECTION_ID( ). After your application is done with the pseudotemporary table, you can either drop it or let a cleanup process remove it instead. Having the connection ID in the table name makes it easy to determine which tables are not in use anymore—you can get a list of active connections from SHOW PROCESSLIST and compare it to the connection IDs in the table names.*

Using real tables instead of temporary tables has other benefits, too. For example, it makes it easier to debug your applications, because you can see the data the applications are manipulating from another connection. If you used a temporary table, you wouldn't be able to do that as easily.

Real tables do have some overhead temporary tables don't, however: it's slower to create them because the *.frm* files associated with these tables must be synced to disk. You can disable the sync_frm option to speed this up, but it's more dangerous.

If you do use temporary tables, you should ensure that the Slave_open_temp_tables status variable is 0 before shutting down a slave. If it's not 0, you're likely to have problems restarting the slave. The proper procedure is to run STOP SLAVE, examine the variable, and only then shut down the slave. If you examine the variable before stopping the slave processes, you're risking a race condition.

Not Replicating All Updates

If you misuse SET SQL_LOG_BIN=0 or don't understand the replication filtering rules, your slave might not execute some updates that have taken place on the master.

---

* *mk-find*—yet another tool in Maatkit—can remove pseudotemporary tables easily with the *--pid* and *--sid* options.

Sometimes you want this for archiving purposes, but it's usually accidental and has bad consequences.

For example, suppose you have a replicate_do_db rule to replicate only the sakila database to one of your slaves. If you execute the following commands on the master, the slave's data will become different from the data on the master:

```
mysql> USE test;
mysql> UPDATE sakila.actor ...
```

Other types of statements can even cause replication to fail with an error because of nonreplicated dependencies.

Lock Contention Caused by InnoDB Locking Selects

InnoDB's SELECT statements are normally nonlocking, but in certain cases they do acquire locks. In particular, INSERT ... SELECT locks all the rows it reads from the source table by default. MySQL needs the locks to ensure that the statement produces the same result on the slave when it executes there. In effect, the locks serialize the statement on the master, which matches how the slave will execute it.

You might encounter lock contention, blocking, and lock wait timeouts because of this design. One way to alleviate the problems is not to hold a transaction open longer than needed, so the locks cause less blocking. You can release the locks by committing the transaction as soon as possible on the master.

It can also help to keep your statements short, by breaking up large statements into several smaller ones. This is a very effective way to reduce lock contention, and even when it's hard to do, it's often worth it.

Another workaround is to replace INSERT ... SELECT statements with a combination of SELECT INTO OUTFILE followed by LOAD DATA INFILE on the master. This is fast and doesn't require locking. It is admittedly a hack, but it's sometimes useful anyway. The biggest issues are choosing a unique name for the output file, which must not already exist, and cleaning up the output file when you're done with it. You can use the CONNECTION_ID( ) technique we discussed in "Missing Temporary Tables" on page 394, earlier in this chapter, to ensure that the filename is unique, and you can use a periodic job (*crontab* on Unix, scheduled tasks on Windows) to purge unused output files after the connections that created them are finished with them.

You might be tempted to try to disable the locks instead of using these workarounds. There is a way to do so, but it's not a good idea for most scenarios, because it makes it possible for your slave to fall silently out of sync with the master. It also makes the binary log useless for recovering a server. If, however, you decide that the risks are worth the benefits, the configuration change that accomplishes this is as follows:

```
innodb_locks_unsafe_for_binlog = 1
```

This allows a statement's results to depend on data it doesn't lock. If a second statement modifies that data and then commits before the first statement, the two statements may not produce the same results when you replay the binary log. This is true both for replication and for point-in-time recovery.

To see how locking reads prevent chaos, imagine you have two tables: one without rows, and one whose single row has the value 99. Two transactions update the data. Transaction 1 inserts the second table's contents into the first table, and transaction 2 updates the second (source) table, as depicted in Figure 8-16.

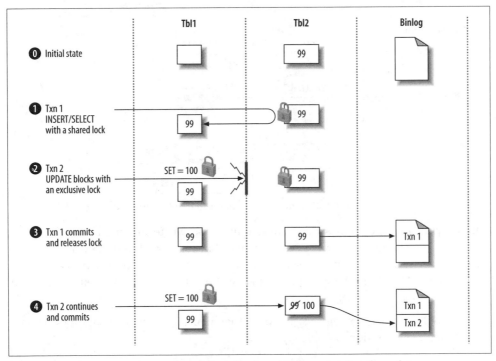

Figure 8-16. Two transactions update data, with shared locks to serialize the updates

Step 2 in this sequence of events is very important. In it, transaction 2 tries to update the source table, which requires it to place an exclusive (write) lock on the rows it wants to update. An exclusive lock is incompatible with any other lock, including the shared lock transaction 1 has placed on that row, so transaction 2 is forced to wait until transaction 1 commits. The transactions are serialized in the binary log in the order they committed, so replaying these transactions in binary log (commit) order will give the same results.

On the other hand, if transaction 1 doesn't place a shared lock on the rows it reads for the INSERT, no such guarantee exists. Study Figure 8-17, which shows a possible sequence of events without the lock.

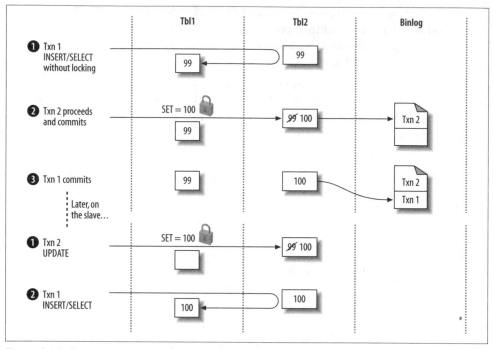

Figure 8-17. Two transactions update data, but without a shared lock to serialize the updates

The absence of locks allows the transactions to be written to the binary log in an order that will produce different results when that log is replayed, as you can see in the illustration. MySQL logs transaction 2 first, so it will affect transaction 1's results on the slave. This didn't happen on the master. As a result, the slave will contain different data than the master.

We strongly suggest, for most situations, that you leave the `innodb_locks_unsafe_for_binlog` configuration variable set to 0.

Writing to Both Masters in Master-Master Replication

Writing to both masters is generally not a good idea. If you're trying to make it safe to write to both masters at the same time, some of the problems have solutions, but not all.

In MySQL 5.0, two server configuration variables help address the problem of conflicting `AUTO_INCREMENT` primary keys. The variables are `auto_increment_increment` and `auto_increment_offset`. You can use them to "stagger" the numbers the servers generate, so they interleave rather than collide.

However, this doesn't solve all the problems you'll have with two writable masters. It solves only the autoincrement problem, which is probably just a small subset of the conflicting writes you're likely to have. In fact, it actually adds several new problems:

- It makes it harder to move servers around in the replication topology.
- It wastes key space by potentially introducing gaps between numbers.
- It doesn't help unless all your tables have AUTO_INCREMENT primary keys, and it's not always a good idea to use AUTO_INCREMENT primary keys universally.

You can generate your own nonconflicting primary key values. One way is to create a multicolumn primary key and use the server ID for the first column. This works well, but it makes your primary keys larger, which has a compound effect on secondary keys in InnoDB.

You can also use a single-column primary key, and use the "high bits" of the integer to store the server ID. A simple left-shift (or multiplication) and addition can accomplish this. For example, if you're using the 8 most significant bits of an unsigned BIGINT (64-bit) column to hold the server ID, you can insert the value 11 on server 15 as follows:

```
mysql> INSERT INTO test(pk_col, ...) VALUES( (15 << 56) + 11, ...);
```

If you convert the result to base 2 and pad it out to 64-bits wide, the effect is easier to see:

```
mysql> SELECT LPAD(CONV(pk_col, 10, 2), 64, '0') FROM test;
+------------------------------------------------------------------+
| LPAD(CONV(pk_col, 10, 2), 64, '0')                               |
+------------------------------------------------------------------+
| 0000111100000000000000000000000000000000000000000000000000001011 |
+------------------------------------------------------------------+
```

The problem with this method is that you need an external way to generate key values, because AUTO_INCREMENT can't do it for you. Don't use @@server_id in place of the constant value 15 in the INSERT, because you'll get a different result on the slave.

You can also turn to pseudorandom values using a function such as MD5( ) or UUID( ), but these can be bad for performance—they're big, and they're essentially random, which is bad for InnoDB in particular. (Don't use UUID( ) unless you generate the values in the application, because UUID( ) doesn't replicate correctly with statement-based replication.)

It's a hard problem to solve, and we usually recommend redesigning your application so that you have only one writable master instead.

Excessive Replication Lag

Replication lag is a frequent problem. No matter what, it's a good idea to design your applications to tolerate some lag on the slaves. If the system can't function with lagging slaves, replication may not be the correct architecture for your application. However, there are some steps you can take to help slaves keep up with the master.

The single-threaded nature of MySQL replication means it's relatively inefficient on the slave. Even a fast slave with lots of disks, CPUs, and memory can easily fall behind a master, because the slave's single thread usually uses only one CPU and disk efficiently. In fact, each slave typically needs to be at least as powerful as the master.

Locking on the slaves is also a problem. Other queries running on a slave might set locks that block the replication thread. Because replication is single-threaded, the replication thread won't be able to do other work while it waits.

Replication tends to fall behind in two ways: spikes of lag followed by catching up, or staying steadily behind. The former is usually caused by single queries that run for a long time, but the latter can crop up even when there are no long queries.

Unfortunately, at present the only way to tell how close your slave is to its capacity is to examine empirical evidence. If your load were perfectly uniform at all times, your slaves would perform nearly as well at 99% capacity as at 10% capacity, and when they reached 100% capacity, they'd abruptly begin to fall behind. In reality, the load is unlikely to be steady, so when a slave is close to its write capacity, you'll probably see increased replication lag during times of peak load.

This is a warning sign! It probably means you are dangerously close to pushing your slaves so hard that they can't catch up during the times of off-peak load. A crude gauge of how close you are to the ceiling is to deliberately stop a slave's SQL thread for a while, then restart it and see how long it takes to catch up again.

The patches Google has released (see "Synchronous MySQL replication" on page 451) also contain a SHOW USER STATISTICS command that can show the replication user's Busy_time. This is the percentage of the time the slave thread spent processing queries. This is another good way to track how much headroom the slave SQL thread has.

Logging queries on a slave and using a log analysis tool to see what's really slow is one of the best things to do when slaves can't keep up. Don't rely on your instincts about what's slow, and don't base your opinion on how queries perform on the master, because slaves and masters have very different performance profiles. The best way to do this analysis is to enable the slow query log on a slave for a while. The standard MySQL slow query log doesn't log slow queries the slave thread executes, so you can't see which queries are slow when they're replicated. The microsecond slow-log patch solves this issue. You can read more about the slow query log and that patch in "MySQL Profiling" on page 63.

There's not much you can tweak or tune on a slave that can't keep up, aside from buying faster disks and CPUs. Most of the options involve disabling some things that cause extra work on the slave to try to reduce its load. One easy change is to configure InnoDB to flush changes to disk less frequently, so transactions commit more quickly. You can accomplish this by setting innodb_flush_log_at_trx_commit to 2. You can also disable binary logging on the slave, set innodb_locks_unsafe_for_binlog to 1, and set delay_key_write to ALL for MyISAM. These settings trade safety for speed, though. If you promote a slave to be a master, make sure to reset these settings to safe values.

Don't duplicate the expensive part of writes

Rearchitecting your application and/or optimizing your queries are often the best ways to help the slaves keep up. Try to minimize the amount of work that has to be duplicated through your system. Any write that's expensive on the master will be replayed on every slave. If you can move the work off the master onto a slave, only one of the slaves will have to do the work. You can then push the write results back up to the master, for example, with LOAD DATA INFILE.

Here's an example. Suppose you have a very large table that you summarize into a smaller table for frequent processing:

```
mysql> REPLACE INTO main_db.summary_table (col1, col2, ...)
    -> SELECT col1, sum(col2, ...)
    -> FROM main_db.enormous_table GROUP BY col1;
```

If you perform that operation on the master, every slave will have to repeat the enormous GROUP BY query. If you do enough of this, the slaves will not be able to keep up. Moving the number crunching to one of the slaves can help. On the slave, perhaps in a special database reserved for the purpose of avoiding conflicts with the data being replicated from the master, you can run the following:

```
mysql> REPLACE INTO summary_db.summary_table (col1, col2, ...)
    -> SELECT col1, sum(col2, ...)
    -> FROM main_db.enormous_table GROUP BY col1;
```

Now you can use SELECT INTO OUTFILE, followed by LOAD DATA INFILE on the master, to move the results back up to the master. Voilà—the duplicated work is reduced to a simple LOAD DATA INFILE. If you have N slaves, you have just saved $N - 1$ enormous GROUP BY queries.

The problem with this strategy is dealing with stale data. Sometimes it's hard to get consistent results by reading on the slave and writing on the master (a problem we address in detail in the next chapter). If it's hard to do the read on the slave, you can simplify and still save your slaves a lot of work. If you separate the REPLACE and SELECT parts of the query, you can fetch the results into your application and then insert them back into the master. First, perform the following query on the master:

```
mysql> SELECT col1, sum(col2, ...) FROM main_db.enormous_table GROUP BY col1;
```

You can then insert the results back into the summary table by repeating the following query for every row in the result set:

```
mysql> REPLACE INTO main_db.summary_table (col1, col2, ...) VALUES (?, ?, ...);
```

Again, you've spared the slaves from the large GROUP BY portion of the query; separating the SELECT from the REPLACE means that the SELECT part of the query isn't replayed on every slave.

This general strategy—saving the slaves from the expensive portion of a write—can help in many cases where you have queries whose results are expensive to calculate but cheap to handle once they've been calculated.

Do writes in parallel outside of replication

Another tactic for avoiding excessive lag on the slaves is to circumvent replication. Any writes you do on the master must be serialized on the slave, so it makes sense to think of "serialized writes" as a scarce resource. Do all your writes need to flow from the master to the slave? How can you reserve your slave's limited serialized write capacity for the writes that really need to be done via replication?

Thinking of it in this light may help you prioritize writes. In particular, if you can identify some writes that are easy to do outside of replication, you can parallelize writes that would otherwise claim precious write capacity on the slave.

One great example is data archiving, which we discussed earlier in this chapter. OLTP archiving queries are often simple single-row operations. If you're just moving unneeded rows from one table to another, there might be no reason these writes have to be replicated to slaves. Instead, you can disable binary logging for the archiving statements, and then run separate but identical archiving processes on the master and slaves.

It might sound crazy to copy the data to another server yourself instead of letting replication do it, but it can actually make sense for some applications. This is especially true if an application is the only source of updates to a certain set of tables. Replication bottlenecks often center around a small set of tables, and if you can handle just those tables outside of replication, you may be able to speed it up significantly.

Prime the cache for the slave thread

If you have the right kind of workload, you might benefit from parallelizing I/O on slaves by prefetching data into memory. This technique is not well known, but we know of some large applications that benefit from it.

The idea is to use a program that reads slightly ahead of the slave's SQL thread in the relay logs and executes the queries as SELECT statements. This causes the server to fetch some of the data from the disk into memory, so when the slave's SQL thread executes the statement from the relay log, it doesn't need to wait for data to be fetched from disk. In effect, the SELECT parallelizes I/O that the slave SQL thread must normally do serially. While one statement is changing data, the next statement's data is being fetched from disk into memory.

How far ahead of the slave SQL thread the program should stay may vary. You can try a few seconds, or an equivalent number of bytes in the relay log. If you get too far ahead, the data you're fetching into the caches will be flushed out again by the time the SQL thread needs it.

Let's look at an example of how to rewrite statements to take advantage of this approach. Consider the following query:

```
mysql> UPDATE sakila.film SET rental_duration=4 WHERE film_id=123;
```

The following SELECT retrieves the same row and columns:

```
mysql> SELECT rental_duration FROM sakila.film WHERE film_id=123;
```

This technique won't work unless you have the right workload characteristics and hardware configuration. The following conditions might indicate that it'll work:

- The slave SQL thread is I/O-bound, but the slave server isn't I/O-bound overall. A completely I/O-bound server won't benefit from prefetching, because it won't have any idle hard drives to do the fetching.

- The working set is much larger than memory (which is why the SQL thread spends a lot of time waiting for I/O). If your working set fits in memory, prefetching won't help, because your server will "warm up" after a while and I/O waits will be rare.

- The slave has a lot of disk drives. The people we know who use this tactic have eight or more drives per slave. It might work with fewer, but you'll need at least two to four drives.

- You use a storage engine with row-level locking, such as InnoDB. Attempting this on a MyISAM table will probably make the slave's SQL thread and the prefetch thread contend for table locks, slowing things down even more. (However, if you have many tables and the writes are distributed among them, in theory you might even be able to speed up replication on MyISAM tables using this technique.)

An example workload that benefits from prefetching is one with a lot of widely scattered single-row UPDATE statements, which are typically high-concurrency on the master. DELETE statements may also benefit. INSERT statements are less likely to benefit from this approach—especially when rows are inserted sequentially—because the end of the index will already be "hot" from previous inserts.

If a table has many indexes, it might not be possible to prefetch all the data the statement will modify. The UPDATE statement may modify every index, but the SELECT will typically read only the primary key and one secondary index, in the best case. The UPDATE will still need to fetch other indexes for modification. That decreases how effective this tactic can be on tables with many indexes.

You can use *iostat* to see whether you have free hard drives that could be servicing prefetch requests. Look at the queue size and service time (see the previous chapter for examples). A small queue shows that something at a higher level is serializing requests. A large queue shows a high load—the type you won't typically get from a slave SQL thread when you have many disks. If the service time is large, it means too many requests are being submitted to the disk at once.

This technique is not a silver bullet. There are many reasons why it might not work for you or might even cause more problems. You should attempt it only if you know your hardware and operating system well. We know some people for whom this approach increased replication speed by 300% to 400%, but we've tried it ourselves and found it doesn't always work. Getting the parameters right is important, but there isn't always a right combination of parameters. Sometimes filesystem and/or kernel behaviors can defeat parallel I/O, too. Your mileage will vary!

The *mk-slave-prefetch* tool, which is part of Maatkit, is one implementation of the ideas we've described in this section.

Oversized Packets from the Master

Another hard-to-trace problem in replication can occur when the master's `max_allowed_packet` size doesn't match the slave's. In this case, the master can log a packet the slave considers oversized, and when the slave retrieves that binary log event, it may suffer from a variety of problems. These include an endless loop of errors and retries, or corruption in the relay log.

Limited Replication Bandwidth

If you're replicating over limited bandwidth, you can enable the `slave_compressed_protocol` option on the slave (available in MySQL 4.0 and newer). When the slave connects to the master, it will request a compressed connection—the same compression any MySQL client connection can use. The compression engine used is *zlib*, and our tests show it can compress some textual data to roughly a third of its original size. The tradeoff is that extra CPU time is required to compress the data on the master and decompress it on the slave.

If you have a slow link with a master on one side and many slaves on the other side, you might want to colocate a distribution master with the slaves. That way only one server connects to the master over the slow link, reducing the bandwidth load on the link and the CPU load on the master.

No Disk Space

Replication can indeed fill up your disks with binary logs, relay logs, or temporary files, especially if you do a lot of `LOAD DATA INFILE` queries on the master and have `log_slave_updates` enabled on the slave. The more a slave falls behind, the more disk space it is likely to use for relay logs that have been retrieved from the master but not yet executed. You can prevent these errors by monitoring disk usage and setting the `relay_log_space` configuration variable.

Replication Limitations

MySQL replication can fail or get out of sync, with or without errors, just because of its inherent limitations. A fairly large list of SQL functions and programming practices simply won't replicate reliably (we've mentioned many of them in this chapter). It's hard to ensure that none of these finds a way into your production code, especially if your application or team is large.[*]

Another issue is bugs in the server. We don't want to sound negative, but most major versions of the MySQL server have historically had some bugs in replication, especially in the first releases of the major version. New features, such as stored procedures, have usually caused more problems.

For most users, this is not a reason to avoid new features. It's just a reason to test carefully, especially when you upgrade your application or MySQL. Monitoring is also important; you need to know when something causes a problem.

MySQL replication is complicated, and the more complicated your application is, the more careful you need to be. However, if you learn how to work with it, it works quite well.

How Fast Is Replication?

A common question about replication is "How fast is it?" The short answer is that it's generally very fast, and it runs as quickly as MySQL can copy the events from the master and replay them. If you have a slow network and very large binary log events, the delay between binary logging and execution on the slave might be perceptible. If your queries take a long time to run and you have a fast network, you can generally expect the query time on the slave to contribute more to the time it takes to replicate an event.

A more complete answer requires measuring every step of the process and deciding which steps will take the most time in your application. Some readers may care only that there's usually very little delay between logging events on the master and copying them to the slave's relay log. For those who would like more details, we did a quick experiment.

We elaborated on the process described in the first edition of this book, and methods used by Giuseppe Maxia,[†] to measure replication speed with high precision. We built a nondeterministic UDF that returns the system time to microsecond precision (see "User-Defined Functions" on page 230 for the source code):

---

[*] Alas, MySQL doesn't have a `forbid_operations_unsafe_for_replication` option.

[†] See *http://datacharmer.blogspot.com/2006/04/measuring-replication-speed.html*.

```
mysql> SELECT NOW_USEC()
+---------------------------+
| NOW_USEC()                |
+---------------------------+
| 2007-10-23 10:41:10.743917 |
+---------------------------+
```

This lets us measure replication speed by inserting the value of NOW_USEC() into a table on the master, then comparing it to the value on the slave.

We measured the delay by setting up two instances of MySQL on the same server to avoid inaccuracies caused by the clock. We configured one instance as a slave of the other, then ran the following queries on the master instance:

```
mysql> CREATE TABLE test.lag_test(
    ->    id INT NOT NULL AUTO_INCREMENT PRIMARY KEY,
    ->    now_usec VARCHAR(26) NOT NULL
    -> );
mysql> INSERT INTO test.lag_test(now_usec) VALUES( NOW_USEC() );
```

We used a VARCHAR column because MySQL's built-in time types can't store times with subsecond resolution (although some of its time functions can do subsecond calculations). All that remained was to compare the difference between the slave and the master. A Federated table is an easy way to do this. On the slave, we ran:

```
mysql> CREATE TABLE test.master_val (
    ->    id INT NOT NULL AUTO_INCREMENT PRIMARY KEY,
    ->    now_usec VARCHAR(26) NOT NULL
    -> ) ENGINE=FEDERATED
    ->    CONNECTION='mysql://user:pass@127.0.0.1/test/lag_test';
```

A simple join and the TIMESTAMPDIFF() function show the microseconds of lag between the time the query executed on the master and the slave:

```
mysql> SELECT m.id, TIMESTAMPDIFF(FRAC_SECOND, m.now_usec, s.now_usec) AS usec_lag
    -> FROM test.lag_test as s
    ->    INNER JOIN test.master_val AS m USING(id);
+----+----------+
| id | usec_lag |
+----+----------+
|  1 |      476 |
+----+----------+
```

We inserted a 1,000 rows into the master with a Perl script, with a 10-millisecond delay between row insertions to prevent the master and slave instances from fighting each other for CPU time. We then built a temporary table containing the lag of each event:

```
mysql> CREATE TABLE test.lag AS
    > SELECT TIMESTAMPDIFF(FRAC_SECOND, m.now_usec, s.now_usec) AS lag
    -> FROM test.master_val AS m
    ->    INNER JOIN test.lag_test as s USING(id);
```

Next, we grouped the results by lag time to see what the most frequent lag times were:

```
mysql> SELECT ROUND(lag / 1000000.0, 4) * 1000 AS msec_lag, COUNT(*)
    -> FROM lag
    -> GROUP BY msec_lag
    -> ORDER BY msec_lag;
+----------+----------+
| msec_lag | COUNT(*) |
+----------+----------+
|   0.1000 |      392 |
|   0.2000 |      468 |
|   0.3000 |       75 |
|   0.4000 |       32 |
|   0.5000 |       15 |
|   0.6000 |        9 |
|   0.7000 |        2 |
|   1.3000 |        2 |
|   1.4000 |        1 |
|   1.8000 |        1 |
|   4.6000 |        1 |
|   6.6000 |        1 |
|  24.3000 |        1 |
+----------+----------+
```

The results show that most small queries take less than 0.3 milliseconds to replicate, from execution time on the master to execution time on the slave.

The part of replication this *doesn't* measure is how soon an event arrives at the slave after being logged to the binary log on the master. It would be nice to know this, because the sooner the slave receives the log event, the better. If the slave has received the event, it can provide a copy if the master crashes.

Although our measurements don't show exactly how long this part of the process takes, in theory it should be extremely fast (i.e., bounded only by the network speed). The MySQL binlog dump process does *not* poll the master for events, which would be inefficient and slow. Instead, the master notifies the slave of events. Reading a binary log event from the master is a blocking network call that begins sending data practically instantaneously after the master logs the event. Thus, it's probably safe to say the event will reach the slave as quickly as the slave thread can wake up and the network can transfer the data.

The Future of MySQL Replication

MySQL replication has a number of shortcomings that MySQL AB plans to address in the future. Third parties have already built some of the features and fixes. For example, Google has released a set of custom patches to the MySQL server that add semisynchronous replication capabilities and many other features (see "Synchronous MySQL replication" on page 451 for more on this).

Another possible addition is support for multimaster replication—i.e., a single slave with more than one master. This is likely to be a difficult problem to solve and will probably require conflict detection and resolution capabilities. The row-based replication in MySQL 5.1 is a step in that direction. Row-based replication might also let multiple threads apply events on the slave in the future, relieving the single-threaded bottleneck.

There are plans to integrate the online backup API with replication and to allow a MySQL server to automatically configure itself as another server's slave.

Data consistency and correctness guarantees are lacking in MySQL at present. According to a poll on MySQL's web site, the single most requested feature is an online consistency check to show whether a slave has the same data as its master. MySQL AB has a worklog open on this task, with a basic description of how it'll be done. Many people have also requested enhancements to the binary log format to ensure corruption can be detected, and MySQL AB has acknowledged this as an important task.

These and many other improvements should make MySQL replication more powerful and reliable in the future. It's encouraging to look back over the last few years and see the changes that have been made during that time. However, it's worth noting that most of the features the first edition of this book predicted never appeared, even though some of them were partially implemented—for instance, failsafe replication is in the MySQL codebase, but it is an abandoned project.

Scaling and High Availability

This chapter shows you how to build a MySQL architecture that can grow very large while remaining fast and reliable.

Most scaling problems don't give advance warning; they just appear suddenly one day. If you don't have a plan to scale your application, you'll probably have to work hard just to keep it responsive. Companies that can't scale their applications often fail completely. It's ironic, but true: too much success can kill your business.

You must also be able to ensure that your application stays up in all circumstances. Many things could interfere, but the most common problems will probably be ordinary hardware and software failures. Your application should treat these as routine and preferably handle them automatically.

The demands for scaling and high availability often go together. High availability isn't as important when the application is small, for several reasons: it usually runs on a single server, so a server failure is less likely; because it is small, downtime is less likely to cost a lot of money; and the smaller user base is more likely to tolerate downtime. But when you grow to 10 times the number of servers, your probability of a server failing is 10 times higher, and you probably have many more users with higher expectations.

You can make MySQL scale well if you choose the right architecture and implement it well. The same is true for guaranteeing high availability. In this chapter, we break these concepts apart as much as possible, so we can consider them separately. We begin with an overview of the terminology, then tackle scaling and high availability in two major parts (we also take a look at load balancing along the way). We begin each part with a section on requirements, because defining your primary business requirements as soon as possible is critical to running a large application successfully. Those requirements will have a great impact on the application's design and architecture. Then we move through a discussion of possible techniques and solutions, covering the advantages and drawbacks of each.

Terminology

The first step is to understand the concepts clearly. People often use terms such as "scalability" and "performance" as synonyms in casual conversation, but they're really very different. Here are our definitions of the key terms we use throughout this chapter:

Performance
> The application's ability to meet a certain goal, such as a desired response time, level of throughput, or any of the other metrics we discussed in Chapter 2.

Capacity
> The total load the application can handle. We talk more about what "load" means later in this section.

Scalability
> The application's ability to maintain performance as it becomes larger by some metric (more servers, for example). When we write about performance in a broad sense, we mean capacity and scalability together.

Availability
> The percentage of time the application is able to respond to requests. This is usually measured in "nines"; for example, "five nines" means the application is available 99.999% of the time, which translates to roughly five minutes of downtime per year. (This is very high availability for most applications.)

Fault tolerance
> The application and overall system's ability to handle failures gracefully. Even a system designed for high availability can fail. When it does, a fault-tolerant application can continue to provide as much functionality as possible, rather than being entirely unavailable.

Scalability is the most difficult concept to explain clearly. Here's an analogy:

- Performance is how fast the car is.
- Capacity is how high the speed limit is, and how many lanes the highway has.
- Scalability is the degree to which you can add more cars and more highways, without slowing traffic.
- Availability is how often a highway or lane is drivable.

In this analogy, scalability depends on factors such as how well the interchanges are designed, how many cars have accidents or break down, and whether the cars change lanes a lot—but generally *not* on how powerful the car engines are.

In other words, *scalability is the ability to add capacity as needed without reducing performance*. The key phrase is "ability to add." Even if your MySQL architecture is scalable, your application might not be. If it's hard to add more capacity for any reason, your application isn't scalable.

Fault tolerance depends on the application's ability to function partially when a component fails. Being fault-tolerant is not the same thing as being self-healing, which refers to an application's ability to restore or maintain full functionality in the event of a failure. Fault tolerance is often an important component of scalability, because you have to plan for it in your application's design. If you don't design components so you can disable them easily and so they can handle the failure of other components, a problem might cause more of the application to fail than necessary. Fault tolerance also requires a clean separation between components, which is difficult to achieve unless you build it in from the start.

If scalability is the ability to add capacity, and capacity is how much load an application can handle, then scalability is also the ability to handle more and more load. "Load" is actually a complicated concept, because it depends on the application. Here are some common load metrics for a typical "social networking" site (an application that's a good example for many of the concepts we discuss):

Quantity of data

The sheer volume of data your application can accumulate is one of the most common scaling challenges. This is particularly an issue for many of today's web applications, which never delete any data. Social networking sites, for example, typically never delete old messages or comments.

Number of users

Even if each user has only a small amount of data, if you have a lot of users it adds up—and the data size can grow disproportionately faster than the number of users. Many users generally means more transactions too, and the number of transactions also might not be proportional to the number of users. Finally, many users can mean increasingly complex queries, especially if queries depend on the number of relationships among users. (The number of relationships is bounded by ($N * (N-1)$) / 2, where N is the number of users.)

User activity

Not all user activity is equal, and user activity is not constant. If your users suddenly become more active, for example, because of a new feature they like, your load can increase significantly. User activity isn't just a matter of the number of page views, either—the same number of page views can cause more work if part of the site that requires a lot of work to generate becomes more popular. Some users are much more active than others, too: they may have many more friends, messages, or photos than the average user.

Size of related datasets

If there are relationships among users, the application might need to run queries and computations on entire groups of related users. This is more complex than just working with individual users and their data. Social networking sites often face challenges due to popular groups or users who have many friends.

Scaling MySQL

Placing all of your application's data in a single MySQL instance simply is not an approach that will scale well. Sooner or later you'll hit performance bottlenecks caused by an increased load on the server. The traditional solution in many types of applications is to buy more powerful servers. This is what's known as "scaling vertically" or "scaling up." The opposite approach is to divide your work across many computers, which is usually called "scaling horizontally" or "scaling out." Most applications also have some data that's rarely or never needed and that can be purged or archived. We call this approach "scaling back," just to give it a name that matches the other strategies. Finally, some database products support scaling through *federation*, which allows you to access remote data as though it's local. MySQL's support for this is limited.

The dream scenario for scaling is a single logical database that can hold as much data, serve as many queries, and grow as large as you need it to. Many people's first thought is to create a "cluster" or "grid" that handles this seamlessly, so the application doesn't need to do any dirty work or know that the data really lives in many servers instead of just one. MySQL's NDB Cluster technology can support this to a degree, but it doesn't perform well for most web applications, and it has quite a few limitations. That's why most large applications built on MySQL are scaled in other ways. We discuss scaling by clustering at the end of this part of the chapter.

Planning for Scalability

The typical symptom of poor scalability is difficulty keeping up with increased load. This usually shows up as reduced performance in the form of slow queries, a shift in workload from CPU-bound to I/O-bound, contention among concurrent queries, and increasing latency. Common culprits are increased query complexity, or a portion of the data or index that used to fit into memory but no longer does. You may see a change in certain types of queries and not others. For example, long or complex queries often show the strain before smaller queries.

If your application is scalable, you can simply plug in more servers to handle the load, and the performance problems will disappear. If it's not scalable, you may find yourself concentrating on the performance problems, trying to tune servers, and so forth. This is focusing on symptoms, not the root cause. You can avoid this by planning for scalability.

The hardest part of scalability planning is estimating how much load you'll need to handle. You don't need to get it exactly right, but you need to be within an order of magnitude. If you overestimate, you'll waste resources on development, but if you underestimate, you'll be unprepared for the load.

You also need to estimate your schedule approximately right—that is, you need to know where the "horizon" is. For some applications, a simple prototype could work fine for a few months, giving you a chance to raise capital and build a more scalable architecture. For other applications, you might need your current architecture to provide enough capacity for two years.

Here are some questions you can ask yourself to help plan for scalability:

- How complete is your application's functionality? A lot of the scaling solutions we suggest can make it harder to implement certain features. If you haven't yet implemented some of your application's core features, it might be hard to see how you can build them in a scaled application. Likewise, it could be hard to decide on a scaling solution before you've seen how these features will really work.

- What is your expected peak load? Your application should work even at peak load. What would happen if your site makes the front page of Yahoo! News or Slashdot? Even if your application isn't a popular web site, you can still have peak loads. For example, if you're an online retailer, the holiday season is a time of peak load—especially the infamous online shopping days such as the few weeks before Christmas. In the U.S., the weekend before Mother's Day is often a peak time for online florists.

- If you rely on every part of your system to handle the load, what would happen if part of it fails? For example, if you rely on replication slaves to distribute the read load, can you still keep up if one of them fails? Do you need to disable some functionality to do so? You can build in some spare capacity to help alleviate these concerns.

Buying Time Before Scaling

In a perfect world, it would be nice to be able to plan ahead, have enough developers, never run into budget limitations, and so on. In the real world, things are usually more complicated, and you'll need to make some compromises as you scale an application. In particular, you might need to put off big application changes for a while. Before we get deep into the details of scaling MySQL, here are some things you might be able to do now, before you make major scaling efforts:

Optimize performance
   You can often get significant performance improvements from relatively simple changes, such as indexing tables correctly or using a different storage engine. If you're facing performance limitations now, one of the first things you should do is enable and analyze the slow query log, and then see which queries you can optimize. See "Logging queries" on page 64 for more on this topic.

There is a point of diminishing returns. After you've fixed most of the major problems, it gets harder and harder to improve performance through query optimizations. Each new optimization makes less of a difference and requires more effort, and they often make your application much more complicated.

Buy more powerful hardware

Upgrading your servers, or adding more of them, can sometimes work well. Especially for an application that's early in its lifecycle, it's often a good idea to buy a few more servers. The alternative might be to try to keep the application running on a single server. Although a beautiful, elegant design might make this possible, if it would take three people a month to build that design, you might find it more practical just to buy some more servers. This is especially true if time is critical and developers are scarce.

Buying more hardware works well if your application is either small or designed so it can use more hardware well. This is common for new applications, which are usually very small or reasonably well designed. For larger, older applications, buying more hardware might not work, or might be too expensive. For example, going from 1 to 3 servers isn't a big deal, but going from 100 to 300 is a different story—it's very expensive. At that point, it's worth a lot of time and effort to get as much performance as possible out of your existing systems.

Scaling Up

Scaling up can work for a while, but if your application grows very large, it won't work.

The first reason is money. Regardless of what software you're running on the server, at some point, scaling up will become a bad financial decision. There's a certain range of hardware that offers the best price-to-performance ratio. Outside that range, the hardware tends to become more proprietary and unusual, and correspondingly more expensive. This means there's a practical limit on how far up you can afford to scale.

Economics aside, MySQL itself doesn't tend to scale vertically very well, because it's hard to get it to use many CPUs and disks effectively. Exactly how much hardware you can use effectively is very specific to your workload, the type of hardware you're using, and your operating system. As a rough guide, we think around 8 CPUs and 14 disks is the limit with current versions of MySQL.* Many people have problems with less hardware than that.

---

* Large amounts of memory are not as much of a problem, as long as you're using a 64-bit operating system and hardware. There are still some limitations, but they're not as severe and obvious. We discussed memory usage at length in Chapter 7.

Even if your master server can use many CPUs effectively, there's little chance that you'll be able to build a slave server that's powerful enough to keep up. A heavily loaded master can easily do more work than a slave server with the same hardware can handle, because the slave's replication thread can't use multiple CPUs and disks efficiently.

Furthermore, you can't scale up indefinitely, because even the most powerful computers have limits. Single-server applications usually run into read limits first, especially if they run complicated read queries. Such queries are single-threaded inside MySQL, so they'll use only one CPU, and money can't buy them much more performance. The fastest server-grade CPUs you can buy are only a couple of times faster than commodity CPUs. Adding many CPUs or CPU cores won't help the slow queries run faster. The server will also begin to run into memory limits as your data becomes too large to cache effectively. This will usually show up as heavy disk usage, and disks are one of the slowest parts of modern computers.

Application scalability is often a problem, too. Application-specific design choices, or limitations caused by the workload, can limit how much hardware you can use effectively.

For these reasons, we recommend that you don't plan to scale up, or at least not indefinitely. If you know your application will grow very large, it's fine to buy a more powerful server for the short term while you work on another solution. However, in general, you'll ultimately have to scale out, which brings us to our next topic.

Scaling Out

The simplest and most common way to scale out is to distribute your data across several servers with replication, and then use the slaves for read queries. This technique can work well for a read-heavy application. It has drawbacks, such as cache duplication, but even that might not be a severe problem if the data size is limited. We wrote quite a bit about these issues in the previous chapter, and we return to them later in this one.

The other common way to scale out is to *partition* your workload across multiple "nodes." Exactly how you partition the workload is an intricate decision. Recall our "dream system" that automatically scales invisibly and infinitely—this is not what people typically build with MySQL. Most large MySQL applications don't automate the partitioning, at least not completely. In this section, we take a look at some of the possibilities for partitioning and explore their strengths and drawbacks.

A *node* is the functional unit in your MySQL architecture. If you're not planning for redundancy and high availability, a node might be one server. If you're designing a redundant system with failover, a node is generally one of the following:

- A master-master replication topology, with an active server and a passive replication slave
- A master and many slaves
- An active server that uses a distributed replicated block device (DRBD) for a standby
- A SAN-based "cluster"

In most cases, all servers within a node should have the same data. We like the master-master replication architecture for two-server active-passive nodes. See "Master-Master in Active-Passive Mode" on page 365 for more on this topology.

Functional partitioning

Functional partitioning, or division of duties, means dedicating different nodes to different tasks. We've mentioned some similar approaches before; for example, we wrote about how to design different servers for OLTP and OLAP workloads in the previous chapter. Functional partitioning usually takes that strategy even further by dedicating individual servers or nodes to different applications, so each contains only the data its particular application needs.

We're using the word "application" a bit broadly here. We don't mean a single computer program, but a set of related programs that's easily separated from other, unrelated programs. For example, if you have a web site with distinct sections that don't need to share data, you can partition by functional area on the web site. It's common to see portals that tie the different areas together; from the portal, you can browse to the news section of the site, the forums, the support area and knowledge base, and so on. The data for each of these functional areas could be on a dedicated MySQL server. Figure 9-1 depicts this arrangement.

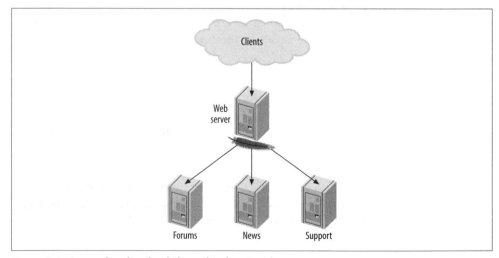

Figure 9-1. A portal and nodes dedicated to functional areas

If the application is huge, each functional area can also have its own dedicated web server, but that's less common.

Another possible functional partitioning approach is to split a single application's data by determining sets of tables that you never join to each other. If it becomes necessary, you can usually perform a few such joins either in the application or with Federated tables if they're not performance-critical. There are a few variations on this approach, but they have the common property that each type of data can be found on only a single node. This is not a common way to partition data, because it's very difficult to do effectively and it doesn't offer any advantages over other methods.

In the final analysis, you still can't scale functional partitioning indefinitely, because each functional area must scale vertically if it is tied to a single MySQL node. One of the applications or functional areas is likely to eventually grow too large, forcing you to find a different strategy. And if you take functional partitioning too far, it can be harder to change to a more scalable design later.

Data sharding

Data sharding[*] is the most common and successful approach for scaling today's very large MySQL applications. You shard the data by splitting it into smaller pieces, or shards, and storing them on different nodes.

Sharding works well when combined with some type of functional partitioning. Most sharded systems also have some "global" data that isn't sharded at all (say, lists of cities). This global data is usually stored on a single node, often behind a cache such as *memcached*.

In fact, most applications shard only the data that needs it—typically, the parts of the dataset that will grow very large. Suppose you're building a blogging service. If you expect 10 million users, you might not need to shard the user registration information because you might be able to fit all of the users (or the active subset of them) entirely in memory. If you expect 500 million users, on the other hand, you should probably shard this data. The user-generated content, such as posts and comments, will almost certainly require sharding in either case, because these records are much larger and there are many more of them.

Large applications might have several various logical datasets that you can shard differently. You can store them on different sets of servers, but you don't have to. You can also shard the same data multiple ways, depending on how you access it. We show an example of this approach later.

---

[*] Sharding is also called "splintering" and "partitioning," but we use the term "sharding" to avoid confusion. Google calls it sharding, and if it's good enough for Google, it's good enough for us.

Sharding is dramatically different from the way most applications are designed initially, and it can be difficult to change an application from a monolithic data store to a sharded architecture. That's why it's much easier to build an application with a sharded data store from the start if you anticipate that it will eventually need one.

Most applications that don't build in sharding from the beginning go through stages as they get larger. For example, you can use replication to scale read queries on your blogging service until it doesn't work any more. Then you can split the service into three parts: users, posts, and comments. You can place these on different servers (functional partitioning) and perform the joins in the application. Figure 9-2 shows the evolution from a single server to functional partitioning.

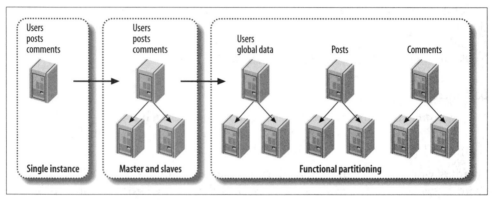

Figure 9-2. From a single instance to a functionally partitioned data store

Finally, you can shard the posts and comments by the user ID, and keep the user information on a single node. If you keep a master-slave configuration for the global node and use master-master pairs for the sharded nodes, the final data store might look like Figure 9-3.

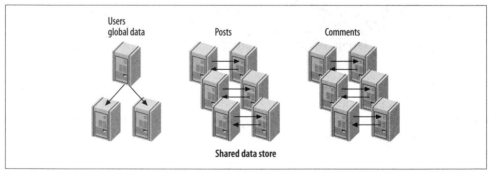

Figure 9-3. A data store with one global node and six master-master nodes

If you know in advance that you'll need to scale very large, and you know the limitations of functional partitioning, you might choose to skip the steps in the middle and go straight from a single node to a sharded data store.

Sharded applications often have a database abstraction library that eases the communication between the application and the sharded data store. Such libraries usually don't hide the sharding completely, because the application usually knows something about a query that the data store doesn't.

Too much abstraction can cause inefficiencies, such as querying all nodes for data that lives on a single node. This is one reason MySQL's NDB Cluster storage engine often performs poorly for web applications: it hides the fact that it must query many nodes and makes it look as though there's just a single server.

A sharded data store may feel like an elegant solution, but it's hard to build. So why choose this architecture? The answer is simple: if you want to scale your write capacity, you *must* partition your data. You cannot scale write capacity if you have only a single master, no matter how many slaves you have. Sharding, for all its drawbacks, is our preferred solution to this problem.

A completely automated, high-performance, transparent way to partition data and make it look like it lives on a single server would be wonderful, but it doesn't exist yet. In the future, MySQL's NDB Cluster storage engine might be fast and robust enough to work well for this purpose.

Choosing a partitioning key

The most important challenge with sharding is finding and retrieving data. How you find data depends on how you shard it. There are many ways to do this, and some are better than others.

The goal is to make your most important and frequent queries touch as few shards as possible. The most important part of that process is choosing a *partitioning key* (or keys) for your data. The partitioning key determines which rows should go onto each shard. If you know an object's partitioning key, you can answer two questions:

- Where should I store this data?
- Where can I find the data I need to fetch?

We'll show you a variety of ways to choose and use a partitioning key later. For now, let's look at an example. Suppose we do as MySQL's NDB Cluster does, and use a hash of each table's primary key to partition the data across all the shards. This is a very simple approach, but it doesn't scale well because it frequently requires you to check all shards for the data you want. For example, if you want user 3's blog posts, where can you find them? They are probably scattered evenly across all shards, because they're partitioned by the primary key, not by the user.

Cross-shard queries are worse than single-shard queries, but as long as you don't touch too many shards, they might not be too bad. The worst case is when you have no idea where the desired data is stored, and you need to scan every shard to find it.

A good partitioning key is usually the ID of a very important entity in the database. These IDs identify the *unit of sharding*. For example, if you partition your data by a user ID or a client ID, the unit of sharding is the user or client.

A good way to start is to diagram your data model with an entity-relationship diagram, or an equivalent tool that shows all the entities and their relationships. Try to lay out the diagram so that the related entities are close together. You can often inspect such a diagram visually and find candidates for partitioning keys that you'd otherwise miss. Don't just look at the diagram, though; consider your application's queries as well. Even if two entities are related in some way, if you seldom or never join on the relationship, you can break the relationship to implement the sharding.

Some data models are easier to shard than others, depending on the degree of connectivity in the entity-relationship graph. Figure 9-4 depicts an easily sharded data model on the left, and one that's difficult to shard on the right.

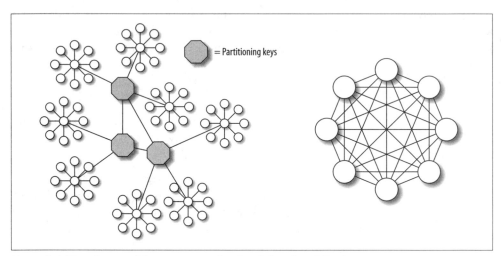

Figure 9-4. Two data models, one easy to shard and the other difficult[a]

[a] Thanks to the HiveDB project and Britt Crawford for contributing these elegant diagrams.

The data model on the left is easy to shard because it has many connected subgraphs consisting mostly of nodes with just one connection, and you can "cut" the connections between the subgraphs relatively easily. The model on the right is hard to shard, because there are no such subgraphs. Most data models look more like the lefthand diagram than the righthand one.

Multiple partitioning keys. Complicated data models make data sharding more difficult. Many applications have more than one partitioning key, especially if there are two or more important "dimensions" in the data. In other words, the application might need to see an efficient, coherent view of the data from different angles. This means you might need to store at least some data twice within the system.

For example, you might need to shard your blogging application's data by both the user ID and the post ID, because these are two common ways the application looks at the data. Think of it this way: you frequently want to see all posts for a user, and all comments for a post. But sharding by user doesn't help you find comments for a post, and sharding by post doesn't help you find posts for a user. If you need both types of queries to touch only a single shard, you'll have to shard both ways.

Just because you need multiple partitioning keys doesn't mean you'll need to design two completely redundant data stores. Let's look at another example: a social networking book club web site, where the site's users can comment on books. The web site can display all comments for a book, as well as books a user has read and commented on.

You might build one sharded data store for the user data and another for the book data. Comments have both a user ID and a post ID, so they cross the boundaries between shards. Instead of completely duplicating comments, you can store the comments with the user data. Then you can store just a comment's headline and ID with the book data. This might be enough to render *most* views of a book's comments without accessing both data stores, and if you need to display the complete comment text, you can retrieve it from the user data store.

Querying across shards

Most sharded applications have at least some queries that need to aggregate or join data from multiple shards. For example, if the book club site shows the most popular or active users, it must by definition access every shard. Making such queries work well is the most difficult part of implementing data sharding, because what the application sees as a single query needs to be split up and executed in parallel as many queries, one per shard. A good database abstraction layer can help ease the pain, but even then such queries are so much slower and more expensive than in-shard queries that aggressive caching is usually necessary as well.

Some languages, such as PHP, don't have good support for executing multiple queries in parallel. A common way to work around this is to build a helper application, often in C or Java, to execute the queries and aggregate the results. The PHP application then queries the helper application, which is often a web service.

Cross-shard queries can also benefit from summary tables. You can build them by traversing all shards and storing the results redundantly on each shard when they're complete. If duplicating the data on each shard would be too wasteful, you can consolidate the summary tables onto another data store, so they're stored only once.

Non-sharded data often lives in the "global" node, with heavy caching to shield it from the load.

Some applications use essentially random sharding when perfectly even data distribution is important, or when there is no good partitioning key. A distributed search application is a good example. In this case, cross-shard queries and aggregation are the norm, not the exception.

Querying across shards isn't the only thing that's harder with sharding. Maintaining data consistency is also difficult. Foreign keys won't work across shards, so the normal solution is to check as needed in the application. It's possible to use XA transactions, but this is uncommon in practice because of the overhead. See "Distributed (XA) Transactions" on page 262 for more on this topic.

You can also design cleanup processes that run intermittently. For example, if a user's book club account expires, you don't have to remove it immediately. You can write a periodic job to remove the user's comments from the per-book shard. You can also build a checker script that runs periodically and makes sure the data is consistent across the shards.

Allocating data, shards, and nodes

Shards and nodes don't have to have a one-to-one relationship. It's often a good idea to make a shard's size much smaller than a node's capacity, so you can store multiple shards on a single node.

Keeping each shard small helps keep the data manageable. It makes it easier to do database backups and recovery, and if the tables are small, it can ease jobs such as schema changes. For example, suppose you have a 100 GB table that you can either store as it is or split into 100 shards of 1 GB tables, which you would store on a single node. Now suppose you want to add an index to the table(s). This would take much longer on a 100 GB shard than it would on all the 1 GB shards combined, because the 1 GB shards fit completely in memory. You also might need to make the data unavailable while ALTER TABLE is running, and blocking 1 GB of data is much better than blocking 100 GB.

Smaller shards are easier to move around, too. This makes it easier to reallocate capacity and rebalance the shards among the nodes. Moving a shard is generally not an efficient process. You typically need to put the affected shard into read-only mode (a feature you'll need to build into your application), extract the data, and move it to another node. This usually involves using *mysqldump* to export the data and *mysql* to reload it. (If you're using MyISAM, you can just copy the files; see Chapter 11 for more on this.)

In addition to moving shards between nodes, you might need to think about moving data between shards, preferably without interrupting service for the whole application. If your shards are large, it will be harder to balance capacity by moving entire shards around, so you'll probably need a way to move the individual bits of data (for example, a single user) between shards. Moving data between shards is usually a lot more complicated than just moving shards, so it's best not to do it if possible. That's why we recommend keeping the shard size manageable.

The relative size of your shards depends on the application's needs. As a rough guide, a "manageable size" for us is one that keeps tables small enough that we can perform regular maintenance jobs, such as `ALTER TABLE`, `CHECK TABLE`, or `OPTIMIZE TABLE`, within 5 or 10 minutes.

If you make your shards too small, you might end up with too many tables, which can cause problems with the filesystem or MySQL's internal structures. See "The Table Cache" on page 279 for more on this. Small shards might also increase the number of cross-shard queries you need to make.

Arranging shards on nodes. You'll need to decide how you want to arrange the shards on a node. Here are some common methods:

- Use a single database per shard, and use the same name for each shard's database. This method is typical when you want each shard to mirror the original application's structure. It can work well when you're making many application instances, each of which is aware of only one shard.

- Place tables from several shards into one database, and include the shard number in each table's name (e.g., `bookclub.comments_23`). A single database can hold multiple shards in this configuration.

- Use a single database per shard, and include all the application's tables in the database. Include the shard number in the database name but not the table name (e.g., the tables might be named `bookclub_23.comments`, `bookclub_23.users`, and so on). This is common when an application connects to a single database and doesn't specify the database name in any of its queries. The advantage is that you don't need to customize the queries per shard, and it can ease the transition to sharding for an application that uses only one database.

- Use a single database per shard, and include the shard number in both the database and table names (e.g., the table name would become `bookclub_23.comments_23`).

If you include the shard number in the table name, you'll need some way to insert the shard number into templated queries. Typical practices include special "magic" placeholder values in queries, `sprintf()`-style formatting specifications such as `%s`, and string interpolation with variables. Here is one way you can create templated queries in PHP:

```
$sql = "SELECT book_id, book_title FROM bookclub_%d.comments_%d... ";
$res = mysql_query(sprintf($sql, $shardno, $shardno), $conn);
```

You could also just use string interpolation:

```
$sql = "SELECT book_id, book_title FROM bookclub_$shardno.comments_$shardno ...";
```

```
$res = mysql_query($sql, $conn);
```

This is easy to build into a new application, but it might be harder for existing applications. When we're building new applications and query templating isn't an issue, we like to use a single database per shard, with the shard number in both the database and table name. It adds some complexity for jobs such as scripting ALTER TABLE, but it has advantages too:

- You can move a shard easily with *mysqldump* if it's completely contained in a single database.
- Because a database is a directory in the filesystem, you can manage a shard's files easily.
- It's easy to find out how large the shard is if it isn't mixed up with other shards.
- The globally unique table names help avoid mistakes. If table names are the same everywhere, it's easy to accidentally query the wrong shard because you connected to the wrong node, or import one shard's data into another shard's tables.

You might want to consider whether your application's data has any *shard affinity*. You might benefit from placing certain shards "near" each other (on the same server, on the same subnet, in the same data center, or on the same switch) to exploit some similarity in the data access patterns. For example, you can shard by user and then place users from the same country into shards on the same nodes.

Adding sharding support to an existing application often results in one shard per node. This simplification helps limit how much you need to change the application's queries. Sharding is usually a pretty disruptive change for an application, so it makes sense to simplify where possible. If you shard so each node looks like a miniature copy of the whole application's data, you might not have to change most of the queries or worry about routing queries to the desired node.

Fixed allocation

There are two main ways to allocate data to the shards: the *fixed* and *dynamic* allocation strategies. Both require a partitioning function that takes a row's partitioning key as input and returns the shard that holds the row.*

Fixed allocation uses a partitioning function that depends only on the partitioning key's value. Hash functions and modulus are good examples. These functions map each value of the partitioning key into a limited number of "buckets" that can hold the data.

---

* We're using "function" in its mathematical sense here to refer to a mapping from the input (domain) to the output (range). As you'll see, you can create such a function in many ways, including using a lookup table in your database.

Suppose you want 100 buckets, and you want to find out where to put user 111. If you're using a modulus, the answer is easy: 111 modulus 100 is 11, so you should place the user into shard 11.

If, on the other hand, you're using the CRC32( ) function for hashing, the answer is 81:

```
mysql> SELECT CRC32(111) % 100;
+-------------------+
| CRC32(111) % 100  |
+-------------------+
|                81 |
+-------------------+
```

The primary advantages of a fixed strategy are simplicity and low overhead. You can also hardcode it into the application.

However, a fixed allocation strategy has disadvantages, too:

- If the shards are large and there are few of them, it can be hard to balance the load across shards.

- Fixed allocation doesn't let you decide where to store each piece of data, which is important for applications that don't have a very uniform load on the unit of sharding. Some pieces of data are much more active than others, and if many of those happen to fall into the same shard, a fixed allocation strategy doesn't let you ease the strain by moving some of them to another shard. This is not as much of a problem when you have many small pieces of data in each shard, because the law of large numbers will help even things out.

- It's usually harder to change the sharding, because it requires reallocating existing data. For example, if you've sharded by a hash function modulus 10, you'll have 10 shards. If the application grows and the shards get too large, you might want to increase the number of shards to 20. That will require rehashing everything, updating a lot of data, and moving data between shards.

Because of these limitations, we usually prefer dynamic allocation for new applications. But if you're sharding an existing application, you might find it easier to build a fixed allocation strategy instead of a dynamic one, because it's simpler.

We sometimes use fixed allocation even for new projects. One example where it worked well is at BoardReader (*http://www.boardreader.com*), a forum search engine some of the authors built. This site indexes a very large amount of data. We were tempted to shard the forums by a hash of the site ID. This would have placed all of a site's forums in one shard, which would have been good for queries that access data from many of a site's forums—for example, the query that finds a site's most popular forums. However, some sites have thousands of forums with tens or hundreds of millions of messages. The shards would have been too large to manage had we used that scheme, so we chose to shard by a hash of the forum's ID instead.

Dynamic allocation

The alternative to fixed allocation is a dynamic allocation that you store separately, as a per-unit-of-sharding mapping. An example is a two-column table of user IDs and shard IDs:

```
CREATE TABLE user_to_shard (
   user_id INT NOT NULL,
   shard_id INT NOT NULL,
   PRIMARY KEY (user_id)
);
```

The table itself is the partitioning function. Given a value of the partitioning key (the user ID), you can find the shard ID. If the row doesn't exist, you can pick the desired shard and add it to the table. You can also change it later—that's what makes this a dynamic allocation strategy.

Dynamic allocation adds overhead to the partitioning function, because it requires a call to an external resource, such as a *directory server* (a data storage node that stores the mapping). Such an architecture often needs more layers for efficiency. For example, you can use a distributed caching system to store the directory server's data in memory, because in practice it doesn't change all that much.

The biggest advantage of dynamic allocation is fine-grained control over where the data is stored. This makes it easier to allocate data to the shards evenly and gives you a lot of flexibility to accommodate changes you don't foresee.

A dynamic mapping also lets you build multiple levels of sharding strategies on top of the simple key-to-shard mapping. For example, you can build a dual mapping that assigns each unit of sharding to a group (e.g., a group of users in the book club), and then keeps the groups together on a shard where possible. This lets you take advantage of shard affinities, so you can avoid cross-shard queries.

If you use a dynamic allocation strategy, you can have imbalanced shards. This can be useful when your servers aren't all equally powerful, or when you want to use some of them for different purposes, such as archived data. If you also have the ability to rebalance shards at any time, you can maintain a one-to-one mapping of shards to nodes without wasting capacity. Some people prefer the simplicity of one shard per node. (But remember, there are advantages to keeping shards small.)

Dynamic allocation and smart use of shard affinities can prevent your cross-shard queries from growing as you scale. Imagine a cross-shard query in a data store with four nodes. In a fixed allocation, any given query may require touching all shards, but a dynamic allocation strategy might let you run the same query on only three of the nodes. This might not seem like a big difference, but consider what will happen when your data store grows to 400 shards: the fixed allocation will require querying 400 shards, while the dynamic allocation might still require querying only 3.

Dynamic allocation lets you make your sharding strategy as complex as you wish. Fixed allocation doesn't give you as many choices.

Mixing dynamic and fixed allocation. You can use a mixture of fixed and dynamic allocation, which is often helpful and sometimes required. Dynamic allocation works well when the directory mapping isn't too large. If there are many units of sharding, it may not work so well.

An example is a system that's designed to store links between web sites. Such a site needs to store tens of billions of rows, and the partitioning key is the combination of source and target URLs. (Just one of the two URLs may have hundreds of millions of links, so neither URL is selective enough by itself.) However, it's not feasible to store all of the source and target URL combinations in the mapping table, because there are many of them, and each URL requires a lot of storage space.

One solution is to concatenate the URLs and hash them into a fixed number of buckets, which you can then map dynamically to shards. If you make the number of buckets large enough—say, a million—you'll be able to fit quite a few of them into each shard. The result is that you get most of the benefits of dynamic sharding, without having a huge mapping table.

Explicit allocation

A third allocation strategy is to let the application choose each row's desired shard explicitly when it creates the row. This is harder to do with existing data, so it's not very common when adding sharding to an application. However, it can be helpful sometimes.

The idea is to encode the shard number into the ID, similar to the technique we showed for avoiding duplicate key values in master-master replication. (See "Writing to Both Masters in Master-Master Replication" on page 398 for more details.)

For example, suppose your application wants to create user 3 and assign it to shard 11, and you've reserved the 8 most significant bits of a BIGINT column for the shard number. The resulting ID value is (11 << 56) + 3, or 792633534417207299. The application can easily extract the user ID and the shard ID later. Here's an example:

```
mysql> SELECT (792633534417207299 >> 56) AS shard_id,
    -> 792633534417207299 & ~(11 << 56) AS user_id;
+----------+---------+
| shard_id | user_id |
+----------+---------+
|       11 |       3 |
+----------+---------+
```

Now suppose you want to create a comment for this user and store it in the same shard. The application can assign the comment ID 5 for the user, and combine the value 5 with the shard ID 11 in the same way.

The benefit of this approach is that each object's ID carries its partitioning key along with it, whereas other approaches usually require a join or another lookup to find the partitioning key. If you want to retrieve a certain comment from the database, you don't need to know which user owns it; the object's ID tells you where to find it. If the object were sharded dynamically by user ID, you'd have to find the comment's user, then ask the directory server which shard to look on.

Another solution is to store the partitioning key together with the object in separate columns. For example, you'd never refer just to comment 5, but to comment 5 belonging to user 3. This approach will probably make some people happier, because it doesn't violate first normal form; however, the extra column causes more overhead, coding, and inconvenience. (This is one case where we feel there's an advantage to storing two values in a single column.)

The drawback of explicit allocation is that the sharding is fixed, and it's harder to balance shards. On the other hand, this approach works well with the combination of fixed and dynamic allocation. Instead of hashing to a fixed number of buckets and mapping these to nodes, you encode the bucket as part of each object. This gives the application control over where the data is located, so it can place related data together on the same shard.

BoardReader uses a variation of this technique: it encodes the partitioning key in the Sphinx document ID. This makes it easy to find each search result's related data in the sharded data store. See Appendix C for more on Sphinx.

We've described mixed allocation because we've seen cases where it's useful, but normally we don't recommend it. We like to use dynamic allocation when possible, and avoid explicit allocation.

Rebalancing shards

If necessary, you can move data to different shards to rebalance the load. For example, many readers have probably heard developers from large photo-sharing sites or popular social networking sites mention their tools for moving users to different shards.

The ability to move data between shards has its benefits. For example, it can help you upgrade your hardware by enabling you to move users off the old shard onto the new one without taking the whole shard down or making it read-only.

However, we like to avoid rebalancing shards if possible, because it can disrupt service to your users. Moving data between shards also makes it harder to add features to the application, because new features might have to include an upgrade to the rebalance script. If you keep your shards small enough, you might not need to do this; you can often rebalance the load by moving entire shards, which is easier than moving part of a shard (and more efficient, in terms of cost per row of data).

One strategy that works well is to assign new data to shards randomly. When a shard gets full enough, you can set a flag that tells the application not to give it any new data. You can then flip the flag back if you want more data on that shard in the future.

Suppose you install a new MySQL node and place 100 shards on it. To begin, you set their flags to 1, so the application knows they're ready for new data. Once they each have enough data (10,000 users each, for example), you set their flags to 0. Then, if the node becomes underloaded after a while because of abandoned accounts, you can reopen some of the shards and add new users to them.

If you upgrade the application and add features that make each shard's query load higher, or if you just miscalculated the load, you can move some of the shards to new nodes to ease the load. The drawback is that an entire shard might be read-only or offline while you do this. It's up to you and your users to decide whether that's acceptable.

Generating globally unique IDs

When you convert a system to use a sharded data store, you frequently need to generate globally unique IDs on many machines. A monolithic data store often uses `AUTO_INCREMENT` columns for this purpose, but by default the `AUTO_INCREMENT` feature is designed to run on a single server that can easily guarantee uniqueness.

There are several ways to solve this problem:

Use `auto_increment_increment` *and* `auto_increment_offset`
> These two server settings instruct MySQL to increment `AUTO_INCREMENT` columns by a desired value and to begin numbering from a desired offset. For example, in the simplest case with two servers, you can configure the servers to increment by two, set one server's offset to one, and set the other's to two (you can't set either value to zero). Now one server's columns will always contain even numbers, and the other's will always contain odd numbers. The setting applies to all tables in the server.
>
> Because of its simplicity and lack of dependency on a central node, this is a popular way to generate values, but it requires you to be careful with your server configurations. It's easy to accidentally configure servers so that they generate duplicate numbers, especially if you move them into different roles as you add more servers, or when you recover from failures.

Create a table in the global node
> You can create a table with an `AUTO_INCREMENT` column in your global database node, and applications can use this to generate unique numbers.

Use memcached
> There's an `incr( )` function in the *memcached* API that can increment a number atomically and return the result.

Allocate numbers in batches

The application can request a batch of numbers from a global node, use all the numbers, and then request more.

Use a combination of values

You can use a combination of values, such as the shard ID and an incrementing number, to make each server's values unique. See the discussion of this technique in the previous section.

Use dual-column AUTO_INCREMENT *keys*

This works only for MyISAM tables:

```
mysql> CREATE TABLE inc_test(
    ->    a INT NOT NULL,
    ->    b INT NOT NULL AUTO_INCREMENT,
    ->    PRIMARY KEY(a, b)
    -> ) ENGINE=MyISAM;
mysql> INSERT INTO inc_test(a) VALUES(1), (1), (2), (2);
mysql> SELECT * FROM inc_test;
+---+---+
| a | b |
+---+---+
| 1 | 1 |
| 1 | 2 |
| 2 | 1 |
| 2 | 2 |
+---+---+
```

Use GUID values

You can generate globally unique values with the UUID( ) function. Beware, though: this function does not replicate correctly, although, it works fine if your application selects the value into its own memory and then uses it as a literal in statements. GUID values are large and nonsequential, so they don't make good primary keys for InnoDB tables. See "Inserting rows in primary key order with InnoDB" on page 117.

The MySQL developers have created a UUID_SHORT( ) function that returns shorter, sequential values that should work better as a primary key. Future versions of the MySQL server may include this code, but at the time of this writing, it has not yet been released.

If you use a global allocator to generate values, be careful that the single point of contention doesn't create a bottleneck for your application.

Although the *memcached* approach can be very fast (tens of thousands of values per second), it isn't persistent. Each time you restart the *memcached* service, you'll need to initialize the value in the cache. This could require you to find the maximum value that's in use across all shards, which might be very slow and difficult to do atomically.

If you use a table in MySQL, one way to do it is to create a single-row MyISAM table with an AUTO_INCREMENT column that you access outside of a transaction for speed.

You can either let the table grow as you add rows, or limit the table to a single row and use REPLACE:

```
CREATE TABLE single_row (
    col1 int NOT NULL AUTO_INCREMENT,
    col2 int NOT NULL,
    PRIMARY KEY(col1),
    UNIQUE KEY(col2)
) ENGINE=MyISAM;
```

You can use this table to generate values as follows:

```
mysql> REPLACE INTO single_row(col2) VALUES(1);
```

After this statement finishes executing, you can use the MySQL API's mysql_insert_id( ) function to retrieve the generated value. How you do this will vary between languages, but here's an example in Perl:

```
my $sth = $dbh->prepare('REPLACE INTO single_row(col2) VALUES(1)');
while ( my $item = @work_to_do ) {
    $sth->execute( );
    my $id = $dbh->{mysql_insert_id};
    # Do the work...
}
```

You should not use another query, such as SELECT LAST_INSERT_ID( ), to retrieve the value. This requires another round-trip to the server, which makes it less efficient.

Tools for sharding

One of the first things you'll have to do when designing a sharded application is write code for querying multiple data sources.

It's generally a poor design to expose the multiple data sources to the application without any abstraction, because it can add a lot of code complexity. It's better to hide the data sources behind an abstraction layer. This layer might handle the following tasks:

- Connecting to the correct shard and querying it
- Distributed consistency checks
- Aggregating results across shards
- Cross-shard joins
- Locking and transaction management
- Creating shards (or at least discovering new shards on the fly) and rebalancing shards if you have time to implement this

You might not have to build your own sharding infrastructure from scratch. There are several tools and systems that either provide some of the necessary functionality or are specifically designed to implement a sharded architecture. At the most basic level, you can use a tool such as MySQL Proxy to abstract some of the complexity of the multiple data sources. Depending on how MySQL Proxy evolves in the future, it could become a key part of many sharded data stores.

One database abstraction layer with sharding support that exists already is Hibernate Shards (*http://shards.hibernate.org*), an extension to the open source Hibernate object-relational mapping (ORM) library, which is written in Java. Google developed Hibernate Shards as one of its famous 20% projects and then contributed the code to the community. It provides shard-aware implementations of the Hibernate Core interfaces, so applications don't necessarily have to be redesigned to use a sharded data store; in fact, they may not even have to be aware that they're using one. Hibernate Shards is a good way to store and retrieve data across many servers transparently, but it doesn't provide some features, such as rebalancing shards and aggregating query results. It uses a fixed allocation strategy to allocate data to the shards.

Another sharding system is HiveDB (*http://www.hivedb.org*), an open source framework for sharding MySQL that tries to implement sharding's core ideas in a clear and concise way. HiveDB is written in Java and was designed from the ground up for creating, using, and managing a sharded data store. It has several features other systems don't support, such as creating shards and moving data between shards (rebalancing). HiveDB uses dynamic allocation and refers to sharding as "horizontal partitioning."

Sphinx is a full-text search engine, not a sharded data storage and retrieval system, but it is still useful for some types of queries across sharded data stores. It can query remote systems in parallel and aggregate the results, which is one of the harder things to do with a sharded data store. (You can read more about Sphinx in Appendix C.)

Scaling Back

One of the simpler ways to deal with an increasing data size and workload is to archive and purge unneeded data. Depending on your workload, you may be able to realize significant gains from archiving and purging data you don't need. This doesn't replace the need to scale horizontally, but it can be part of a short-term strategy to buy time and should probably be part of a long-term strategy to cope with large data volumes.

Here are some things to think about when designing archiving and purging strategies:

Impact on the application
> A well-designed archiving strategy can move data away from a heavily loaded OLTP server without impacting transaction processing noticeably. The key is to make it efficient to find the rows to remove, and to remove them in small chunks. You'll usually need to balance the number of rows you archive at once

with the size of a transaction to find a good compromise between lock contention and transactional overhead. You should design your archive jobs to yield to transactional processing jobs when necessary.

Which rows to archive

You can purge or archive data once you know you'll never refer to it again, but you can also design your application to archive seldom-accessed data. You can store the archived data adjacent to the core tables and access it through views, or even move it to another server entirely.

Depth first or breadth first?

Data relationships make archiving and purging more complex. A well-designed archiving job keeps the data logically consistent, or at least as consistent as the application needs, without involving multiple tables in huge transactions.

Deciding which tables to archive first is always a challenge when there are relationships among the tables. You'll have to consider the impact of "orphaned" or "widowed" rows while archiving. It's usually a matter of deciding whether to violate foreign keys (you can disable InnoDB foreign key constraints with SET FOREIGN_KEY_CHECKS=0) or to leave "dangling pointer" records temporarily. Which is preferable depends on how your application views the data. If the application views a particular set of related tables from the top down, you should probably archive them in the same order. For example, if your application always examines orders before invoices, archive the orders first; your application shouldn't see the orphaned invoices, and you can archive them next.

Avoiding data loss

If you're archiving between servers, you probably shouldn't do distributed transactions, and you may be archiving into MyISAM or another nontransactional storage engine anyway. Therefore, to avoid data loss, you should insert into the destination before deleting from the source. It might also be a good idea to write archived data to a file along the way. You should design your archive jobs so you can kill and restart them at will, without causing inconsistencies or index-violation errors.

Unarchiving

You can often trim a lot more data by archiving with an unarchiving strategy. This helps because it lets you archive data you're not sure you'll need, with the option of bringing it back later. If you can identify a few points of entry where your system can check whether it needs to retrieve some archived data, it might be fairly easy to implement such a strategy. For example, if you archive possibly inactive users, the entry point might be the login process. If a login fails because there's no such user, you can check the archive and see whether the user exists there, retrieve the user from the archive, and process the login.

Maatkit contains a tool that can help you archive and/or purge MySQL tables efficiently. It does not offer any support for unarchiving, however.

Keeping active data separate

Even if you don't actually move stale data away to another server, many applications can benefit from separating active and inactive datasets. This helps with cache efficiency, and it enables you to use different kinds of hardware or application architectures for the active and inactive data. Here are some ways to accomplish this:

Splitting tables into parts

It's often smart to split tables, especially if the entire table won't fit in memory. For example, you can split the users table into active_users and inactive_users. You might think this isn't necessary because the database will cache only the "hot" data anyway, but that depends on your storage engine. If you use InnoDB, caching works a page at a time. If you can fit 100 users on a page and only 10% of your users are active, that probably makes every page "hot" from InnoDB's point of view—yet 90% of each "hot" page will be wasted space. Splitting the table in two could improve your memory usage dramatically.

The Falcon storage engine has row-level caching, which should help make the cache more efficient. However, that doesn't mean Falcon tables won't benefit from an active/inactive split too. Falcon caches its indexes a page at a time, so having a mixture of active and inactive data will make its index cache less efficient.

MySQL partitioning

MySQL 5.1 offers natively partitioned tables, which can help keep the most recent data in memory. See "Merge Tables and Partitioning" on page 253 for more about partitioning.

Time-based data partitioning

If your application continually gets new data, it's likely that the newest data will be far more active than the older data. For example, we know of one blog service whose traffic is mostly from posts and comments created in the last seven days. Most of its updates are to the same set of data. As a result, they keep this data entirely in memory, with replication to keep a recoverable copy on disk if there's a failure. The rest of the data lives forever in another location.

We've also seen designs that store each user's data in shards on two nodes. New data goes to the "active" node, which has a lot of memory and fast disks. This data is optimized for very fast access. The other node stores older data, with very large (but slower) disks. The application assumes that it's not likely to need the older data. This is a good assumption for a lot of applications, which might be able to satisfy 90% or more of requests from only the most recent 10% of the data.

You can implement this sharding policy easily with dynamic sharding. For example, your sharding directory's table definition might look something like the following:

```
CREATE TABLE users (
    user_id              int unsigned not null,
    shard_new            int unsigned not null,
    shard_archive        int unsigned not null,
    archive_timestamp timestamp,
    PRIMARY KEY (user_id)
);
```

An archive script can move older data from the active node to the archive node, updating the archive_timestamp column when it moves a user's data to the archive node. The shard_new and shard_archive columns tell you which shard numbers hold the data.

Scaling by Clustering

Clustering is another way of scaling by distributing load across many servers. The term "clustering" is overloaded with several meanings in the computing field, but in general a clustered system consists of several hosts on a local area network configured to appear as a single server. A variation on clustering is federation—that is, accessing remote servers as though they're local, thus creating one giant "virtual server" that really acts as a proxy to many servers.

Clustering

MySQL's NDB Cluster storage engine is a distributed, in-memory, shared-nothing storage engine with synchronous replication and automatic data partitioning across the nodes. It has a completely different performance profile from other MySQL storage engines, and it performs best with specialized hardware. Although it is a very high-performance way to store data for some applications, it is not yet a good high-performance solution for most web applications.

NDB Cluster is good for applications that have relatively little data and execute simple queries. Good uses for it include storing web site sessions, file-storage metadata, and so forth. It performs very poorly for complex queries, including joins. Essentially, any query that's not a single-table indexed lookup requires inter-node communication and therefore is slow.

NDB Cluster is a transactional system, but it does not have MVCC support, and reads are locking. It also does not do any deadlock detection. If there's a deadlock, NDB resolves it with a timeout. The combination of locking reads and timeout-based deadlock resolution means it may not be a good solution for interactive multiuser applications or web applications.

You can implement a variety of other clustering solutions on top of, in front of, or underneath MySQL. One example is Continuent (*http://www.continuent.com*),[*]

---

[*] Or its makers' open source offering, Sequoia, available at *http://sequoia.continuent.org*.

which offers synchronous replication, load balancing, and failover for MySQL via a middleware layer.

Federation

Federation is another term with many meanings. In the database world, it generally means accessing one server's data from another server. Microsoft SQL Server's distributed views are one example.

MySQL provides limited support for federation via the Federated storage engine. Like NDB Cluster, it works best for very simple lookups, though it is also an acceptable way to perform INSERT queries on another server. Its current architecture makes DELETE and UPDATE queries less efficient—much less efficient, in the worst case.

The Federated engine performs very badly with joins and large SELECT queries. For example, a GROUP BY query retrieves all the data from a table and uses mysql_store_result* to fetch that data from the remote server into the local server's memory. This can cause a lot of trouble as the application's data size grows. Federated tables can also make replication more complicated, because a single update can execute on multiple servers.

Load Balancing

The basic idea behind load balancing is simple: to share the workload as evenly as possible among a collection of servers. The usual way to do this is to place a load balancer (often a specialized piece of hardware) in front of the servers. The load balancer then routes incoming connections to the least busy available server. Figure 9-5 shows a typical load-balancing setup for a large web site, with one load balancer for the HTTP traffic and another for MySQL traffic.

Load balancing has five common goals:

Scalability
> If you've designed your systems properly, you can add capacity by adding more servers to a node. But when you add more servers, you have to balance the load among them.

Efficiency
> Load balancing helps you use resources more efficiently because you have control over how requests are routed. This is particularly important if your servers aren't all equally powerful: you can direct more work to the powerful machines.

Availability
> A smart load-balancing solution uses the servers that are available at each moment.

---

* See "The MySQL Client/Server Protocol" on page 161 for more about mysql_store_result.

Transparency

Clients don't need to know about the load-balancing setup. They don't have to care about how many machines are behind the load balancer, or what their names are; the load balancer makes it so the clients see a single virtual server.

Consistency

If your application is stateful (database transactions, web site sessions, etc.), the load balancer should direct related requests to a single server so that the state isn't lost between requests. This relieves the application of having to keep track of which server it's connected to.

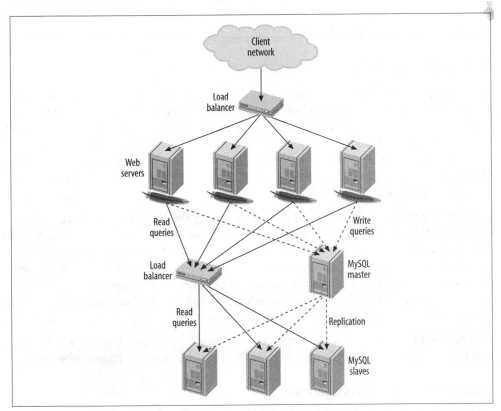

Figure 9-5. Typical load-balancing architecture for a read-intensive web site

In the MySQL world, load-balancing architectures are often tightly coupled with sharding and replication. You can mix and match load-balancing and high-availability solutions and place them at whatever level is appropriate within your application. For example, you can load balance across multiple nodes in a MySQL cluster. You can also load balance across data centers, and within each data center you might have a sharded architecture, each node of which is actually a master-master replication pair with many slaves that are load balanced yet again. The same is true of high-availability strategies; you can have multiple levels of failover in an architecture.

Load balancing has many nuances. For example, one of the challenges is managing read/write policies. Some load-balancing technologies do this themselves, whereas others require the application to be aware of which nodes are readable and writable.

You should consider these factors when you decide how to implement load balancing. A wide variety of load-balancing solutions are available, ranging from peer-based implementations such as Wackamole (*http://www.backhand.org/wackamole/*) to Domain Name System (DNS), LVS (Linux Virtual Server; *http://www. linuxvirtualserver.org*), hardware load balancers, MySQL Proxy, and managing the load balancing in the application.

Connecting Directly

Some people automatically associate load balancing with a central system that's inserted between the application and the MySQL servers. This isn't the only way to load balance, though. You can load balance and yet still connect directly from the application to the MySQL servers. In fact, centralized load-balancing systems usually work well only when there's a pool of servers the application can treat as interchangeable. If the application needs to make a decision such as whether it's safe to perform a read from a slave server, it usually needs to connect directly to the server.

Besides making special-case logic possible, handling the load-balancing decisions in the application can actually be very efficient. For example, if you have two identical slaves, you can choose to use one of them for all queries that touch certain shards and the other for queries that touch other shards. This makes good use of the slaves' memory, because each of them caches only a portion of the data from its disks in memory. If one of the slaves fails, the other still has all the data required to serve queries to both shards.

The following sections discuss some common ways to connect directly from the application, and some of the things you should consider as you evaluate each option.

Splitting reads and writes in replication

MySQL replication gives you multiple copies of your data and lets you choose whether to run a query on the master or a slave. The primary difficulty is how to handle stale data on the slave, because replication is asynchronous. You should also treat slaves as read-only, but the master can handle both read and write queries.

You usually have to modify your application so that it's aware of these concerns.[*] The application can then use the master for writes and split the reads between the

---

[*] If you can use MySQL Proxy to split your queries, you might not need to change the application.

master and the slaves; it can use the slaves when possibly stale data doesn't matter and use the master for data that has to be up-to-date.

If you use a master-master pair with an active and a passive master, the same considerations hold. In this configuration, though, only the active server should receive writes. Reads can go to the passive server if it's OK to read potentially stale data.

The biggest problem is how to avoid artifacts caused by reading stale data. The classic artifact is when a user makes some change, such as adding a comment to a blog post, then reloads the page but doesn't see the change because the application read stale data from a slave.

Some of the most common methods of splitting reads and writes are as follows:

Query-based split

The simplest split is to direct all writes and any reads that can never tolerate stale data to the active or master server. All other reads go to the slave or passive server. This strategy is easy to implement, but in practice it won't use the slave as often as it could, because very few read queries can always tolerate stale data.

Stale-data split

This is a minor enhancement of the query-based split strategy. Relatively little extra work is required to make the application check the slave's lag and decide whether or not its data is too stale to read. Many reporting applications can use this strategy: as long as the nightly data load has finished replicating to the slave, they don't care whether its data is 100% in sync with the master's.

Session-based split

A slightly more sophisticated way to decide whether a read can go to a slave is to note whether the user has changed any data. The user doesn't have to see the most up-to-date data from other users but should see his or her own changes. You can implement this at the session level by flagging the session as having made a change and directing the user's read queries to the master for a certain period of time after that.

You can combine this with replication lag monitoring; if the user changed some data 10 seconds ago and no slave is more than 5 seconds behind, it's safe to read from a slave. It's a very good idea to select one of the slaves and use it for the whole session, though, or the user might see strange effects caused by some of the slaves being farther behind than others.

Version-based split

This is similar to session-based splitting: you can track version numbers and/or timestamps for objects, and read the object's version or timestamp from the slave to determine whether its data is fresh enough to use. If the slave's data is too old, you can read the fresh data from the master. You can also increment the top-level item's version number even when the object itself doesn't change, which simplifies staleness checks (you need to look in only one place—at the top-level item). For example, you can update the user's version if he or she posts a new blog entry. This will cause reads to go to the master.

Reading the object's version from the slave adds overhead, which you can reduce with caching. We discuss caching and object versioning further in the next chapter.

Global version/session split

This is a variation on version- and session-based splits. When the application performs a write, it runs SHOW MASTER STATUS after the transaction commits. It stores the master's log coordinates in the cache as the modified object's and/or session's version number. Then, when the application connects to the slave, it runs SHOW SLAVE STATUS and compares the slave's coordinates to the stored version. If the slave has advanced to at least the point at which the master committed the transaction, the slave is safe to use for the read.

Most read/write splitting solutions require monitoring the slave lag and using it to decide where to direct reads. If you do this, be aware that the Seconds_behind_master column from SHOW SLAVE STATUS is not a reliable way to monitor slave lag. See "Measuring Slave Lag" on page 379 for details.

If pure scalability is your goal and you don't care how much hardware it takes, you can keep things simpler and either not use replication or use it only for high availability and not for load balancing. That might let you avoid the complexity of splitting reads between the master and slaves. Some people think this makes sense; others think it wastes hardware. This division reflects differing goals: do you want scalability only, or both scalability and efficiency? If you want efficiency too, and thus want to use the slaves for something other than just keeping a copy of the data, you'll probably have to deal with some added complexity.

Changing the application configuration

One way you can distribute load is to reconfigure your application. For example, you can configure several machines to share the load of generating large reports. Each machine's configuration can instruct it to connect to a different MySQL slave and generate reports for every *N*th customer or site.

This system is generally very simple to implement, but if it requires any code changes—including changes to configuration files—it becomes brittle and unwieldy. Anything hardcoded that you have to change on every server, or change in a central location and "publish" via file copies or source-control update commands, is inherently limited. If you store the configuration in the database and/or a cache, you can avoid the need to publish code changes.

Changing DNS names

A crude load-balancing technique, but one that works well for some simple applications, is to create DNS names for various purposes. You can then write a periodic job to monitor the MySQL servers, and point the names at different servers as appropriate. The simplest implementation is to have one DNS name for the read-only servers and one for the writable server. If the slaves are keeping up with the master, you can change the read-only DNS name to point to the slaves; when they fall behind, you can point it back to the master.

The DNS technique is very easy to implement, but it has many drawbacks. The biggest problem is that DNS is not completely under your control:

- DNS changes are not instantaneous. It can take a long time for DNS changes to propagate throughout a network or between networks.
- DNS data is cached in various places, and expiry times are advisory, not mandatory.
- DNS changes might require an application or server restart to take effect fully.
- It's not a good idea to use multiple IP addresses for a DNS name and rely on round-robin behavior to balance requests. The round-robin behavior isn't always predictable.
- DNS changes are not atomic.
- The DBA may not always have direct access to DNS.

Unless the application is very simple, it's dangerous to rely on a system that's not controllable. You can improve your control a little by making changes to /etc/hosts instead of DNS. When you publish a change to this file, you know the change has taken effect. This is better than waiting for a cached DNS entry to expire, but it is still not ideal.

We usually advise people to build for zero reliance on DNS. It's a good idea to avoid it even for simple applications, because you never know how large your application will grow.

Moving IP addresses

Some load-balancing solutions rely on moving virtual IP addresses* between servers, which can work very well. This may sound similar to making DNS changes, but it's not the same thing. Servers don't listen for network traffic to a DNS name; they listen for traffic to a specific IP address, so moving IP addresses allows DNS names to remain static. You can force IP address changes to be noticed very quickly and atomically via Address Resolution Protocol (ARP) commands.

---

* Virtual IP addresses aren't connected to any specific computer or network interfaces; they "float" between computers.

Two systems that use this technique are Wackamole and LVS. For example, they let you have a single IP address associated with a role such as "read-only," and they take care of moving the IP address between machines as needed. Wackamole can manage many IP addresses and ensures that one and only one machine is listening on each address in the pool. Wackamole is unique in that the service is peer-based, which helps eliminate a single point of failure.

One handy technique is to assign a fixed IP address to each physical server. This IP address defines the server itself and never changes. You can then use a virtual IP address for each logical "service." These can move between servers easily, which makes it easy to move services and application instances around without reconfiguring the application. This is a nice feature, even if you don't move IP addresses a lot for load balancing or high availability.

Introducing a Middleman

So far, the techniques we've discussed all assume your application is communicating directly with MySQL servers. However, many load-balancing solutions introduce a middleman whose job is to act as a proxy for the network traffic. The middleman accepts all traffic on one side and directs it to the desired server on the other, then routes the responses back to the originating machine. Sometimes the middleman is a piece of hardware, and sometimes it's software.* Figure 9-6 illustrates this architecture. Such solutions generally work very well, although unless you make the load balancer itself redundant, they add a single point of failure.

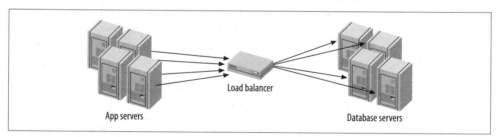

Figure 9-6. A load balancer that acts as a middleman

Load balancers

There is a wide variety of load-balancing hardware and software on the market, but few of the offerings are designed specifically for balancing load to MySQL servers.†

---

* You can configure LVS so it is involved only when an application needs to create a new connection, and it isn't a middleman after that.

† We mentioned some of the software implementations (Sequoia, Continuent) earlier in the chapter; there's also DBIx::DBCluster for Perl, and SQL Relay (*http://sqlrelay.sourceforge.net*) for a language-independent solution.

Web servers need load balancing much more often, so many general-purpose load-balancing devices have special features for HTTP and only a few basic features for everything else.

> An exception is MySQL Proxy, which is a good way to help divide reads and writes for some applications. It adds complexity and some overhead, but it also gives a lot of flexibility and lets you use scripting for custom read/write splits. MySQL Proxy is relatively new, but already there are many tutorials and examples of how to use it for custom load balancing online. Because it can peek inside the conversations it's relaying, this tool can potentially do very complicated query routing.

MySQL connections are just normal TCP/IP connections, so you can use general-purpose load balancers for MySQL. However, the lack of MySQL-specific features does add some limitations:

- Unless the load balancer is aware of MySQL's true load, it's unlikely to *balance load* so much as *distribute requests*. Not all queries are equal, but general-purpose load balancers usually treat all requests as equal.

- Most load balancers know how to inspect an HTTP request and "stick a session" to a server to preserve session state on one web server. MySQL connections are stateful too, but the load balancer is unlikely to know how to "stick" all connection requests from a single HTTP session to a single MySQL server. This results in a loss of efficiency (if a single session's requests all go to the same MySQL server, the server's cache will be more efficient).

- Connection pooling and persistent connections can interfere with a load balancer's ability to distribute connection requests. For example, suppose a connection pool opens its configured number of connections, and the load balancer distributes them among the existing four MySQL servers. Now say you add two more MySQL servers. Because the connection pool isn't requesting any new connections, they'll sit idle. The connections in the pool also might end up being unfairly distributed among the servers, so some are overloaded and others are underloaded. You can work around these problems by expiring the connections in the pool at various levels, but that's complicated and difficult to do. Connection pooling solutions work best when they do their own load balancing.

- Most general-purpose load balancers know how to do health and load checks only for HTTP servers. A simple load balancer can verify that the server accepts connections on a TCP port, which is the bare minimum. A better load balancer can make an HTTP request and check the response code to determine whether the web server is running well. MySQL doesn't accept HTTP requests to port 3306, though, so you'll have to build a custom health check. You can install HTTP server software on the MySQL server and point the load balancer at a custom script that actually checks the MySQL server's status and returns an appropriate status code.* The most important things to check are the operating system load (generally by looking at */proc/loadavg*), the replication status, and the number of MySQL connections.

Load-balancing algorithms

There are many different algorithms to determine which server should receive the next connection. Each vendor uses different terminology, but this list should provide an idea of what's available:

Random

The load balancer directs each request to a server selected at random from the pool of available servers.

Round-robin

The load balancer sends requests to servers in a repeating sequence: A, B, C, A, B, C, etc.

Least connections

The next connection goes to the server with the fewest active connections.

Fastest response

The server that has been handling requests the fastest receives the next connection. This can work well when the pool contains a mix of fast and slow machines. However, it's very tricky with SQL when the query complexity varies widely. Even the same query can perform very differently under different circumstances, such as when it's served from the query cache or when the server's caches already contain the needed data.

Hashed

The load balancer hashes the connection's source IP address, which maps it to one of the servers in the pool. Each time a connection request comes from the same IP address, the load balancer sends it to the same server. The bindings change only when the number of machines in the pool does.

Weighted

The load balancer can combine and weight several of the other algorithms. For example, you may have single- and dual-CPU machines. The dual-CPU machines are roughly twice as powerful, so you can tell the load balancer to send them an average of twice as many requests.

The best algorithm for MySQL depends on your workload. The least-connections algorithm, for example, might flood new servers when you add them to the pool of available servers—just when their caches aren't warmed up yet. The authors of this book's first edition experienced that problem firsthand.

---

* Actually, if your coding kung fu is up to the task of writing a program to listen on port 80, or if you configure *xinetd* to invoke your program, you don't even need to install a web server.

You'll need to experiment to find the best performance for your workload. Be sure to consider what happens in extraordinary circumstances as well as in the day-to-day norm. It is under extraordinary circumstances—such as high load, schema changes, or an unusual number of servers going offline—when you can least afford something going terribly wrong.

We've described only instant-provisioning algorithms, which don't queue connection requests. Sometimes algorithms that use queuing can be more efficient. For example, an algorithm might maintain a given concurrency on the database server, such as allowing no more than N active transactions at the same time. If there are too many active transactions, the algorithm can put a new request in a queue and serve it from the first server that becomes "available" according to the criteria. Some connection pools support queuing algorithms.

Adding and removing servers in the pool

Adding a new server to the pool is usually not as simple as plugging it in and notifying the load balancer of its existence. You might think it'll be OK as long as it doesn't get flooded with connections, but that's not always true. Sometimes you can add load to a server slowly, but some servers whose caches are cold might be so slow that they shouldn't get *any* queries for a while.

When a server's caches are cold, even simple queries can take a long time to complete. If it takes 30 seconds to return the data a user needs to see for a page view, the server is unusable even for a small amount of traffic. You can avoid this problem by mirroring SELECT traffic from an active server for a while before you notify the load balancer about the new server. You can do this by reading and replaying the active server's log files on the newly started server.

You should configure the servers in the connection pool so that there is enough unused capacity to let you take servers out for maintenance, or to handle the load when servers fail. You need more than just "enough" capacity on each server.

Make sure your configuration limits are high enough to work when servers are out of the pool. For example, if you find that each MySQL server typically has 100 connections, you should set max_connections to 200 on each server in the pool. Then, even if half the servers fail, the pool should be able to handle the same number of connections as a whole.

Load Balancing with a Master and Multiple Slaves

The most common replication topology is a single master with multiple slaves. It can be difficult to move away from this architecture. Many applications assume there's a single destination for all writes, or that all data will always be available on a single server. Though this is not the most scalable architecture, there are ways you can use it to good effect with load balancing. This section examines some of those techniques:

Functional partitioning

You can stretch capacity quite a bit by configuring slaves or groups of slaves for particular purposes. Common functions you might consider separating are reporting and analytics, data warehousing, and full-text searching. You can find more ideas in "Custom Replication Solutions" on page 371.

Filtering and data partitioning

You can partition data among otherwise similar slaves with replication filters (see "Replication Filters" on page 360). This strategy can work well as long as your data is already separated into different databases or tables on the master. Unfortunately, there's no built-in way to filter at the level of individual rows. However, you could implement a row-level filtering scheme by replicating into a distribution master and using Blackhole tables with triggers to insert the rows into different tables based on a column's value.

You can even do more exotic things, such as replicating into Federated tables, but this will probably turn into a mess. Federated tables introduce interserver dependencies that are generally best avoided.

Even if you don't partition the data amongst the slaves, you can improve cache efficiency by partitioning reads instead of distributing them randomly. For instance, you might direct all reads for users whose names begin with the letters A–M to a given slave, and all reads for users whose names begin with N–Z to another slave. This helps use each machine's cache more fully, because repeated reads are more likely to find the relevant data in the cache. In the best case, where there are no writes, this strategy effectively gives you a total cache size the same as the two machine's cache sizes combined. In comparison, if you distribute the reads randomly among the slaves, every machine's cache essentially duplicates the data, and your total effective cache size is only as big as a single slave's cache, no matter how many slaves you have.

Moving parts of writes to a slave

The master doesn't always have to do all the work involved in writes. You can save a significant amount of redundant work for the master *and* the slaves by decomposing write queries and running parts of them on slaves. See "Excessive Replication Lag" on page 399 for more on this topic.

Guaranteeing a slave is caught up

If you want to run a certain process on the slave, and it needs to know that its data is current as of a certain point in time—even if it has to wait a while for that to happen—you can use the MASTER_POS_WAIT( ) function to block until the slave catches up to the desired point on the master. Alternatively, you can use a replication heartbeat to check for up-to-dateness, though this doesn't provide subsecond granularity. See "Measuring Slave Lag" on page 379 for more on this technique.

Write synchronization

You can also use `MASTER_POS_WAIT( )` to make sure your writes actually reach one or more slaves. If your application needs to emulate synchronous replication to guarantee data safety, it can cycle between each slave, running `MASTER_POS_WAIT( )` on each. This creates a "synchronization barrier" that can take a long time to pass if any of the slaves is far behind in replication, so it's a good idea to use it only when absolutely necessary. (You can also wait until just one slave receives the event if your goal is only to ensure that some slave has the event.)

High Availability

Most people consider a system to be available if it is responding to users. Availability might be a little more complex than that, however. An application can be responding, yet in "degraded" mode, if part of it has failed but it has enough built-in fault tolerance to continue running. You may also place an application in read-only mode for maintenance or in case of an emergency; whether this counts toward its "uptime" is up to you. Most users of photo-sharing sites, for instance, don't mind a brief period when they're unable to upload new photos; on the other hand, an ATM user doesn't want to see a "read-only for maintenance" message. The web site can be considered up, but the ATM is down.

Implementing high availability is actually very simple: you build in redundancy, and make your systems bring replacements online when something fails. The hard part is doing this quickly and reliably.

Planning for High Availability

Applications have vastly different availability needs. Before you set your heart on a certain uptime goal, ask yourself what you really need to achieve. Each increment of availability usually costs far more than the previous one; the ratio of availability to effort and cost is nonlinear.

The most important principle of high availability is to find and eliminate single points of failure in your system. Think through your application and try to identify any such points. Is it a hard drive, a server, a switch or router, or the power for one rack? Are your machines all in one data center, or are your "redundant" data centers provided by the same company? Any point in your system that isn't redundant is a single point of failure. Other common single points of failure are reliance on services such as DNS, a single network provider (check that your redundant network connections are really connected to different Internet backbones), and a single power grid.

Try to understand all of the components that affect availability, take a balanced view of the risks, and work on the biggest ones first. Some people work hard to build software that can handle any kind of hardware failure, but bugs in this kind of software can cause more downtime than it saves. Some people build "unsinkable" systems with all kinds of redundancy, but they forget that the data center can lose power or connectivity. Or maybe they completely forget about the possibility of malicious attackers or programmer mistakes that delete or corrupt data—a careless DROP TABLE can cause downtime, too.

You can identify high-priority risks by calculating your risk exposure, which is the probability of failure multiplied by the cost of failure. A simple spreadsheet of risks—with columns for the probability, the cost, the exposure—can help you prioritize your efforts.

You can't always eliminate single points of failure. Making a component redundant might not be possible because of some limitation you can't work around, such as a geographic, budgetary, or timing constraint.

Next, think about switching (or failing over) to a standby system in the event of a failure, upgrade, application modification, or scheduled maintenance. Anything that makes part of your application unavailable might require a failover plan, and you need to identify how fast that failover needs to be.

A related question is how quickly you need to replace the failed component after a failover. Until you restore the system's depleted standby capacity, you have less redundancy and extra risk. Thus, having a standby doesn't eliminate the need for timely replacement of failed components. How quickly can you build a new standby server, install its operating system, and give it a fresh copy of your data? Do you have enough standby machines? You might need more than one.

Another consideration is whether you'll lose any data, even if your application doesn't go offline. If a server has a truly catastrophic failure, you might lose at least some data, such as the last few transactions that were written to the (now lost) binary log and didn't make it to a slave's relay log. Can you tolerate this? Most applications can; the alternatives are usually expensive, complex, or have some performance overhead. For example, you can use Google's synchronous replication patches (more on this later), or you can place the binary log on a device that's replicated by DRBD so you won't lose it even if the system fails completely.

A clever application architecture can often reduce your availability needs, at least for part of the system, and thus make high availability easier to achieve. Separating critical and noncritical parts of your application can save you a lot of work and money, because it's much easier to provide redundancy and high availability for a smaller system.

In general, making an application highly available and preventing data loss is difficult and expensive past a certain point, so we advise setting realistic goals and avoiding overengineering. Fortunately, the effort required to build two or three nines of uptime may not be that high, depending on the application.

Adding Redundancy

Adding redundancy to your system can take two forms: adding spare capacity and duplicating components.

It's actually quite easy to add spare capacity—you can use any of the techniques we've mentioned throughout this chapter. One way to increase availability is to create a cluster or pool of servers and add a load-balancing solution. If one server fails, the other servers take over its load. It is generally a good idea to underutilize your components if you can, because it gives you much more "headroom" to handle performance problems caused either by increased load or by component failures.

For many purposes, you will need to duplicate components and have a standby ready to take over if the main component fails. A duplicated component can be a simple as a spare network card, router, or hard drive—whatever you think is most likely to fail.

Duplicating entire MySQL servers is a little harder, because a server is useless without its data. That means you must ensure that your standby servers have access to the primary server's data. The following sections discuss some ways you can accomplish this.

Shared-storage architectures

Shared storage is a way to remove some single points of failure, usually with a SAN (see "Storage Area Networks" on page 325 for more on this). With this strategy, the active server mounts the filesystem and operates normally. If the active server dies, the standby server can mount the same filesystem, perform any necessary recovery operations, and start MySQL on the failed server's files. This process is logically no different from fixing the failed server, except that it's much faster because the standby server is already booted and ready to go. Filesystem checks and InnoDB recovery are the biggest delays you're likely to encounter.

Shared storage helps eliminate some data loss scenarios, but it is still a single point of failure. If it goes down, the whole system goes down. And if the failure corrupts your data files, the standby server might not be able to recover anyway. We highly recommend using InnoDB or another transactional storage engine with shared storage. A crash will almost certainly corrupt MyISAM tables, and repairing them can take a long time.

Replicated-disk architectures

A replicated disk is another way to keep your data safe in case of a catastrophic failure on a master server. The disk replication most commonly used for MySQL is DRBD (*http://www.drbd.org*), in combination with the tools from the Linux-HA project (more on this later).

DRBD is synchronous, block-level replication implemented as a Linux kernel module. It copies every block from a primary device over a network card to another server's block device (the secondary device), and writes it there before committing the block on the primary device.*

DRBD runs only in active-passive mode. The passive device is a hot standby, and you cannot access it—not even in read-only mode—unless it becomes primary. Because writes must complete on the secondary device before the writes on the primary are considered complete, the secondary device must perform at least as well as the primary, or it will limit write performance on the primary. Also, if you're using DRBD to have an interchangeable standby in the event that the primary fails, the standby server's hardware should match the primary server's.

If the active server fails, you can promote the secondary device to be the primary. Because DRBD replicates the disk at the block layer, however, the filesystem may become inconsistent. This means it's best to use a journaling filesystem for fast recovery. Once recovery is complete, MySQL will probably need to run its own recovery as well. If the first server recovers, it resyncs its device with the new primary device and assumes the secondary role.

In terms of how you actually implement failover, DRBD is similar to a SAN: you have a hot standby machine, and you make it begin serving from the same data as the failed machine. The biggest difference is that it is replicated storage—not shared storage—so with DRBD you're serving a replicated copy of the data, while with a SAN you're serving the same data from the same physical device as the failed machine. In both cases, the MySQL server's caches will be empty when you start it on the standby machine. In contrast, a replication slave's caches are likely to be at least partially warmed up.

DRBD has some nice features and capabilities that can prevent problems common to clustering software. An example is split-brain syndrome, which occurs when two nodes promote themselves to primary simultaneously. You can configure DRBD so it won't let split-brain syndrome happen. However, DRBD isn't a perfect solution for every need. Let's take a look at its drawbacks:

- DRBD's failover is not subsecond. It will generally require at least five seconds to promote the secondary device to primary, not including any necessary filesystem and MySQL recovery.

- It's expensive because you must run it in active-passive mode. The hot standby server's replicated device is not usable for any other tasks while it's in passive mode. Whether this is really a shortcoming depends on your point of

---

* You can actually adjust the level of synchronization for DRDB. You can set it to be asynchronous, to wait until the remote device receives the data, or to block until the remote device writes the data to disk. Also, it is strongly recommended to dedicate a network card to DRBD.

view. If you want truly high availability and can't tolerate degraded service when there's a failure, you can't place more than one machine's worth of load on any two machines, because if you did, you wouldn't be able to handle the load if one of them failed. You can use the standby server for something else, such as a replication slave, but you'll still waste some resources.

- It's practically unusable for MyISAM tables, because they take too long to check and repair. MyISAM is not a good choice for any installation that requires high availability; use InnoDB or another storage engine that has good recovery performance instead.

- It does not replace backups. If your data becomes corrupt on disk due to malicious interference, mistakes, bugs, or hardware failures, DRBD will not help: the replicated data will be a perfect copy of the corrupted original. You need backups (or time-delayed MySQL replication) to protect against these problems.

Our favorite way to use DRBD is to replicate only the device that holds the binary logs. If the active node fails, you can start a log server on the passive node and use the recovered binary logs to bring all of the failed master's slaves up to the latest binary log position (see "Creating a log server" on page 374). You can then choose one of the slaves and promote it to master, replacing the failed system.

Synchronous MySQL replication

In synchronous replication, a transaction cannot complete on the master until it commits on one or more slave servers. There are various levels of synchronous replication, which have several common names. MySQL does not offer synchronous replication at the time of this writing, but there are third-party solutions. One such solution is Google's internal patches.

Google has an extensive set of patches for MySQL and InnoDB, which add many extra features. Among them is semisynchronous replication, which causes a replication master to wait until at least one slave has received the event before it commits a transaction. Google has released its patches for MySQL 4.0.26 and 5.0.37. You can download the patches and several related tools at *http://code.google.com/p/google-mysql-tools*.

Another option is Solid Information Technology's high-availability technology, which it has ported to solidDB for MySQL. This solution has several advantages over MySQL replication, including:

- The slave cannot fall behind the master.

- Solid uses multiple threads for writing on the slave, improving replication performance in many scenarios.

- The "safeness" level during replication is user-configurable. In 1-Safe mode, transactions return once they are committed on the master. In 2-Safe mode, transactions do not return until after they have also been committed on the slave, providing an extra level of safety in the event of a failure.

However, it works only with the solidDB storage engine, not with MyISAM, InnoDB, or any other storage engine. Solid may port more of its high-availability technology for a future release.

In addition to these two variations on the MySQL server itself, you can use a middleware solution such as Continuent.

Failover and Failback

Failover is the process of removing a failed server and using another server instead. This is one of the most important parts of a high-availability architecture.

Before we go any further, let's define a few terms. We use "failover" in a standard way; some people use "fallback" as a synonym. Sometimes people also say "switchover" to denote a switch that's planned instead of a response to a failure.

We also use the term "failback" to indicate the reverse of failover. If you have failback capability, failover can be a two-way process: when server A fails and server B replaces it, you can repair server A and fail back to it.

Failover comes in many flavors. We've already discussed several of them, because load balancing and failover are similar in many ways, and the line between them is a bit fuzzy. In general, we think a full failover solution, at a minimum, needs to be able to monitor and automatically replace a server. This should ideally be transparent to the application. Load balancing need not provide this capability.

In the Unix world, failover is usually accomplished with the tools provided by the High Availability Linux project (*http://linux-ha.org*), which—despite their creator's name, run on many Unix-like operating systems. The heartbeat tool provides monitoring, and various other tools accomplish IP takeover and load-balancing functionality. You can combine them with DRBD and/or LVS.

The most important part of failover is failback. If you can't switch back and forth between servers at will, failover is a dead end and only postpones downtime. This is why we like symmetrical replication topologies, such as the dual-master configuration, and we dislike ring replication with three or more co-masters. If the configuration is symmetrical, failover and failback are the same operation in opposite directions. (It's worth mentioning that DRBD has built-in failback capabilities.)

In some applications, it's critical that failover and failback be as fast and atomic as possible. Even when it's not, it's still a good idea not to rely on things that are out of your control, such as DNS changes or application configuration files. Some of the worst problems don't show up until a system becomes larger, when issues such as forced application restarts and the need for atomicity rear their heads. Anyone who's ever tried to atomically update code across many servers knows it's difficult.

Because load balancing and failover are closely related, and the same piece of hardware or software often serves both purposes, we suggest that any load-balancing technique you choose provide failover capabilities as well. This is the real reason we suggested you avoid DNS or code changes for load balancing. If you use these strategies for load balancing, you'll create extra work: you'll have to rewrite the affected code later when you need high availability.

The following sections discuss some common failover techniques.

Promoting a slave or switching roles

Promoting a slave to a master, or switching the active and passive roles in a master-master replication setup, is an important part of many failover solutions for MySQL. See "Changing Masters" on page 382 for detailed explanations of how to accomplish this.

Virtual IP addresses or IP takeover

You can achieve high availability by assigning a logical IP address to a MySQL instance that you expect to perform certain services. If the MySQL instance fails, you can move the IP address to a different MySQL server. This is essentially the same approach we wrote about earlier, in "Moving IP addresses" on page 441, except that now we're using it to provide failover instead of load balancing.

The benefit of this approach is its transparency for the application. It will abort existing connections, but it doesn't require you to change your application's configuration. It is also possible to move the IP address atomically, so all applications see the change at the same time. This can be especially important when a server is "flapping" between available and unavailable states.

The downsides are as follows:

- You need to either define all IP addresses on the same network segment, or use network bridging.
- Changing the IP address requires root access to the system.
- Sometimes you need to update address resolution protocol (ARP) caches. Some network devices may cache ARP entries for too long, and may not instantly switch an IP address to a different MAC address.
- You need to make sure the network hardware supports fast IP takeover. Some hardware requires MAC address cloning for this to work properly.
- It's possible for a server to keep its IP address even though it's not fully functional, so you may need to physically shut it down or disconnect it from the network.

Floating IP addresses and IP takeover work well for failover between machines that are local to each other—that is, on the same subnet.

The MySQL Master-Master Replication Manager

The MySQL Master-Master Replication Manager tool (*http://code.google.com/p/ mysql-master-master*), or *mmm* for short, is a set of scripts that perform monitoring, failover, and management of master-master replication configurations. Despite its name, it can automate the failover process for other topologies as well, including simple master-slave and master-master configurations with one or many slaves. It uses the abstraction of a *role*, such as reader or writer, and a mixture of permanent and floating IP addresses. It notices when a server fails and reassigns IP addresses to "move the roles" if necessary. It can also help with planned failover for maintenance and other tasks.

The usual setup is a pair of co-master MySQL servers, with an *mmmd_agent* process running on each one. You need to configure each with some basic information, such as IP addresses, usernames, and passwords. Each of the *mmmd_agent* processes is aware of its peer.

There's also a separate monitoring node. This shouldn't run on the same hardware as either of the co-masters. It watches both nodes and handles failover—that is, moving the writer role. There are a total of three virtual IP addresses you can use to connect to the MySQL servers: two for the reader role and one for the writer. You can use the *mmm_control* program to view and control the MySQL instances and to move the writer role as desired.

You can combine *mmm* with other techniques (such as Google's semisynchronous replication patches, which we mentioned earlier in this chapter) to further increase reliability and availability.

Middleman solutions

You can use proxies, port forwarding, network address translation (NAT), and hardware load balancers for failover and failback. However, they do introduce a single point of failure themselves, and you'll need to make them redundant to avoid that problem.

One of the nice things you can do with such a solution is make a remote data center appear to be on the same network as your application. This lets you use techniques such as floating IP addresses to make your application begin communicating with an entirely different data center. You can configure each application server in each data center to connect through its own middleman, each of which routes traffic to the machines in the active data center. Figure 9-7 illustrates this configuration.

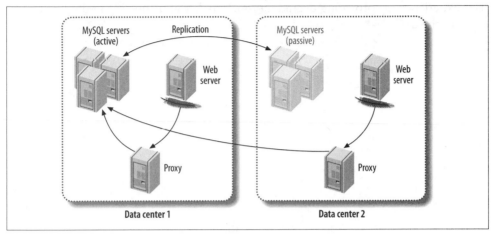

Figure 9-7. Using MySQL Proxy to route MySQL connections across data centers

If the active data center's MySQL installation fails entirely, the middleman can route the traffic to the pool of servers in the other data center, and the application never needs to know the difference.

The major disadvantage of this configuration is the high latency between the Apache server in one data center and the MySQL servers in the other data center. To alleviate this problem, you can run the web server in redirect mode. This will redirect traffic to the data center that houses the pool of active MySQL servers. You can also achieve this with an HTTP proxy.

Figure 9-7 shows MySQL Proxy as the means of connecting to the MySQL servers, but you can combine this approach with many middleman architectures, such as LVS and hardware load balancers.

Handling failover in the application

Sometimes it's easier or more flexible to let the application handle failover. For example, if the application experiences an error that isn't normally detected by an outside observer, such as an error message indicating database corruption, it can handle the failover process itself.

Although integrating the failover process into the application may seem attractive, it tends not to work well. Most applications have many components, such as *cron* jobs, configuration files, and scripts written in different programming languages.

Integrating failover into the application can therefore become unwieldy, especially as the application grows and becomes more complicated.

However, it's a good idea to build monitoring into your application and let it *initiate* the failover process if it needs to. The application should also be able to manage the user experience, by providing degrading functionality and showing appropriate messages to the user.

Application-Level Optimization

This book would not be complete without a chapter on optimizing the applications that connect to MySQL, because they are frequently to blame for many performance problems that seem to be caused by MySQL. We focus mostly on optimizing MySQL in this book, but we don't want you to miss the bigger picture. There is no way to optimize MySQL enough to compensate for poor application design. In fact, sometimes the answer is to take operations entirely out of MySQL and do them in the application or use other tools, which may offer much better performance.

This chapter isn't a reference for how to build a high-performance application, but we hope it will help you avoid some common mistakes that can hurt MySQL's performance. We focus on web applications, because MySQL is so often used for them.

Application Performance Overview

The search for faster performance begins very simply: the application is taking too long to respond to requests, and you need to do something about it. But what exactly is the problem? The common bottlenecks are slow queries, locks, CPU saturation, network latency, and file I/O. Any of these can become a problem if the application is misconfigured or uses resources inappropriately.

Find the Source of the Problem

The first task is to find the culprit. This will be much easier if you've added profiling capabilities to your application. If you've done this but you can't see what's causing the slow performance, you may need to add more profiling calls. Look for places where a resource is either slow or requested many times.

If your application is waiting because it's CPU-bound and you have high concurrency, the "lost time" we mentioned in "Profiling an Application" on page 55 might be the problem. For this reason, it's sometimes helpful to profile under limited concurrency conditions.

Network latency can use up a lot of time, even on a local network. Application-level profiling already includes the network latency, so you should be able to see the effects of network round-trips in your profiling system. For example, if a page executes 1,000 queries, just half a millisecond of network latency will add up to half a second of response time. This is a lot for a high-performance application.

If your application-level profiling is thorough, it should not be hard to find the source of your problem. If you don't have profiling built in, add it if possible. If you can't add it, try some of the suggestions in "When You Can't Add Profiling Code" on page 76. This might be easier and faster than chasing dead-end theories about what's causing the slowdown.

Look for Common Problems

We see the same problems over and over again in applications, often because people have used poorly designed off-the-shelf systems or popular frameworks that simplify development. Although it's sometimes easier and faster to use something you didn't build yourself, it also adds risk if you don't really know what it's doing under the hood. Here's a list of things you should check:

- What's using the CPU, disk, network, and memory resources on each of the machines involved? Do the numbers look reasonable to you? If not, check the basics for the applications that are hogging resources. Configuration is sometimes the simplest way to solve problems. For example, if Apache runs out of memory because it creates 1,000 worker processes that each need 50 MB of memory, you can configure the application to require fewer Apache workers. You can also configure the system to use less memory for each process.

- Is the application really using all the data it's getting? Fetching 1,000 rows but displaying only 10 and throwing away the rest is a common mistake. (However, if the application caches the other 990 rows for later use, it might be an intentional optimization.)

- Is the application doing processing that ought to be done in the database, or vice versa? Two examples are fetching all rows from a table to count them and doing complex string manipulations in the database. Databases are good at counting rows, while application languages are good at regular expressions. Use the best tool for the job.

- Is the application doing too many queries? Object-relational mapping (ORM) query interfaces that "protect programmers from having to write SQL" are often to blame. The database server is designed to match data from multiple tables. Remove the nested loops in the code and write a join instead.

- Is the application doing too few queries? We know, we just said doing too many queries can be a problem. But sometimes "manual joins" and similar practices can be a *good* idea, because they can permit more granular and efficient caching, less locking (especially for MyISAM), and sometimes even faster execution when you emulate a hash join in application code (MySQL's nested loop join method is not always efficient).

- Is the application connecting to MySQL unnecessarily? If you can get the data from the cache, don't connect.

- Is the application connecting too many times to the same MySQL instance, perhaps because different parts of the application open their own connections? It's usually a better idea to reuse the same connection throughout.

- Is the application doing a lot of "garbage" queries? A common example is selecting the desired database before each query. It might be a good idea to always connect to a specific database and use fully qualified names for tables. (This also makes it easier to analyze queries from the log or via SHOW PROCESSLIST, because you can execute them without needing to change the database.) "Preparing" the connection is another common problem. The Java driver in particular does a lot of things during preparation, most of which you can disable. Another common garbage query is SET NAMES UTF8, which is the wrong way to do things anyway (it does not change the client library's character set; it affects only the server). If your application uses a specific character set for most of its work, you can avoid the need to change the character set by configuring it as the default.

- Does the application use a connection pool? This can be both a good and a bad thing. It helps limit the number of connections, which is good when connections aren't used for many queries (Ajax applications are a typical example). However, it can have side effects, such as applications interfering with each other's transactions, temporary tables, connection-specific settings, and user-defined variables.

- Does the application use persistent connections? These can result in way too many connections to MySQL. They're generally a bad idea, except if the cost of connecting to MySQL is very high because of a slow network, if the connection will be used only for one or two fast queries, or if you're connecting so frequently that you're running out of local port numbers on the client (see "Network Configuration" on page 328 for more about this). If you configure MySQL correctly, you may not need persistent connections. Use skip-name-resolve to prevent reverse DNS lookups and ensure that thread_cache is set high enough.

- Is the application holding connections open even when it's not using them? If so—particularly if it connects to many servers—it may be consuming connections that other processes need. For example, suppose you're connecting to 10 MySQL servers. Getting 10 connections from an Apache process isn't a problem, but only one of them will really be doing anything at any given time. The other nine will spend a lot of time in the Sleep state. If one server slows down, or there's a long network call, the other servers can suffer because they're out of connections. The solution is to control how the application uses connections.

For example, you can batch operations to each MySQL instance in turn, and close each connection before querying the next one. If you're doing time-consuming operations, such as calls to a web service, you can even close the MySQL connection, perform the time-consuming work, then reopen the MySQL connection and continue working with the database.

The difference between persistent connections and connection pooling can be confusing. Persistent connections can cause the same side effects as connection pooling, because a reused connection is stateful in either case.

However, connection pools don't usually result in as many connections to the server, because they queue and share connections among processes. Persistent connections, on the other hand, are created on a per-process basis and can't be shared among processes.

Connection pools also allow more control over connection policies than shared connections. You can configure a pool to autoextend, but the usual practice is to queue connection requests when the pool is completely busy. This makes the connection requests wait on the application server, rather than overload the MySQL server with too many connections.

There are many ways to make queries and connections faster, but the general rule is that avoiding them altogether is better than trying to speed them up.

Web Server Issues

Apache is the most popular server software for web applications. It works well for many purposes, but when used badly it can consume a lot of resources. The most common issues are keeping its processes alive too long, and using it for a mixture of purposes instead of optimizing it separately for each type of work.

Apache is usually used with mod_php, mod_perl, and mod_python in a "prefork" configuration. Preforking dedicates a process for each request. Because the PHP, Perl, and Python scripts can be demanding, it's not uncommon for each process to use 50 or 100 MB of memory. When a request completes, it returns most of this memory to the operating system, but not all of it. Apache keeps the process open and reuses it for future requests. This means that if the next request is for a static file, such as a CSS file or an image, you'll wind up with a big fat process serving a simple request. This is why it's dangerous to use Apache as a general-purpose web server. It *is* general-purpose, but if you specialize it, you'll get much better performance.

The other major problem is that processes can be kept busy for a long time if you have Keep-Alive enabled. And even if you don't, some of the processes might be staying alive too long, "spoon-feeding" content to a client that is fetching the data slowly.[*]

---

[*] Spoon-feeding occurs when a client makes an HTTP request but then doesn't fetch the result quickly. Until the client fetches the entire result, the HTTP connection—and thus the Apache process—stays alive.

People also often make the mistake of leaving the default set of Apache modules enabled. You can trim Apache's footprint by removing modules you don't need. It's simple: just review the Apache configuration file and comment out unwanted modules, then restart Apache. You can also remove unused PHP modules from your *php. ini* file.

The bottom line is that if you create an all-purpose Apache configuration that faces the Web directly, you're likely to end up with many heavyweight Apache processes. These will waste resources on your web server. They can also keep a lot of connections open to MySQL, wasting resources on MySQL too. Here are some ways you can reduce the load on your servers:[*]

- Don't use Apache to serve static content, or at least use a different Apache instance. Popular alternatives are *lighttpd* and *nginx*.

- Use a caching proxy server, such as Squid or Varnish, to keep requests from ever reaching your web servers. Even if you can't cache full pages on this level, you may be able to cache most of a page and use technologies such as edge side includes (ESI; see *http://www.esi.org*) to embed the small dynamic portion of the page into the cached static portion.

- Set an expiration policy on both dynamic and static content. You can use caching proxies such as Squid to invalidate content explicitly. Wikipedia uses this technique to remove articles from caches when they change.

- Sometimes you might need to change the application so that you can use longer expiration times. For example, if you tell the browser to cache CSS and JavaScript files forever and then release a change to the site's HTML, the pages might render badly. You can version the files explicitly with a unique filename for each revision. For example, you can customize your web site publishing script to copy the CSS files to */css/123_frontpage.css*, where *123* is the Subversion revision number. You can do the same thing for image filenames—never reuse a filename, and your pages will never break when you upgrade them, no matter how long the browser caches them.

- Don't let Apache spoon-feed the client. It's not just slow; it also makes denial-of-service attacks easy. Hardware load balancers typically do buffering, so Apache can finish quickly and the load balancer can spoon-feed the client from the buffer. You can also use *lighttpd*, Squid, or Apache in event-driven mode in front of the application.

- Enable *gzip* compression. It's very cheap for modern CPUs, and it saves a lot of traffic. If you want to save on CPU cycles, you can cache and serve the compressed version of the page with a lightweight server such as *lighttpd*.

---

[*] A good book on how to optimize web applications is *High Performance Web Sites* by Steve Souders (O'Reilly). Though it's mostly about how to make web sites faster from the client's point of view, the practices he advocates are good for your servers, too.

- Don't configure Apache with a Keep-Alive for long-distance connections, because that will keep fat Apache processes alive for a long time. Instead, let a server-side proxy handle the Keep-Alive, and shield Apache from the client. It's OK to configure the connections between the proxy and Apache with a Keep-Alive, because the proxy will use only a few connections to fetch data from Apache. Figure 10-1 illustrates the difference.

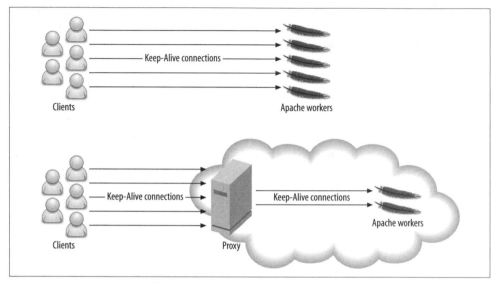

Figure 10-1. A proxy can shield Apache from long-lived Keep-Alive connections, resulting in fewer Apache workers

These tactics should keep Apache processes short-lived, so you don't end up with more processes than you need. However, some operations may still cause an Apache process to stay alive for a long time and consume a lot of resources. An example is a query to an external resource that has high latency, such as a remote web service. This problem is often unsolvable.

Finding the Optimal Concurrency

Every web server has an *optimal concurrency*—that is, an optimal number of concurrent connections that will result in requests being processed as quickly as possible, without overloading your systems. A little trial and error can be required to find this "magic number," but it's worth the effort.

It's common for a high-traffic web site to handle thousands of connections to the web server at the same time. However, only a few of these connections need to be actively processing requests. The others may be reading requests, handling file uploads, spoon-feeding content, or simply awaiting further requests from the client.

As concurrency increases, there's a point at which the server reaches its peak throughput. After that, the throughput levels off and often starts to decrease. More importantly, the response time (latency) starts to increase.

To see why, consider what happens when you have a single CPU and the server receives 100 requests simultaneously. One second of CPU time is required to process each request. Assuming a perfect operating system scheduler with no overhead, and no context switching overhead, the requests will need a total of 100 CPU seconds to complete.

What's the best way to serve the requests? You can queue them one after another, or you can run them in parallel and switch between them, giving each request equal time before switching to the next. In both cases, the throughput is one request per second. However, the average latency is 50 seconds if they're queued (concurrency = 1), and 100 seconds if they're run in parallel (concurrency = 100). In practice, the average latency would be even higher for parallel execution, because of the switching cost.

For a CPU-bound workload, the optimal concurrency is equal to the number of CPUs (or CPU cores). However, processes are not always runnable, because they make blocking calls such as I/O, database queries, and network requests. Therefore, the optimal concurrency is usually higher than the number of CPUs.

You can estimate the optimal concurrency, but it requires accurate profiling. It's usually easier to experiment with different concurrency values and see what gives the peak throughput without degrading response time.

Caching

Caching is vital for high-load applications. A typical web application serves a lot of content that costs much more to generate than it costs to cache (including the cost of checking and expiring the cache), so caching can usually improve performance by orders of magnitude. The trick is to find the right combination of granularity and expiration policies. You also need to decide what content to cache and where to cache it.

A typical high-load application has many layers of caching. Caching doesn't just happen in your servers: it happens at every step along the way, including the user's web browser (that's what content expiration headers are for). In general, the closer the cache is to the client, the more resources it saves and the more effective it is. Serving an image from the browser's cache is better than serving it from the web server's memory, which is better than reading it from the server's disk. Each type of cache has unique characteristics, such as size and latency; and we examine some of them in the following sections.

You can think about caches in two broad categories: *passive caches* and *active caches*. Passive caches do nothing but store and return data. When you request something from a passive cache, either you get the result or the cache tells you "that doesn't exist." An example of a passive cache is *memcached*.

In contrast, an active cache does something when there's a miss. It usually passes your request on to some other part of the application, which generates the requested result. The active cache then stores the result and returns it. The Squid caching proxy server is an active cache.

When you design your application, you usually want your caches to be active (also called *transparent*), because they hide the check-generate-store logic from the application. You can build active caches on top of passive caches.

Caching Doesn't Always Help

You need to make sure that caching really improves performance, because it might not help at all. For example, in practice it's often faster to serve content from *lighttpd*'s memory than to serve it from a caching proxy. This is especially true if the proxy's cache is on disk.

The reason is simple: caching has its own overhead. There's the overhead of checking the cache, and serving the data from the cache if there's a hit. There's also the overhead of invalidating the cache and storing data in it. Caching is helpful only if these costs are less than the cost of generating and serving the data without a cache.

If you know the costs of all these operations, you can calculate how much the cache helps. The cost without the cache is the cost of generating the data for each request. The cost with the cache is the cost of checking the cache, plus the probability of a cache miss times the cost of generating the data, plus the probability of a cache hit times the cost of serving the data from the cache.

If the cost with the cache is lower than without, it's an improvement, but that's not guaranteed. Also bear in mind that, as in the case of serving data from *lighttpd*'s memory rather than from the proxy's on-disk cache, some caches are cheaper than others.

Caching Below the Application

The MySQL server has its own internal caches, and you can build your own cache and summary tables too. You can custom design your cache tables so that they're most useful for filtering, sorting, joining to other tables, counting, or any other purpose. Cache tables are also more persistent than many application-level caches, because they'll survive a server restart.

We wrote about these cache strategies in Chapters 3 and 4, so in this chapter, we focus on caching at the application level and above.

Application-Level Caching

An application-level cache typically stores data in memory on the same machine, or across the network in another machine's memory.

Application-level caching can be more efficient than caching at a lower level, because the application can store partially computed results in the cache. Thus, the cache saves two types of work: fetching the data, and doing computations on it. A good example is blocks of HTML text. The application can generate HTML snippets such as the top news headlines, and cache them. Subsequent page views can then simply insert this cached text into the page. In general, the more you process the data before you cache it, the more work you save when there's a cache hit.

The disadvantage is that the cache hit rate can be lower, and the cache can use more memory. Suppose you need 50 different versions of the top news headlines, so the user sees different content depending on where she lives. You'll need enough memory to store all 50 of them, fewer requests will hit any given version of the headlines, and invalidation can be more complicated.

There are many types of application caches. Here are a few:

Local caches

These caches are usually small and live only in the process's memory for the duration of the request. They're useful for avoiding a repeated request for a resource when it's needed more than once. There's nothing fancy about this type of cache: it's usually just a variable or hash table in the application code. For example, suppose you need to display a user's name, and you know the user's ID. You can build a get_name_from_id( ) function and add caching to it like this:

```php
<?php
function get_name_from_id($user_id) {
    static $name; // static makes the variable persist
    if ( !$name ) {
        // Fetch name from database
    }
    return $name;
}
?>
```

If you're using Perl, the Memoize module is the standard way to cache the results of function calls:

```perl
use Memoize qw(memoize);
memoize 'get_name_from_id';
sub get_name_from_id {
    my ( $user_id ) = @_;
    my $name = # get name from database
    return $name;
}
```

These techniques are simple, but they can save your application a lot of work.

Local shared-memory caches

These caches are medium-size (a few GB), fast, and hard to synchronize across multiple machines. They're good for small, semi-static bits of data. Examples include lists of the cities in each state, the partitioning function (mapping table) for a sharded data store, or data that you can invalidate with time-to-live (TTL) policies. The biggest benefit of shared memory is that accessing it is very fast—usually much faster than accessing any type of remote cache.

Distributed memory caches

The best-known example of a distributed memory cache is *memcached*. Distributed caches are much larger than local shared-memory caches and are easy to grow. Only one copy of each bit of cached data is created, so you don't waste memory and introduce consistency problems by caching the same data many places. Distributed memory is great for storing shared objects, such as user profiles, comments, and HTML snippets.

These caches have much higher latency than local shared-memory caches, though, so the most efficient way to use them is with multiple-get operations (i.e., getting many objects in a single round-trip). They also require you to plan how you'll add more nodes, and what to do if one of the nodes dies. In both cases, the application needs to decide how to distribute or redistribute cached objects across the nodes.

Consistent caching is important to avoid performance problems when you add a server to or remove a server from your cache cluster. There's a consistent caching library for *memcached* at *http://www.audioscrobbler.net/development/ketama/*.

On-disk caches

Disks are slow, so caching on disk is best for persistent objects, objects that are hard to fit in memory, or static content (pregenerated custom images, for example).

One very useful trick with on-disk caches and web servers is to use 404 error handlers to catch cache misses. Suppose your web application shows a custom-generated image in the header, based on the user's name ("Welcome back, John!"). You can refer to the image as */images/welcomeback/john.jpg*. If the image doesn't exist, it will cause a 404 error and trigger the error handler. The error handler can generate the image, store it on the disk, and either issue a redirect or just stream the image back to the browser. Further requests will just return the image from the file.

You can use this trick for many types of content. For example, instead of caching the latest headlines as a block of HTML, you can store them in a JavaScript file and then refer to */latest_headlines.js* in the web page's header.

Cache invalidation is easy: just delete the file. You can implement TTL invalidation by running a periodic job that deletes files created more than *N* minutes ago.

And if you want to limit the cache size, you can implement a least recently used (LRU) invalidation policy by deleting files in order of their last access time.

Invalidation based on last access time requires you to enable the access time option in your filesystem's mount options. (You actually do this by omitting the noatime mount option.) If you do this, you should use an in-memory filesystem to avoid a lot of disk activity. See "Choosing a Filesystem" on page 331 for more on this topic.

Cache Control Policies

Caches create the same problem as denormalizing your database design: they duplicate data, which means there are multiple places to update the data, and you have to figure out how to avoid reading bad data. The following are several of the most common cache control policies:

TTL (time to live)
> The cached object is stored with an expiration date; you can either remove the object with a purge process when that date arrives, or leave it until the next time something accesses it (at which time you should replace it with a fresh version). This invalidation policy is best for data that changes rarely or doesn't have to be fresh.

Explicit invalidation
> If stale data is not acceptable, the process that updates the source data can invalidate the old version in the cache. There are two variations of this policy: *write-invalidate* and *write-update*. The write-invalidate policy is simple: you just mark the cached data as expired (and optionally purge it from the cache). The write-update policy involves a little more work, because you have to replace the old cache entry with the updated data. However, it can be very beneficial, especially if it is expensive to generate the cached data (which the writer process might already have). If you update the cached data, future requests won't have to wait for the application to generate it. If you do invalidations in the background, such as TTL-based invalidations, you can generate new versions of the invalidated data in a process that's completely detached from any user request.

Invalidation on read
> Instead of invalidating stale data when you change the source data from which it's derived, you can store some information that lets you determine whether the data has expired when you read it from the cache. This has a significant advantage over explicit invalidation: it has a fixed cost that you can spread out over time. Suppose you invalidate an object upon which a million cached objects depend. If you invalidate on write, you have to invalidate a million things in the cache in one hit, which could take a long time even if you have an efficient way to find them. If you invalidate on read, the write can complete immediately, and

each of a million reads will be delayed slightly. This spreads out the cost of the invalidation and helps avoid spikes of load and long latencies.

One of the simplest ways to do invalidation on read is with *object versioning*. With this approach, when you store an object in the cache, you also store the current version number or timestamp of the data upon which it depends. For example, suppose you're caching statistics about a user's blog posts, including the number of posts the user has made. When you cache the blog_stats object, you store the user's current version number with it, because the statistics are dependent on the user.

Whenever you update some data that also depends on the user, you update the user's version number. Suppose the user's version is initially 0, and you generate and cache the statistics. When the user publishes a blog post, you increase the user's version to 1 (you'd store this with the blog post too, though we don't really need it for this example). Then, when you need to display the statistics, you compare the cached blog_stats object's version to the cached user's version. Because the user's version is greater than the object's version, you know that the statistics are stale and you need to recompute them.

This is a pretty coarse way to invalidate content, because it assumes that every bit of data that's dependent on the user also interacts with all other data. That's not always true. If a user edits a blog post, for example, you'll increment the user's version, and that will invalidate the stored statistics even though the statistics (the number of blog posts) didn't really change. The tradeoff is simplicity. A simple cache invalidation policy isn't just easier to build, it might be more efficient too.

Object versioning is a simplified approach to a *tagged cache*, which can handle more complex dependencies. A tagged cache knows about different kinds of dependencies and tracks versions separately for each of them. To return to the book club example from the previous chapter, you could make the cached comments dependent on the user's version and the book's version by tagging the comments with these version numbers: user_ver=1234 and book_ver=5678. If either version changes, you'd refresh the cached comments.

Cache Object Hierarchies

Storing objects in a cache hierarchically can help with retrieval, invalidation, and memory usage. Instead of caching just objects, you can cache the object IDs, as well as the groups of object IDs that you commonly retrieve together.

A search result on an e-commerce web site is a good example of this technique. A search might return a list of matching products, complete with names, descriptions, thumbnail photos, and prices. Caching the entire list would be inefficient: other searches would be likely to include some of the same products, resulting in duplicate data and wasted memory. That strategy would also make it hard to find and invalidate search results when a product's price changes, because you'd have to look inside each list to see which ones include the updated product.

Instead of caching the list, you can cache minimal information about the search, such as the number of results returned and a list of product IDs. You can then cache each product separately. This solves both problems: it doesn't duplicate any results, and it makes it easy to invalidate the cache at the granularity of individual products.

The drawback is that you have to retrieve multiple objects from the cache, instead of getting the entire search result at once. However, storing the list of product IDs for the search result makes this efficient. Now a cache hit returns the list of IDs, which you can use for a second call to the cache. The second call can return multiple products if the cache lets you get multiple results with a single call (*memcached* supports this through the mget( ) call).

If you're not careful, this approach could cause odd results. Suppose you use a TTL policy to invalidate search results, and you invalidate individual products explicitly when they change. Now imagine that a product's description changes so it no longer contains the keywords that matched a search, but the search isn't old enough to have expired from the cache. Your users will see stale search results, because the cached search will refer to the product even though it no longer matches the search keywords.

This isn't usually a problem for most applications. If your application can't tolerate it, you can use version-based caching and store the product versions with the results when you perform a search. When you find a search result in the cache, you can compare each product's version in the search results to the current (cached) version. If any product is stale, you can repeat the search and recache the results.

Pregenerating Content

In addition to caching bits of data at the application level, you can prerequest some pages with background processes and store the results as static pages. If your pages are dynamic, you can pregenerate parts of the pages and use a technique such as server-side includes to build the final pages. This can help to reduce the size and cost of the pregenerated content, because you might otherwise duplicate a lot of content due to minor variations in how the constituent pieces are assembled into the final page.

Caching pregenerated content can take a lot of space, and it's not always possible to pregenerate everything. As with any form of caching, the most important pieces of content to pregenerate are those that are requested the most, so you can do on-demand generation with the 404 error handlers we mentioned earlier in this chapter.

Pregenerated content sometimes benefits from being stored on an in-memory file-system to avoid disk I/O.

Extending MySQL

If MySQL can't do what you need, one possibility is to extend its capabilities. We won't show you how to do that, but we want to mention some of the possibilities. If you're interested in exploring any of these avenues further, there are good resources online, and there are books available on many of the topics.

When we say "MySQL can't do what you need," we mean two things: MySQL can't do it at all, or MySQL can do it, but in a slow or awkward way that's not good enough. Either is a reason to look at extending MySQL. The good news is that MySQL is becoming more and more modular and general-purpose. For example, MySQL 5.1 has a lot of useful plug-in functionality; it even allows storage engines to be plug-ins, so you don't need to compile them into the server.

Storage engines are a great way to extend MySQL for a special purpose. Brian Aker has written a skeleton storage engine and a series of articles and presentations about how to get started writing your own storage engine. This has formed the basis for several of the major third-party storage engines. Many companies are writing their own internal storage engines now, as you'll see if you follow the MySQL internals mailing list. For example, Friendster uses a special storage engine for social graph operations, and we know of another company that built a custom engine for fuzzy searches. A simple custom storage engine isn't very hard to write.

You can also use a storage engine as an interface to another piece of software. A good example of this is the Sphinx storage engine, which interfaces with the Sphinx full-text search software (see Appendix C).

MySQL 5.1 also allows full-text search parser plug-ins, and you can write UDFs (see Chapter 5), which are great for CPU-intensive tasks that have to run in the server's thread context and are too slow or clumsy in SQL. You can use them for administration, service integration, reading operating system information, calling web services, synchronizing data, and much more.

MySQL Proxy is another option that's great if you want to add your own functionality to the MySQL protocol. And Paul McCullagh's scalable blob-streaming infrastructure project (*http://www.blobstreaming.org*) opens up a range of new possibilities for storing large objects in MySQL.

Because MySQL is free, open source software, you can even hack the server itself if it doesn't do what you need. We know of companies that have extended the server's parser grammar, for example. Third parties have submitted many interesting MySQL extensions in the areas of performance profiling, scalability, and new features in recent years. The MySQL developers are very responsive and helpful when people want to extend MySQL. They're available via the mailing list *internals@lists.mysql.com* (see *http://lists.mysql.com* to subscribe), MySQL forums, or the *#mysql-dev* IRC channel on freenode.

Alternatives to MySQL

MySQL is not necessarily the solution for every need. It's often much better to do some work completely outside MySQL, even if MySQL can theoretically do what you want.

One of the most obvious examples is storing data in a traditional filesystem instead of in tables. Image files are the classic case: you can put them into a BLOB column, but this is rarely a good idea.* The usual practice is to store images or other large binary files on the filesystem and store the filenames inside MySQL; the application can then retrieve the files from outside of MySQL. In a web application, you accomplish this by putting the filename in the <img> element's src attribute.

Full-text searching is something else that's best handled outside of MySQL—MySQL doesn't perform these searches as well as Lucene or Sphinx (see Appendix C).

The NDB API can also be useful for certain tasks. For instance, although MySQL's NDB Cluster storage engine isn't (yet) well suited for storing all of a high-performance web application's data, it's possible to use the NDB API directly for storing web site session data or user registration information. You can learn more about the NDB API at *http://dev.mysql.com/doc/ndbapi/en/index.html*. There's also an NDB module for Apache, *mod_ndb*, which you can download at *http://code.google. com/p/mod-ndb/*.

Finally, for some operations—such as graph relationships and tree traversals—a relational database just isn't the right paradigm. MySQL isn't good for distributed data processing, because it lacks parallel query execution capabilities. You'll probably want to use other tools for this purpose (possibly in combination with MySQL).

---

* There are advantages to using MySQL replication to distribute images quickly to many machines, and we know of some applications that use this technique.

CHAPTER 11
Backup and Recovery

It's easy to focus on "getting real work done" and neglect backup and recovery. What's urgent is often not important, and what's important is often not urgent. Backups are important for high performance as well as for disaster recovery. You need to plan and design for backups from the start so that they don't cause downtime or reduced performance.

If you don't plan for backups and build them in early, you'll usually create a bolt-on solution later. At that point, you might find that you've made decisions that rule out the best way to handle high-performance backups. For example, you might set up a server and then realize you really want LVM so that you can take filesystem snapshots—but it's too late. You also might not notice some important performance impacts of configuring your systems for backups. And if you don't plan for and practice recovery, it won't go smoothly when you need to do it.

Backup systems are like monitoring and alerting systems: most system administrators have reinvented them at one time or another. This is a shame, because there is good, well-supported, flexible backup software out there—some of it open source and free. We encourage you to use the parts of these systems that make sense for you.

We aren't going to cover all parts of a well-designed backup and recovery solution in this chapter. The subject is big enough to fill a book, and in fact there are several books devoted to it.* We skim over some topics, and focus on solutions for high-performance MySQL. In contrast to the first edition of this book, we assume many readers are using InnoDB in addition to or instead of MyISAM. This makes some backup scenarios more complicated.

---

* We think W. Curtis Preston's *Backup & Recovery* (O'Reilly) is a good choice.

Overview

We begin this chapter with a review of some terminology and a discussion of various issues you should bear in mind when planning your backup and recovery solutions, including potential requirements. We then present an overview of the various technologies and methods for making backups and explore techniques for restoring data and recovering from disasters. Finally, we discuss a selection of the available backup tools, and we close the chapter with some examples of how to build your own backup utilities.

Terminology

Before we begin, let's clarify some key terms. First, you'll often hear about so-called hot, warm, and cold backups. People generally use these terms to denote a backup's impact: "hot" backups aren't supposed to require any server downtime, for example. The problem is that these terms don't mean the same things to everyone. Some tools even use the word "hot" in their names, but definitely don't perform what we consider to be hot backups. We try to avoid these terms and instead tell you how much a specific technique or tool interrupts your server.

Two other confusing words are *restore* and *recover*. We use them in specific ways in this chapter. Restoring means retrieving data from a backup and either loading it into MySQL or placing the files where MySQL expects them to be. Recovery generally means the entire process of rescuing a system, or part of a system, after something has gone wrong. This includes restoring data from backups, as well as all the steps necessary to make a server fully functional again, such as restarting MySQL, changing the configuration, warming up the server's caches, and so on.

To many people, recovery just means fixing corrupted tables after a crash. This is not the same as recovering an entire server. A storage engine's recovery reconciles its data and log files. It makes sure the data files contain only the modifications made by committed transactions, and it replays transactions from the log files that have not yet been applied to the data files. If you use a transactional storage engine, this may be part of the overall recovery process, or even part of making backups. However, it's not the same as the recovery you might need to do after an accidental DROP TABLE, for example.

It's All About Recovery

If all goes well, you'll never need to think about recovery. But when you do, the best backup system in the world won't help. Instead, you'll need a great recovery system.

The problem is it's easier to make your backup systems work smoothly than to build good recovery processes and tools. Here's why:

- Backups come first. You can't recover unless you've first backed up, so your attention naturally focuses on backups when building a system. It's important to counter this tendency by planning for recovery first. In fact, you shouldn't build your backup systems until you figure out your recovery requirements.

- Backups are routine. This makes you focus on automating and fine-tuning the backup process, often without thinking of it. Five-minute tweaks to your backup process may not seem important, but are you applying the same attention to recovery, day in and day out? You should intentionally practice your recovery procedure until it is as smooth and bug-free as your backup process.

- Backups aren't usually made under extreme pressure, but recovery is usually a crisis situation. It's hard to overstate how important this is.

- Security often gets in the way. If you're doing offsite backups, you're probably encrypting the backup data or taking other measures to protect it. It's easy to focus on how damaging it would be for your data to be compromised, and lose sight of how damaging it is when nobody can unlock your encrypted volume to recover your data—or when you need to extract a single file from a monolithic encrypted file.

- One person can plan, design, and implement backups, especially with the excellent tools available. That person might not be available when disaster strikes. You need to train several people and plan for coverage, so you're not asking an unqualified person to recover your data.

Here's an example we've seen in the real world: a customer reported that backups became lightning fast when the *-d* option was added to *mysqldump*, and wanted to know why no one had mentioned how much that option could speed up the backup process. If this customer had tried to restore the backups, it would have been hard to miss the reason: the *-d* option dumps no data! The customer was focused on backups, not recovery, so was completely unaware of this problem.

When you start thinking about recovery, it's a good idea to define your requirements before you do anything else. Here are some of the things you should consider:

- How much data can you lose without serious consequences? Do you need point-in-time recovery, or is it acceptable to lose whatever work has happened since your last regular backup? Are there legal requirements?

- How fast does recovery have to be? What kind of downtime is acceptable? What impacts (e.g., partial unavailability) can your application and users accept, and how will you build in the capability to continue functioning when those scenarios happen?

- What do you need to recover? Common requirements are to recover a whole server, a single database, a single table, or just specific transactions or statements.

Write down your answers to these questions, add them to your system's documentation, and keep them in mind as you read the rest of this chapter. Doing this exercise first will help you focus on recovery as you plan your backups. Keeping it with the rest of your documentation will help when you need to retrace your steps later.

Backup Myth #1: "I Use Replication As a Backup."

This is a mistake we see quite often. A replication slave is not a backup. Neither is a RAID array. To see why, consider this: will they help you get back all your data if you accidentally execute DROP DATABASE on your production database? RAID and replication don't pass even this simple test. Not only are they not backups, they're not a substitute for backups. Nothing but backups fill the need for backups.

Topics We Won't Cover

Backing up MySQL is in many ways just a specialized case of the more general problem of backup and recovery. We want to focus on high-performance MySQL, but it's a little hard not to include material about lots of other topics too, especially because we've seen so many people struggling with the same backup and recovery problems. Here are some points we decided not to include:

- Security (who can access the backup, who has privileges to restore data, whether the files need to be encrypted)
- Where to store the backups, including how far away from the source they should be (on a different disk, a different server, or offsite), and how to move the data from the source to the destination
- Retention policies, auditing, legal requirements, and related subjects
- Storage solutions and media, compression, and incremental backups
- Storage formats (but we'll say this much: avoid proprietary backup formats)
- Monitoring and reporting on your backups
- Backup capabilities built into storage layers, or particular devices such as prefabricated file servers

These are important topics. You should read a book on backups if you are unfamiliar with them.

The Big Picture

Before we go into great detail on all of the available options, here's our opinion on what most people are likely to need for a backup and recovery solution. You can view these recommendations as a starting point, or a direction toward which you can work:

- Raw backups are practically a must-have for large databases: they're fast, which is very important. Snapshot-based backups are our favorite, but InnoDB Hot Backup is a good alternative if you use only InnoDB tables.

- Back up your binary logs for point-in-time recovery.

- Keep several backup generations, and keep binary log files long enough that you can restore from them.

- Test your backups and recovery process periodically by going through the entire recovery process.

- Create logical backups (probably from the raw backups, for efficiency) periodically. Make sure you keep enough binary logs to recover from your last logical backup.

- Test your raw backups, if possible, to make sure they're useful for recovery. If you can, test them during the backup process, before you copy them to the destination.

- Think hard about security. What happens if someone compromises your server—can he then get access to the backup server too, or vice versa?

- Monitor your backups and backup processes independently from the backup tools themselves. You need external verification that they're OK.

- Be smart about how you copy files between machines. There are much more efficient ways to copy files than *scp* or *rsync*. You can read more about this in Appendix A.

Why Backups?

If you're building a high-performance system that relies on MySQL, it's important to make backups. Here are a few reasons:

Disaster recovery

Disaster recovery is what you do when hardware fails, a nasty bug corrupts your data, or your server and its data become unavailable or unusable for some other reason (the potential reasons are many and varied—use your imagination). Although the odds of any particular disaster striking are fairly low, taken together they add up. You need to be ready for everything from someone accidentally connecting to the wrong server to type ALTER TABLE,* to the building burning down, to a malicious attacker or a MySQL bug.

---

* Baron still remembers doing this as a developer at an e-commerce site by typing the command into the wrong window. It was the DBA team's fault; they shouldn't have given developers privileges on the live servers. Really!

People changing their minds

You'd be surprised how often we've seen the need to recover at least some data as it existed at some point. For some applications, this might happen even more often than disasters (for example, if an important customer intentionally deletes some data and then wants it back).

Auditing

Sometimes you need to know what your data or schema looked like at some point in the past. You might be involved in a lawsuit, for example, or you might discover a bug in your application and need to see what the code used to do (sometimes just having your code in version control isn't enough).

Testing

One of the easiest ways to test on realistic data is to periodically refresh a test server with the latest production data. If you're making backups, it's easy; just use the backup.

Check your assumptions. For example, do you assume your shared hosting provider is backing up the MySQL server provided with your account? Although shared hosting isn't really relevant to high performance, we want to point out that such assumptions can bite. (In case you were wondering, many hosting providers don't back up MySQL servers, and others just do a file copy while the server is running, which probably creates a corrupt backup that's useless.)

Considerations and Tradeoffs

Backing up MySQL is harder than it looks. At its most basic, a backup is just a copy of the data, but your application's needs, MySQL's storage engine architecture, and your system configuration can make it difficult to make a copy of your data.

What Can You Afford to Lose?

Knowing how much data you can afford to lose will guide your backup strategy. Do you need point-in-time recovery capability, or is it enough to recover to last night's backup and lose whatever work has been done since then? If you need point-in-time recovery, you can probably make a regular backup and make sure the binary log is enabled, so you can restore that backup and recover to the desired point by replaying the binary log.

Generally, the more you can afford to lose, the easier it is to do backups. If you have very strict requirements, it's harder to ensure you can recover everything. There are even different flavors of point-in-time recovery. A "soft" point-in-time recovery requirement means you'd like to be able to recreate your data so that it's "close enough" to where it was when the problem happened. A "hard" requirement means you can never tolerate the loss of a committed transaction, even if something terrible happens (such as the server catching fire). This requires special techniques, such as keeping your binary log on a separate SAN volume or using DRBD disk replication. You can read more about these approaches in Chapter 9.

Online or Offline Backups?

If you can get away with it, shutting down MySQL to make a backup is the easiest, safest, and overall best way to get a consistent copy of the data with minimal risk of corruption or inconsistency. If you shut down MySQL, you can copy the data without any complications from things such as dirty buffers in the InnoDB buffer pool or other caches. You don't need to worry about your data being modified while you're trying to back it up, and because the server isn't under load from the application, you can make the backup more quickly.

However, taking a server offline is more expensive than it might seem. Even if you can minimize the downtime, shutting down and restarting MySQL can take a long time under demanding loads and high data volumes:

- If you have a lot of dirty buffers in the InnoDB buffer pool—that is, a lot of data that's been modified in memory but not yet written to disk—InnoDB can take a long time to flush the modified data to disk. You can influence InnoDB's shutdown time with the `innodb_fast_shutdown` configuration variable, which controls how InnoDB treats the buffer pool and inserts buffer at shutdown,* but this just shifts work around; it doesn't eliminate it. Thus, you can't significantly decrease the shutdown and restart cycle time this way. You can sometimes do so by configuring other aspects of InnoDB, but those changes have much broader performance effects. See "Tuning MySQL's I/O Behavior" on page 281 for more on this.

- Restarting can take a long time, too. Opening all the tables and warming up the caches can be a slow process, especially if you have lots of tables and data. If you set `innodb_fast_shutdown=2` to make InnoDB shut down quickly, InnoDB will have to perform its recovery process before it starts fully. Even after your server appears to be fully started, it can take a long time for it to be warmed up and ready to use.

Consequently, if you're building for high performance, you'll almost certainly need to design your backups so that they don't require the production server to be taken offline. Depending on your consistency requirements, though, making a backup while the server is online can still mean interrupting service significantly.

For example, one of the most cited backup methods begins with FLUSH TABLES WITH READ LOCK. This tells MySQL to flush† and lock all tables, and also flushes the query

---

* The insert buffer is stored in the InnoDB tablespace files, along with all other data; a background thread eventually merges inserted records into the tables where they belong.

† Flushing tables flushes MyISAM's data, but not InnoDB's, to disk.

cache. That can take a while to complete. (Exactly how long is unpredictable; it will be longer if the global read lock has to wait for a long-running statement to finish, or if you have many tables.) Until the locks are released, you can't change any data on the server. FLUSH TABLES WITH READ LOCK is not as expensive as shutting down, because most of your caches are still in memory and the server is still "warm," but it's relatively disruptive.

If this is a problem, you'll have to find an alternative. One method we use is to make a backup from a replication slave, which is one of a pool of slaves that can be cycled in and out pretty cheaply. We come back to this topic, and other considerations for online and offline backups, later in this chapter. For now, we'll just say this: online backups that don't interrupt service are difficult in MySQL at present.

Logical or Raw Backups?

There are two major ways to back up MySQL's data: with a *logical backup* (also called a "dump") and by copying the *raw files*. A logical backup contains the data in a form that MySQL can interpret either as SQL or as delimited text.* The raw files are the files as they exist on disk.

Each method of copying the data has advantages and disadvantages.

Logical backups

Logical backups have the following advantages:

- They're normal files that you can manipulate and inspect with editors and command-line tools such as *grep* and *sed*. This can be very helpful when restoring data, or when you just want to inspect the data without restoring.
- They're easy to restore. You can just pipe them into *mysql* or use *mysqlimport*.
- You can back up and restore across the network—that is, on a different machine from the MySQL host.
- They can be very flexible because *mysqldump*—the tool most people prefer to use to make them†—can accept lots of options, such as a WHERE clause to restrict what rows are backed up.
- They're storage engine-independent. Because you create them by extracting data from the MySQL server, they abstract away differences in the underlying data

---

* Logical backups produced by *mysqldump* are not always text files. SQL dumps can contain many different character sets, and can even include binary data that's not valid character data at all. Lines can be too long for many editors, too. Still, many such files will contain data a text editor can open and read, especially if you run *mysqldump* with the *--hex-blob* option.

† There are other choices, including tools that can do parallel dumps and restores, but this is the most popular tool.

storage. Thus, you can back up from InnoDB tables and restore to MyISAM tables with very little work. You can't do this with raw file copies.

- If you specify the right options to *mysqldump*, in many cases, you can even import your logical backups into another database server, such as PostgreSQL.
- They can help avoid data corruption. If your disk drives are failing and you copy the raw files, you'll make a corrupt backup, and unless you check the backup, you won't notice it and it'll be unusable later. If the data MySQL has in memory is *not* corrupt, you can sometimes get a trustworthy logical backup when you can't get a good raw file copy.

Logical backups have their shortcomings, though:

- The server has to do the work of generating them, so they use more CPU cycles.
- Logical backups can be bigger than the underlying files in some cases.* The ASCII representation of the data isn't always as efficient as the way the storage engine stores the data. For example, an integer requires 4 bytes to store, but when written in ASCII, it can require up to 12 characters. You can often compress the files effectively, but this uses more CPU resources.
- The loss of precision in floating-point representations may prevent accurate restoration from dump files. (Google's patches to the MySQL server include a patch to *mysqldump* that works around this.)
- Restoring from a logical backup requires MySQL to load and interpret the statements and rebuild indexes, which piles more work onto the server.

The biggest disadvantages are really the cost of dumping the data from MySQL and the cost of loading data back in via SQL statements.

Raw backups

Raw backups have the following advantages:

- Raw file backups simply require you to copy the desired files somewhere else for backup. The raw files don't require any extra work to generate.
- Restoring raw backups can be simpler, depending on the storage engine. For MyISAM, it can be as easy as just copying the files into their destinations. InnoDB, however, requires you to stop the server and possibly take other steps as well.
- Raw backups are generally pretty portable across platforms, operating systems, and MySQL versions.
- It can be faster to restore raw backups, because the MySQL server doesn't have to execute any SQL or build indexes. If you have InnoDB tables that don't fit entirely in the server's memory, it can be *much* faster to restore raw files.

---

* In our experience, logical backups are generally smaller than raw backups, but they aren't always.

Here are some disadvantages of raw backups:

- InnoDB's raw files are often far larger than the corresponding logical backups. The InnoDB tablespace typically has lots of unused space. Quite a bit of space is also used for purposes other than storing table data (the insert buffer, the rollback segment, and so on).

- Raw backups are not always portable across platforms, operating systems, and MySQL versions. Filename case sensitivity and floating-point formats are places where you might encounter trouble. You might not be able to move files to a system whose floating-point format is different (however, the vast majority of processors use the IEEE floating-point format).

Raw backups are generally easier and more efficient. You should not rely on them for long-term retention or legal requirements, though; you must make logical backups at least periodically.

Don't consider a backup (especially a raw backup) to be good until you've tested it. For InnoDB, that means starting a MySQL instance and letting InnoDB recovery run, then running CHECK TABLES. You can skip this, or just run *innochecksum* on the files, but we don't recommend it. For MyISAM, you should run CHECK TABLES or use *myisamchk*.

Another smart option is to use a blend of the two approaches: make raw copies, then start a MySQL server instance and use it to create logical backups from the raw copies. This gives you the advantages of both approaches, without unduly burdening the production server during the dump. It's especially convenient if you have the ability to take filesystem snapshots—you can take a snapshot, copy the snapshot to another server and release it, then test the raw files and perform a logical backup.

What to Back Up

Your recovery requirements will dictate what you need to back up. The simplest strategy is to just back up your data and table definitions, but this is a bare minimum approach. You generally need a lot more to recover a server for use in production. Here are some things you might consider including with your MySQL backups:

Nonobvious data
> Don't forget data that's easy to overlook: your binary logs and InnoDB transaction logs, for example.

Code
> A modern MySQL server can store a lot of code, such as triggers and stored procedures. If you back up the mysql database, you'll back up much of this code, but then it will be hard to restore a single database in its entirety, because some of the "data" in that database, such as stored procedures, will actually be stored in the mysql database.

Replication configuration

If you are recovering to a server that is involved in replication, you should include in your backups whatever replication files you'll need for that—e.g., binary logs, relay logs, log index files, and the *.info* files. At a minimum, you should include the output of SHOW MASTER STATUS and/or SHOW SLAVE STATUS. It's also helpful to issue FLUSH LOGS so MySQL starts a new binary log. It's easier to do point-in-time recovery from the beginning of a log file than the middle.

Server configuration

If you have to recover from a real disaster—say, if you're building a server from scratch in a new data center after an earthquake—you'll appreciate having the server's configuration files included in the backup.

Selected operating system files

As with the server configuration, it's important to back up any external configuration that is essential to a production server. On a Unix server, this might include your *cron* jobs, user and group configurations, administrative scripts, and *sudo* rules.

These recommendations quickly translate into "back up everything" in many scenarios. If you have a lot of data, however, this can get expensive, and you might have to be smarter about how you do your backups. In particular, you might want to back up different data into different backups. For example, you can back up data, binary logs, and operating system and system configuration files separately.

Incremental backups

A common strategy for dealing with too much data is to do regular incremental backups. Here are some ideas:

- Back up your binary logs. This is the simplest, the most widely used, and overall the best way to make incremental backups.

- Don't back up tables that haven't changed. Some storage engines, such as MyISAM, record the last time each table was modified. You can see these times by inspecting the files on disk or by running SHOW TABLE STATUS. If you use InnoDB, a trigger can help you keep track of the last changes by recording the change times in a small "last changed time" table. You need to do this only on tables that change infrequently, so the cost should be minimal. A custom backup script can easily determine which tables have changed.

  If you have "lookup" tables that contain data such as lists of month names in various languages or abbreviations for states or regions, it can be a good idea to place them into a separate database, so you don't have to back them up all the time.

- Don't back up rows that haven't changed. If a table is INSERT-only, such as a table that logs hits to a web page, you can add a TIMESTAMP column and back up only rows that have been inserted since the last backup. You can also use the Merge storage engine to good effect so that older data lives in static tables.

- Don't back up some data at all. Sometimes this makes a lot of sense—for example, if you have a data warehouse that's built from other data and is technically redundant, you can merely back up the data you used to build the warehouse, instead of the data warehouse itself. This can be a good idea even if it's very slow to "recover" by rebuilding the warehouse from the original files. Avoiding the backups can add up over time to much greater savings than the potentially faster recovery time you'll gain by having a full backup. You can also opt not to back up some temporary data, such as tables that hold web site session data.

- Back up just the changes to the binary log. You can use *rdiff* to get binary deltas of your binlogs and back up just the changes made since the last backup (periodically doing a full backup as well). Another useful tool we've used is *rdiff-backup*, which combines *rdiff* and *rsync* functionality into a complete backup solution. Or you can just use FLUSH LOGS to begin a new binary log after each backup, so you don't need to do binary deltas at all.

- Back up just the changes to the data files. This is like backing up differences in your binary logs. Common Unix tools for this purpose are, again, *rdiff* and *rdiff-backup*. This strategy is helpful for extremely large databases that don't change much. Suppose you have a terabyte of data, only 50 GB of which changes every day. It might be a good idea to back up binary differences daily, and just do a full backup once in a while. The benefit is that you can apply the binary differences to the full backup in a sequential disk read/write operation much faster than you can apply a binary log. The binary difference backup itself might be slower than making a full backup, though.

The drawback of incremental backups is increased complexity during recovery. If you have do recovery under stress, you'll appreciate being able to restore just one backup instead of having to apply incremental backups one after the other. If you can do full backups, we suggest that you do so for simplicity's sake.

Regardless, you definitely need to do full backups occasionally—we suggest at least weekly. You can't expect to recover from a year's worth of incremental backups. Even a week is a lot of work and risk.

Storage Engines and Consistency

MySQL's choice of storage engines can make backups significantly more complicated. The issue is how to get a consistent backup with any given storage engine.

There are actually two kinds of consistency to think about: *data consistency* and *file consistency*.

Data consistency

When you do backups, you must ensure that your data is point-in–time consistent. For example, in an e-commerce database, you need to make sure your invoices and payments are consistent with each other. Recovering a payment without its corresponding invoice, or vice versa, is bound to cause trouble!

If you're making online backups (from a running server), you need to make sure you get a consistent backup of all related tables. That means you can't just lock and back up tables one at a time—which in turn means your backups might be more intrusive than you'd like. If you're not using a transactional storage engine, you have no choice but to use LOCK TABLES on all the tables you want to back up together, and release the lock only when all the related tables have been backed up.

InnoDB's MVCC capabilities can help. You can begin a transaction, dump a group of related tables, and commit the transaction. (You should not use LOCK TABLES if you're using a transaction to get a consistent backup, because it commits your transaction implicitly—see the MySQL manual for details.) As long as you're using the REPEATABLE READ transaction isolation level, this will give you a perfectly consistent, point-in-time snapshot of the data that doesn't block further work from happening on your server while the backup is being made.

However, this approach doesn't protect you from poorly designed application logic. Suppose your e-commerce store inserts a payment, commits the transaction, and then inserts the invoice in a different transaction. Your backup process might start between those two operations, backing up the payment and not the invoice. This is why you have to design transactions carefully to group related operations together.

You can also get a consistent logical backup of InnoDB tables with *mysqldump*, which supports a *--single-transaction* option that does what we just described. However, this can cause a very long transaction, which might have an unacceptably high overhead on some workloads.

Tools that support "backup sets," such as ZRM (discussed later) or Maatkit's *mk-parallel-dump*, can help you back up related sets of tables easily.

File consistency

It's also important that each file is internally consistent—e.g., that the backup doesn't reflect a file's state partway through a big UPDATE statement—and that all the files you're backing up are consistent with each other. If you don't get internally consistent files, you'll have a nasty surprise when you try to restore them (they'll probably be corrupt). And if you copy related files at different times, they won't be consistent with each other. MyISAM's .*MYD* and .*MYI* files are an example.

With a nontransactional storage engine such as MyISAM, your only option is to lock and flush the tables. That means using either a combination of LOCK TABLES and FLUSH TABLES, so the server flushes its in-memory changes to disk, or FLUSH TABLES WITH READ LOCK. Once the flush is complete, you can safely do a raw copy of MyISAM's files.

With InnoDB, it's actually a little harder to ensure the files are consistent on disk. Even if you do a FLUSH TABLES WITH READ LOCK, InnoDB keeps working in the background: its insert buffer, log, and write threads continue to merge changes to its log and tablespace files. These threads are asynchronous by design—doing this work in background threads is what helps InnoDB achieve high concurrency—so they are independent of LOCK TABLES. Thus, you need to make sure not only that each file is internally consistent, but that you copy the log and tablespace files at the same instant. If you make a backup while a thread is changing a file, or back up the log files at a different point in time from the tablespace files, you can again end up with a corrupt system after recovery. You can avoid this problem in two ways:

- Wait until InnoDB's purge and insert buffer merge threads are done. You can watch the output of SHOW INNODB STATUS and copy the files when there are no more dirty buffers or pending writes. However, this approach might take a long time; it also involves too much guesswork and might not be safe, because of InnoDB's background threads. Consequently, we don't recommend it.

- Take a consistent snapshot of the data and log files with a system such as LVM. You *must* snapshot the data and log files consistently with respect to each other; it's no good to snapshot them separately. We discuss LVM snapshots later in this chapter.

Once you have copied the files elsewhere, you can release the locks and let the MySQL server run normally again.

Replication

The popular wisdom is that MySQL replication is fantastic for backups. There's merit to using replication as part of an overall backup strategy, but it's not the be-all and end-all of backups, as it's often said to be.

The biggest advantage to backing up from a slave is that it doesn't interrupt the master or place extra load on it. This is a good reason to set up a slave server, even if you don't need it for load balancing or high availability. If money is a concern, you can always use the backup slave for other purposes too, such as reporting—as long as you don't write to it and thus change the data you're trying to back up. The slave doesn't have to be dedicated to backups; it just has to be able to catch up to the master in time to make your next backup in the event that its other roles make it fall behind in replication at times.

When you make a backup from a slave, save all the information about the replication processes, such as the slave's position on the master. This is useful for cloning new slaves, reapplying binary logs to the master to get point-in-time recovery, promoting the slave to a master, and more. Also be sure that no temporary tables are open if you stop your slave, because they might keep you from restarting replication. You can read more about this in "Missing Temporary Tables" on page 394.

Intentionally delaying replication on one of your slaves can be very useful for recovering from some disaster scenarios. Suppose you delay replication by an hour. If an unwanted statement runs on the master, you have an hour to notice it and stop the slave before it repeats the event from its relay log. You can then promote the slave to master and replay some relatively small number of log events, skipping the bad statements. This can be much faster than the point-in-time recovery technique we discuss later. The *mk-slave-delay* script from Maatkit can help with this.

The slave might not have the same data as the master. Many people assume slaves are exact copies of their masters, but in our experience, data mismatches on slaves are common, and MySQL has no way to detect this problem. Backing up wrong or corrupt data on the slave will not result in a useful backup. See "Determining Whether Slaves Are Consistent with the Master" on page 380 for more on how to ensure a slave's data is the same as its master's. Chapter 8 also contains advice on how to keep your slaves from becoming different from the master.

Having a replicated copy of your data may help protect you from problems such as disk meltdowns on the master, but there's no guarantee. Replication is *not* a backup.

Managing and Backing Up Binary Logs

Your server's binary logs are one of the most important things you can back up. They are necessary for point-in-time recovery, and because they're usually smaller than your data, they're easier to back up frequently. If you have a backup of your data at some point and all the binary logs since then, you can replay the binary logs and "roll forward" changes made since the last full backup.

MySQL uses the binary log for replication, too. That means that your backup and recovery policy often interacts with your replication configuration.

Binary logs are "special." If you lose your data, you really don't want to lose them as well. To minimize the chances of this happening, you can keep them on a separate volume. It's OK to do this even if you want to snapshot the binary logs with LVM. For extra safety, you can keep them on a SAN or replicate them to another device with DRBD. You can read more about this in Chapter 9.

It's a good idea to back up binary logs frequently. If you can't afford to lose more than 30 minutes' worth of data, back them up at least every 30 minutes. You can also use a read-only replication slave with *--log_slave_updates*, for an extra degree of safety. The log positions won't match the master's, but it's usually not hard to find the right positions for recovery.

Here's our recommended server configuration for binary logging:

```
log_bin         = mysql-bin
sync_binlog     = 1
innodb_support_xa = 1 # MySQL 5.0 and newer only
innodb_safe_binlog    # MySQL 4.1 only, roughly equivalent to innodb_support_xa
```

There are several other configuration options for the binary log, such as options to limit the size of each log. You can learn more about these in the MySQL manual.

The Binary Log Format

The binary log consists of a sequence of events. Each event has a fixed-size header that contains a variety of information, such as the current timestamp and default database. You can use the *mysqlbinlog* tool to inspect a binary log's contents, and it prints out some of the header information. Here's an example of the output:

```
1  # at 277
2  #071030 10:47:21 server id 3  end_log_pos 369   Query   thread_id=13   exec_time=0
   error_code=0
3  SET TIMESTAMP=1193755641/*!*/;
4  insert into test(a) values(2)/*!*/;
```

Line 1 contains the byte offset within the log file (in this case, 277).

Line 2 contains the following items:

- The date and time of the event, which MySQL also uses to generate the SET TIMESTAMP statement.

- The server ID of the originating server, which is necessary to prevent endless loops in replication and other problems.

- The end_log_pos, which is the byte offset of the next event. This value is incorrect for most of the events in a multistatement transaction. MySQL copies the events into a buffer on the master during such transactions, but it doesn't know the next log event's position when it does so.

- The event type. Our sample's type is Query, but there are many different types.

- The thread ID of the thread that executed the event on the originating server, which is important for auditing as well as for executing the CONNECTION_ID( ) function.

- The exec_time, whose true meaning is unclear even to some of the MySQL developers we asked about it. It generally records how long the statement took to execute, but under some conditions it can have strange values. For example, it will have very large values in the relay log on a slave whose I/O thread is far behind the master, even if the statements executed quickly on the master. It's a good idea not to rely on this value.

- Any error code the event raised on the originating server. If the event causes a different error when replayed on a slave, replication will fail as a safety precaution.

Any further lines contain the SQL needed to replay the event. User-defined variables and any other special settings, such as the timestamp in effect when the statement executed, also appear here.

 If you're using the row-based logging available in MySQL 5.1, the event won't be SQL. Instead, it's a non-human-readable "image" of the modifications the statement made to the table.

Purging Old Binary Logs Safely

You'll need to decide on a log expiration policy to keep MySQL from filling your disk with binary logs. How large your logs grow depends on your workload and the logging format (row-based logging, available in MySQL 5.1, results in larger log entries). We suggest you keep logs as long as they're useful if possible. Keeping them is helpful for setting up replication slaves, analyzing your server's workload, auditing, and point-in-time recovery from your last full backup. Consider all of these needs when you decide how long you want to keep your logs.

A common setup is to use the expire_logs_days variable to tell MySQL to purge logs after a while. This variable isn't available until MySQL 4.1; prior to this version, you had to purge binary logs manually. Thus, you might see advice to remove old binary logs with a *cron* entry such as the following:

```
0 0 * * * /usr/bin/find /var/log/mysql -mtime +N -name "mysql-bin.[0-9]*" | xargs rm
```

Although this was the only way to purge the logs prior to MySQL 4.1, don't do this in MySQL 4.1 and newer! Removing the logs with *rm* will cause the *mysql-bin.index* status file to become out of sync with the files on disk, and some statements, such as SHOW MASTER LOGS, will begin failing silently. Changing the *mysql-bin.index* file by hand won't fix the problem, either. Instead, use a *cron* command such as the following:

```
0 0 * * * /usr/bin/mysql -e "PURGE MASTER LOGS BEFORE CURRENT_DATE - INTERVAL N DAY"
```

The expire_logs_days setting takes effect upon server startup or when MySQL rotates the binary log, so if your binary log never fills up and rotates, the server will not purge older entries. It decides which files to purge by looking at their modification times, not their contents.

Backing Up Data

As with most topics, there are better and worse ways to actually make a backup—and the obvious ways are sometimes not so good. The trick is to maximize your network, disk, and CPU capacity to make backups as fast as possible. This is a balancing act, and you'll have to experiment to find the "sweet spot."

Specific advice is hard to give, so we show you some more general techniques.

Making a Logical Backup

The first thing to realize about logical backups is that they are not all created equal. There are actually two kinds of logical backups: SQL dumps and delimited files.

SQL dumps

SQL dumps are what most people are familiar with, as they're what *mysqldump* creates by default. For example, dumping a small table with the default options will produce the following (abridged) output:

```
$ mysqldump test t1
-- [Version and host comments]

/*!40101 SET @OLD_CHARACTER_SET_CLIENT=@@CHARACTER_SET_CLIENT */;
-- [More version-specific comments to save options for restore]


--
-- Table structure for table `t1`
--

DROP TABLE IF EXISTS `t1`;
CREATE TABLE `t1` (
  `a` int(11) NOT NULL,
  PRIMARY KEY  (`a`)
) ENGINE=MyISAM DEFAULT CHARSET=latin1;


--
-- Dumping data for table `t1`
--

LOCK TABLES `t1` WRITE;
/*!40000 ALTER TABLE `t1` DISABLE KEYS */;
INSERT INTO `t1` VALUES (1);
/*!40000 ALTER TABLE `t1` ENABLE KEYS */;
UNLOCK TABLES;
/*!40103 SET TIME_ZONE=@OLD_TIME_ZONE */;

/*!40101 SET SQL_MODE=@OLD_SQL_MODE */;
-- [More option restoration]
```

The dump file contains both the table structure and the data, all written out as valid SQL commands. The file begins with comments that set various MySQL options. These are present either to make the restore work more efficiently or for compatibility and correctness. Next you can see the table's structure, and then its data. Finally, the script resets the options it changed at the beginning of the dump.

The dump's output is executable for a restore operation. This is convenient, but *mysqldump*'s default options aren't great for making a huge backup (we delve into *mysqldump*'s options in more detail later).

mysqldump is not the only tool that can make SQL logical backups. You can also create them with phpMyAdmin, for example. What we'd really like to point out here is not so much problems with any particular tool, but rather the shortcomings of doing monolithic SQL logical backups in the first place. Here are the main problem areas:

Schema and data stored together
> Although this is convenient if you want to restore from a single file, it makes things difficult if you need to restore only one table, or want to restore only the data. You can alleviate this concern by dumping twice—once for data, once for schema—but you'll still have the next problem.

Huge SQL statements
> It's a lot of work for the server to parse and execute all of the SQL statements. This is a relatively slow way to load data.

A single huge file
> Most text editors can't edit large files or files with very long lines. Although you can sometimes use command-line stream editors—such as *sed* or *grep*—to pull out the data you need, it's preferable to keep the files small.

Logical backups are expensive
> There are more efficient ways to get data out of MySQL than sending it over the client/server protocol as a result set.

These limitations mean that SQL dumps quickly become unusable as tables get large. There's another option, though: export data to delimited files.

Delimited file backups

You can use the SELECT INTO OUTFILE SQL command to create a logical backup of your data in a delimited file format. (You can dump to delimited files with *mysqldump*'s *--tab* option, which runs the SQL command for you.) Delimited files contain the raw data represented in ASCII, without SQL, comments, and column names. Here's an example that dumps into comma-separated values (CSV) format, which is a good *lingua franca* for tabular data:

```
mysql> SELECT * INTO OUTFILE '/tmp/t1.txt'
    -> FIELDS TERMINATED BY ',' OPTIONALLY ENCLOSED BY '"'
    -> LINES TERMINATED BY '\n'
    -> FROM test.t1;
```

The resulting file is more compact and easier to manipulate with command-line tools than a SQL dump file, but the biggest advantage of this approach is the speed of backing up and restoring. You can load the data back into the table with LOAD DATA INFILE, with the same options used to dump it:

```
mysql> LOAD DATA INFILE '/tmp/t1.txt'
    -> INTO TABLE test.t1
    -> FIELDS TERMINATED BY ',' OPTIONALLY ENCLOSED BY '"'
    -> LINES TERMINATED BY '\n';
```

Here's an informal test we did to demonstrate the backup and restore speed difference between SQL files and delimited files. We adapted some production data for this test. The table we're dumping from looks like the following:

```
CREATE TABLE load_test (
    col1 date NOT NULL,
    col2 int NOT NULL,
    col3 smallint unsigned NOT NULL,
    col4 mediumint NOT NULL,
    col5 mediumint NOT NULL,
    col6 mediumint NOT NULL,
    col7 decimal(3,1) default NULL,
    col8 varchar(10) NOT NULL default '',
    col9 int NOT NULL,
    PRIMARY KEY (col1,col2)
) ENGINE=InnoDB;
```

The table has 15 million rows and uses about 700 MB on disk. Table 11-1 compares the performance of the two backup and restore methods. You can see there's a large speed difference in the restore times for the test.

Table 11-1. Backup and restore times for SQL and delimited dumps

Method	Dump size	Dump time	Restore time
SQL dump	727 MB	102 sec	600 sec
Delimited dump	669 MB	86 sec	301 sec

The SELECT INTO OUTFILE method has some limitations, though:

- You can back up only to a file on the machine on which the MySQL server is running. (You can roll your own SELECT INTO OUTFILE by writing a program that reads a SELECT result and writes it to disk, which is an approach we've seen some people take.)

- MySQL must have permission to write to the directory where the file is written, because the MySQL server—not the user running the SQL command—is what writes the file.

- For security reasons, you can't overwrite an existing file, no matter what the file's permissions are.

- You can't dump directly to a compressed file.

Parallel dump and restore

It's often much faster to back up and restore in parallel on a system with multiple CPUs. By "in parallel," we mean dumping or restoring multiple tables at once, not multiple programs working on the same table. Two programs loading data into a single table at the same time generally doesn't work well.

You don't need fancy tools to back up and restore in parallel; you can do it manually by running multiple instances of a backup tool. However, there are some tools and scripts specifically designed for this purpose, such as *mk-parallel-dump* from Maatkit and *mysqlpdump* (*http://www.fr3nd.net/projects/mysqlpdump/*). At the time of this writing, these tools are relatively new. However, benchmarks indicate that *mk-parallel-dump* can be several times faster than simply using *mysqldump* for backups.

In MySQL 5.1, *mysqlimport* has support for importing in multiple threads at once. You can use the 5.1 version of *mysqlimport* on earlier versions of MySQL.

Parallel dumps and restores might actually take longer if you use too high a degree of parallelism. Additionally, they may cause more data fragmentation, which can impact the system's performance.

Filesystem Snapshots

Filesystem snapshots are a great way to make online backups. Snapshot-capable filesystems can create a consistent image of their contents at an instant in time, which you can then use to make a backup. Snapshot-capable filesystems and appliances include FreeBSD's filesystem, the ZFS filesystem, GNU/Linux's Logical Volume Manager (LVM), and many SAN systems and file-storage solutions, such as NetApp storage appliances.

Don't confuse a snapshot with a backup. Taking a snapshot is simply a way of reducing the time for which locks must be held; after releasing the locks, you must copy the files to the backup. In fact, you can optionally take snapshots on InnoDB without even acquiring locks. We show you two ways to use LVM to make backups of an all-InnoDB system, with your choice of minimal or zero locking.

 Lenz Grimmer's *mylvmbackup* is a ready-to-use Perl script for creating MySQL backups with LVM. See "Backup Tools" on page 511, later in this chapter, for more details.

How LVM snapshots work

LVM uses copy-on-write technology to create a snapshot—i.e., a logical copy of an entire volume at an instant in time. It's a little like MVCC in a database, except it keeps only one old version of the data.

Notice we didn't say a *physical* copy. A logical copy appears to contain all the same data as the volume you snapshotted, but initially it contains no data. Instead of copying the data to the snapshot, LVM simply notes the time at which you created the snapshot, then reads the data from the original volume when you request it from the snapshot. So, the initial copy is basically an instantaneous operation, no matter how large a volume you're snapshotting.

When something changes the data in the original volume, LVM copies the affected blocks to an area reserved for the snapshot before it writes any changes to them. LVM doesn't keep multiple "old versions" of the data, so additional writes to blocks that are changed in the original volume don't require any further work for the snapshot. In other words, only the first write to each block causes a copy-on-write to the reserved area.

Now, when you request these blocks in the snapshot, LVM reads the data from the copied blocks instead of from the original volume. This lets you continue to see the same data in the snapshot without blocking anything on the original volume. Figure 11-1 depicts this arrangement.

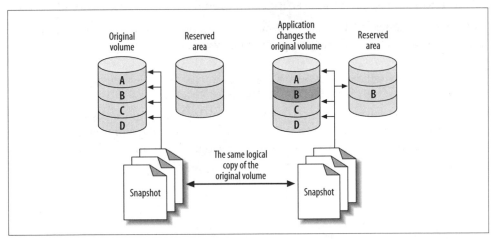

Figure 11-1. How copy-on-write technology reduces the size needed for a volume snapshot

The snapshot creates a new logical device in the /dev directory, and you can mount this device just as you would mount any other.

You can theoretically snapshot an enormous volume and consume very little physical space with this technique. However, you need to set aside enough space to hold all the blocks you expect to be updated in the original volume while you hold the snapshot open. If you don't reserve enough copy-on-write space, the snapshot will run out of space, and the device will become unavailable. The effect is like unplugging an external drive: any backup job that's reading from the device will fail with an I/O error.

Prerequisites and configuration

It's almost trivial to create a snapshot, but you need to ensure that your system is configured in such a way that you can get a consistent copy of *all* the files you want to back up at a single instant in time. First, make sure your system meets these conditions:

- All InnoDB files (InnoDB tablespace files and InnoDB transaction logs) must be on a single logical volume (partition). You need absolute point-in-time consistency, and LVM can't take consistent snapshots of more than one volume at a time. (This is an LVM limitation; some other systems do not have this problem.)

- If you need to back up the table definitions too, the MySQL data directory must be in the same logical volume. If you use another method to back up table definitions, such as a schema-only backup into your version control system, you may not need to worry about this.

- You must have enough free space in the volume group to create the snapshot. How much you need will depend on your workload. When you set up your system, leave some unallocated space so that you'll have room for snapshots later.

LVM has the concept of a *volume group*, which contains one or more logical volumes. You can see the volume groups on your system as follows:

```
# vgs
  VG   #PV #LV #SN Attr   VSize   VFree
  vg     1   4   0 wz--n- 534.18G 249.18G
```

This output shows a volume group that has four logical volumes distributed across one physical volume, with about 250 GB free. The *vgdisplay* command gives more detail if you need it. Now let's take a look at the logical volumes on the system:

```
# lvs
  LV    VG   Attr   LSize   Origin Snap% Move Log Copy%
  home  vg   -wi-ao  40.00G
  mysql vg   -wi-ao 225.00G
  tmp   vg   -wi-ao  10.00G
  var   vg   -wi-ao  10.00G
```

The output shows that the mysql volume has 225 GB of space. The device name is /dev/vg/mysql. This is just a name, even though it looks like a filesystem path. To add to the confusion, there's a symbolic link from the file of the same name to the real device node at */dev/mapper/vg-mysql*, which you can see with the *ls* and *mount* commands:

```
# ls -l /dev/vg/mysql
lrwxrwxrwx 1 root root 20 Sep 19 13:08 /dev/vg/mysql -> /dev/mapper/vg-mysql
# mount | grep mysql
/dev/mapper/vg-mysql on /var/lib/mysql type reiserfs (rw,noatime,notail)
```

Armed with this information, you're ready to create a filesystem snapshot.

Creating, mounting, and removing an LVM snapshot

You can create the snapshot with a single command. You just need to decide where to put it and how much space to allocate for copy-on-write. Don't hesitate to use more space than you think you'll need. LVM doesn't use the space you specify right away; it just reserves it for future use, so there's no harm in reserving lots of space, unless you need to leave space for other snapshots at the same time.

Let's create a snapshot just for practice. We'll give it 16 GB of space for copy-on-write, and we'll call it backup_mysql:

```
# lvcreate --size 16G --snapshot --name backup_mysql /dev/vg/mysql
  Logical volume "backup_mysql" created
```

We deliberately called the volume backup_mysql instead of mysql_ backup so that tab completion would be unambiguous. This helps avoid the possibility of tab completion causing you to accidentally delete the mysql volume group. Little details like this can really help avoid catastrophe. At least one of this book's authors has been burned by hasty tab completion with LVM snapshots.

Now let's see the newly created volume's status:

```
# lvs
  LV            VG   Attr   LSize   Origin Snap%  Move Log Copy%
  backup_mysql  vg   swi-a- 16.00G  mysql   0.01
  home          vg   -wi-ao 40.00G
  mysql         vg   owi-ao 225.00G
  tmp           vg   -wi-ao 10.00G
  var           vg   -wi-ao 10.00G
```

Notice that the snapshot's attributes are different from the original device's, and that the display shows a little extra information: its origin and how much of the allocated 16 GB is currently being used for copy-on-write. It's a good idea to monitor this as you make your backup, so you can see if the device is getting full and is about to fail. You can monitor your device's status with a monitoring system such as Nagios:

```
# watch 'lvs | grep backup'
```

As you saw from the output of *mount* earlier, the mysql volume contains a ReiserFS filesystem. That means the snapshot volume does too, and you can mount and use it just like any other filesystem:

```
# mkdir /tmp/backup
# mount /dev/mapper/vg-backup_mysql /tmp/backup
# ls -l /tmp/backup/mysql
total 5336
-rw-r----- 1 mysql mysql        0 Nov 17  2006 columns_priv.MYD
-rw-r----- 1 mysql mysql     1024 Mar 24  2007 columns_priv.MYI
-rw-r----- 1 mysql mysql     8820 Mar 24  2007 columns_priv.frm
-rw-r----- 1 mysql mysql    10512 Jul 12 10:26 db.MYD
-rw-r----- 1 mysql mysql     4096 Jul 12 10:29 db.MYI
-rw-r----- 1 mysql mysql     9494 Mar 24  2007 db.frm
... omitted ...
```

This is just for practice, so we'll unmount and remove the snapshot now with the *lvremove* command:

```
# umount /tmp/backup
# rmdir /tmp/backup
# lvremove --force /dev/vg/backup_mysql
    Logical volume "backup_mysql" successfully removed
```

LVM snapshots for online backups

Now that you've seen how to create, mount, and remove snapshots, you can use them to make backups. First, let's look at how to back up an InnoDB database without stopping the MySQL server. Connect to the MySQL server and flush the tables to disk with a global read lock, then get the binary log coordinates:

```
mysql> FLUSH TABLES WITH READ LOCK; SHOW MASTER STATUS;
```

Record the output from SHOW MASTER STATUS, and make sure you keep the connection to MySQL open so the lock doesn't get released. You can then take the LVM snapshot and immediately release the read lock, either with UNLOCK TABLES or by closing the connection. Finally, mount the snapshot and copy the files to the backup location. If you script this process, you can get the lock time down to a few seconds.

The major problem with this approach is that it may take a while to get the read lock, especially if there are long-running queries. All queries will be blocked while the connection waits for the global read lock, and it's impossible to predict how long this will take.

Lock-free InnoDB backups with LVM snapshots

Lock-free backups are only a little different. The distinction is that you don't do a FLUSH TABLES WITH READ LOCK. This means there won't be any guarantee that your MyISAM files will be consistent on disk, but if you use only InnoDB, that's probably not an issue. You'll still have some MyISAM tables in the mysql system database, but if your workload is typical, they're unlikely to be changing at the moment you take the snapshot.

If you think the mysql system tables might be changing, you can lock and then flush them. You shouldn't have any long-running queries on these tables, so this will normally be very fast:

```
mysql> LOCK TABLES mysql.user READ, mysql.db READ, ...;
mysql> FLUSH TABLES mysql.user, mysql.db, ...;
```

You're not getting a global read lock, so you won't be able to get anything useful from SHOW MASTER STATUS. However, when you start MySQL on the snapshot (to verify your backup's integrity), you'll see something like the following in the log file:

```
InnoDB: Doing recovery: scanned up to log sequence number 0 40817239
InnoDB: Starting an apply batch of log records to the database...
InnoDB: Progress in percents: 3 4 5 6 ...[omitted]... 97 98 99
InnoDB: Apply batch completed
InnoDB: Last MySQL binlog file position 0 3304937, file name /var/log/mysql/mysql-
bin.000001
070928 14:08:42  InnoDB: Started; log sequence number 0 40817239
```

Filesystem Snapshots and InnoDB

InnoDB's background threads continue to work even if you've locked all tables, so it is probably still writing to its files even as you take the snapshot. Also, because InnoDB hasn't performed its shutdown sequence, the snapshot's InnoDB files will look just as though the server has lost power unexpectedly.

This is not a problem, because InnoDB is an ACID system. At any instant (such as the instant you take the snapshot), every committed transaction is either in the InnoDB data files or in the log files. When you start MySQL after restoring the snapshot, InnoDB will run its recovery process, just as though the server had lost power. It will look in the transaction log for any committed transactions that haven't yet been applied to the data files and apply them, so you won't lose any transactions. This is why it's mandatory to snapshot the InnoDB data and log files together.

This is also why you should test your backups when you make them. Start an instance of MySQL, point it at the new backup, let InnoDB's recovery run, and check all the tables. This way you won't back up corrupted data without knowing it (the files could be corrupt for any number of reasons). Another benefit to this practice is that restoring from the backup will be faster in the future, because you've already run the recovery process.

You can optionally run this process on the snapshot before even copying it to the backup, but that can add quite a bit of overhead. Just be sure you plan for it. (More on this later.)

InnoDB logs the MySQL binary log position corresponding to the point to which it has recovered. This is the binary log position you can use for point-in-time recovery.

This approach to lock-free backups with snapshots has a twist in MySQL 5.0 and newer. These MySQL versions use XA to coordinate transactions between InnoDB and the binary log. If you restore the backup to a server with a different `server_id` from the one on which the backup was made, the server might find prepared transactions from a server whose ID doesn't match its own. In this case, the server can become confused, and it's possible for transactions to become stuck in PREPARED status upon recovery. This rarely happens, but it is possible. This is why you should always verify your backup before you consider it a success. It may not be recoverable!

If you're taking the snapshot from a slave, InnoDB recovery will also print some lines that look like these:

```
InnoDB: In a MySQL replication slave the last master binlog file
InnoDB: position 0 115, file name mysql-bin.001717
```

In some versions of MySQL, this output shows you the master's binary log coordinates (as opposed to the slave's binary log coordinates) at the point to which InnoDB has recovered, which can be very useful for making backups from slaves or cloning slaves from other slaves. However, in MySQL 5.0 and newer, the values are untrustworthy.

Planning for LVM backups

LVM snapshot backups aren't free. The more your server writes to the original volume, the more overhead they cause. When the server modifies many distinct blocks in random order, the disk head has to seek back and forth to the copy-on-write space and write the old version of the data there. Reading from the snapshot also has overhead, because LVM really reads most of the data from the original volume. It reads from the copy-on-write space only as needed; thus, a logically sequential read from the snapshot actually causes the disk head to move back and forth.

You should plan for this to happen. What it really means is that both the original volume and the snapshot will perform worse than usual for both reads and writes—possibly much worse if you use a lot of copy-on-write space. This can slow down both your MySQL server and the process of copying the files for the backup.

The other important thing to plan for is allocating enough space for the snapshot. We take the following approach:

- Remember that LVM needs to copy each modified block to the snapshot only once. When MySQL writes a block in the original volume, it copies the block to the snapshot, then makes a note of the copied block in its exception table. Future writes to this block will not cause any further copies to the snapshot.

- If you use only InnoDB, consider how InnoDB writes data. Because it writes all data twice, at least half of InnoDB's write I/O goes to the doublewrite buffer, log files, and other relatively small areas on disk. These reuse the same disk blocks over and over, so they'll have an initial impact on the snapshot, but after that they'll stop causing writes to the snapshot.

- Next, estimate how much of your I/O will be writing to blocks that haven't yet been copied to the snapshot, as opposed to modifying the same data again and again. Be generous with your estimate. This is how much extra I/O you expect the snapshot to cause. (Add in a little for the LVM process itself.)

- Use *vmstat* or *iostat* to gather statistics on how many blocks your server writes per second. You can learn more about these tools in Chapter 7.

- Measure (or estimate) how long it will take to copy your backup to another location: in other words, how long you need to keep the LVM snapshot open.

Let's suppose you've estimated that half of your writes will cause writes to the snapshot's copy-on-write space, and your server writes 10 MB per second. If it takes an hour (3,600 seconds) to copy the snapshot to another server, you will need $1/2 \times 10$ MB$\times$ 3,600, or 18 GB of space for the snapshot. Err on the side of caution, and add some extra space as well.

Sometimes it's easy to calculate how much data will change while you keep the snapshot open. Let's return to an example we've used in several other places. The Board-Reader forum search engine has about 1 TB of InnoDB tables per storage node. However, we know the biggest cost is loading new data. About 10 GB of new data is added per day, so 50 GB should be plenty of space for the snapshot. This estimate doesn't always work, though. At one point, we had a long-running ALTER TABLE that changed each shard one after the other, which modified much more than 50 GB of data; while this was running, we weren't able to make the backup.

Other uses and alternatives

You can use snapshots for more than just backups. For example, they can be a useful way to take a "checkpoint" just before a potentially dangerous action. Some systems, such as ZFS, let you promote the snapshot to the original filesystem. This makes it easy to roll back to the point at which you took the snapshot.

Filesystem snapshots aren't the only way to get an instantaneous copy of your data, either. Another option is a *RAID split*: if you have a three-disk software RAID mirror, for example, you can remove one disk from the mirror and mount it separately. There's no copy-on-write penalty, and it's easy to promote this kind of "snapshot" to be the master copy if necessary.

Recovering from a Backup

Recovery is what really matters. In this section, we focus on MySQL-specific aspects of recovery and assume you know how to handle the other parts of your environment. Perform "fire drills" routinely, so you know how to back up and recover your data when there's a real emergency. Above all, test your backups.

How you recover your data depends on how you backed it up. You might need to take some or all of the following steps:

- Stop the MySQL server.
- Take notes on the server's configuration and file permissions.
- Move the data from the backup into the MySQL data directory.
- Make configuration changes.
- Change file permissions.
- Restart the server with limited access, and wait for it to start fully.
- Reload logical backup files.
- Examine and replay binary logs.
- Verify what you've restored.
- Restart the server with full access.

We demonstrate how to do each of these steps as needed in the following sections. We also add notes specific to certain backup methods or tools in sections about those methods or tools later in this chapter.

 If there's a chance you'll need the current versions of your files, *don't replace them with the files from the backup*. For example, if your backup includes the binary logs, and you need to replay binary logs for point-in-time recovery, don't overwrite the current binary logs with older copies from the backup. Rename them or move them elsewhere if necessary.

Limiting Access to MySQL

During recovery, it's often important to make MySQL inaccessible to everything except the recovery process. This is hard to guarantee in complex systems. We like to start MySQL with the *--skip-networking* and *--socket=/tmp/mysql_recover.sock* options to ensure that it is unavailable to existing applications until we've checked it and brought it back online. This is especially important for logical backups, which are loaded in pieces.

Restoring Raw Files

Restoring raw files tends to be pretty straightforward—which is another way of saying there aren't many options. This can be a good or a bad thing, depending on your recovery requirements. The usual procedure is simply to copy the files into place.

Whether you need to shut down MySQL depends on the storage engine. MyISAM's files are generally independent from one another, and simply copying each table's *.frm*, *.MYI*, and *.MYD* files works well, even if the server is running. The server will find the table as soon as anyone queries it or otherwise it makes the server look for it (for example, by executing SHOW TABLES). If the table is open when you copy in these files, it'll probably cause trouble, so before doing so, you should either drop or rename the table, or use LOCK TABLES and FLUSH TABLES to close it.

InnoDB is another matter. If you're restoring a traditional InnoDB setup, where all tables are stored in a single tablespace, you'll have to shut down MySQL, copy or move the files into place, and then restart. You also need to ensure that InnoDB's transaction log files match its tablespace files. If the files don't match—for example, if you replace the tablespace files but not the transaction log files—InnoDB may refuse to start. This is one reason it's crucial to back up the transaction log along with the data files.

If you're using the newer InnoDB file-per-table feature (innodb_file_per_table), InnoDB stores the data and indexes for each table in a *.ibd* file, which is like a combination of MyISAM's *.MYI* and *.MYD* files. You can back up and restore individual tables by copying these files, and you can do it while the server is running, but it's not as simple as with MyISAM. The individual files are not independent from InnoDB as a whole. Each *.ibd* file has internal information that tells InnoDB how the file is related to the main (shared) tablespace. When you restore such a file, you have to tell InnoDB to "import" the file.

There are many restrictions on this process, which you can read about in the MySQL manual section on using per-table tablespaces. The biggest is that you can only restore a table to the server from which you backed it up. It's not impossible to back up and restore tables in this configuration, but it's trickier than you might think.

All this complexity means that restoring raw files can be very tedious, and it's easy to get it wrong. A good rule of thumb is that the harder and more complex your recovery procedure becomes, the more you need to protect yourself with logical backups as well. It's always a good idea to have a logical backup, in case something goes wrong and you can't convince MySQL to use your raw backups.

Starting MySQL after restoring raw files

There are a few things you'll need to do before you start the MySQL server you're recovering.

The first and most important thing, and one of the easiest to forget, is to check your server's configuration and make sure the restored files have the correct owner and permissions, *before* you try to start the MySQL server. These attributes must be exactly right, or MySQL may not start. The attributes vary from system to system, so check your notes to see exactly what you'll need to set. You typically want the *mysql* user and group to own the files and directories, which you want to be readable and writable by that user and group but no others.

We also suggest watching the MySQL error log while the server starts. On a Unix-style system, you can watch the file like this:

```
$ tail -f /var/log/mysql/mysql.err
```

The exact location of the error log will vary. Once you're monitoring the file, you can start the MySQL server and watch for errors. If all goes well, you'll have a nicely recovered server once MySQL starts.

Watching the error log is even more important in newer MySQL versions. Older versions wouldn't start if InnoDB had an error, but in newer versions the server will start anyway and just disable InnoDB. Even if the server seems to start without trouble, you should run SHOW TABLE STATUS in each database, then check the error log again.

Restoring Logical Backups

If you're restoring logical backups instead of raw files, you need to use the MySQL server itself to load the data back into the tables, as opposed to using the operating system to simply copy files into place.

Before you load that dump file, however, take a moment to consider how large it is, how long it'll take to load, and anything you might want to do before you start, such as notifying your users or disabling part of your application. Disabling binary logging might be a good idea, unless you need to replicate the restoration to a slave: a huge dump file is hard enough for the server to load, and writing it to the binary log adds even more (possibly unnecessary) overhead. Loading huge files also has consequences for some storage engines. For example, it's not a good idea to load 100 GB of data into InnoDB in a single transaction, because of the huge rollback segment that will result. You should load in manageable chunks and commit the transaction after each chunk.

There are two kinds of restoration you might do, which correspond to the two kinds of logical backups you can make.

Loading SQL files

If you have a SQL dump, the file will contain executable SQL. All you need to do is run it. Assuming you backed up the Sakila sample database and schema into a single file, the following is a typical command you might use to restore it:

```
$ mysql < sakila-backup.sql
```

You can also load the file from within the *mysql* command-line client with the SOURCE command. Although this is mostly a different way of doing the same thing, it makes some things easier. For example, if you're an administrative user in MySQL, you can turn off binary logging of the statements you'll execute from within your client connection, and then load the file without needing to restart the MySQL server:

```
mysql> SET SQL_LOG_BIN = 0;
mysql> SOURCE sakila-backup.sql;
mysql> SET SQL_LOG_BIN = 1;
```

If you use SOURCE, be aware that an error won't abort a batch of statements, as it will by default when you redirect the file into *mysql*.

If you compressed the backup, don't separately decompress and load it. Instead, decompress and load it in a single operation. This is much faster:

```
$ gunzip -c sakila-backup.sql.gz | mysql
```

If you want to load a compressed file with the SOURCE command, see the discussion of named pipes in the next section.

What if you want to restore only a single table (for example, the actor table)? If your data has no line breaks, it's not hard to restore the data if the schema is already in place:

```
$ grep 'INSERT INTO `actor`' sakila-backup.sql | mysql sakila
```

Or, if the file is compressed:

```
$ gunzip -c sakila-backup.sql.gz | grep 'INSERT INTO `actor`'| mysql sakila
```

If you need to create the table as well as restore the data, and you have the entire database in a single file, you'll have to edit the file. This is why many people like to dump each table into its own file. Most editors can't deal with huge files, especially if they're compressed. Besides, you don't want to actually edit the file itself—you just want to extract the relevant lines—so you'll probably have to do some command-line work. It's easy to use *grep* to pull out only the INSERT statements for a given table, as we did in the previous commands, but it's harder to get the CREATE TABLE statement. Here's a *sed* script that extracts the paragraph you need:

```
$ sed -e '/./{H;$!d;}' -e 'x;/CREATE TABLE `actor`/!d;q' sakila-backup.sql
```

That's pretty cryptic, we admit. If you have to do this kind of work to restore data, your backups are poorly designed. With a little planning, it's possible to prevent a situation in which you're panicked and trying to figure out how *sed* works. Just back up each table into its own file, or, better yet, back up the data and schema separately.

Loading delimited files

If you dumped the data via SELECT INTO OUTFILE, you'll have to use LOAD DATA INFILE with the same parameters to restore it. You can also use *mysqlimport*, which is a wrapper around LOAD DATA INFILE. It relies on naming conventions to determine where to load a file's data.

We hope you dumped your schema, not just your data. If so, it's a SQL dump, and you can use the techniques outlined in the previous section to load it.

There's a great optimization you can use with LOAD DATA INFILE. It must read directly from a file, so you might think you have to decompress the file before loading it, which is very slow and disk-intensive. However, there's a way around that, at least on systems that support FIFO "named pipe" files, such as GNU/Linux. First, create a named pipe and stream the decompressed data into it:

```
$ mkfifo /tmp/backup/default/sakila/payment.fifo
$ chmod 666 /tmp/backup/default/sakila/payment.fifo
$ gunzip -c /tmp/backup/default/sakila/payment.txt.gz > /tmp/backup/default/sakila/
payment.fifo
```

Notice we're using a greater-than character (>) to redirect the decompressed output into the *payment.fifo* file—not a pipe symbol, which creates anonymous pipes between programs. The *payment.fifo* file is a named pipe, so there's no need for an anonymous one.

The pipe will wait until some program opens it for reading from the other end. Here's the neat part: the MySQL server can read the decompressed data from the pipe, just like any other file. Don't forget to disable binary logging if appropriate:

```
mysql> SET SQL_LOG_BIN = 0; -- Optional
    -> LOAD DATA INFILE '/tmp/backup/default/sakila/payment.fifo'
    -> INTO TABLE sakila.payment;
Query OK, 16049 rows affected (2.29 sec)
Records: 16049  Deleted: 0  Skipped: 0  Warnings: 0
```

Once MySQL is done loading the data, *gunzip* will exit, and you can delete the named pipe. You can use this same technique to load compressed files from within the MySQL command-line client with the SOURCE command.

Why Test Backups?

One of the authors recently changed a column from DATETIME to TIMESTAMP to save space and make processing faster, as recommended in Chapter 3. The resulting table definition looked like the following:

```
CREATE TABLE tbl (
    col1 timestamp NOT NULL,
    col2 timestamp NOT NULL default CURRENT_TIMESTAMP
        on update CURRENT_TIMESTAMP,
    ... more columns ...
);
```

This table definition causes a syntax error on MySQL 5.0.40, the server version from which it was created. You can dump it, but you can't reload it. Odd, unforeseen errors such as this one are among the reasons why it's important to test your backups. You never know what will prevent you from restoring your data!

Point-in-Time Recovery

The most common way to do point-in-time recovery with MySQL is to restore your last full backup and then replay the binary log from that time forward (sometimes called "roll-forward recovery"). As long as you have the binary log, you can recover to any point you wish. You can even recover a single database without too much trouble.

A common scenario is undoing the effects of a harmful statement, such as a DROP TABLE. Let's see a simplified example of how to do that, using only MyISAM tables. Suppose that at midnight, the backup job ran the equivalent of the following statements, which copied the database elsewhere on the same server:

```
mysql> FLUSH TABLES WITH READ LOCK;
    -> server1# cp -a /var/lib/mysql/sakila /backup/sakila;
```

```
mysql> FLUSH LOGS;
    -> server1# mysql -e "SHOW MASTER STATUS" --vertical > /backup/master.info;
mysql> UNLOCK TABLES;
```

Then, later in the day, suppose someone ran the following statement:

```
mysql> USE sakila;
mysql> DROP TABLE sakila.payment;
```

For the sake of illustration, we assume that we can recover this database in isolation (that is, that no tables in this database were involved in cross-database queries). We also assume that we didn't notice the offending statement until some time later. The goal is to recover everything that's happened to the database, except for that statement. That is, we must also preserve all the modifications that have been made to other tables, including after that statement was run.

This isn't all that hard to do. First, we stop MySQL to prevent further modifications and restore just the sakila database from the backup:

```
server1# /etc/init.d/mysql stop
server1# mv /var/lib/mysql/sakila /var/lib/mysql/sakila.tmp
server1# cp -a /backup/sakila /var/lib/mysql
```

We disable normal connections by adding the following to the server's *my.cnf* file while we work:

```
skip-networking
socket=/tmp/mysql_recover.sock
```

Now it's safe to start the server:

```
server1# /etc/init.d/mysql start
```

The next task is to find which statements in the binary log we want to replay, and which we want to skip. As it happens, the server has created only one binary log since the backup at midnight. We can examine this file with *grep* and find the offending statement:

```
server1# mysqlbinlog --database=sakila /var/log/mysql/mysql-bin.000215 | grep -B
3 -i 'drop table sakila.payment'
# at 352
#070919 16:11:23 server id 1 end_log_pos 429   Query   thread_id=16   exec_time=0
error_code=0
SET TIMESTAMP=1190232683/*!*/;
DROP TABLE sakila.payment/*!*/;
```

The statement we want to skip is at position 352 in the log file, and the next statement is at position 429. We can replay the log up to position 352, and then from 429 on, with the following commands:

```
server1# mysqlbinlog --database=sakila /var/log/mysql/mysql-bin.000215
--stop-position=352 | mysql -uroot -p
server1# mysqlbinlog --database=sakila /var/log/mysql/mysql-bin.000215
--start-position=429 | mysql -uroot -p
```

Now all we have to do is check the data just to be sure, stop the server and undo the changes to *my.cnf*, and restart the server.

More Advanced Recovery Techniques

Replication and point-in-time recovery use the same mechanism: the server's binary log. This means replication can be a helpful tool during recovery, in some not-so-obvious ways. We show you some of the possibilities in this section. This isn't an exhaustive list, but it should give you some ideas about how to design recovery processes for your needs. Remember to script and rehearse anything you think you'll need to do during recovery.

Delayed replication for fast recovery

As we mentioned earlier in this chapter, having a delayed replication slave can make point-in-time recovery much faster and easier if you notice the accident before the slave executes the offending statement.

The procedure is a little different from that outlined in the preceding section, but the idea is the same. You stop the slave, then use START SLAVE UNTIL to replay events until just before the statement you want to skip. Next, you execute SET GLOBAL SQL_SLAVE_SKIP_COUNTER=1 to skip the bad statement. Set it to a value higher than 1 if you want to skip several events (or simply use CHANGE MASTER TO to advance the slave's position in the log).

All you have to do then is execute START SLAVE and let the slave run until it is finished executing its relay logs. Your slave has done all the tedious work of point-in-time recovery for you. Now you can promote the slave to master, and you've recovered with very little interruption.

Even if you don't have a delayed replication slave to speed recovery, slaves can be useful because they fetch the master's binary logs onto another machine. If your master's disk fails, a slave's relay logs might be the only place you'll have a reasonably up-to-date copy of the master's binary logs. (It's even safer to keep the binary logs on a SAN or replicate them with DRBD, as discussed in Chapter 9.)

Recovering with a log server

There's another way to use replication for recovery: set up a log server. (See "Creating a log server" on page 374 for more details on how to do this.)

A log server is more flexible and easier to use for recovery than *mysqlbinlog*, not only because of the START SLAVE UNTIL option, but also because of the replication rules you can apply (such as replicate-do-table). With a log server, you can do much more complex filtering than you'd be able to do otherwise.

For example, a log server lets you recover a single table easily. This is a lot harder to do correctly with *mysqlbinlog* and command-line tools—in fact, it's hard enough that we advise you not to try.

Let's suppose our careless developer dropped the same table as before, and we want to recover it without reverting the whole server to last night's backup. Here's how to do this with a log server:

1. Let the server you need to recover be called server1.

2. Recover last night's backup to another server, called server2. Run the recovery process on this server to avoid the risk of making things worse if you make a mistake in recovery.

3. Set up a log server to serve server1's binary logs, following the directions in "Creating a log server" on page 374. (It might be a good idea to copy the logs away to another server and set up the log server there, just to be extra careful.)

4. Change server2's configuration file to include the following:

        replicate-do-table=sakila.payment

5. Restart server2, then make it a slave of the log server with CHANGE MASTER TO. Configure it to read from the binary log coordinates of last night's backup. Don't run START SLAVE yet.

6. Examine the output of SHOW SLAVE STATUS on server2 and verify that everything is correct. Measure twice, cut once!

7. Find the binary log position of the offending statement, and execute START SLAVE UNTIL to replay events until just before that position on server2.

8. Stop the slave process on server2 with STOP SLAVE. It should now have the table as it existed just before it was dropped.

9. Copy the table from server2 to server1.

This process is possible only if the table isn't the target of any multitable UPDATE, DELETE, or INSERT statements. Any such statements will execute against a different database state than the one that existed when the binary log events were logged, so the table will probably end up containing different data than it should.

InnoDB Recovery

InnoDB checks its data and log files every time it starts to see whether it needs to perform its recovery process. However, InnoDB's recovery isn't the same thing we've been talking about in the context of this chapter. It's not recovering backed-up data; instead, it's applying transactions from the logs to the data files and rolling back uncommitted modifications to the data files.

Exactly how InnoDB recovery works is a little too complicated to describe here. We focus instead on how to actually perform recovery when InnoDB has a serious problem.

Most of the time InnoDB is very good at fixing problems. Unless there is a bug in MySQL or your hardware is faulty, you shouldn't have to do anything out of the ordinary, even if your server loses power. InnoDB will just perform its normal recovery upon startup, and all will be well. In the log file, you'll see messages like the following:

```
InnoDB: Doing recovery: scanned up to log sequence number 0 40817239
InnoDB: Starting an apply batch of log records to the database...
```

InnoDB prints progress messages in percents into the log file. Some people report not seeing these until the whole process is done. Be patient; there is no way to hurry the process. Killing and restarting will just make it take longer.

If there's a severe problem with your hardware, such as memory or disk corruption, or if you run into a bug in MySQL or InnoDB, you might have to intervene and either force recovery or prevent the normal recovery from happening.

Causes of InnoDB corruption

InnoDB is generally pretty robust. It is built to be reliable, and it has a lot of built-in sanity checks to prevent, find, and fix corrupted data—much more so than some other storage engines. However, it can't protect itself against everything.

At a minimum, InnoDB relies on unbuffered I/O calls and fsync() calls not returning until the data is safely written to physical media. If your hardware doesn't deliver these, InnoDB can't protect your data, and a crash can cause corruption.

Many InnoDB corruption problems are hardware-related (e.g., corrupted page writes caused by power failures or bad memory). However, misconfigured hardware is a much bigger source of problems in our experience. Common misconfigurations include enabling the writeback cache on a RAID card that doesn't have a battery backup unit, or enabling the writeback cache on hard drives themselves. These mistakes will cause the controller or drive to lie and say the fsync() completed, when the data is in fact only in the writeback cache, not on disk. In other words, the hardware doesn't provide the guarantees InnoDB needs to keep your data safe.

Sometimes machines are configured this way by default, because it gives better performance—which may be fine for some purposes, but not for a transactional database server. You should always check a machine if you didn't set it up yourself.

You can also get corruption if you run InnoDB on network-attached storage (NAS), because completing a fsync() to such a device just means the device received the data. The data is safe if InnoDB crashes, but not necessarily if the NAS device crashes.

Sometimes the corruption is worse than other times. Severe corruption can crash InnoDB or MySQL, but less severe corruption might just mean some transactions are lost because the log files weren't really synced to disk.

How to recover corrupted InnoDB data

There are three major types of InnoDB corruption, and each requires a different level of effort to recover the data:

Secondary index corruption
> You can often fix a corrupt secondary index with OPTIMIZE TABLE; alternatively, you can use SELECT INTO OUTFILE, drop and recreate the table, then use LOAD DATA INFILE. These processes fix the corruption by building a new table, and hence rebuilding the affected index.

Clustered index corruption
> You may need to use the innodb_force_recovery settings to dump the table (more on this later). Sometimes the dump process crashes InnoDB; if this happens, you may need to dump ranges of rows to skip the corrupted pages that are causing the crash. A corrupt clustered index is more severe than a corrupt secondary index because it affects the data rows themselves, but it's still possible to fix just the affected tables in many cases.

Corrupt system structures
> System structures include the InnoDB transaction log, the undo log area of the tablespace, and the data dictionary. This type of corruption is likely to require a complete dump and restore, because much of InnoDB's inner workings may be affected.

You can usually repair a corrupted secondary index without losing any data. However, the other two scenarios often involve at least some data loss. If you have a backup, you're probably better off restoring that backup rather than trying to extract data from corrupt files.

If you must try to extract the data from the corrupted files, the general process is to try to get InnoDB up and running, then use SELECT INTO OUTFILE to dump the data. If your server has already crashed and you can't even start InnoDB without crashing it, you can configure it to prevent the normal recovery and background processes from running. This might let you start the server and make a logical backup with reduced or no integrity checking.

The innodb_force_recovery parameter controls which kinds of operations InnoDB will do at startup and during normal operation. The normal value is 0, and you can increase it up to 6. The MySQL manual documents the exact behavior of each option; we won't duplicate that information here, but we will note that you can increase the value to as high as 4 with little danger. At this setting, you may lose some data on pages that have corruption; if you go higher, you may extract bad data from corrupted pages, or increase the risk of a crash during the SELECT INTO OUTFILE. In other words, levels up to 4 do no harm to your data, but they might miss opportunities to fix problems; levels 5 and 6 are more aggressive at fixing problems but risk doing harm.

When you set `innodb_force_recovery` to a value greater than 0, InnoDB is essentially read-only, but you can still create and drop tables. This prevents further corruption, and it makes InnoDB relax some of its normal checks so it doesn't intentionally crash when it finds bad data. In normal operations, this is a safeguard, but you don't want it when you're recovering. If you need to force InnoDB recovery, it's a good idea to configure MySQL not to allow normal connection requests until you're finished.

If InnoDB's data is so corrupt that you can't start MySQL at all, you can use the InnoDB Recovery Toolkit to extract data directly from the tablespace pages. These tools were developed by some of this book's authors and are freely available at *http:// code.google.com/p/innodb-tools/*.

 We usually don't mention specific bugs in MySQL, but there's a pretty severe bug in many versions of MySQL that prevents you from performing recovery when `innodb_force_recovery` is defined. You can track the bug's status at *http://bugs.mysql.com/28604*. If you get the error "Incorrect key file" while trying to dump a corrupt InnoDB table, read that bug report and see if it's the problem. If so, you may be able to use MySQL 5.0.22 to dump the data. Hopefully, you'll never need to worry about this.

Backup and Recovery Speed

Next to correctness, speed is the most important concern for backing up and recovering high-performance systems. Here are some things to consider:

Lock time
How long do you need to hold locks, such as the global FLUSH TABLES WITH READ LOCK, while backing up?

Backup time
How long does it take to copy the backup to the destination?

Backup load
How much does it impact the server's performance to copy the backup to the destination?

Recovery time
How long does it take to copy your backup image from its storage location to the MySQL server, replay binary logs, and so on?

The biggest tradeoff is backup time versus backup load. You can often improve one at the other's expense; for example, you can prioritize the backup at the expense of causing more performance degradation on the server.

You can also design your backups to take advantage of load patterns. For instance, if your server is only 50% loaded for 8 hours during the night, you can try to design your backups to load the server less than 50% and still complete within 8 hours.

You can accomplish this in many ways: for example, you can use *ionice* and *nice* to prioritize the copy or compression operations, use different compression levels, or compress the data on the backup server instead of the MySQL server. You can also use O_DIRECT or *madvice* to bypass the operating system's cache for the copy operations, so they don't pollute the server's caches.

In general, it's a good bit faster and requires less work to do raw copies than logical backups. However, logical backups are an important supplement, because raw files aren't as portable, aren't restorable indefinitely, and can have corruption that's hard to detect. If you do periodic logical backups from a raw file copy, you can get the best of both worlds for relatively little extra effort.

Backup Tools

Anything beyond simply stopping the server, restoring the data, and restarting the server can get pretty involved. It's essential to rehearse and script these actions. The following sections introduce some tools that are useful for backup and recovery, both for scripting and for one-shot dumps and restores.

The first edition of this book said, "If you have a complex configuration or unusual needs, there's a chance that none of these alone will do the job for you. Instead, you'll need to build a custom solution." Times have changed, and today we'd advise against scripting your own backup tools unless it's really necessary. There's a good chance that some preexisting tool will fit your needs nicely, and if not, you may be able to modify one to do what you need.

Still, some of the more complicated backup scenarios will necessitate custom scripting, so we've included some basic how-to advice at the end of the chapter.

mysqldump

The most popular program for creating logical backups of data and schema is *mysqldump*. *mysqldump* is provided with the server, so you don't even need to install it. It's a general-purpose tool that can be used for many tasks, such as copying a table from one server to another:

```
$ mysqldump --host=server1 test t1 | mysql --host=server2 test
```

We've shown several examples of how to create logical backups with *mysqldump* throughout this chapter. By default, it outputs a script containing all the commands needed to create a table and fill it with data; there are also options to output views, stored routines, and triggers. Here are some more examples of typical usage:

- To make a logical backup of everything on a server to a single file:

```
$ mysqldump --all-databases > dump.sql
```

- To make a logical backup of only the Sakila sample database:

    `$ mysqldump --databases sakila > dump.sql`

- To make a logical backup of only the `sakila.actor` table:

    `$ mysqldump sakila actor > dump.sql`

You can use the *--result-file* option to specify an output file, which can help prevent newline conversion on Windows:

`$ mysqldump sakila actor --result-file=dump.sql`

The default options for *mysqldump* aren't all that good for serious backup purposes. You'll probably want to specify some options explicitly to change the output. Here are options we use frequently to make *mysqldump* more efficient and make its output easier to use:

--opt
> Enables a group of options that disable buffering (which could make your server run out of memory), write more data into fewer SQL statements in the dump, so they'll load more efficiently, and do some other useful things. Read your version's help for the details. If you disable this group of options, *mysqldump* will store each table you dump in its memory before writing it to the disk, which is impractical for large tables.

--allow-keywords, --quote-names
> Make it possible to dump and restore tables that use reserved words as names.

--complete-insert
> Makes it possible to move data between tables that don't have identical columns.

--tz-utc
> Makes it possible to move data between servers in different time zones.

--lock-all-tables
> Uses FLUSH TABLES WITH READ LOCK to get a globally consistent backup.

--tab
> Dumps files with SELECT INTO OUTFILE, which is very fast to dump and to restore.

--skip-extended-insert
> Causes each row of data to have its own INSERT statement. This can help you selectively restore certain rows if necessary. The cost is larger files that are more expensive to import into MySQL; you should enable this only if you need it.

If you use the *--databases* or *--all-databases* options to *mysqldump*, the resulting dump's data will be consistent within each database, because *mysqldump* will lock and dump all tables a database at a time. However, tables from different databases may not be consistent with each other. Using the *--lock-all-tables* option solves this problem.

mysqlhotcopy

mysqlhotcopy is a Perl script included in standard MySQL server downloads. It was designed for MyISAM tables, and in our opinion it does *not* do "hot" backups, because it locks all tables before copying them. Although it used to be one of the most popular options for backups on a live server, it is less popular these days. Many high-performance installations are moving away from MyISAM, and even if you're using only MyISAM, filesystem snapshots are often less intrusive because they can lock the data for a shorter time.

As an example, we created a copy of the Sakila sample database using all MyISAM tables. To back up this database to */tmp*, we ran the following command:

```
$ mysqlhotcopy sakila_myisam /tmp
```

This created a *sakila_myisam* subdirectory in */tmp* that contained all the tables from the database:

```
$ ls -l /tmp/sakila_myisam/
total 3632
-rw-rw---- 1 mysql mysql   8694 2007-09-28 09:57 actor.frm
-rw-rw---- 1 mysql mysql   5016 2007-09-28 09:57 actor.MYD
-rw-rw---- 1 mysql mysql   7168 2007-09-28 09:57 actor.MYI
... omitted ...
-rw-rw---- 1 mysql mysql   8708 2007-09-28 09:57 store.frm
-rw-rw---- 1 mysql mysql     18 2007-09-28 09:57 store.MYD
-rw-rw---- 1 mysql mysql   4096 2007-09-28 09:57 store.MYI
```

It copied the data, index, and table definition files for each table in the database. To save space, you can use the *--noindices* option to back up only the first 2,048 bytes of each *.MYI* file, which is all MySQL needs to reconstruct the indexes later. If you use this option, you'll need to rebuild the indexes after restoring the files. You can either use *myisamchk* with the *--recover* option, or use the REPAIR TABLE SQL command.

mysqlhotcopy is pretty complicated and not all that flexible, so a lot of people roll their own scripts to do essentially the same job in a slightly different way.

 mysqlhotcopy will copy the *.ibd* data files when InnoDB is configured with innodb_file_per_table, but that's useless. Don't let this give you a false sense of security; it is not a safe way to back up your InnoDB data.

InnoDB Hot Backup

The InnoDB Hot Backup, *ibbackup*, is a commercial tool distributed by the makers of InnoDB (Innobase). Using it does not require stopping MySQL, setting locks, or interrupting normal database activity (though it will cause some extra load on your server). It can also compress backups.

Configure *ibbackup* by providing it with a configuration file matching your production server's *my.cnf* file, but with a different data directory. The tool reads both configuration files and copies the InnoDB files from the production server to the location specified in the second configuration file:

```
$ ibbackup /etc/my.cnf /etc/ibbackup.cnf
```

To restore the backup, shut down MySQL and run the following command:

```
$ ibbackup --restore /etc/ibbackup.cnf
```

There's one small problem: *ibbackup* copies only the InnoDB files, not the table definition or other necessary files. Innobase also provides an *innobackup* helper script that wraps file copies, table locks, and *ibbackup* into a single command that can back up table definitions and MyISAM files as well as the InnoDB files. Unlike *ibbackup* by itself, this does interrupt normal processing, because it uses FLUSH TABLES WITH READ LOCK. It is free software.

In our opinion, LVM's snapshot capabilities are more convenient and useful for InnoDB backups than *ibbackup*. One of LVM's great conveniences is that you don't need to make a second copy of your data on the filesystem—you can create a snapshot, perform InnoDB recovery on it if you wish, and then send it directly to the backup destination.

LVM and *ibbackup* generally have comparable performance, depending on how you've configured the backup and whether you have a write-intensive workload. In that case, there will be a lot of copy-on-write overhead for LVM. On the other hand, *ibbackup* may not scale linearly with data size. It works by copying the data files page-by-page, then applying the log file to the copied data files to "recover" them to a single point in time that corresponds to the end of the backup process.

mk-parallel-dump

This tool is part of Maatkit (*http://maatkit.sourceforge.net*). It performs several backup operations at the same time.

By default, *mk-parallel-dump* acts as a multithreaded wrapper around *mysqldump*, but it can also perform tab-separated exports with SELECT INTO OUTFILE. It defaults to one thread per CPU, so the more CPUs you have, the faster it generally works. It can also back up each table in chunks of a desired size, which makes restore operations much faster for InnoDB tables. The benefit is that you can avoid an enormous transaction when restoring. A large transaction can cause InnoDB's tablespace to grow very large and increases rollback time if there's an error.

The tool also has some nice features, such as the ability to do incremental backups and group tables into logical backup sets. Benchmarks indicate a significant speed boost from doing logical backups in parallel.

Maatkit also contains *mk-parallel-restore*, a companion program to do multithreaded imports. Both tools make good use of Unix idioms such as pipes and FIFO devices to reduce the impact of compressing and decompressing files.

mylvmbackup

Lenz Grimmer's *mylvmbackup* (*http://lenz.homelinux.org/mylvmbackup/*) is a Perl script to help automate MySQL backups via LVM snapshots. It gets a global read lock, creates a snapshot, and releases the lock. It then compresses the data with *tar* and removes the snapshot. It names the tarball according to the timestamp at which the backup was made.

Zmanda Recovery Manager

Zmanda Recovery Manager for MySQL, or ZRM (*http://www.zmanda.com*), is the most comprehensive of the backup and recovery tools we mention here. It comes in both free (GPL) and commercial versions. The enterprise edition comes with a management console that provides a graphical web-based interface for configuration, backup, verification, recovery, reporting, and scheduling. It can also back up MySQL Cluster, and it has all the usual benefits (such as support).

The open source edition is not crippled in any way, but it doesn't include some of the extra niceties, such as the web-based console. It's perfectly usable if you're comfortable at the command line. For example, you can still schedule and check backups at the command prompt.

ZRM is actually more of a "backup coordinator" than a single tool. It wraps its own functionality around standard tools and techniques, such as *mysqldump* and LVM snapshots, and it stores the data in standard formats, so there's no need to buy proprietary software to restore a backup. One of its nice features is its unified recovery mechanism, which works the same way regardless of how the backup was made.

Figure 11-2 shows the enterprise version's calendar overview of MySQL backups and the binary log analyzer, which Zmanda calls the "Database Events Viewer." It is essentially a search tool for your binary logs; you can use ordinary search syntax to find events, which makes it easier to restore to a certain log event or point in time.

Installing and testing ZRM

Zmanda's web site claims it takes about 15 minutes to install, perform, and verify a backup; set up and verify a daily schedule; and perform a restoration. As a test, we installed ZRM from scratch on a laptop running Ubuntu. The ZRM package itself is a tiny download, and we installed it with *sudo dpkg -i mysql-zrm_1.2.1_all.deb*. There were several prerequisites, but they were easy to install with *sudo apt-get -f install*. The process took less than a minute.

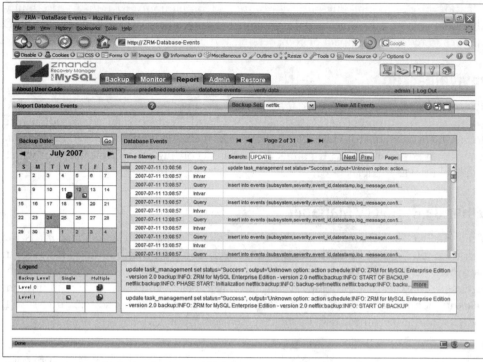

Figure 11-2. ZRM's backup calendar and binary log search interface

We followed the instructions on the web site to configure the backup set, which, in our case, was a logical backup of the Sakila sample database. This took about three minutes. Then we typed the following command to begin the backup:

```
# mysql-zrm-scheduler --now --backup-set dailyrun
```

The backup took just a moment, and the resulting file was stored in */var/lib/mysql-zrm/dailyrun*. We then ran it again and deliberately caused some errors for ZRM, such as killing some of its child processes and giving it the wrong login parameters. It correctly detected the errors and noted them in the backup emails it sent. Details were logged to the expected system log location.

Finally, we dropped the `sakila` database and restored it from the last successful backup with the following commands:

```
# mysql-zrm-reporter --show restore-info --where backup-set=dailyrun
# mysql-zrm-restore --backup-set dailyrun --source-directory
/var/lib/mysql-zrm/dailyrun/20070930134242/
```

In general, ZRM is a well-designed system with good error checking that automates much of the tedious work of backups and recovery. And, as its name indicates, it is designed from the bottom up for recovery.

R1Soft

R1Soft (*http://www.r1soft.com*) offers a product called Continuous Data Protection that is similar to filesystem snapshots, except that when it copies a snapshot to another server, it copies only the blocks that have changed. You can use it to roll back to multiple past versions of your data. It is commercial software.

MySQL Online Backup

MySQL online backup isn't a tool; it's a feature that's being developed for MySQL 5.2 (currently in alpha) and is likely to be released in MySQL 6.0.

The interface is a new BACKUP DATABASE SQL statement, which writes a consistent snapshot from each table to a file at high speed. It uses either a default driver that can back up any storage engine, or a driver implemented for a particular storage engine to do the backup more efficiently. The default driver blocks other SQL statements, but native drivers can perform the backup without blocking. Restore functionality is also included.

At the time of this writing, the project has an initial implementation in the 5.2 source tree and a respectable list of features completed, but there are also many features that have yet to be implemented, such as a native driver for MyISAM and consistent backups across storage engines.

Online backup is much anticipated, and when it's complete, it is likely to be one of the most important ways to back up MySQL.

Comparison of Backup Tools

Table 11-2 provides a quick summary of some of the backup methods we discussed in this chapter.

Table 11-2. Characteristics of backup tools

	mylvmbackup	mysqldump	mk-parallel-dump	mysqlhotcopy	ibbackup
Blocks processing?	Optional	Yes	Yes	Yes	No
Logical or raw	Raw	Logical	Logical	Raw	Raw
Engines	All	All	All	MyISAM/Archive	InnoDB
Speed	Very good	Slow	Good	Very good	Very good
Remote backups	No	Yes	Yes	No	No
Availability	Free	Free	Free	Free	Commercial
License	GPL	GPL	GPL	GPL	Proprietary

Scripting Backups

We've advised you not to reinvent the wheel if an existing system will work for you, but you still might need to either roll your own or modify an existing script. Here are some of the kinds of backup configurations we've seen in the real world:

- Backing up many servers onto some number of backup servers, which have large, cheap hard drives without RAID. The backup script allocates different volumes for each backup, based on which servers have enough space. It also ensures that different backup generations go on different servers, so losing any single server isn't a big deal.

- Slicing a backup archive into pieces, encrypting them, and storing them outside the data center, on Amazon's S3 service or another large storage service.

- Integrating recovery with replication, so you can reclone a slave from a backup.

Rather than showing you a sample program, which would necessarily have a lot of scaffolding that just takes up space on the page, we list the ingredients that go into a typical backup script and show you code snippets for a Perl script. You can view these as building blocks that you can snap together to create your own script. We show them in roughly the order you'll need to use them:

Sanity checking

Make life easier on yourself and your teammates—turn on strict error checking and use English variable names:

```
use strict;
use warnings FATAL => 'all';
use English qw(-no_match_vars);
```

If you script in Bash, you can enable stricter variable checking too. The following will raise an error when there's an undefined variable in a substitution or when a program exits with an error:

```
set -u;
set -e;
```

Command-line arguments

Every script needs to accept command-line arguments. If you find yourself hard-coding configuration such as usernames and passwords, you really should be working at a higher level.

```
use Getopt::Long;
Getopt::Long::Configure('no_ignore_case', 'bundling');
GetOptions( .... );
```

Connecting to MySQL

The standard Perl DBI library is nearly ubiquitous, and it provides a lot of power and flexibility. Read the Perldoc (available online at *http://search.cpan.org*) for details on how to use it.

```
use DBI;
$dbh = DBI->connect(
        'DBI:mysql:;host=localhost', 'user', 'pass', {RaiseError => 1 });
```

For command-line scripting, read the *--help* text for the standard *mysql* program. It has a lot of options to make it friendly for scripting. For example, here's how to iterate over a list of databases in Bash:

```
for DB in `mysql --skip-column-names --silent --execute 'SHOW DATABASES'`
do
    echo $DB
done
```

Stopping and starting MySQL

The best way to stop and start MySQL is to use your operating system's preferred method, such as running the */etc/init.d/mysql* init script or the service control (on Windows). It's not the only way, though. You can shut down the database from Perl, with an existing database connection:

```
$dbh->func("shutdown", 'admin');
```

You shouldn't rely on MySQL being shut down when this command completes—it may only be in the process of shutting down. You can also stop MySQL from the command line:

```
$ mysqladmin shutdown
```

Getting lists of databases and tables

Every backup script asks MySQL for a list of databases and tables. Beware of entries that aren't really databases, such as the *lost+found* directory in some journaling filesystems and the INFORMATION_SCHEMA. Make sure your script is ready to deal with views, too, and be aware that SHOW TABLE STATUS can take a really long time when you have lots of data in InnoDB:

```
mysql> SHOW DATABASES;
mysql> SHOW /*!50002 FULL*/ TABLES FROM <database>;
mysql> SHOW TABLE STATUS FROM <database>;
```

Locking, flushing, and unlocking tables

You're bound to need to lock and/or flush one or more tables. You can either lock the desired tables by naming them all, or just lock everything globally:

```
mysql> LOCK TABLES <database.table> READ [, ...];
mysql> FLUSH TABLES;
mysql> FLUSH TABLES <database.table> [, ...];
mysql> FLUSH TABLES WITH READ LOCK;
mysql> UNLOCK TABLES;
```

Be very careful about race conditions when getting lists of tables and locking them. New tables could be created, or tables could be dropped or renamed. If you lock and back them up one at a time, you won't get consistent backups.

Flushing binary logs

It's handy to ask the server to begin a new binary log (do this after locking the tables, but before taking a backup):

```
mysql> FLUSH LOGS;
```

It makes recovery and incremental backups easier if you don't have to think about starting in the middle of a log file. This does have some side effects with regard to flushing and reopening logs and potentially destroying old log entries, so be careful you're not throwing away data you need.

Getting binary log positions

Your script should get and record both the master and slave status—even if the server is just a master or just a slave:

```
mysql> SHOW MASTER STATUS;
mysql> SHOW SLAVE STATUS;
```

Issue both statements and ignore any errors you get, so your script gets all the information possible.

Dumping data

Your two best options are to use *mysqldump* or SELECT INTO OUTFILE.

Copying data

Use one of the methods we showed throughout the chapter.

These are the building blocks of any backup script. The hard part is to script the recovery. If you want inspiration for how to do this well, take a look at the source code for ZRM. Its scripts do some smart things, such as keeping metadata with each backup to make it easier to restore.

Security

Keeping MySQL secure is critical to protecting your data's integrity and privacy. Just as you have to protect Unix or Windows login accounts, you need to ensure that MySQL accounts have good passwords and only the privileges they need. Because MySQL is often used on a network, you also need to consider the security of the host that runs MySQL, who has access to it, and what someone could learn by sniffing traffic on your network.

MySQL has a nonstandard security and privilege system that lets you do a lot of specialized tasks. It's built around a set of simple rules, but there are many complicated exceptions and special cases, so it can be hard to understand. In this chapter, we look at how MySQL's permissions work and how you can control who has access to your data. The MySQL manual has thorough documentation on privileges, so we just explain the confusing concepts and show you how to do some common tasks that might otherwise be hard to learn. We also consider some of the basic operating system and network security measures you can employ to keep the bad guys out of your databases. Finally, we discuss encryption and running MySQL in a highly restricted environment.

Terminology

Before we begin, let's define a few terms that may be confusing. We use them to mean specific things in this chapter:

Authentication
> Who are you? MySQL authenticates you with a username, a password, and the host from which you are connecting. Knowing who you are is a prerequisite to determining your privileges.

Authorization
> What are you allowed to do? Shutting down the server, for example, requires that you have the SHUTDOWN privilege. In MySQL, authorization applies to global

privileges, which aren't associated with any specific schema objects (such as tables or databases).

Access control

What data are you allowed to see and/or manipulate? When you try to read or modify data, MySQL checks to see that you've been granted permission to see or change the columns you are selecting. Unlike global privileges, access controls apply to specific data, such as a particular database, table, or column.

Privileges and permissions

These terms mean roughly the same thing—a privilege or permission is how MySQL represents an authorization or access right.

Account Basics

MySQL accounts aren't like accounts in most systems, because MySQL considers the origin of a login attempt to be part of the authentication. In contrast, a Unix login attempt is usually authenticated with just a username and a password. In other words, a Unix account's primary key is the username, whereas in MySQL it's the username and location (usually a hostname, IP address, or wildcard).

As we'll see, having a location associated with the account adds complexity to an otherwise simple system. The user *joe* who logs in from *joe.example.com* may not be the same as the *joe* who logs in from *sally.example.com*. From MySQL's point of view, they can be completely different users, with different passwords and privileges. On the other hand, they could be the same user. It depends on how you've configured the accounts.

Privileges

MySQL uses your account information (username, password, and location) to authenticate you. Once it has done so, it must decide what you're allowed to do. It does this by consulting your *privileges*, which are usually named after the SQL queries they let you execute. For example, you need the SELECT privilege on a table to retrieve data from it.

There are two kinds of privileges: those that are associated with objects (such as tables, databases, and views), and those that aren't. *Object-specific privileges* grant you access to specific objects. For example, they control whether you can retrieve data from a table, alter a table, create a view in a database, or create a trigger. MySQL 5.0 and newer have many additional object-specific privileges, because of the introduction of views, stored procedures, and other new features.

Global privileges, on the other hand, let you perform functions such as shutting down the server, executing FLUSH commands, running various SHOW commands, and viewing other users' queries. In general, the global privileges let you do things to the server, and the object-based privileges let you do things to the server's contents (although that distinction is not always sharply defined). Each global privilege has far-reaching security implications, so be very cautious when granting any of them!

MySQL privileges are Boolean: a privilege is either granted or not. Unlike some other database systems, MySQL doesn't have the notion of explicitly denied privileges. Revoking a privilege doesn't forbid the user to perform an action; it merely removes the privilege to perform the action if it exists.

MySQL's privileges are also hierarchical, with a twist or two. We explain this in a bit.

The Grant Tables

MySQL uses a series of *grant tables* to store users and their privileges. The tables are ordinary MyISAM tables* that live in the mysql database. Storing the security information in grant tables makes a lot of sense, but it also means that if the server isn't configured correctly, any user can make security changes by altering the data in those tables!

MySQL's grant tables are the heart of its security system. MySQL now gives you nearly full control of security with the GRANT, REVOKE, and DROP USER privileges (which we discuss later). However, manipulating the grant tables used to be the only means of performing certain tasks. For instance, in old MySQL versions, the only way to remove a user completely was to DELETE that user from the user table, then FLUSH PRIVILEGES.

We don't recommend changing the grant tables directly, but you should still understand how they work so you can debug unexpected behavior. We encourage you to examine the grant table structures with DESCRIBE or SHOW CREATE TABLE, especially after you use GRANT and REVOKE to change privileges. You'll learn more from doing that than from reading about them.

Here are the grant tables in the order in which MySQL consults them when checking whether a user is authorized to do a specific operation:

user
> Each row contains a user account (the username, hostname, and encrypted password) and the user's global privileges. MySQL 5.0 adds optional per-user limits, such as the number of connections the user is allowed to have.

db
> Each row contains database-level privileges for a specific user.

---

* And they must remain ordinary MyISAM tables. Don't change their storage engine to anything else.

host

Each row contains privileges to one database for a user connecting from a given host. The entries are "merged" with entries in db when checking database-level access. Though we list it as a grant table, the GRANT and REVOKE commands never modify the host table. You can only add and remove entries manually.

We recommend that you do not use this table to prevent maintenance problems and confusing behavior later.

tables_priv

Each row contains table-level privileges for a specific user and table. It also contains view privileges.

columns_priv

Each row contains column-level privileges for a specific user and column.

procs_priv *(new in MySQL 5.0)*

Each row contains privileges for a specific user and stored routine (stored procedure or function).

How MySQL Checks Privileges

MySQL checks the privileges from the grant tables in the order we listed them in the previous section. The server stops checking when it finds a match that grants the desired privilege. That is, if it finds a matching entry in the db table that grants the desired access, it will not consult the tables_priv table at all. Figure 12-1 illustrates this process.

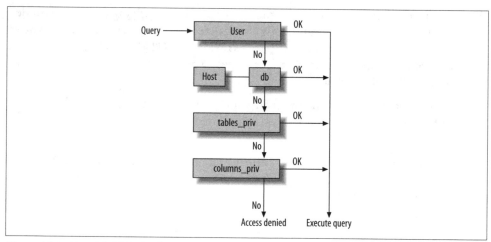

Figure 12-1. How MySQL checks privileges

MySQL determines which privileges apply by issuing the equivalent of a SELECT statement against the cached grant tables. This virtual statement's WHERE clause contains the columns of each table's primary key. Some of the columns allow pattern matches, and many of them have "magical" meanings when they have special values, such as when they're empty. Consult the MySQL manual for details.

You could spend a lot of time learning about the grant tables and how they work, and that knowledge might occasionally come in handy. However, we wouldn't recommend putting in all that time unless it's absolutely necessary. Instead, read the next section. Delving deeply into the grant tables is worthwhile only if you find a situation that you can't set up (or that is too complex to set up) with the GRANT and REVOKE commands.

Adding, Removing, and Viewing Grants

The recommended way to add user accounts and add and remove privileges in MySQL is via the GRANT and REVOKE commands, which are well documented in the MySQL manual. They provide a simple syntax for making most changes without needing to understand the underlying grant tables and their various matching rules. You can add a new user account or a privilege with GRANT, but REVOKE can remove only privileges, not accounts; you'll need to use DROP USER to remove a user account.

You can use SHOW GRANTS to see a user's grants. The result is the syntax required to recreate the same account with its current privileges. For example, here's what a default installation on a Debian system shows after logging in as *root*:

```
mysql> SHOW GRANTS;
+--------------------------------------------------------------------+
| Grants for root@localhost                                          |
+--------------------------------------------------------------------+
| GRANT ALL PRIVILEGES ON *.* TO 'root'@'localhost' WITH GRANT OPTION |
+--------------------------------------------------------------------+
```

This statement shows the grants for the user that executed it by default, so it's an easy way to see who you're logged in as and what your current privileges are. The user shown here has all privileges, but there's no password, which means that user can log in without specifying a password.* That's very insecure! This is one of the first things you should check for when setting up a fresh MySQL installation.

If you want to see the grants for a different user, you'll need to specify the username and hostname for that particular user. For example, the same Debian system has the following entries in the user table:

---

* The only mitigating factor is that this user cannot log in from any other host, but that's not much of a security measure.

```
| repl             | %         |
| root             | 127.0.0.1 |
| root             | kanga     |
| debian-sys-maint | localhost |
| root             | localhost |
+------------------+-----------+
```

Notice there are three *root* accounts! If you want to see the grants for a specific one, you must specify both the username and hostname. The default hostname is %, so omitting the hostname will cause an error:

```
mysql> SHOW GRANTS FOR root;
ERROR 1141 (42000): There is no such grant defined for user 'root' on host '%'
```

If you issue a GRANT for a user without specifying a hostname, you effectively grant to *user@'%'* (e.g., any host).

There's nothing to prevent you from using normal INSERT, UPDATE, and DELETE queries to manipulate the grant tables directly, but sticking to the GRANT and REVOKE commands insulates you from changes in those tables. It is also easy to make very bad mistakes when modifying the tables directly. For instance, MySQL doesn't stop you from changing the tables to contain data it doesn't know how to interpret. The GRANT and REVOKE commands are the recommended way of managing privileges and are likely to remain so.

If you do decide to manipulate the grant tables by hand rather than using the GRANT and REVOKE commands, you must tell MySQL that you've done so by issuing a FLUSH PRIVILEGES command, which refetches and recaches the accounts and privileges in the tables. Any changes you make to the grant tables with an INSERT or other generic command may go unnoticed until you restart the server or run FLUSH PRIVILEGES.

Setting Up MySQL Privileges

Let's look at an example of how to create appropriate user accounts and privileges for a fictional organization, *widgets.example.com*. We'll assume you're logging into a freshly installed MySQL instance and have deleted all default accounts with DROP USER. Be sure to check the mysql.user table to make sure you got them all.

MySQL does not support roles or groups, which you may be familiar with from other database servers. MySQL supports only users.

The basic idiom is to use combinations of these three commands:

```
GRANT [privileges] ON [objects] TO [user];
GRANT [privileges] ON [objects] TO [user] IDENTIFIED BY [password];
REVOKE [privileges] ON [objects] FROM [user];
```

Here's an overview of the types of accounts you may need to create and the privileges you should set for them:

Password Security

We use the intentionally cute "p4ssword" for purposes of illustration, but it's not a good password for real installations. Just because MySQL passwords aren't stored in plain text doesn't mean you can be careless about password complexity. Anyone who can connect to your MySQL server can run a brute-force attack against it in an attempt to discover passwords, and in MySQL there aren't as many sophisticated ways to detect and prevent this as there are with other types of passwords, such as Unix passwords. MySQL also doesn't provide any way for an administrator to enforce good password standards. You can't link MySQL against *libcrack* and demand that passwords meet its criteria, no matter how cool that idea may be. There are many good tools and web sites out there that can help you and your users generate strong passwords—we recommend that you use one of them.

System administrator account

In most large organizations, you have two important administrator roles. The *system administrators* manage the "physical" server, including the operating system, Unix login accounts, etc., and the *database administrators* concentrate on the database server. How you allocate the administrator accounts is up to you— you might want to just keep things simple and ask anyone who needs to do administrative tasks to log into MySQL as a superuser, or you might want to create a separate account for each person who needs administrative access. We keep it simple to begin with and create a super-privileged user named *root* (after the traditional Unix superuser):

```
mysql> GRANT ALL PRIVILEGES ON *.* TO 'root'@'localhost'
    -> IDENTIFIED BY 'p4ssword' WITH GRANT OPTION;
```

Database administrator accounts

When more than one DBA has access to MySQL, it's sometimes a good idea to give each one a separate account rather than having them share the root account. This setup provides greater accountability and auditability:

```
mysql> GRANT ALL PRIVILEGES ON *.* TO 'john'@'localhost'
    -> IDENTIFIED BY 'p4ssword' WITH GRANT OPTION;
```

Per-employee accounts

The average *widgets.example.com* employee is a customer service representative responsible for entering orders taken over the phone, updating existing orders, and so on. Let's assume that Tera, a customer service representative, logs into a custom application that passes her username and password through to the MySQL server for any activity. The command to create Tera's account might look like this:

```
mysql> GRANT INSERT,UPDATE PRIVILEGES ON widgets.orders
    -> TO 'tera'@'%.widgets.example.com'
    -> IDENTIFIED BY 'p4ssword';
```

Tera must provide her username and password to the application, which then lets her add new orders or update existing orders. However, she can't go back and delete entries, etc. In this configuration, every employee of *widgets.example. com* that needs to enter an order into the system has her own individual database access. Instead of a shared "application account," each employee's transactions are logged under her own username, and each employee has only the privileges she needs to enter or work with orders.

Simulated groups

MySQL doesn't provide any functionality for user groups or roles, as they're variously known in other database servers. Sometimes it makes sense to create an account named after a particular employee or application role, such as *custserv* or *analyst*, but we won't do that in this example.

Logging, write-only access

It is common to use MySQL as the backend for logging various types of data. Whether you have Apache recording every request in MySQL or you're keeping track of when your doorbell rings, logging is a write-only application that probably needs to write to only a single database or table. You can create a logging account with a command like this:

```
mysql> GRANT INSERT ON logs.* TO 'logger'@'%.widgets.example.com'
    -> IDENTIFIED BY 'p4ssword';
```

This command adds a row to the user table, but because we specified no global (*.*) privileges, all the privilege columns in the resulting row in user will contain N. The only purpose of the row here is to let the user connect from any host and provide a password. Because we specified a privilege that applies to a specific database, the interesting bits were added to the db table, where the resulting row's columns will all contain N, except for the Insert_priv column, which will contain Y.

Backups

A backup user who will do backups via *mysqldump* will typically need only SELECT and LOCK TABLES privileges. If the user will do tab-delimited dumps with the *--tab* option to *mysqldump*, or via SELECT INTO OUTFILE, you will also need to grant that user the FILE privilege. Here's a sample backup user who can connect only from the local host:

```
mysql> GRANT SELECT, LOCK TABLES, FILE ON *.* TO 'backup'@'localhost'
    -> IDENTIFIED BY 'p4ssword';
```

To guarantee consistency many backup operations use FLUSH TABLES WITH READ LOCK, which requires the RELOAD privilege as well. This privilege also permits several other common operations, such as FLUSH LOGS.

Operations and monitoring

There may be times when you'll want to give someone or something (e.g., a user or some monitoring software at a network operations center, or NOC) access to your MySQL server for the purposes of maintenance or troubleshooting. This user account needs to be able to connect, issue the KILL and SHOW commands, and shut down the server. Because this ability is very powerful, it has to be limited to a single host. This means that even if an unauthorized user compromises the password, that user will have to be in the NOC to do anything. This statement accomplishes that:

```
mysql> GRANT PROCESS, SHUTDOWN on *.*
    -> TO 'noc'@'monitorserver.noc.widgets.example.com'
    -> IDENTIFIED BY 'p4ssword';
```

You might also need to grant the SUPER privilege, which lets the user execute SHOW INNODB STATUS.

Privilege Changes in MySQL 4.1

MySQL 4.1 introduced a new, much more secure password hashing scheme. However, you can still use the old password hashing scheme in the newer versions (even MySQL 5.0 and newer). We recommend against this, because the old-style password hashing is easy to crack. If you care about security, use MySQL 4.1 or newer and stick to the new scheme.

Some GNU/Linux distributions configure MySQL to use old-style password hashing by default, for compatibility with older client programs. Check your default configuration for the old_passwords option. If you want the MySQL server to reject any attempts to connect with an old-style, insecure password, you can set the secure_auth option in the server's configuration file. There's a similar option for client programs, which will prevent them from trying to send passwords to the server in the old format even if the server asks for it. This can be a good idea, because the old format is easy to sniff and crack.

New-style passwords begin with an asterisk, so you can tell them apart readily with visual inspection. In most cases, user accounts that were upgraded from older MySQL versions will authenticate fine. However, when a pre-MySQL 4.1 client program tries to connect to a newer MySQL server with a user account whose password is stored in the new format, it won't be able to connect. To fix this problem, you can either set the account's password back to the old-style hashing manually with OLD_PASSWORD( ), or upgrade the client program's MySQL client library.

Privilege Changes in MySQL 5.0

MySQL 5.0 added a few new kinds of privileges and changed some existing behaviors slightly. This section gives an overview of the changes. Before you upgrade to any new MySQL version, you should read the release notes to learn what's new and what's changed.

Stored routines

As we discussed in Chapter 5, MySQL 5.0 added support for stored routines. These can execute in two security contexts: as the definer (i.e., the user who defined the routine) or the invoker (i.e., the user who invokes the routine).

Stored routines are commonly used as proxies to grant specific rights to tables where users don't have any rights assigned directly. The usual idiom is to create a privileged user, then create the routines with that user as their definer, and give them the SQL SECURITY DEFINER characteristic. Table 12-1 illustrates how a stored procedure allows users to execute statements with another user's privileges.

Table 12-1. The security context for statements inside a stored procedure

User who calls the procedure	Security context for statements	
	With SQL SECURITY INVOKER	With SQL SECURITY DEFINER and DEFINER=LegalStaff
LegalStaff	LegalStaff	LegalStaff
HumanResources	HumanResources	LegalStaff
CustomerService	CustomerService	LegalStaff

This approach lets you grant or deny access to tables based on who the user is, and at the same time grant permission to perform specific actions on tables—the actions encapsulated in the stored procedure—when you don't want the user to access the tables directly. For instance, say you want some private legal data in a set of tables (such as the status of a contract with an outside party) to be visible only to the legal staff, but your customer service representatives need to be able to update a particular column in these tables. You can deny SELECT privileges for the tables to everyone but the legal staff, and then write a stored procedure to permit everyone to update the desired column and use SQL SECURITY DEFINER to make it run with *LegalStaff*'s privileges. This is rather like using SUID privileges in Unix-like operating systems.

The namespace of stored routines is per schema (database), so you can have db1.func_1( ) and db2.func_1( ) without a naming conflict.

MySQL checks privileges for each statement within the stored routine. The privilege to execute the routine doesn't provide a blanket authorization for the statements inside it. The statements inside are checked against either the definer's or the invoker's privileges, depending on whether you created the routine with SQL SECURITY DEFINER or SQL SECURITY INVOKER.

Triggers

MySQL 5.0 also added support for triggers, which require special privileges to execute if they're not defined with the SQL SECURITY DEFINER characteristic. This can have confusing effects, such as the following error message when trying to run UPDATE, INSERT, or DELETE queries on a table:

```
mysql> INSERT INTO ...;
ERROR 1142 (42000): Access denied; you need the SUPER privilege for this operation
```

If the trigger isn't created with the SQL SECURITY DEFINER characteristic the user who inserts into the table must have the SUPER privilege to execute the trigger, which is why the error message seems to say the SUPER privilege is required to insert into the table. (MySQL 5.1 includes a TRIGGER privilege, which should make this error message a little less confusing.)

MySQL checks privileges for the statements inside a trigger just as it does for a stored routine.

Views

Like stored procedures and triggers, you can execute views with the privileges of either the definer or the invoker. Definer privileges let you give a user access to a view but not to the underlying tables.

This lets you implement row-level security, but also restrict access to columns. We believe this is a better solution than specifying column-level privileges with GRANT, as it is much easier to maintain. If you put the views in a separate database, you can simply grant database-level privileges to users, rather than having to maintain privileges on individual tables or views. Figure 12-2 shows the difference between granting access to particular columns with GRANT and extracting the relevant columns into a view.

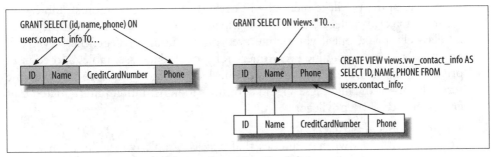

Figure 12-2. Simplifying access to particular columns by defining a view

On the left side of Figure 12-2, the DBA issues a GRANT statement granting fine-grained access to individual columns. This slows down all database accesses and requires separate GRANT statements for each table that requires column-level permission checking.

On the right side of Figure 12-2, the DBA creates a new database named views to hold a series of views. He then creates a view containing the columns from the table where he wants users to have fine-grained privileges. Any such views can be stored in views, and the single GRANT statement grants access efficiently.

Privileges on the INFORMATION_SCHEMA tables

The official SQL standards define a set of views, collectively known as the INFORMATION_SCHEMA tables, which give you information about databases, tables, and other parts of your database server. MySQL tries to follow these standards as closely as possible. As a result, the server manages privileges for these tables automatically, and it's best not to define any privileges explicitly. If a user without the appropriate privileges attempts to access rows or values in these tables, MySQL will not show the rows and will return NULL for the values. For example, a user will not be able to see tables in the INFORMATION_SCHEMA.TABLES view unless she has some privileges for those tables. This is analogous to MySQL's SHOW TABLES behavior: MySQL will not show tables for which the user has no privileges.

Privileges and Performance

Privileges may not seem very related to performance, but they can actually cause performance problems in certain circumstances. Here are some things to think about:

Too many privileges
> If you have a very large number of entries in your grant tables, the overhead can be significant. Each privilege adds to the work the server must do when checking whether a user can execute a statement. Privileges also consume memory.

Privileges that are too fine-grained
> Each level of the privilege hierarchy in MySQL (user, database, host, table, and column) makes privilege checks more expensive. Checking for global privileges is relatively quick, but if you define even one column privilege, the server will potentially have to examine every query for global, database, table, and column privileges (recall from "How MySQL Checks Privileges" on page 524 that the server begins at the highest level and continues looking until it finds a match that grants the necessary privilege).

Column privileges and the query cache
> At the time of this writing, queries that access a table with column privileges cannot be served from the query cache. We suggest using views instead of column privileges, as discussed in the previous section, to avoid this and other problems with column privileges.

By default, MySQL does both a forward and a reverse DNS lookup when authenticating users. Adding skip_name_resolve to your *my.cnf* file will disable this. This can be good for both security and performance, because it speeds up connections, reduces reliance on DNS servers, and reduces susceptibility to denial-of-service attacks.

The side effect of this change is that it prevents you from defining users with host-names in the Host column. These user definitions will just stop working. Instead, you must use IP addresses (but you can still use wildcards, such as *192%*). You can also use the special value *localhost* even when skip_name_resolve is enabled.

Common Problems and Solutions

Because the MySQL manual covers privileges thoroughly, we decided to limit this section of the book to a discussion of common needs, gotchas, and unexpected behavior, so you can use it as a quick-reference manual or for troubleshooting. The following sections describe frequently asked questions, common tasks, and puzzling situations we've encountered.

Errors When Connecting

Mailing lists, forums, and IRC channels are jam-packed with users having trouble connecting to MySQL servers. There are dozens of reasons for these problems, ranging from TCP connections failing because skip_networking is defined in *my.cnf*, to bind_address being set to an IP address that doesn't match the server's, to mistakes with the GRANT statement, to firewalls. We can't cover all the reasons here, but the MySQL manual has a section dedicated to this topic.

Connecting through localhost versus 127.0.0.1

The *localhost* hostname is usually an alias for the IP address 127.0.0.1, but MySQL has slightly different default behavior. When you specify the hostname *localhost* as a connection parameter, it tries by default to connect through a Unix socket* instead of via TCP/IP, as you might expect. Thus, the following command will connect over a Unix socket:

```
$ mysql --host=localhost
```

This is a somewhat unfortunate design decision, because it doesn't behave as people expect; however, it's too late to change it because doing so would break compatibility with older applications and client libraries. If you want to connect via TCP/IP to the machine on which you're running, you have two choices: specify an IP address instead of the hostname, or specify the protocol explicitly. Either of the following two commands will connect via TCP/IP:

```
$ mysql --host=127.0.0.1
$ mysql --host=localhost --protocol=tcp
```

---

* *localhost* isn't special on Windows, but . is; it means to connect via a named pipe.

On a related note, if you attempt to connect to the forwarded TCP port on *localhost* when setting up SSH tunneling, you'll find that it doesn't work. You have to use TCP to connect to a port, so you must use the IP address 127.0.0.1 instead. We discuss SSH tunneling later in the chapter.

This hostname is special in another way, too: MySQL won't try to match *localhost* against a % wildcard. In other words, it is not redundant to specify permissions for *user@'%'* and *user@localhost*.

Using temporary tables safely

MySQL doesn't have special privileges for temporary tables, other than the CREATE TEMPORARY TABLE privilege. Once a temporary table is created, the user's normal table-level privileges apply. This means that a user might be able to create a temporary table, but then be denied the right to add more columns, alter the table, and add indexes (or even to SELECT from it). However, granting these rights might let the user harm real tables, which you don't want.

The solution is to disallow these privileges except in a special database reserved for temporary tables:

```
mysql> CREATE DATABASE temp;
mysql> GRANT SELECT, INSERT, UPDATE, DELETE, DROP, ALTER, INDEX,
    -> CREATE TEMPORARY TABLES ON temp.* TO analyst@'%';
```

Disallowing passwordless access

MySQL allows passwordless access. An account without a password is one whose row in the user table contains an empty string in the password column. You can create such an account with a GRANT statement that has no IDENTIFIED BY clause.

You can't completely disallow passwordless access in MySQL, but if you have control over the machines from which the users connect, you can add an entry in the [client] section of *my.cnf* as follows:

```
password
```

This will cause programs that read this file by default (which includes all the programs MySQL distributes, unless they're instructed otherwise) to always prompt the user for a password. In MySQL 5.0 and newer, you can set the server's SQL mode to NO_AUTO_CREATE_USER to prevent GRANT from creating users without a password, but it's possible for a determined user to work around this.

Remember, a user whose password in the mysql.user table is an empty string is a user without a password, not a user with an empty password.

Disabling anonymous users

MySQL also allows anonymous users: any entry in the grant tables whose User column contains the empty string defines privileges for anonymous users. Be careful of such entries, as SHOW GRANTS will not show the resulting privileges. We think it's best to remove these entries. You can run the MySQL-provided *mysql_secure_installation* program to do this.

Remember to quote hostnames separately

It's easy to forget to quote usernames and hostnames separately. The following command doesn't do what it looks like it should:

```
mysql> GRANT USAGE ON *.* TO 'fred@%';
```

It looks like it creates an account for a user named *fred* who can connect from anywhere, but in fact it creates a user named *fred@%*. The correct syntax is as follows (note that the user and host are quoted separately):

```
mysql> GRANT USAGE ON *.* TO 'fred'@'%';
```

Don't reuse usernames

MySQL considers users with the same username but different hosts to be entirely different users. It may seem helpful that you can grant a user completely different privileges depending on where the connection attempt originated, but in our experience it's rarely a good idea to do this. The potential for confusion or problems far outweighs the benefits. It's much simpler to treat usernames as though they should be unique, and use the Host column to restrict *where users can connect from*, rather than *what they can do once connected*. For example, you might decide that you want to allow connections only from the local machine, only from the local network, or only from a specific subnet. This is a reasonable security precaution, though a firewall is a much safer way to restrict connection attempts (we discuss this more later).

Just because MySQL allows a lot of flexibility doesn't mean it will make your life easier. We think it's better to keep it simple.

Granting SELECT allows SHOW CREATE TABLE

Granting the SELECT privilege lets a user execute SHOW CREATE TABLE, which shows the SQL command that will recreate a table. This is usually fine, but sometimes it can show sensitive details. The most obvious case is for Federated tables in MySQL 5.0: the user will be able to see the username and password by which the engine connects to the remote server. (MySQL 5.1 adds a separate mechanism for managing remote connections for Federated tables.)

Don't grant privileges on the mysql database

If you grant privileges on the mysql database, a user might be able to update her own privileges, view other users' privileges (which opens the door to easy password-guessing attacks), or even rename or change the tables MySQL needs to run. There's no need to give ordinary users *any* access to these tables—even read-only access. That means the following is a bad idea, because it grants privileges globally:

```
mysql> GRANT ... ON *.* ...;
```

If a user has permission to modify the tables in the mysql database, that user should also have the GRANT option. Otherwise, it will be possible for the user to drop privileges by deleting rows, yet to be unable to add them back. One of this book's authors once accidentally removed every user in the system this way, and had to shut down the MySQL server and restore the users by starting the server with the *--skip_grant_tables* option.

Don't grant the SUPER privilege freely

The SUPER privilege lets a user do superuser operations (such as changing data on a server that's configured to be read-only), as you might expect, but it also has one extra behavior: MySQL will reserve one connection for a user with the SUPER privilege, even if it has reached its max_connections limit. This lets you connect and administer the server even when it won't accept any more normal client connections.

You should try to avoid granting the SUPER privilege to too many users, but this can be difficult as it's needed for several other common purposes (such as purging master logs).

Granting privileges on wildcarded databases

MySQL's database pattern matching doesn't let you specify "all databases except these." That means it can be tedious to omit privileges for the mysql database. A good naming convention can help: just name all databases with a common prefix and grant privileges to the wildcarded database name. For example:

```
mysql> GRANT ... ON `analysis%`.* TO 'analyst' ...;
```

Unfortunately, MySQL doesn't have true schemas, which would help with this problem. Naming conventions can ease some of the pain, though. Note that you must quote the database name as an identifier (with backticks) in the GRANT statement.

This is also a useful technique for setting up a shared hosting environment. Most such environments restrict users to databases whose names begin with their own username and an underscore. The underscore is a wildcard pattern, so you must escape it in the GRANT statement. For example, you might use a command like this to set up a new hosting account for a user named *sunny*:

```
mysql> GRANT ... ON `sunny\_%`.* TO 'sunny' ...;
```

You probably should not grant the SHOW DATABASES privilege in a shared hosting environment. This will ensure that users don't see databases to which they don't have access—the less they know, the better.

Revoking specific privileges

If you grant privileges globally, you can't revoke them nonglobally:

```
mysql> GRANT SELECT ON *.* TO 'user';
mysql> SHOW GRANTS FOR user;
+-----------------------------------+
| Grants for user@%                 |
+-----------------------------------+
| GRANT SELECT ON *.* TO 'user'@'%' |
+-----------------------------------+
mysql> REVOKE SELECT ON sakila.film FROM user;
ERROR 1147 (42000): There is no such grant defined for user 'user' on host '%' on
table 'film'
```

This privilege was granted globally and can only be revoked globally; attempting to revoke it from a specific table causes MySQL to complain that there's no table-level privilege matching the specified criteria.

Users can connect even after REVOKE

Suppose you revoke every privilege for a user:

```
mysql> REVOKE ALL PRIVILEGES ON...;
```

The user will still be able to connect, because REVOKE doesn't remove user accounts; it just removes privileges. You have to use DROP USER to remove the account entirely (or, in old MySQL versions, DELETE the row from the mysql.user table).

If you merely revoke all privileges, SHOW GRANTS will show that the user still has the USAGE privilege. You can't revoke this privilege, because it's a synonym for "no privileges." It simply means the user can connect to MySQL.

When you can't grant or revoke a privilege

In addition to the GRANT option, you must have the privilege you're trying to grant or revoke. This safeguard prevents users from escalating each other's permissions. If you're trying to revoke ALL PRIVILEGES, you must have the CREATE USER privilege.

Invisible privileges

SHOW GRANTS doesn't really show all the privileges for a user: it merely shows the privileges explicitly assigned to that user. A user may have other permissions, perhaps because of permissions granted to anonymous users. For example, default MySQL installations grant privileges on the test database, and databases whose names begin with test_, to every user! Let's look at an example. First, we log in as *root* and create a user with no privileges:

```
mysql> GRANT USAGE ON *.* TO 'restricted'@'%' IDENTIFIED BY 'p4ssword';
mysql> SHOW GRANTS FOR restricted;
```

```
+----------------------------------------------------+
| Grants for restricted@%                            |
+----------------------------------------------------+
| GRANT USAGE ON *.* TO 'restricted'@'%' IDENTIFIED BY |
| PASSWORD '*544F2E9C6390E7D5A5E0A508679188BBF7467B57' |
+----------------------------------------------------+
```

Looks good; the user seems to be able to connect but do nothing else. That's not the whole story, though. To prove it, just log in as that user and run SHOW DATABASES:

```
$ mysql -u restricted -pp4ssword
mysql> SHOW DATABASES;
+--------------------+
| Database           |
+--------------------+
| information_schema |
| test               |
+--------------------+
```

This server also contains a copy of the Sakila sample database, which isn't listed because the user doesn't have the SHOW DATABASES privilege, but the test database is listed. In fact, as you can see here, the new user has privileges to that database and all tables in it:

```
mysql> USE test;
mysql> SHOW TABLES;
+----------------+
| Tables_in_test |
+----------------+
| heartbeat      |
+----------------+
mysql> SELECT * FROM heartbeat;
+----+---------------------+
| id | ts                  |
+----+---------------------+
|  1 | 2007-10-28 21:31:08 |
+----+---------------------+
```

The user account can't just read from the tables; it also has most other privileges. In fact, it can even create a new database:

```
mysql> CREATE DATABASE test_muah_ha_ha;
Query OK, 1 row affected (0.01 sec)
```

The culprit is two rows in the mysql.db table:

```
mysql> SELECT * FROM mysql.db\G
*************************** 1. row ***************************
                Host: %
                  Db: test
                User:
          Select_priv: Y
... omitted ...
```

```
*************************** 2. row ***************************
            Host: %
              Db: test\_%
            User:
     Select_priv: Y
... omitted ...
```

Notice that the User columns are blank, which means anonymous users—in effect, all users—have these privileges, even though they don't appear in the SHOW GRANTS[*] output. The moral of this story is that SHOW GRANTS doesn't always show you everything. Sometimes you still need to know how to read and interpret the grant tables.

This isn't the only way a user's privileges can behave strangely, though. Because hostname and database matching prefer the most specific match first, grants for a less specific match will be hidden even when they're more permissive.

Consider the following scenario: instead of adopting a naming convention as we suggested earlier and using the principle of least privileges, a lazy DBA decides to take the reverse approach. He grants all privileges for a user, and then overrides undesired privileges by hiding privileges in the mysql database with a row whose privilege columns are all set to N:

```
mysql> GRANT USAGE ON *.* TO 'gotcha'@'%' IDENTIFIED BY 'p4ssword';
mysql> GRANT ALL PRIVILEGES ON `%`.* TO 'gotcha'@'%';
mysql> INSERT INTO mysql.db(Host, DB, User) VALUES('%', 'mysql', 'gotcha');
mysql> FLUSH PRIVILEGES;
```

Because the mysql pattern is more specific than the % pattern, the lazy DBA reasons that the user should be denied privileges such as SELECT in the mysql database. And indeed, this is the case:

```
mysql> SELECT * FROM mysql.user;
ERROR 1142 (42000): SELECT command denied to user 'gotcha'@'localhost' for table
'user'
```

The problem is that this privilege scheme sets a trap for anyone who changes that user's privileges in the future. It's very easy to mistakenly remove the mysql-specific privileges, which unmasks the elevated privileges in that database. In other words, removing privileges can actually grant *more* privileges! This scheme is not nearly as clever as it seems, and in fact it's dangerous. It also doesn't show up in SHOW GRANTS, so it's easy to miss.

You can play similar games with hostname matching, with the same consequences. For example, if you want to allow the *gotcha* user to connect from all but a specific hostname, you can't do it by specifying a "negated hostname pattern," because no

---

[*] This example illustrates one of the "magic" values in MySQL's privilege tables. The empty string in the User column can indicate an anonymous user, which is how MySQL will authenticate you if you connect with a nonexistent username, or it can indicate that the privilege applies to everyone.

such thing exists in MySQL. The only way to do this is to create a user with the same username, but specify the blocked hostname and a bogus password:

```
mysql> GRANT USAGE ON *.* TO 'gotcha'@'denied.com' IDENTIFIED BY 'bogus';
```

Now when *gotcha* tries to connect from this hostname, MySQL will try to authenticate against the gotcha@denied.com row in the user table and will deny the login because the password doesn't match. This "solution" can turn out to be very dangerous, however, if someone thinks this entry in the table is a mistake and removes it, or disables hostname lookups for performance reasons, or perhaps if the user compromises reverse DNS. In any of these cases, the user will be able to connect as *gotcha@'%'*.

We advise you to avoid hidden privileges and "clever tricks" such as the schemes we just showed. Instead, adopt a common-sense approach, don't try to do anything fancy with privileges if you don't need to, and follow best practices such as the principle of least privileges.

Obsolete privileges

MySQL doesn't clean up old privileges when you remove objects. For example, let's say you've done the following:

```
mysql> GRANT ALL PRIVILEGES ON my_db.* TO analyst;
```

And you later run this command:

```
$ mysqladmin drop my_db
```

It would be nice if MySQL destroyed the GRANT as a result, but the privileges will actually remain in the db table. If you later create another database with the same name, the privileges will still exist; this may cause problems, as you may not even remember that the *analyst* account ever had any privileges.

In MySQL 5.0 and newer, the INFORMATION_SCHEMA tables can help you find obsolete privileges. For example, you can use an exclusion join query to find privileges that reference nonexistent databases:

```
mysql> SELECT d.Host, d.Db, d.User
    -> FROM mysql.db AS d
    ->     LEFT  OUTER JOIN INFORMATION_SCHEMA.SCHEMATA AS s
    ->         ON s.SCHEMA_NAME LIKE d.Db
    -> WHERE s.SCHEMA_NAME IS NULL;
+------+---------+------+
| Host | Db      | User |
+------+---------+------+
| %    | test\_% |      |
+------+---------+------+
```

You can write similar queries against any of the other tables in INFORMATION_SCHEMA. In earlier MySQL versions, you have to search for obsolete privileges manually, or write a script to do it for you.

MySQL will let you create database-level privileges for databases that don't exist, but it won't let you grant table-level privileges for tables that don't exist. If you need to do this, you'll have to insert rows directly into `mysql.tables_priv`.

Operating System Security

Even the most well thought out and secure grant tables will do you little good if an attacker can get root access to your server. With unlimited access, the user could simply copy all your data files to another machine running MySQL.[*] Doing so would effectively give the attacker an identical copy of your database.

Data theft isn't the only threat to guard against, though. A creative attacker may decide that it's more fun to make subtle changes to your data over the course of weeks or even months. Depending on how long you keep backups and how much time passes before you notice the data corruption, such an attack could be devastating.

Guidelines

The general guidelines discussed here aren't a comprehensive guide to system security. If you are serious about security—and you should be—we recommend a copy of *Practical Unix and Internet Security* by Simson Garfinkel et al. (O'Reilly). That said, here are some ideas for maintaining good security on your database servers:

Don't run MySQL from a privileged account
> The root user on Unix and the system (administrator) user on Windows possess ultimate control over the system. If someone finds a security bug in MySQL and you're running it as a privileged user, the attacker can gain extensive access to your server. The installation instructions are quite clear about this, but it bears repeating: create a separate account, usually *mysql*, for the purpose of running MySQL.

Keep your operating system up-to-date
> All operating system vendors (Microsoft, Sun, Red Hat, Novell, etc.) provide notifications when a security-related update is available. Find your vendor's mailing list and subscribe to it. Pay special attention to the security list for MySQL itself, as well as anything that may interact directly with the database, such as PHP or Perl.

Restrict logins on the database host
> Does every developer building a MySQL-based application need an account on the server? Certainly not; only system and database administrators need

---

[*] Remember: MyISAM data files are portable across operating systems and CPU architectures (provided the CPU's floating-point format is also the same).

accounts on the machine. All the developers need to be able to do is issue queries against the database remotely using TCP/IP.

Separate production from everything else

Separate your production environment from your development and testing environments. It's best to use entirely different physical servers. The security and access requirements for a production server are completely different from those of a development server, so it makes sense to physically separate them. This also prevents mistakes and makes management and maintenance easier. It requires that you create proper procedures and tools from the very beginning, such as ways to transfer data between servers.

Have your server audited

Many larger organizations have internal auditors who can assess the security of a server and make recommendations for improving it. If you aren't lucky enough to have access to auditors, you can hire a security consultant to perform the audit.

Use the strongest means available

You can use techniques such as chrooting, jails, zones, or virtual servers to isolate MySQL even more

Keeping your backups on a different server is another important security measure. If someone breaks into your server, you'll need to reinstall the operating system from an untainted source. Once that's done, you'll be faced with the task of having to restore all the data. If you have time, you might want to compare the compromised server to a known good backup in an effort to determine how the attacker gained entry.

Network Security

It's always best to isolate your servers and make them inaccessible, but you may need to have a MySQL server that is accessible to clients not located on the same host. We look at several techniques you can use to limit such a server's exposure.

Even if you use your server only on an internal network at your organization, you should take steps to keep data away from prying eyes. After all, some of the most serious security threats in a company actually come from the inside.

Keep in mind that this information is only a starting point in the process of ensuring that your MySQL servers are well protected. There are numerous good network security books available, including *Building Internet Firewalls* by Elizabeth D. Zwicky et al., and *TCP/IP Network Administration* by Craig Hunt (both from O'Reilly). If you're serious about network security, do yourself a favor and pick up a book on the topic (after you finish this one!).

As with operating system security, having a third-party audit of your network done can be quite helpful in spotting weaknesses before someone exploits them.

Localhost-Only Connections

If you use MySQL in an application that resides on the same host (as is common with small and mid-size web sites), there's a good chance you won't need to allow any access to MySQL over the network. Eliminating the need to accept external connections reduces the number of ways an attacker can get access to your MySQL server.

Disabling network access limits your ability to make administrative changes remotely (adding users, rotating logs, etc.), so you'll need to either log into the MySQL server via SSH, or install a web-based application that lets you make those changes. The remote login requirement can be difficult on some Windows systems, but there are other remote-access alternatives. One solution to the problem might be to install *phpMyAdmin*. But beware, because it has been known to have security flaws too!

The skip_networking option tells MySQL not to listen on any TCP socket, but it will still allow connections on a Unix socket. Starting MySQL without networking support is simple. Just place the following option in the [mysqld] section of your *my.cnf* file:

```
[mysqld]
skip_networking
```

The skip_networking option has some inconvenient side effects: it prevents you from using tools such as *stunnel* for secure remote connectivity and replication, and it doesn't let Java applications connect (Connector/J will connect only through TCP/IP). An alternative is to configure MySQL as follows:

```
[mysqld]
bind_address=127.0.0.1
```

This enables TCP connections, but only from the local machine, so it's both secure and convenient. Some popular GNU/Linux distributions have switched to this configuration by default.

A MySQL slave server configured with skip_networking is an interesting configuration. Because it initiates its connection to the master, the slave still gets all its data updates, but because no TCP connections are permitted, you can have a more secure "backup replica" that can't be remotely tainted. You can't use such a slave in a failover configuration, though: no other client could connect to it.

Firewalling

As with any other network-based service, it is important that you allow connections only from authorized hosts. You can use MySQL's GRANT command to restrict the hosts from which users can connect, but it's a good idea to have more than one level of protection. Having multiple ways to filter connections means that a single mistake, such as a typo in a GRANT command, won't allow connections from unauthorized hosts. Using a firewall to filter connections at the network level gives you extra security.*

In many organizations, network security is administered by a different group of people from those developing applications. This helps further reduce the risk that a single person's change can expose a server.

The most secure approach to use when firewalling a machine is to deny all connections by default. Then you can add rules that allow access to the few services other hosts may need to access. For a system limited to providing a MySQL server, you should allow connections only to TCP port 3306 (MySQL's default) and possibly to a remote login service such as SSH (typically on TCP port 22).

No default route

Consider not having a default route configured on your firewalled MySQL servers. That way, even if the firewall configuration is compromised and someone tries to contact your MySQL server from the outside, the packets will never get back to them. They'll never leave your local network.

Let's say your MySQL server is 192.168.0.10, and the local network has a 255.255.255.0 netmask. In this configuration, any packet from 192.168.0.0/24 is considered "local" because it can be reached directly via the attached network interface (probably *eth0* or the host operating system's equivalent). Traffic from any other address will have to be directed to a gateway to reach its final destination, and because there is no default route, there is no way for those packets to find their gateway and get to their destination.

If you must allow a select few outside hosts to access your otherwise firewalled server, add static routes for them. Doing so ensures that the server responds to as few outside hosts as possible.

The practice of not configuring a default route isn't foolproof, and it protects you more from firewall configuration mistakes than from a full compromise. However, every little bit helps.

---

* For our purposes, a firewall is simply a device that network traffic passes through for the purposes of filtering and possibly routing. Whether it's a "real" firewall, a router, or an old 486 PC doesn't matter.

MySQL in a DMZ

Simply firewalling MySQL servers isn't secure enough for many installations. If one of your web or application servers is compromised, an attacker could use that server to attack a MySQL server directly. Once the attacker gains access to a single computer on the firewalled network, all the other servers on that network are reachable with relatively few restrictions in most configurations.*

Moving the MySQL servers to their own separate network segment, which isn't accessible from the outside, can improve security. For instance, imagine a LAN containing the web or other application servers and a firewall. Behind the firewall, on a different physical network segment and a different logical subnet, is one or more MySQL server(s). The application servers have restricted access to the MySQL servers: all of their traffic must first pass through the firewall, which you can configure in a very restrictive way. If someone gains access to the application server but the firewall permits traffic only to port 3306 on the MySQL servers, the intruder won't be able to launch an attack on other services that may be running on the MySQL server, such as SSH.

You might even put the application servers either in the DMZ or in their own separate DMZ. Is that going too far? Maybe. As is always the case in security matters, you may need to trade safety measures for convenience; however, you should be aware of the risks you're taking in doing so.

Connection Encryption and Tunneling

Any time you need to communicate with a MySQL server across a network that is public (such as the Internet) or otherwise open to traffic sniffing (as many wireless networks are), consider using some form of encryption. Doing so can make it far more difficult for anyone who might try to intercept the connection and either sniff or spoof the data.

As an added benefit, many encryption algorithms result in a compressed data stream. So, not only are your data more secure, but you're also using the available network bandwidth more optimally.

Although our discussion focuses on a client accessing a MySQL server, the client could be another MySQL server. This is common when using MySQL's built-in replication: each slave server connects to the master with the same protocol normal MySQL clients use.

---

* That's not entirely true. Many modern network switches let you configure multiple Virtual LANs (VLANs) on a single physical network. Machines that aren't on the same VLAN may not be able to talk to each other.

Virtual private networks

A company with two or more offices in distant locations may set up a virtual private network (VPN) between them, using a variety of technologies. A common solution is for the external routers at each office to encrypt all traffic destined for another office. In such a situation, there's little to worry about. All the traffic is already being encrypted as it is sent out over whichever public or private network happens to connect the offices.

Does the VPN preclude the necessity of applying a MySQL-specific solution? Not necessarily. In the event that the VPN must be disabled for some reason, it would be nice if MySQL's network traffic remained secret. Configuring MySQL to allow connections only from the VPN IP addresses should solve this problem: if the VPN is disabled, the MySQL server won't be reachable.

SSL in MySQL

As of version 4.1, MySQL has native support for Secure Sockets Layer (SSL)—the same technology that keeps your credit card number safe when buying books on Amazon.com or airline tickets from your favorite travel site. Specifically, MySQL uses the freely available yaSSL library (or OpenSSL in older builds).

Some binary versions of MySQL don't have SSL enabled by default. To check your server, simply inspect the have_openssl variable:

```
mysql> SHOW VARIABLES LIKE 'have_openssl';
+---------------+-------+
| Variable_name | Value |
+---------------+-------+
| have_openssl  | NO    |
+---------------+-------+
```

If it says NO, you'll need to compile your own MySQL server or get a different version. If it says YES, whole new levels of database access security are opened to the administrator. How you use them will depend on the security needs of your particular application.

At the most basic level, you may wish to allow only encrypted sessions, relying on the SSL protocol to protect the user's password. You can require a user to connect via SSL with optional arguments to the GRANT command:

```
mysql> GRANT ... IDENTIFIED BY 'p4ssword' REQUIRE SSL;
```

That GRANT, however, doesn't place any restrictions on the SSL certificate the connecting client uses. As long as the client and the MySQL server can negotiate an SSL session, MySQL won't check the client certificate's validity.

You can require minimal checking of the client certificate with the REQUIRE x509 option:

```
mysql> GRANT ... IDENTIFIED BY 'p4ssword' REQUIRE x509;
```

This requires that the client certificate be at least verifiable against the CA certificates the MySQL server has been set up to recognize.

One step up might be to permit only a specific client certificate to access the database. You can do that with the REQUIRE SUBJECT syntax:

```
mysql> GRANT ... IDENTIFIED BY 'p4ssword'
    -> REQUIRE SUBJECT "/C=US/ST=New York/L=Albany/O=Widgets
Inc./CN=client-ray.example.com/emailAddress=raymond@example.com";
```

Maybe you don't care specifically what client license is used but only that it be one issued with your organization's CA certificate. In this case, you might use the REQUIRE ISSUER syntax to do something like the following:

```
mysql> GRANT ... IDENTIFIED BY 'p4ssword'
    -> REQUIRE ISSUER "/C=US/ST=New+20York/L=Albany/O=Widgets
Inc./CN=cacert.example.com/emailAddress=admin@example.com";
```

For the ultimate in authentication, you can combine the two clauses to require both the issuer and subject to be predefined values. For example, you can require Raymond to use the specific certificate issued with your organization's CA certificate as follows:

```
mysql> GRANT ... IDENTIFIED BY 'p4ssword'
    -> REQUIRE SUBJECT "/C=US/ST=New York/L=Albany/O=Widgets
Inc./CN=client-ray.example.com/emailAddress=raymond@example.com"
    -> AND ISSUER "/C=US/ST=New+20York/L=Albany/O=Widgets
Inc./CN=cacert.example.com/ emailAddress=admin@example.com";
```

One other minor SSL-related option is the CIPHER requirement option, which lets the administrator permit only "trusted" (strong) encryption ciphers to be used. SSL is cipher independent, and the potentially strong SSL encryption can be invalidated if a really weak cipher is used to protect the data being transferred. You can restrict the choice of protocols to a set you consider to be secure by issuing a command like the following:

```
mysql> GRANT ... IDENTIFIED BY 'p4ssword'
    -> REQUIRE CIPHER "EDH-RSA-DES-CBC3-SHA";
```

Managing individual client certificates may seem like excellent security, but it can be an administrative nightmare. When you create a client certificate, you have to assign it an expiration date—preferably something not too far in the future. You want its life to be long enough that you're not constantly having to regenerate a new certificate, but short enough that if the certificate falls into the hands of a hostile entity it won't have access to your data for too long.

In a small environment with a couple of employees, it may be very easy to keep track of individual certificate ownership. But when your organization scales upward to hundreds or thousands of employees with certificates, keeping track of which certificates expire when and making sure that client certificates don't expire before they've been replaced can become quite cumbersome.

Some organizations solve this problem with a combination of REQUIRE ISSUER and a series of monthly client certificates that they distribute via a trusted distribution path, such as a company intranet. Clients can download and connect to the MySQL server with certificates that are good for a month or two. This way, if an employee loses access to the company intranet, or a partner is no longer given access to the monthly key, even if the administrator isn't told to remove that user's access her ability to connect will naturally expire in a predetermined schedule.

SSH tunneling

If you're using an older version of MySQL or simply don't want the hassle of setting up SSL support, consider using SSH instead. If you use Linux or Unix, there's a good chance you're already using SSH to log into remote machines.* What a lot of people don't know is that you can use SSH to establish an encrypted tunnel between two hosts.

SSH tunneling is best illustrated with an example. Let's suppose that you want an encrypted connection from a GNU/Linux workstation to the MySQL server running on *db.example.com*. On the workstation, you execute the following command:†

```
$ ssh -N -f -L 4406:db.example.com:3306
```

This establishes a tunnel between TCP port 4406 on the workstation and port 3306 on *db.example.com*. You can now connect to MySQL through the tunnel from the workstation by doing this:

```
$ mysql -h 127.0.0.1 -P 4406
```

SSH is a very powerful tool that can do far more than this simple example illustrates. *Stunnel* is another tool for creating secure tunnels, but without a login/shell component. It's also a good substitute for a VPN in some cases.

TCP Wrappers

You can compile MySQL with support for TCP wrappers on Unix systems. If a full-blown firewall isn't an option, TCP wrappers provide a basic level of defense: you can gain additional control over which hosts MySQL will or will not talk to without having to change your grant tables. Some operating systems, such as Debian GNU/Linux, build MySQL this way by default.

---

* A variant of OpenSSH is available for Windows clients, and Putty is also popular (*http://www.chiark.greenend.org.uk/~sgtatham/putty/*). There is a full tutorial on how to set up SSH tunnels to connect to MySQL machines at *http://www.vbmysql.com/articles/security/sshtunnel.html*.

† Assuming SSH version 2 is installed. SSH version 1 has no *-N* option. See your SSH documentation for details.

To use TCP wrappers, you need to build MySQL from source and pass the *--with-libwrap* option to *configure* so that it will know where to find the proper header files on your operating system:

```
$ ./configure --with-libwrap=/usr/local/tcp_wrappers
```

Assuming you have an entry in your */etc/hosts.deny* file that denies all connections by default:

```
# deny all connections
ALL: ALL
```

you can explicitly add MySQL to your */etc/hosts.allow* file:

```
# allow mysql connections from hosts on the local network
mysqld: 192.168.1.0/255.255.0.0 : allow
```

The only other catch is that you need an appropriate entry in */etc/services* for MySQL. If you don't already have one, add a line such as the following:

```
mysql    3306/tcp  # MySQL Server
```

If you are running MySQL on a nonstandard port, use that number instead of 3306.

TCP wrappers add some overhead, such as reverse DNS lookups. This creates a dependency on the DNS subsystem, which you might not want.

Automatic Host Blocking

MySQL provides some help in preventing network-based attacks: if it notices too many bad connections from a particular host, it starts blocking connections from that host. The server variable max_connection_errors determines how many bad connections MySQL will allow before it begins blocking. A "bad connection" is any connection attempt that doesn't complete (i.e., result in a valid MySQL session). Bad passwords are often the culprit, but network problems can lead to bad connections too.

When MySQL blocks a host, it logs a message that looks like this:

```
Host 'host.badguy.com' blocked because of many connection errors.
Unblock with 'mysqladmin flush-hosts'
```

As that message indicates, you can use the *mysqladmin flush-hosts* command to unblock the host, presumably after you have figured out why that host was having problems connecting and have addressed the relevant issue. The *mysqladmin flush-hosts* command simply executes a FLUSH HOSTS SQL command, which empties MySQL's host cache tables. This unblocks *all* blocked hosts; there's no way to unblock a single host.

If you find that this becomes a common problem for some reason, you can set the max_connection_errors variable in the *my.cnf* file to a relatively high number to avoid hosts being blocked:

```
max_connection_errors=999999999
```

It isn't possible to set max_connection_errors to 0 and disable the check entirely, and you wouldn't really want to do that anyway. It's better to find and resolve the underlying problem.

Data Encryption

In applications that store sensitive data, such as banking records, you may want to store the data in an encrypted format. This makes it very difficult for unauthorized people to use the data even if they have physical access to your server. A full discussion of the relative merits of encryption algorithms and techniques is beyond the scope of this book, but we will take a quick look at some of the relevant topics.

Hashing Passwords

In less sensitive applications, you may need to protect just a small amount of information, such as a password database for another application. Passwords really shouldn't be stored in the clear, so they are commonly encrypted in applications. But rather than using encryption, it may be wise to follow the lead of most Unix systems and even MySQL itself: use a hashing algorithm on the passwords and store the results in your table.

Unlike traditional encryption, which can be reversed, a good hash function is a one-way process that can't be undone. The only way to determine the password that generated a particular hash value is to use a very computationally expensive brute-force attack (trying all possible combinations of input).

MySQL provides three user functions for hashing passwords: ENCRYPT( ), SHA1( ), and MD5( ).[*] The best way to see the results of each function is to try them all on the same source text. Let's see how the string p4ssword hashes in the three functions:

```
mysql> SELECT MD5('p4ssword'), ENCRYPT('p4ssword'), SHA1('p4ssword')\G
*************************** 1. row ***************************
    MD5('p4ssword'): 93863810133ebebe6e4c6bbc2a6ce1e7
ENCRYPT('p4ssword'): dDCjeBzIycENk
   SHA1('p4ssword'): fbb73ec5afd91d5b503ca11756e33d21a9045d9d
```

---

[*] MySQL's ENCRYPT( ) simply calls the C library's crypt( ) function. On some Unix variants, crypt( ) is an MD5 implementation, making it no different from MD5( ). On others, it is the traditional DES encryption algorithm.

Each function returns a fixed-length alphanumeric string that you can store in a `CHAR` column. To cope with the possibility of mixed-case characters in the result of `ENCRYPT( )`, it's best to declare the column `CHAR BINARY`.

 Never use MySQL's internal `PASSWORD( )` function in applications. The result is not the same in all MySQL versions.

Storing hashed data is as easy as:

```
mysql> INSERT INTO user_table (user, pass) VALUES ('user', MD5('p4ssword') );
```

To verify *user*'s password, run a `SELECT` query to see if the supplied username and password match. In Perl for example, you can do this:

```
my $sth = $dbh->prepare('SELECT * FROM user_table '
        . 'WHERE user = ? AND pass = MD5(?)');
$sth->execute($username, $password);
```

Password hashing is an easy-to-use and relatively secure way to store passwords in a database without them being easily recoverable. For a slightly better approach that makes dictionary attacks more difficult, you can combine the username and password for the hash, so it depends on more variables:

```
my $sth = $dbh->prepare('SELECT * FROM user_table '
        . 'WHERE user = ? AND pass = SHA1(CONCAT(?, ?))');
$sth->execute($username, $username, $password);
```

The only trouble is the possible security risk caused by sending the password to MySQL in plain text; it could be written in plain text to the disk in the logs, and it's visible in the process list. You could store the password as a user variable to reduce the risk a little bit, or move the hashing into the application to avoid it entirely. There are encryption functions or libraries in most programming languages. We look at application-level encryption shortly.

Encrypted Filesystems

Because MySQL's various storage engines all store their data as regular files on whatever filesystem you may be using, it's possible to use an encrypted filesystem. Most popular operating systems have at least one encrypted filesystem available (either free or commercial).

The main advantage of this approach is that you don't have to do anything special for MySQL to take advantage of it. Because all the encryption and decryption takes place outside MySQL, it just performs reads and writes without any knowledge of what's happening under the hood. All you need to do is make sure you store your data and logs on the proper filesystem. From your application's point of view, there's nothing special about this arrangement either.

There are a few downsides to using an encrypted filesystem with MySQL. First of all, because you're encrypting all the data, indexes, and logs, there will be a fair amount of CPU overhead involved in encrypting and decrypting the data. If you're thinking about using an encrypted filesystem, be sure to perform good benchmarks, so you understand how it behaves under heavy load.

Also, be sure that you don't decrypt the data when you make backups of it. This isn't a hard rule to follow, but it's easy to forget to do.

A final concern is that an encrypted filesystem provides no protection against people who get access to the server that has the data. Because the server that mounts the filesystem transparently decrypts it, anyone with access to the server can read the data—and make decrypted copies of it.

Application-Level Encryption

A more common approach to encryption is to build it into the application (or middleware). When the application needs to store sensitive data, it first encrypts the data and then stores the result in MySQL. Conversely, when it retrieves encrypted data from MySQL, it must decrypt it.

This approach provides a lot of flexibility. It doesn't tie you to a particular file-system, operating system, or even database (if your code is written in a generic fashion), and it gives the application designer the freedom to choose the encryption algorithm that's most appropriate (balancing speed and strength) for the data being stored.

Because the data is encrypted, backups are very easy. No matter where you copy the data, it is encrypted. However, this also means that access to the data must go through software that understands how to decrypt it. You can't just fire up the *mysql* command-line tool and begin issuing queries.

Application-level encryption is often a good solution, but it does have some drawbacks. For example, it's much harder for MySQL to effectively index encrypted data, and it's much harder to optimize MySQL's performance when you're working with encrypted data.

Design issues

The freedom and flexibility we mentioned have interesting implications for database design. One issue is that you must ensure that the column types you're using are appropriate for the type of encryption you're using. Some algorithms produce blocks of data with fixed minimum sizes. That means you may need a column that can hold 256 bytes just to hold a piece of data that was significantly smaller than that before encryption. Also, many popular encryption libraries produce binary data, so you'll need to create columns that can store binary data. As an alternative, you can convert the binary data to a hex or base-64 representation, but that will require more space and time.

Deciding exactly what data should and shouldn't be encrypted isn't easy, either. You need to balance security against making the information in your tables difficult to query. For example, you might have an account table that represents bank accounts and contains the following columns:

- id
- type
- status
- balance
- overdraft_protection
- date_established

Which columns does it make sense to encrypt? If you encrypt the balance, which seems reasonable, it will be difficult to answer common reporting questions. For example, you might try to write the following query to find the minimum, maximum, and average balance of accounts of each account type:

```
mysql> SELECT MIN(balance), MAX(balance), AVG(balance)
    -> FROM account GROUP BY type;
```

But the results will be meaningless. MySQL doesn't know what the encrypted balance column means, so it will just try to perform those functions on the encrypted data.

The solution is for your application to read all the rows from the account table and do the math for the report you need. That may not be terribly difficult, but it's annoying. Not only are you reimplementing functionality MySQL already provides, you're also slowing down the process considerably.

What all this boils down to is a tradeoff between security and the advantages of using a relational database in the first place. Any column that contains encrypted data is basically useless to MySQL's built-in functions, because they need to operate on unencrypted data. Similar problems arise in query optimization. For instance, in an unencrypted setup, you can easily find all the accounts with a balance greater than $100,000:

```
mysql> SELECT * FROM account WHERE balance > 100000;
```

If there is an index on the balance column and it's not encrypted, MySQL can use the index to find the desired rows. But if the data is encrypted, you'll have to fetch all the rows into your application, decrypt them, and then filter them.

Encrypting and decrypting inside MySQL

That said, you can store encrypted values inside MySQL and encrypt and decrypt them as needed with its built-in functions. The best functions to use for this purpose are AES_ENCRYPT( ) and AES_DECRYPT( ), which convert strings to encrypted binary strings and back again. They are symmetric: the key you use for encryption is the same key you use for decryption. For example:

```
mysql> SET @key       := 's3cret';
mysql> SET @encrypted := AES_ENCRYPT('sensitive data', @key);
mysql> SELECT AES_DECRYPT(@encrypted, @key);
+------------------------------+
| AES_DECRYPT(@encrypted, @key) |
+------------------------------+
| sensitive data               |
+------------------------------+
```

We didn't show the encrypted value because it is binary ones and zeros and will appear simply as garbled characters.

This approach doesn't solve all the problems we've mentioned, though. For one thing, it doesn't avoid the indexing issues; additionally, the data you're trying to encrypt will still be in plain text in the SQL query, and it will still be logged into the server's log (assuming it is activated). However, we did show one step you can take to help reduce the risk of other users seeing your secret data: store the encryption key in a user variable. There are more secure ways to actually set the variable's value, too. For example, you can place the variable in a stored procedure and call the stored procedure to set its value, and then restrict access to the stored procedure. This makes it harder for other users to determine the key's value.

Source Code Modification

If you're looking for a more flexible approach than either encrypted filesystems or application-based encryption, you can always build a custom solution. The source code for MySQL is freely available under the GNU General Public License.

This sort of work requires that you either know C++ or hire someone who does. Beyond that, you'll be looking to create your own storage engine with native encryption support, or you might find it easier to extend an existing one with encryption.

MySQL in a chrooted Environment

Running a server in a chrooted environment greatly enhances overall system security on a Unix system. It does this by setting up an isolated environment in which files outside of a given directory are no longer accessible. That way, even if a security flaw is found in the server and exploited, the potential for damage is limited to the files in that directory, which should only be the files for that particular application.

If you want your MySQL application to run in a chrooted environment, you'll have to begin by either compiling MySQL from source or unpacking and installing the binary package MySQL AB provides. Many administrators do this as a matter of course, but it's an absolute must for a chrooted application: many prepackaged MySQL installations put some files in */usr/bin*, some in */var/lib/mysql*, etc., but all the files in a chrooted installation need to reside under the same directory structure.

What we tend to do is to create a */chroot* directory where all our chrooted applications will live. To do this, you can configure your MySQL installation as follows:

```
$ ./configure --prefix=/chroot/mysql
```

Then compile MySQL as you normally would, and let the installation procedure install the MySQL files in the */chroot/mysql* tree.

The next thing to do is a little magic, to make everything happier. *chroot* actually stands for *change root*. If you enter:

```
$ chroot /chroot/mysql
```

the / directory is now actually */chroot/mysql*. Because both the chrooted server and the non-chrooted client use the files, it's important to set up the filesystem so that both the server and the clients can find the files they need. An easy solution to this problem is to do the following:

```
$ cd /chroot/mysql
$ mkdir chroot
$ cd chroot
$ ln -s /chroot/mysql mysql
```

This creates a symbolic directory path, */chroot/mysql/chroot/mysql*, which actually points to */chroot/mysql*. Now, even if the application is chrooted and trying to get to */chroot/mysql*, it will reach the proper directory. Meanwhile, if the client application is running outside the chroot environment, it can find the files it needs.

The last step is to send the proper commands to *mysqld_safe*, so that the MySQL server can start itself up and *chroot* to the proper directory. To do this, you might enter something like the following:

```
$ mysqld_safe --chroot=/chroot/mysql --user=1001
```

You'll notice we used the Unix UID of the MySQL user (1001), instead of *--user=mysql*. This is because in the chrooted environment, the MySQL server may no longer be able to query your authentication backend to do username-to-UID lookups.[*]

There are some caveats when using a chrooted MySQL server. LOAD DATA INFILE and other commands that access filenames directly may behave significantly differently from what you expect, because the server no longer considers / to be the filesystem

---

[*] From our experience in testing this, it might be as simple as copying *libnss** to your MySQL library directory in the chrooted environment, but from a practical standpoint, it's probably best not to worry about such things and to just enter the UID directly in your startup script.

root. So, if you tell it to load data from *tmp/filename*, you should be sure that the file is actually */chroot/mysql/tmp/filename*, or MySQL won't be able to find it.

A chrooted environment is only one way to partially isolate MySQL. There are others, such as FreeBSD jails, Solaris Zones, and virtualization.

MySQL Server Status

You can answer many questions about a MySQL server by inspecting its status. MySQL exposes information about server internals in two main ways: the newest is the standard INFORMATION_SCHEMA database, and the more traditional is a series of SHOW commands (which MySQL continues to support even though the INFORMATION_SCHEMA database is the preferred mechanism for new features). Some information you can get via SHOW commands isn't found in the INFORMATION_SCHEMA tables yet.

The challenges for you are determining what is relevant to your problem, how to get the information you need, and how to interpret it. Although MySQL lets you see a lot of information about what's going on inside the server, it's not always easy to use that information. Understanding it requires patience, experience, and ready access to the MySQL manual.

There are some tools that can help you understand the server status in various contexts, such as monitoring and profiling, and we mention a few of those in the next chapter. However, you should still understand the values at a high level—at a minimum, what the categories of values are—and know how to get them from the server.

This chapter explains many of the status commands and their output. When we've covered a topic in detail elsewhere, we refer you to that part of the book.

System Variables

MySQL exposes many system variables through the SHOW VARIABLES SQL command, as variables you can use in expressions, or with *mysqladmin variables* at the command line. From MySQL 5.1, you can also access them through tables in the INFORMATION_SCHEMA database.

These variables represent a variety of configuration information, such as the server's default storage engine (storage_engine), the available time zones, the connection's collation, and startup parameters. We explained how to set and use system variables in Chapter 6.

SHOW STATUS

The SHOW STATUS command shows server status variables in a two-column name/value table. Unlike the server variables we mentioned in the previous section, these are read-only. You can view the variables by either executing SHOW STATUS as a SQL command or executing *mysqladmin extended-status* as a shell command. If you use the SQL command, you can use LIKE and WHERE to limit the results; the LIKE does a standard pattern match on the variable name. The commands return a table of results, but you can't sort it, join it to other tables, or do other standard things you can do with MySQL tables.

> We use the term "status variable" to refer to a value from SHOW STATUS and the term "system variable" to refer to a server configuration variable.

The behavior of SHOW STATUS changed greatly in MySQL 5.0, but you might not notice unless you're paying close attention. Instead of just maintaining one set of global variables, MySQL now maintains some variables globally and some on a per-connection basis. Thus, SHOW STATUS contains a mixture of global and session variables. Many of them have dual scope: there's both a global and a session variable, and they have the same name. SHOW STATUS also now shows session variables by default, so if you were accustomed to running SHOW STATUS and seeing global variables, you won't see them anymore; now you have to run SHOW GLOBAL STATUS instead.*

In MySQL 5.1 and newer, you can select values directly from the INFORMATION_SCHEMA.GLOBAL_STATUS and INFORMATION_SCHEMA.SESSION_STATUS tables.

There are hundreds of status variables in a MySQL 5.0 server, and newer versions include even more. Most either are counters or contain the current value of some status metric. Counters increment every time MySQL does something, such as initiating a full table scan (Select_scan). Metrics, such as the number of open connections to the server (Threads_connected), may increase and decrease. Sometimes there are several variables that seem to refer to the same thing, such as Connections (the number of connection attempts to the server) and Threads_connected; in this case, the variables are related, but similar names don't always imply a relationship.

Counters are stored as unsigned integers. They use 4 bytes on 32-bit builds and 8 bytes on 64-bit builds, and they wrap back to 0 after reaching their maximum values. If you're monitoring the variables incrementally, you might need to watch for and correct the wrap; you should also be aware that if your server has been up for a long time, you might see lower values than you expect simply because the variable's values have wrapped around to zero. (This is very rarely a problem on 64-bit builds.)

---

* There's a gotcha waiting here: if you use an old version of *mysqladmin* on a new server, it won't use SHOW GLOBAL STATUS, so it won't display the "right" information.

The best way to look at many of these variables is to see how much their values change over the course of a few minutes. You can use *mysqladmin extended-status -r -i 5* or *innotop*.

The following is an overview—not an exhaustive list—of the different categories of variables you'll see in SHOW STATUS. For full details on a given variable, you should consult the MySQL manual, which helpfully documents them at *http://dev.mysql. com/doc/en/mysqld-option-tables.html*. When we discuss a set of related variables whose name begins with a common prefix, we refer to the group collectively as "The *<prefix>*_* variables."

Thread and Connection Statistics

These variables track connection attempts, aborted connections, network traffic, and thread statistics:

- Connections, Max_used_connections, Threads_connected
- Aborted_clients, Aborted_connects
- Bytes_received, Bytes_sent
- Slow_launch_threads, Threads_cached, Threads_created, Threads_running

If Aborted_connects isn't zero, it may mean that you have network problems or that someone is trying to connect and failing (perhaps because they're specifying the wrong password or an invalid database). If this value gets too high, it can have serious side effects: it can cause MySQL to block a host. See Chapter 12 for more on this.

Aborted_clients has a similar name but a completely different meaning. If this value increments, it usually means there's been an application error, such as the programmer forgetting to close MySQL connections properly before terminating the program. This is not usually indicative of a big problem.

A useful metric is how many threads are created per second (Threads_created/ Uptime). If this value is not close to zero, it may mean your thread cache is too small and new connections aren't able to find free threads to use from the thread cache.

It's most useful to look at the values of all these variables and metrics over the course of the last several minutes, not over the entire uptime of the server.

Binary Logging Status

The Binlog_cache_use and Binlog_cache_disk_use status variables show how many transactions have been stored in the binary log cache, and how many transactions were too large for the binary log cache and so had their statements stored in a temporary file. We explained how to size the binary log cache in Chapter 6.

Command Counters

The `Com_*` variables count the number of times each type of SQL or C API command has been issued. For example, `Com_select` counts the number of `SELECT` statements, and `Com_change_db` counts the number of times a connection's default database has been changed, either with the `USE` statement or via a C API call. The `Questions` variable counts the total number of queries and commands the server has received. However, it doesn't quite equal the sum of all the `Com_*` variables, because of query cache hits, closed and aborted connections, and possibly other factors.

The `Com_admin_commands` status variable may be very large. It counts not only administrative commands, but ping requests to the MySQL instance as well. These requests are issued through the C API and typically come from client code, such as the following Perl code:

```
my $dbh = DBI->connect(...);
while ( $dbh && $dbh->ping ) {
   # Do something
}
```

These ping requests are "garbage" queries. They probably don't load the server very much, but they're still a waste. We've seen ORM systems that ping the server before each query, which is pointless. We've also seen database abstraction libraries that change the default database before every query, which will show up as a very large number of `Com_change_db` commands. It's best to eliminate both practices.

Temporary Files and Tables

You can view the variables that count how many times MySQL has created temporary tables and files with:

```
mysql> SHOW GLOBAL STATUS LIKE 'Created_tmp%';
```

Handler Operations

The handler API is the interface between MySQL and its storage engines. The `Handler_*` variables count handler operations, such as the number of times MySQL asks a storage engine to read the next row from an index. Studying your server's `Handler_*` variables can give insight into what kinds of work your server does most. `Handler_*` variables are useful for profiling queries as well. You can view these variables with:

```
mysql> SHOW GLOBAL STATUS LIKE 'Handler_%';
```

MyISAM Key Buffer

The Key_* variables contain metrics and counters about the MyISAM key buffer. You can view these variables with:

```
mysql> SHOW GLOBAL STATUS LIKE 'Key_%';
```

See Chapter 6 for a detailed explanation of how to analyze and tune the key caches.

File Descriptors

If you mainly use the MyISAM storage engine, it's important to watch file descriptor statistics, because they tell you how often MySQL opens each table's *.frm*, *.MYI*, and *.MYD* files. InnoDB keeps all data in its tablespace files, so if you mainly use InnoDB, these variables aren't as important. You can view the Open_* variables with:

```
mysql> SHOW GLOBAL STATUS LIKE 'Open_%';
```

Chapter 6 explains in detail how to tune the settings that influence these variables.

Query Cache

You can inspect the query cache by looking at the Qcache_* status variables. All the variables in this group are important if you rely on your query cache for performance. To inspect them, use:

```
mysql> SHOW GLOBAL STATUS LIKE 'Qcache_%';
```

There's a detailed explanation of how to tune the query cache in Chapter 5.

SELECT Types

The Select_* variables are counters for certain types of SELECT queries. They can help you see the ratio of SELECT queries that use various query plans. Unfortunately, there are no such status variables for other kinds of queries, such as UPDATE and REPLACE; however, you can look at the Handler_* status variables (discussed earlier) for insight into the performance of non-SELECT queries. To see all the Select_* variables, use:

```
mysql> SHOW GLOBAL STATUS LIKE 'Select_%';
```

In our judgment, the Select_* status variables can be ranked as follows, in order of ascending cost:

Select_range
  The number of joins that scanned an index range on the first table.

Select_scan
  The number of joins that scanned the entire first table. There is nothing wrong with this if every row in the first table should participate in the join; it's only a

bad thing if you don't want all the rows and there is no index to find the ones you wanted.

Select_full_range_join
> The number of joins that used a value from table *n* to retrieve rows from a range of the reference index in table *n* + 1. Depending on the query, this can be more or less costly than Select_scan.

Select_range_check
> The number of joins that reevaluate indexes in table *n* + 1 for every row in table *n* to see which is least expensive. This generally means no indexes in table *n* + 1 are useful for the join. This query plan has very high overhead.

Select_full_join
> A cross join, or a join without any criteria to match rows in the tables. The number of rows examined is the product of the number of rows in each table. This is usually a very bad thing.

The last two variables should not increase rapidly on a well-tuned server. You can sometimes spot a badly optimized workload by comparing the ratio of these two counters to the total number of SELECT queries your server is processing (Com_select). If either is more than a few percent of the total, you probably need to optimize your queries and/or schema.

A related status variable is Slow_queries. The patches we've developed for the slow query log can help you see whether a query required a full join, whether it was served from the query cache, and so on. See "Finer control over logging" on page 65 for more information.

Sorts

We covered a lot of MySQL's sorting optimizations in Chapters 3 and 4, so you should have a good idea of how sorting works. When MySQL can't use an index to retrieve rows presorted, it has to do a filesort, and it increments the Sort_* status variables. Aside from Sort_merge_passes, you can influence these values only by adding indexes that MySQL can use for sorting. Sort_merge_passes depends on the sort_buffer_size server variable (not to be confused with the myisam_sort_buffer_size server variable). MySQL uses the sort buffer to hold a chunk of rows for sorting. When it's finished sorting them, it merges these sorted rows into the result, increments Sort_merge_passes, and fills the buffer with the next chunk of rows to sort. If the sort buffer is too small, it will have to do this many times, and the value of the status variable will be large.

You can see all the Sort_* variables with:

```
mysql> SHOW GLOBAL STATUS LIKE 'Sort_%';
```

MySQL increments the Sort_scan and Sort_range variables when it reads sorted rows from the results of a filesort and returns them to the client. The difference is merely that the first is incremented when the query plan causes Select_scan to increment (see the preceding section), and the second is incremented when Select_range increments. There is no implementation or cost difference between the two; they merely indicate the type of query plan that caused the sort.

Table Locking

The Table_locks_immediate and Table_locks_waited variables tell you how many locks were granted immediately and how many had to be waited for. If you see many threads in the Locked state in SHOW FULL PROCESSLIST, check these variables. Be aware, however, that they show only server-level locking statistics, not storage engine locking statistics. See Appendix D for more about debugging locks.

Secure Sockets Layer (SSL)

The Ssl_* variables show how the server is configured for SSL if applicable. You can see all the SSL variables with:

```
mysql> SHOW GLOBAL STATUS LIKE 'Ssl_%';
```

InnoDB-Specific

The Innodb_* variables show some of the data included in SHOW INNODB STATUS, discussed later in this chapter. The variables can be grouped together by name: Innodb_buffer_pool_*, Innodb_log_*, and so on. We discuss InnoDB's internals more when we examine SHOW INNODB STATUS.

These variables are available in MySQL 5.0 and newer, and they have an important side effect: they create a global lock and traverse the entire InnoDB buffer pool before releasing the lock. In the meantime, other threads run into the lock and block until it is released. This skews some status values, such as Threads_running, so they will appear higher than normal (possibly much higher, depending on how busy your server is). The same effect happens when you run SHOW INNODB STATUS or access these statistics via the INFORMATION_SCHEMA tables (in MySQL 5.0 and newer, SHOW STATUS and SHOW VARIABLES are mapped to queries against the INFORMATION_SCHEMA tables behind the scenes).

These operations can, therefore, be expensive in these versions of MySQL—checking the server status too frequently (e.g., once a second) causes significant overhead. Using SHOW STATUS LIKE doesn't help, because it retrieves the full status and then post-filters it.

Plug-in-Specific

MySQL 5.1 and newer support pluggable storage engines and provide a mechanism for storage engines to register their own status and configuration variables with the MySQL server. You may see some plug-in-specific variables if you're using a pluggable storage engine.

Miscellaneous

Some other status variables include the following:

Delayed_*, Not_flushed_delayed_rows
> These variables are counters and metrics for INSERT DELAYED queries.

Last_query_cost
> This variable shows the query optimizer's query plan cost for the last query run. We discussed the query plan cost in Chapter 4.

Ndb_*
> This variable show NDB Cluster configuration information, if applicable.

Slave_*
> This variable apply if the server is a replication slave. The Slave_open_temp_tables variable is particularly important for statement-based replication. See "Missing Temporary Tables" on page 394 for more about replication and temporary tables.

Tc_log_*
> This counter are for a server that acts as the coordinator for XA transactions. See "Distributed (XA) Transactions" on page 262 for details.

Uptime
> This variable shows the server's uptime, in seconds.

A good way to get a feel for your overall workload is to compare values within a group of related status variables—for example, look at all the Select_* variables together, or all the Handler_* variables. If you're using *innotop*, this is easy to do in Command Summary mode, but you can also do it manually with a command like *mysqladmin extended -r -i60 | grep Handler_*. Here's what *innotop* shows for the Select_* variables on one server we checked:

```
_____ Command Summary _____ __
Name                    Value   Pct      Last Incr  Pct
Select_scan             756582  59.89%          2   100.00%
Select_range            497675  39.40%          0   0.00%
Select_full_join          7847  0.62%           0   0.00%
Select_full_range_join    1159  0.09%           0   0.00%
Select_range_check           1  0.00%           0   0.00%
```

The first two columns of values are since the server was booted, and the last two are since the last refresh (10 seconds ago, in this case). The percentages are over the total of the values shown in the display, not over the total of all queries.

Even though this server has a relatively low percentage of full joins, it might be worth looking into why there are any at all.

SHOW INNODB STATUS

The InnoDB storage engine exposes a lot of information about its internals in the output of SHOW ENGINE INNODB STATUS, or its simpler synonym, SHOW INNODB STATUS. Unlike most of the SHOW commands, its output consists of a single string, not rows and columns. It is divided into sections, each of which shows information about a different part of the InnoDB storage engine. Some of the output is most useful for InnoDB developers, but much of it is interesting—or even essential—if you're trying to understand and tune InnoDB for high performance.

 InnoDB often prints out 64-bit numbers in two pieces: the high 32 bits and the low 32 bits. An example is a transaction ID, such as TRANSACTION 0 3793469. You can calculate the 64-bit number's value by shifting the first number left 32 bits and adding it to the second one. We show some examples later.

The output includes some average statistics, such as fsync( ) calls per second. These show average activity since the last time the output was generated, so if you're examining these values, make sure you wait 30 seconds or so between samples to give the statistics time to accumulate. The output is not all generated at a single point in time, so not all averages that appear in the output are calculated over the same time interval. Also, InnoDB has an internal reset interval that is unpredictable and varies between versions; you should examine the output to see the time over which the averages were generated, because it will not necessarily be the same as the time between samples.

There's enough information in the output to calculate averages for most of the statistics manually if you want. However, a monitoring tool such as *innotop*—which does incremental differences and averages for you—is very helpful here.

Header

The first section is the header, which simply announces the beginning of the output, the current date and time, and how long it has been since the last printout. Line 2 shows the current date and time. Line 4 shows the time frame over which the averages were calculated, which is either the time since the last printout or the time since the last internal reset:

```
1  =======================================
2  070913 10:31:48 INNODB MONITOR OUTPUT
3  =======================================
4  Per second averages calculated from the last 49 seconds
```

SEMAPHORES

If you have a high-concurrency workload, you may want to pay attention to the next section, SEMAPHORES. It contains two kinds of data: event counters and, optionally, a list of current waits. If you're having trouble with bottlenecks, you can use this information to help you find the bottlenecks. Unfortunately, knowing what to do about them is a little more complex, but we give some advice later in this chapter. Here is some sample output for this section:

```
1  ----------
2  SEMAPHORES
3  ----------
4  OS WAIT ARRAY INFO: reservation count 13569, signal count 11421
5  --Thread 1152170336 has waited at ./../include/buf0buf.ic line 630 for 0.00 seconds
   the semaphore:
6  Mutex at 0x2a957858b8 created file buf0buf.c line 517, lock var 0
7  waiters flag 0
8  wait is ending
9  --Thread 1147709792 has waited at ./../include/buf0buf.ic line 630 for 0.00 seconds
   the semaphore:
10 Mutex at 0x2a957858b8 created file buf0buf.c line 517, lock var 0
11 waiters flag 0
12 wait is ending
13 Mutex spin waits 5672442, rounds 3899888, OS waits 4719
14 RW-shared spins 5920, OS waits 2918; RW-excl spins 3463, OS waits 3163
```

Line 4 gives information about the operating system wait array, which is an array of "slots." InnoDB reserves slots in the array for semaphores, which the operating system uses to signal threads that they can go ahead and do the work they're waiting to do. This line shows how many times InnoDB has needed to use operating system waits. The reservation count indicates how often InnoDB has allocated slots, and the signal count measures how often threads have been signaled via the array. Operating system waits are costly relative to spin waits, as we'll see momentarily.

Lines 5 through 12 show the InnoDB threads that are currently waiting for a mutex. The example shows two waits, each beginning with the text "-- Thread <num> has waited..." This section should be empty unless your server has a high-concurrency workload that causes InnoDB to resort to operating system waits. The most useful thing to look at, unless you're familiar with InnoDB source code, is the filename at which the thread is waiting. This gives you a hint where the hot spots are inside InnoDB. For example, if you see many threads waiting at a file called *buf0buf.ic*, you have buffer pool contention. The output indicates how long the thread has been waiting, and the "waiters flag" shows how many waiters are waiting for the mutex.

The text "wait is ending" means the mutex is actually free already, but the operating system hasn't scheduled the thread to run yet.

You might wonder what exactly InnoDB is waiting for. InnoDB uses mutexes and semaphores to protect critical sections of code by restricting them to only one thread at a time, or to restrict writers when there are active readers, and so on. There are many critical sections in InnoDB's code, and under the right conditions any of them could appear here. Gaining access to a buffer pool page is one you might see commonly.

After the list of waiting threads, lines 13 and 14 show more event counters. Line 13 shows several counters related to mutexes, and line 14 is for read/write shared and exclusive locks. In each case, you can see how often InnoDB has resorted to an operating system wait.

InnoDB has a multiphase wait policy. First, it tries to spin-wait for the lock. If this doesn't succeed after a preconfigured number of spin rounds (specified by the innodb_sync_spin_loops configuration variable), it falls back to the more expensive and complex wait array.*

Spin waits are relatively low-cost, but they burn CPU cycles by checking repeatedly if a resource can be locked. This isn't as bad as it sounds, because there are typically free CPU cycles while the processor is waiting for I/O. And even if there aren't any free CPU cycles, spin waits are often much less expensive than the alternative. However, spinning monopolizes the processor when another thread might be able to do some work.

The alternative to a spin wait is for the operating system to do a context switch, so another thread can run while the thread waits, then wake the sleeping thread when it is signaled via the semaphore in the wait array. Signaling via a semaphore is efficient, but the context switch is expensive. These can add up quickly: thousands of them per second can cause a lot of overhead.

You can try to strike a balance between spin waits and operating system waits by changing the innodb_sync_spin_loops system variable. Don't worry about spin waits unless you see many (perhaps in the range of hundreds of thousands) spin rounds per second. There's more advice on how to tune this part of InnoDB in Chapter 6.

LATEST FOREIGN KEY ERROR

The next section, LATEST FOREIGN KEY ERROR, doesn't appear unless your server has had a foreign key error. There are many places in the source code that can generate this output, and it varies depending on the kind of error. Sometimes it's a transaction and the parent or child rows it was looking for while trying to insert, update, or

---

* The wait array was changed to be much more efficient in MySQL 5.1.

delete a record. At other times it's a type mismatch between tables while InnoDB was trying to add or delete a foreign key, or alter a table that already had a foreign key.

This section's output is very helpful for debugging the exact causes of InnoDB's often vague foreign key errors. Let's look at some examples. First, we create two tables with a foreign key between them, and insert a little data:

```
CREATE TABLE parent (
    parent_id int NOT NULL,
    PRIMARY KEY(parent_id)
) ENGINE=InnoDB;

CREATE TABLE child (
    parent_id int NOT NULL,
    KEY parent_id (parent_id),
    CONSTRAINT child_ibfk_1 FOREIGN KEY (parent_id) REFERENCES parent (parent_id)
) ENGINE=InnoDB;

INSERT INTO parent(parent_id) VALUES(1);
INSERT INTO child(parent_id) VALUES(1);
```

There are two basic classes of foreign key errors. Adding, updating, or deleting data in a way that would violate the foreign key causes the first class of errors. For example, here's what happens when we delete the row from the parent table:

```
DELETE FROM parent;
ERROR 1451 (23000): Cannot delete or update a parent row: a foreign key constraint
fails (`test/child`, CONSTRAINT `child_ibfk_1` FOREIGN KEY (`parent_id`) REFERENCES
`parent` (`parent_id`))
```

The error message is fairly straightforward, and you'll get similar messages for all errors caused by adding, updating, or deleting nonmatching rows. Here's the output from SHOW INNODB STATUS:

```
1  ------------------------
2  LATEST FOREIGN KEY ERROR
3  ------------------------
4  070913 10:57:34 Transaction:
5  TRANSACTION 0 3793469, ACTIVE 0 sec, process no 5488, OS thread id 1141152064
   updating or deleting, thread declared inside InnoDB 499
6  mysql tables in use 1, locked 1
7  4 lock struct(s), heap size 1216, undo log entries 1
8  MySQL thread id 9, query id 305 localhost baron updating
9  DELETE FROM parent
10 Foreign key constraint fails for table `test/child`:
11 ,
12   CONSTRAINT `child_ibfk_1` FOREIGN KEY (`parent_id`) REFERENCES `parent` (`parent_
   id`)
13 Trying to delete or update in parent table, in index `PRIMARY` tuple:
14 DATA TUPLE: 3 fields;
15  0: len 4; hex 80000001; asc     ;; 1: len 6; hex 00000039e23d; asc    9 =;; 2: len
    7; hex 000000002d0e24; asc     - $;;
16
17 But in child table `test/child`, in index `parent_id`, there is a record:
```

```
18  PHYSICAL RECORD: n_fields 2; compact format; info bits 0
19    0: len 4; hex 80000001; asc      ;; 1: len 6; hex 000000000500; asc      ;;
```

Line 4 shows the date and time of the last foreign key error. Lines 5 through 9 show details about the transaction that violated the foreign key error; we explain more about these lines later. Lines 10 through 19 show the exact data InnoDB was trying to change when it found the error. A lot of this output is the row data converted to printable formats; we say more about this later, too.

So far, so good, but there's another class of foreign key error that can be much harder to debug. Here's what happens when we try to alter the parent table:

```
ALTER TABLE parent MODIFY parent_id INT UNSIGNED NOT NULL;
ERROR 1025 (HY000): Error on rename of './test/#sql-1570_9' to './test/parent'
(errno: 150)
```

This is less than clear, but the SHOW INNODB STATUS text sheds some light on it:

```
 1  ------------------------
 2  LATEST FOREIGN KEY ERROR
 3  ------------------------
 4  070913 11:06:03 Error in foreign key constraint of table test/child:
 5  there is no index in referenced table which would contain
 6  the columns as the first columns, or the data types in the
 7  referenced table do not match to the ones in table. Constraint:
 8  ,
 9    CONSTRAINT child_ibfk_1 FOREIGN KEY (parent_id) REFERENCES parent (parent_id)
10  The index in the foreign key in table is parent_id
11  See http://dev.mysql.com/doc/refman/5.0/en/innodb-foreign-key-constraints.html
12  for correct foreign key definition.
```

The error in this case is a different data type. Foreign-keyed columns must have *exactly* the same data type, including any modifiers (such as UNSIGNED, which was the problem in this case). Whenever you see error 1025 and don't understand why, the best place to look is in SHOW INNODB STATUS.

LATEST DETECTED DEADLOCK

Like the foreign key section, the LATEST DETECTED DEADLOCK section appears only if your server has had a deadlock.

A deadlock is a cycle in the waits-for graph, which is a data structure of row locks held and waited for. The cycle can be arbitrarily large. InnoDB detects deadlocks instantly, because it checks for a cycle in the graph every time a transaction has to wait for a row lock. Deadlocks can be quite complex, but this section shows only the last two transactions involved, the last statement executed in each of the transactions, and the locks that created the cycle in the graph. You don't see other transactions that may also be included in the cycle, nor do you see the statement that may have really acquired the locks earlier in a transaction. Nevertheless, you can usually find out what caused the deadlock by looking at this output.

There are actually two types of InnoDB deadlocks. The first, which is what most people are accustomed to, is a true cycle in the waits-for graph. The other type is a waits-for graph that is too expensive to check for cycles. If InnoDB has to check more than a million locks in the graph, or if it recurses through more than 200 transactions while checking, it gives up and says there's a deadlock. These numbers are hardcoded constants in the InnoDB source, and you can't configure them (though you can change them and recompile InnoDB if you wish). You'll know when exceeding these limits causes a deadlock, because you'll see "TOO DEEP OR LONG SEARCH IN THE LOCK TABLE WAITS-FOR GRAPH" in the output.

InnoDB prints not only the transactions and the locks they held and waited for, but also the records themselves. This information is mostly useful to the InnoDB developers, but there's currently no way to disable it. Unfortunately, it can be so large that it runs over the length allocated for output and prevents you from seeing the sections that follow. The only way to remedy this is to cause a small deadlock to replace the large one, or to use a patch one of this book's authors developed, which is available at *http://lists.mysql.com/internals/35174*.

Here's a sample deadlock:

```
 1  ------------------------
 2  LATEST DETECTED DEADLOCK
 3  ------------------------
 4  070913 11:14:21
 5  *** (1) TRANSACTION:
 6  TRANSACTION 0 3793488, ACTIVE 2 sec, process no 5488, OS thread id 1141287232
    starting index read
 7  mysql tables in use 1, locked 1
 8  LOCK WAIT 4 lock struct(s), heap size 1216
 9  MySQL thread id 11, query id 350 localhost baron Updating
10  UPDATE test.tiny_dl SET a = 0 WHERE a <> 0
11  *** (1) WAITING FOR THIS LOCK TO BE GRANTED:
12  RECORD LOCKS space id 0 page no 3662 n bits 72 index `GEN_CLUST_INDEX` of table
    `test/tiny_dl` trx id 0 3793488 lock_mode X waiting
13  Record lock, heap no 2 PHYSICAL RECORD: n_fields 4; compact format; info bits 0
14   0: len 6; hex 000000000501 ...[ omitted ] ...
15
16  *** (2) TRANSACTION:
17  TRANSACTION 0 3793489, ACTIVE 2 sec, process no 5488, OS thread id 1141422400
    starting index read, thread declared inside InnoDB 500
18  mysql tables in use 1, locked 1
19  4 lock struct(s), heap size 1216
20  MySQL thread id 12, query id 351 localhost baron Updating
21  UPDATE test.tiny_dl SET a = 1 WHERE a <> 1
22  *** (2) HOLDS THE LOCK(S):
23  RECORD LOCKS space id 0 page no 3662 n bits 72 index `GEN_CLUST_INDEX` of table
    `test/tiny_dl` trx id 0 3793489 lock mode S
24  Record lock, heap no 1 PHYSICAL RECORD: n_fields 1; compact format; info bits 0
25   0: ... [ omitted ] ...
26
27  *** (2) WAITING FOR THIS LOCK TO BE GRANTED:
```

```
28   RECORD LOCKS space id 0 page no 3662 n bits 72 index `GEN_CLUST_INDEX` of table
     `test/tiny_dl` trx id 0 3793489 lock_mode X waiting
29   Record lock, heap no 2 PHYSICAL RECORD: n_fields 4; compact format; info bits 0
30     0: len 6; hex 000000000501 ...[ omitted ] ...
31
32   *** WE ROLL BACK TRANSACTION (2)
```

Line 4 shows when the deadlock occurred, and lines 5 through 10 show information about the first transaction involved in the deadlock. We explain the meaning of this output in detail in the next section.

Lines 11 through 15 show the locks transaction 1 was waiting for when the deadlock happened. We've omitted some of the information that's useful only for debugging InnoDB on line 14. The important thing to notice is line 12, which says this transaction wanted an exclusive (X) lock on GEN_CLUST_INDEX* on the test.tiny_dl table.

Lines 16 through 21 show the second transaction's status, and lines 22 through 26 show the locks it held. There are several records listed on line 25, which we've removed for brevity. One of these was the record for which the first transaction was waiting. Finally, lines 27 through 31 show the locks for which it was waiting.

A cycle in the waits-for graph occurs when each transaction holds a lock the other wants and wants a lock the other holds. InnoDB doesn't show all the locks held and waited for, but it shows enough to help you determine what indexes the queries were using, which is valuable in determining whether you can avoid deadlocks.

If you can get both queries to scan the same index in the same direction, you can often reduce the number of deadlocks, because queries can't create a cycle when they request locks in the same order. This is sometimes easy to do. For example, if you need to update a number of records within a transaction, sort them by their primary key in the application's memory, then update them in that order—then they can't deadlock. At other times, however, it can be infeasible (such as when you have two processes that need to work on the same table but are using different indexes).

Line 32 shows which transaction was chosen as the deadlock victim. InnoDB tries to choose the transaction it thinks will be easiest to roll back, which is the one with the fewest updates.

This information can be valuable to monitor and log for analysis. Maatkit's *mk-deadlock-logger* tool is a convenient way to do this. It's also very helpful to examine the general log, find all the queries from the threads involved, and see what really caused the deadlock. Read the next section to see where to find the thread ID in the deadlock output.

---

* This is the index InnoDB creates internally when you don't specify a primary key.

TRANSACTIONS

This section contains a little summary information about InnoDB transactions, followed by a list of the currently active transactions. Here are the first few lines (the header):

```
1  ------------
2  TRANSACTIONS
3  ------------
4  Trx id counter 0 80157601
5  Purge done for trx's n:o <0 80154573 undo n:o <0 0
6  History list length 6
7  Total number of lock structs in row lock hash table 0
```

The output varies depending on the MySQL version, but it includes at least the following:

- Line 4: the current transaction identifier, which is a system variable that increments for each new transaction.

- Line 5: the transaction ID to which InnoDB has purged old MVCC row versions. You can see how many old versions haven't yet been purged by looking at the difference between this value and the current transaction ID. There's no hard and fast rule as to how large this number can safely get. If nothing is updating any data, a large number doesn't mean there's unpurged data, because all the transactions are actually looking at the same version of the database. On the other hand, if many rows are being updated, one or more versions of each row is staying in memory. The best policy for reducing overhead is to ensure that transactions commit when they're done instead of staying open a long time, because even an open transaction that doesn't do any work keeps InnoDB from purging old row versions.

  Also in line 5: the undo log record number InnoDB's purge process is currently working on, if any. If it's "0 0", as in our example, the purge process is idle.

- Line 6: the history list length, which is the number of unpurged transactions in the undo space in InnoDB's data files. When a transaction performs updates and commits, this number increases; when the purge process removes the old versions, it decreases. The purge process also updates the value in line 5.

- Line 7: the number of lock structs. Each lock struct usually holds many row locks, so this is not the same as the number of rows locked.

The header is followed by a list of transactions. Current versions of MySQL don't support nested transactions, so there's a maximum of one transaction per client connection at a time, and each transaction belongs to only a single connection. Each transaction has at least two lines in the output. Here's a sample of the minimal information you'll see about a transaction:

```
1  ---TRANSACTION 0 3793494, not started, process no 5488, OS thread id 1141152064
2  MySQL thread id 15, query id 479 localhost baron
```

The first line begins with the transaction's ID and status. This transaction is "not started," which means it has committed and not issued any more statements that affect transactions; it's probably just idle. Then there's some process and thread information. The second line shows the MySQL process ID, which is also the same as the Id column in SHOW FULL PROCESSLIST. This is followed by an internal query number and some connection information (also the same as what you can find in SHOW FULL PROCESSLIST).

Each transaction can print much more information than that, though. Here's a more complex example:

```
1  ---TRANSACTION 0 80157600, ACTIVE 4 sec, process no 3396, OS thread id 1148250464,
   thread declared inside InnoDB 442
2  mysql tables in use 1, locked 0
3  MySQL thread id 8079, query id 728899 localhost baron Sending data
4  select sql_calc_found_rows * from b limit 5
5  Trx read view will not see trx with id>= 0 80157601, sees <0 80157597
```

Line 1 in this sample shows the transaction has been active for four seconds. The possible states are "not started," "active," "prepared," and "committed in memory" (once it commits to disk, the state will change to "not started"). You may also see information about what the transaction is currently doing, though this example doesn't show that. There are over 30 string constants in the source that can be printed here, such as "fetching rows," "adding foreign keys," and so on.

The "thread declared inside InnoDB 442" text on line 1 means the thread is doing some operation inside the InnoDB kernel and has 442 "tickets" left to use. In other words, the same SQL query is allowed to reenter the InnoDB kernel 442 more times. The ticket system limits thread concurrency inside the kernel to prevent thread thrashing on some platforms. Even if the thread's state is "inside InnoDB," the thread might not necessarily be doing all its work inside InnoDB; the query might be processing some operations at the server level and just interacting with the InnoDB kernel in some way. You might also see that the transaction's status is "sleeping before joining InnoDB queue" or "waiting in InnoDB queue."

The next line you may see shows how many tables the current statement has used and locked. InnoDB doesn't normally lock tables, but it does for some statements. Locked tables can also show up if the MySQL server has locked them at a higher level than InnoDB. If the transaction has locked any rows, there will be a line showing the number of lock structs (again, not the same thing as row locks) and the heap size; you can see examples of this in the earlier deadlock output. In MySQL 5.1 and newer, this line also shows the actual number of row locks the transaction holds.

The heap size is the amount of memory used to hold row locks. InnoDB implements row locks with a special table of bitmaps, which can theoretically use as little as one bit per row it locks. Our tests have shown that it generally uses no more than four bits per lock.

The third line in this example has a little more information than the second line in the previous sample: at the end of the line is the thread status, "Sending data." This is the same as what you'll see in the Command column in SHOW FULL PROCESSLIST.

If the transaction is actively running a query, the query's text (or, in some MySQL versions, just an excerpt of it) will come next, in this case in line 4.

Line 5 shows the transaction's read view, which indicates the range of transaction identifiers that are definitely visible and definitely invisible to the transaction because of versioning. In this case, there's a gap of four transactions between the two numbers. These four transactions may or may not be visible. When InnoDB executes a query, it must check the visibility of any rows whose transaction identifiers fall into this gap.

If the transaction is waiting for a lock, you'll also see the lock information just after the query. There are examples of this in the earlier deadlock sample as well. Unfortunately, the output doesn't say which other transaction *holds* the lock for which this transaction is waiting.

If there are many transactions, InnoDB may limit the number it prints to try to keep the output from growing too large. You'll see "…truncated…" if this happens.

FILE I/O

The FILE I/O section shows the state of the I/O helper threads, along with performance counters:

```
 1  --------
 2  FILE I/O
 3  --------
 4  I/O thread 0 state: waiting for i/o request (insert buffer thread)
 5  I/O thread 1 state: waiting for i/o request (log thread)
 6  I/O thread 2 state: waiting for i/o request (read thread)
 7  I/O thread 3 state: waiting for i/o request (write thread)
 8  Pending normal aio reads: 0, aio writes: 0,
 9   ibuf aio reads: 0, log i/o's: 0, sync i/o's: 0
10  Pending flushes (fsync) log: 0; buffer pool: 0
11  17909940 OS file reads, 22088963 OS file writes, 1743764 OS fsyncs
12  0.20 reads/s, 16384 avg bytes/read, 5.00 writes/s, 0.80 fsyncs/s
```

Lines 4 through 7 show the I/O helper thread states. Lines 8 through 10 show the number of pending operations for each helper thread, and the number of pending fsync() operations for the log and buffer pool threads. The abbreviation "aio" means "asynchronous I/O." Line 11 shows the number of reads, writes, and fsync() calls performed. These are good variables to monitor with a trending and graphing system such as those we mention in the next chapter. Absolute values will vary with your workload, so it's more important to monitor how they change over time. Line 12 shows per-second averages over the time interval shown in the header section.

The pending values on lines 8 and 9 are good ways to detect an I/O-bound application. If most of these types of I/O have some pending operations, the workload is probably I/O-bound.

On Windows, you can adjust the number of I/O helper threads with the `innodb_file_io_threads` configuration variable, so you may see more than one read and write thread. However, you'll always see at least these four threads on all platforms:

Insert buffer thread
 Responsible for insert buffer merges (i.e., records being merged from the insert buffer into the tablespace)

Log thread
 Responsible for asynchronous log flushes

Read thread
 Performs read-ahead operations to try to prefetch data InnoDB predicts it will need

Write thread
 Flushes dirty buffers

INSERT BUFFER AND ADAPTIVE HASH INDEX

This section shows the status of the INSERT BUFFER AND ADAPTIVE HASH INDEX:

```
1  -----------------------------------
2  INSERT BUFFER AND ADAPTIVE HASH INDEX
3  -----------------------------------
4  Ibuf for space 0: size 1, free list len 887, seg size 889, is not empty
5  Ibuf for space 0: size 1, free list len 887, seg size 889,
6  2431891 inserts, 2672643 merged recs, 1059730 merges
7  Hash table size 8850487, used cells 2381348, node heap has 4091 buffer(s)
8  2208.17 hash searches/s, 175.05 non-hash searches/s
```

Line 4 shows information about the insert buffer's size, the length of its "free list," and its segment size. The text "for space 0" seems to indicate the possibility of multiple insert buffers—one per tablespace—but that was never implemented, and this text has been removed in recent MySQL versions. There's only one insert buffer, so line 5 is really redundant. Line 6 shows statistics about how many buffer operations InnoDB has done. The ratio of merges to inserts gives a good idea of how efficient the buffer is.

Line 7 shows the adaptive hash index's status. Line 8 shows how many hash index operations InnoDB has done over the time frame mentioned in the header section. The ratio of hash index lookups to non-hash index lookups is another good efficiency metric, because hash lookups are faster than non-hash lookups. This is advisory information; you can't configure the adaptive hash index.

LOG

This section shows statistics about InnoDB's transaction LOG subsystem:

```
1  ---
2  LOG
3  ---
4  Log sequence number 84 3000620880
5  Log flushed up to   84 3000611265
6  Last checkpoint at  84 2939889199
7  0 pending log writes, 0 pending chkp writes
8  14073669 log i/o's done, 10.90 log i/o's/second
```

Line 4 shows the current log sequence number, and line 5 shows the point up to which the logs have been flushed. The log sequence number is just the number of bytes written to the log files, so you can use it to calculate how much data in the log buffer has not yet been flushed to the log files. In this case, it is 9,615 bytes (13000620880 − 13000611265). Line 6 shows the last checkpoint (a checkpoint identifies an instant at which the data and log files were in a known state, and can be used for recovery). Lines 7 and 8 show pending log operations and statistics, which you can compare to values in the FILE I/O section to see how much of your I/O is caused by your log subsystem relative to other causes of I/O.

BUFFER POOL AND MEMORY

This section shows statistics about InnoDB's BUFFER POOL AND MEMORY (see Chapter 6 for information on how to tune the buffer pool):

```
1  ----------------------
2  BUFFER POOL AND MEMORY
3  ----------------------
4  Total memory allocated 4648979546; in additional pool allocated 16773888
5  Buffer pool size    262144
6  Free buffers        0
7  Database pages          258053
8  Modified db pages   37491
9  Pending reads 0
10 Pending writes: LRU 0, flush list 0, single page 0
11 Pages read 57973114, created 251137, written 10761167
12 9.79 reads/s, 0.31 creates/s, 6.00 writes/s
13 Buffer pool hit rate 999 / 1000
```

Line 4 shows the total memory allocated by InnoDB, and how much of that amount is allocated in the additional memory pool.

Lines 5 through 8 show buffer pool metrics, in units of pages. The metrics are the total buffer pool size, the number of free pages, the number of pages allocated to store database pages, and the number of "dirty" database pages. InnoDB uses some pages in the buffer pool for lock indexes, the adaptive hash index, and other system structures, so the number of database pages in the pool will never equal the total pool size.

Lines 9 and 10 show the number of pending reads and writes (i.e., the number of logical reads and writes InnoDB needs to do for the buffer pool). These values will not match values in the FILE I/O section, because InnoDB might merge many logical operations into a single physical I/O operation. LRU stands for "least recently used"; it's a method of freeing space for frequently used pages by flushing infrequently used ones from the buffer pool. The flush list holds old pages that need to be flushed by the checkpoint process, and single page writes are independent page writes that won't be merged.

Line 8 in this output shows that the buffer pool contains 37491 dirty pages, which need to be flushed to disk at some point (they have been modified in memory but not on disk). However, line 10 shows that no flushes are scheduled at the moment. This is not a problem; InnoDB will flush them when it needs to.

Line 11 shows how many pages InnoDB has read, created, and written. The pages read and written values refer to data that's read into the buffer pool from disk or vice versa. The pages created value refers to pages that InnoDB allocates in the buffer pool without reading their contents from the data file, because it doesn't care what the contents are (for example, they might have belonged to a table that has since been dropped).

Line 13 reports the buffer pool hit rate, which measures the rate at which InnoDB finds the pages it needs in the buffer pool. This is a cache efficiency metric. It measures hits since the last InnoDB status printout, so if the server has been quiet since then, you'll see "No buffer pool page gets since the last printout." Because of how InnoDB is designed, you can't compare the InnoDB buffer pool hit rate directly to MyISAM's key buffer hit rate.

ROW OPERATIONS

This section shows ROW OPERATIONS and miscellaneous InnoDB statistics:

```
 1  --------------
 2  ROW OPERATIONS
 3  --------------
 4  0 queries inside InnoDB, 0 queries in queue
 5  1 read views open inside InnoDB
 6  Main thread process no. 10099, id 88021936, state: waiting for server activity
 7  Number of rows inserted 143, updated 3000041, deleted 0, read 24865563
 8  0.00 inserts/s, 0.00 updates/s, 0.00 deletes/s, 0.00 reads/s
 9  ---------------------------
10  END OF INNODB MONITOR OUTPUT
11  ============================
```

Line 4 shows how many threads are inside the InnoDB kernel (we referred to this in our discussion of the TRANSACTIONS section). Queries in the queue are threads InnoDB is not admitting into the kernel yet to restrict the number of threads concurrently executing. Queries can also be sleeping before they go into the queue to wait, as discussed earlier.

Line 5 shows how many read views InnoDB has open. A read view is a consistent MVCC "snapshot" of the database's contents as of the point the transaction started. You can see whether a specific transaction has a read view in the TRANSACTIONS section.

Line 6 shows the kernel's main thread status. The possible status values in MySQL 5.0.45 and 5.1.22 are as follows:

- archiving log (if log archive is on)
- doing background drop tables
- doing insert buffer merge
- flushing buffer pool pages
- flushing log
- making checkpoint
- purging
- reserving kernel mutex
- sleeping
- suspending
- waiting for buffer pool flush to end
- waiting for server activity

Lines 7 and 8 show statistics on the number of rows inserted, updated, deleted, and read, and per-second averages of these values. These are good numbers to monitor if you want to watch how much work InnoDB is doing.

The SHOW INNODB STATUS output ends with lines 9 through 13. If you don't see this text, you probably have a very large deadlock that's truncating the output.

SHOW PROCESSLIST

The process list is the list of connections, or threads, that are currently connected to MySQL. SHOW PROCESSLIST lists the threads, with information about each thread's status. For example:

```
mysql> SHOW FULL PROCESSLIST\G
*************************** 1. row ***************************
     Id: 61539
   User: sphinx
   Host: se02:58392
     db: art136
Command: Query
   Time: 0
  State: Sending data
```

```
     Info: SELECT a.id id, a.site_id site_id, unix_timestamp(inserted) AS
inserted,forum_id, unix_timestamp(p
*************************** 2. row ***************************
       Id: 65094
     User: mailboxer
     Host: db01:59659
       db: link84
  Command: Killed
     Time: 12931
    State: end
     Info: update link84.link_in84 set url_to =
replace(replace(url_to,'&amp;','&'),'%20','+'), url_prefix=repl
```

There are several tools (such as *innotop*) that can show you an updating view of the process list.

The Command and State columns are where the thread's "status" is really indicated. Notice that the first of our processes is running a query and sending data while the second has been killed, probably because it took a very long time to complete and someone deliberately terminated it with the KILL command. A thread can remain in this state for some time, because a kill may not complete instantly. For example, it may take a while to roll back the thread's transaction.

SHOW FULL PROCESSLIST (with the added FULL keyword) shows the full text of each query, which is otherwise truncated after 100 characters.

SHOW MUTEX STATUS

SHOW MUTEX STATUS returns detailed InnoDB mutex information and is mostly useful for gaining insight into scalability and concurrency problems. Each mutex protects a critical section in the code, as explained previously.

The output varies depending on the MySQL version and compile options. Sometimes you get the names of the mutexes and several columns of output for each; sometimes you just get a filename, a line, and a number. You may need to write a script to aggregate the output, which can be very large. Here's a single line of sample output:

```
*************************** 1. row ***************************
        Mutex: &(buf_pool->mutex)
       Module: buf0buf.c
        Count: 95
   Spin_waits: 0
  Spin_rounds: 0
     OS_waits: 0
    OS_yields: 0
OS_waits_time: 0
```

You can inspect the output to help determine which parts of InnoDB are bottlenecks. Having many CPUs, for example, can cause bottlenecks. MySQL has recently fixed many InnoDB scalability problems on multi-CPU systems, but some problems with mutexes remain. Typical ones we've seen people encounter are AUTO_INCREMENT locks, which are global per table and protected by a mutex in InnoDB, and the insert buffer. Anywhere there's a mutex, there's a potential for contention.

The columns in the output are as follows:

Mutex
: The mutex name.

Module
: The source file where the mutex is defined.

Count
: How many times something has requested the mutex.

Spin_waits
: How many times InnoDB chose to spin-wait for the mutex to be free. Recall that InnoDB first tries a spin wait and then falls back to an operating system wait.

Spin_rounds
: How many times InnoDB checked whether the mutex was free in a spin wait.

OS_waits
: How many times InnoDB fell back to an operating system wait for the mutex.

OS_yields
: How many times the thread waiting for the mutex yielded to the operating system so another thread could run.

OS_waits_time
: If the timed_mutexes system variable is set to 1, this is the number of milliseconds spent waiting.

You can find the hot spots by comparing the relative size of the counters. There are three main strategies for easing the bottlenecks: try to avoid InnoDB's weak points, try to limit concurrency, or try to balance between CPU-intensive spin waits and resource-intensive operating system waits. For more advice on tuning InnoDB's concurrency, see "InnoDB Concurrency Tuning" on page 296.

Replication Status

MySQL has several commands for monitoring replication. On a master server, SHOW MASTER STATUS shows the master's replication status and configuration:

```
mysql> SHOW MASTER STATUS\G
*************************** 1. row ***************************
            File: mysql-bin.000079
        Position: 13847
    Binlog_Do_DB:
Binlog_Ignore_DB:
```

The output includes the master's current binary log position. You can get a list of binary logs with SHOW BINARY LOGS:

```
mysql> SHOW BINARY LOGS
+------------------+-----------+
| Log_name         | File_size |
+------------------+-----------+
| mysql-bin.000044 |     13677 |
...
| mysql-bin.000079 |     13847 |
+------------------+-----------+
36 rows in set (0.18 sec)
```

To view the events in the binary logs, use SHOW BINLOG EVENTS.

On a slave server, you can view the slave's status and configuration with SHOW SLAVE STATUS. We won't include the output here, because it's a bit verbose, but we will note a few things about it. First, you can see the status of both the slave I/O and slave SQL threads, including any errors. You can also see how far behind the slave is in replication. Finally, for purposes of backups and cloning slaves, there are three sets of binary log coordinates in the output:

Master_Log_File/Read_Master_Log_Pos
> The position at which the I/O thread is reading in the master's binary logs.

Relay_Log_File/Relay_Log_Pos
> The position at which the SQL thread is executing in the slave's relay logs.

Relay_Master_Log_File/Exec_Master_Log_Pos
> The position at which the SQL thread is executing in the master's binary logs. This is the same logical position as Relay_Log_File/Relay_Log_Pos, but it's in the slave's relay logs instead of the master's binary logs. In other words, if you look at these two positions in the logs, you will find the same log events.

INFORMATION_SCHEMA

The INFORMATION_SCHEMA database is a set of system views defined in the SQL standard. MySQL implements many of the standard views and adds some others. In MySQL 5.1, many of the views correspond to MySQL's SHOW commands, such as SHOW FULL PROCESSLIST and SHOW STATUS. However, there are also some views that have no corresponding SHOW command.

The beauty of the INFORMATION_SCHEMA views is that you can query them with standard SQL. This gives you much more flexibility than the SHOW commands, which produce result sets that you can't aggregate, join, or otherwise manipulate with standard SQL. Having all this data available in system views makes it possible to write interesting and useful queries.

For example, what tables have a reference to the actor table in the Sakila sample database? The consistent naming convention makes this relatively easy to determine:

```
mysql> SELECT TABLE_NAME FROM INFORMATION_SCHEMA.COLUMNS
    -> WHERE TABLE_SCHEMA='sakila' AND COLUMN_NAME='actor_id'
    -> AND TABLE_NAME <> 'actor';
+------------+
| TABLE_NAME |
+------------+
| actor_info |
| film_actor |
+------------+
```

We needed to find tables with multiple-column indexes for several of the examples in this book. Here's a query for that:

```
mysql> SELECT TABLE_NAME, GROUP_CONCAT(COLUMN_NAME)
    -> FROM INFORMATION_SCHEMA.KEY_COLUMN_USAGE
    -> WHERE TABLE_SCHEMA='sakila'
    -> GROUP BY TABLE_NAME, CONSTRAINT_NAME
    -> HAVING COUNT(*) > 1;
+---------------+------------------------------------+
| TABLE_NAME    | GROUP_CONCAT(COLUMN_NAME)          |
+---------------+------------------------------------+
| film_actor    | actor_id,film_id                   |
| film_category | film_id,category_id                |
| rental        | customer_id,rental_date,inventory_id |
+---------------+------------------------------------+
```

You can also write more complex queries, just as you would against any ordinary tables. The MySQL Forge (*http://forge.mysql.com*) is a great place to find and share queries against these views. There are samples to find duplicate or redundant indexes, find indexes with very low cardinality, and much, much more.

The biggest drawback is that the views are sometimes very slow compared to the corresponding SHOW commands. They typically fetch all the data, store it in a temporary table, then make the temporary table available to the query. For many monitoring, troubleshooting, and tuning purposes, it's faster to simply type the SHOW command, rather than type the full SQL to select the data from the views.

The views also aren't updatable at the time of this writing. Although you can retrieve server settings from them, you can't update them to influence the server's configuration. In practice, these limitations mean you'll still need to use the SHOW and SET commands for configuration, even though the INFORMATION_SCHEMA views are very useful for other tasks.

Tools for High Performance

The MySQL server distribution doesn't include tools for many common tasks, such as monitoring the server or comparing data between servers. Fortunately, MySQL's devoted community has made a wide variety of tools available, reducing the need to roll your own. Many companies also provide commercial alternatives or supplements to MySQL's own tools.

This chapter covers some of the most popular and important productivity tools for MySQL. We divide the tools into categories: interface, monitoring, analysis, and utilities.

Interface Tools

Interface tools help you run queries, create tables and users, and perform other routine tasks. This section gives a brief description of some of the most popular tools for these purposes. You can generally do all or most of the jobs they're used for with SQL queries or commands; the tools we discuss here just add convenience, help you avoid mistakes, and speed up your work.

MySQL Visual Tools

MySQL AB distributes a set of visual tools that includes MySQL Query Browser, MySQL Administrator, MySQL Migration Toolkit, and MySQL Workbench. These are all freely available, and you can download and install them as a bundle. They run on all popular desktop operating systems. These tools previously had many annoying quirks, but MySQL AB recently made an effort to find and fix bugs in all four of them.

MySQL Query Browser can be used for tasks such as running queries, creating tables and stored procedures, exporting data, and browsing database structures. It has integrated documentation on MySQL's SQL commands and functions. It is most useful for those who develop and query MySQL databases.

MySQL Administrator is focused on server administration and is therefore most useful for DBAs, not developers or analysts. It helps automate tasks such as creating backups, creating users and assigning privileges, and viewing server logs and status information. It includes some basic monitoring functionality, such as graphing status variables, but is not as flexible as the interactive monitoring tools presented later in this chapter. It also doesn't record the statistics for later analysis, which many other monitoring tools are designed to do.

The bundle also includes MySQL Migration Toolkit, which helps migrate databases from other systems to MySQL, and the MySQL Workbench modeling tool.

The benefits of MySQL's own tools are that they're free, they're now quite good quality, and they run on most desktop operating systems. They have a simple feature set that's adequate for many tasks. The standout features are the user management and backup features in MySQL Administrator and the integrated documentation in MySQL Query Browser.

The primary drawback of these tools is that they are somewhat simplistic, without all the bells and whistles power users may come to appreciate and demand. A complete description, including screenshots, is available on MySQL's web site at *http://www.mysql.com/products/tools/*.

 MySQL Workbench was recently rewritten from scratch and is now available in both free and commercial versions. The free version is not feature-crippled, but the commercial version includes some plug-ins that help automate tasks so that they require less manual work. At the time of this writing, the new version of the MySQL Workbench tool is still in beta.

SQLyog

SQLyog is the most popular visual tool for MySQL. It is well designed to support DBA and developer productivity. The full feature list is too large to include here, but here are some highlights:

- Code autocompletion to help you write queries more quickly
- The ability to connect over SSH tunnels to remotely hosted servers
- Visual tools and wizards to help with common tasks like building queries
- The ability to schedule tasks such as backups, data imports, and data synchronization
- Keyboard shortcuts
- Schema comparisons, offering access to properties of objects such as tables and views
- User management

SQLyog also has all the standard features you'd expect, such as a schema editor. It is available only for Microsoft Windows, in a full-featured edition for a price and in a limited-functionality edition for free. More information about SQLyog is available at *http://www.webyog.com*.

phpMyAdmin

phpMyAdmin is a popular administration tool that runs on a web server and gives you a browser-based interface to your MySQL servers. It has a lot of nice features for querying and administration. Its main advantages are platform independence, a large feature set, and access through a browser. Browser-based access is nice if you're away from your usual environment and a browser is all you have. For example, you can install phpMyAdmin on hosted servers where you have only FTP access and therefore can't run the *mysql* client or any other programs for a shell.

phpMyAdmin is certainly a handy tool that can be just what you need for a lot of situations. Be very careful when installing it on systems that are accessible to the Web, however, because if your server isn't secured properly, you could hardly give an attacker a better way in.

phpMyAdmin's detractors say it has too many features and is too large and complex. phpMyAdmin is hosted on SourceForge.net, where it is consistently ranked one of the top projects. More information is available at *http://sourceforge.net/projects/phpmyadmin/*.

Monitoring Tools

Monitoring MySQL is a topic that almost deserves its own book: it's a large and complicated task, with different applications often having different requirements. However, we can direct you to some of the better tools and resources on the subject.

"Monitoring" is one of those terms people tend to overload with several meanings, assuming others know what they're talking about. However, in our experience, most MySQL shops need to do many different kinds of monitoring.

We focus on tools for noninteractive monitoring and interactive monitoring. Noninteractive monitoring usually involves an automated system that takes measurements and potentially alerts the administrator when some parameter is out of its safe range. Interactive monitoring tools let you watch a server in real time. We present these two categories of tools separately in the following sections.

You might also be interested in other distinctions between tools, such as those that monitor passively (such as *innotop*) versus the active ones that can send alerts or initiate actions (for example, Nagios); or perhaps you're looking for a tool that creates an information warehouse, rather than one that just displays current statistics. We indicate each tool's qualities as we go.

Noninteractive Monitoring Systems

Many monitoring systems are not designed specifically to monitor the MySQL server. Instead, they are general-purpose systems designed to periodically check the status of many kinds of resources, from machines to routers to software (such as MySQL). They usually have some kind of plug-in architecture and often come with ready-made plug-ins for MySQL. Some such systems can record the status of the systems they monitor and graph it via web interfaces. Many can also send alerts or initiate an action when something they're monitoring fails or exceeds a safe limit.

You generally install such a system on its own server and use it to monitor other servers. If you're using it to monitor important systems, it will quickly become a critical part of your infrastructure, so you may need to take extra steps, such as making the monitoring system itself redundant with failover.

An automated monitoring system that records history and shows trends can be a lifesaver when a MySQL instance slows down under increasing load or experiences other troubles. Fixing problems often requires knowing what has changed, which requires knowing your server's history and thus recording that history. A system that alerts you when something looks awry can warn you before disaster strikes and help focus your troubleshooting efforts if it does.

Homegrown systems

Many organizations start by building their own monitoring and alert systems. This usually works OK when there are few systems to monitor and few people involved. However, when the organization becomes larger and more complex and more members of the system administration staff get involved, homegrown monitoring systems tend to break down. They might flood mailboxes with thousands of email messages every time there's a network outage, or they might fail silently and not alert anyone of a critical problem. Duplicate or redundant notifications are a frequent issue with homegrown systems and can be an obstacle to getting any work done.

If you are considering writing a monitoring tool yourself—even something as simple as a *cron* job that checks a query and emails someone when there's a problem—you should give this some thought. It's probably a better idea to invest the time and energy into learning one of the systems mentioned in the following sections. Even though some of these systems have a steep learning curve and might not seem worth the initial investment, they will save you time and energy in the long run, and your organization will be better off. Implementing one of them, even if it's done poorly at first, will ultimately prove preferable to implementing your own system. At the very least, in the long run, you will have gained experience and competence in using a standard monitoring system.

Nagios

Nagios (*http://www.nagios.org*) is an open source monitoring and alerting system that periodically checks services you define and compares the results to default or explicit limits. If the results are outside the limits, Nagios can execute a program and/or alert someone to the trouble. Nagios's contact and alert system lets you escalate alerts to different contacts, change alerts or send them to different places depending on the time of day and other conditions, and honor scheduled downtime. Nagios also understands dependencies between services, so it won't bother you about a MySQL instance being down when it notices the server is unreachable because a router in the middle is down, or when it finds that the host server itself is down.

Nagios can run any executable file as a plug-in, provided it accepts the right arguments and gives the right output. As a result, Nagios plug-ins exist in many languages, including the shell, Perl, Python, Ruby, and other scripting languages. There's even a web site, *http://www.nagiosexchange.org*, devoted to sharing and categorizing plug-ins. And if you can't find a plug-in that does exactly what you need, it's simple to create your own. A plug-in just needs to accept standard arguments, exit with an appropriate status, and optionally print output for Nagios to capture.

Nagios can monitor just about anything you can measure, on many operating systems, via several methods (including active checks, remotely executed plug-ins, and passive checks that merely accept status data "pushed" from other systems). It has a web interface as well, which you can use to check status, view graphs and visualizations of your network and its status, schedule planned downtime, and much more.

Nagios's major shortcoming is its daunting complexity. Even once you've learned it well, it is hard to maintain. It also keeps its entire configuration in files, which have a special syntax that is easy to get wrong, and they are labor-intensive to modify as your systems grow and evolve. Finally, its graphing, trending, and visualization capabilities are limited. Nagios can store some performance and other data in a MySQL server and generate graphs from it, but not as flexibly as some other systems.

There are several books devoted to Nagios; we like Wolfgang Barth's *Nagios System and Network Monitoring* (No Starch Press).

Alternatives to Nagios

Although Nagios is the most popular general-purpose monitoring and alerting software,* there are several open source alternatives:

---

* Perhaps because once you've installed and configured Nagios, you never want to think about monitoring systems again.

Zenoss

Zenoss is written in Python and has a browser-based user interface that uses Ajax to make it faster and more productive. It can autodiscover resources on the network, and it folds monitoring, alerting, trending, graphing, and recording historical data into a unified tool. Zenoss uses SNMP to gather data from remote machines by default but can also use SSH, and it has support for Nagios plug-ins. More information is available at *http://www.zenoss.com.*

Hyperic HQ

Hyperic HQ is a Java-based monitoring system that is targeted more toward so-called enterprise monitoring than most of the other systems in its class. Like Zenoss, it can autodiscover resources and supports Nagios plug-ins, but its logical organization and architecture are different, and it is a little "bulkier." Whether this suits you will depend on your preferences and what you are trying to monitor. More information can be found at *http://www.hyperic.com.*

OpenNMS

OpenNMS is written in Java and has an active developer community. It has the usual features, such as monitoring and alerting, but adds graphing and trending capabilities as well. Its goals are high performance and scalability, automation, and flexibility. Like Hyperic, it is intended for enterprise monitoring of large, critical systems. For more information, see *http://www.opennms.org.*

Groundwork Open Source

Groundwork Open Source is actually based on Nagios, and it combines Nagios and several other tools into one system with a portal interface. Perhaps the best way to describe it is as the system you might build in-house if you were an expert in Nagios, Cacti, and a host of other tools and had a lot of time to integrate them seamlessly together. See *http://www.groundworkopensource.com* for more information.

Zabbix

Zabbix is an open source monitoring system similar in many respects to Nagios but with some key differences. For example, it stores all configuration and other data in a database, not in configuration files. It also stores more types of data than Nagios and can thus generate better trending and history reports. Its network graphing and visualization capabilities are superior to Nagios's, and many people find it easier to configure and more flexible. It is also said to stand up to much heavier loads than Nagios. On the other hand, Zabbix has a more limited community than Nagios, and its alerting capabilities aren't as advanced. See *http://www.zabbix.com* for more information.

MySQL Monitoring and Advisory Service

MySQL's own monitoring solution is designed specifically to monitor MySQL instances, and it can monitor some key aspects of the host machine as well. It is not open source, and it requires a MySQL Enterprise subscription.

A major advantage of this service over Nagios is that it offers a prebuilt set of rules, or "advisors," that examine many aspects of server performance, status, and configuration. It can also suggest solutions to the problems it notices, instead of just letting the system administrator figure out what's wrong. It has a well-designed dashboard that shows status information for all your servers at once.

Though it would be possible to use Nagios or another system to monitor the same statistics, it would be a fair amount of work to write the necessary plug-ins and configure Nagios to monitor each of the scores of metrics the MySQL Monitoring and Advisory Service provides out of the box.

The disadvantage of this product is that you can't monitor the rest of your network with it; it is designed for monitoring only MySQL. It also requires an agent to be installed on each system it monitors. This is distasteful to some MySQL administrators, who like to keep their servers trimmed down to the bare essentials.

More information is available at *http://www.mysql.com/products/enterprise/advisors. html*.

MONyog

MONyog (*http://www.webyog.com*) is a lightweight, agentless monitoring system that takes a different approach from the tools previously mentioned. It is designed to run on a desktop system, where it starts an HTTP listener on an unused port. You can point your browser at this port to see information on your MySQL servers, rendered by a combination of JavaScript and Flash. The underlying implementation uses a JavaScript engine, and all configuration is done via a JavaScript object model.

MONyog is actually both interactive and noninteractive, so you might want to examine its capabilities for both kinds of monitoring.

RRDTool-based systems

Although it's not strictly a monitoring system, RRDTool (*http://www.rrdtool.org*) is important enough to mention here. Many organizations use some kind of script or program—often homemade—to extract information from servers and save them in round-robin database (RRD) files. RRD files are an elegant solution for many situations that require recording and graphing data. They automatically aggregate incoming data, interpolate missing values in case the incoming values are not delivered when expected, and have powerful graphing tools that generate beautiful, distinctive graphs. Several RRDTool-based systems are available.

The Multi Router Traffic Grapher, or MRTG (*http://oss.oetiker.ch/mrtg/*), is the quintessential RRDTool-based system. It is really designed for recording network traffic, but it can be extended to record and graph other things as well.

Munin (*http://munin.projects.linpro.no*) is a system that gathers data for you, puts it into RRDTool, and then generates graphs of the data at several levels of granularity. It creates static HTML files from the configuration, so you can browse them and view trends easily. It is easy to define a graph; you just create a plug-in script whose command-line help output has some special syntaxes Munin recognizes as graphing instructions. Munin's disadvantages include the requirement to load an agent on each system it monitors, and simplified one-size-fits-all configuration and graphing options that might not be flexible enough for some needs.

Cacti (*http://www.cacti.net*) is another popular graphing and trending system. It works by fetching data from systems, storing it in RRD files, then graphing the data with RRDTool via a PHP web interface, which is also the configuration and management interface (configuration data is stored in a MySQL server). It is template-driven, so you can define templates and then apply them to your systems. It can fetch data from SNMP or custom scripts.

Cricket (*http://cricket.sourceforge.net*) is a Cacti-like system written in Perl, but with a file-based configuration system. Ganglia (*http://ganglia.sourceforge.net*) is also similar to Cacti, but it's designed to monitor clusters and grids of systems, so you can view data from many servers in aggregate and drill down to the individual servers if you wish. (Cacti and Cricket can't show aggregated data.)

These systems can all be used to gather, record, and graph data and report on MySQL systems, with various degrees of flexibility and for slightly different purposes. They all lack a really flexible means of alerting someone when something is wrong, and some of them don't even have a concept of "wrong." Some people view this as an advantage, feeling it is better to separate the jobs of recording, graphing, and alerting; in fact, Munin is specifically designed to use Nagios as the alerting system. However, for others it's a drawback. Another disadvantage is the time and effort you may need to invest to install and configure a system that almost meets your needs, but not quite.

Finally, you should consider your future needs. RRD files don't let you query the data by SQL or other standard means, and nor do they store data at a fine granularity forever by default. Many MySQL administrators are unwilling to accept these limitations and opt to store historical data in a relational database instead. A lot of DBAs also want more customized and flexible ways to record data, so they end up writing their own systems or tweaking an existing one.

Whether RRDTool-based systems are a good match for your organization will be a matter of personal choice, availability of the skills needed to administer the system, and your organization's requirements.

Interactive Tools

Interactive tools are those you can start on demand and use to get a continually updating view of what's happening in your server. We concentrate on *innotop* (*http:// innotop.sourceforge.net*), but there are several others, such as *mtop* (*http://mtop. sourceforge.net*), *mytop* (*http://jeremy.zawodny.com/mysql/mytop/*), and some web-based clones of *mytop*.

innotop

Baron Schwartz, one of this book's authors, wrote *innotop*. Despite its name, it is not limited to monitoring InnoDB internals. This tool was inspired by *mytop* but offers much more functionality. It has many modes to monitor all kinds of MySQL internals, including all the information available in SHOW INNODB STATUS, which it parses into its component parts. It lets you monitor multiple MySQL instances simultaneously, and it is very configurable and extensible.

Some of its features include:

- A transaction list that displays current InnoDB transactions
- A query list that shows currently running queries
- A list of current locks and lock waits
- Summaries of server status and variables to show the relative magnitudes of values
- Modes to display information about InnoDB internals, such as its buffers, deadlocks, foreign key errors, I/O activity, row operations, semaphores, and more
- Replication monitoring, with master and slave statuses displayed together
- A mode to view arbitrary server variables
- Server grouping to help you organize many servers easily
- Noninteractive mode for use in command-line scripting

It's easy to install *innotop*. You can either install it from your operating system's package repository or download it from *http://innotop.sourceforge.net*, unpack it, and run the standard make install routine:

```
perl Makefile.PL
make install
```

Once you've installed it, execute *innotop* at the command line, and it will walk you through the process of connecting to a MySQL instance. It can read your *~/.my.cnf* option files, so you may not need to do anything but type your server's hostname and press Enter a few times. Once connected, you'll be in T (InnoDB Transaction) mode, and you should see a list of InnoDB transactions, as shown in Figure 14-1.

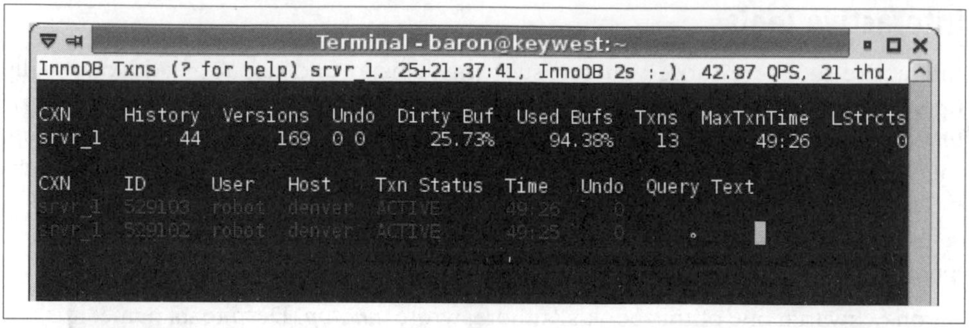

Figure 14-1. innotop in T (Transaction) mode

By default, *innotop* applies filters to reduce the clutter (as with everything in *innotop*, you can define your own or customize the built-in filters). In Figure 14-1, most of the transactions have been filtered out to show only active transactions. You can press the i key to disable the filter and fill the screen with as many transactions as will fit.

innotop displays a header and a main thread list in this mode. The header shows some overall InnoDB information, such as the length of the history list, the number of unpurged InnoDB transactions, the percentage of dirty buffers in the buffer pool, and so forth.

The first key you should press is the question mark (?), to see the help screen. This screen's contents will vary depending on what mode *innotop* is in, but it always displays every active key, so you can see all possible actions. Figure 14-2 shows the help screen in T mode.

We won't go through all of its other modes, but as you can see from the help screen, *innotop* has a lot of features.

The only other thing we cover here is some basic customization to show you how to monitor whatever you please. One of *innotop*'s strengths is its ability to interpret user-defined expressions, such as Uptime/Questions to derive a queries-per-second metric. It can display the result since the server was started and/or incrementally since the last sample.

This makes it easy to add your own columns to its tabular displays. For example, the Q (Query List) mode has a header that shows some overall server information. Let's see how to modify it to monitor how full the key cache is. Start *innotop* and press Q to enter Q mode. The result will look like Figure 14-3.

The screenshot is truncated because we're not interested in the query list for this exercise; we care only about the header.

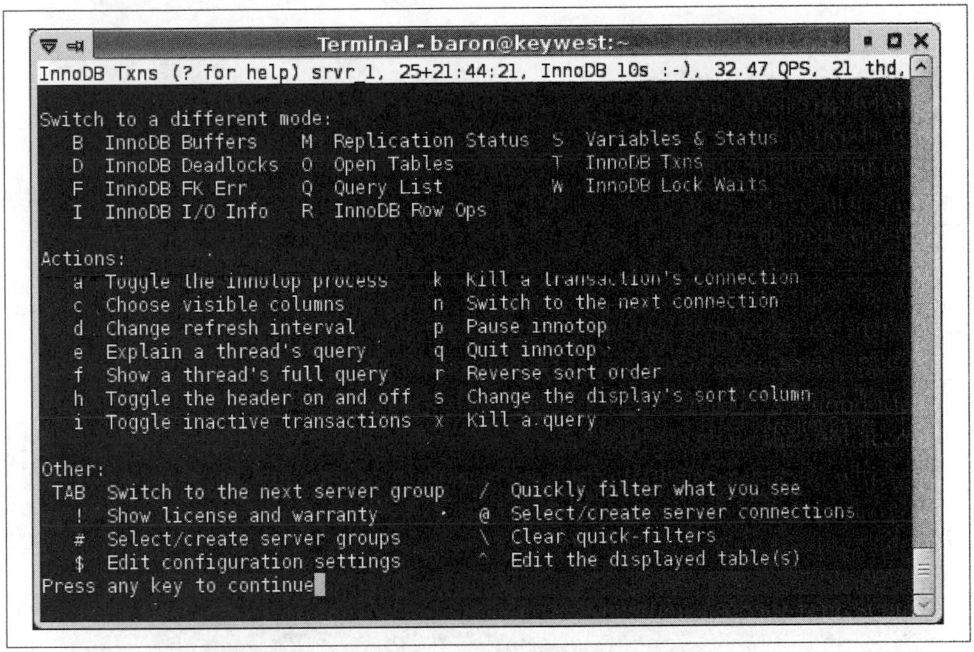

Figure 14-2. innotop help screen

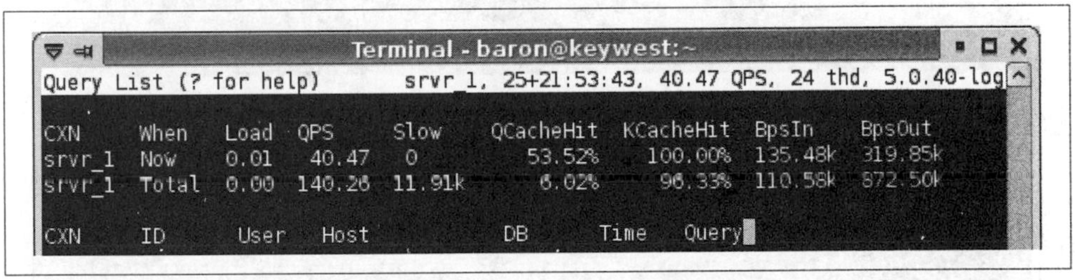

Figure 14-3. innotop in Q (Query List) mode

The header shows statistics for "Now" (which measures incremental activity since the last time *innotop* refreshed itself with new data from the server) and "Total" (which measures all activity since the MySQL server started 25 days ago). Each column in the header is derived from an equation involving values from SHOW STATUS and SHOW VARIABLES. The default headers shown in Figure 14-3 are built-in, but it's easy to add your own. All you have to do is add a column to the header "table." Press the ^ key to start the table editor, then enter q_header at the prompt to edit the header table (Figure 14-4). Tab completion is built-in, so you can just press q and then Tab to complete the word.

After this, you'll see the table definition for the Q mode header (Figure 14-5). The table definition shows the table's columns. The first column is selected. We could move the selection around, reorder and edit the columns, and do several other things

Figure 14-4. Adding a header (start)

(press ? to see a full list), but we're just going to create a new column. Press the n key and type the column name (Figure 14-6).

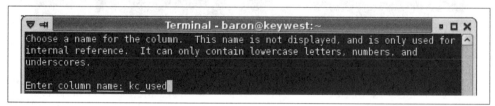

Figure 14-5. Adding a header (choices)

Figure 14-6. Adding a header (naming column)

Next, type the column's header, which will appear at the top of the column (Figure 14-7). Finally, choose the column's source. This is an expression that *innotop* compiles into a function internally. You can use names from SHOW VARIABLES and SHOW STATUS as though they're variables in an equation. We use some parentheses and Perl-ish "or" defaults to prevent division by zero, but otherwise this equation is pretty straightforward. We also use an *innotop* transformation called percent( ) to format the resulting column as a percentage; check the *innotop* documentation for more on that. Figure 14-8 shows the expression.

Figure 14-7. Adding a header (text for column)

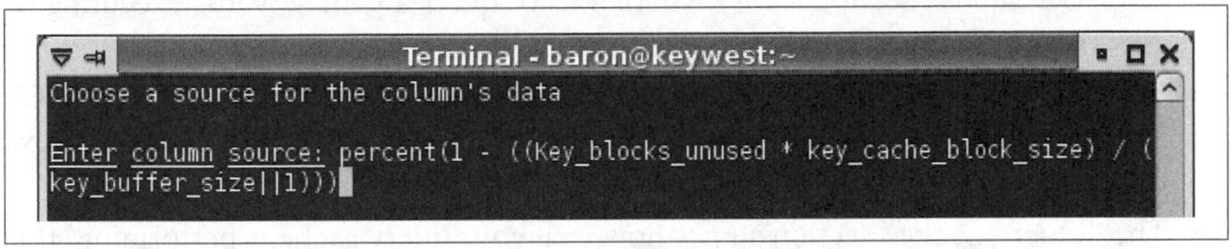

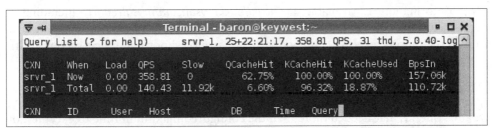

Figure 14-8. Adding a header (expression to calculate)

Press Enter, and you'll see the table definition just as before, but with the new column added at the bottom. Press the + key a few times to move it up the list, next to the key_buffer_hit column, and then press q to exit the table editor. Voilà: your new column, nestled between KCacheHit and BpsIn (Figure 14-9). It's easy to customize *innotop* to monitor what you want. You can even write plug-ins if it really can't do what you need. There's more documentation at *http://innotop.sourceforge.net*.

Figure 14-9. Adding a header (result)

Analysis Tools

Analysis tools help you automate the tedious job of inspecting servers and looking for areas that might benefit from optimization or tuning. These tools can be a great way to get started tackling performance problems. If one of them raises an obvious issue, you can focus your efforts there and perhaps solve the problem more quickly.

HackMySQL Tools

Daniel Nichter maintains a web site called HackMySQL, where he hosts some useful MySQL tools. *mysqlreport* is a Perl script that examines the server's SHOW STATUS output, transforms it into an easy-to-read report, and prints it out. You can read this report much more quickly than you can examine SHOW STATUS, and it is quite thorough.

Here's an overview of the major parts of the report, as of version 3.23:

- The "Key" section shows how your keys (indexes) are being used. If these values are not healthy, you probably need to tune your key cache settings.

- The "Questions" section shows what kinds of queries your server is executing to give you an idea of where the load is concentrated.

- The "SELECT and Sort" section shows what kinds of query plans and sort strategies your server runs most often. This section can show problems with indexing or poorly optimized queries.

- The "Query Cache" section shows how well your query cache is performing. If it is not performing well, you may need to tune the settings or, if your workload doesn't benefit from caching, even disable the cache.

- Several sections show information about tables, locks, connections, and network traffic. Problems here usually indicate a poorly tuned server.

- Three sections show InnoDB performance metrics and settings. Problems here might indicate bad server settings, hardware problems, or query or schema optimization issues.

More information is available at *http://hackmysql.com/mysqlreport*, including a detailed tutorial on how to interpret reports. It's worth taking the time to learn how to read the reports, especially if you frequently troubleshoot unfamiliar servers. With practice, you can scan a report and immediately pick out problems.

mysqlsla (the MySQL Statement Log Analyzer) is another useful tool. You can use it to analyze the general log of all queries executed on the server, the slow query log (that is, queries that needed more than the configured maximum time to execute), or any other log. It accepts several log formats and can analyze many logs at once. See "Finer control over logging" on page 65 for more on analyzing MySQL's log files.

Other programs at the site can help you analyze a server's index usage and examine MySQL-related network traffic.

Maatkit Analysis Tools

Maatkit is another of Baron Schwartz's creations. It is a collection of command-line tools, all written in Perl and designed to provide important functionality that MySQL's products don't supply. It is available at *http://maatkit.sourceforge.net* and includes a mixture of analysis tools and utilities.

One of the analysis tools is *mk-query-profiler*, which can execute queries while it watches your server's status variables. It prints out a detailed, easy-to-read report on the differences before and after a query. This report gives you a deeper understanding of your query's performance impact than execution time alone.

You can pipe queries into *mk-query-profiler*'s standard input, specify one or more files of queries, or simply ask it to observe your server without running any queries (this can be helpful while you're running an external application). You can also make it execute shell commands instead of queries.

mk-query-profiler's report is divided into sections. By default, the profiler prints a batch summary, but you can also get a report on each query or selected queries in the batch, which you can easily compare with the included *mk-profile-compact* helper tool.

Here are the report's major sections:

- The "Overall stats" section lists basics such as execution time, number of commands, and network traffic.
- The "Table and index accesses" section shows how many of the various types of execution plans the batch caused. If you see many table scans, it probably means you don't have indexes well suited to the queries.
- The "Row operations" section shows you how many low-level handler and/or InnoDB operations the batch caused. Poor query plans may cause many more low-level operations.
- The "I/O operations" section shows how much memory and disk traffic the batch caused. A companion section shows InnoDB-specific data operations.

All told, this report gives detailed insight into how much and what type of work the server does, which is much more valuable than just measuring how long queries take. For example, it can help you choose between two queries that run in about the same time on a small dataset under low load, but that might run very differently with a lot of data or under high load. It can also validate whether your optimizations are working. In this sense, it's like a miniature benchmark tool.

There are several other analysis tools in the toolkit:

mk-visual-explain
> Reconstructs the query execution plan from EXPLAIN and displays it as a tree, which many people find more readable. This is especially helpful as query plans become more complex; we have seen EXPLAIN output require hundreds of lines, and it's nearly impossible to understand at that length. *mk-visual-explain* is also useful as a teaching tool, or when you're trying to learn how to read EXPLAIN output.

mk-duplicate-key-checker
> Identifies duplicate or redundant indexes and foreign keys, which can be very bad for performance. See "Redundant and Duplicate Indexes" on page 127 for more on this.

mk-deadlock-logger
> Watches for InnoDB deadlocks and records them in a file or table.

mk-heartbeat
> Measures replication lag accurately, without needing to check SHOW SLAVE STATUS (which is not always correct). It keeps moving averages over the last 1, 5, and 15 minutes by default. This is a more complete and configurable implementation of the heartbeat script mentioned in the first edition of this book.

MySQL Utilities

Several tools have sprung up to fill gaps in the functionality provided by the MySQL server and its accompanying command-line tools. This section discusses a few of those.

MySQL Proxy

The MySQL Proxy project is developed and maintained by MySQL AB, is licensed under the GPL, and will probably be distributed with the MySQL server in the future. At the time of this writing, it is less than a year old and is in very rapid development.* You can currently find it on the Community section of *http://www.mysql. com*, and documentation is available in the MySQL manual.

The core concept is a stateful application that understands the MySQL client/server protocol and can sit between a client and server, transparently relaying their messages. A client application can connect to it exactly as though it were a server. The proxy can then create a connection to a real MySQL server and act as a man in the middle.

This functionality alone could be used for many applications (e.g., load balancing and failover), but the proxy goes a step further. It understands the client/server protocol, so it can inspect the queries and responses. It also has a built-in Lua interpreter, so you can write custom scripts and do nearly anything you can imagine to queries and responses. Here are a few of the possibilities:

- Rewriting or filtering queries. For example, you can pass commands to the proxy itself by writing a script to recognize them and do something instead of passing the query to the server.

- Generating new result sets that appear to have come from the MySQL server, or discarding those the server did generate.

---

* MySQL Proxy is evolving quickly, so this information is likely to be outdated by the time you read this book.

- Dynamically tuning the MySQL server based on what it observes. For example, the proxy can enable or disable the slow query log, or it can keep track of query statistics and show response time histograms in response to a query.

- Injecting queries every time a transaction commits (for example, to create a global transaction identifier).

There's working code for all of these, which you can download from online articles and source code repositories. The possibilities are almost limitless, and creative users will certainly find uses for the proxy that we haven't yet imagined. If you're having trouble thinking of what to do with it, we suggest reading some articles by Giuseppe Maxia or Jan Kneschke.

Dormando's Proxy for MySQL

Another GPL proxy project that appeared around the same time as MySQL Proxy (and actually offered Lua scripting first) is Dormando's Proxy for MySQL. It was in part a response to the MySQL Proxy project, which was unreleased at the time and whose eventual licensing was uncertain. Like MySQL Proxy, it is changing rapidly, so you should check the latest release to see its true status. Its web site is *http://www.consoleninja.net/code/dpm/*.

Maatkit Utilities

We mentioned Maatkit earlier while listing analysis tools, but it includes a number of utility scripts too. The most important of the tools are *mk-table-checksum* and *mk-table-sync*, which we wrote about in "Determining Whether Slaves Are Consistent with the Master" on page 380. Aside from the tools we listed earlier, Maatkit includes the following:

mk-archiver
  Runs purging and archiving jobs to help keep your tables free of unwanted data. This tool is designed to move data without affecting OLTP queries, but you can also use it to build a data warehouse or find and remove stale data. It can write data to a file and/or another table on any MySQL instance. It has a plug-in mechanism that makes it easy to customize jobs; for example, you could use a plug-in to build summary tables on a data warehouse while inserting the data into a log table.

mk-find
  Similar to the Unix *find* command, but for MySQL databases and tables.

mk-parallel-dump

Does multithreaded logical backups, breaking each table into chunks of the desired size, for faster backups on systems with many CPUs or disks. In fact, you can use this as a multithreaded wrapper around any tool, so it's also useful for doing multithreaded CHECK TABLE or OPTIMIZE TABLE operations (for example). Many types of jobs benefit from parallelization on systems with more than one CPU and disk.

mk-parallel-restore

The companion program to *mk-parallel-dump*: loads files into MySQL in parallel. This tool can load delimited files directly via LOAD DATA INFILE, or delegate SQL files to the *mysql* client program. It is a smart wrapper around many load operations, such as loading compressed files through named pipes.

mk-show-grants

Canonicalizes, negates, separates, and sorts GRANT statements for easy command-line manipulation. One interesting application is to store your database privileges into a version-control system without getting spurious changesets.

mk-slave-delay

Makes a slave lag behind its master, which is convenient for disaster recovery. If a destructive SQL statement executes on the master, you can stop the slave before it applies that statement, replay the binary log up to the statement, and promote it to master. This is typically faster than reloading the last backup and then replaying a day's worth of binary logs.

mk-slave-prefetch

Implements the techniques discussed in "Prime the cache for the slave thread" on page 402. On some workloads, it can help replication run more quickly on the slave.

mk-slave-restart

Restarts a slave after an error.

mk-table-checksum

Checksums table contents efficiently on one or many servers in parallel, or propagates checksum queries through replication to verify the integrity of your slaves.

mk-table-sync

Finds the differences between tables efficiently, and generates a minimal set of SQL commands to resolve them. It can also operate through replication.

Baron adds new tools frequently, so this list is probably out-of-date. Downloads and up-to-date documentation are always available at *http://maatkit.sourceforge.net*.

Sources of Further Information

If you find yourself doing a lot of repetitive or error-prone manual work with MySQL, someone might already have created a tool or script to ease your load. Finding the tool is another matter. We've learned about many of our favorite tools from reading the Planet MySQL blog aggregator (*http://www.planetmysql.org*) and the MySQL Forge community site (*http://forge.mysql.com*). These are great resources for learning about MySQL in general. There are also mailing lists, IRC channels, and forums where you can often get answers from friendly gurus (but search the archives first!).

Conferences are another important place we've learned about MySQL tools and techniques. Even if you can't attend conferences, you can frequently download slide decks or watch videos online.

Further information on some of the more complex tools, such as Nagios, can also be found in books dedicated to those tools. These resources go into much more detail than we can in this chapter.

Transferring Large Files

Copying, compressing, and decompressing huge files (often across a network) are common tasks when administering MySQL, initializing servers, cloning slaves, and performing backups and recovery operations. The fastest and best ways to do these jobs are not always the most obvious, and the difference between good and bad methods can be significant. This appendix shows some examples of how to copy a large backup image from one server to another using common Unix utilities.

It's common to begin with an *uncompressed* file, such as one server's InnoDB tablespace and log files. You also want the file to be decompressed when you finish copying it to the destination, of course. The other common scenario is to begin with a *compressed* file, such as a backup image, and finish with a decompressed file.

If you have limited network capacity, it's usually a good idea to send the files across the network in compressed form. You might also need to do a secure transfer, so your data isn't compromised; this is a common requirement for backup images.

Copying Files

The task, then, is to do the following efficiently:

1. (Optionally) compress the data.
2. Send it to another machine.
3. Decompress the data into its final destination.
4. Verify the files aren't corrupted after copying.

We've benchmarked various methods of achieving these goals. The rest of this appendix shows you how we did it and what we found to be the fastest way.

For many of the purposes we've discussed in this book, such as backups, you might want to consider which machine to do the compression on. If you have the network bandwidth, you can copy your backup images uncompressed and save the CPU resources on your MySQL server for queries.

A Naive Example

We begin with a naïve example of how to send an uncompressed file securely from one machine to another, compress it en route, and then decompress it. On the source server, which we call server1, we execute the following:

```
server1$ gzip -c /backup/mydb/mytable.MYD > mytable.MYD.gz
server1$ scp mytable.MYD.gz root@server2:/var/lib/myql/mydb/
```

And then, on server2:

```
server2$ gunzip /var/lib/mysql/mydb/mytable.MYD.gz
```

This is probably the simplest approach, but it's not very efficient because it serializes the steps involved in compressing, copying, and decompressing the file. Each step also requires reads from and writes to disk, which is slow. Here's what really happens during each of the above commands: the *gzip* performs both reads and writes on server1, the *scp* reads on server1 and writes on server2, and the *gunzip* reads and writes on server2.

A One-Step Method

It's more efficient to compress and copy the file and then decompress it on the other end in one step. This time we use SSH, the secure protocol upon which SCP is based. Here's the command we execute on server1:

```
server1$ gzip -c /backup/mydb/mytable.MYD | ssh root@server2
"gunzip -c - > /var/lib/mysql/mydb/mytable.MYD"
```

This usually performs much better than the first method, because it significantly reduces disk I/O: the disk activity is reduced to reading on server1 and writing on server2. This lets the disk operate sequentially.

You can also use SSH's built-in compression to do this, but we've shown you how to compress and decompress with pipes because they give you more flexibility. For example, if you didn't want to decompress the file on the other end, you wouldn't want to use SSH compression.

You can improve on this method by tweaking some options, such as adding *–1* to make the *gzip* compression faster. This usually doesn't lower the compression ratio much, but it can make it much faster, which is important. You can also use different compression algorithms. For example, if you want very high compression and don't care about how long it takes, you can use *bzip2* instead of *gzip*. If you want very fast compression, you can instead use an LZO-based archiver. The compressed data might be about 20% larger, but the compression will be around five times faster.

Avoiding Encryption Overhead

SSH isn't the fastest way to transport data across the network, because it adds the overhead of encrypting and decrypting. If you don't need encryption, you can just copy the "raw" bits over the network with *netcat*. You invoke this tool as *nc* for non-interactive operations, which is what we want.

Here's an example. First, let's start listening for the file on port 12345 (any unused port will do) on server2, and uncompress anything sent to that port to the desired data file:

```
server2$ nc -l -p 12345 | gunzip -c - > /var/lib/mysql/mydb/mytable.MYD
```

On server1, we then start another instance of *netcat*, sending to the port on which the destination is listening. The *-q* option tells *netcat* to close the connection after it sees the end of the incoming file. This will cause the listening instance to close the destination file and quit:

```
server1$ gzip -c - /var/lib/mysql/mydb/mytable.MYD | nc -q 1 server2 12345
```

An even easier technique is to use *tar*, so filenames are sent across the wire, eliminating another source of errors and automatically writing the files to their correct locations. The *z* option tells *tar* to use *gzip* compression and decompression. Here's the command to execute on server2:

```
server2$ nc -l -p 12345 | tar xvzf -
```

And here's the command for server1:

```
server1$ tar cvzf - /var/lib/mysql/mydb/mytable.MYD | nc -q 1 server2 12345
```

You can assemble these commands into a single script that will compress and copy lots of files into the network connection efficiently, then decompress them on the other side.

Other Options

Another option is *rsync*. *rsync* is convenient because it makes it easy to mirror the source and destination and because it can restart interrupted file transfers, but it doesn't tend to work as well when its binary difference algorithm can't be put to good use. You might consider using it for cases where you know most of the file doesn't need to be sent—for example, for finishing an aborted *nc* copy operation.

You should experiment with file copying when you're not in a crisis situation, because it will take a little trial and error to discover the fastest method. Which method performs best will depend on your system. The biggest factors are how many disk drives, network cards, and CPUs you have, and how fast they are relative to each other. It's a good idea to monitor *vmstat -n 5* to see whether the disk or the CPU is the speed bottleneck.

If you have idle CPUs, you can probably speed up the process by running several copy operations in parallel. Conversely, if the CPU is the bottleneck and you have lots of disk and network capacity, omit the compression. As with dumping and restoring, it's often a good idea to do these operations in parallel for speed. Again, monitor your servers' performance to see if you have unused capacity. Trying to over-parallelize may just slow things down.

File Copy Benchmarks

For the sake of comparison, Table A-1 shows how quickly we were able to copy a sample file over a standard 100 Mb/S Ethernet link on a LAN. The file was 738 MB uncompressed and compressed to 100 MB with *gzip*'s default options. The source and destination machines had plenty of available memory, CPU resources, and disk capacity; the network was the bottleneck.

Table A-1. Benchmarks for copying files across a network

Method	Time (seconds)
rsync without compression	71
scp without compression	68
nc without compression	67
rsync with compression (-z)	63
gzip, *scp*, and *gunzip*	60 (44 + 10 + 6)
ssh with compression	44
nc with compression	42

Notice how much it helped to compress the file when sending it across the network—the three slowest methods didn't compress the file. Your mileage will vary, however. If you have slow CPUs and disks and a gigabit Ethernet connection, reading and compressing the data might be the bottleneck, and it might be faster to skip the compression.

By the way, it's often much faster to use fast compression, such as *gzip --fast*, than to use the default compression levels, which use a lot of CPU time to compress the file only slightly more. Our test used the default compression level.

The last step in transferring data is to verify that the copy didn't corrupt the files. You can use a variety of methods for this, such as *md5sum*, but it's rather expensive to do a full scan of the file again. This is another reason why compression is helpful: the compression itself typically includes at least a cyclic redundancy check (CRC), which should catch any errors, so you get error checking for free.

Using EXPLAIN

This appendix shows you how to invoke EXPLAIN to get information about the query execution plan, and how to interpret the output. The EXPLAIN command is the main way to find out how the query optimizer decides to execute queries. This feature has many limitations and doesn't always tell the truth, but its output is the best information available, and it's worth studying, so you can make an educated guess about how your queries are executed.

Invoking EXPLAIN

To use EXPLAIN, simply add the word EXPLAIN just before the SELECT keyword in your query. MySQL will set a flag on the query. When it executes the query, the flag causes it to return information about each step in the execution plan, instead of executing it. It returns one or more rows, which show each part of the execution plan and the order of execution.

Here's the simplest possible EXPLAIN result:

```
mysql> EXPLAIN SELECT 1\G
*************************** 1. row ***************************
           id: 1
  select_type: SIMPLE
        table: NULL
         type: NULL
possible_keys: NULL
          key: NULL
      key_len: NULL
          ref: NULL
         rows: NULL
        Extra: No tables used
```

There's one row in the output per table in the query. If the query joins two tables, there will be two rows of output. An aliased table counts as a separate table, so if you join a table to itself, there will be two rows in the output. The meaning of "table" is fairly broad here: it can mean a subquery, a UNION result, and so on. You'll see later why this is so.

There are two important variations on EXPLAIN:

- EXPLAIN EXTENDED appears to behave just like a normal EXPLAIN, but it tells the server to "reverse compile" the execution plan into a SELECT statement. You can see this generated statement by running SHOW WARNINGS immediately afterward. The statement comes directly from the execution plan, not from the original SQL statement, which by this point has been reduced to a data structure. It will not be the same as the original statement in most cases. You can examine it to see exactly how the query optimizer has transformed the statement. EXPLAIN EXTENDED is available in MySQL 5.0 and newer, and it adds an extra filtered column in MySQL 5.1 (more on that later).

- EXPLAIN PARTITIONS shows the partitions the query will access, if applicable. It is available only in MySQL 5.1 and newer. See "Partitioned Tables" on page 257 for details on partitions.

It's a common mistake to think that MySQL doesn't execute a query when you add EXPLAIN to it. In fact, if the query contains a subquery in the FROM clause, MySQL actually executes the subquery, places its results into a temporary table, and then finishes optimizing the outer query. It has to process all such subqueries before it can optimize the outer query fully, which it must do for EXPLAIN. This means EXPLAIN can actually cause a great deal of work for the server if the statement contains expensive subqueries or views that use the TEMPTABLE algorithm.

Bear in mind that EXPLAIN is an approximation, nothing more. Sometimes it's a good approximation, but at other times, it can be very far from the truth. Here are some of its limitations:

- EXPLAIN doesn't tell you anything about how triggers, stored functions, or UDFs will affect your query.

- It doesn't work for stored procedures, although you can extract the queries manually and EXPLAIN them individually.

- It doesn't tell you about ad-hoc optimizations MySQL does during query execution.

- Some of the statistics it shows are estimates and can be very inaccurate.

- It doesn't show you everything there is to know about a query's execution plan. (The MySQL developers are adding more information when possible.)

- It doesn't distinguish between some things with the same name. For example, it uses "filesort" for in-memory sorts and for temporary files, and it displays "Using temporary" for temporary tables on disk and in memory.

- It can be misleading. For example, it can show a full index scan for a query with a small LIMIT. (MySQL 5.1's EXPLAIN shows more accurate information about the number of rows to be examined, but earlier versions don't take LIMIT into account.)

Rewriting Non-SELECT Queries

MySQL explains only `SELECT` queries, not stored routine calls or `INSERT`, `UPDATE`, `DELETE`, or any other statements. However, you can rewrite some non-`SELECT` queries to be `EXPLAIN`-able. To do this, you just need to convert the statement into an equivalent `SELECT` that accesses all the same columns. Any column mentioned must be in a `SELECT` list, a join clause, or a `WHERE` clause.

For example, suppose you want to rewrite the following `UPDATE` statement to make it `EXPLAIN`-able:

```
UPDATE sakila.actor
    INNER JOIN sakila.film_actor USING (actor_id)
SET actor.last_update=film_actor.last_update;
```

The following `EXPLAIN` statement is *not* equivalent to the `UPDATE`, because it doesn't require the server to retrieve the `last_update` column from either table:

```
mysql> EXPLAIN SELECT film_actor.actor_id
    -> FROM sakila.actor
    ->     INNER JOIN sakila.film_actor USING (actor_id)\G
*************************** 1. row ***************************
           id: 1
  select_type: SIMPLE
        table: actor
         type: index
possible_keys: PRIMARY
          key: PRIMARY
      key_len: 2
          ref: NULL
         rows: 200
        Extra: Using index
*************************** 2. row ***************************
           id: 1
  select_type: SIMPLE
        table: film_actor
         type: ref
possible_keys: PRIMARY
          key: PRIMARY
      key_len: 2
          ref: sakila.actor.actor_id
         rows: 13
        Extra: Using index
```

This difference is very important. The output shows that MySQL will use covering indexes, for example, which it can't use when retrieving and updating the `last_updated` column. The following statement is much closer to the original:

```
mysql> EXPLAIN SELECT film_actor.last_update, actor.last_update
    -> FROM sakila.actor
    ->     INNER JOIN sakila.film_actor USING (actor_id)\G
*************************** 1. row ***************************
           id: 1
  select_type: SIMPLE
```

```
          table: actor
           type: ALL
  possible_keys: PRIMARY
            key: NULL
        key_len: NULL
            ref: NULL
           rows: 200
          Extra:
*************************** 2. row ***************************
             id: 1
    select_type: SIMPLE
          table: film_actor
           type: ref
  possible_keys: PRIMARY
            key: PRIMARY
        key_len: 2
            ref: sakila.actor.actor_id
           rows: 13
          Extra:
```

Rewriting queries like this is not an exact science, but it's often good enough to help you understand what a query will do.

It's important to understand that there is no such thing as an "equivalent" read query to show you the plan for a write query. A SELECT query needs to find only one copy of the data and return it to you. Any query that modifies data must find and modify all copies of it, in all indexes. This will often be much more expensive than what appears to be an equivalent SELECT query.

The Columns in EXPLAIN

EXPLAIN's output always has the same columns (except for EXPLAIN EXTENDED, which adds a filtered column in MySQL 5.1, and EXPLAIN PARTITIONS, which adds a partitions column). The variability is in the number and contents of the rows. However, to keep our examples clear, we don't always show all columns in this appendix.

In the following sections, we show you the meaning of each of the columns in an EXPLAIN result. Keep in mind that the rows in the output come in the order in which MySQL actually executes the parts of the query, which is not always the same as the order in which they appear in the original SQL.

The id Column

This column always contains a number, which identifies the SELECT to which the row belongs. If there are no subqueries or unions in the statement, there is only one SELECT, so every row will show a 1 in this column. Otherwise, the inner SELECT statements generally will be numbered sequentially, according to their positions in the original statement.

MySQL divides SELECT queries into simple and complex types, and the complex types can be grouped into three broad classes: simple subqueries, so-called derived tables (subqueries in the FROM clause),[*] and UNIONs. Here's a simple subquery:

```
mysql> EXPLAIN SELECT (SELECT 1 FROM sakila.actor LIMIT 1) FROM sakila.film;
+----+-------------+-------+...
| id | select_type | table |...
+----+-------------+-------+...
|  1 | PRIMARY     | film  |...
|  2 | SUBQUERY    | actor |...
+----+-------------+-------+...
```

Subqueries in the FROM clause and UNIONs add more complexity to the id column. Here's a basic subquery in the FROM clause:

```
mysql> EXPLAIN SELECT film_id FROM (SELECT film_id FROM sakila.film) AS der;
+----+-------------+------------+...
| id | select_type | table      |...
+----+-------------+------------+...
|  1 | PRIMARY     | <derived2> |...
|  2 | DERIVED     | film       |...
+----+-------------+------------+...
```

As you know, this query is executed with a temporary table. MySQL internally refers to the temporary table by its alias (der) within the outer query, which you can see in the ref column in more complicated queries.

Finally, here's a UNION query:

```
mysql> EXPLAIN SELECT 1 UNION ALL SELECT 1;
+------+--------------+------------+...
| id   | select_type  | table      |...
+------+--------------+------------+...
|  1   | PRIMARY      | NULL       |...
|  2   | UNION        | NULL       |...
| NULL | UNION RESULT | <union1,2> |...
+------+--------------+------------+...
```

Note the extra row in the output for the result of the UNION. UNION results are always placed into a temporary table, and MySQL then reads the results back out of the temporary table. The temporary table doesn't appear in the original SQL, so its id column is NULL. In contrast to the preceding example (illustrating a subquery in the FROM clause), the temporary table that results from this query is shown as the last row in the results, not the first.

So far this is all very straightforward, but mixtures of these three categories of statements can cause the output to become more complicated, as we'll see a bit later.

---

[*] The statement "a subquery in the FROM clause is a derived table" is true, but "a derived table is a subquery in the FROM clause" is false. The term "derived table" has a broader meaning in SQL.

The select_type Column

This column shows whether the row is a simple or complex SELECT (and if it's the latter, which of the three complex types it is). The value SIMPLE means the query contains no subqueries or UNIONs. If the query has any such complex subparts, the outermost part is labeled PRIMARY, and other parts are labeled as follows:

SUBQUERY
> A SELECT that is contained in a subquery in the SELECT list (in other words, not in the FROM clause) is labeled as SUBQUERY.

DERIVED
> The value DERIVED is used for a SELECT that is contained in a subquery in the FROM clause, which MySQL executes recursively and places into a temporary table. The server refers to this as a "derived table" internally, because the temporary table is derived from the subquery.

UNION
> The second and subsequent SELECTs in a UNION are labeled as UNION. The first SELECT is labeled as though it is executed as part of the outer query. This is why the previous example showed the first SELECT in the UNION as PRIMARY. If the UNION were contained in a subquery in the FROM clause, its first SELECT would be labeled as DERIVED.

UNION RESULT
> The SELECT used to retrieve results from the UNION's temporary table is labeled as UNION RESULT.

In addition to these values, a SUBQUERY and a UNION can be labeled as DEPENDENT and UNCACHEABLE. DEPENDENT means the SELECT depends on data that is found in an outer query; UNCACHEABLE means something in the SELECT prevents the results from being cached with an Item_cache. (Item_cache is undocumented; it is not the same thing as the query cache, athough it can be defeated by some of the same types of constructs, such as the RAND( ) function.)

The table Column

This column shows which table the row is accessing. In most cases, it's straightforward: it's the table, or its alias if the SQL specifies one.

You can read this column from top to bottom to see the join order MySQL's join optimizer chose for the query. For example, you can see that MySQL chose a different join order than the one specified for the following query:

```
mysql> EXPLAIN SELECT film.film_id
    -> FROM sakila.film
    ->    INNER JOIN sakila.film_actor USING(film_id)
    ->    INNER JOIN sakila.actor USING(actor_id);
+----+------------+-----------+...
```

```
| id | select_type | table     |...
+----+-------------+-----------+...
|  1 | SIMPLE      | actor     |...
|  1 | SIMPLE      | film_actor |...
|  1 | SIMPLE      | film      |...
+----+-------------+-----------+...
```

Remember the left-deep tree diagrams we showed in "The execution plan" on page 172? MySQL's query execution plans are always left-deep trees. If you flip the plan on its side, you can read off the leaf nodes in order, and they'll correspond directly to the rows in EXPLAIN. The plan for the preceding query looks like Figure B-1.

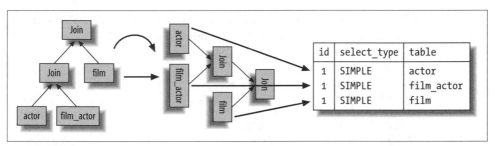

Figure B-1. How the query execution plan corresponds to the rows in EXPLAIN

Derived tables and unions

The table column becomes much more complicated when there is a subquery in the FROM clause or a UNION. In these cases, there really isn't a "table" to refer to, because the temporary table MySQL creates exists only while the query is executing.

When there's a subquery in the FROM clause, the table column is of the form <derivedN>, where N is the subquery's id. This is always a "forward reference"—in other words, N refers to a later row in the EXPLAIN output.

When there's a UNION, the UNION RESULT table column contains a list of ids that participate in the UNION. This is always a "backward reference," because the UNION RESULT comes after all of the rows that participate in the UNION. If there are more than about 20 ids in the list, the table column may be truncated to keep it from getting too long, and you won't be able to see all the values. Fortunately, you can still deduce which rows were included, because you'll be able to see the first row's id. Everything that comes between that row and the UNION RESULT is included in some way.

An example of complex SELECT types

Here's a nonsense query that serves as a fairly compact example of some of the complex SELECT types:

```
1  EXPLAIN
2  SELECT actor_id,
3     (SELECT 1 FROM sakila.film_actor WHERE film_actor.actor_id =
4        der_1.actor_id LIMIT 1)
```

```
5  FROM (
6      SELECT actor_id
7      FROM sakila.actor LIMIT 5
8  ) AS der_1
9  UNION ALL
10 SELECT film_id,
11     (SELECT @var1 FROM sakila.rental LIMIT 1)
12 FROM (
13     SELECT film_id,
14         (SELECT 1 FROM sakila.store LIMIT 1)
15     FROM sakila.film LIMIT 5
16 ) AS der_2;
```

The LIMIT clauses are just for convenience, in case you wish to execute the query without EXPLAIN and see the results. Here is the result of the EXPLAIN:

```
+------+---------------------+------------+...
| id   | select_type         | table      |...
+------+---------------------+------------+...
|  1   | PRIMARY             | <derived3> |...
|  3   | DERIVED             | actor      |...
|  2   | DEPENDENT SUBQUERY  | film_actor |...
|  4   | UNION               | <derived6> |...
|  6   | DERIVED             | film       |...
|  7   | SUBQUERY            | store      |...
|  5   | UNCACHEABLE SUBQUERY | rental    |...
| NULL | UNION RESULT        | <union1,4> |...
+------+---------------------+------------+...
```

We've been careful to make each part of the query access a different table, so you can see what goes where, but it's still hard to figure out! Taking it from the top:

- The first row is a forward reference to der_1, which the query has labeled as <derived3>. It comes from line 2 in the original SQL. To see which rows in the output refer to SELECT statements that are part of <derived3>, look forward...

- ...to the second row, whose id is 3. It is 3 because it's part of the third SELECT in the query, and it's listed as a DERIVED type because it's nested inside a subquery in the FROM clause. It comes from lines 6 and 7 in the original SQL.

- The third row's id is 2. It comes from line 3 in the original SQL. Notice that it comes after a row with a higher id number, suggesting that it is executed afterward, which makes sense. It is listed as a DEPENDENT SUBQUERY, which means its results depend on the results of an outer query (also known as a correlated subquery). The outer query in this case is the SELECT that begins in line 2 and retrieves data from der_1.

- The fourth row is listed as a UNION, which means it is the second or later SELECT in a UNION. Its table is <derived6>, which means it's retrieving data from a subquery in the FROM clause and appending to a temporary table for the UNION. As before, to find the EXPLAIN rows that show the query plan for this subquery, you must look forward.

- The fifth row is the der_2 subquery defined in lines 13, 14, and 15 in the original SQL, which EXPLAIN refers to as <derived6>.

- The sixth row is an ordinary subquery in <derived6>'s SELECT list. Its id is 7, which is important...

- ...because it is greater than 5, which is the seventh row's id. Why is this important? Because it shows the boundaries of the <derived6> subquery. When EXPLAIN outputs a row whose SELECT type is DERIVED, it represents the beginning of a "nested scope." If a subsequent row's id is smaller (in this case, 5 is smaller than 6), it means the nested scope has closed. This lets us know that the seventh row is part of the SELECT list that is retrieving data from <derived6>—i.e., part of the fourth row's SELECT list (line 11 in the original SQL). This example is fairly easy to understand without knowing the significance and rules of nested scopes, but sometimes it's not so easy. The other notable thing about this row in the output is that it is listed as an UNCACHEABLE SUBQUERY because of the user variable.

- Finally, the last row is the UNION RESULT. It represents the stage of reading the rows from the UNION's temporary table. You can begin at this row and work backward if you wish; it is returning results from rows whose ids are 1 and 4, which are in turn references to <derived3> and <derived6>.

As you can see, the combination of these complicated SELECT types can result in EXPLAIN output that's pretty difficult to read. Understanding the rules makes it easier, but there's no substitute for practice.

Reading EXPLAIN's output often requires you to jump forward and backward in the list. For example, look again at the first row in the output. There is no way to know just by looking at it that it is part of a UNION. You'll only see that when you read the last row of the output.

The type Column

The MySQL manual says this column shows the "join type," but we think it's more accurate to say the *access type*—in other words, how MySQL has decided to find rows in the table. Here are the most important access methods, from worst to best:

ALL
> This is what most people call a table scan. It generally means MySQL must scan through the table, from beginning to end, to find the row. (There are exceptions, such as queries with LIMIT or queries that display "Using distinct/not exists" in the Extra column.)

index
> This is the same as a table scan, except MySQL scans the table in index order instead of the rows. The main advantage is that this avoids sorting; the biggest

disadvantage is the cost of reading an entire table in index order. This usually means accessing the rows in random order, which is very expensive.

If you also see "Using index" in the Extra column, it means MySQL is using a covering index (see Chapter 3) and scanning only the index's data, not reading each row in index order. This is much less expensive than scanning the table in index order.

range

A range scan is a limited index scan. It begins at some point in the index and returns rows that match a range of values. This is better than a full index scan because it doesn't go through the entire index. Obvious range scans are queries with a BETWEEN or > in the WHERE clause.

When MySQL uses an index to look up lists of values, such as IN( ) and OR lists, it also displays it as a range scan. However, these are quite different types of accesses, and they have important performance differences. See the sidebar "What Is a Range Condition?" on page 134 for more information.

The same cost considerations apply for this type as for the index type.

ref

This is an index access (sometimes called an index lookup) that returns rows that match a single value. However, it might find multiple rows, so it's a mixture of a lookup and a scan. This type of index access can happen only on a non-unique index or a nonunique prefix of a unique index. It's called ref because the index is compared to some reference value. The reference value is either a constant or a value from a previous table in a multiple-table query.

The ref_or_null access type is a variation on ref. It means MySQL must do a second lookup to find NULL entries after doing the initial lookup.

eq_ref

This is an index lookup that MySQL knows will return at most a single value. You'll see this access method when MySQL decides to use a primary key or unique index to satisfy the query by comparing it to some reference value. MySQL can optimize this access type very well, because it knows it doesn't have to estimate ranges of matching rows or look for more matching rows once it finds one.

const, system

MySQL uses these access types when it can optimize away some part of the query and turn it into a constant. For example, if you select a row's primary key by placing its primary key into the WHERE clause, MySQL can convert the query into a constant. It then effectively removes the table from the join execution.

NULL

This access method means MySQL can resolve the query during the optimization phase and will not even access the table or index during the execution stage.

For example, selecting the minimum value from an indexed column can be done by looking at the index alone and requires no table access during execution.

The possible_keys Column

This column shows which indexes could be used for the query, based on the columns the query accesses and the comparison operators used. This list is created early in the optimization phase, so some of the indexes listed might be useless for the query after subsequent optimization phases.

The key Column

This column shows which index MySQL decided to use to optimize the access to the table. If the index doesn't appear in possible_keys, MySQL chose it for another reason—for example, it might choose a covering index even when there is no WHERE clause.

In other words, possible_keys reveals which indexes can help *make row lookups efficient*, but key shows which index the optimizer decided to use to *minimize query cost* (see "The Query Optimization Process" on page 164 for more on the optimizer's cost metrics). Here's an example:

```
mysql> EXPLAIN SELECT actor_id, film_id FROM sakila.film_actor\G
*************************** 1. row ***************************
           id: 1
  select_type: SIMPLE
        table: film_actor
         type: index
possible_keys: NULL
          key: idx_fk_film_id
      key_len: 2
          ref: NULL
         rows: 5143
        Extra: Using index
```

The key_len Column

This column shows the number of bytes MySQL will use in the index. If MySQL is using only some of the index's columns, you can use this value to calculate which columns it uses. Remember that MySQL can use only the leftmost prefix of the index. For example, sakila.film_actor's primary key covers two SMALLINT columns, and a SMALLINT is two bytes, so each tuple in the index is four bytes. Here's a sample query:

```
mysql> EXPLAIN SELECT actor_id, film_id FROM sakila.film_actor WHERE actor_id=4;
...+------+---------------+---------+---------+...
...| type | possible_keys | key     | key_len |...
...+------+---------------+---------+---------+...
...| ref  | PRIMARY       | PRIMARY | 2       |...
...+------+---------------+---------+---------+...
```

Based on the key_len column in the result, you can deduce that the query performs index lookups with only the first column, the actor_id. When calculating column usage, be sure to account for character sets in character columns:

```
mysql> CREATE TABLE t (
    ->    a char(3) NOT NULL,
    ->    b int(11) NOT NULL,
    ->    c char(1) NOT NULL,
    ->    PRIMARY KEY (a,b,c)
    -> ) ENGINE=MyISAM DEFAULT CHARSET=utf8 ;
mysql> INSERT INTO t(a, b, c)
    ->    SELECT DISTINCT LEFT(TABLE_SCHEMA, 3), ORD(TABLE_NAME),
    ->       LEFT(COLUMN_NAME, 1)
    ->    FROM INFORMATION_SCHEMA.COLUMNS:
mysql> EXPLAIN SELECT a FROM t WHERE a='sak' AND b = 112;
...+------+---------------+---------+---------+...
...| type | possible_keys | key     | key_len |...
...+------+---------------+---------+---------+...
...| ref  | PRIMARY       | PRIMARY | 13      |...
...+------+---------------+---------+---------+...
```

The length of 13 bytes in this query is the sum of the lengths of the a and b columns. Column a is three characters, which in utf8 require up to three bytes each, and column b is a four-byte integer.

MySQL doesn't always show you how much of an index is really being used. For example, if you perform a LIKE query with a prefix pattern match, it will show that the full width of the column is being used.

The key_len column shows the maximum possible length of the indexed fields, not the actual number of bytes the data in the table used. MySQL will always show 13 bytes in the preceding example, even if column a happens to contain no values more than one character long. In other words, key_len is calculated by looking at the table's definition, not the data in the table.

The ref Column

This column shows which columns or constants from preceding tables are being used to look up values in the index named in the key column. Here's an example that shows a combination of join conditions and aliases. Notice that the ref column reflects how the film table is aliased as f in the query text:

```
mysql> EXPLAIN
    -> SELECT STRAIGHT_JOIN f.film_id
    -> FROM sakila.film AS f
    ->    INNER JOIN sakila.film_actor AS fa
    ->       ON f.film_id=fa.film_id AND fa.actor_id = 1
    ->    INNER JOIN sakila.actor AS a USING(actor_id);
...+-------+...+--------------------+---------+-----------------------+...
...| table |...| key                | key_len | ref                   |...
...+-------+...+--------------------+---------+-----------------------+...
...| a     |...| PRIMARY            | 2       | const                 |...
...| f     |...| idx_fk_language_id | 1       | NULL                  |...
...| fa    |...| PRIMARY            | 4       | const,sakila.f.film_id|...
...+-------+...+--------------------+---------+-----------------------+...
```

The rows Column

This column shows the number of rows MySQL estimates it will need to read to find
the desired rows. This number is *per loop in the nested-loop join plan*. That is, it's not
just the number of rows MySQL thinks it will need to read from the table; it is the
number of rows, on average, MySQL thinks it will have to read to find rows that satisfy the criteria in effect at that point in query execution. (The criteria include constants given in the SQL as well as the current columns from previous tables in the
join order.)

This estimate can be quite inaccurate, depending on the table statistics and how
selective the indexes are. It also doesn't reflect LIMIT clauses in MySQL 5.0 and earlier. For example, the following query will not examine 1,022 rows:

```
mysql> EXPLAIN SELECT * FROM sakila.film LIMIT 1\G
...
        rows: 1022
```

You can calculate roughly the number of rows the entire query will examine by multi-
plying all the rows values together. For example, the following query might examine
approximately 2,600 rows:

```
mysql> EXPLAIN
    -> SELECT f.film_id
    -> FROM sakila.film AS f
    ->    INNER JOIN sakila.film_actor AS fa USING(film_id)
    ->    INNER JOIN sakila.actor AS a USING(actor_id);
...+------+...
...| rows |...
...+------+...
...|  200 |...
...|   13 |...
...|    1 |...
...+------+...
```

Remember, this is the number of rows MySQL thinks it will examine, not the number of rows in the result set. Also realize that there are many optimizations, such as join buffers and caches, that aren't factored into the number of rows shown. MySQL will probably not have to actually read every row it predicts it will. MySQL also doesn't know anything about the operating system or hardware caches.

The filtered Column

This column is new in MySQL 5.1 and appears when you use EXPLAIN EXTENDED. It shows a pessimistic estimate of the percentage of rows that will satisfy some condition on the table, such as a WHERE clause or a join condition. If you multiply the rows column by this percentage, you will see the number of rows MySQL estimates it will join with the previous tables in the query plan. At the time of this writing, the optimizer uses this estimate only for the ALL, index, range, and index_merge access methods.

To illustrate this column's output, we created a table as follows:

```
CREATE TABLE t1 (
    id INT NOT NULL AUTO_INCREMENT,
    filler char(200),
    PRIMARY KEY(id)
);
```

We then inserted 1,000 rows into this table, with random text in the filler column. Its purpose is to prevent MySQL from using a covering index for the query we're about to run:

```
mysql> EXPLAIN EXTENDED SELECT * FROM t1 WHERE id < 500\G
*************************** 1. row ***************************
           id: 1
  select_type: SIMPLE
        table: t1
         type: ALL
possible_keys: PRIMARY
          key: NULL
      key_len: NULL
          ref: NULL
         rows: 1000
     filtered: 49.40
        Extra: Using where
```

MySQL could use a range access to retrieve all rows with IDs less than 500 from the table, but it won't because that would eliminate only about half the rows. It thinks a table scan is less expensive. As a result, it uses a table scan and a WHERE clause to filter out rows. It knows how many rows the WHERE clause will remove from the result, because of the range access cost estimates. That's why the 49.40% value appears in the filtered column.

The Extra Column

This column contains extra information that doesn't fit into other columns. The MySQL manual documents most of the many values that can appear here; we have referred to many of them throughout this book.

The most important values you might see frequently are as follows:

"Using index"
> This indicates that MySQL will use a covering index to avoid accessing the table (see "Covering Indexes" on page 120). Don't confuse covering indexes with the index access type.

"Using where"
> This means the MySQL server will post-filter rows after the storage engine retrieves them. Many WHERE conditions that involve columns in an index can be checked by the storage engine when (and if) it reads the index, so not all queries with a WHERE clause will show "Using where." Sometimes the presence of "Using where" is a hint that the query can benefit from different indexing.

"Using temporary"
> This means MySQL will use a temporary table while sorting the query's result.

"Using filesort"
> This means MySQL will use an external sort to order the results, instead of reading the rows from the table in index order. MySQL has two filesort algorithms, which you can read about in "Optimizing for filesorts" on page 300. Either type can be done in memory or on disk. EXPLAIN doesn't tell you which type of filesort MySQL will use, and it doesn't tell you whether the sort will be done in memory or on disk.

"range checked for each record (index map: N)"
> This value means there's no good index, and the indexes will be reevaluated for each row in a join. N is a bitmap of the indexes shown in possible_keys and is redundant.

Visual EXPLAIN

MySQL's developers have said that they'd like EXPLAIN's output to be formatted as a tree, showing a more accurate representation of the execution plan. MySQL's users have wished for such an improvement as well. As it is, EXPLAIN is a somewhat awkward way to see the execution plan; a tree structure doesn't fit very well into a tabular output. The awkwardness is highlighted by the large number of possible values for the Extra column, as well as by UNION. UNION is quite unlike every other kind of join MySQL can do, and it doesn't fit well into EXPLAIN.

It's possible, with a good understanding of the rules and particularities of EXPLAIN, to work backward to a tree-formatted execution plan. This is quite tedious, though, and it's best left to an automated tool. Maatkit (see Chapter 14) contains *mk-visual-explain*, which is such a tool.

Using Sphinx with MySQL

Sphinx (*http://www.sphinxsearch.com*) is a free, open source, full-text search engine, designed from the ground up to integrate well with databases. It has DBMS-like features, is very fast, supports distributed searching, and scales well. It is also designed for efficient memory and disk I/O, which is important because they're often the limiting factors for large operations.

Sphinx works well with MySQL. It can be used to accelerate a variety of queries, including full-text searches; you can also use it to perform fast grouping and sorting operations, among other applications. Additionally, there is a pluggable storage engine that lets a programmer or administrator access Sphinx directly through MySQL. Sphinx is especially useful for certain queries that MySQL's general-purpose architecture doesn't optimize very well for large datasets in real-world settings. In short, Sphinx can enhance MySQL's functionality and performance.

The source of data for a Sphinx index is usually the result of a MySQL SELECT query, but you can build an index from an unlimited number of sources of varying types, and each instance of Sphinx can search an unlimited number of indexes. For example, you can pull some of the documents in an index from a MySQL instance running on one remote server, some from a PostgreSQL instance running on another server, and some from the output of a local script through an XML pipe mechanism.

In this appendix, we explore some use cases where Sphinx's capabilities enable enhanced performance, show a summary of the steps needed to install and configure it, explain its features in detail, and discuss several examples of real-world implementations.

Overview: A Typical Sphinx Search

We start with a simple but complete Sphinx usage example to provide a starting point for further discussion. We use PHP because of its popularity, although APIs are available for a number of other languages too.

Assume that we're implementing full-text searching for a comparison-shopping engine. Our requirements are to:

- Maintain a searchable full-text index on a product table stored in MySQL
- Allow full-text searches over product titles and descriptions
- Be able to narrow down searches to a given category if needed
- Be able to sort the result not only by relevance, but by item price or submission date

We begin by setting up a data source and an index in the Sphinx configuration file:

```
source products
{
    type        = mysql
    sql_host    = localhost
    sql_user    = shopping
    sql_pass    = mysecretpassword
    sql_db      = shopping
    sql_query   = SELECT id, title, description, \
                    cat_id, price, UNIX_TIMESTAMP(added_date) AS added_ts \
                    FROM products
    sql_attr_uint       = cat_id
    sql_attr_float      = price
    sql_attr_timestamp  = added_ts
}

index products
{
    source    = products
    path      = /usr/local/sphinx/var/data/products
    docinfo   = extern
}
```

This example assumes that the MySQL shopping database contains a products table with the columns we request in our SELECT query to populate our Sphinx index. The Sphinx index is also named products. After creating a new source and index, we run the *indexer* program to create the initial full-text index data files and then (re)start the *searchd* daemon to pick up the changes:

```
$ cd /usr/local/sphinx/bin
$ ./indexer products
$ ./searchd --stop
$ ./searchd
```

The index is now ready to answer queries. We can test it with Sphinx's bundled *test.php* sample script:

```
$ php -q test.php -i products ipod

Query 'ipod ' retrieved 3 of 3 matches in 0.010 sec.
Query stats:
    'ipod' found 3 times in 3 documents
```

```
Matches:
1. doc_id=123, weight=100, cat_id=100, price=159.99, added_ts=2008-01-03 22:38:26
2. doc_id=124, weight=100, cat_id=100, price=199.99, added_ts=2008-01-03 22:38:26
3. doc_id=125, weight=100, cat_id=100, price=249.99, added_ts=2008-01-03 22:38:26
```

The final step is to add searching to our web application. We need to set sorting and filtering options based on user input and format the output nicely. Also, because Sphinx returns only document IDs and configured attributes to the client—it doesn't store any of the original text data—we need to pull additional row data from MySQL ourselves:

```php
 1  <?php
 2  include ( "sphinxapi.php" );
 3  // ... other includes, MySQL connection code,
 4  // displaying page header and search form, etc. all go here
 5
 6  // set query options based on end-user input
 7  $cl = new SphinxClient ();
 8  $sortby = $_REQUEST["sortby"];
 9  if ( !in_array ( $sortby, array ( "price", "added_ts" ) ) )
10      $sortby = "price";
11  if ( $_REQUEST["sortorder"]=="asc" )
12      $cl->SetSortMode ( SPH_SORT_ATTR_ASC, $sortby );
13  else
14      $cl->SetSortMode ( SPH_SORT_ATTR_DESC, $sortby );
15  $offset = ($_REQUEST["page"]-1)*$rows_per_page;
16  $cl->SetLimits ( $offset, $rows_per_page );
17
18  // issue the query, get the results
19  $res = $cl->Query ( $_REQUEST["query"], "products" );
20
21  // handle search errors
22  if ( !$res )
23  {
24      print "<b>Search error:</b>" . $cl->GetLastError ();
25      die;
26  }
27
28  // fetch additional columns from MySQL
29  $ids = join ( ",", array_keys ( $res["matches"] ) );
30  $r = mysql_query ( "SELECT id, title FROM products WHERE id IN ($ids)" )
31      or die ( "MySQL error: " . mysql_error() );
32  while ( $row = mysql_fetch_assoc($r) )
33  {
34      $id = $row["id"];
35      $result["matches"][$id]["sql"] = $row;
36  }
37
38  // display the results in the order returned from Sphinx
39  $n = 1 + $offset;
40  foreach ( $result["matches"] as $id=>$match )
41  {
```

```
42      printf ( "%d. <a href=details.php?id=%d>%s</a>, USD %.2f<br>\n",
43          $n++, $id, $match["sql"]["title"], $match["attrs"]["price"] );
44  }
45
46  ?>
```

Even though the snippet just shown is pretty simple, there are a few things worth highlighting:

- The SetLimits( ) call tells Sphinx to fetch only the number of rows that the client wants to display on a page. It's cheap to impose this limit in Sphinx (unlike in MySQL's built-in search facility), and the number of results that would have been returned without the limit are available in $result['total_found'] at no extra cost.

- Because Sphinx only *indexes* the title column and doesn't *store* it, we must fetch that data from MySQL.

- We retrieve data from MySQL with a single combined query for the whole document batch using the clause WHERE id IN (...), instead of running one query for each match (which would be inefficient).

- We inject the rows pulled from MySQL into our full-text search result set, to keep the original sorting order. We explain this more in a moment.

- We display the rows using data pulled from both Sphinx and MySQL.

The row injection code, which is PHP-specific, deserves a more detailed explanation. We couldn't simply iterate over the result set from the MySQL query, because the row order can (and in most cases actually will) be different from that specified in the WHERE id IN (...) clause. PHP hashes (associative arrays), however, keep the order in which the matches were inserted into them, so iterating over $result["matches"] will produce rows in the proper sorting order as returned by Sphinx. To keep the matches in the proper order returned from Sphinx (rather than the semirandom order returned from MySQL), therefore, we inject the MySQL query results one by one into the hash that PHP stores from the Sphinx result set of matches.

There are also a few major implementation and performance differences between MySQL and Sphinx when it comes to counting matches and applying a LIMIT clause. First, LIMIT is cheap in Sphinx. Consider a LIMIT 500,10 clause. MySQL will retrieve 510 semirandom rows (which is slow) and throw away 500, whereas Sphinx will return the IDs that you will use to retrieve the 10 rows you actually need from MySQL. Second, Sphinx will always return the exact number of matches it actually found in the result set, no matter what's in the LIMIT clause. MySQL can't do this efficiently (see "Optimizing SQL_CALC_FOUND_ROWS" on page 194 for details).

Why Use Sphinx?

Sphinx can complement a MySQL-based application in many ways, bolstering performance where MySQL is not a good solution and adding functionality MySQL can't provide. Typical usage scenarios include:

- Fast, efficient, scalable, relevant full-text searches
- Optimizing WHERE conditions on low-selectivity indexes or columns without indexes
- Optimizing ORDER BY ... LIMIT *N* queries and GROUP BY queries
- Generating result sets in parallel
- Scaling up and scaling out
- Aggregating partitioned data

We explore each of these scenarios in the following sections. This list is not exhaustive, though, and Sphinx users find new applications regularly. For example, one of Sphinx's most important uses—scanning and filtering records quickly—was a user innovation, not one of Sphinx's original design goals.

Efficient and Scalable Full-Text Searching

MySQL's full-text search capability[*] is fast for smaller datasets but performs badly when the data size grows. With millions of records and gigabytes of indexed text, query times can vary from a second to more than 10 minutes, which is unacceptable for a high-performance web application. Although it's possible to scale MySQL's full-text searches by distributing the data in many locations, this requires you to perform searches in parallel and merge the results in your application.

Sphinx works significantly faster than MySQL's built-in full-text indexes. For instance, it can search over 1 GB of text within 10 to 100 milliseconds—and that scales linearly up to 10–100 GB per CPU. Sphinx also has the following advantages:

- It can index data stored with InnoDB and other engines, not just MyISAM.
- It can create indexes on data combined from many source tables, instead of being limited to columns in a single table.
- It can dynamically combine search results from multiple indexes.
- In addition to indexing textual columns, its indexes can contain an unlimited number of numeric *attributes*, which are analogous to "extra columns." Sphinx attributes can be integers, floating-point numbers, and Unix timestamps.
- It can optimize full-text searches with additional conditions on attributes.

---

[*] See "Full-Text Searching" on page 244.

- Its phrase-based ranking algorithm helps it return more relevant results. For instance, if you search a table of song lyrics for "I love you, dear," a song that contains that exact phrase will turn up at the top, before songs that just contain "love" or "dear" many times.

- It makes scaling out much easier. For more on scaling, see Chapter 9 and "Scaling" on page 632, later in this appendix.

Applying WHERE Clauses Efficiently

Sometimes you'll need to run SELECT queries against very large tables (containing millions of records), with several WHERE conditions on columns that have poor index selectivity (i.e., return too many rows for a given WHERE condition) or could not be indexed at all. Common examples include searching for users in a social network and searching for items on an auction site. Typical search interfaces let the user apply WHERE conditions to 10 or more columns, while requiring the results to be sorted by other columns. See "An Indexing Case Study" on page 131 for an example of such an application and the required indexing strategies.

With the proper schema and query optimizations, MySQL can work acceptably for such queries, as long as the WHERE clauses don't contain too many columns. But as the number of columns grows, the number of indexes required to support all possible searches grows exponentially. Covering all the possible combinations for just four columns strains MySQL's limits. It becomes very slow and expensive to maintain the indexes, too. This means it's practically impossible to have all the required indexes for many WHERE conditions, and you have to run the queries without indexes.

More importantly, even if you can add indexes, they won't give much benefit unless they're selective. The classic example is a gender column, which isn't much help because it typically selects half of all rows. MySQL will generally revert to a full table scan when the index isn't selective enough to help it.

Sphinx can perform such queries much faster than MySQL. You can build a Sphinx index with only the required columns from the data. Sphinx then allows two types of access to the data: an indexed search on a keyword or a full scan. In both cases, Sphinx applies *filters*, which are its equivalent of a WHERE clause. Unlike MySQL, which decides internally whether to use an index or a full scan, Sphinx lets you choose which access method to use.

To use a full scan with filters, specify an empty string as the search query. To use an indexed search, add pseudokeywords to your full-text fields while building the index and then search for those keywords. For example, if you wanted to search for items in category 123, you'd add a "category123" keyword to the document during indexing and then perform a full-text search for "category123." You can either add keywords to one of the existing fields using the CONCAT() function, or create a special full-text field for the pseudokeywords for more flexibility. Normally, you should use filters for nonselective values that cover over 30% of the rows, and fake keywords for selective ones that select 10% or less. If the values are in the 10–30% gray zone, your mileage may vary, and you should use benchmarks to find the best solution.

Sphinx will perform both indexed searches and scans faster than MySQL. Sometimes Sphinx actually performs a full scan faster than MySQL can perform an index read.

Finding the Top Results in Order

Web applications frequently need the top *N* results in order. As we discussed in "Optimizing LIMIT and OFFSET" on page 193, this is hard to optimize in MySQL.

The worst case is when the WHERE condition finds many rows (let's say 1 million) and the ORDER BY columns aren't indexed. MySQL uses the index to identify all the matching rows, reads the records one by one into the sort buffer with semirandom disk reads, sorts them all with a filesort, and then discards most of them. It will temporarily store and process the entire result, ignoring the LIMIT clause and churning RAM. And if the result set doesn't fit in the sort buffer, it will need to go to disk, causing even more disk I/O.

This is an extreme case, and you might think it happens rarely in the real world, but in fact the problems it illustrates happen often. MySQL's limitations on indexes for sorting—using only the leftmost part of the index, not supporting loose index scans, and allowing only a single range condition—mean many real-world queries can't benefit from indexes. And even when they can, using semirandom disk I/O to retrieve rows is a performance killer.

Paginated result sets, which usually require queries of the form SELECT ... LIMIT *N, M*, are another performance problem in MySQL. They read *N* + *M* rows from disk, causing a large amount of random I/O and wasting memory resources. Sphinx can accelerate such queries significantly by eliminating the two biggest problems:

Memory usage

Sphinx's RAM usage is always strictly limited, and the limit is configurable. Sphinx supports a result set offset and size similar to the MySQL LIMIT *N, M* syntax but also has a max_matches option. This controls the equivalent of the "sort buffer" size, on both a per-server and a per-query basis. Sphinx's RAM footprint is guaranteed to be within the specified limits.

I/O

If attributes are stored in RAM, Sphinx does not do any I/O at all. And even if attributes are stored on disk, Sphinx will perform sequential I/O to read them, which is much faster than MySQL's semirandom retrieval of rows from disks.

You can sort search results by a combination of relevance (weight), attribute values, and (when using GROUP BY) aggregate function values. The sorting clause syntax is similar to a SQL ORDER BY clause:

```
<?php
$cl = new SphinxClient ();
$cl->SetSortMode ( SPH_SORT_EXTENDED, 'price DESC, @weight ASC' );
// more code and Query( ) call here...
?>
```

In this example, price is a user-specified attribute stored in the index, and @weight is a special attribute, created at runtime, that contains each result's computed relevance. You can also sort by an arithmetic expression involving attribute values, common math operators, and functions:

```
<?php
$cl = new SphinxClient ();
$cl->SetSortMode ( SPH_SORT_EXPR, '@weight + log(pageviews)*1.5' );
// more code and Query( ) call here...
?>
```

Optimizing GROUP BY Queries

Support for everyday SQL-like clauses would be incomplete without GROUP BY functionality, so Sphinx has that too. But unlike MySQL's general-purpose implementation, Sphinx specializes in solving a practical subset of GROUP BY tasks efficiently. This subset covers the generation of reports from big (1–100 million row) datasets when one of the following cases holds:

- The result is only a "small" number of grouped rows (where "small" is on the order of 100,000 to 1 million rows).

- Very fast execution speed is required and approximate COUNT(*) results are acceptable, when many groups are retrieved from data distributed over a cluster of machines.

This is not as restrictive as it might sound. The first scenario covers practically all imaginable time-based reports. For example, a detailed per-hour report for a period of 10 years will return fewer than 90,000 records. The second scenario could be expressed in plain English as something like "as quickly and accurately as possible, find the 20 most important records in a 100-million-row sharded table."

These two types of queries can accelerate general-purpose queries, but you can also use them for full-text search applications. Many applications need to display not only full-text matches, but some aggregate results as well. For example, many search result pages show how many matches were found in each product category, or display a graph of matching document counts over time. Another common requirement is to group the results and show the most relevant match from each category.

Sphinx's group-by support lets you combine grouping and full-text searching, eliminating the overhead of doing the grouping in your application or in MySQL.

As with sorting, grouping in Sphinx uses fixed memory. It is slightly (10% to 50%) more efficient than similar MySQL queries on datasets that fit in RAM. In this case, most of Sphinx's power comes from its ability to distribute the load and greatly reduce the latency. For huge datasets that could never fit in RAM, you can build a special disk-based index for reporting, using inline attributes (defined later). Queries against such indexes execute about as fast as the disk can read the data—about 30–100 MB/sec on modern hardware. In this case, the performance can be many times better than MySQL's, though the results will be approximate.

The most important difference from MySQL's GROUP BY is that Sphinx may, under certain circumstances, yield approximate results. There are two reasons for this:

- Grouping uses a fixed amount of memory. If there are too many groups to hold in RAM and the matches are in a certain "unfortunate" order, per-group counts might be smaller than the actual values.

- A distributed search sends only the aggregate results, not the matches themselves, from node to node. If there are duplicate records in different nodes, per-group distinct counts might be greater than the actual values, because the information that can remove the duplicates is not transmitted between nodes.

In practice, it is often acceptable to have fast approximate group-by counts. If this isn't acceptable, it's often possible to get exact results by tuning the daemon and client application carefully.

You can generate the equivalent of COUNT(DISTINCT <attribute>), too. For example, you can use this to compute the number of distinct sellers per category in an auction site.

Finally, Sphinx lets you choose criteria to select the single "best" document within each group. For example, you can select the most relevant document from each domain, while grouping by domain and sorting the result set by per-domain match counts. This is not possible in MySQL without a complex query.

Generating Parallel Result Sets

Sphinx lets you generate several results from the same data simultaneously, again using a fixed amount of memory. Compared to the traditional SQL approach of either running two queries (and hoping that some data stays in the cache between runs) or creating a temporary table for each search result set, this yields a noticeable improvement.

For example, assume you need per-day, per-week, and per-month reports over a period of time. To generate these with MySQL you'd have to run three queries with different GROUP BY clauses, processing the source data three times. Sphinx, however, can process the underlying data once and accumulate all three reports in parallel.

Sphinx does this with a *multi-query* mechanism. Instead of issuing queries one by one, you batch several queries and submit them in one request:

```php
<?php
$cl = new SphinxClient ();
$cl->SetSortMode ( SPH_SORT_EXTENDED, "price desc" );
$cl->AddQuery ( "ipod" );
$cl->SetGroupBy ( "category_id", SPH_GROUPBY_ATTR, "@count desc" );
$cl->AddQuery ( "ipod" );
$cl->RunQueries ();
?>
```

Sphinx will analyze the request, identify query parts it can combine, and parallelize the queries where possible.

For example, Sphinx might notice that only the sorting and grouping modes differ, and that the queries are otherwise the same. This is the case in the sample code just shown, where the sorting is by price but the grouping is by category_id. Sphinx will create several sorting queues to process these queries. When it runs the queries, it will retrieve the rows once and submit them to all queues. Compared to running the queries one by one, this eliminates several redundant full-text search or full scan operations.

Note that generating parallel result sets, although it's a common and important optimization, is only a particular case of the more generalized multi-query mechanism. It is not the *only* possible optimization. The rule of thumb is to combine queries in one request where possible, which generally allows Sphinx to apply internal optimizations. Even if Sphinx can't parallelize the queries, it still saves network round-trips. And if Sphinx adds more optimizations in the future, your queries will use them automatically with no further changes.

Scaling

Sphinx scales well both horizontally (scaling out) and vertically (scaling up).

Sphinx is fully distributable across many machines. All the use cases we've mentioned can benefit from distributing the work across several CPUs.

The Sphinx search daemon (*searchd*) supports special *distributed indexes*, which know which local and remote indexes should be queried and aggregated. This means scaling out is a trivial configuration change. You simply partition the data across the nodes, configure the master node to issue several remote queries in parallel with local ones, and that's it.

You can also scale up, as in using more cores or CPUs on a single machine to improve latency. To accomplish this, you can just run several instances of *searchd* on a single machine and query them all from another machine via a distributed index. Alternatively, you can configure a single instance to communicate with itself so that the parallel "remote" queries actually run on a single machine, but on different CPUs or cores.

In other words, with Sphinx a single query can be made to use more than one CPU (multiple concurrent queries will use multiple CPUs automatically). This is a major difference from MySQL, where one query always gets one CPU, no matter how many are available. Also, Sphinx does not need any synchronization between concurrently running queries. That lets it avoid mutexes (a synchronization mechanism), which are a notorious MySQL performance bottleneck on multi-CPU systems.

Another important aspect of scaling up is scaling disk I/O. Different indexes (including parts of a larger distributed index) can easily be put on different physical disks or RAID volumes to improve latency and throughput. This approach has some of the same benefits as MySQL 5.1's partitioned tables, which can also partition data into multiple locations. However, distributed indexes have some advantages over partitioned tables. Sphinx uses distributed indexes both to distribute the load and to process all parts of a query in parallel. In contrast, MySQL's partitioning can optimize some queries (but not all) by pruning partitions, but the query processing will not be parallelized. And even though both Sphinx and MySQL partitioning will improve query throughput, if your queries are I/O-bound, you can expect linear latency improvement from Sphinx on all queries, whereas MySQL's partitioning will improve latency only on those queries where the optimizer can prune entire partitions.

The distributed searching workflow is straightforward:

1. Issue remote queries on all remote servers.
2. Perform sequential local index searches.
3. Read the partial search results from the remote servers.
4. Merge all the partial results into the final result set, and return it to the client.

If your hardware resources permit it, you can search through several indexes on the same machine in parallel, too. If there are several physical disk drives and several CPU cores, the concurrent searches can run without interfering with each other. You can pretend that some of the indexes are remote and configure *searchd* to contact itself to launch a parallel query on the same machine:

```
index distributed_sample
{
    type = distributed
    local = chunk1 # resides on HDD1
    agent = localhost:3312:chunk2 # resides on HDD2, searchd contacts itself
}
```

From the client's point of view, distributed indexes are absolutely no different from local indexes. This lets you create "trees" of distributed indexes by using nodes as proxies for sets of other nodes. For example, the first-level node could proxy the queries to a number of the second-level nodes, which could in turn either search locally themselves or pass the queries to other nodes, to an arbitrary depth.

Aggregating Sharded Data

Building a scalable system often involves *sharding* (partitioning) the data across different physical MySQL servers. We discussed this in depth in "Data sharding" on page 417.

When the data is sharded at a fine level of granularity, simply fetching a few rows with a selective WHERE (which should be fast) means contacting many servers, checking for errors, and merging the results together in the application. Sphinx alleviates this problem, because all the necessary functionality is already implemented inside the search daemon.

Consider an example where a 1 TB table with a billion blog posts is sharded by user ID over 10 physical MySQL servers, so a given user's posts always go to the same server. As long as queries are restricted to a single user, everything is fine: we choose the server based on user ID and work with it as usual.

Now assume that we need to implement an archive page that shows the user's friends' posts. How are we going to display page 50, with entries 981 to 1000, sorted by post date? Most likely, the various friends' data will be on different servers. With only 10 friends, there's about a 90% chance that more than 8 servers will be used, and that probability increases to 99% if there are 20 friends. So, for most queries, we will need to contact all the servers. Worse, we'll need to pull 1,000 posts from *each* server and sort them all in the application. Following the suggestions we've made in Chapter 10 and elsewhere, we'd trim down the required data to the post ID and timestamp only, but that's still 10,000 records to sort in the application. Most modern scripting languages consume a lot of CPU time for that sorting step alone. In addition, we'll either have to fetch the records from each server sequentially (which will be slow) or write some code to juggle the parallel querying threads (which will be difficult to implement and maintain).

In such situations, it makes sense to use Sphinx instead of reinventing the wheel. All we'll have to do in this case is set up several Sphinx instances, mirror the frequently accessed post attributes from each table—in this example, the post ID, user ID, and timestamp—and query the master Sphinx instance for entries 981 to 1000, sorted by post date, in approximately three lines of code. This is a much smarter way to scale.

Architectural Overview

Sphinx is a standalone set of programs. The two main programs are:

indexer

> A program that fetches documents from specified sources (e.g., from MySQL query results) and creates a full-text index over them. This is a background batch job, which sites usually run regularly.

searchd

> A daemon that serves search queries from the indexes *indexer* builds. This provides the runtime support for applications.

The Sphinx distribution also includes native *searchd* client APIs in a number of programming languages (PHP, Python, Perl, Ruby, and Java, at the time of this writing), and the SphinxSE, which is a client implemented as a pluggable storage engine for MySQL 5.0 and newer. The APIs and SphinxSE allow a client application to connect to *searchd*, pass it the search query, and fetch back the search results.

Each Sphinx full-text index can be compared to a table in a database; in place of rows in a table, the Sphinx index consists of *documents*. (Sphinx also has a separate data structure called a *multivalued attribute*, discussed later.) Each document has a unique 32-bit or 64-bit integer identifier that should be drawn from the database table being indexed (for instance, from a primary key column). In addition, each document has one or more full-text fields (each corresponding to a text column from the database) and numerical attributes. Like a database table, the Sphinx index has the same fields and attributes for all of its documents. Table C-1 shows the analogy between a database table and a Sphinx index.

Table C-1. Database structure and corresponding Sphinx structure

Database structure	Sphinx structure
```CREATE TABLE documents (id` int(11) NOT NULL auto_increment,     title` varchar(255), content` text,     group_id` int(11), added` datetime, PRIMARY KEY (id));```	```index documents document ID title field, full-text indexed content field, full-text indexed group_id attribute, sql_attr_uint added` attribute, sql_attr_timestamp```

Sphinx does not store the text fields from the database but just uses their contents to build a search index.

Installation Overview

Sphinx installation is straightforward and typically includes the following steps:

1. Building the programs from sources:

    ```
    $ configure && make && make install
    ```

2. Creating a configuration file with definitions for data sources and full-text indexes

3. Initial indexing

4. Launching *searchd*

After that, the search functionality is immediately available for client programs:

```php
<?php
include ( 'sphinxapi.php' );
$cl = new SphinxClient ();
$res = $cl->Query ( 'test query', 'myindex' );
// use $res search result here
?>
```

The only thing left to do is run *indexer* regularly to update the full-text index data. Indexes that *searchd* is currently serving will stay fully functional during reindexing: *indexer* will detect that they are in use, create a "shadow" index copy instead, and notify *searchd* to pick up that copy on completion.

Full-text indexes are stored in the filesystem (at the location specified in the configuration file) and are in a special "monolithic" format, which is not well suited for incremental updates. The normal way to update the index data is to rebuild it from scratch. This is not as big a problem as it might seem, though, for the following reasons:

- Indexing is fast. Sphinx can index plain text (without HTML markup) at a rate of 4–8 MB/sec on modern hardware.

- You can partition the data in several indexes, as shown in the next section, and reindex only the updated part from scratch on each run of *indexer*.

- There is no need to "defragment" the indexes—they are built for optimal I/O, which improves search speed.

- Numeric attributes can be updated without a complete rebuild.

A future version will offer an additional index backend, which will support real-time index updates.

Typical Partition Use

Let's discuss partitioning in a bit more detail. The simplest partitioning scheme is the *main* + *delta* approach in which two indexes are created to index one document collection. *Main* indexes the whole document set, while *delta* indexes only documents that have changed since the last time the main index was built.

This scheme matches many data modification patterns perfectly. Forums, blogs, email and news archives, and vertical search engines are all good examples. Most of the data in those repositories never changes once it is entered, and only a tiny fraction of documents are changed or added on a regular basis. This means the delta index is small and can be rebuilt as frequently as required (e.g., once every 1–15 minutes). This is equivalent to indexing just the newly inserted rows.

You don't need to rebuild the indexes to change attributes associated with documents—you can do this online via *searchd*. You can mark rows as deleted by simply setting a "deleted" attribute in the main index. Thus, you can handle updates by marking this attribute on documents in the main index, then rebuilding the delta index. Searching for all documents that are not marked as "deleted" will return the correct results.

Note that the indexed data can come from the results of any SELECT statement; it doesn't have to come from just a single SQL table. There are no restrictions on the SELECT statements. That means you can preprocess the results in the database before they're indexed. Common preprocessing examples include joins with other tables, creating additional fields on the fly, excluding some fields from indexing, and manipulating values.

Special Features

Besides "just" indexing and searching through database content, Sphinx offers several other special features. Here's a partial list of the most important ones:

- The searching and ranking algorithms take word positions and the query phrase's proximity to the document content into account.
- You can bind numeric attributes to documents, including multivalued attributes.
- You can sort, filter, and group by attribute values.
- You can create document snippets with search query keyword highlighting.
- You can distribute searching across several machines.
- You can optimize queries that generate several result sets from the same data.
- You can access the search results from within MySQL using SphinxSE.
- You can fine-tune the load Sphinx imposes on the server.

We covered some of these features earlier. This section covers a few of the remaining features.

Phrase Proximity Ranking

Sphinx remembers word positions within each document, as do other open source full-text search systems. But unlike most other ones, it uses the positions to rank matches and return more relevant results.

A number of factors might contribute to a document's final rank. To compute the rank, most other systems use only keyword frequency: the number of times each keyword occurs. The classic BM25 weighting function* that virtually all full-text search systems use is built around giving more weight to words that either occur frequently in the particular document being searched or occur rarely in the whole collection. The BM25 result is usually returned as the final rank value.

In contrast, Sphinx also computes query phrase proximity, which is simply the length of the longest verbatim query subphrase contained in the document, counted in words. For instance, the phrase "John Doe Jr" queried against a document with the text "John Black, John White Jr, and Jane Dunne" will produce a phrase proximity of 1, because no two words in the query appear together in the query order. The same query against "Mr. John Doe Jr and friends" will yield a proximity of 3, because three query words occur in the document in the query order. The document "John Gray, Jane Doe Jr" will produce a proximity of 2, thanks to its "Doe Jr" query subphrase.

By default, Sphinx ranks matches using phrase proximity first and the classic BM25 weight second. This means that verbatim query quotes are guaranteed to be at the very top, quotes that are off by a single word will be right below those, and so on.

When and how does phrase proximity affect results? Consider searching 1,000,000 pages of text for the phrase "To be or not to be." Sphinx will put the pages with verbatim quotes at the very top of search results, whereas BM25-based systems will first return the pages with the most mentions of "to," "be," "or," and "not"—pages with an exact quote but only a few instances of "to" will be buried deep in the results.

Most major web search engines today rank results with keyword positions as well. Searching for a phrase on Google will likely put perfect or near-perfect phrase matches at the very top, followed by the "bag of words" documents.

However, analyzing keyword positions requires additional CPU time, and sometimes you might need to skip it for performance reasons. There are also cases when phrase ranking produces undesired, unexpected results. For example, searching for tags in a cloud is better without keyword positions: it makes no difference whether the tags from the query are next to each other in the document.

To allow for flexibility, Sphinx offers a choice of ranking modes. Besides the default mode of proximity plus BM25, you can choose from a number of others that include

---

* See *http://en.wikipedia.org/wiki/Okapi_BM25* for details.

BM25-only weighting, fully disabled weighting (which provides a nice optimization if you're not sorting by rank), and more.

Support for Attributes

Each document may contain an unlimited number of numeric attributes. Attributes are user-specified and can contain any additional information required for a specific task. Examples include a blog post's author ID, an inventory item price, a category ID, and so on.

Attributes enable efficient full-text searches with additional filtering, sorting, and grouping of the search results. In theory, they could be stored in MySQL and pulled from there every time a search is performed. But in practice, if a full-text search locates even hundreds or thousands of rows (which is not many), retrieving them from MySQL is unacceptably slow.

Sphinx supports two ways to store attributes: inline in the document lists or externally in a separate file. Inlining requires all attribute values to be stored in the index many times, once for each time a document ID is stored. This inflates the index size and increases I/O, but reduces use of RAM. Storing the attributes externally requires preloading them into RAM upon *searchd* startup.

Attributes normally fit in RAM, so the usual practice is to store them externally. This makes filtering, sorting, and grouping very fast, because accessing data is a matter of quick in-memory lookup. Also, only the externally stored attributes can be updated at runtime. Inline storage should be used only when there is not enough free RAM to hold the attribute data.

Sphinx also supports *multivalued attributes* (MVAs). MVA content consists of an arbitrarily long list of integer values associated with each document. Examples of good uses for MVAs are lists of tag IDs, product categories, and access control lists.

Filtering

Having access to attribute values in the full-text engine allows Sphinx to filter and reject candidate matches as early as possible while searching. Technically, the filter check occurs after verification that the document contains all the required keywords, but before certain computationally intensive calculations (such as ranking) are done. Because of these optimizations, using Sphinx to combine full-text searching with filtering and sorting can be 10 to 100 times faster than using Sphinx for searching and then filtering results in MySQL.

Sphinx supports two types of filters, which are analogous to simple WHERE conditions in SQL:

- An attribute value matches a specified range of values (analogous to a `BETWEEN` clause, or numeric comparisons).

- An attribute value matches a specified set of values (analogous to an `IN( )` list).

If the filters will have a fixed number of values ("set" filters instead of "range" filters), and if such values are selective, it makes sense to replace the integer values with "fake keywords" and index them as full-text content instead of attributes. This applies to both normal numeric attributes and MVAs. We see some examples of how to do this later.

Sphinx can also use filters to optimize full scans. Sphinx remembers minimum and maximum attribute values for short continuous row blocks (128 rows, by default) and can quickly throw away whole blocks based on filtering conditions. Rows are stored in the order of ascending document IDs, so this optimization works best for columns that are correlated with the ID. For instance, if you have a row-insertion timestamp that grows along with the ID, a full scan with filtering on that timestamp will be very fast.

The SphinxSE Pluggable Storage Engine

Full-text search results received from Sphinx almost always require additional work involving MySQL—at the very least, to pull out the text column values that the Sphinx index does not store. As a result, you'll frequently need to `JOIN` search results from Sphinx with other MySQL tables.

Although you can achieve this by sending the result's document IDs to MySQL in a query, that strategy leads to neither the cleanest nor the fastest code. For high-volume situations, you should consider using SphinxSE, a pluggable storage engine that you can compile into MySQL 5.0 or newer, or load into MySQL 5.1 or newer as a plug-in.

SphinxSE lets programmers query *searchd* and access search results from within MySQL. The usage is as simple as creating a special table with an `ENGINE=SPHINX` clause (and an optional `CONNECTION` clause to locate the Sphinx server if it's at a non-default location), and then running queries against that table:

```
mysql> CREATE TABLE search_table (
    ->    id        INTEGER NOT NULL,
    ->    weight    INTEGER NOT NULL,
    ->    query     VARCHAR(3072) NOT NULL,
    ->    group_id  INTEGER,
    ->    INDEX(query)
    -> ) ENGINE=SPHINX CONNECTION="sphinx://localhost:3312/test";
Query OK, 0 rows affected (0.12 sec)

mysql> SELECT * FROM search_table WHERE query='test;mode=all' \G
```

```
*************************** 1. row ***************************
     id: 123
 weight: 1
  query: test;mode=all
group_id: 45
1 row in set (0.00 sec)
```

Each SELECT passes a Sphinx query as the query column in the WHERE clause. The Sphinx *searchd* server returns the results. The SphinxSE storage engine then translates these into MySQL results and returns them to the SELECT statement.

Queries may include JOINs with any other tables stored using any other storage engines.

The SphinxSE engine supports most searching options available via the API, too. You can specify options such as filtering and limits by plugging additional clauses into the query string:

```
mysql> SELECT * FROM search_table WHERE query='test;mode=all;
    -> filter=group_id,5,7,11;maxmatches=3000';
```

Per-query and per-word statistics that are returned by the API are also accessible through SHOW STATUS:

```
mysql> SHOW ENGINE SPHINX STATUS \G
*************************** 1. row ***************************
  Type: SPHINX
  Name: stats
Status: total: 3, total found: 3, time: 8, words: 1
*************************** 2. row ***************************
  Type: SPHINX
  Name: words
Status: test:3:5
2 rows in set (0.00 sec)
```

Even when you're using SphinxSE, the rule of thumb still is to allow *searchd* to perform sorting, filtering, and grouping—i.e., to add all the required clauses to the query string rather than use WHERE, ORDER BY, or GROUP BY. This is especially important for WHERE conditions. The reason is that SphinxSE is only a client to *searchd*, not a full-blown built-in search library. Thus, you need to pass everything that you can to the Sphinx engine to get the best performance.

Advanced Performance Control

Both indexing and searching operations could impose a significant additional load on either the search server or the database server. Fortunately, a number of settings let you limit the load coming from Sphinx.

An undesired database-side load can be caused by *indexer* queries that either stall MySQL completely with their locks or just occur too quickly and hog resources from other concurrent queries.

The first case is a notorious problem with MyISAM, where long-running reads lock the tables and stall other pending reads and writes—you can't simply do SELECT * FROM big_table on a production server, because you risk disrupting all other operations. To work around that, Sphinx offers *ranged queries*. Instead of configuring a single huge query, you can specify one query that quickly computes the indexable row ranges and another query that pulls out the data step by step, in small chunks:

```
sql_query_range  = SELECT MIN(id),MAX(id) FROM documents
sql_range_step   = 1000
sql_query        = SELECT id, title, body FROM documents \
                     WHERE id>=$start AND id<=$end
```

This feature is extremely helpful for indexing MyISAM tables, but it should also be considered when using InnoDB tables. Although InnoDB won't just lock the table and stall other queries when running a big SELECT *, it will still use significant machine resources because of its MVCC architecture. Multiversioning for a thousand transactions that cover a thousand rows each can be less expensive than a single long-running million-row transaction.

The second cause of excessive load happens when *indexer* is able to process the data more quickly than MySQL provides it. You should also use ranged queries in this case. The sql_ranged_throttle option forces *indexer* to sleep for a given time period (in milliseconds) between subsequent ranged query steps, increasing indexing time but easing the load on MySQL.

Interestingly enough, there's a special case when you can tune Sphinx to achieve exactly the opposite effect: that is, improve indexing time by placing *more* load on MySQL. When the connection between the *indexer* box and the database box is 100 Mbps, and the rows compress well (which is typical for text data), the MySQL compression protocol can improve overall indexing time. That comes at a cost of more CPU time spent on both the MySQL and *indexer* sides to compress and uncompress the rows transmitted over the network, respectively. However, overall indexing time could be up to 20–30% less because of greatly reduced network traffic.

Search clusters can suffer from occasional overload, too, so Sphinx provides a few ways to help avoid *searchd* going off on a spin.

First, a max_children option simply limits the total number of concurrently running queries and tells clients to retry when that limit is reached.

Then there are query-level limits. You can specify that query processing stop either at a given threshold of matches found or a given threshold of elapsed time, using the SetLimits( ) and SetMaxQueryTime( ) API calls, respectively. This is done on a per-query basis, so you can ensure that more important queries always complete fully.

Finally, periodic *indexer* runs can cause bursts of additional I/O that will in turn cause intermittent *searchd* slowdowns. To prevent that, options that limit *indexer* disk I/O exist. max_iops enforces a minimal delay between I/O operations that ensures that no more than `max_iops` disk operations per second will be performed. But even a single operation could be too much; consider a 100-MB `read( )` call as an example. The `max_iosize` option takes cares of that, guaranteeing that the length of every disk read or write will be under a given boundary. Larger operations are automatically split into smaller ones, and these smaller ones are then controlled by `max_iops` settings.

Practical Implementation Examples

Each of the features we've described can be found successfully deployed in production. The following sections review several of these real-world Sphinx deployments, briefly describing the sites and some implementation details.

Full-Text Searching on Mininova.org

A popular torrent search engine, Mininova.org, provides a clear example of how to optimize "just" full-text searching. Sphinx replaced several MySQL slaves using MySQL built-in full-text indexes, which were unable to handle the load. After the replacement, the search servers were underloaded; the current load average is now in the 0.3–0.4 range.

Here are the database size and load numbers:

- The site has a small database, with about 300,000–500,000 records and about 300–500 MB of index.
- The site load is quite high: about 8–10 million searches per day at the time of this writing.

The data mostly consists of user-supplied filenames, frequently without proper punctuation. For this reason, prefix indexing is used instead of whole-word indexing. The resulting index is several times larger than it would otherwise be, but it is still small enough that it can be built quickly and its data can be cached effectively.

Search results for the 1,000 most frequent queries are cached on the application side. About 20–30% of all queries are served from the cache. Because of the "long tail" query distribution, a larger cache would not help much more.

For high availability, the site uses two servers with complete full-text index replicas. The indexes are rebuilt from scratch every few minutes. Indexing takes less than one minute, so there's no point in implementing more complex schemes.

The following are lessons learned from this example:

- Caching search results in the application helps a lot.

- There might be no need to have a huge cache, even for busy applications. A mere 1,000 to 10,000 entries can be enough.

- For databases on the order of 1 GB in size, simple periodic reindexing instead of more complicated schemes is OK, even for busy sites.

Full-Text Searching on BoardReader.com

Mininova is an extreme high-load project case—there's not that much data, but there are a lot of queries against that data. BoardReader (*http://www.boardreader. com*) was initially just the opposite: a forum search engine that performed many fewer searches on a much larger dataset. Sphinx replaced a commercial full-text search engine, which took up to 10 seconds per query to search through a 1 GB collection. Sphinx allowed BoardReader to scale greatly, both in terms of data size and query throughput.

Here's some general information:

- There are more than 1 billion documents and 1.5 TB of text in the database.

- There are about 500,000 page views and between 700,000 and 1 million searches per day.

At the time of this writing, the search cluster consists of six servers, each with four logical CPUs (two dual-core Xeons), 16 GB of RAM, and 0.5 TB of disk space. The database itself is stored on a separate cluster. The search cluster is used only for indexing and searching.

Each of the six servers runs four *searchd* instances, so all four cores are used. One of the four instances aggregates the results from the other three. That makes a total of 24 *searchd* instances. The data is distributed evenly across all of them. Every *searchd* copy carries several indexes over approximately 1/24 of the total data (about 60 GB).

The search results from the six "first-tier" *searchd* nodes are in turn aggregated by another *searchd* running on the frontend web server. This instance carries several purely distributed indexes, which reference the six search cluster servers but have no local data at all.

Why have four *searchd* instances per node? Why not have only one *searchd* instance per server, configure it to carry four index chunks, and make it contact itself as though it's a remote server to utilize multiple CPUs, as we suggested earlier? Having four instances instead of just one has its benefits. First, it reduces startup time. There are several gigabytes of attribute data that need to be preloaded in RAM; starting several daemons at a time lets us parallelize that. Second, it improves availability. In the event of *searchd* failures or updates, only 1/24 of the whole index is inaccessible, instead of 1/6.

Within each of the 24 instances on the search cluster, we use time-based partitioning to reduce the load even further. Many queries need to be run only on the most recent data, so the data is divided into three disjoint index sets: data from the last week, from the last three months, and from all time. These indexes are distributed over several different physical disks on a per-instance basis. This way, each instance has its own CPU and physical disk drive and won't interfere with the others.

Local *cron* jobs update the indexes periodically. They pull the data from MySQL over the network but create the index files locally.

Using several explicitly separated "raw" disks proved to be faster than a single RAID volume. Raw disks give control over which files go on which physical disk. That is not the case with RAID, where the controller decides which block goes on which physical disk. Raw disks also guarantee fully parallel I/O on different index chunks, but concurrent searches on RAID are subject to I/O stepping. We chose RAID 0, which has no redundancy, because we don't care about disk failures; we can easily rebuild the indexes on the search nodes. We could also have used several RAID 1 (mirror) volumes to give the same throughput as raw disks while improving reliability.

Another interesting thing to learn from BoardReader is how Sphinx version updates are performed. Obviously, the whole cluster cannot be taken down. Therefore, backward compatibility is critical. Fortunately, Sphinx provides it—newer *searchd* versions usually can read older index files, and they are always able to communicate to older clients over the network. Note that the first-tier nodes that aggregate the search results look just like clients to the second-tier nodes, which do most of the actual searching. Thus, the second-tier nodes are updated first, then the first-tier ones, and finally the web frontend.

Lessons learned from this example are:

- The Very Large Database Motto: partition, partition, partition, parallelize.
- On big search farms, organize *searchd* in trees with several tiers.
- Build optimized indexes with a fraction of the total data where possible.
- Map files to disks explicitly rather than rely on the RAID controller.

Optimizing Selects on Sahibinden.com

Sahibinden.com, a leading Turkish online auction site, had a number of performance problems, including full-text search performance. After deploying Sphinx and profiling some queries, it was found that Sphinx could perform many of the frequent application-specific queries with filters faster than MySQL—even when there was an index on one of the participating columns in MySQL. Besides, using Sphinx for non-full-text searches resulted in unified application code that was simpler to write and support.

MySQL was underperforming because the selectivity on each individual column was not enough to reduce the search space significantly. In fact, it was almost impossible to create and maintain all the required indexes, because too many columns required them. The product information tables had about 100 columns, each of which the web application could technically use for filtering or sorting.

Active insertion and updates to the "hot" products table slowed to a crawl, because of too many index updates.

For that reason, Sphinx was a natural choice for *all* the SELECT queries on the product information tables, not just the full-text search queries.

Here are the database size and load numbers for the site:

- The database contains about 400,000 records and 500 MB of data.
- The load is about 3 million queries per day.

To emulate normal SELECT queries with WHERE conditions, the Sphinx indexing process included special keywords in the full-text index. The keywords were of the form __CAT*N*___, where *N* was replaced with the corresponding category ID. This replacement happened during indexing with the CONCAT( ) function in the MySQL query, so the source data was not altered.

The indexes needed to be rebuilt as frequently as possible. We settled on rebuilding them every minute. A full reindexing took 9–15 seconds on one of many CPUs, so the *main + delta* scheme discussed earlier was not necessary.

The PHP API turned out to spend a noticeable amount of time (7–9 milliseconds per query) parsing the result set when it had many attributes. Normally, this overhead would not be an issue because the full-text search costs, especially over big collections, would be higher than the parsing cost. But in this specific case, we also needed non-full-text queries against a small collection. To alleviate the issue, the indexes were separated into pairs: a "lightweight" one with the 34 most frequently used attributes, and a "complete" one with all 99 attributes.

Other possible solutions would have been to use SphinxSE or to implement a feature to pull only the specified columns into Sphinx. However, the workaround with two indexes was by far the fastest to implement, and time was a concern.

The following are the lessons learned from this example:

- Sometimes, a full scan in Sphinx performs better than an index read in MySQL.
- For selective conditions, use a "fake keyword" instead of filtering on an attribute, so the full-text search engine can do more of the work.
- APIs in scripting languages can be a bottleneck in certain extreme but real-world cases.

Optimizing GROUP BY on BoardReader.com

An improvement to the BoardReader service required counting hyperlinks and building various reports from the linking data. For instance, one of the reports needed to show the top *N* second-level domains linked to during the last week. Another counted the top *N* second- and third-level domains that linked to a given site, such as YouTube. The queries to build these reports had the following common characteristics:

- They always group by domain.
- They sort by count per group or by the count of distinct values per group.
- They process a lot of data (up to millions of records), but the result set with the best groups is always small.
- Approximate results are acceptable.

During the prototype-testing phase, MySQL took up to 300 seconds to execute these queries. In theory, by partitioning the data, splitting it across servers, and manually aggregating the results in the application, it would have been possible to optimize the queries to around 10 seconds. But this is a complicated architecture to build; even the partitioning implementation is far from straightforward.

Because we had successfully distributed the search load with Sphinx, we decided to implement an approximate distributed GROUP BY with Sphinx, too. This required preprocessing the data before indexing to convert all the interesting substrings into standalone "words." Here's a sample URL before and after preprocessing:

```
source_url      = http://my.blogger.com/my/best-post.php
processed_url    = my$blogger$com, blogger$com, my$blogger$com$my,
                   my$blogger$com$my$best, my$blogger$com$my$best$post.php
```

Dollar signs ($) are merely a unified replacement for URL separator characters so that searches can be conducted on any URL part, be it domain or path. This type of preprocessing extracts all "interesting" substrings into single keywords that are the fastest to search. Technically, we could have used phrase queries or prefix indexing, but that would have resulted in bigger indexes and slower performance.

Links are preprocessed at indexing time using a specially crafted MySQL UDF. We also enhanced Sphinx with the ability to count distinct values for this task. After that, we were able to move the queries completely to the search cluster, distribute them easily, and reduce query latency greatly.

Here are the database size and load numbers:

- There are about 150–200 million records, which becomes about 50–100 GB data after preprocessing.
- The load is approximately 60,000–100,000 GROUP BY queries per day.

The indexes for the distributed GROUP BY were deployed on the same search cluster of 6 machines and 24 logical CPUs described previously. This is a minor complementary load to the main search load over the 1.5 TB text database.

Sphinx replaced MySQL's exact, slow, single-CPU computations with approximate, fast, distributed computations. All of the factors that introduce approximation errors are present: the incoming data frequently contains too many rows to fit in the "sort buffer" (we use a fixed RAM limit of 100K rows), we use COUNT(DISTINCT), and the result sets are aggregated over the network. Despite that, the results for the first 10 to 1000 groups—which are actually required for the reports—are from 99% to 100% correct.

The indexed data is very different from the data that would be used for an ordinary full-text search. There are a huge number of documents and keywords, even though the documents are very small. The document numbering is nonsequential, because it uses a special numbering convention (source server, source table, and primary key) that does not fit in 32 bits. The huge amount of search "keywords" was also causing frequent CRC32 collisions (Sphinx uses CRC32 to map keywords to internal word IDs). For these reasons, we were forced to use 64-bit identifiers everywhere internally.

The current performance is satisfactory. For the most complex domains, queries normally complete in 0.1 to 1.0 seconds.

The following are the lessons learned from this example:

- For GROUP BY queries, some precision can be traded for speed.
- With huge textual collections or moderately sized special collections, 64-bit identifiers might be required.

Optimizing Sharded JOIN Queries on Grouply.com

Sphinx's MVA support is a fairly new feature, but users have already found clever uses for it. Grouply.com built a Sphinx-based solution to search its multimillion-record database of tagged messages. The database is split across many physical servers for massive scalability, so it may be necessary to query tables that are located on different servers. Arbitrary large-scale joins are impossible because there are too many participating servers, databases, and tables.

Grouply.com uses Sphinx's MVA attributes to store message tags. The tag list is retrieved from a Sphinx cluster via the PHP API. This replaces multiple sequential SELECTs from several MySQL servers. To reduce the number of SQL queries as well, certain presentation-only data (for example, a small list of users who last read the message) is also stored in a separate MVA attribute and accessed through Sphinx.

Two key innovations here are using Sphinx to prebuild JOIN results and using its distributed capabilities to merge data scattered over many shards. This would be next to impossible with MySQL alone. Efficient merging would require partitioning the data over as few physical servers and tables as possible, but that would hurt both scalability and extensibility.

Lessons learned from this example are:

- Sphinx can be used to aggregate highly partitioned data efficiently.
- MVAs can be used to store and optimize prebuilt JOIN results.

Conclusion

We've discussed the Sphinx full-text search system only briefly in this appendix. To keep it short, we intentionally omitted discussions of many other Sphinx features, such as HTML indexing support, ranged queries for better MyISAM support, morphology and synonym support, prefix and infix indexing, and CJK indexing. Nevertheless, this appendix should give you some idea of how Sphinx can solve many different real-world problems efficiently. It is not limited to full-text searching; it can solve a number of difficult problems that would traditionally be done in SQL.

Sphinx is neither a silver bullet nor a replacement for MySQL. However, in many cases (which are becoming common in modern web applications), it can be used as a very useful complement to MySQL. You can use it to simply offload some work, or even to create new possibilities for your application.

Download it at *http://www.sphinxsearch.com*—and don't forget to share your own usage ideas!

APPENDIX D

Debugging Locks

Any system that uses locks to control shared access to resources can be hard to debug when a lock contention issue crops up. Perhaps you're trying to add a column to a table, or just trying to run a query, when suddenly you find that your queries are blocked because something else is locking the table or rows you're trying to use. This appendix shows you what to do when you encounter these situations in MySQL. Often all you will want to do is find out why your query is blocked, but sometimes you will want to know what's blocking it, so you know which process to kill. This appendix shows you how to achieve both goals.

Lock Waits at the Server Level

A lock wait can happen at either the server level or the storage engine level.[*] (Application-level locks could be a problem too, but we're focusing on MySQL.)

The MySQL server itself uses several types of locks. If a query is waiting for a lock at the server level, you can see evidence of it in the output of SHOW PROCESSLIST. In addition to server-level locks, any storage engine that supports row-level locks, such as InnoDB, implements its own locks, at least at the time of this writing. In MySQL 5.0 and earlier versions, the server is unaware of such locks, and they're mostly hidden from users and database administrators. Future versions may expose more of these locks at the server level, probably through pluggable INFORMATION_SCHEMA tables.

Here are the kinds of locks the MySQL server uses:

Table locks

> Tables can be locked with explicit read and write locks. There are a couple of variations on these locks, such as local read locks. You can learn about the varia-

---

[*] Refer to Figure 1-1 in Chapter 1 if you need to refresh your memory on the separation between the server and the storage engines.

tions in the LOCK TABLES section of the MySQL manual. In addition to these explicit locks, queries acquire implicit locks on tables for their durations.

Global locks

There is a single global read lock that can be acquired with FLUSH TABLES WITH READ LOCK.

Name locks

Name locks are a type of table lock that the server creates when it renames or drops a table.

String locks

You can lock and release an arbitrary string server-wide with GET_LOCK( ) and its associated functions.

We examine each of these lock types in more detail in the following sections.

Table Locks

Table locks can be either explicit or implicit. You create explicit locks with LOCK TABLES. For example, if you execute the following command in a *mysql* session, you'll have an explicit lock on sakila.film:

```
mysql> LOCK TABLES sakila.film READ;
```

If you then execute the following command in a different session, the query will hang and not complete:

```
mysql> LOCK TABLES sakila.film WRITE;
```

You can see the waiting thread in the first connection:

```
mysql> SHOW PROCESSLIST\G
*************************** 1. row ***************************
     Id: 7
   User: baron
   Host: localhost
     db: NULL
Command: Query
   Time: 0
  State: NULL
   Info: SHOW PROCESSLIST
*************************** 2. row ***************************
     Id: 11
   User: baron
   Host: localhost
     db: NULL
Command: Query
   Time: 4
  State: Locked
   Info: LOCK TABLES sakila.film WRITE
2 rows in set (0.01 sec)
```

Notice that thread 11's state is Locked. There is only one place in the MySQL server's code where a thread enters that state: when it tries to acquire a table lock and another thread has the table locked. Thus, if you see this, you know the thread is waiting for a lock in the MySQL server, not in the storage engine.

Explicit locks, however, are not the only type of lock that might block such an operation. As we mentioned earlier, the server implicitly locks tables during queries. An easy way to show this is with a long-running query, which you can create easily with the SLEEP( ) function:

```
mysql> SELECT SLEEP(30) FROM sakila.film LIMIT 1;
```

If you try again to lock sakila.film while that query is running, the operation will hang because of the implicit lock, just as it did when you had the explicit lock. You'll be able to see the effects in the process list, as before:

```
mysql> SHOW PROCESSLIST\G
*************************** 1. row ***************************
     Id: 7
   User: baron
   Host: localhost
     db: NULL
Command: Query
   Time: 12
  State: Sending data
   Info: SELECT SLEEP(30) FROM sakila.film LIMIT 1
*************************** 2. row ***************************
     Id: 11
   User: baron
   Host: localhost
     db: NULL
Command: Query
   Time: 9
  State: Locked
   Info: LOCK TABLES sakila.film WRITE
```

In this example, the implicit read lock for the SELECT query blocks the explicit write lock requested by LOCK TABLES. Implicit locks can block each other, too.

You may be wondering about the difference between implicit and explicit locks. Internally, they are the same type of structure, and the same MySQL server code controls them. Externally, you can control explicit locks yourself with LOCK TABLES and UNLOCK TABLES.

When it comes to storage engines other than MyISAM, however, there's one very important difference between them. When you create a lock explicitly, it does what you tell it to, but implicit locks are hidden and "magical." The server creates and releases implicit locks automatically as needed, and it tells the storage engine about them. Storage engines "convert" these locks as they see fit. For example, InnoDB has rules about what type of InnoDB table lock it should create for a given server-level table lock. This can make it hard to understand what locks InnoDB is really creating behind the scenes.

In MySQL 5.0 and 5.1, the server manages server-level table locks in a deadlock-free manner, by creating and releasing them all at the same time, and all in the same internally defined order. In MySQL 6.0, it is possible to add more locks without releasing your existing locks, so it may be possible to create deadlocks on table-level locks. However, this functionality is incomplete at the time of this writing, so the ultimate behavior is unknown.

Finding out who holds a lock

If you see a lot of processes in the Locked state, your problem might be that you're trying to use MyISAM or a similar storage engine for a high-concurrency workload. This can block you from performing an operation manually, such as adding an index to a table. If an UPDATE query is queued and waiting for a lock on a MyISAM table, even a SELECT query won't be allowed to run. (You can read more about MySQL's lock queuing and priorities in the MySQL manual.)

In some cases, it can become clear that some connection has been holding a lock on a table for a very long time and just needs to be killed (or a user needs to be admonished not to hold up the works!). But how can you find out which connection that is?

There's currently no SQL command that can show you which thread holds the table locks that are blocking your query. If you run SHOW PROCESSLIST, you can see the processes that are waiting for locks, but not which processes hold those locks. Fortunately, there's a *debug* command (which it's not possible to run through SQL) that can print information about locks into the server's error log. You can use the *mysqladmin* utility to run the command:

```
$ mysqladmin debug
```

The output includes a lot of debugging information, but near the end you'll see something like the following. We created this output by locking the table in one connection, then trying to lock it again in another:

```
Thread database.table_name Locked/Waiting    Lock_type

7       sakila.film         Locked - read    Read lock  without concurrent inserts
8       sakila.film         Waiting - write  Highest priority write lock
```

You can see that thread 8 is waiting for the lock thread 7 holds.

The *mysqladmin debug* command prints out more information if MySQL is compiled with debugging enabled, but it prints the locks and some other useful information no matter what.

The Global Read Lock

The MySQL server also implements a global read lock. You can obtain this lock as follows:

```
mysql> FLUSH TABLES WITH READ LOCK;
```

If you now try to lock a table in another session, it will hang as before:

```
mysql> LOCK TABLES sakila.film WRITE;
```

How can you tell that this query is waiting for the global read lock and not a table-level lock as before? Look at the output of SHOW PROCESSLIST:

```
mysql> SHOW PROCESSLIST\G
...
*************************** 2. row ***************************
     Id: 22
   User: baron
   Host: localhost
     db: NULL
Command: Query
   Time: 9
  State: Waiting for release of readlock
   Info: LOCK TABLES sakila.film WRITE
```

Notice that the query's state is Waiting for release of readlock. This is your clue that the query is waiting for the global read lock, not a table-level lock.

MySQL provides no way to find out who holds the global read lock.

Name Locks

Name locks are a type of table lock that the server creates when it renames or drops a table. A name lock conflicts with an ordinary table lock, whether implicit or explicit. For example, if we use LOCK TABLES as before, and then in another session try to rename the locked table, the query will hang, but this time not in the Locked state:

```
mysql> RENAME TABLE sakila.film2 TO sakila.film;
```

As before, the process list is the place to see the locked query, which is in the Waiting for table state:

```
mysql> SHOW PROCESSLIST\G
...
*************************** 2. row ***************************
     Id: 27
   User: baron
   Host: localhost
     db: NULL
Command: Query
   Time: 3
  State: Waiting for table
   Info: rename table sakila.film to sakila.film 2
```

You can see the effects of a name lock in the output of SHOW OPEN TABLES, too:

```
mysql> SHOW OPEN TABLES;
+-----------+-----------+--------+-------------+
| Database  | Table     | In_use | Name_locked |
+-----------+-----------+--------+-------------+
| sakila    | film_text |      3 |           0 |
| sakila    | film      |      2 |           1 |
| sakila    | film2     |      1 |           1 |
+-----------+-----------+--------+-------------+
3 rows in set (0.00 sec)
```

Notice that both names (the original and the new name) are locked. sakila.film_text is locked because there's a trigger on sakila.film that refers to it, which illustrates another way locks can insinuate themselves into places you might not expect. If you query sakila.film, the trigger causes you to implicitly touch sakila.film_text, and therefore to implicitly lock it. It's true that the trigger really doesn't need to fire for the rename, and thus technically the lock isn't required, but that's the way it is: MySQL's locking is sometimes not as fine-grained as you might like.

MySQL doesn't provide any way to find out who holds name locks, but this usually isn't a problem because they're generally held for only a very short time. When there's a conflict, it is generally because a name lock is waiting for a normal table lock, which you can view with *mysqladmin debug*, as shown earlier.

User Locks

The final type of lock implemented in the server is the user lock, which is basically a named mutex. You specify the string to lock and the number of seconds to wait before the lock attempt should time out:

```
mysql> SELECT GET_LOCK('my lock', 100);
+--------------------------+
| GET_LOCK('my lock', 100) |
+--------------------------+
|                        1 |
+--------------------------+
1 row in set (0.00 sec)
```

This attempt returned success immediately, so this thread now has a lock on that named mutex. If another thread tries to lock the same string, it will hang until it times out. This time the process list shows a different state:

```
mysql> SHOW PROCESSLIST\G
*************************** 1. row ***************************
     Id: 22
   User: baron
   Host: localhost
     db: NULL
Command: Query
   Time: 9
  State: User lock
```

```
Info: SELECT GET_LOCK('my lock', 100)
```

The User lock state is unique to this type of lock. MySQL provides no way to find out who holds a user lock.

Lock Waits in Storage Engines

Locks at the server level can be quite a bit easier to debug than locks in storage engines. Storage engine locks differ from one storage engine to the next, and the engines may not provide any means to inspect their locks. We focus mostly on InnoDB in this appendix, because it's currently the most popular storage engine that implements its own locks.

InnoDB Lock Waits

InnoDB exposes some lock information in the output of SHOW INNODB STATUS. If a transaction is waiting for a lock, the lock will appear in the TRANSACTIONS section of the output from SHOW INNODB STATUS. For example, if you execute the following commands in one session, you will acquire a write lock on the first row in the table:

```
mysql> SET AUTOCOMMIT=0;
mysql> BEGIN;
mysql> SELECT film_id FROM sakila.film LIMIT 1 FOR UPDATE;
```

If you now run the same commands in another session, your query will block on the lock the first session acquired on that row. You can see the effects in SHOW INNODB STATUS (we've abbreviated the results for clarity):

```
1  LOCK WAIT 2 lock struct(s), heap size 1216
2  MySQL thread id 8, query id 89 localhost baron Sending data
3  SELECT film_id FROM sakila.film LIMIT 1 FOR UPDATE
4  ------- TRX HAS BEEN WAITING 9 SEC FOR THIS LOCK TO BE GRANTED:
5  RECORD LOCKS space id 0 page no 194 n bits 1072 index `idx_fk_language_id` of table
   `sakila/film` trx id 0 61714 lock_mode X waiting
```

The last line shows that the query is waiting for an exclusive (lock_mode X) lock on page 194 of the table's idx_fk_language_id index. Eventually, the lock wait timeout will be exceeded, and the query will return an error:

```
ERROR 1205 (HY000): Lock wait timeout exceeded; try restarting transaction
```

Unfortunately, without seeing who holds the locks, it's hard to figure out which transaction is causing the problem. You can often make an educated guess by looking at which transactions have been open a very long time; alternatively, you can activate the InnoDB lock monitor, which will show up to 10 of the locks each transaction holds. To activate the monitor, you create a magically named table with the InnoDB storage engine:*

```
mysql> CREATE TABLE innodb_lock_monitor(a int) ENGINE=INNODB;
```

When you issue this query, InnoDB begins printing a slightly enhanced version of the output of SHOW INNODB STATUS to standard output at intervals (the interval varies, but it's usually several times per minute). On most systems, this output is redirected to the server's error log; you can examine it to see which transactions hold which locks. To stop the lock monitor, drop the table.

Here's the relevant sample of the lock monitor output:

```
1   ---TRANSACTION 0 61717, ACTIVE 3 sec, process no 5102, OS thread id 1141152080
2   3 lock struct(s), heap size 1216
3   MySQL thread id 11, query id 108 localhost baron
4   show innodb status
5   TABLE LOCK table `sakila/film` trx id 0 61717 lock mode IX
6   RECORD LOCKS space id 0 page no 194 n bits 1072 index `idx_fk_language_id` of table
    `sakila/film` trx id 0 61717 lock_mode X
7   Record lock, heap no 2 PHYSICAL RECORD: n_fields 2; compact format; info bits 0
8   ... omitted ...
9
10  RECORD LOCKS space id 0 page no 231 n bits 168 index `PRIMARY` of table `sakila/film`
    trx id 0 61717 lock_mode X locks rec but not gap
11  Record lock, heap no 2 PHYSICAL RECORD: n_fields 15; compact format; info bits 0
12  ... omitted ...
```

Notice that line 3 shows the MySQL thread ID, which is the same as the value in the Id column in the process list. Line 5 shows that the transaction has an implicit exclusive table lock (IX) on the table. Lines 6 through 8 show the lock on the index. We've omitted the information on line 8 because it's a dump of the locked record and is pretty verbose. Lines 9 through 11 show the corresponding lock on the primary key (a FOR UPDATE lock must lock the row, not just the index).

It's undocumented, but when the lock monitor is activated the extra information appears in the output of SHOW INNODB STATUS too, so you don't actually have to look in the server's error log to see the lock information.

Toward more usable lock output

The lock monitor is not optimal, for several reasons. The primary problem is that the lock information is very verbose, because it includes hex and ASCII dumps of the records that are locked. It fills up the error log, and it can easily overflow the fixed-size output of SHOW INNODB STATUS. This means you might not get the information you're looking for in later sections of the output (see "LATEST DETECTED DEAD-LOCK" on page 569 for more on this). InnoDB also has a hardcoded limit to the number of locks it prints per transaction—after printing 10 locks, it will not print any more, which means you may not even see any information on the lock you want.

---

* InnoDB honors several "magical" table names as instructions. Current practice is to use dynamically settable server variables, but InnoDB has been around a long time, so it still has some old behaviors.

To top it all off, even if what you're looking for is there, it's hard to find it in all that lock output. (Just try it on a busy server, and you'll see!)

Two things can make the lock output more usable. The first is a patch one of this book's authors wrote for InnoDB and the MySQL server. The patch removes the verbose record dumps from the output, includes the lock information in the output of SHOW INNODB STATUS by default (so the lock monitor doesn't need to be activated), and adds dynamically settable server variables to control the verbosity and how many locks should be printed per transaction. You can get the patch for MySQL 5.0 at *http://lists.mysql.com/internals/35174*.

The second option is to use *innotop* to parse and format the output. Its Lock mode shows locks, aggregated neatly by connection and table, so you can see quickly which transactions hold locks on a given table. This is not a foolproof method of finding which transaction is blocking a lock, as that would require examining the dumped records to find the precise record that's locked. However, it's much better than the usual alternatives, and it's good enough for many purposes.

InnoDB developers have told us they're working on exporting InnoDB information into INFORMATION_SCHEMA tables for a future release, but this code isn't in any public release yet. In the future, this will probably be the preferred way to expose lock information.

Falcon Lock Waits

The Falcon transactional storage engine, which is part of the MySQL 6.0 alpha release at the time of this writing, exports its transaction information to an INFORMATION_SCHEMA table. You can use this to find the cause of a lock wait very easily with a SQL command:

```
mysql> SELECT a.THREAD_ID AS blocker, a.STATEMENT AS blocking_query,
    ->     b.THREAD_ID AS blocked, b.STATEMENT AS blocked_query
    -> FROM INFORMATION_SCHEMA.FALCON_TRANSACTIONS AS a
    ->     INNER JOIN INFORMATION_SCHEMA.FALCON_TRANSACTIONS AS b ON
    ->     a.ID = b.WAITING_FOR
    -> WHERE b.WAITING_FOR > 0;
+---------+----------------+---------+----------------------------+
| blocker | blocking_query | blocked | blocked_query              |
+---------+----------------+---------+----------------------------+
|       4 |                |       5 | SELECT * FROM tbl FOR UPDATE |
+---------+----------------+---------+----------------------------+
```

This type of diagnostic information should make life much easier for MySQL database administrators in the future!

Index

Symbols

* (asterisk), passwords beginning with, 529
% (percent sign), default hostname, 526, 534
? (question mark), parameters in prepared statements, 225
'...' (quotes), for hostnames and usernames, 535

A

ab tool, 42
Aborted_clients status variable, 301, 559
Aborted_connects status variable, 301, 559
access control, 522
access time, of hard disk, 315, 316
accounts, 522
    adding, 525, 526
    anonymous, disabling, 534
    privileges associated with
        displaying, 525
        for running MySQL, 541
        types of, 522
    removing, 525
    for replication, creating, 347
    stored in grant tables, 523
    types of, 526
ACID test, 7
active caches, 463
active monitoring, 585
adaptive hash indexes, 103, 575
administration, software for, 584, 585

administrator account
    database, 527
    system, 527
AES_DECRYPT() function, 554
AES_ENCRYPT() function, 554
Aker, Brian (functions for memcached), 230
algebraic equivalence rules, for query optimizations, 167
ALTER TABLE command, 138
    improving performance of, 145–148
    table conversions using, 30
analysis tools, 595–598
ANALYZE TABLE command, 137
Analyzing state, of query, 164
anonymous users, disabling, 534
Apache web server, 460–462
application-level caching, 465–467
application-level encryption, 552–554
applications
    joins performed in, 159
    performance of
        caching for, 463–469
        extending MySQL for, 470
        optimal concurrency, finding, 462
        problems with, finding, 457–460
        web server problems, 460–463
    profiling, 55–63, 457
Archive storage engine, 21, 29
archiving data
    for scalability, 432–435
    replication for, 372
    utility for, 599
asterisk (*), passwords beginning with, 529
Atomicity, in ACID test, 7

attributes support, in Sphinx, 638
auditing, backups for, 477
authentication, 3, 521
authorization, 521
    (see also privileges)
auto_increment_increment variable, 364
auto_increment_offset variable, 364
AUTOCOMMIT mode, 11
autogenerated schemas, 96
automatic host blocking, 549
availability, high, 409, 410, 447–456
    adding redundancy, 449
    failover and failback for, 452–456
    IP addresses, moving, 453
    IP takeover for, 453
    masters, switching roles of, 453
    middleman solutions for, 454
    MySQL Master-Master Replication
        Manager tool for, 454
    planning for, 447
    replicated-disk architectures for, 449
    replication for, 345
    shared-storage architectures for, 449
    slave, promoting, 453
    synchronous replication for, 451

B

Background Patrol Read, 320
Backup & Recovery (Preston), 472
backup accounts, 528
BACKUP DATABASE command, 517
backups, 472–477
    for auditing, 477
    of binary logs, 476, 486–488
    choosing storage engine based on, 25
    "cold" backups, 473
    copying files between machines, 476
    data and file consistency of, 483–485
    delimited file backups, 490
    for disaster recovery, 476
    filesystem snapshots, 492–499
    "hot" backups, 473
    importance of, 472, 476
    incremental, 482
    location of, 542
    logical backups, 476, 479
        creating, 489–492, 511, 517
        restoring, 502–504
    LVM snapshots, 492–499
    monitoring, 476

    offline, 478
    online, 478
    parallel dump and restore, 491
    RAID as, 475
    raw backups, 476, 480, 500
    recommendations for, 475
    replication for, 345, 475, 485
    replication slave initialization using, 353
    scripting, 518–520
    security of, 476
    by shared hosting provider, 477
    snapshot-based backups, 476
    speed of, 510
    SQL dumps, 489
    testing, 476, 481, 504
    for testing purposes, 477
    tools for, 511–517, 600
    "warm" backups, 473
    what data to include in, 477, 481–483
    (see also recovery)
Barth, Wolfgang (*Nagios System and Network
        Monitoring*), 587
battery backup unit (BBU), 324, 327
BBU (battery backup unit), 324, 327
BENCHMARK( ) function, 45
benchmarking, 32
    automating, 41
    before configuring server, 270
    changing parameters of, 40
    common mistakes in, avoiding, 37
    concurrency measurements, 36
    data set for, 38
    designing benchmarks, 38
    errors during, 38
    examples of, 44–54
    full-stack, 33, 42
    goals for, determining, 34–37
    interference by other jobs, 40
    latency, 35
    of migrations, 40
    number of times to run, 41
    queries for, 39
    realistic scenarios for, 37
    reasons for, 33
    repeatability of, 39, 40
    results of
        accuracy of, 39
        analyzing, 41
        documenting, 39
        unusual, 41
    scalability measurements, 35

single-component, 33, 34, 43
standard benchmarks, when to use, 38
tools for, 42–45
  ab tool, 42
  BENCHMARK( ) function, 45
  Database Test Suite, 43, 51–53
  http_load tool, 42, 44
  JMeter, 42
  MySQL Benchmark Suite
    (sql-bench), 43, 53
  mysqlslap tool, 43
  Super Smack, 44
  sysbench tool, 43, 46–50
transactions per time unit
    (throughput), 34
warming up system before, 38
BIGINT type, 82
binary log events, replication, 345
binary logs
  backing up, 476, 486–488
  flushing, InnoDB, 294
  format of, 487
  purging, 488
  for replication, 345, 354
  status of, 581
  status variables for, 559
bind_address variable, 543
binlog dump process, 346
Binlog_cache_disk_use status variable, 301,
    559
Binlog_cache_use status variable, 301, 559
binlog_do_db variable, 360
binlog_ignore_db variable, 360, 373
BIT type, 91
bit-packed data types, 91–93
Blackhole storage engine, 22, 29
"blob streaming" infrastructure, PBXT, 24
BLOB types, 86, 298–301
books and publications
  Backup & Recovery (Preston), 472
  Building Internet Firewalls (Zwicky
    et al.), 542
  High Performance Web Sites
    (Souders), 461
  MySQL documentation, 559
  MySQL Stored Procedure Programming
    (Harrison, Feuerstein), 217
  Nagios System and Network Monitoring
    (Barth), 587
  Practical Unix and Internet Security
    (Garfinkel et al.), 541

TCP/IP Network Administration
    (Hunt), 542
Boolean full-text searches, 247
B-Tree indexes, 97–101
  limitations of, 100
  when to use, 99
buffer pool, 271, 277
BUFFER POOL AND MEMORY section,
    SHOW INNODB STATUS
    output, 576
buffer pool, status of, 576
Building Internet Firewalls (Zwicky
    et al.), 542
bulletin boards, storage engines suited
    for, 28
Bytes_received status variable, 302
Bytes_sent status variable, 302

C

CACHE INDEX command, 275
cache miss rate, 314
cache tables, 142–145
cache units, 313
caches, CPU, 309
caching, 463–469
  active caches, 463
  application-level, 465–467
  below application level, 464
  control policies for, 467
  memory requirements for, 274–281
  object hierarchies for, 468
  passive caches, 463
  pregenerating content for, 469
  reads and writes affected by, 311
  (see also specific caches)
caching proxy server, 461
Cacti tool, 329, 590
capacity, 410
CD-ROM applications, storage engines
    suited for, 28
certificates, SSL (see SSL)
CHANGE MASTER TO command, 349,
    352, 382, 383
CHAR type, 84–86
CHAR_LENGTH( ) function, 242
CHARACTER SET clause, 239
character sets, 237–240
  character length affected by, 242
  choosing, 240, 243
  client/server communication of, 238
  comparison of values between, 239

architecture of, 308
number of, 306–309, 414
profiling usage of, tools for, 63
saturation of, 306–309
speed of, 306–308
crash recovery, choosing storage engine
based on, 26
CREATE TEMPORARY TABLE
command, 21
CREATE USER privilege, 537
Created_tmp* status variables, 560
Created_tmp_disk_tables status
variable, 302
Created_tmp_tables status variable, 302
Cricket tool, 590
CSV storage engine, 21, 29
current waits, status of, 566
CURRENT_DATE( ) function, caching not
used for, 205
CURRENT_USER( ) function, caching not
used for, 205
cursors, 224

D

data archiving (see archiving data)
data consistency, with backups, 484
data dictionary, 280
data distribution, replication for, 344
data encryption (see encryption)
data files (see files)
data fragmentation, 138
data sharding, 417–419
aggregating data with Sphinx, 634, 648
arranging shards on nodes, 423
dynamic allocation of data to shards, 426
explicit allocation of data to shards, 427
fixed allocation of data to shards, 424
fixed and dynamic allocation, 427
globally unique IDs needed for, 429–431
partitioning function for, 424
partitioning keys for, 419–421
querying across shards, 421
rebalancing shards, 428
size of shards, 422
in Sphinx, 636
time-based data partitioning, 434
tools for, 431
unit of sharding for, 420
data synchronization (see replication)

data types
autogenerated schemas choosing, 96
optimal, 80
bit-packed, 91–93
choosing, 81
date and time, 82, 90
for identifier columns, 93
nullable, 81
real numbers, 83
size of, 81, 86
strings, 84–90
whole numbers, 82
database
files for, 326–328
host for, restricting logins on, 541
migrating to MySQL, 584
privileges for, 535
storage location of, 14
database administrator accounts, 527
Database Test Suite, 43, 51–53
date and time data types, 90
high-resolution support, 91
optimal, choosing, 82
DATETIME type, 82, 90
db table, 523
dbt2 tool, Database Test Suite, 51–53
deadlocks, 9
monitoring, 598
status of, 569–571
debug command, mysqladmin, 653
debugging (see troubleshooting)
DECIMAL type, 83
decompressing files, 603–606
DEFAULT keyword
for configuration variables, 268
for MyISAM recovery, 282
default route, not having, for firewall, 544
DELAY_KEY_WRITE option, 18
delay_key_write variable, 281, 296
delayed key writes, MyISAM, 18
DELAYED option, 196
delayed replication, for recovery, 506
Delayed_* status variables, 564
DELETE command, EXPLAIN command
with, 609
delimited file backups, 490, 503
denormalization, 139, 140–142
DETERMINISTIC option, 219
development, software for, 584
directio( ) function, 289

network-attached storage (NAS), 326
next-key locking strategy, InnoDB, 19
Nichter, Daniel (HackMySQL tools web
    site), 595
nondeterministic functions, caching not used
    for, 205
noninteractive mode, 591
noninteractive monitoring tools, 586–590
nonrepeatable read, 8
normalization, 139–140, 141
Not_flushed_delayed_rows status
    variable, 564
NOW() function, caching not used for, 205
NOW_USEC() UDF, 230
NPTL (Native POSIX Threads Library), 334
NTFS filesystem, 333
nullable data types, 81

O

O_DIRECT flag, 289
O_DSYNC flag, 290
O_SYNC flag, 289
object hierarchies, for caching, 468
object versioning, 468
Object-relational mapping (ORM), 96
object-specific privileges, 522
obsolete privileges, 540
offline backups, 478
OFFSET clause, optimizing, 193
OLAP (online analytical processing),
    separating from OLTP, 372
OLD_PASSWORD() function, 529
old_passwords variable, 529
OLTP (online transaction processing)
    performance of, measuring, 35
    separating from OLAP on different
        slaves, 372
    sysbench tool for, 49–50
on-controller cache (RAID cache), 323
on-disk caches, 466
online analytical processing (OLAP), 372
online backups, 478
online transaction processing (see OLTP)
Open_* status variables, 561
Open_files status variable, 303
Open_tables status variable, 303
Opened_tables status variable, 280, 303
OpenNMS tool, 588
OpenSSL library, 546
operating system
    backing up files on, 482

choosing, 330
    memory requirements for, 273
    profiling, 76–79
    security of, 541
    status of, monitoring, 336–341
        for CPU-bound server, 339
        for idle server, 341
        for I/O-bound server, 340
        iostat tool, 338–339
        for swapping server, 341
        vmstat tool, 336
    updating, importance of, 541
operating system waits, 566
operations accounts, 528
OProfile tool, 78
optimal concurrency, 462
optimization
    BLOB columns, 298–301
    cache tables, 142–145
    counter tables, 144
    of CPUs, 306–309
    data types, 80
        bit-packed, 91–93
        choosing, 81
        date and time, 82, 90
        for identifier columns, 93
        nullable, 81
        real numbers, 83
        size of, 81, 86
        strings, 84–90
        whole numbers, 82
    denormalization, 139, 140–142
    of filesorts, 176, 300
    filesystem for, choosing, 331–333
    fragmentation, reducing, 138
    of full-text searching, 251–252
    index corruption, repairing, 136
    index statistics, updating, 136
    of memory-to-disk ratio, 314–317
    of multiple disk volumes, 327
    of network configuration, 328–330
    normalization, 139–140, 141
    operating system for, choosing, 330
    of RAID, 317–325
    of slave hardware, 317
    of sorts, 135, 176
    summary tables, 142–145
    table corruption, repairing, 136
    TEXT columns, 298–301
    (see also availability, high; load balancing;
        performance; scaling; server
        configuration)

OPTIMIZE TABLE command, 138
optimizer_prune_level variable, 198
optimizer_search_depth variable, 197
order processing, storage engines suited
  for, 27
ORM (object-relational mapping), 96

P

packed (prefix-compressed) indexes, 126
packet loss, 328
packet sniffers, for profiling, 76
parallel dump and restore, 491
parallel execution, not supported, 185
parallel result sets, Sphinx tool for, 631
partitioned data (see data sharding)
partitioned tables, 253, 257–262
  advantages of, 258
  examples of, 259
  limitations of, 260
  queries against, optimizing, 261
  for scalability, 434
  types of, 258
partitioning keys, for data sharding, 419–421
partitioning, functional, 415, 416, 446
passive caches, 463
passive monitoring, 585
passwordless access, disallowing, 534
passwords
  hashing, 529, 550
  security of, 527
pattern matching, limitations of, 536
PBXT (Primebase XT) storage engine, 23, 29
  locking in, 14
  MVCC supported by, 12
percent sign (%), default hostname, 526, 534
percentile response times, 35
performance, 306, 410, 413
  of ALTER TABLE command, 145–148
  of application
    caching for, 463–469
    extending MySQL for, 470
    optimal concurrency, finding, 462
    problems with, finding, 457–460
    web server problems, 460–463
  application level profiling affecting, 57
  autogenerated schemas affecting, 96
  of backup and recovery, 510
  of character sets and collations, 241–244
  of cursors, 224

development complexity increased by
    improving, 145
  of distributed (XA) transactions, 263, 264
  of DNS, avoiding reliance on, 329
  of EXPLAIN command, 608
  of file copies, 606
  of foreign keys, 252
  of full-text searching, 249–252
  of indexes
    building quickly, 148
    clustered indexes, 110–119
    covering indexes, 120–124
    duplicate indexes, 127–129
    index scans for sorts, 124–126
    isolating columns, 106
    locking and, 129–131
    packed indexes, 126
    prefix indexes, 107–110
    redundant indexes, 127–129
    sorting, 135
  of locks, 5
  of merge tables, 255
  of OLTP, measuring, 35
  of partitioned tables, 261
  of prepared statements, 226
  privileges affecting, 532
  of queries
    data access, analyzing, 152–157
    optimizations for specific types
      of, 188–195
    optimizer for, 3, 165–188, 195, 203
    query cache for, 164
    restructuring queries for, 157–160
    (see also query cache)
  of replication, 405–407
  server configuration benefits for, 265
  of server variables set
      dynamically, 268–270
  in Sphinx, controlling, 641
  of stored code, 217–223
  swapping affecting, 334
  of temporary tables, 298
  tools for
    analysis tools, 595–598
    Dormando's Proxy for MySQL
      tool, 599
    interface tools, 583–585
    Maatkit tools, 599
    monitoring tools, 585–595
    MySQL Proxy, 598

queries
  accelerating (see Sphinx tool)
  access methods used by, 155
  analyzing, 152–157, 596, 598
  character sets affecting, 241–244
  client/server protocol for, 161–164
  collations affecting, 241–244
  consistent formatting of, importance
    of, 205
  COUNT( ) queries, 167, 188–190
  DISTINCT clauses, 191
  execution of, 160, 178
  execution plan for, 172, 178
    (see also EXPLAIN command)
  execution time of, 154
  GROUP BY clause, 191, 630, 646
  IN( ) list comparisons, 169
  index-covered queries, 121
  joins
    decomposition of, 159
    execution strategy for, 170–172
    optimizations for, 167, 173–176, 190
    STRAIGHT_JOIN option, 196
  LIMIT clause, 193, 194
  MAX( ) queries, 167, 187
  MIN( ) queries, 167, 187
  monitoring, 591
  OFFSET clause, 193
  optimizations for specific types
    of, 188–195
  optimizer for, 3, 165–170
    dynamic optimizations, 166
    early termination by, 168
    hint options for, 194, 195, 203
    index statistics used by, 170
    join optimizations by, 173–176
    join strategy used by, 170–172
    limitations of, 165, 179–188
    optimizations performed by, 167–169
    sort optimizations used by, 176
    static optimizations, 166
    system variables affecting, 197
    table statistics used by, 170
  parser for, 165
  of partitioned tables, 261
  prepared statements for, 225
    limitations of, 229
    optimizing, 227
    SQL interface for, 227
  preprocessor for, 165
  profiling, 71–74

  restructuring, 157–160
    breaking into multiple queries, 157
    join decomposition, 159
    reducing rows returned by, 158
  results returned by, 178
  rows examined by, 154–157
  rows returned by, 153, 154, 158
  software for, 583
  states of, 163
  subqueries, 168, 191
  subqueries, correlated, 179–183
  UNION clause, 183, 194, 254
  WHERE clause, 169, 628
query cache, 3, 164, 204–209
  cache hits
    checking for, 205
    improving, 213, 216
  cache misses, reasons for, 209
  column privileges not using, 532
  disabling, 211, 216
  enabling, 211
  excluding queries from, 216
  fragmentation in, 208, 212
  helpfulness of, determining, 209–211
  hit rate of, 209
  locks affecting, 212
  memory use by, 206–209, 211
  not using for query, 71
  overhead added by, 206
  pruning of, 213, 216
  removing all queries and results
    from, 213
  result sets in, size of, 212
  size of, 269
    allocated, 211
    performance affected by, 206
    potential, 211
  status variables for, 561
  tuning, 211–213
query logs, 64–70
query plan cost, status variable for, 564
Query state, 163
query_cache_limit variable, 212
query_cache_min_res_unit variable, 207,
    210, 211, 212
query_cache_size variable, 211, 216, 267,
    269
query_cache_type variable, 211
query_cache_wlock_invalidate variable, 212
query-based split, 439

question mark (?), parameters in prepared statements, 225

Questions status variable, 560

quotes ('...'), for hostnames and usernames, 535

R

R1Soft, 517

RAID (Redundant Arrays of Inexpensive Disks), 317–325
  as backups, 475
  BBU (battery backup unit), 324, 327
  configuration, 322–325
  crash testing script for, 324
  failure of, 320
  hardware, balancing with software, 321
  levels of, 318–320
  monitoring, 320
  stripe chunk size for, 322

RAID cache, 323

random I/O, 310

random, load-balancing algorithm, 444

range condition, 134

range partitioning, 258

ranged queries, in Sphinx, 641

raw backups, 476, 480, 500

READ COMMITTED isolation level, 8, 14

read locks, 4

READ UNCOMMITTED isolation level, 8, 14

read_buffer_size variable, 269, 270

read_only variable, 354

read_rnd_buffer_size variable, 270

read-around writes, 276

reading (see I/O)

read-mostly tables, storage engines suited for, 27

read-only slaves, 373

read-only tables, storage engines suited for, 27

real numbers, data types for, 83

records_in_range( ) function, 136

recovery, 473–475, 499–510
  delayed replication for, 506
  disaster recovery, 476
  with InnoDB, 507–510
  limiting MySQL access during, 500
  log server for, 506
  logical backups, restoring, 502–504
  point-in-time recovery, 504

raw files, restoring, 500

speed of, 510

redundancy, adding, for high availability, 449

Redundant Arrays of Inexpensive Disks (see RAID)

redundant indexes, 127–129, 597

ReiserFS filesystem, 332, 333

relay log, 346

relay_log variable, 349

relay_log_space_limit variable, 355

relay-log.info file, 358

RELOAD privilege, 528

REPAIR TABLE command, 136

REPEATABLE READ isolation level, 8, 14

replicate_* variables, 360

replicate_ignore_db variable, 372

replicated-disk architectures, 449

replication, 343–346
  accounts for, creating, 347
  for backups, 345, 475, 485
  capacity planning for, 376–378
  configuration for, 348
    backing up, 482
    recommended, 353
  CPUs affecting, 307
  delayed, for recovery, 506
  files used by, 357
  filtering for, 360
  for scalability, 415
  future of, 407
  limitations of, 405
  for load balancing, 438
  monitoring, 378, 591, 598
  performance of, 405–407
  row-based, 343, 356
  Sandbox script for experimentation with, 352
  scaling reads using, 344
  scaling writes using, 344, 377
  setting up, 347–355, 360
  slave lag, measuring, 379
  slave server
    changing master of, 382
    consistency with master, determining, 380
    delaying (lagging), 600
    hardware for, 317
    initializing from another server, 352
    as master of other slaves, 359
    prefetch for, 600

storage_engine variable, 557
stored code
    advantages of, 217
    comments in, 224
    disadvantages of, 218
    events, 222
    language constructs used in, 217
    library of, 217
    stored functions, 219
    stored procedures, 219, 228
    triggers, 220–222
stored functions, 219
stored procedures, 219, 228
stored routines, privileges used with, 530
strace tool, 76, 78
STRAIGHT_JOIN option, 196
string locks, 651
strings
    data types for, 84–90
    for identifier columns, 94
Stunnel tool, 548
subqueries
    correlated, optimization of, 179–183
    optimizations for, 168, 191
summary tables, 142–145
SUPER privilege
    for operations and monitoring
        accounts, 529
    and read_only option, 354
    for triggers, 531
    when to grant, 536
Super Smack, 44
surrogate keys, 117
swapping, 334, 341
sync_binlog variable, 294, 328, 354
synchronization of data (see replication)
synchronous replication, for high
    availability, 451
sysbench tool, 43, 46–50
system administrator account, 527
system security, 541
system variables
    affecting query optimizer, 197
    exposing, 557

T

table cache, 269, 279
table conversions, between storage
    engines, 30
table definition cache (see data dictionary)
table locks, 5, 149, 650, 651–653

concurrency level of, 14
    as potential bottleneck, 149
    status variables for, 563
table statistics, 170
table_cache variable, 268
table_cache_size variable, 269
table_definition_cache variable, 280
Table_locks_immediate status variable, 563
Table_locks_waited status variable, 304, 563
table_open_cache variable, 280
tables
    checksums of, 600
    corruption of, 136
    filename of, 14
    information about, displaying, 14
    storage engine used by, determining, 14
    synchronizing, 600
tables_priv table, 524
tablespace, InnoDB, 19, 290–293
tagged cache, 468
tar command, 605
Tc_log_* status variables, 564
TCP wrappers, 548
TCP/IP Network Administration (Hunt), 542
tcpdump tool, 76
temporary files, status variables for, 560
temporary tables
    avoiding, 87
    compared to Memory tables, 21
    improving performance of, 298
    privileges for, 534
    status variables for, 560
TEMPTABLE algorithm, for views, 232
TEXT types, 86, 298–301
thread cache, 269, 278
thread libraries, 334
thread_cache_size variable, 269, 278
threaded discussion forums, storage engines
    suited for, 28
threads (see connections to MySQL)
threads benchmark, sysbench tool, 50
Threads_connected status variable, 279, 558
Threads_created status variable, 278, 304,
    559
throughput, 34, 307, 315
time data types (see date and time data types)
time to live (TTL), cache control policy, 467
time-based data partitioning, 434
TIMESTAMP type, 90
    compared to DATETIME type, 82
    high-resolution support, 91

About the Authors

Baron Schwartz is a software engineer who lives in Charlottesville, Virginia and goes by the online handle of "Xaprb," which is his first name typed in QWERTY on a Dvorak keyboard. When he's not busy solving a fun programming challenge, Baron relaxes with his wife, Lynn, and dog, Carbon. He blogs about software engineering at *http://www.xaprb.com/blog*.

Peter Zaitsev, a former manager of the High Performance Group at MySQL AB, now runs the *mysqlperformanceblog.com* site. He specializes in helping administrators fix issues with web sites handling millions of visitors a day, dealing with terabytes of data using hundreds of servers. He is used to making changes and upgrades both to hardware and software (such as query optimization) in order to find solutions. Peter also speaks frequently at conferences.

Vadim Tkachenko is coowner of Percona Inc., a company specializing in MySQL performance consulting. He was a performance engineer at MySQL AB. As an expert in multithreaded programming and synchronization, his primary tasks were benchmarks, profiling, and finding bottlenecks. He also worked on a number of features for performance monitoring and tuning, and getting MySQL to scale well on multiple CPUs.

Jeremy D. Zawodny and his two cats moved from Northwest Ohio to Silicon Valley in late 1999, so he could work for Yahoo!—just in time to witness the dot-com bubble bursting firsthand. He spent eight and half years at Yahoo!, helping to put MySQL and other open source technologies to use in fun, interesting, and often very big ways.

In recent times, he's rediscovered his love of aviation, earning a private pilot glider license in early 2003 and his commercial pilot rating in 2005. Since then he's spent far too much of his free time flying gliders out of Hollister, California and the Lake Tahoe area. He also flies single engine light airplanes now and then, coowning a Citabria 7KCAB and Cessna 182. Occasional consulting work helps to pay for his flying addiction.

Jeremy lives in the San Francisco Bay Area of California with his wonderful wife and their four cats. He blogs at *jeremy.zawodny.com/blog*.

Arjen Lentz was born in Amsterdam but has lived in Queensland, Australia since the turn of the millennium, sharing his life these days with his beautiful daughter Phoebe and black cat Figaro. Originally a C programmer, Arjen was employee #25 at MySQL AB (2001–2007). After a brief break in 2007, Arjen founded Open Query (*http://openquery.com.au*), which develops and provides its own data management training and consulting services in the Asia Pacific region and beyond. Arjen also regularly speaks at conferences and user groups. In his abundance of spare time, Arjen indulges in cooking, gardening, reading, camping, and exploring the RepRap. Visit his weblog at *http://arjen lentz.livejournal.com*.

Derek J. Balling has been a Linux system administrator since 1996. He has helped build and maintain server infrastructure for companies like Yahoo!, and institutions like Vassar College. He has also written articles for *The Perl Journal* and a number of online magazines, and he serves on the Program Committee for the LISA (Large Installation System Administration) Conference. He is employed as the Data Center manager for Answers.com.

When not working on computer-related issues, Derek enjoys spending time with his wife, Debbie, and their posse of animals (four cats and a dog). He also makes his opinion known on current events or whatever is annoying him lately on his blog at *http://blog.megacity.org*.

Colophon

The animal on the cover of *High Performance MySQL* is a sparrow hawk (*Accipiter nisus*), a small woodland member of the falcon family found in Eurasia and North Africa. Sparrow hawks have a long tail and short wings; males are bluish-gray with a light brown breast, and females are more brown-gray and have an almost fully white breast. Males are normally somewhat smaller (11 inches) than females (15 inches).

Sparrow hawks live in coniferous woods and feed on small mammals, insects, and birds. They nest in trees and sometimes on cliff ledges. At the beginning of the summer, the female lays four to six white eggs, blotched red and brown, in a nest made in the boughs of the tallest tree available. The male feeds the female and their young.

Like all hawks, the sparrow hawk is capable of bursts of high speed in flight. Whether soaring or gliding, the sparrow hawk has a characteristic flap-flap-glide action; its large tail enables the hawk to twist and turn effortlessly in and out of cover.

The cover image is a 19th-century engraving from the Dover Pictorial Archive. The cover font is Adobe ITC Garamond. The text font is Linotype Birka; the heading font is Adobe Myriad Condensed; and the code font is LucasFont's TheSansMonoCondensed.

Related Titles from O'Reilly

Database

The Art of SQL

Database in Depth

FileMaker Pro 9: The Missing Manual

Head First SQL

High Performance MySQL

Learning MySQL

Learning PHP and MySQL, *2nd Edition*

Learning SQL

Learning SQL on SQL Server 2005

Managing & Using MySQL, *2nd Edition*

MySQL Cookbook, *2nd Edition*

MySQL in a Nutshell

MySQL Pocket Reference, *2nd Edition*

MySQL Reference Manual

MySQL Stored Procedure Programming

Oracle Essentials, 4th *Edition*

Oracle PL/SQL Best Practices, *2nd Edition*

Oracle PL/SQL Language Pocket Reference, *4th Edition*

Practical PostgreSQL

Programming SQL Server 2005

The Relational Database Dictionary

SQL Cookbook

SQL in a Nutshell, *2nd Edition*

SQL Pocket Guide, *2nd Edition*

SQL Tuning

Understanding MySQL Internals

Our books are available at most retail and online bookstores.

To order direct: 1-800-998-9938 • *order@oreilly.com* • *www.oreilly.com*

Online editions of most O'Reilly titles are available by subscription at *safari.oreilly.com*